of Our Time

POLAR ORTHOGRAPHIC PROJECTION

AMERICA'S
FOREIGN POLICY

AMERICA'S FOREIGN POLICY

edited, with an introduction and notes, by

HAROLD KARAN JACOBSON

UNIVERSITY OF MICHIGAN

 RANDOM HOUSE · NEW YORK

to

KNUTE, ERIC, AND KRISTOFFER

—*may our decisions help make their world
free and peaceful*

First Printing

© Copyright, 1960, by Harold K. Jacobson

*All rights reserved under International and Pan-American Copyright
Conventions. Published in New York by Random House, Inc., and
simultaneously in Toronto, Canada, by Random House of Canada, Limited.*

Library of Congress Catalog Card Number: 60-6196

Manufactured in the United States of America by the Colonial Press Inc.

FOREWORD

This anthology results from the conviction that one of the most significant contributions political scientists as teachers can make to United States foreign policy is to assist in clarifying and raising the level of public debate. Ideally, the informed segments of the public would explore policy alternatives as fully and as rationally as possible, and their choice would then be based on this consideration. To do this they need facts about the contemporary world, but more important they need analytical skill. They need to be able to isolate value judgments and to subject assumptions to the most rigorous possible analysis. This skill can only be gained through training and practice. This anthology is designed for such training. After presenting selections dealing with the framework of policy-making and the contemporary environment of world politics, it juxtaposes contrasting and at times conflicting analyses of present foreign policy problems in the hope that their intellectual substructure will thereby be made more apparent. It does not attempt to present a chronology or description of United States policy, but rather, various analyses of it. As far as possible these analyses are reproduced in their entirety, to give the full flavor of their arguments.

My debts for assistance are many. I am grateful to my teachers for the intellectual ferment they created and to my students for their critical insights which have redounded to my benefit. One teacher, Marshall M. Knappen, particularly deserves mention. His strength of character and deep concern for public understanding of foreign policy have since undergraduate days been a continuing source of inspiration. I especially want to thank Inis L. Claude, Jr., my colleague at the University of Michigan, and Charles D. Lieber of Random House, both of whom have contributed helpful advice and counsel through all stages of this project. Responsibility, of course, is mine alone.

H. K. J.
Department of Political Science
University of Michigan

Table of Contents

MAPS

AMERICA'S
FOREIGN POLICY

Chapter I

INTRODUCTION—THE PUBLIC DEBATE AND FOREIGN POLICY

Seldom in United States history has public understanding of foreign policy been both so vitally necessary and so difficult to achieve as at the present time. Faced first with the fascist challenge to its existence, and then with the implacable yet subtle threat posed by Soviet communism, the United States has been forced to come out of its isolationist shell and to become the leader of a coalition of widely differing states. America's new role imposes unforeseen and vast burdens and requires patience and skill; informed public support, the product of a meaningful public debate, is a prerequisite for the development and execution of adequate policies.

While the United States' new tasks demand public understanding, the circumstances under which they were assumed make this difficult. The transformation in the foreign policy of the United States in the two decades since the beginning of the Second World War has occurred at a bewildering pace. America has moved from an era in which Charles A. Lindbergh could say, and many would listen and agree, that the United States had no interest in the nascent holocaust in Europe, to an era in which developments everywhere—the pronouncement of a tribal chief in Africa, a change in the United Kingdom's defense structure, the decision to decentralize planning in the U.S.S.R.—all seem to vitally affect our interests. In 1939 many thought that the only moral course for the United States was to attempt to preserve its neutrality and believed that great sacrifice should be made to this end, but today equal numbers condemn others' neutralism in the cold war as immoral. Alliances were seriously viewed as "entangling" and morally repugnant in 1939; twenty years later the United States had formal commitments to aid in the defense of over forty states. Foreign assistance programs, almost unheard of then, now seem to be a permanent feature of American life. Universities which used to have one or two courses dealing with international affairs now feel justified in establishing whole schools to train those who look forward to overseas duties. In the brief span of twenty years the United States has moved from a period in which its involvement in world politics was spasmodic and partial, and its policies were largely negative, to one in which its involvement is continual and total, and its policies must necessarily be positive and forward-looking.

Not only have the broad outlines of United States foreign policy been radically transformed in the past two decades, the separate strands which make up these outlines have also undergone vast and swift changes. The United States' two major enemies in 1945 were two of our most important allies in 1955. China, the state in Eastern Asia which had long held our sympathies and on which we pinned our hopes for the preservation of postwar peace and stability in Eastern Asia, fell under communist rule and became violently hostile toward us, even to the extent of waging war against United States troops in Korea. Our friendship turned to animosity and we refused to extend diplomatic recognition to the new regime and blocked its admission to the United Nations. America's official attitude toward the Soviet Union vacillated from regarding it as a vicious state which attacked hapless smaller states in Eastern Europe, to seeing it as a major ally which might even have elements of democracy, to finally viewing it as our principal totalitarian enemy. Official estimates of Soviet capabilities followed a similar zig-zag movement punctuated by such events as the slow pace of the Finnish campaigns, the heroic defense of Stalingrad and Moscow, the need for lend-lease equipment to make up deficiencies in transport and other equipment, the explosion of an atomic weapon in 1949, the observed shoddiness of postwar consumer goods, and the launching of the earth satellites.

Although it is true that no public was, or could be, prepared for understanding the international politics of the mid-twentieth century, the United States' historical experience left the American public singularly ill equipped. Assumptions which seemed appropriate in 1939 have little significance in the present world, and many of those of 1945 are just as outmoded. In 1939 we attempted to interpret international politics with theories derived from our own history, and in so doing we relied primarily on the record prior to 1914. In the period between the two world wars, despite our own involvement in the First and its settlement, we lapsed into habits of thinking of an earlier age. As a people, Americans were not used to continually facing political tensions or to "living with" disagreeable but for the moment insoluble problems. A fertile continent with an open frontier and the absence of powerful neighbors made our past exceedingly happy; since the early nineteenth century we had not faced a serious external challenge and many of our internal problems were solved through the opportunities provided by relatively rapid economic growth and westward expansion. On the basis of our experience as we interpreted it, some Americans in the interwar period underestimated the strength of conflict in international relations. They optimistically thought that conflict could significantly be mitigated and possibly ultimately even eliminated. They suggested solutions based on our internal experience, ignoring the factors which made them successful here, but which were lacking in international politics. Others, particularly in the Thirties, thought that the conflicts they could not help but see were the result of petty and insignificant quarrels over issues of no concern to us and therefore felt it proper and necessary to abstain.

We were jarred into reality in 1940 and 1941 by the dangerous plight of Britain and the Japanese attack. But although the public involvement in the Second World War probably impressed many with the need for military preparedness, beyond this it did little immediately to facilitate sophisticated understanding of the postwar world. The pace was too rapid and immediate demands too pressing for reflective thinking. There was the inevitable emotionalism caused by wartime passions. The government, facing unforeseen and unfamiliar problems, was not always equipped to give the public adequate guidance. And some of its pronouncements, because of the exigencies of domestic politics, the necessity of mobilizing a sometimes lethargic people most of whom were accustomed to devoting themselves almost exclusively to private matters, and the problems of holding together an alliance of disparate states, were less candid and forthright than they might have been; difficult problems were glossed over and events given their most optimistic interpretation. Thus, the theories we held at the close of the Second

World War are almost equally inadequate to interpret present events as those of 1939.

The subtle nature of the challenge posed by Soviet communism compounded the already difficult problem of achieving public understanding of present world politics. The historical record and the U.S.S.R.'s present demands clearly demonstrate Soviet expansionism. Most people in the United States are aware of the threat this poses, but too often we interpret it exclusively in short-range, military terms. Soviet ideology gives believers a dedicated sense of mission. They are convinced of the validity of their system and of its ultimate triumph, and they unceasingly use all means to advance its cause. While the U.S.S.R. poses military dangers, they are not of the same sort that were present in the Thirties, and in addition, it poses other dangers as well. We frequently ignore the attractions the Soviet Union has for many in other parts of the world. Elements of the ideal society held out by Soviet communists command wide appeal and, unlike the nazi, the communist utopia contains few obviously morally repugnant features. Further, the U.S.S.R. has a remarkable record of economic growth. The costs of the Soviet system in terms of human values, although horribly real, are not always easy to point out to people in underdeveloped areas. Combating Soviet communism therefore requires a long-range, multi-faceted approach. It requires positive and dynamic policies, which even with the best foresight, may not always succeed. Above all meeting the Soviet challenge requires working with other states, making compromises to their interests and at least recognizing the existence of interpretations differing from our own. These requirements are not easy for a people unaccustomed to continual involvement in foreign affairs and possible frustration, and for a people who have always thought in terms of the freedom of action associated with "going it alone."

Perhaps even with the complex nature of the Soviet threat, public adjustment to the transformation in United States foreign policy would not have been unduly difficult, had not the problem been multiplied manifold by just as radical and as rapid changes in the environment of international affairs. World politics in the mid-twentieth century are significantly different from earlier eras.

Perhaps the most dramatic change has been in weapons technology. The explosive power of weapons has been increased almost beyond comprehension. One ten-megaton thermonuclear weapon, which can be delivered to its target quickly by a high-speed aircraft or a missile, has the destructive force in terms of blast and heat effects of 2.2 times all the bombs dropped on Germany during the Second World War, or 4.7 times those dropped on Japan. In addition, this weapon has immediate and long-range fall-out effects which (although they would vary with its construction, the level of detonation, and prevailing wind conditions) could cause awesome harm. It is possible for the immediate fall-out effects of one ten-megaton weapon to contaminate for a short period an area as large as New York, New Jersey, and Pennsylvania combined. New developments in delivery systems are equally startling. An intercontinental ballistic missile can travel from the heart of the U.S.S.R. to the heart of the United States in approximately thirty minutes. A shorter-range missile which can be fired under water from a submarine, making its base almost undetectable, can travel 1,500 miles in about fifteen minutes. The introduction, already in process, of weapon systems embodying these new developments into the armed forces of the United States and the Union of Soviet Socialist Republics must have altered the future of warfare; how, no one can be certain. Even if these weapon systems are never used, they will have an impact on world politics. Further, it appears that the future will bring continuing technological developments which will vitally affect the nature of warfare, and will have equally unpredictable consequences. All that is clear is that these developments have done little if anything to diminish political differences between states. Indeed, political tensions between the U.S.S.R. and the U.S.A. and also between other states in the years since the first atomic bomb was dropped on Hiroshima have been just as great, if not greater than in previous periods.

Although developments in weapons technology may provide the most dramatic changes in the world environment, these are certainly not the only changes, nor perhaps even the most important. It may be more important that since the end of the Second World War over twenty states have achieved independence. This number grows annually, and soon colonial status—at least in the nineteenth-century sense—will no longer exist. These newly independent states are located in Africa and Asia. They have attempted at their Bandung Conference in 1955 and elsewhere to form a rough unity in world politics. They are committed to accelerating the liquidation of colonial rule and are hypersensitive about their own political and economic independence. Their memory of Western imperialism is frequently more influential in determining their conduct than any perception of a Soviet threat.

Above all these new Asian and African states are determined rapidly to develop their own economies, and in this they are joined by other economically underdeveloped states throughout the world. These states have all undergone what has aptly been described as a "revolution of rising expectations." Improved communications have made possible comparisons of their material standards with those of others, independence has given them a new sense of control, and both developments have contributed to undermining traditional social patterns which previously blocked innovations. All these factors have led to a growing demand for rapid economic growth in the underdeveloped areas of the world. The motives for this are mixed; the perceived political benefits are frequently desired even more strongly than economic ones.

Because of the development of international institutions based on the principles of sovereign equality and majority rule, and because of the strength of the tensions between the United States and the Soviet Union, Asian, African, and other economically underdeveloped states have been able to exert more influence in contemporary international affairs than their present physical strength would indicate. In the United Nations General Assembly the Asian and African states alone comprise a bloc which, if it acts as a unit, because of the two-thirds rule can prevent the adoption of any resolution. To both East and West the allegiance of the underdeveloped states appears as one of the principal stakes of the cold war. For these reasons, the underdeveloped states have been able to gain acceptance of the proposition that they are entitled to rapid economic development and to substantial international assistance to facilitate this process. The movement toward economic development in these areas is already in progress, but its outcome is hardly apparent at this time. In terms of human welfare, if material standards are raised significantly throughout the world, this movement may well be the most important feature of the twentieth century. It is also its most staggering task.

Another significant but less obvious change in the world environment is the collapse of the political system which gave the world some semblance of stability during the greater part of the nineteenth century, and which parenthetically was one of the reasons why the United States suffered no serious external threat in these years. From 1815 to 1914 the major European powers constituted a political system which dominated world politics and which because of mutual rivalries and ambitions was able to maintain a sort of equilibrium within itself which served to prevent major wars and to preserve the independence of the participants. This European political system collapsed before or during the First World War, and as yet no mechanism has been established which can perform comparable functions. Moral revulsion against the old system because of its associations with the origins of the war and doubts about its practical achievements ruled out its reëstablishment, and even had the desire existed to reëstablish the European political system, conditions had probably so changed by 1919 that it would have been impossible. The institutions created to take its place, the League of Nations and the United Nations, have never been capable of performing the same tasks. It may be that for the present period no system can.

Internal changes in states have also had an impact on the environment of foreign relations. Probably the two most important are the advent of mass participation in the governmental process and the increased role of governments in economic affairs. The modern great powers, whether democratic or not, all rely on mass support; entire populations are involved emotionally and otherwise in decision-making. This creates a tendency to phrase foreign policy in ideological terms and to simplify complex issues. The result frequently is that demands are increased and policy made more rigid. At the same time, governments have vastly increased their activities in the economic field. The severe depression of the Thirties produced the conviction that this tragedy must not be repeated and also a school of economic thought, the Keynesian, which prescribed the preventative of increased governmental functions. Since most states have at least partly accepted this recommendation, the separation between politics and economics, if it was ever possible, is clearly unthinkable today. Disputes which might have been confined to two business firms in the past are now major matters of state. And governmental attempts to pursue full employment policies at home have important repercussions on the international scene.

These swift and basic alterations of the world environment make the development of public understanding even more vital but also more difficult to achieve. Ours is an age of change; indications point to the next years bringing still more new developments. Success in world politics will partly depend on how adequately and rapidly policies adjust to new situations. Our changing world, however, is not one that is easy to comprehend, and without comprehension appropriate policies cannot be formulated.

The materials for developing public understanding of United States foreign policy and the environment in which it operates are extensive. In spite of the recurring objections of various foreign policy professionals that not enough coverage is given the United Nations or some other facet of international relations, few can deny the abundance of available data, if only the public chooses to utilize it. The press, radio, and television all provide a detailed chronology of events and ample commentary and interpretation. Even the most casual viewer is exposed to some facts concerning international politics, and if an individual chooses, the opportunities for gaining information are almost limitless. A twist of the dial would have brought Nikita Khrushchev into his home with a presentation specifically designed for the American audience months before the Soviet leader's celebrated visit to the United States. There is more literature on international politics than can be read, even if one did nothing else. It ranges from the simplest analysis to the most sophisticated, utilizing advanced mathematical tools. Radio and television present a countless parade of statesmen, scholars, and journalists expounding their views.

There are ample explanations of official United States policy: speeches of the President and Secretary of State, press releases, and official Department of State publications are the most obvious sources. Admittedly their use creates certain problems, but these are not insuperable. Any official pronouncement is intended to have at least three effects. It is intended to explain policy, and thereby increase public understanding and attempt to gain support. An official pronouncement is also intended to convey certain meanings to other states: in this sense any statement itself comprises what has been called "declaratory policy." In dealing with future contingencies it may be useful for diplomatists not to be entirely explicit, since doubt and bluff both have their uses in international politics. Therefore, "declaratory policy" and "actual policy" may not be identical. Yet there are limits to the possible divergence, for if "declaratory policy" varies too much from "actual policy" the effectiveness of both is diminished. Finally, an official pronouncement in a democracy will have important internal political repercussions, and those in power will always try to make these as favorable as possible. But there are limits here too, for too great a discrepancy between an official's promises and claims and reality is subject to easy detection. While the other purposes of official pronouncements frequently dilute their explanatory content, the core must be left, and it does not require extreme sophistication to separate the shadow of foreign policy from its substance.

Statements of alternative policies are not as readily available, but for the interested citizen they can be found with ease. Members of the opposition have no difficulty obtaining forums for their views in the press and other media. Here again one must separate politically motivated claims from actuality. Journalists and scholars provide another source of criticism and new ideas, and their products can easily be acquired.

This wealth of information, however, has produced neither a highly articulated debate on foreign policy, nor even a well-informed public. In the public debate basic issues are all too often obscured either in a maze of seemingly daily crises, for which blame is loudly and variously assessed but only infrequently pin-pointed; or by emphasis on personalities, whose relationship to policy is seldom clearly defined. Public opinion polls constantly create surprise at the large segments of the population who seem unaware of major aspects of foreign policy. Considering this situation, an eminent American journalist, Walter Lippmann, in his book *The Public Philosophy* questioned the ability of a democracy to cope with present world problems, and advocated greater executive authority in the formulation of foreign policy. Similarly a distinguished diplomatic historian, Dexter Perkins, in an article in a widely respected journal,* concluded that the public discussion of foreign policy in Presidential campaigns has achieved little positive good, and has possibly had harmful effects. Should we infer that it is impossible to formulate foreign policy in a democratic fashion?

This anthology does not accept that conclusion. It is based on the premise that foreign policy not only should, but can be made through democratic processes. Belief in democratic principles is ultimately a value choice which one either accepts or rejects. But who is more qualified than the individual himself to express his own desires, and what fairer method than majority rule can be found to collectively determine which desires shall be implemented? If valid, these principles must apply equally to all areas of governmental activity including foreign affairs. In the present complex world how could one possibly separate foreign from domestic policy? A steel strike today will have more impor-

* "Foreign Policy in Presidential Campaigns," *Foreign Affairs*, Vol. XXXV, No. 2 (January, 1957), pp. 213-224.

tant consequences for America's position in world politics than many occurrences abroad. Further, to exclude foreign policy from the democratic process would be to exclude many of our era's most vital problems, among them the roughly two-thirds of the federal budget devoted to major national security matters. A system following this practice could hardly be called democratic.

Acceptance of the premise that foreign policy should and can be made democratically does not, however, imply a belief that all foreign policy issues should be subjected to wide and intensive public debate. Obviously some issues are suitable, others are not. The necessity of keeping some information confidential imposes certain limits, the public's lack of technical competence creates others, and the desirability of allowing diplomatists sufficient freedom to meet rapidly changing tactical situations erects still more. Probably the question of whether or not in the face of Soviet pressures the United States garrison in Berlin needs reinforcement is an issue that is not suitable for public debate. The general public lacks both the current information on the status of our own and opposing forces and the technical knowledge of military strategy to discuss this problem intelligently. Nor is the question whether increased United States economic assistance to India should be used to assist development of the small machine-tool industry or for support of the river waters program susceptible to public debate. Few could realistically evaluate the alternative benefits and costs. It would probably also be inappropriate for the public to attempt to define precisely exact United States responses to possible future Soviet moves. To do so might preclude the adoption of policies which, however disadvantageous they might appear now, might be appropriate and fruitful in changed and perhaps unforeseen circumstances.

But the necessary information is available and the public is competent to discuss the principal issues of foreign policy. This is all that an operational definition of democracy would require. Such questions as the adequacy of the United States defense effort; the appropriateness of the division of available military resources between competing air, land, and sea forces; the merits of increasing or decreasing foreign assistance programs; the wisdom of the relative allocation between military and economic assistance, and between various recipient countries; and the general posture the United States should adopt vis-à-vis Soviet actions, all surely can and must be discussed. Admittedly these larger questions are comprised of several smaller ones, and the line between what is and is not suitable for public debate is difficult to draw: its exact location must vary with circumstances. Yet this distinction can be made, and to make foreign policy in a democratic fashion does not require that every detail be decided in the open forum. It requires only that the major issues which will significantly affect the citizenry be so determined.

Acceptance of the premise that foreign policy should and can be made democratically also does not imply that all must participate equally in the formulation of foreign policy. The obvious factor of time would preclude this. Democracy requires only that all have equal access to the policy process. Few gainfully employed citizens can devote more than a small portion of each day to the analysis of foreign policy problems and many have only limited interest in such questions. On most foreign policy issues those who lack the time or the interest to be informed must rely primarily on the judgment of opinion leaders whose analyses they trust: governmental officials, representatives of political parties and interest groups, and independent observers and commentators. Those in the public who are more aware of events—the informed public—must also rely on opinion leaders, but in addition they can make their own analyses and scrutinize the more sophisticated arguments involved. The strength of democracy depends on the ability of opinion leaders and the quality of their analyses, and the size and capabilities of the informed public. The public debate on foreign policy, the basic source of meaningful understanding and support, must largely be conducted by opinion leaders before the informed public. The opinion leaders must structure the debate. In most instances only they can originate proposals for action and they also must be responsible for most critiques. The role of the informed public is to listen to their proposals and critiques, to evaluate them and to support those individuals and policies they favor. To the limited extent that the marketplace analogy is applicable, in the public debate on foreign policy the informed public are the consumers of the products of the opinion leaders. The role of the general public in the public debate is to set boundaries, to broadly delimit the range of acceptable alternatives. They are only involved when these are established or reëstablished, or when matters of special interest to them are considered. In a sense, they hold a residual veto power. In the busy and complex modern world specialization is necessary; a "town meeting" concept of democracy would hardly be appropriate for a state of over one hundred and seventy million people in the middle of the twentieth century; indeed the "town meeting" concept may not even have adequately described those New England gatherings from which the term is derived. If all have equal access to the governmental process and can influence decisions when they feel it is necessary, the requirements of democracy are met.

Nor does acceptance of the premise that foreign policy should and can be made democratically imply uncritical acceptance of the present situation. To the contrary, the present public debate falls far short of ideal criteria. If this is so, despite a willingness to accept limits on debate and differential participation, what is desired? Certainly not unanimity. To expect this would be both utopian and antidemocratic. Even though broad consensus concerning basic values exists in the United States, value differences are at stake in many policy decisions. Foreign aid and trade for example intimately involve many economic interests. And in the realm of human affairs, who can be so certain of his knowledge that he will not allow the possibility of differing interpretations? Further, the democratic system is a prescription for the arrangement of compromise between conflicting views, not for the creation of unanimity.

What is desired is that the public debate be as clear, precise, and rational as possible. The ideal public debate would be based on logic and free from emotion. It would carefully and meaningfully scrutinize foreign policy recommendations. Any such recommendation, or choice from competing alternatives, rests ultimately upon value preferences and assumptions about reality. All courses of action will involve costs, possible gains and losses, and risks. In choosing a particular course one expresses a preference for certain values over others, and even the values that one hopes to achieve, are given different weights. Assumptions also must be made about the impact of particular actions upon future events. For instance, those who argue that the United States should give greater support to Algerian independence in the United Nations, must make assumptions about the effects of this action upon the Algerian situation itself, upon France, and the North Atlantic Alliance, upon other colonial and anticolonial states, and upon the U.S.S.R. and its allies. Will the total effect of the action be to promote human freedom and stability, or will it narrow the opportunities for self-expression and increase international tensions? Methods will probably never be adequate nor knowledge sufficient to give conclusive answers to such questions, yet in the real world of foreign policy they must be answered daily. Without assumptions, action is impossible. The ideal public debate would clearly develop the value choices and assumptions implicit in every policy alternative so that the merits and liabilities of each proposal could fully be considered and courses of action rationally chosen. It would make people painfully aware of the value choices which must be made and are too often overlooked and would subject every assumption to the most rigorous possible analysis, something presently seldom done. Responsibility for achieving these ideal standards rests with opinion leaders, who structure the debate, and the informed public, the most active and frequent audience. The integrity and analytical skills of these two groups determine the level of the public debate.

Whether or not the public debate in the United States on foreign policy will ever achieve ideal standards is moot. While present debates are closer approximations than those of two decades ago, the need for and direction of further improvement is apparent.

FOR FURTHER READING:

Thomas A. Bailey, *The Man in the Street* (New York: The Macmillan Company, 1948).

William G. Carleton, *The Revolution in American Foreign Policy* (New York: Random House, rev. ed., 1957).

Robert A. Dahl, *A Preface to Democratic Theory* (Chicago: University of Chicago Press, 1956).

Dorothy Fosdick, *Common Sense and World Affairs* (New York: Harcourt, Brace and Company, 1955).

Norman Graebner, *The New Isolationism* (New York: The Ronald Press, 1956).

William Reitzel, Morton A. Kaplan, and Constance G. Coblenz, *United States Foreign Policy, 1945-1955* (Washington, D.C.: The Brookings Institution, 1956).

Chapter II

THE DEMOCRATIC PROCESS

A clear understanding of the democratic process is a necessary foundation for an effective public debate on foreign policy. Only through this can the public's role adequately be perceived. In democracies, as in all regimes, there is an obvious distinction between those who have political power and those who do not, between the governors and the governed. What distinguishes a democracy from other regimes is the nature of the relationships between those in power and their constituents. The copybook maxims defining these are well known. We have always assumed their validity and their general application in the United States. However, in recent years, especially with regard to foreign affairs, both the utility and the feasibility of these maxims have increasingly been questioned.

These doubts stem from two sources. Some commentators such as Walter Lippmann fear that democracies, and especially the United States, may not be adequate to the challenges of the mid-twentieth century. They derive their concern from the dismal failure of democracies in the period between the two world wars to take measures to insure their own security; this record is extrapolated into the present more dangerous era with frightening consequences. These commentators doubt the ability of the public to understand its long-range interests, and urge giving greater authority to professionals and the Executive branch in the formulation of foreign policy. The other source of questioning is social science. Increasing efforts in social science are being devoted to empirical research, and this has proved many of the copy-

17

book maxims on democracy demonstrably false. Public opinion polls indicate, for example, that approximately 30 per cent of the population is unaware of most foreign policy issues and another 45 per cent, aware but uninformed.* A New York *Times* survey published March 23, 1959, during the height of the Berlin crisis indicated that almost 40 per cent of those interviewed did not know that Berlin was an enclave in communist territory, an obviously crucial fact. Many have been led to question whether foreign policy can be formulated in a democratic fashion with such large areas of public ignorance. Some have sought to eliminate this ignorance through public education, but their efforts have not been notably successful.

In the first selection in this chapter, Lester B. Pearson, former Secretary of State for External Affairs of Canada, an individual with long experience in formulating and executing foreign policy in a democratic setting, and a friendly but not uncritical observer of United States democracy, attempts to answer the doubts which stem from the record of the Thirties. His is the classic defense of democracy, that the majority may not always be right, but that it knows its own desires better than anyone else. His historical examples are useful correctives to all too frequent tendencies to evaluate the record of democracies by abstract and unreal criteria, ignoring what other types of regimes have done, and to become so immersed in the dangers of our own age as to forget that there were also grave crises in earlier periods. His plea for individual responsibility seems to come closer to constructive advice than any criticism of institutional machinery. In adopting Edmund Burke's position on representation, however, he leaves open the question of how responsibility is to be enforced.

Gabriel A. Almond in the second selection is more concerned with this. Professor Almond's *The American People and Foreign Policy*, from which this extract is taken, is an attempt to integrate the findings of recent social science with traditional democratic theory, and to suggest a feasible method for improving the democratic process as it applies to foreign policy. Two of the terms he uses require explanation. His "elite" is the group referred to as "opinion leaders" in the previous chapter, those public officials and others who have access to important communications media and who structure the public debate. His "attentive

---

* Martin Kriesberg, "Dark Areas of Ignorance," pp. 49-64 in Lester Markel (ed.), *Public Opinion and Foreign Policy* (New York: Harper and Brothers, 1949), pp. 51-52.

public" is that group previously referred to as the "informed public"; the segment of the population interested in and informed about foreign policy. Almond's thesis is that the "elites" debate foreign policy alternatives before the "attentive public" and that the "general" or "mass" public reacts largely in terms of oversimplified moods, historically vacillating from a desire to participate in international affairs, to a desire to withdraw, and from idealism to cynicism. His concept of democracy is based on a division of labor. Particular note should be made of the role given interest groups in his analysis and recommendations: they play a significant part in enforcing responsibility.

Political parties are another device through which responsibility can be enforced. Our governmental system, however, places severe limits on the possible extent of partisan differences concerning foreign affairs. Positive action in international affairs inevitably requires bipartisan collaboration. A two-thirds majority in the Senate is necessary for ratification of any treaty, and it is unlikely that any party alone would have this strength. Further, a President usually cannot rely on all members of his party to support his programs in Congress and must consequently seek support elsewhere. These pressures are even greater when Congress is controlled by the opposition party, as it was in 1947 and 1948 and has been again since 1954. There are, of course, virtues to the necessity of bipartisan collaboration. It gives United States policy a consistency which might not otherwise exist, and a united America no doubt appears stronger to the outside world than it would if torn by partisan strife over foreign policy issues, but there are also costs which are frequently overlooked. Two political scientists with widely differing viewpoints, Willmoore Kendall of Yale University, a conservative, and James MacGregor Burns of Williams College, a liberal, analyze these costs in the last two selections. Both agree on the need for a more intensive and articulate public debate on foreign policy.

Democracy and the Power of Decision*

by Lester B. Pearson

The enlargement of the scope and scale of our international problems has been accompanied by—some say hopelessly complicated by—the increase within democratic states of the number of people who take part in determining the essential decisions of foreign policy. The vast majority of them do this indirectly, though decisively, through their votes. A growing number intervene more directly through the agencies that influence opinion, agencies such as press, radio, or television which can remove—or create—prejudice and ignorance. Increasing also, in certain forms of democratic rule, is the intervention of the individual member or committee of the legislature in the day-to-day decisions on and administration of foreign policy, something which has been traditionally the main responsibility of the executive.

Popular participation in foreign policy decisions in some form is, of course, inherent in the nature of the democratic process. This is as it should be. Nowadays, in free and democratic countries, foreign policy must not only seek to protect and advance the interests of all the citizens, but its principles and its major moves must carry their understanding and consent as well. Until comparatively recently, even in Western societies, decisions in this field were usually taken by a single ruler, or a few members of a ruling class. Sometimes, indeed, policies sought only to serve the interests of those few. Today it is very different. We are all concerned now. We are all masters and all servants. We are also all experts!

Those who today fear the confusing intellectual and emotional effect of legislative and popular intervention in the execution of foreign policy, who complain about the alleged prejudices and the unwise purposes that inspire much of this intervention, should not forget that selfish and unprincipled influences could also be and often were exerted in former years in the highly centralized government of a monarchy or a small group. The palace favourite, the courtier, or even the clown could, I suspect, often operate to obstruct good and wise decisions, or alter and confuse a carefully thought out foreign policy in the same way that mass

* From *Democracy in World Politics*, pp. 96-123, by Lester B. Pearson. Copyright 1955 by Princeton University Press and reprinted with their permission.

opinion and mass appeal can today. Countermeasures in those earlier days by the monarch's wise and patient foreign minister against a palace clique may, however, have been easier and more effective—though entailing no doubt greater personal physical risk—than those which a Secretary of State or a Foreign Minister can take today against a newspaper columnist, a radio commentator, or a legislative subcommittee!

Democracy may make for more numerous and more varied interventions in the control and execution of foreign policy. Autocracy certainly makes for more deep-set and sinister intrigue—as Moscow is our witness. A Secretary of State may lose some prestige and power if a legislative committee thinks he is a "deviationist" from what they feel to be wise and patriotic policy. A Foreign Commissar will lose far more than prestige if he finds himself in the same dilemma and running counter to the views of one or two or three dictators.

The fact remains, however, even though some of the worries caused by it may be unfounded, that the views and attitudes of millions of people, informed, misinformed, and uninformed, now play an important part in the formulation of policies.

It is often argued that the mass of people, in whom rests this final power, find it peculiarly difficult to face up fully to their responsibilities and to take the hard decisions, the wise rather than the opportunist ones, which may be required. Certainly history affords many instances of democratic inadequacy in this regard.

Twenty-three hundred years ago, in the pure, if restricted, democracy of Greece, there was a face-to-face relationship between people and leaders, the kind that television is reintroducing, at times with somewhat dubious results. Direct contact of this kind didn't always make for conviction, however, in those days, any more than it does today. You will recall how Demosthenes tried in vain to rouse the Athenian Assembly to the threat from Philip of Macedon, and how he failed, just as Sir Winston Churchill failed in the 1930's to rouse the British Parliament to the threat of the Nazis.

Thucydides tells us how, in 427 B.C., Cleon told the Assembly, "I have often before now realized that a democracy is incapable of empire. . . ." The reason for this incapacity, Cleon suggested, is that the members of the Assembly forget that other people are not like themselves. "The most alarming feature in the case," he asserted, "is the constant change of policies, and seeming ignorance of the fact that bad laws which are never changed are better for a city than good ones that have no authority." Cleon went on to describe his public—and to their face—in these terms:

> The persons to blame are you, who are so foolish as to institute these debates: you go to see an oration as you would to see a sight, you take your facts on hearsay and judge of the practicability of a project by the wit of its advocates, and trust for the truth about past events not to your eyes but to your ears—to some clever critic's words.

It has a contemporary ring, except that politicians today do not often talk like that to their electors.

Twenty-six centuries or so later Mr. Walter Lippmann, analyzing as "a field of equations" the series of interdependent choices with which government policy makers are faced, concluded that

> faced with these choices between the hard and the soft, the normal propensity of democratic governments is to please the largest number of voters. The pressure of the electorate is normally for the soft side of the equations.[1]

From this Mr. Lippmann draws the depressing conclusion that it is safer for a democratic politician to be wrong before it has become popular to be right, and tempting for him to keep in step with opinion rather than with events.

Mr. Lippmann is inclined to blame this on the pressure of mass opinion on government, on the contradictory character of mass purpose in using this pressure to attain policy objectives. To him "public opinion becomes less realistic as the mass to whom information must be conveyed and argument addressed grows larger and more heterogeneous."[2] This, he feels, accounts in large part for the conflicting and confusing nature of the pressures developed. These also tend to grow more and more passionate and insistent and dominating; and, according to Mr. Lippmann, "where mass opinion dominates, there is a morbid derangement of the true function of power."

It is not necessary to agree with the whole of Mr. Lippmann's thesis on this matter to admit that he has put his finger on a danger that certainly *can* result from this increase in direct popular determination and control of policy. Such control, if not exercised with responsibility and restraint, can undoubtedly facilitate that type of moral and intellectual

---

[1] Walter Lippmann, *The Public Philosophy*, pp. 45-46, Atlantic, Little Brown, 1955.
[2] Walter Lippmann, *The Public Philosophy*, p. 39.

deterioration which, throughout history, has preceded and been the effective cause of the overthrow, from within or without, of great societies.

It will help us to understand this danger if we look at one or two aspects of international politics during the last fifty years. One way of learning is trial and error, and we have had a heap of both. But experience in itself, though a valuable channel to wisdom, is no guarantee of it. It should moreover be measured less in how much happens around one than in the quality and intensity of awareness. You may remember Napoleon's comment when someone recommended one of his officers to him for promotion on the ground that he had been through an exceptional number of campaigns. "My horse," Napoleon is reported to have replied, "has been through even more." As Frederick the Great asked searchingly of his generals: "What good is your experience, if you have not reflected on it?"

If we are to reflect on and benefit from our experience, the first step must be to recall it. May I do so in relation to one matter.

Thirty years ago the thinking of many people in the United States was isolationist. A great number, perhaps the majority of Americans, felt remote from what was going on in Europe and were far from unhappy about that remoteness. They were, if not indifferent, apparently unaware that their own fate might be involved in these far-away matters.

Canadians, because of their history and traditions, though not immune from isolationism, have never felt to the same extent this remoteness from Europe. Canada's entry into war in 1914 and in 1939 was a result (and also, of course, a cause) of this attitude. Nevertheless there were many Canadians in the thirties, as there were more Americans, who hoped that they could sail by the European sirens, their ears stopped with the tax bills and their eyes blinded by the tears of the last great war.

In the twenties and thirties Canadian Governments, however, had another motive, no less compelling, for avoiding European entanglements. This lay in the profound differences of opinion held by various sections of the Canadian people, about the rights and wrongs of European issues and their concern for us. There were, of course, some Canadians, as there were many Americans, who shared the comfortable illusion that the oceans would suffice to protect us, and that our country could remain secure and untouched, outside any European conflict. But Canadian Governments in the 1930's sought to avoid acceptance of

political and security responsibilities in Europe or in the old League of
Nations, less because they really thought that they could thereby avoid
future military commitments if war came, than because they knew that
any expression of opinion more precise than pious generalities would
involve them immediately in domestic political difficulties at home.

If, in the decade before the Second World War, North America was
ineffective in world politics, either through a false sense of security or
through the weakness which profound divergences of opinion are apt to
bring, the performance of the democracies of Europe was no more
creditable and possibly even less so. They were closer to the danger, yet
they refused to see it. In many countries this refusal was reinforced by
a sort of paralysis of the will which was almost as disastrous as wrong
headedness and wrong policies. Intellectual error and inadequacy played
their part, of course; but a sort of moral blindness was, I think, primarily
responsible for the rot. It was not so much that people did not know
that a willingness to accept risks is sometimes necessary to the victories
of peace as well as of war, but that, necessary or not, they were unwilling to assume the responsibilities and sacrifices that action would involve.

In the 1930's the Western democracies reached a nadir which had
little or nothing to do with political institutions at home or diplomatic
method abroad, relatively little to do even with the state of knowledge
or intellect, a nadir which indicated something more like moral bankruptcy of societies and of the men who compose them.

In foreign relations and in domestic affairs, too, the 1930's reached a
low point. Technically, great progress was made, but a society can be
advanced in a technical field and backward in others. The depression
was certainly no mere technical matter, with its insulting paradox of
idle and hungry men in the midst of abundant resources; and it illustrated, I suggest, a failure of moral insight and social purpose in our
society. It seemed almost to be forgotten that men are the most important of any nation's resources, and their welfare the purpose of the economic process.

Then came a cruel and brutal but liberating experience. The development at the end of the thirties of an over-riding and coherent social
purpose (even though that purpose had to arise from a war which the
democracies a few years earlier might have prevented) drove home to
governments and people the lesson that for societies any objective

which is both physically possible and passionately desired is financially and politically possible also.

If I recall these ills of democratic society in the 1930's, which one might sum up as *malaise* in foreign policy and depression at home, it is to illustrate the point that no amount of democracy is a guarantee, in internal or external politics, either of good judgment as to methods or of a sound sense of direction as to ends.

It will also remind us of the speed with which a rot can spread when too many people in democratic societies forget their own standards.

Recall of the 1930's serves, finally, to counter present discouragements by reminding us that we have made great progress since then (though not without the appalling cost of war) on the return to political vitality and health.

The malady which Mr. Lippmann warns us against, of indecisiveness, reluctance to face reality or take the necessary but hard decisions, is not, as I see it, inherent in democracy as a political or constitutional system. It is, rather, the result of an internal derangement within individual men. This malady, which is contagious, can hit *any* society if enough men in positions of political influence abdicate their own responsibilities in favour of their special or selfish or superficial interests.

For this purpose, the key difference between a representative democracy and other forms of political society is that in the former every citizen as an elector is in a position to influence a decision; the attitudes of more people have an immediate and significant bearing on political events. When the moral tone of the majority is sound this is a source of strength, a reserve on which the society can draw and which will tend to remove the second-rate or shoddy from elected positions of power. In autocratic or oligarchic societies, on the other hand, the moral and intellectual flabbiness of only a few men in the seats of power will lead to the disintegration of great empires, as it did in 1917 in Czarist Russia.

Democracies are not, then, as I see it, more susceptible than other societies to the political disease which destroys civilizations, and which I have described as a loss of character and a weakening of moral fibre.

The demagogue, for instance, is merely the democratic version of the sycophantic courtier of absolute monarchy. He can reach more people but not, I suggest, bring as much decisive influence to bear on policy. His roars into the microphone are not as effective in this regard as the whisper in the monarch's or the despot's ear.

Just as absolute rulers, however, could be a prey to hypocrisy and insincerity in courtiers, who told the king not what they believed but what they thought the ruler wished to hear, so democracies can never be wholly immune against the same unamiable characteristics in those who seek position or power.

The disease, of course, occurs not only in demagogic politicians. It can develop in a foreign service, or a civil service, or in any other organization of government or of business, if officers shape their reports and recommendations not on their own honest judgment of a situation but on their estimate of whether a particular recommendation is likely to be popular and to earn them advancement now, or be unpopular ten years later, and earn them dismissal then.

This is an occupational hazard which the man of honesty and strength and moral courage will take in his stride.

Similarly, there is nothing in the theory or practice of democratic government which requires a public servant to speak or vote or act contrary to his own judgment of the nation's best interests. Politics has been well called "the art of the possible," and it is not only reasonable but useful and indeed indispensable that the practising politician should, before reaching a decision, make an estimate of the public acceptability of any given course; usually he will be right to adapt his timing and method of presentation to it. But that is a very different thing from acting against his own best judgment of what, all factors considered, the national interest requires. To do this latter is a form of betrayal.

The essential political principle of democracy is what is called responsible government: the provision that the government, if its exercise of power is not approved, can be removed from office by the electorate. This provision is in no sense based on the assumption, demonstrably false in the light of even short periods of history, that the opinion of the majority on every issue is invariably right; but rather on the sound theory that the most appropriate, though possibly not the most expert, judge of good cooking is not the man in the kitchen but the man in the dining room.

So far as I am aware, no democratic constitution beyond the town-meeting level has ever provided that the government should follow majority opinion on each issue that arises. What they do provide, on the contrary, is that the government is accountable either to a legislature or, at intervals of a few years, directly to an electorate. While the persistent flaunting of the conviction of the majority would render government impossible, there is no constitutional or political necessity for governments to be at the mercy of transient tempers or to be directed by opinion polls or by popular pressures into courses which they know to be wrong.

One of the best servants that a democracy has ever had, it seems to me, was Edmund Burke. It is worth recalling once again what he said to his electors at the Guildhall in Bristol, when they sought in midterm to harness him to their opinion on individual issues:

> . . . I did not obey your instructions. No. I conformed to the instructions of truth and Nature, and maintained your interest, against your opinions, with a constancy that became me. A representative worthy of you ought to be a person of stability. I am to look, indeed, to your opinions—but to such opinions as you and I *must* have five years hence. I was not to look to the flash of the day. I knew that you chose me, in my place, along with others, to be a pillar of the state, and not a weathercock on the top of the edifice, exalted for my levity and versatility, and of no use but to indicate the shiftings of every fashionable gale.

That was in 1780. His electors had already been given notice six years earlier of his conception—I submit a sound one—of his duty as a Member of Parliament. Listen to this:

> Certainly, Gentlemen, it ought to be the happiness and glory of a representative to live in the strictest union, the closest correspondence, and the most unreserved communication with his constituents. Their wishes ought to have great weight with him; their opinions high respect; their business unremitted attention. It is his duty to sacrifice his repose, his pleasure, his satisfactions, to theirs—and above all, ever, and in all cases, to prefer their interest to his own.
>
> But his unbiased opinion, his mature judgment, his enlightened conscience, he ought not to sacrifice to you, to any man, or to any set of men living. These he does not derive from your pleasure—no, nor from the laws and the Constitution. They are a trust from Providence, for the abuse of which he is deeply answerable. Your representative owes you, not his industry only, but his judgment; and he betrays, instead of serving you, if he sacrifices it to your opinion.

Burke certainly disagreed with the theory that members of the legislature should consider themselves merely agents of their electors, bound to echo local prejudices or to vote in response to pressure from a lobby of local interests. He unhesitatingly told his constituents:

. . . Parliament is a deliberative assembly of *one* nation, with *one* interest, that of the whole—where not local purposes, not local prejudices, ought to guide, but the general good, resulting from the general reason of the whole. You choose a member, indeed; but when you have chosen him, he is not a member of Bristol, but he is a member of *Parliament*. If the local constituent should have an interest or should form an hasty opinion evidently opposite to the real good of the rest of the community, the member for that place ought to be as far as any other from any endeavour to give it effect.

This may sound, in 1955, like a counsel of perfection. Yet Burke's words were merely a prescription of what has always been essential for the political health of any democratic society. Its basic ingredient is, and always will be, not so much political form or constitutional structure, as the character of individuals. What Burke told his electors was put more briefly by an American who asserted "I'd rather be right than be President."

In emphasizing that the determining factor in making democracy work is the character of individual men, I do not of course mean to minimize the value of constitutional devices and political institutions. One of the values of such institutions is precisely that they crystallize and embody the political insights of the past and thus help to transmit to the future the wisdom, restraint, and character of former generations. . . .

Whatever the relative merits of its various forms, experience during the past thirty years has shown major instances when *all* types of democracy have shirked commitments and refused to make the hard, necessary decisions which the situation required. On the other hand, since 1947 most of the great democracies, and notable among them the most powerful of all, the United States of America, have assumed responsibilities and accepted burdens unprecedented in time of peace.

The essential point to grasp is that there exists for democracies in world politics a set of issues which does not change with and is not determined by external situations, and which has little to do with diplomatic methods or constitutional procedures. This is what I might call the climate, the character, the moral basis, of our society. It would be foolish to say that our future in world politics depends exclusively on ourselves, for we are not alone. But it seems to me beyond question that that future, in foreign policy as elsewhere, will depend to a much greater extent on this internal factor than on anything else—on our quality as peoples, on what we believe in, and on what we really stand for.

The more I see of the policies and processes of government, the more remarkable it seems to me that serious and intelligent men could ever have brought themselves to propound or to accept the doctrine of historical determinism in any of its forms: the suggestion that we are slaves of fate and playthings of destiny. Such a view is only comprehensible when the human intellect loses its moral bearings.

Such a surrender is, of course, the essence of all theories of determinism. It not only blurs but blots out the whole question. For precisely what gives significance to life and history and politics is the possibility which men and nations always possess, though they by no means always use it, of acting creatively in their environment rather than merely reacting to it. To some extent, of course, all men transmit to the future impulses determined by the conditioning of the past, or respond almost mechanically to impulses from outside. But men can do more than this. If they will, they can always in some degree transform the situation in which they find themselves. They can take creative action which, while tailor-made, as it were, to fit the environment, is in no sense merely a product of it.

The whole of our belief in the possibility of constructive action, whether by men or nations, is of course based on the assumption that man, and his mind, are more than merely products of heredity and environment, that he does have this possibility of contact with the unconditioned realm of the spirit. Public opinion and political judgment, therefore, are bound to reflect among other things the level of a people's moral insight and spiritual stature. This is as true in international as in domestic affairs.

I have often heard it said, as I am sure you have, and particularly regarding foreign policies, that governments pursue their national interest irrespective of moral considerations. This verdict, I think, begs most of the real questions. Of course governments pursue the national interest as they conceive it. That is their duty. The real questions are, however, first, how accurately governments (or people) can discern what is the real national interest, and second, how wisely they act in trying to reach the goals which they set. But here moral, even more than political, insight is required to decide where your real interest lies, and how to achieve it.

The foreign policy of a democracy is thus in large part a product and a test of the moral insight of a whole people.

In stressing the decisive relation of moral considerations to effective judgment—in international affairs as in other fields of activity—I am not, of course, suggesting that all political and diplomatic questions should be regarded as issues between right and wrong. Far from it. A moral approach to problems does not require that we should see all of them in simple terms of challenges to righteousness, or of black and white.

Indeed the contrary is true, and gray is the prevailing shade. This should induce humility and tolerance. . . .

An arrogant Pharisaism and smug satisfaction with one's own superior righteousness, in a person or in a nation, are not only unamiable qualities, they are not conducive to clear political judgment. The man whose humility and moral sensitivity is *least* highly developed is most likely to confuse principle with questions of fact or expediency, and to make an easy subconscious identification of his own viewpoint with the cause of right.

Furthermore, self-righteousness in international affairs is likely to lead to rigidity of thought and intolerance of other views. This often prevents a wise understanding of complex and changing situations, and tends to make diplomacy captive and inflexible. . . .

When societies disintegrate—as several societies, European and Asian, have disintegrated during the past forty years under totalitarian pressure—the real explanation is that pointed out long ago by a Hebrew prophet: "Where there is no vision the people perish." We are far too apt to pigeonhole this in our minds as a moral exhortation rather than to recognize it for the hardheaded political observation that it is.

If this is true, then the greatest danger to our civilization today lies not outside, but within. . . .

It is, I think, clear that during the first four decades of this century the vision of Western society was weakened. The results are apparent enough to anyone who will take the trouble to reflect honestly on the history of our times.

But the deepest tradition of our civilization is precisely the capacity for creative response and renewal. It is possible, and may indeed be probable, that the trend has now turned, that man may be moving, even if somewhat unsteadily, toward a rebirth. We cannot afford much unsteadiness in the nuclear era, of course. But it is, I think, reasonable to believe that within democratic society during the past few years progress has on the whole been in the right direction.

If today we are justified in being cautiously optimistic, one ground for this lies, I think, in the very scale and profundity of the challenges which face us.

One advantage from external threats, as any good historian will point out, is that they may be used to prompt constructive responses, that they may lead to efforts and achievements which were in any case desirable but which, without the pressure from outside, men would have been too indolent or too shortsighted to undertake. Such pressure may thus sometimes be recognized later as an asset, leading to the development of habits and institutions of cooperation which remain to give men life and growth long after the challenge which impelled them has subsided or been destroyed.

The union in the 1760's of the thirteen American colonies, in reaction against pressure from Britain, is one example of this creative response. Confederation of the Canadian colonies a century later is another, prompted as it was to no small extent by fear of expansion from our powerful southern neighbours who at that time seemed to us flushed with visions of "manifest destiny" on a continental scale.

Certain recent examples also stand out. North American economic assistance after 1945 for the reconstruction of the democracies of Western Europe would, in any case, have been desirable, but it might not have been forthcoming on any adequate scale had it not been for the threat of Soviet imperialism in Eastern Europe.

In the development of North Atlantic cooperation in other fields, and in the habits of consultation to which it gives rise, there can without too much fancy be discerned a trend toward the revitalization of the old sense of community of Western Christendom. These things may prove of use to men long after the defence needs of this generation have receded.

Similarly, cooperation between civilizations, including substantial economic and technical aid, while desirable in itself, is made easier of achievement by consciousness of external danger. If we survive the present tensions, it is, I think, not at all inconceivable that the contacts now being established under pressure may prove fruitful and constructive long after the external stimulus has disintegrated or subsided.

More important, however, than any other factor is, I repeat, the internal response; for a healthy society depends essentially on subjective factors, and the fundamental characteristics of a civilization are not institutions but how people feel, the way they think, above all the things they consider worth doing.

Life has always faced men with two fundamental questions: what to do, and how to do it. This is the age-old question of ends and means, always interdependent, always subject to derangement if priority is placed on methods rather than on the selection of goals.

"How?" is, of course, a technical question; and in all technical areas except the social sciences the West has, during the past half-century, produced triumphant answers. Indeed it is often suggested that the cure for most of our political and economic problems lies in putting behind the social sciences something of the same emphasis and energy and imagination that have paid off so strikingly in the natural science fields.

But there is, I think, more to it than this. What is really needed is rather to pay more attention to the primary question of goals: of *what* is worth doing.

This brings us into the field of values, where the emphasis is less on the mind than on the will, less on method than on the choice of ends. What is needed here—as I have already said—is vision accompanied by a hard-headed sense of reality. The two can and should go together.

The true realist is the man who sees things both as they are and as they can be. In every situation there is the possibility of improvement, in every life the hidden capacity for something better. True realism involves a dual vision, both sight and insight. To see only half the situation, either the actual or the possible, is to be not a realist but in blinkers. Of the two visions, the latter is the rarer, and the more important. But to be whole, and to be effective, we need both.

It is a fundamental principle of *all* the great religions of man, that values have objective existence—that they are, indeed, aspects of a reality which is universal and absolute. Recognition that these values can be only partially apprehended by individual men, only partially embodied in any particular piece of matter, only provisionally expressed in any given law or work of art, has taught us, or should have done, the necessity of tolerance and understanding.

Where erosion is at work, however, these qualities of tolerance relapse into indifference, into a lazy assumption that one view, one taste, one response is as good as another, with the corollary that none matters much. As a result, we sink into an uncritical acceptance of the shoddy and the second rate. This can be as great a danger as prejudice and in-tolerance, for it strikes at the very root of growth and healthy development.

I do not wish to close, however, on a note of pessimism or gloom. So may I return to where I began: to history, which provides a useful corrective to our worries and our present discontents and shows us that, while there is today great need for wisdom and resolution, there is no cause for defeatism or dismay.

Man, faced with the sad memories and the grim consequences of his failures to live peaceably with other men, has many times accepted as inevitable the prophecies of a doom that he has somehow managed to escape. Pessimistic speculation, or indeed *any* speculation, about the future is always a risky intellectual pursuit. In the eighteenth century the British Empire was considered lost beyond salvation at the dawn of its greatest hour. "I dare not marry; the future is so dark and unsettled," said William Wilberforce in 1790. Twenty-five years later, after Napoleon's new order had collapsed on the field of Waterloo as the old guard charged into the sunset and died, the confusion and turmoil seemed to many to presage total domination of Europe by the Czar's Muscovite hordes, whose presence aroused in the minds of Western Europeans emotions that have a familiar echo today. But in only a few years the Cossacks had retired to the Don, and Europe was given another chance to work out its salvation. Some thirty years later, on his deathbed in the midst of that enviable if somewhat stuffy era of calm and contentment which we have called Victorian, the great Duke of Wellington sighed, "I thank God that I am spared the ruin that is gathering around us."

The fact is that, to every challenge given by the threat of death and destruction, there has always been the response from free men, "It shall not be." By these responses man has not only saved himself, but has ensured his future.

May it be so again this time, as we face the awful and the glorious possibilities of the nuclear age.

Consensus in a World of Crisis*

by Gabriel A. Almond

The "crisis of Western man" has become a common theme among learned men. Theologians decry the secularization of modern life, the decline of religious feeling, and the rise of materialism and "scientism." College presidents deplore the rise of vocationalism and the decay of humanist cultural ideals. Critics of the arts struggle against the domination of "mass" standards of taste and the crumbling of esthetic discrimination. Sociologists and social philosophers are troubled by the breakdown of older forms of community relations and the costs of urban industrial civilization in human isolation and insecurity. Business leaders and economists caution against the consequences of the decline of the risk-taking mentality and the emergence of security as a dominant social value. Psychiatrists and psycho-anthropologists comment on the competitiveness of modern life and the impairment of human relations which it entails. This is but a partial summary of the modern jeremiad.

One of the most interesting interpretations of the modern crisis of the spirit, an interpretation which brings into focus many of the problems with which we have been concerned, is the "privatization" hypothesis of Ernst Kris and Nathan Leites. These writers propose that in the mass societies of the twentieth century, politics and public affairs have come to impinge ever more closely on the life of the common man. In a formal sense, the masses determine the basic political decisions which affect them, and they are encouraged by their leaders to believe that they actually exercise such power. But the complexity of modern economic and political decisions and the professionalization of the decision-making process has created the feeling that in actuality the masses can neither *understand* nor *influence* the very events upon which their life and happiness is known to depend." [1] There has been, according to this view, an increasing sense of "incompetence" among the masses. Thus, in contrast to the era of political decentralization, when the average man is said to have had a sense of relatedness to, and understanding of,

---

* From *The American People and Foreign Policy*, pp. 226-244, by Gabriel A. Almond, copyright, 1950, by Harcourt, Brace and Company, Inc. and reprinted with their permission.

[1] E. Kris and N. Leites, "Trends in Twentieth Century Propaganda," in *Psychoanalysis and the Social Sciences*, 1947, pp. 393 ff.

politics, contemporary Americans (and Western Europeans) have a sense of dependence upon, and distrust of, remote elites and decision-makers. This sense of powerlessness and suspicion is not discharged constructively in the form of "critical distrust" and critical evaluation of policy proposals and decisions. It cannot be expressed in constructive ways because the ordinary individual lacks the knowledge and analytical ability to evaluate policy in an age of complex interdependence. "He [the common man] therefore regressively turns to projective distrust: He fears, suspects and hates what he cannot understand and master." [2] He projects his own feelings of hostility and resentment, continually fed by his sense of powerlessness and of being a tool manipulated for purposes other than his own, on his leaders. In the mind of the common man the leadership groups become malevolent, cynical, self-seeking and corrupt. In conclusion, these writers suggest that if "the appropriate education on a vast enough scale and at a rapid enough rate is not provided for, the distrust and privatization of the masses may become a fertile soil for totalitarian management."

In the present state of knowledge it is impossible to accept or reject such a hypothesis. We have seen that, particularly in relation to foreign policy, the feeling of powerlessness among Americans is widespread. But these feelings of powerlessness are most marked among the lower-income and lower-educational strata. They are less characteristic of the "attentive public" which feels itself capable of exercising in some measure the kind of "critical distrust" which represents a sound response to the modern political division of labor. Instead of withdrawing into private rancor and suspicion, the attentive public subjects policy to more or less-informed criticism. Furthermore, with the broadening of educational opportunity and the general rise in the standard of living in the course of the past decades, it would seem that this attentive public has expanded.

It is indeed an arguable point as to whether Americans have been withdrawing from political involvement. In some areas we may perhaps speak of an increasing sense of political involvement and relatedness. Thus if we take the moral tone of American political life in the past half century, we find a genuine decline in the cruder forms of corruption and manipulation. The urban public of today is more effectively related to urban politics than was the case in the era of the "shame of the

---

[2] *Ibid.*, p. 402.

cities." But it is not related to politics in any direct sense of the term. It is related to politics through a *division of labor*. What broke the hold of the older and grosser forms of urban political corruption was the rise of effective civic elites capable of competing with the politicians, and the broadening of the attentive public through educational opportunity and rising standards of living.

There is a certain tendency to treat the nineteenth century in the United States as a utopian age of mass political involvement. Actually this was the era during which de Tocqueville called the United States "blessed" because it did not need a foreign policy. In his judgment, had the United States been involved in world politics, her survival would have been seriously threatened by the instability of the American democracy, its intense involvement in private affairs, and its proclivities for evangelistic interventions. The nineteenth century also was the era of the great waves of evangelism and complacency in urban politics. This was attributable to a kind of privatism which was perhaps stronger in the nineteenth century than it is today.

Actually political involvement in the United States in the era before the first world war tended to take the form either of evangelistic political religiosity or hard and narrow interest calculation. There was, as we have already seen, a certain cyclical fluctuation from the one mood to the other. What seems to be developing today is a disenchantment with all sweeping ideals and, in addition, a rejection of the older forms of narrow interest calculation. Thus in the first world war the United States joined the Allies in a mood of sweeping idealism. The disenchantment that followed in the next decade was in part a consequence of the collapse of these exorbitant hopes. In the second world war a more wary people rejected millennial aspirations. There was less willingness to accept general slogans and a greater resistance to propaganda. The mood responses of soldiers asked to fight,[3] and of civilians asked to sacrifice, were generally couched in simple terms of defense against aggression.

In this, as in other areas, there has undoubtedly been a decline in belief in general principles and ideals and a preference for interest calculation with the self as the starting point. But this tendency does not necessarily lead to political withdrawal and bitterness. It may lead into a broadening rationality in which the interdependence of individual

---

[3] Samuel A. Stouffer *et al.*, *The American Soldier: Adjustment During Army Life*, Princeton University Press, 1949, Vol. I, pp. 431 ff.

and social action is recognized and in which there is a sober respect for the inevitability of division of labor in the making of complex policy decisions. Those writers who view the political apathy of the masses as a simple manifestation of social pathology have perhaps overlooked a number of essential aspects of the problem.

If we take any of the great problems of American foreign policy—such as the control of atomic energy, or the problem of Western European or Ear Eastern stability and security—we have to recognize that even the most highly trained specialists have to act in the dark and on the basis of anxious guess-work. There is indeed a constructive sense of economy of effort in the reaction of the "common man" who refuses to involve himself and to accumulate knowledge about these problems. Would he be in any better position to evaluate policy if he were able to pass the information tests posed by the public opinion researchers? Suppose all adult Americans knew the name of their Secretary of State, could locate Iran on a blank map, could identify the raw materials from which fissionable materials are derived, and could list the permanent members of the Security Council in alphabetical order, could they then make a sound decision whether military aid under the North Atlantic Pact should be a billion dollars or a billion and a half? This approach to the problem of public information operates on a kind of "Quiz Kids" standard. Anyone who has gone through the experience of trying to analyze a policy is aware of the fact that in the first period of concentrated effort, increased knowledge results in increased confusion and indecision. Since the great mass of the public lacks the time, energy, and training necessary for more than the most superficial consideration of foreign policy problems, widespread mass ignorance and indifference are hardly to be viewed as simple pathologies.

Mass indifference toward problems of foreign policy is partly justified by the great proliferation of interest organizations in the past fifty years or so. The public is not only represented in the formal political sense by a variety of elected officials, but there are few groups of any size in the United States today which do not have their interest representation. *Mass inattention* to problems of public policy is accompanied by the *accentuation* of *elite attention*. The trade-union leader, the agricultural lobbyist or propagandist, the official of the Chamber of Commerce is "paid" to look out for the interests of the worker, farmer, or businessman. There is, undoubtedly, considerable distrust among the masses of their political and interest representation, a distrust which is largely sound and healthy. Pressure group leaders are agents, and there can be little question that they bear watching. Anyone who has had experience with agency relationships becomes aware of the constructive value of distrust and lack of confidence.

In the last half century the American population has developed a political structure adapted to an era of mass democracy and social interdependence. The implications of these developments have been accepted with great reluctance and in the form of an "under-the-counter" transaction. The myth of democratic spontaneity and mass control still holds sway "above the counter," only to trouble the literal minds of young people, and older people who have resisted the impact of experience.

These considerations are of significance for public information policy. Only recently an analysis of the results of a foreign information campaign in Cincinnati showed that even a heavy concentration of information through the mass media of communication had no perceptible effects.[4] According to the criteria used by the polling organization, approximately the same percentages of respondents were informed and ignorant after the campaign, as before.

What accounts for this mass immunity to information on foreign policy problems? The public information specialist who operates through the mass media reasons by analogy from the success of advertising. Advertisers get enormous results from radio, newspaper and periodical advertising, while information on the United Nations distributed through the same media appears to get no results at all. The point seems to be that the masses are already predisposed to want automobiles, refrigerators, and toothpaste, but they are not predisposed to want information about the United Nations or the control of atomic energy. Such information has no immediate utility or meaning.

What this and other studies suggest is that there is no mass market for detailed information on foreign affairs. The general public looks for *cues* for *mood responses* in public discussion of foreign policy. It does not listen to the content of discussion but to its tone. A presidential statement that a crisis exists will ordinarily be registered in the form of apprehension. A reassuring statement will be received with complacency reactions. In both cases the reaction has no depth and no structure.

But if there is no "quantity" market for information about foreign

---

[4] National Opinion Research Center, University of Chicago, *Cincinnati Looks at the United Nations*, Report 37; *Cincinnati Looks Again*, Report 37 A.

affairs, there is an important quality market. And it is through this quality market that an articulate and broad foreign policy consensus can be shaped and maintained. Through a disciplined democratic elite and a broad attentive public, foreign policy moods may be contained and gross fluctuations in attitude checked. No slick public relations campaign will "do the trick." The side-show barker who can appeal to well-established appetites will get the "cash," but little more than self-intoxication results from a grass roots campaign in Middletown, Ohio, "to relate Middletowners to the world in which we live." We are dealing with a complex political structure which has special points of access. If we shout at the wall, we can take a certain satisfaction in a ringing echo. But if we come up closer, we can find openings through which a quiet word might reach a listening ear.

An effective approach to public information on foreign policy questions will therefore be selective and qualitative. It will be directed toward enlarging the attentive public and training the elite cadres. This is not to suggest that the mass public is to be overlooked or neglected. A sound information program will confront the common man continually with opportunities to be informed and involved in foreign policy decisions. There should be a standing invitation for him to join the attentive public if and when he is ready to make the essential sacrifices of time and energy. The repetition of slogans and occasional promotional campaigns directed at the mass public through the mass media have the primary consequence of minimizing the complexities of the problem and encouraging self-deception.

The containment of mass moods and the broadening and qualitative improvement of the attentive public may be approximated through a bettering of elite selection and training. Our efforts ought to be directed toward the articulate points in the political structure. Both a democratic and effective foreign policy may be shaped and maintained as long as we have trained and disciplined elites competing for influence before an attentive public. These elites constitute an elaborate system of representation; they are (although in quite different ways and degrees) responsible to mass constituencies.

We have already referred to the shortcomings of the various American elites—politicians, bureaucrats, pressure group leaders, journalists, social scientists, and the like. If we set as our standard of elite performance in foreign policy the objectives of democratic discipline, ideological consensus, and the development of a systematic and integrative mentality,

we are led inevitably to the two primary training elites—the teachers
and the clergy. These elites appear to fall short of fulfilling their tasks
in a number of respects. Teachers and clergymen tend to be the bearers
of moral and political idealism. They are susceptible to millennial hopes,
and thereby lay the groundwork for cynical rejections and disillusion-
ments among their charges. In this respect they contribute to American
moral dualism; they are responsible in part for the persistence of instability in American opinion. They set up aspirations which cannot be
fulfilled, and inculcate principles of conduct which cannot be effective.

There is no short cut to the improvement of the educational and
religious elites. What might be proposed are such changes in the training of teachers and the clergy as will make it increasingly difficult for
the practitioners of these professions to evade political reality. Few
clergymen and teachers even in the purely formal sense study "politics."
They are rarely called upon to confront the real problems of military
and political security. An already strong penchant for escapism, which
often lies at the basis of their choice of these professions, is encouraged
by curricula badly adapted to the broad character-molding and ideal-
setting function these elites are called on to perform.

It is the special task of the educational elites—and particularly in
higher education—to develop those analytical and integrative modes of
thought so essential in policy-makers. The institutions of higher learning—and the social sciences in particular—have a potential function
which cannot be sufficiently emphasized. The attentive public is largely
a college-educated public, and the political, interest, and communications elites are also largely college trained. It is in the social sciences in
the universities that a democratic ideological consensus can be fostered
and a democratic elite discipline encouraged.

One of the factors responsible for the indiscipline of the democratic
elites and for the persistence of ideological confusion, is the absence of a
coherent theory of society and politics. The aim of such a theory would
be to clarify the value premises and conflicts of the politically significant
cultures and social groupings of our time. This is not to suggest that all
conflicts will be resolved once the social sciences achieve a measure of
theoretical clarity. What this would facilitate would be a type of discussion of public policy issues in which premises would be explicit and
consequences of alternative policies comparatively clear. Developments
in the social sciences in this direction would make it increasingly diffi-

cult for the policy and opinion elites to produce those magnificent in-consistencies, *non sequiturs,* and frequent elisions of logical analysis which confuse and obscure the public debate of important policy ques-tions. A democratic discipline and a democratic consensus do not call for full and continuous agreement. What they require are a rational statement of the alternatives and a consensus as to the mode of selec-tion among them. A homogeneous training in this kind of policy analy-sis might contribute to the development of a common language among the various elite sectors, a common method of problem-setting and prob-lem-solving.

Among the interest elites perhaps the most important objective is to moderate the rigid assertion of narrow interest by the insight and analytical clarity of the specialist. Sound interest representation is one of the most important methods of clarifying policy alternatives. The various interest positions can hardly be imagined in the detached study of the scholar, or adequately asserted by the politician who represents a heterogeneous constituency. The foreign policy orientations of interest groups would be greatly improved if these special points of view were screened through the minds of persons who have analytical familiarity with alternative foreign policies, persons who can set special interest advocacy in the context of social and political consequences. Efforts to foster such a development are hardly utopian, since the pressure groups themselves have begun to set the pattern of relying on specialists. It does not follow, of course, that the mere inclusion of such specialists will lead to a broader and more flexible conception of interest representa-tion. Specialists, particularly where they have lost contact with their professions, often become mere interest advocates, using their skills to make more impressive cases for policies which have not been subjected to any analysis at all. Nevertheless, the presence of foreign policy special-ists on the staffs of pressure groups cannot fail in the long run to make some improvement in the policy-making processes of these organiza-tions. They introduce certain delays in action and complexities of in-sight and detail which act as barriers to the simple extension of group interest into the foreign policy arena. A sound information program on foreign policy will encourage this process of professionalization among the pressure group elites, will maintain continued contact with these specialists, and will endeavor to keep alive their professional standards.

This conception of professionalism—in the sense of the dignity of the calling—is the hallmark of a mature democratic elite. In a totalitarian society the elites acquire their dignity through the fulfillment of commands which in turn are derived from authoritative interpretations of the totalitarian mission. In this sense, they perform a duty which is specific and compulsory.

The democratic elites cannot appeal to this doctrine of authoritative mission and command. Though they are subject to the control of employers, the fluctuations of markets, and the choices of constituents, they have an area of discretion in defining their missions. There is room for conscience. From what sources do they derive their vocational criteria? The essence of the conception of professionalism—whether it be in politics, law, administration, journalism, scholarship, or the arts—is that the function of the particular calling sets certain standards of performance. Thus in journalism certain criteria flow from the task of providing information about significant events. Providing misinformation is a violation of the calling, just as a biased selection of information deviates from the standard of "getting out the news." It is not accidental that the controversies over the ethics of journalism turn on this question of whether the "news" has been fairly represented. Both the press and the critics of the press agree on the principle that the press has a *task*, and that this task involves giving a valid representation of significant events. The development of professionalism, as distinguished from the simple exercise of certain skills, involves this constant evaluation of performance according to the criteria set by the calling itself.

Thus we may say of the various foreign policy elites—in government, in the mass media, in academic life, and in the voluntary associations— that professionalism involves a constant search for the most adequate policy means to realize the values of their clienteles, whether they serve humanity, nations, social classes, religious movements, or age and sex groups.

If the intellectual and emotional energies of the elites are genuinely freed to pursue the implications of these value preferences, there comes a point where the values of humanity, nation, and class begin to converge, where common values begin to take their place beside the special ones. This is the "end of the rainbow" of the great rational consensual aspirations of Western man; it is to be sought in the modern era not by democratic spontaneity, but by democratic professionalism.

The dignity of the political calling rests on responsibility to the constituency, however this may be conceived, and to the values to which it aspires.[5] The dignity of the social-scientific calling rests on the clarification of value premises, the analysis of the adequacy of means, and the consequences of social action.[6] The dignity of the journalistic calling rests on the truthful representation of significant happenings. The dignity of the interest-group calling derives from the responsible representation of special interest in the context of political and social consequences. These elite values are more or less felt by those who perform these tasks. But the conditions affecting the exercise of these callings vary greatly in the degree of discretion left open to the individual practitioner. Perhaps the academic elites are least pressed with the urgency of routine and least restricted in the formulation of their goals. Those of us who would facilitate the development of this professionalism among the democratic elites will find that the starting point lies in the training of character and intellect. And a special responsibility attaches to those who have the task of interpreting man and his institutions to the new elite generations.

The argument so far advanced has had to do primarily with the tactics of a public information program in the sphere of foreign affairs. It has suggested an approach through political structure rather than through mass campaigns, through qualitative changes at key points rather than through quantitative information. But what of the substantive problems of American opinion on foreign affairs?

Perhaps the gravest general problem confronting policy-makers is that of the instability of mass moods, the cyclical fluctuations which stand in the way of policy stability. Such stabilization may in part be achieved by the kind of elite discipline which has already been discussed. But there is evidence which suggests that the era of great fluctuations in American opinion may have passed, that some balance between the poles of American moods on foreign affairs may have been approximated. The comparative sobriety of American participation in World War II and the comparatively moderate decline in interest in foreign affairs in the postwar period substantiate such a hypothesis. Perhaps the contemporary American neither soars to such heights nor falls to such depths as has been the case in the past. The impact of historical experience has placed a ceiling on hopes and a floor on disappointment.

But even moderate fluctuations of moods may have serious con-

---

[5] H. H. Gerth and C. Wright Mills, *From Max Weber: Essays in Sociology*, Oxford University Press, 1946, pp. 77 ff.
[6] *Ibid.*, pp. 129 ff.

sequences. While it is difficult to believe that the present readiness for foreign policy commitments will ever be supplanted by the kind of withdrawal which occurred after World War I, even a moderate return of complacency may seriously undermine the effectiveness of foreign policy. Such complacency affords opportunities to special interest elites to weaken the effect of foreign policy programs by the introduction of special exceptions and by penny-wise economies.

Thus the consequence of fluctuations in Soviet pressure may take the form of moderate American fluctuations in readiness to sacrifice. It is probably unrealistic to hope that such irrationalities in American foreign policy can be eliminated by any available means. On the other hand, there is a certain tendency to attribute to the Soviet elites a degree of policy discretion which their actual power situation is hardly likely to tolerate. To what extent and for what periods of time can the Soviet and Communist elites put on a conciliatory front without seriously weakening their own power position? American resolution cannot be greatly affected by mere verbal conciliation, and the Communists cannot accept a genuine stabilization without seriously weakening the dynamism and unity of their *movement*.

There are problems of American opinion which arise from the special attitudes and feelings of the various social groupings in the United States. The lower-income, unskilled labor, and the relatively uneducated groups present the most serious problems. These are the social groupings which seem to fit the "privatization" hypothesis of Kris and Leites. The evidence suggests that among the poor and ignorant of the cities and the countryside there are widespread feelings of powerlessness, of resentment, and bitterness, which produce a certain susceptibility to activist movements—whether they take the form of radical utopianism or reactionary nationalism. Democracy of participation and opportunity has never reached these elements in any adequate way. It is simple enough to say that we must reach these groups with propaganda and information, that we must lighten these dark areas of ignorance by short-run steps of one kind or another. All such direct approaches are bound to be of limited value at best. These groups lack both the motivation and the intellectual skills to make such information meaningful.

Only in the long-run and indirect ways can the lower-income groups be effectively related to American political life. This can be done through the spread of educational and social opportunity and the development of effective interest organization among them. The swift development of trade-union organization in the past fifteen years has produced elites and small attentive publics within certain sectors of this lower-income stratum. But there are still large groups which are inarticulate and unorganized—notably, the Negroes, the foreign born, and the rural poor. A sound democratic strategy would be directed at the creation of trained elites among these groups. But even these developments would represent a mere beginning. We should anticipate among these elites psychological phenomena quite comparable to the behavior of the new elites among the dependent peoples of the world. Only partly accepted in the established elite structure, they tend to be unstable, anxious, and insecure. They are, in the language of Kurt Lewin, "uncertain of their psychological ground." [7] Since these lower-income and lower-educational groups constitute so serious a problem, efforts at elite improvement and at establishing attentive strata should be concentrated in these areas. And yet, most of our efforts at present are directed toward the middle- and upper-class elements.

While it has been possible to identify an "attentive stratum" among the American public, relatively little is known about its dimensions and characteristics. We know that it is "informed" and that it possesses some of the details essential to the understanding of public policy; but the criteria employed are minimal and quantitative in character. We know that it is largely a college-educated stratum, but here again we have little information about its emotional and intellectual characteristics. The truth of the matter is that we know extremely little about the characteristics of the attentive public and the American elites save that they exist according to our criteria. An effective campaign directed toward stabilizing and articulating foreign policy moods requires thorough investigation and analysis before objectives and means can be established. The present analysis merely opens the problem for discussion.

The academic and religious elites have already been cited as the bearers of moral wishful thinking. The strata most susceptible to such thinking are the younger generations and women. Here again, quantitative campaigns through the mass media are of quite limited value. The approach has to be through the civic elites of the younger generations and the feminine organizational elites. Both of these groups are largely college products. If it were to become increasingly difficult for young people of either sex to complete their educations without confronting

[7] Kurt Lewin, *Resolving Social Conflicts*, Harper, 1948, pp. 145 ff.

historical and political reality, the problem of youthful and feminine idealism might in part take care of itself.

The pessimism and bitterness among the older age groups is a problem of another order. It cannot be solved by intellectual training; it raises questions fundamental to American culture. American culture stresses instrumental knowledge, activism, accomplishment, success. The old in America, the potential bearers of mature wisdom, are pushed from the focus of attention as symbols of the meaninglessness of human effort and death. There is something deeply moving in the modern discovery of the neuroses of old age and in the utopian security movements of the older generations of the last twenty years. Such problems as these can only be resolved when the panic and urgency of American culture subside and honest relationships with tragedy and death are established.

Finally, we come to the shadow cast over human expectations through the discovery of the "unconventional" weapons of modern military technology. Since the beginning of the nineteenth century the physical security anxieties[8] of nations and peoples have risen, as their capacity for destruction has increased. By reason of geographic accident, Americans have been protected from the world struggle for power. They have tended to view the older peoples of the world as living in the fallen state of power politics. Americans now too have eaten of the forbidden fruit and have been driven from Eden. But they have registered the increased risks and costs of political life only in an oblique way. They have repressed the personal meanings and implications of these developments.

The absence of overt concern should not conceal the fact that we are sitting on feelings of strong potential force which events may release with the most serious consequences. When the Soviet Union comes to the point of being able to reach the United States with modern weapons of destruction, the period of short-run American security will have run out. The psychological mechanisms which have produced a certain overt complacency in a world hardly suited to this mood will no longer control. Public opinion unprepared for the power game with such prohibitive stakes may either force premature decisions or delay timely ones.

There is, of course, a dilemma confronting efforts at preparing Americans for risks such as these. A premature mass campaign in the absence of an immediate threat might create "wolf, wolf" reactions, which would reduce the effectiveness of appeals at a later and more threatening

---

[8] John Herz, "Idealist Internationalism and the Security Dilemma," *World Politics*, Vol. II, No. 2 (January 1950), pp. 157-180.

time. At the same time, failure to prepare for these contingencies would leave us vulnerable to possible future panic.

Perhaps the wisest procedure at this stage of comparative American safety would be directed at the twofold aim of creating general public confidence that future contingencies are being planned for by the responsible agencies, and indoctrinating the elite groups in the military and civilian defense problems of the future. This is, perhaps, the only kind of psychological "fire drill" which is possible today. It might insure that possible future decisions will fall on a comparatively prepared public soil and that American policy will neither be forced nor restrained by the sudden welling of mass anxiety. A psychological policy for atomic war or threat of war cannot be effectively improvised. This is not at all to suggest that atomic war is inevitable. But anyone who would argue against such proposals for psychological preparation has the task of proving that there is no possibility whatever of atomic warfare.

There is a kind of hope which springs from the mastery of emotion and feeling, like that of the child who discovers that a frustration is bearable, or a terrifying risk within the scope of his competence. Such hope begins with the resistance of self-deception. It is as different from the willful selection of the favorable omen as it is from the protective selection of despair as a defense against disappointment. In this sense, the long road of foreign policy is not without hope. While it does not hold out the prospect of a joyous homecoming, a militant resistance to tyranny need not lead inevitably to disaster. History is full of examples of the crumbling of impressive façades.

It is human to aspire to a degree of security which is somehow commensurate to the risk. But if such security cannot be attained, we shall have to accept a lesser goal and live with our risks as best we can.

Bipartisanship and Majority-Rule Democracy*

by Willmoore Kendall

The major purpose of this article is to answer the question, "What are the merits of bipartisanship in foreign policy as seen from the point of

* From *American Perspective*, Vol. IV, No. 2 (Spring 1950), pp. 146-156. Copyright 1950 by the Foundation for Foreign Affairs, Inc. Reprinted by permission of the Foundation for Foreign Affairs and Willmoore Kendall.

view of the majority-rule democrat?" But for reasons which will become clear, I shall be obliged to raise and try to answer two further questions, namely: (1) What is bipartisanship in foreign policy and (2) what hypothesis can we offer to explain the appearance and swift rise to popularity of this kind of proposal in this period of American history rather than in some previous period?

[I]

What is it, then that the proponents of bipartisanship want? Mary Follett has written somewhere that we must maintain a sharp distinction between what a man *thinks* he is doing, what he *says* he is doing, and what he *is* doing. Following the applicable parts of her advice, I will try to distinguish here between what the proponents of bipartisanship say they want and the state of affairs it tends to bring about or perpetuate. The proponents of bipartisanship are honorable men and the question of distinguishing between what they want and what they say they want does not arise.

To find out what they say they want, let us call a few of the proponents to the witness box to speak for themselves. Mr. Ernest A. Gross, who was then Assistant Secretary of State for Congressional Relations, reads from a piece he wrote in the *Department of State Bulletin* in October 1949. "Bipartisan foreign policy exists," he tells us, "when there is a sustained sincere effort *to reach agreement on* objectives and on courses of action . . . the end in view is to achieve agreement on a sound and publicly supported [foreign] policy . . . [to] *make it* virtually impossible for 'momentous divisions' to occur in our foreign affairs . . ." [1] Bipartisanship, then, is a state of affairs in which we all (or perhaps only some of us?), make a sustained sincere effort to "reach agreement" on objectives and courses of action. And what the proponent of bipartisanship "objectives" says he wants is, presumably, to bring about that state of affairs. Is this a good idea, regardless of the extent of our disagreement? Mr. Gross has anticipated the question and is ready with his reply: "This is all the more necessary when serious differences of opinion exist within Congressional parties." Why is it

---

[1] "What is a Bipartisan Foreign Policy?", *Department of State Bulletin*, XXI (October 3, 1949), 504-505. The *italics*, here and throughout the article are the writer's and are intended to direct the reader's attention to phrases that bear especially on the thesis presented.

a good idea? Because "national security demands that *continuity and consistency* [in foreign policy] survive changes in administration." [2]

We can dismiss Mr. Gross and place him in the general category of "not very helpful," but not until we give him an opportunity to say why he applies to it so strange a name (etymologically speaking) as "bipartisanship." "The evolution of a successful foreign policy is better assured if it is founded on the support of like-minded statesmen, whatever their party affiliation." [3] The reader can supply the missing step: since ours is a two-party system, the phrase "like-minded statesmen, whatever their party affiliation" equals "like-minded statesmen" of both parties. And a policy supported by such like-minded statesmen becomes a "bipartisan" foreign policy.

Listen next to Mr. Hamilton Fish Armstrong who is a little easier to follow. For him, bipartisanship "exists" where "political leaders . . . rule out partisan considerations *in trying to reach agreement* on basic national objectives [in foreign policy] . . ." [4] Since "partisan" might mean "of or pertaining to personal preferences" or "of or pertaining to party," Mr. Armstrong must be a little more precise. It appears that the reference of "partisan" must be to "party" for his point seems to be that where you have bipartisanship, "party leaders" do not "press differences to the point where the goal itself is brought into jeopardy." [5]

Mr. Armstrong will be a little more precise if we but concede him a distinction he wishes to draw between "basic objectives" and the "methods" for attaining them, and if we but grasp the point that bipartisanship is a modification of our "party system" which "normally requires that there be debate *both* as to objectives and as to methods." [6] Mr. Armstrong—one wonders why—does not spell out the clear implication: under bipartisanship you do *something other than* debate both objectives and methods. (What you do will be explained later in interrogating Mr. Lippmann.) We may permit Mr. Armstrong one parting word as to why he favors bipartisanship. "It is," he says, "a healthy and perhaps necessary condition of American security [not only in wartime but] in normal times as well."

The next witness, Mr. Harold Laski, differs from the first two in that

---

[2] *Ibid.*
[3] *Ibid.*
[4] "Foreign Policy and Party Politics," *The Atlantic*, April 1947.
[5] *Ibid.*
[6] *Ibid.*

there is a visible connection between what he is describing and the manifest content of the word "bipartisanship." (Both Mr. Gross and Mr. Armstrong would have done better with "nonpartisanship.") "From the San Francisco Conference onwards," Mr. Laski explains, "American foreign policy has been made by the President in conjunction with a small body of advisers, chosen in part from Senators of *the* rival party . . ." [7] Or again, "The scale on which its power has compelled the abandonment of isolationism in the United States, has also made it necessary for the President to give to American foreign policy an institutional basis which *transcends the boundaries of the party he temporarily leads* . . . That means that no President can afford to repeat the mistake Woodrow Wilson made over the Treaty of Versailles . . . A bipartisan foreign policy [is now] imperative . . ." [8] In other words —and Mr. Laski is more specific than most writers on the subject— bipartisanship "exists" when the President associates with him, in the making of foreign policy, some leaders of the opposition party. This is, perhaps, as realistic a definition as we shall find.

Laski is equally realistic as to whether those leaders of the opposition party should regard their being associated with the President as an unmixed blessing. "An attempt to continue bipartisan relations when the President's party is in control of Congress *would tie the hands of the opposition, to a degree that might easily be fatal not only to its right to criticism, but also to its ability to pull over to its side an effective public opinion.*" [9] Mr. Laski—just this once, for he must not presume upon our generosity—goes into the category of "very helpful."

Our next expert is Mr. Blair Bolles, a toiler in the vineyard of bipartisanship ever since 1943. What he says he wants now, and says we are well along toward having, is "systematic inter-party cooperation in dealing with foreign affairs." [10] He sees this as committing the party in power, or at least the President, to (a) soliciting the "opposition's" views on impending actions in international affairs, and (b) assigning members of the opposition as United States delegates to the United Nations and to certain diplomatic negotiations, and (c) soliciting op-

---

[7] "The American President and Foreign Relations," *The Journal of Politics,* II (February 1949), 171-205.

[8] *Ibid.*

[9] *Ibid.*

[10] "Bipartisanship in American Foreign Policy," *Foreign Policy Reports,* January 1, 1949.

position support for policy legislation sponsored by the party in power.

What good things does all this promise us? "If bipartisanship *engendered real unity and continuity* in policy, foreign governments would be able to predict the course the United States would follow in international relationships." [11] What obligation does bipartisanship impose upon the opposition party, correlative to the three obligations imposed upon the party in power? This he does not choose to answer directly. But in another context we get a hint. Mr. Bolles explains that bipartisanship has "suffered" up to the present time from a malady that he terms "limited territorial application," whereas it "probably should apply to the whole surface of the earth in order to achieve maximum effect." [12] Our policies with regard to the occupation of Japan, for example, as also our plans respecting Western Germany, have been formulated without participation by the Republicans. These policies and plans "are not bipartisan, *but Republicans refrain from discussing them.*" Again we must supply the missing step: what the Republicans don't understand is that it is *only* the policies and plans which are really and truly bipartisan that they are supposed to refrain from discussing.

We come at last to Mr. Lippmann who has done more than anyone else to create the aura of sanctity that now surrounds bipartisanship in foreign policy. We listen to him at a moment when he is trying to clear up any possible misunderstandings as to how far he is prepared to go with bipartisanship. Not that he is any less in favor of bipartisanship than he has always been: "It is evident that partisan politics should stop at the water's edge . . . National unity is essential in our main transactions with foreign powers . . ." [13] But Mr. Lippmann's candidate for the presidency, Mr. Thomas Dewey, had been raising questions about the disposition of the Italian colonies, and the high priests of bipartisanship had accused him of showing precisely the "partisan" interest in the suffrage of the American-Italian voters that we have been taught to regard as appropriate to our pre-bipartisan past. Mr. Lippmann, obligated to choose on this occasion between bipartisanship and Mr. Dewey, does not hesitate: he will have both and to this end he will redefine bipartisanship.

"The bipartisan understanding cannot be," he explains, ". . . an

---

[11] *Ibid.*

[12] *Ibid.*

[13] *New York Herald-Tribune*, August 24, 1948.

agreement to unite the parties by *ignoring differing views and suppressing debate* . . ." [14] What then is it? It is "an understanding to accept and abide faithfully by the decisions arrived at after prolonged and thorough debate"; it "covers" only "national commitments that have been settled by the normal constitutional processes of the American government." It "has never been meant"—and here we must arrive by inference at what *has* been meant—"that private consultation was to take the place of public debate in *determining* the great commitments of the country." The inference? Where bipartisanship does *not* extend, matters are still to be settled by public debate; where it *does* extend, they are settled by "private consultation." In short, Mr. Dewey, because of the nature of the subject he had in hand was right in rejecting "the idea that . . . American policy in . . . [an] *unsettled* field of foreign affairs can be determined privately and without public debate."

The reader will have to take this writer's word that the assembling of further quotes from the literature of bipartisanship would be unprofitable. We should only find slight variations in the themes that have already been illustrated in the foregoing paragraphs.

Definitions of bipartisanship vary to some extent from proponent to proponent, which is to say that there is something less than full agreement as to the character and/or geographical reference of the foreign policy decisions bipartisanship has been—or should be—extended to cover. There is something less than full agreement again as to what bipartisanship requires in the way of institutional implementation, and as to the reciprocal rights and duties it confers and imposes upon those concerned with foreign policy decisions. But we must not leap to the conclusion that the writers whom I have been citing, and a host of other writers that might have been cited in their stead, are not enlisted in a common cause, or that they do not have a common body of doctrine. They are and they do have a common cause—at least to the extent of justifying the following comments:

1. All of them favor a fundamental and at least a partly accomplished revision of what we may call our traditional frontier treaty with regard to the making of foreign policy. ("Traditional frontier treaty" is a short expression for the sharing, among the President and the parties and the party leadership and the electorate, of powers and responsibilities in the field of foreign affairs.)

---

[14] *Ibid.*

Few of the proponents of bipartisanship would accompany Joseph and Stewart Alsop to the length of describing bipartisanship as a "great, permanent constitutional amendment." [15] But none of them makes any secret of the alleged fact that it constitutes a sharp break with past practices in the making of foreign policy.

2. They are all demanding revision in one and the same direction, i.e., the incorporation in the frontier treaty of some set of rules or "understandings" that can be counted on to assure that one of two things shall happen in the United States: either (a) basic national objectives in foreign policy are always given such shape as to enjoy general support, or (b) general support is always forthcoming for current basic national objectives in foreign policy.

3. They all place an extremely high valuation upon something called "unity" or "agreement," at least upon "basic objectives" in the sphere of foreign affairs.

4. While they speak sometimes as if the desired unity or agreement were unity or agreement on the part of the electorate, their practical proposals always tend to fix attention upon the relation between the President and his party, on the one hand, and either (a) the other of the two great parties or (b) all or some of the Congressional leadership of the other of the two great parties—whereof the term "bipartisanship."

5. Their vocabulary does not appear to include such phrases as "the bureaucracy" or "the permanent officials in the Department of State"; i.e., they persistently ignore the impact of what it is now fashionable to call "the planners" in the formulation of foreign policy.

6. They all use language (Mr. Gross' "to achieve agreement" is typical) that betrays the fact, and their knowledge of the fact, that the present situation in the United States is one of *disunity*, of *disagreement*, concerning basic objectives in foreign policy.

7. There appears to be no way in which the positive aspect of their proposals can be fully stated and defended without exposing a negative aspect to which none of them seems eager to draw attention: *Insofar as foreign policy is bipartisan, it is foreign policy arrived at via private consultation rather than via open debate*—or that, to put the same thing in another way, *the rules appropriate to bipartisanship automatically become "gag" rules as far as all-out discussion of the matters to which*

---

[15] *New York Herald-Tribune*, August 2, 1948.

they are applied is concerned. And the proponents of bipartisanship do not—I deliberately choose an unprejudicial form of words—give any evidence of the kind of distaste for this negative aspect that the majority-rule democrat *necessarily and as a matter of course* feels for it.

I wish space permitted full discussion of each of these points. Since it does not, I shall deal only in passing with 1, 2, 4, and 5, and fix attention primarily upon 3, 6, and 7.

[II]

The majority-rule democrat need have no quarrel with the pride of place assigned to "unity" or "agreement" in our writers' scale of values. The connection—inescapable, in his view—between majority-rule and democracy poses baffling problems both theoretical and practical save as majority-rule tries constantly to transform itself into unanimity-rule— save as the majority and its leaders sincerely seek to carry the minorities and their leaders along with them. Let us, then, have unity in foreign policy—if we can get it without sacrificing too much of too many of the other items in our scale of values. And let us not press, on this occasion at least, any objections the majority-rule democrat may have to all this preoccupation with unity in foreign policy rather than unity in public policy foreign *and* domestic.[16] But it cannot be over-emphasized that unity is a large order in what my friend Dankwart Rustow calls a "low consensus society," i.e., a society where for all that you may *want* unity what you *have* is disunity—which is the kind of society that the proponents of bipartisanship tacitly concede our society to be.[17] For failing a miracle of the kind it would take in order to get Mr. James Burnham and Mr. Henry Wallace mobilized behind one and the same set of basic national objectives *vis-à-vis* the Soviet Union, you must in such a society either:

(a) write off the achievement of unity as pie in the sky and accept and live with the fact of disunity, inching forward toward your destiny in full awareness that some people are getting their way and others are not.

Or, if you are not prepared to do that,

---

[16] Cf. Harry S. Truman, as quoted in *The New York Herald-Tribune* on June 17, 1948, on the occasion of a speech in Emporia, Kansas: "Domestic issues can be fought out on the basis of their merits. The foreign policy of the United States must be the policy of the whole United States . . ."

[17] By speaking always of unity and agreement as something to be achieved.

(b) create, through one kind or another of optical illusion, an *appearance* of unity sufficiently convincing to distract attention from the fact of disunity.

And this, as I see it, is *the* issue between the majority-rule democrat and the proponent of bipartisanship from which all other issues we might draw between them are ultimately derivative. In the eyes of the former, bipartisanship—in the present circumstances of American life—is precisely a formula for creating the appearance, the optical illusion, of a kind of unity that we know in our hearts (though we may prefer to "repress" the knowledge) to be not only unachievable but inconceivable.

The majority-rule democrat of course chooses the first horn of the above dilemma: accept and live with the fact of disunity. He also accepts the fact that nobody has ever yet discovered any democratic alternative to majority-rule save that of the Palestinian *kibutzim*, namely: postpone decisions (including what we may call the "decision by default" to carry on with existing policy) until you have talked matters through to a to-all-intents-and-purposes unanimous sense of the meeting. The majority-principle, or some version of the unanimity principle, but on either showing the process of settling "basic national objectives" in a democracy, is a matter of continuous all-out public debate. This public debate *canvasses all the realistic alternatives* and *ventilates all the arguments*, with the understanding that the ultimate decisions lie with *the electorate, which imposes its preferences upon the President and the bureaucracy* through its elected representatives in the Congress. The majority-rule democrat can acquiesce in no other kind of frontier treaty among the elements I have listed above.

I hasten to add that I should be the last to suggest that we have had any such frontier treaty in America within the memory of living man. To leave the reader with any such impression would be to encourage him to miss the point about bipartisanship. The concept of bipartisanship cannot be understood save as a recipe for preventing the canvass of all the alternatives and the ventilation of all the arguments by the electorate. But it is *not* a new formula, *not* a modification of the "normal operation of our party system." It is merely the American political system as it applies to a particular aspect (foreign policy) of the public, grown strangely aware of itself and strangely articulate about itself.

The common inarticulate premise of the proponents of bipartisanship is, that in the absence of determined and ingenious efforts, the disunity characteristic of American public opinion will bubble up in the form of "momentous divisions" between our two great parties whenever it is given something to get its teeth into. This conjures up the awesome possibility, which as far as I know no proponent of bipartisanship has yet dared to put into words: An election fought over a clear-cut issue and resulting in a popular mandate that no one could disobey without openly defying the great beast. Nothing, of course, could be less realistic. The dissident, who might become the nucleus around which opposition to current Presidential-State Department fiat might form, would need the voice of Stentor in order to get himself heard above the roar of the State Department propaganda machine. He can, at the margin, always be discredited—on the grounds that he is ignorant of information that it would not be in the public interest for the President and the State Department to release to those of us who are less burdened with responsibilities. If these guarantees prove inadequate, he is up against the fact that any "momentous division" he contrives to bring about will be a momentous division, not between the parties, but within his own party and not the kind of momentous division that can be resolved by popular mandate in the next election. Why? Because the political parties we operate in America are the kind of political parties that, by definition, have hearts large enough to take in, accommodate, and neutralize *any* not-too-disreputable point of view about public policy. If the President is a knowing fellow—and this is the great tactical principle upon which the proponents of bipartisanship have stumbled —he will have "associated" with this policy (which our writers erroneously identify with that of the President's party) just that number of Vandenbergs he needs in order to create a presumption that the Tafts do not speak for the "opposition" party.

The American political system, in the very form in which it was handed down to us, embodies all the bias against majority-rule it needs in order to deny a police permit to the parade of imaginary horribles with which the proponents of bipartisanship are torturing themselves. It is America's great contribution to the theory of delivering nascent democratic processes stillborn; and those Republicans who, to Mr. Bolles' annoyance, kept right on not discussing, even when the rules of bipartisanship did not tell them to, were behaving just as the system requires them to. It seems highly improbable that that bias requires reworking, at this late moment, by Mr. Hamilton Fish Armstrong or the Brothers Alsop.

The majority-rule democrat will, then, have none of this latest addition to our vocabulary of honorific political terms,[18] regardless of which of the definitions canvassed above may become generally accepted. He will have none of it even in the relatively inoffensive form it takes in the skilled hands of Mr. Lippmann, who *says* he wants all foreign policy decisions fully discussed and debated. Mr. Lippmann limits the application of bipartisanship to a few major policies after the latter have been adopted, but not before he reveals that its effect is to keep issues from being raised. For the majority-rule democrat recognizes bipartisanship as a (conscious or unconscious) attempt on the part of its proponents to put into attractive language, and so reinforce, the most undemocratic features of our political system, namely, those that prevent it from producing real popular decisions on real issues. Nor is that all: the majority-rule democrat sees that the years of self-conscious bipartisanship, these years during which we have all been "for" bipartisanship (and, incidentally, without having debated *its* merits either), have been years during which there has been less presumption than ever of any coincidence between current United States foreign policy and the will of the majority of the American electorate. He also sees that the men who have been stating the case for bipartisan foreign policy are, in the main, men who favor the particular foreign policy bipartisanship appears to have given us. And he suspects that all the fuss about bipartisanship is their tacit recognition that their foreign policy could not stand the test of competition in a free market for foreign policy ideas.

What is the majority-rule democrat's own formula over against that of the proponents of bipartisanship? The discovery of means for channeling into American foreign policy the native good sense of the American electorate.

---

[18] Cf. Joseph and Stewart Alsop, *New York Herald-Tribune*, August 2, 1948: "A crypto-isolationist Republican leader urged making an issue of the Berlin crisis. 'But,' said Senator Vandenberg bluntly, 'that would be treason.'"

Bipartisanship and the Weakness of the Party System*

by James MacGregor Burns

What is a bipartisan foreign policy? Almost everyone seems to define it in his own partisan terms. Administration Democrats seem to support bipartisanship to the extent—but only to the extent—that Senator Vandenberg goes along with the Truman-Acheson foreign policies. Internationally-minded Republicans champion bipartisanship on the understanding that all important foreign policies will be approved by Senator Vandenberg before action is taken. Other Republicans support it to the extent that the State Department clears with a more broadly representative set of GOP leaders in Senate and House. Then there is the Wherry crowd, which under the banner of "no more me-tooism" is out to axe bipartisanship no matter how many people it is cleared with.

How is a bipartisan foreign policy made? In a rough sort of way our government is organized to make partisan policy. The President is the leader of his party; he chooses the Secretary of State, who presumably subscribes to the foreign policies of President and party. This is partisan control. Both House and Senate are organized on party lines; more often than not at least one of the chambers is controlled by the President's party. Here, too, is at least a measure of party control. But our government is not well organized for fashioning bipartisanship. Institutions and procedures are lacking. This becomes clear when one asks certain questions about the mechanics of bipartisanship. Who among the opposition are to share in foreign policy-making—the party leader (if there is one), the Congressional leaders, or some broader set of leaders? What form shall their participation take? Being merely informed of decisions in advance, or really being consulted? Given a suspensive veto or even a final veto? What about the scope of bipartisan action? The opposition leaders to come in on all foreign policies? On only the more important ones? Who is to draw the line?

These questions—and there are many others—are not asked in a carping spirit, but because they suggest some of the basic difficulties and dilemmas of a bipartisan foreign policy. Bipartisanship in foreign policy,

* From *American Perspective*, Vol. IV, No. 2 (Spring 1950), pp. 169-174. Copyright 1950 by the Foundation for Foreign Affairs, Inc. Reprinted by permission of the Foundation for Foreign Affairs and James MacGregor Burns.

as in domestic policy, is wrong in theory for a democratic nation, I suggest; and because it is wrong in theory, a number of practical evils result.

The word "partisanship" seems to have taken on ugly connotations for some, but it is closely linked with our democratic ideals. For these ideals assume that in a free society men will differ, and that they should be allowed and even encouraged to differ. It assumes more—that the democratic system should be so organized that the expression of their differences becomes meaningful in making the decisions that societies must make. This is where parties come in. They present choices. Often these choices are not as meaningful or decisive as we might like, but at least they are choices, expressed in terms of candidates and policies. They are choices, moreover, that have a direct relation with the senti-ments of the great mass of the voters. Like a multitude of other organ-izations, parties find some common denominator among their adherents; their peculiar virtue lies in the breadth of the support that they mobil-ize. To win elections a party must enlist wide backing for a set of poli-cies and for an array of leaders. What seems like a sham battle to some is really an expression of the underlying unity of the voters; within boundaries set by that unity parties enable the voters to make decisions.

A party system not only presents choices, but it performs the related function of limiting the number of choices. The average voter cannot handle a wide array of alternatives any more than he can manage the "long ballot" with its scores of candidates. He needs a mechanism for selecting the crucial national issues awaiting decision and action. Our system—essentially a two-party one—is admirably suited for this select-ing and distilling function. If we had a multi-party system like that in France, there would be some point to bipartisanship, even to "multi-partisanship." Fortunately, we do not; we have a party system that, whatever its defects, can serve as a means for confronting the voter with a manageable set of issues. A healthy two-party system, in short, helps dissipate confusion—and confusion is an enemy of responsible govern-ment.

A third role of a healthy two-party system is to help translate the sentiments of a majority of the voters into governmental action. It is one thing to mobilize this majority at the polls; it is something else again to give effect to majority feeling in public policy-making. Here the party has an advantage, for it works through all the organs of government—

executives, legislators, higher bureaucrats, even judges. In this respect
parties are the institutionalization of majority action; this role is vital
to the extent that one views majority rule as a foundation of democracy.

All this is civics-book democracy; the curious thing is that we like to
throw overboard these ancient maxims when it comes to foreign policy.
Politics, we are told, must stop at the water's edge. Since politics in its
fullest sense cannot stop at any boundary between peoples these days,
we are really being told that party politics cannot be a means of democratic expression and selection except on "domestic" issues. The motives
for keeping foreign policy out of party politics are varied. The psycho-
pathologist may explain the urge in terms of the herd instinct that grips
a community when it stares out at the dark and mysterious world
around it. The political scientist may explain it in terms of the reaction
against the fumbling and awkwardness of party politics by people who
forget that if politics is diverted out of party channels it crops up in
group or factional politics that is not only cumbersome but even antidemocratic. The motive, of course, may be a somewhat more rational
one, such as the fear of parading our nation's internal disunities that
other Powers might use to our disadvantage.

The shift toward bipartisanship in 1946-48, however, came partly in
response to a very practical situation—the divided party control of our
national government during those years. With a Democratic President
and a Republican Congress, the country desperately needed a formula
that would permit decision and action in foreign affairs. The bipartisan
foreign policy provided that formula. It was a means of building a bridge
between parties, between leaders, between organs of government. It
supplied the Administration with both the basis of a consensus and the
impetus for action. Given the initial handicap of a divided government,
some such device as a bipartisan foreign policy was inevitable.

Why, then, do we hang onto bipartisanship in a time of "one-party"
control? Here is the nub of the issue. Democratic Party control of
Presidency and Congress would seem to be the opportunity for restoring
those party forms that, I have argued, are central to a democratic party.
The fact that partisan control of foreign policy has not been wholly
restored seems to indicate that even with one-party "control" our system
of political organization is not equipped to mobilize majority opinion
at the polls and give effect to it in governmental action. Such, indeed,
is the case. The Democratic Party does not really govern today, largely

because it falls apart in Congress under the pulling and hauling of its various wings, economic, sectional, and ideological. In order to enlist support for his policies, Mr. Truman must tap Republican resources, and to do that he must act in terms of a formula—bipartisanship—that enables Republicans to offer support without appearing to desert their party standard. The Republicans would be in a similar position if they held office.

Viewed in these terms, bipartisanship is not the real villain of the piece; it is our system of checks and balances and our political organization that lie at the root of the trouble. In order to act, our government must have more than the support of the majority of the voters operating through the party holding office. It must have the support of the "concurrent majority" that Calhoun analyzed a century ago, acting through two or more parties. The concurrent majority is far greater than a simple majority in size and scope; it embraces diverse groups any one of which might obstruct action if not consulted and won over in advance. The problem is not one of numbers alone. The President needs the cooperation of a majority in the House and sometimes of a two-thirds majority in the Senate, but he also needs help from members of Congress holding strategic positions in the House Appropriations Committee, the Senate Foreign Relations and Appropriations Committees, the House Rules Committee, the conference committees. Thus bipartisanship may help overcome some of the obstacles implicit in our system, especially the obstructionism and sabotage that can disrupt foreign policy-making in Congress.

To explain the attraction of bipartisanship in terms of the nature of our political and constitutional system is not, however, to explain away the evils of bipartisanship. For they are still evils. As long as we have a bipartisan foreign policy its methods of operation will lead to the baffling questions mentioned above. As long as we have it, the voters will not confront a meaningful choice at the polls. They will not know what leaders or what parties to hold responsible for public policies. Unless they are full-time students of politics they will not see much meaning in the Washington kaleidoscope that pictures a confusion of shifting alliances and hybrid coalitions. And the great number of voters organized in the party in power will see their strength frittered away under a policy that tends to represent minorities at the expense of the majority.

In these respects bipartisanship erodes the democratic process. In another sense bipartisanship positively threatens it. The President, the leader of his party, tends by virtue of his enormous powers as Chief Legislator and Chief of State to be the natural instrument for the direction of a bipartisan foreign policy. The danger here is that the President, frustrated as party chief, may veer away from the majority that elected him, from the party that sustained him, in order to respond to some collective national feeling that seems to rise above party politics, however spurious that feeling may be in its apparent unanimity. In the era of the Cold War, ideological conflict, and the H-Bomb, such a tendency may lead to rash adventures. Bipartisanship might not be effective against this danger because the natural channels for the expression of popular disapproval of such a course would already have been blocked off by bipartisan leaders. The opposition party, in particular, would be badly handicapped as instrument for mobilizing sentiment opposed to the party in power, if only because its leaders would have previously committed themselves to the bipartisan policy.

Whatever its defects and dangers, however, bipartisanship in some form or another will be with us as long as our political system retains its present character. How long will that be? This question no one can answer, but it seems safe to say that shifting more and more power over to the President through such practices as bipartisanship will be an easier means of vitalizing our slow-moving political and governmental machinery than doing the hard thinking and hard work that must precede any attempt to change our basic forms for the sake of more partisan—and hence more responsible—control.

FOR FURTHER READING:

Max Beloff, *Foreign Policy and the Democratic Process* (Baltimore: The Johns Hopkins Press, 1955).

Bernard C. Cohen, *The Political Process and Foreign Policy: The Making of the Japanese Peace Settlement* (Princeton: Princeton University Press, 1957).

Cecil V. Crabb, Jr., *Bipartisan Foreign Policy: Myth or Reality?* (Evanston and White Plains: Row, Peterson and Company, 1957).

Robert A. Dahl, *Congress and Foreign Policy* (New York: Harcourt, Brace and Company, 1950).

William Yandell Elliott, *United States Foreign Policy: Its Organization and Control* (New York: Columbia University Press, 1952).

Walter Lippmann, *The Public Philosophy* (Boston: Little, Brown and Company, 1955).

Dexter Perkins, "Foreign Policy in Presidential Campaigns," *Foreign Affairs*, Vol. XXV, No. 2 (January, 1957), pp. 213-224.

Bertrand Russell and others, "Can Foreign Policy Be Democratic?" *American Perspective*, Vol. II, No. 4 (September, 1948), pp. 147-181.

H. Bradford Westerfield, *Foreign Policy and Party Politics: Pearl Harbor to Korea* (New Haven: Yale University Press, 1955).

Henry M. Wriston, *Diplomacy in a Democracy* (New York: Harper and Brothers, 1956).

Chapter III

THE NATURE OF FOREIGN POLICY

If the public debate is to have relevance for the real world, it must be grounded on an adequate conception of the nature of foreign policy. Otherwise it is likely to result in value-laden exhortations which, though unexceptionable, have little relation to the immediate problems of foreign affairs. Confronted with such exhortations professional diplomatists respond either by ignoring the proffered advice or by replying in equally high-sounding and unreal terms. Such unsatisfactory results can only be avoided through full public understanding of the basic aspects of world politics.

Perhaps the most important single fact about United States foreign policy is that it is conducted within a multi-state system, the basic framework of world politics since 1648 and the Peace of Westphalia. In this system the separate units are sovereign, each is supreme within its own territory and largely independent in external relations. There is no central monopoly of coercive power, and systems of law covering all the units must rely on voluntary enforcement. The nature of foreign policy is derived from the implications of the multi-state system.

Analysis of these implications may appropriately begin with consideration of their impact on morality. Moral values form the basis for all decisions; choice in foreign policy as elsewhere is an expression of value preferences. Further, the relationship of morality to foreign policy has recently been a subject of great concern and intensive discussion in the United States. Shortly after John Foster Dulles became Secretary of State a national weekly magazine editorially proclaimed that he was "trying to put foreign policy back on an explicitly moral basis." This statement and others like it and the invidious inferences that could be drawn from them produced numerous rejoinders from those who previously held office. At about the same time a discussion at a somewhat different level was touched off by George F. Kennan's assertion in his *American Diplomacy, 1900-1950* that one of the major causes for the failure of past United States foreign policies was their great emphasis on "moralism." His position found both several supporters and many dissenters among scholars and publicists. The various discussions generated considerable heat and regrettably also some confusion.

The first selection in this chapter is an attempt to deal with this difficult question, to spell out the relationship between morality and foreign policy. In it Arnold Wolfers, Sterling Professor Emeritus of International Relations at Yale University and presently Director of the Washington Center for Foreign Policy Research, eschews offering a prescription for a "moral foreign policy," but instead concentrates on developing a method of applying non-perfectionist moral codes, such as most of us hold, to foreign policy. He develops the relationship between moral values and foreign policy and suggests how one's personal moral code can be used as a basis for evaluating foreign policy and for the selection of courses of action from competing alternatives. He rejects the argument that personal morality has no relationship to foreign affairs and at the same time the argument that relations between states should be judged on the same basis as relations between individuals. His position is that each action must be considered in the light of the circumstances under which it was taken. These determine what is and is not possible. Moral evaluation of foreign policy, as of other human action, must be based on a thorough knowledge of the current circumstances. It is important to note that while Mr. Wolfers recognizes the tendency of the multi-state system to push relations between states toward conflict, he does not assume that the system is the cause of conflict. It is rather, in his view, a factor which tends to make the possible alternatives less attractive from the point of view of most moral systems. Conflict has deeper roots. Thus abolishing the system, even if it were possible, would not eliminate the necessity of morally difficult choices. It is also important to note Mr. Wolfers' argument that however passionately one might desire to have peaceful relations with another state, it may be impossible if one is interested in preserving his basic values. At the same time, he does not feel that considerations of defense necessarily justify any action. Policies can only be adjudged on the basis of detailed knowledge of the prevailing circumstances.

The second selection, by Charles Burton Marshall, a former member of the Policy Planning Staff of the Department of State, attempts to define what is possible in foreign policy, the limits of action, and thereby to provide the broadest sort of knowledge necessary for judging foreign policy. The first limit he suggests is that clearly imposed by the multi-state system—the United States controls only its territory, it cannot ordain circumstances elsewhere, but only influence them. Other restrictions are those imposed by the limited means available to the United States and the human inability to accurately predict future events.

In foreign policy the limits on possible action are great, the range of choices narrow, and the process of choice difficult. Understanding this, however, should not lead to pessimism, but rather to the mature vision appropriate to the real world. Gaining such vision is the first step toward being able to capitalize on the available opportunities.

Statesmanship and Moral Choice*

by Arnold Wolfers

Throughout the ages moralists have expressed horror at the way princes and sovereign states behave toward each other. Behavior which would be considered immoral by any standard can obviously be detected in all realms of life; but nowhere does the contradiction between professed ethical principles and actual behavior appear so patent and universal as in the conduct of foreign relations. Governments spy on each other and lie to each other; they violate pledges and conduct wars, often at the cost of millions of lives and untold misery. No wonder, then, that in western democracies if not elsewhere indignation over such practices should be voiced with vehemence. In our day it frequently expresses itself in wholesale denunciations of the multi-state system on the ground that sovereign states cannot deal with each other except by the use of immoral means, derogatorily called power politics. Some draw the cynical conclusion that morality has no place in international politics, while others would have men fulfill their moral duty by substituting world government for the present immoral political system.

This sweeping moral condemnation of foreign policy as pursued by all nations points to a striking and disturbing contradiction in our public life. Most of our statesmen claim to be pursuing policies of peace and enunciate high moral principles upon which their policy is supposed to be based; they and many publicists praise the democracies for the moral superiority of their conduct of foreign affairs over that of aggressive and ruthless dictators. Yet at the same time many respected students in the field of international relations insist that all sovereign states alike are compelled by the "system" to play the evil game of power politics. The two positions would seem to be incompatible. Either our statesmen and their supporters are deceiving themselves and others or those who without discrimination condemn all power politics as immoral are overstating the case. In a country like the United States where moral passion tends to run high and where the question of morality in politics is a matter of genuine and wide concern, it is important to try to resolve this contradiction.

The idea that power politics are beyond the pale of morality is not

* From *World Politics*, Vol. I, No. 2 (January 1949), pp. 175-195. Reprinted by permission of *World Politics*.

new. Down through the centuries Machiavelli and Machiavellianism have stood for a doctrine which places princes and sovereign states under the rule not of ordinary morality but of the "reason of state," considered an amoral principle peculiar to the realm of politics.[1] German writers have been particularly insistent that ethical standards which apply to private individuals cannot measure the behavior of states which are said to be guided by necessity if not by a *höhere Sittlichkeit*.[2]

The English-speaking world, not seldom accused of comfortably ignoring or hypocritically denying the contradictions between ethics and international politics, has been unwilling on the whole to admit of any peculiar ethics of state behavior. Because states are abstractions, or at best fictitious personalities, it is not the state that decides and acts but always individuals, though they be statesmen. Should their behavior be judged differently from that of other individuals merely because they act for the state? To answer in the affirmative would mean accepting the hardly more palatable idea of a double standard of morality, according to which individuals when acting for themselves shall follow one set of moral principles while the same individuals when conducting their nation's foreign policy shall be bound by another and presumably less stringent code of behavior.[3]

---

[1] One might question whether Machiavelli meant to draw a sharp distinction between the ethics of state behavior, the behavior of "princes," which was his main concern, and the ethics of individual behavior. In the same Chapter XV of *The Prince*, in which he advises the sovereign to learn "how not to be good," he also speaks generally of the condition of man, saying that "whoever abandons what is done for what ought to be done will rather learn to bring about his own ruin than his preservation." He goes on to say that such a man "must necessarily come to grief among so many who are not good."

[2] Friedrich Meinecke's *Die Idee der Staatsräson*, Munich and Berlin, 1925, is a classic study of the relations between ethics and power politics as seen by Machiavelli and his continental disciples down to Treitschke. No similar study has been written on the views of their Anglo-Saxon contemporaries, though Gerhard Ritter, in *Machtstaat und Utopie*, Munich and Berlin, 1914, makes a suggestive beginning to such a study. He contrasts Machiavelli, "pioneer of the continental power state," with Thomas More, "ideological father of the English insular welfare state"—the former setting power above morality (p. 31), the latter seeking the *"Ethisierung und Entdämonisierung der Macht"* (p. 89).

[3] While Hans J. Morgenthau in *Scientific Man vs. Power Politics*, Chicago, University of Chicago Press, 1946, declares that "No civilization can be satisfied with . . . a dual morality" (p. 179), William Ernest Hocking, *The Spirit of World Politics*, New York, Macmillan, 1932, writes that statesmen distrust public opinion in international affairs because the public "takes for granted that the codes (for individuals and for states) are the same." E. H. Carr, *The Twenty Years' Crisis*, London, Macmillan, 1940, in contrast to these authors asserts that most people, while believing that states ought to act morally, do not expect of them the same kind of moral behavior which they expect of themselves and of one another (p. 199).

At first sight the facts seem to bear this out. Do we not condemn and punish citizens for committing the very acts of violence, treaty violation or untruthfulness which we condone in international politics? Are we not constantly struck by the gulf that separates the relatively peaceful and humane life within the national borders of states from the events occurring on the international scene? It is this contrast—more apparent than true, as we shall see—that has led some to demand that statesmen be made to give up their sinful ways and to conform to the rules of behavior expected from individuals in an orderly community. Unfortunately, advice of this kind often proves so patently impractical that instead of inducing statesmen to mend their ways it provokes in them a sense of moral cynicism. What is the use of listening to moral advice, they ask, if statesmanship, capable of mastering the problems which present themselves in practice, is apparently incompatible with morality?

The fundamental discrepancy which seems to exist between the morality of "state" and private behavior would disappear only if it could be shown that politics conducted in a multistate system is not necessarily any more immoral than average private behavior, or that the chief difference pertains not to the degree of immorality prevailing in the two spheres of human action but to the circumstances under which men are required to act. Much of what strikes people as immoral practices of governments may prove to be morally justified by the peculiar and unhappy circumstances which the statesman has to face and which, moreover, he may often be unable to change.

Any ethical perfectionist will be shocked at such a suggestion. He will deny that any action that would be evil under one set of conditions could be morally justified under another. If men are held to be morally bound to act in accordance with an absolute ethic of love such as the Sermon on the Mount, obviously no set of circumstances, even circumstances in which the survival of a nation were at stake, could justify acts such as a resort to violence, untruthfulness, or treaty violation. The concern for self-preservation and power in itself would have to be condemned as evil. This being the case, the ethical perfectionist can offer no advice to statesmen other than that they give up public office and turn their backs on politics. As a matter of fact, in order to be consistent, the perfectionist, as some have pointed out, must give the same advice to private citizens, requiring of them that they abandon their concern for their own welfare, for family or business. If, as Hans Morgenthau holds, "the very act of acting destroys our moral integrity," only a life of saintliness could come close to satisfying perfectionist moral commands.[4]

We must address ourselves exclusively then to the non-perfectionist who demands of man, not that he follow an absolute code of ethical rules—what Max Weber calls the "natural law of absolute imperatives" —but that he make the best moral choice which the circumstances permit.[5]

But surely, it will be objected, no moralist, at least in our culture, could deviate so far from perfectionist standards as to condone even in wartime such inhuman practices as the torture of enemy soldiers or the shooting of hostages. One would wish that this objection would always be valid, but the fact is that the non-perfectionist cannot escape the conclusion that circumstances may justify what superficially appear to be the most despicable kinds of human conduct. Or would he condemn without careful prior investigation all the members of the French Resistance movement who, in the face of brutal Nazi tactics, are said to have answered their enemy in kind? What if they were unable to discover any other alternatives but either to stop in this repulsive fashion the horrors committed by the Nazis or else to leave their friends and their cause unprotected? This does not imply that circumstances morally justify every act of power politics from the violation of the pledged word to aggression and concentration camps; the chances are that in most instances they will not, whether because the cause is unworthy of such extreme sacrifices or because other means are available which will assure morally preferable over-all results. Nor does it mean that where circumstances do justify such acts men may not be guilty of having brought about these circumstances or of having failed to remove them.

There is nothing peculiar to international politics in this impact of circumstance. Our conscience revolts at the idea of men putting other men to death. Yet non-perfectionist moralists throughout the western world agree in condoning the acts of those who kill in self-defense, in obedience to an order to execute a criminal, in war, or possibly in the case of tyrannicide. In other cultures it has been considered morally proper, if not a moral duty, to put the first born, aging parents, or

---

[4] Hans J. Morgenthau, *op. cit.*, p. 189.
[5] See Max Weber's "Politics as a Vocation," in *From Max Weber: Essays in Sociology*, New York, Oxford University Press, 1946, pp. 120 ff.

widows to death. One and the same act, then, will be judged differently depending on the context within which it is performed and depending also, of course, on the ethical standards by which behavior in general is judged.

This is not the place to enter upon the age-old discussion of what the standards of a non-perfectionist ethic should be, nor is such a discussion necessary for our purpose. However much non-perfectionists may disagree on ethical standards and thus on the nature and hierarchy of values, they hold in common the process by which they reach their moral judgments. They start with the conviction that there can be no escape from sacrifices of value whether, as theologians maintain, because of man's original sin and essential corruption, or because of the dilemmas of a world in which man is faced with incompatible moral claims. With this as a basis they hold that men, statesmen and private individuals alike, are morally required to choose among the roads open to them the one which under the circumstances promises to produce the least over-all destruction of value or, positively speaking, points toward the maximization of value.[6]

Moral condemnation, according to non-perfectionist ethics, rests not on the fact that values have been destroyed, however deplorable or downright evil such destruction may be judged. Instead it is based on the conviction either that the action in question rested on false ethical standards or that in terms of agreed ethical standards a less destructive choice could and should have been made.[7]

Thus a private citizen who breaks family ties in order to serve what he considers a higher cause may find himself condemned because his cause

----

[6] Max Weber's "ethic of responsibility" (*op. cit.,* pp. 118 ff.) comes closer to what is here described as a non-perfectionist ethic of maximization of value than it might appear from some of his statements. Weber, it is true, declares that "from no ethics in the world can it be concluded when and to what extent the ethically good purpose 'justifies' the ethically dangerous means and ramification" (p. 121). He is here taking issue with the revolutionary fanatic who from the point of view of an "ethic of ultimate ends" considers every act of violence justified so long as it serves his ultimate end. But when Weber goes on to demand of men that they hold themselves responsible for the consequences of their acts, especially their acts of violence, he does not refute their moral right to "contract with the diabolic powers of violence" which as political men they must do, but implicitly calls on them to choose the road which will minimize the evil consequences for which they bear responsibility.

[7] Hans J. Morgenthau, *op. cit.*, following in the footsteps of Max Weber, also emphasizes the "ethical paradoxes" of politics. "Political ethics," he says, "is indeed the ethics of doing evil" (p. 202). Yet he too concludes that "it is moral judgment," meaning presumably the best a man can morally do "to choose among several expedient actions the least evil one" (p. 203).

is not considered worth the sacrifice or because there were other less costly ways of attaining his end. Similarly a statesman who decides to break off diplomatic negotiations rather than to accept the terms of the opposing side may be judged wrong because he placed undue value on an increment of national prestige which was at stake or because he failed to appreciate properly the dangers involved in his choice of action. There is no difference either in the method of evaluation or in the ethical standards, whether the case be one of political or private behavior. In that sense the ethic of politics is but a part of general ethics. The question which remains to be answered, however, is why the sacrifices of value in international politics should be as widespread, continuous, and shocking in extent as they so obviously are. Is it because the circumstances under which foreign policy is conducted are so different and so unalterably different from those under which private citizens make their choices?

German writers on international politics have emphasized what they consider a unique and all-pervasive circumstance characteristic of interstate relations. Writing in the heyday of German *Realpolitik* Ratzenhofer declared categorically that the relations between sovereign states are unalterably relations of enmity.[8] His assertion reminds one of the no less dogmatic Marxist proposition according to which the relations between capital and labor in a capitalist economy are relations of enemies engaged in a class war.[9]

If one looks at the facts of history and of the contemporary world, one cannot subscribe to this German view. Instead it seems as if the relations between sovereign states no less than the relations between other groups or individuals run the whole gamut from almost complete amity—take Canadian-American or Anglo-Canadian relations—to almost unmitigated enmity, as in the days of war. Amity and enmity appear as the two extreme poles of a wide scale of human relationships. It remains true, however, and a matter of great political and moral consequence, that the multi-state system, for reasons which cannot be analyzed here, has a tendency to push relations between at least some

---

[8] See Gustav Ratzenhofer, *Wesen und Zweck der Politik*, Leipzig, 1893.

[9] Carl Schmitt, in *Der Begriff des Politischen*, Munich, 1932, modifies Ratzenhofer's thesis by declaring that inter-state and, in fact, all truly political relations are in the nature of "friend-foe" relations. While he does not claim that relations between all states at all times are inevitably hostile, he maintains that nations always group themselves as friends and foes and that there could be no such thing as statehood or politics if it were not for the existence of potential enmity, by which he means the possibility of deadly physical combat.

states in the direction of enmity—and, for that matter, more so in our century than in the last. The Nazis certainly saw to it that this would be so. As faithful disciples of Gustav Ratzenhofer, Carl Schmitt and others, they not only believed in the inevitability of international enmity but true to their theoretical assumption conducted German policy in such a way as to arouse the fiercest kind of enmity in most parts of the world.

The concepts of amity and enmity can be usefully employed to shed light on the context within which statesmen are forced to make their choices. They stand for the two opposite and marginal extremes of human relationships. Behavior changes as the relationship approximates one or the other of these poles. The causes of enmity in inter-state relations are significant to the moral problem only to the extent to which statesmen may be responsible for bringing about or for not eliminating enmity, and thus become responsible for the consequences of such enmity.

One can imagine a condition of complete enmity between states. There would be no trace of community between them, no sense of commonly held values or of common interest. Each individual state would have to be looked upon as an entirely separate entity operating in the social vacuum of absolute anarchy. There would exist a state of latent if not actual war all the time, turning diplomacy into warfare with other means. With good reason nations could consider themselves in a constant state of emergency with all the things gravely endangered to which they attached value. It would be a situation, as we know it from the experience of total war, in which the sheer quest for survival would justify almost any course of action. "Out-group morality" of the most extreme type would prevail.

Take the other extreme, that of amity or the "friend-to-friend" relationship. While there would be no complete identification, a sense of community would exist sufficient to eliminate mutual fear and suspicion. There would be no expectation of violence and therefore no need for preparations with which to meet the dangers of conflict. Despite the fact that each state would be sovereign, or rather because each state would be free to handle its own affairs, such friendly nations could behave toward each other according to the codes of "in-group morality" and live in peace with each other.

The more relations between states degenerate toward enmity the more nations are justified in fearing for the things they cherish and the more reason they have to make and require sacrifices by which inimical claims can be defeated. Greater enmity therefore increases the likelihood that Machiavellian practices will become necessary and morally justified. The degree of amity or enmity thus appears as a morally portentous circumstance. While in a state of amity statemen are likely to be able to choose between different avenues toward cooperation, compromise and conciliation. Enmity, however, may preclude such choices and place before the statesman a different set of alternatives. He may be able to take steps which will promise to mitigate if not to eliminate existing enmity. Often, however, he will have to choose between efforts to deter his opponent, thereby neutralizing the effects of enmity, and efforts to defeat him.

This cannot be said to be a peculiarity of international politics or of the multi-state system. The same phenomenon can be found in the relationship between father and son, employer and employee, white and colored man. There may be complete amity between them with no trace of distrust, no shadow of fear, no concern for self-protection, no awareness of conflicting demands or expectations. But here, too, relations may degenerate into fierce hostility for reasons too numerous to detail. Behavior then may change beyond recognition.

Two friends may live in almost perfect harmony. But let suspicion arise that one is seeking to exploit their hitherto harmonious relationship in some treacherous fashion. The other will feel justified in spying on his onetime friend. He may start laying traps. The case may end with one man killing the other. What is important to remember in this connection is that the killer may be judged to have been neither legally nor morally guilty, provided the treachery was flagrant enough. Not only our courts but public opinion in our country recognize the excuses of self-defense and unbearable provocation.

Similarly, strife between such groups as industrialists and workers may lead to property damage, kidnapping, or even open violence. Here, again, moral judgment will take the circumstances into account. Public opinion has been aroused at times by the employment of industrial police in labor disputes and by acts of violence on the part of striking workers. In each case, however, condemnation on the part of fair-minded judges of human behavior has been based not so much on the fact that the group in question used tactics of power politics as on the conviction that the provocation or grievances in a given instance were not sufficient to justify acts of coercion and violence.

It will be objected, and rightly so, that intra-state relations are less likely than inter-state relations to reach a degree of hostility that would call for the use of violence and other Machiavellian devices.[10] The state protects many of the values to which people are attached. The state can also prohibit the use of means to which society is opposed and can enforce its prohibition—though only by the very means which the components of that society have renounced for themselves. This holds true, however, only for well organized states where the government can marshal sufficient authority and police power to prevent family feuds and social or racial conflicts from breaking into the open and degenerating into violence and the use of other Machiavellian means. But while the pacifying influence of such a state and its influence on human behavior should not be minimized, exponents of world statehood tend to exaggerate the case for government.[11] The kind of government and therefore the kind of internal peace which this country enjoys at this time represents the exception rather than the rule. Our government operates under conditions, not wholly state made, of widespread amity between most of the groups that are powerful enough to influence the course of domestic events. It is recognized as legitimate by practically everyone and is ordinarily obeyed not because it has the force of coercion but because its authority is freely accepted. If one looks at the performance of other governments either in the contemporary world or in past periods of history, one finds no lack of examples of governments operating under quite different conditions and with quite different results.

Some governments are strong and ruthless enough to suppress the hostilities that would otherwise break out between warring factions, ethnic, social, or religious, but they do so by means of suppression, often tyrannical or terroristic. Rather than eliminate Machiavellian practices, such governments merely monopolize them. To what extremes of be-

---

[10] Some writers while agreeing that the ethical problems of political and private life are basically the same nevertheless stress the difference, if only quantitative, which makes international power politics the domain of evil *par excellence*. In his earlier works Reinhold Niebuhr stresses the peculiar selfishness and immorality of human communities including the state, as indicated by the title of his book, *Moral Man and Immoral Society*, New York, Charles Scribner's Sons, 1936. Later, however, he places more emphasis on the fact that all life is a "contest of power" and that international war and conflict are but a revelation of the general character of human existence and human sinfulness. (See his *Christianity and Power Politics*, New York, Charles Scribner's Sons, 1940, especially pages 11, 12, and 103.)

[11] Mortimer Adler, *How to Think About War and Peace*, New York, Simon and Schuster, 1944, declares anarchy to be the only cause of war and defines anarchy as "the condition of those who try to live without government" (p. 69).

havior this may lead has been drastically demonstrated by the way modern totalitarian regimes have persecuted the "enemies of the people." Other governments are too weak to control the forces of internal enmity; then there are bloody revolts or civil wars. When that happens enmity often reaches a degree of fierceness which relations between states rarely approximate. Machiavellian practices of the most extreme kind become the order of the day.

Government or statehood, whether national or world-wide, is therefore no panacea against those aspects of power politics which are morally deplorable. The real evil is enmity and its threat to values to which people are devoted.

However, the moralist needs to be reminded of the fact that there is not only no sure way to eliminate the fateful circumstance of enmity but that at a given time there may be no way at all. Certainly the elimination of the multi-state system itself, whether within a region such as Europe or on a world-wide scale is not one of the objectives statesmen are free to choose and therefore morally obliged to choose under all circumstances. Even if a radical change in the existing order were morally desirable because there was reason to suppose that a regional federation or a world government would create circumstances of greater amity than exist today, the psychological prerequisites for a concerted move of major nations toward such a goal are beyond the control of governments.

If it be true that statesmen cannot at all times choose to work for conditions of world-wide amity under world government, is it not their moral duty at least to promote amity at all times and at all costs? Once it is conceded that enmity requires and justifies sacrifices of value often of the most shocking kind, it would seem as if no price paid for amity could be considered too high. Yet statesmen would be rendered incapable of maximizing value if, without respect for the context in which they were forced to operate in a given instance, the quest for amity were taken as the sole measure of their actions. Amity is a condition passionately to be desired; but there are times when efforts to bring it about will lead to disaster. It takes two to make friends. An attempt to establish bonds of friendship may be interpreted as a sign of weakness; the result may be aggression. Again the demands of the opponent may call for sacrifices of value greater than those connected with continued enmity. Firmness and even resort to force may under certain circumstances require less loss of life, less human suffering, less destruction of faith and principle than the most sincere attempt to eliminate the causes of hostility by concessions.

This is not the same as saying that power politics generally preclude the opportunity for persistent and active pursuit of amity—or of justice for that matter. There are many occasions when disputes can be settled peacefully and when enmity can be eliminated or avoided, provided one side at least has enough courage, imagination and initiative. Sometimes a spirit of conciliation or even of generosity can do wonders in evoking a ready and sincere response. Whenever the lines of enmity are not irreparably drawn, there may remain room for moderation and self-restraint, for better understanding of each other's true designs and for fair compromise. While it is true that in the end it needs two to make friends, it is not always the other side which must take the first step.[12]

Only those who extol the value of national "virility" which is supposed to express itself in obstinate resistance to compromise, or those who are afraid of being the suckers will insist that the "necessity of state" is always on the side of toughness and unrelenting assertion of national claims. Harold Nicolson castigates Napoleon for being able to ascribe Castlereagh's "splendid moderation" only to treachery or corruption, to ignorance or folly.[13] Whether moderation is politically practical or suicidal depends on the circumstances. Those who feel called upon to give moral advice to statesmen must be ready, if they are to be true to the tenets of non-perfectionist ethics, to demand restraint of power, charity and forgiveness in one situation, as when feelings of revenge and war passions run high, but to insist on a break with an opponent, if not on the use of violence, when weakness or procrastination threaten to bring on greater evils. If world government were not only practical but would, if established, temper enmities and help nations protect or attain what they rightly value most highly, it would be the moral duty of statesmen to seek to bring it about. As things stand today, however, lack of consensus among the major nations about the

---

[12] Winston Churchill, *The Gathering Storm*, Boston, Houghton Mifflin, 1948, p. 320, testifies admirably to these opportunities for statesmanship. He says "those who are prone by temperament and character to seek sharp and clear-cut solutions of difficult and obscure problems, who are ready to fight whenever some challenge comes from a foreign Power, have not always been right. On the other hand, those whose inclination is to bow their heads, to seek patiently and faithfully for peaceful compromise, are not always wrong. On the contrary, in the majority of instances they may be right, not only morally but from a practical standpoint. How many wars have been averted by patience and persisting good will!"

[13] Harold Nicolson, *The Congress of Vienna*, London, Constable, 1946, p. 236.

desirability of world government as well as about the kind of world government they would accept is so obvious that any attempt to establish such a government today would be more likely to lead to war than to reduce enmity.

To the extent that enmity exists and cannot be eliminated at a given moment it would appear to dictate to the statesman a course of action that will often run counter to his moral preferences. Does this not mean that those exponents of *Realpolitik* are right who claim that the statesman, instead of being able to make moral choices, is left with virtually no leeway, having to bow to the dictates of the "necessity of state"?

It confuses the moral issue to state the case in this way. The "necessities" in international politics and for that matter in all spheres of life do not push decision and action beyond the realm of moral judgment; they rest on moral choice themselves. If a statesman decides that the dangers to the security of his country are so great that a course of action which may lead to war is necessary, he has placed an exceedingly high value on an increment of national security.

Necessities of a similar kind are known to private citizens. Parents may decide that in order to save the family business they must try to get their son to enter the family firm. Although they know that they are asking him to choose a career he abhors, they are ready to sacrifice his happiness to the "necessity of family." A trade union leader who calls a strike which he knows to be ruinous to patrons to whom he is devoted makes and requires a painful sacrifice for the "necessities" of the labor movement. In every such case conflicting values, interests and loyalties call for choices in which what is deemed to be the higher cause or value calls for submission to its necessities.

It is no play on words to say that the necessity or reason of state is but another of these necessities of life which become compelling only as a particular pattern of values is accepted. If the position of the statesman differs from that of private citizens it is because he must take upon himself the responsibility for sacrifices of value in order that others, as a nation, may protect or attain the things which they treasure. He may feel in duty bound to do so even though in a given instance he may disagree with the moral judgment of those to whom he is responsible. In that sense if in no other it may be justifiable to speak of the peculiar "demonic" quality of politics and public office, as Max Weber and other writers frequently do.

There is good reason why the controversy about the relationship between necessity of state and ethical standards should be rife in our culture. It points to a clash between two sets of ethical standards, one Christian or humanistic, the other nationalistic. Nationalistic ethics place what are called vital national interests—and not national survival only—at the very pinnacle of the hierarchy of values. The preservation or attainment of these values—territorial integrity, colonial possessions, *Lebensraum*, treaty rights or economic interests—are therefore assumed to justify the sacrifice of almost every other value whether it be life, generosity, humane treatment of others, truthfulness or obedience to the law. Especially, the interests of other nations count for little, if anything, on a nationalistic scale of values.

While those who adhere to non-perfectionist Christian or humanistic ethical views accept the fact that sacrifices of value are inescapable, as non-nationalists they may nevertheless, in the case of any policy decision, question whether a particular national interest is worth the sacrifices required or could not be protected by a less costly method. This may not seem to hold true when national survival itself is unquestionably at stake. It could properly be said that the multi-state system, since it rests on the co-existence of a multitude of independent states, is incompatible with any ethic which would forbid sacrifices necessary for national survival. Moral advice not to submit to the necessities of survival would not only be advice to commit national suicide but would tend to wreck the multi-state system itself.[14]

As a matter of fact, the controversy between exponents of nationalistic and non-nationalistic ethical standards in our culture is not over the moral right to pay the price of survival. None but the perfectionists or

---

[14] It is not surprising that authors who believe that international politics is essentially a struggle for national survival should reach very pessimistic ethical conclusions. Thus, Nicholas J. Spykman, *America's Strategy in World Politics*, New York, Harcourt Brace, 1942, bases his case on the proposition that "the struggle for power is identical with the struggle for survival" and that states can survive only by constant devotion to power politics. Although the use of power "should be constantly subjected to moral judgments" (p. 12), Spykman concludes that the "statesman can concern himself with values of justice, fairness and tolerance only to the extent that they contribute to or do not interfere with the power objective," meaning the quest for survival. In his further statement that the quest for power is not made for "the achievement of moral values" he is taking issue with those exponents of nationalistic ethics who place supreme moral value on national survival. See also in this connection Mortimer Adler's statement that "so long as national self-preservation remains the dominant end for which prudence must choose means, the principles of morality cannot be reconciled with the counsels of prudence" (*op. cit.*, p. 78).

absolute pacifists deny a nation which is engaged in a life and death struggle the right to make and demand every sacrifice necessary for victory.

But this is not the same as saying that the non-perfectionist must capitulate before every alleged "necessity of state." Nations engaged in international politics are faced with the problem of survival only on rare occasions. How otherwise could it be explained that most of the nations which have attained independence in recent centuries have survived when surely most of them most of the time have been devoted to anything but an unrestrained quest for power? If ever any country did employ Machiavellian principles consciously and methodically it was Hitler's Germany, but with the result that she lost her independence as conclusively as few great nations have done.

As a rule, not survival but other "national interests" are at stake, such as the preservation of outlying bases and possessions, the protection of treaty rights, the restoration of national honor, or the maintenance of economic advantages. While it is a prerequisite of the system that nations attach a high if not the highest value to their survival, the same cannot be said of these other national interests. As a matter of fact, the moral dilemmas with which statesmen and their critics are constantly faced revolve around the question of whether in a given instance the defense or satisfaction of interests other than survival justify the costs in other values. Does the expropriation of American investments abroad, for instance, justify the choice of military intervention rather than of unpromising negotiation? Is it morally preferable to risk a loss of prestige with its possible dangerous consequences for the safety of the country rather than to insist on maintaining a position which threatens to provoke hostilities? In every case the interpretation of what constitutes a vital national interest and how much value should be attached to it is a moral question. It cannot be answered by reference to alleged amoral necessities inherent in international politics; it rests on value judgments.

Even national survival itself, it should be added, is a morally compelling necessity only as long as people attach supreme value to it. In that sense the multi-state system itself depends on a value pattern in which there is an element of nationalism. If at any time those who have the power to decide over the foreign policies of the major countries should come to attach higher value to the attainment of world government than to the preservation of independence, the psychological, though not necessarily all other practical, obstacles to world government would be removed.[15] Until that happens nations are likely to consent to all kinds of Machiavellian practices, however much they may abhor them, whenever they are convinced that their independence can be saved in no other way.

International politics offer some opportunities and temptations for immoral action on a vast and destructive scale; they tend to present themselves in the guise of "necessity of state." Statesmen in command of the machinery by which public opinion can be manipulated may make it appear as if they were acting for the sake of objectives to which the people attach high value when in fact they are out to serve material personal interests or to satisfy personal ambitions for power. Where men wield as much power as they do in international politics there is room for an infinite variety of abuses for which the "necessity of state" can serve as a convenient cloak. Then again, statesmen may sincerely believe that a particular course of action is dictated by vital national interests; but judged by non-nationalistic standards of ethics they may be placing undue value on certain interests of their people or underestimating the value of things not pertaining to their nation which their policy would sacrifice.

While this makes moral criticism and self-criticism imperative, the difficulties which stand in the way of their proper use in international politics need to be emphasized. If it is hard for statesmen to make proper moral choices, it is not any easier for others to do justice to their conduct of foreign policy.

It is a baffling task, almost exceeding human capacity, to compare the value of an increment of national security with the value of human lives, or the value of a continued period of peace with the risks of a more destructive war in the future. Yet the statesman is faced with even more exacting and truly terrifying problems. Forced to make his

---

[15] R. M. MacIver, *The Web of Government*, New York, Macmillan, 1947, suggests that these basic value judgments may change as the old myths of national sovereignty and national interests lose their grip on people, while Arnold Toynbee, *A Study of History*, New York and London, Oxford University Press, 1947 (p. 299), passing moral judgment, denounces the "pagan worship of sovereign nation-states" calling it a monstrous product of the impact of parochialism on the Western Christian Church." See, in this connection, also Harold Lasswell, *World Politics and Personal Insecurity*, New York and London, McGraw-Hill, 1935, who devotes Chapter XI, "In Quest of a Myth: The Problem of World Unity," to the problem of how, by the use of symbols, myths, and other practices, human value judgments might be changed in favor of world unity.

choices whenever a decision is called for, he may have to compare the value of an uncertain chance of greater security with only roughly predictable risks of conflict and destruction. It may be easy with hindsight, and years after the event, to condemn a statesman for having failed to maximize value; but it also becomes increasingly difficult as time goes on to do justice to the inevitable lack of knowledge and foresight under which the decision-maker labored at the time. Yalta is a good example to illustrate this moral problem.[16]

The trouble about much of the moral condemnation of foreign policies and with much of the moral advice tendered to statesmen goes back to a lack of appreciation of the kind of knowledge required for proper and useful moral criticism in international affairs. From a non-perfectionist point of view the circumstances, however technical, have to be taken into consideration; moral conviction and high ideals, much as they are needed to guide moral judgment, cannot by themselves offer an answer. Nor is this true in international politics only. It needs some knowledge of economics to judge whether an industrialist is exploiting his workers; he may be paying the highest wages the traffic will bear. It needs psychological understanding to decide whether in a particular situation divorce represents morally the least evil choice.

Similarly, in international politics where the circumstances are no less involved and technical, moral convictions cannot tell what roads are open to a statesman under the specific conditions under which he is forced to act, nor can they reveal what the political consequences and therefore the relative costs in terms of value of any one of several courses of action are likely to be. Will an alliance provoke war or will the failure to make a commitment tempt an aggressor? Will an appeal to the United Nations in a given case help bring about a peaceful settlement or instead create graver tension, perhaps even going so far as to destroy the organization? Disarmament may be morally the best choice under one set of circumstances; it may be downright evil in another in which it would place a nation—and small nations dependent upon it for their security—at the mercy of an ambitious conqueror. The same holds true for all the other panaceas or devices so dear to the heart of those who are most quickly ready to give moral advice to policy-makers or to condemn them for their actions. In one context it may be right to offer con-

---

[16] See Rudolph A. Winnacker, "Yalta—Another Munich?" in *The Virginia Quarterly Review*, Vol. 24, No. 4 (Autumn, 1948), pp. 521-37.

cessions whereas in another it may constitute "appeasement" with all of
its evil consequences.

There might seem to be one exception to the rule that no general
principle can guide non-perfectionist moral judgment on all occasions.
It might seem proper to assume that the "defensive" side is always right
and that every action is justified and justified only if necessary for the
protection and preservation of values already possessed. Unfortunately,
while individuals can disprove their guilt if they can rightly claim to
have acted in self-defense, the case of nations is far more complex.
Neither the nation's self nor its possessions are clearly circumscribed.
May a nation defend as its self and its possessions only its territorial
integrity and independence, or does the right of self-defense cover a
way of life, national honor, living space, prestige, colonial possessions
and economic rights abroad? *Status quo* powers whose main concern
is the preservation of the values they possess and therefore the defense
of the established order are prone to blame all Machiavellianism on
those nations that seek to bring about change, whether it be revision
of treaties, revolution of the social order or liberation from foreign
domination. Yet, the "offensive" side may have a valid case for insisting
that it has a vital need for things withheld from it and may rightly
value them to a point where any means of attaining them become
morally justified. Those who refuse to make the sacrifices of change or
who, having brought about an unjust distribution of possessions and
power are unwilling to correct it, may be guilty of provoking enmity and
aggression. If the Moslems in India or the Zionists in Palestine resorted
to violence, they were not defending an existing order but were seeking
to establish new and independent national homes through changes in
the existing order. They were not necessarily at fault merely because
they wanted these changes so urgently or because they despaired of any
means short of violence. The *beati possidentes* may be more peaceful
and less inclined to initiate open hostility, but their guilt may lie in
their self-righteous and blind devotion to the *status quo* or in the resentment which they evoke in others.

Despite the difficulties of doing justice to the statesman and of avoiding the pitfalls of politically dangerous as well as morally untenable con-
demnations, men who have non-perfectionist and non-nationalistic
moral convictions dare not evade the task of moral judgment whether of
their own political acts or of the acts of others. Where there is so much

room for moral choices as there is in international politics and where
the destiny of entire nations depends on these choices, attempts to
evade, silence or ignore moral judgment merely play into the hands of
those who relish the uncriticized use or abuse of their power. The Nazi
leaders were helped by the climate of moral cynicism which prevailed
in Germany. It made it easy for them to justify even the most brutal
acts on the grounds of necessity of state or to glorify their freedom from
any "decadent" moral inhibitions.

The world will not fail to suffer from the immoral acts of statesmen
as of other men in the future as it has in the past, nor does it look as
though nations would soon be freed from the bitter consequences of
international enmity, or from the appalling sacrifices inflicted and justified in the name of national interest and survival. A single powerful
government, engaged for whatever reasons, in a policy of aggression and
aggrandizement may force all others into line with its Machiavellian
practices, provided these others have the will to survive. In such cases
moral exhortations and intentions will serve little unless the causes of
such aggression and the dangers inherent in it are removed.

Yet international politics are not beyond the pale of non-nationalistic,
non-perfectionist morality. Statesmen need not be fooling either themselves or others if they contend, as they frequently do, that in specific
instances they have restrained their nation's quest for power; nor need
they apologize if, on occasion they choose a conciliatory or even a generous course of action, though a more egotistical policy would promise
more tangible national benefits. Despite the continued strength of nationalist sentiment in all parts of the world, there is no reason to assume
that people value national benefits only. They often attach a great deal
of value to a good record of international collaboration and at times
applaud a leader who takes risks for the good will, the amity or the
interests of other nations—or seeks to keep his own conscience and
that of his people clear.

This explains why under certain circumstances a national government
might receive the backing of its people even in sacrificing national independence itself, particularly if it were done for the purpose of establishing a better international order, perhaps a world-wide federation. From
the point of view of non-nationalistic ethics such national self-sacrifice
for world government might appear morally justified if there was assurance of enough amity and all-around consent to permit the establishment and functioning of an orderly and humane government of the

world; it might be condemned if it led to world tyranny or world anarchy. There are historical instances when such sacrifice of independence has justified itself in the eyes of almost everybody, as when the thirteen American states federated successfully.

Under the circumstances usually prevailing in a multi-state system painful limitations are set on policies of self-negation, generosity or restraint of power. It would be utopian to expect drastic changes in this respect. But to say that the field of international politics is reserved for selfishness, brutality, self-righteousness or unrestrained ambition for power is not only cynical but manifestly unrealistic.

The Limits of Foreign Policy*

by Charles Burton Marshall

One of the most unforgettable characters I have never met is archy—spelled with a lower-case *a*—the philosophic roach, creature of the imagination of Don Marquis. I recall as an example of this roach's insight an account of a conversation with another insect about the difficulties of livelihood among cockroaches in the face of such circumstances as stringency of food and the unremitting hostility of man, whose hand and sometimes also his foot are against them. The other insect suggests a formula for freedom from want and freedom from fear for cockroaches. This calls for them to quit the towns for the countryside and there to become grasshoppers. At first the simplicity of this suggested solution astounds the roach. Then second thought prompts a request for precise directions for the transformation into grasshoppers. The other insect answers, in sum, that this is a detail for the execution of policy; the general scheme has been indicated, and it is up to others to give it effect, for policy-makers should not have to do everything. The roach sets all this down under the title of "statesmanship," with a suggestion that the account has in it "something analogous to a number of easy schemes for the improvement of the human race."

It does indeed bear such analogy. Nothing comes more easily or does less good than the engaging pastime of thinking up bold and imagina-

---

* From *The Limits of Foreign Policy*, pp. 11-34, by Charles Burton Marshall. Copyright, 1954, by Henry Holt and Company, Inc. By permission of the publishers.

tive schemes for improvement in disregard of the means for realizing them. This is true in all human endeavor. Here I wish to apply the thought to the subject of foreign policy.

I do not need to exhort about the importance of this subject. Foreign policy has a bearing on the duration and the conditions of our lives as individuals. It bears also on profound questions of our destiny as a nation, for the relationships between us and the portions of the world external to our jurisdiction will largely determine whether our national greatness is to be enduring or brief.

That issue is not foreclosed in our favor. No grace inherent in us and no providential gift exempt us from the pitfalls and infirmities attending the course of great nations. Whether, and how long, we shall avoid them will depend in some great and essential portion on our courage and wisdom as a politically organized people in handling our relationships with other peoples in other lands with cultures and loyalties different from ours.

Surely here is a subject of such moment as to deserve our taking great care in thinking about it and discussing it.

Foreign policy does not always receive such care. Indeed it is altogether too often denied it. The sweep of its problems gives foreign policy a special attraction for those—in the words of Shelley's self-description —born with a passion to reform the world. Foreign policy appeals to those inspired by identification with large and high-sounding public causes. Its complexities and subtleties are rich with opportunity for generalizers and obfuscators.

This is consequential. Ours is an accountable government. Acceptability to popular opinion is certainly a factor in the conduct of foreign policy by our government. Popular opinion is not of much, if any, value in helping in the discovery of answers to the problems in this field. It certainly counts, however, in setting bounds to the area of maneuver available to those charged with responsibility. A sound general understanding of the limits of foreign policy, avoiding excessive expectations and the sense of frustration incident to the disappointment of such expectations, is therefore essential to the conduct of a sound foreign policy.

I do not mean to identify lack of public comprehension as the sole brake on progress along wise courses in foreign policy. If it were that, then all that would be necessary in order to achieve wisdom and success would be to do away with accountability in our government and to let magistrates and experts take over unconditional authority with respect to external relations. Magistrates are never worthy of such mastery, however, and experts are never endowed with such expertness. Those who govern and those who counsel them are subject to refractions of view and errors of judgment. The problem is neither how to endow them with unquestioned authority in foreign affairs nor how to render them entirely subservient to the whims and pressures of the particular interests which in sum constitute the public. The problem is how to acquaint Americans in general, whether in government or out of it, with the inherent limits respecting foreign policy so that issues may turn on questions how best for the nation to fill the limits rather than on vain propositions of perfection and destructive self-reproach over failure to achieve it.

I intend in these discourses to put calipers on foreign policy. I wish to stress its limits rather than its magnitudes. I shall do so analytically, concentrating on the inherent character of the subject . . .

As a beginning in laboring the analytic aspects, a loose definition will do. The foreign policy of a state takes form in the courses of action undertaken by authority of the state and intended to affect situations beyond the span of its jurisdiction.

Do not construe too narrowly the meaning of the word *action*. In this field utterance is sometimes a form of action, and pronouncements are deeds when they convey meaning about things intended to be done rather than merely expressing abstractions and moralizations.

Let me emphasize the human and therefore finite character of the political institutions concerned in foreign policy.

The state is an abstract expression representing a body of people occupying a defined territory and politically organized so as to be capable of acting collectively with respect to matters both within that territory and beyond it. Government is the apparatus of decision and execution for such action.

The terms *state* and *government* convey ideas of hugeness, majesty, and impersonality. These overtones should not mislead us. The state—and this is true also of its agent, government—remains, in Plato's phrase, man written large.

It is only man. It is not superman. It is man written large, not limitless. The individual is multiplied in the frame of the state. The individual's limitations are not transcended. The institutions of political life do not add to the dimensions of the human mind. They have no

insights denied to individuals. They produce no wisdom beyond the
compass of man's mind. The intelligence operating in the lines of
decision and execution is but human intelligence. It has the inherent
attributes of contingency, fallibility, and subjectivity. Service to the
state does not bring to the minds of the servants any additional endow-
ments for perceiving the future. For all its majesty, the situation of the
state is still the human situation.

Americans generally recognize the characteristics of intrinsic limitation in respect to the state's role in domestic affairs. Here indeed, in
their precepts if not so much in their practices, the Americans are virtually singular among the nations for their skepticism about the wisdom
and the efficacy of public authority. Americans tend to overlook these
limitations—at least, many Americans tend to do so—in their attitudes
toward the role of the United States in foreign affairs. In this range their
perspectives tend to be thrown off. Americans, said Gertrude Stein, are
brought up "to believe in boundlessness." With respect to nothing else
is this so manifest as it is with respect to their views as to the inherent
capability of the United States government to avail in matters actually
external to its jurisdiction and therefore beyond its control.

I stress the obvious but often overlooked externalness of foreign
policy. The fundamental circumstance giving rise to foreign policy is
that most of the world is outside the United States. The areas in which
our foreign policy has its effects are those lying beyond the range of
our law. They include about fifteen-sixteenths of the world's land surface and contain about sixteen-seventeenths of its peoples. We cannot
ordain the conditions there. The forces do not respond to our fiat. At
best we can only affect them. We exercise only influence, not the
sovereign power to dispose, in those ranges once described by the Supreme Court in a memorable opinion as "this vast external realm, with
its important, complicated, delicate, and manifold problems."

I can recall from my own experience dozens of examples of the
American tendency to disregard limitation of power precisely with
respect to matters beyond the limits of our control.

An exigent lady in the audience in a Midwestern city about three
years ago asked me to outline the course of United States foreign policy
for the next ten years. I denied having a crystal ball. She reduced to five
years the interval concerned in the request. I carefully restated my view
of foreign policy as necessarily being in large part a response to situations arising beyond the national jurisdiction and therefore beyond our

government's control and beyond my modest power to predict. She spurned that answer. She insisted on the predictability of the future in world affairs, given sufficient diligence on the part of those conducting policy. I told her the main surely predictable element of the future was trouble, which was bound to proliferate along our course, though I could not undertake to define all its forms and occasions. The lady answered with scorn for the Department of State for not having worked out a formula for eliminating trouble. . . .

A while back a friend of mine, giving me his personal views on how to handle foreign affairs, drew an analogy from his own business, railroad traffic management. He represented the world as a switchyard, the United States as a locomotive, and all the other nations as boxcars. I remarked on the irrelevancy of his account of railroading technics to foreign affairs. The world is not an organized place like a switchyard. Other nations are not inert vehicles like boxcars. They are corporate entities with purposes of their own. Respecting them the United States disposes no monopoly of power like that of a locomotive among boxcars. All this I explained to my friend. He rejoined with a comment about the mulish unwillingness of the members of the State Department to accept from other walks of life the lessons of how to conduct the nation's affairs.

The same notion of the attainability of perfect foresight in the planning and perfect efficacy in the execution of foreign policy is an ingredient in the abundant schemes put forth by well-meaning groups for a variety of one-shot solutions of the problems of a difficult world. It is reflected also in a way many people have of attributing developments in every quadrant of the globe to some design conceived in Washington.

This underlies a great deal of discussion about the China issue. One hears repeated references to our having lost China—a land never ours to lose. That ancient, complex, and populous land is represented as without a substance of its own—as merely a screen reflecting only what is projected from this side of the Pacific. The course of that remote nation is construed as wholly determinable by American will. From the tone of discussion one might never guess that indigenous impulses and predispositions counted for anything in China's course: for the native army's want of military zeal someone here must be held to account; for an Oriental regime's loss of grip on itself blame must be fixed in Washington.

This mistaken notion of thinking of our policy as the paramount factor in situations beyond our borders is not confined to the China issue. I have heard serious-minded Americans lay at our own doorstep the blame for everything believed by them to be deficient in the internal situations of the Latin American nations.

I believe it worth while to ponder briefly the causes of this tendency to see in disproportion the dimensions of our power in the world, a tendency highly important as a main obstacle to sound thinking about foreign policy.

According to a friend of mine professionally concerned with the study of deeper sources of human behavior, this tendency of individuals to think of the state as if it were omnipotent in the world is an unconsciously chosen way of redressing the sense of their own inadequacy, much as small boys redress their boyishness by vaunting the imagined prowess of their fathers. I shall leave such theory to others better prepared than I to delve into the psyche.

One source of the notion of perfect efficacy in foreign affairs, it seems to me, is consciousness of an extraordinarily successful past. The diplomatic course in the evolution from a colonial beachhead to a power of highest magnitude was one of matchless performance. It is easy to assume this as setting the enduring standard for our conduct in the world.

Faith in law—perhaps I should say excessive faith in legislation—is another factor relevant here. Legislation is law. Law is to be obeyed. An aim legislatively expressed is *ipso facto* achievable. So goes the reasoning. This tempts toward exaggerated notions of the preventive as well as of the positive power of legislation. In both respects this has a bearing on ideas about foreign policy. . . .

The very fact of having a lot of legislation laying down the objectives entertained by the Congress for situations internal to other countries tends to obscure the limits of our jurisdiction—to make us forget that we cannot by our own fiat cure problems arising from the narrowness of the margins of political power within other countries or ordain the easy and immediate consummation of purposes realizable, if at all, only with energetic and purposeful support of other peoples in long spans of time.

Another influence on the American attitude toward foreign affairs might be called faith in engineering—confidence of a limitless power to transform situations by working on the material factors, faith in the achievability of great purposes through applying technics. This relates to our natural pride in the physical development of our country. Popular tradition treasures the notion in the realm of creation all things are possible to those who will them. A recent book by an American assailing his government for suffering the postwar contretemps in Germany dismisses the notion of limitation of American power with the observation, "Americans can do anything." The margins available to us have made this true at least in a poetic sense in the development of our own country. The error arises in the attempt to apply it to situations involving wills other than our own.

This faith in capability to transform through material factors is relevant to a tendency to think loosely about the nature of force, which is physical, and its relation to power in general. By force I mean the capacity to transmit energy and so to expend it as to do vital harm to a foe and also the deterrent, compulsive effect produced by having that capacity. It is only one of many forms of power. For power let us use Count Tolstoi's definition of it as "merely the relation between the expression of someone's will and the execution of that will by others."

Wars occur when nations seek to impose their wills by effecting drastic changes in the ratios of power through radical action in the factors of force. The force factors are susceptible of precision in military planning. The elements are concrete. The speeds of ships, their capabilities for carrying men and cargo, the distances, the fuel requirements of planes and tanks, the fire power of divisions, and so on are knowable factors. The military planning process, insofar as it relates to the ponderables of real or hypothetical campaigns, turns out tidy and complete results. I do not mean that battles and campaigns are fought according to preconceived schedules. I mean only that insofar as advance planning is employed in the military field, the quotients are precise, the columns are even, and the conclusions concrete.

In a course of active hostilities force capabilities may be brought to a ratio of 100 to 0 as between one side and the other by the elimination of resistance in a particular place for a particular time, changing the relationship between antagonists to that between victor and vanquished. Surrender may be complete and unconditional. Victory may appear absolute.

It is easy for the unwary to jump to a conclusion that if all human affairs were laid out with the precision of military plans, then all problems could be brought to as complete solution as can the problem of force in the conduct of a victorious military campaign.

Victory's appearance of absoluteness is transitory. Victory itself is evanescent. It invariably has given way to a substitute unless the victors, like the Romans at Carthage, have obliterated the conquered or undertaken permanently to deprive them of will—in other words, to enslave them, an undertaking likely to prove burdensome and fearsome to the enslavers as well as to the enslaved.

Ascendancy based on force begins to diminish as soon as force ceases to be sole arbiter. The introduction of factors other than force modifies the relationship between conquerors and those conquered. The victor will ceases to be the only active will. The vanquished recover in some degree wills of their own. A mutuality of relationship begins to be renewed. The relationship recovers political character. Victory fades as a circumstance and becomes only a memory. Bold expectations identified with the moment of victory fade away with it.

This accounts for an ancient and recurring cliché—I am old enough to have heard it in the sequels to two world wars—about politicians' having dissipated the glories and benefits of victories achieved by violence. To my view a failure of events to confirm expectations shows something wrong about the expectations rather than something deficient in the facts. The failure of peace to live up to the high hopes of the moment of victory shows something to be deceptive about the hopes—indeed about the concept—of victory itself.

Use of force is an incident. The problems of power are endless. Wars occur. Politics endures. Let us identify as a persistent illusion about power in foreign policy the idea that by dint of planning and perseverance it can be realized in that degree of efficacy seemingly secured in the moment of victory. It is an illusion first in equating all power with force and second in exaggerating the enduring effectiveness of the latter.

In examining the urges and the claims of perfection of solution in foreign policy, let us take note of a characteristic tendency of our times to regard the whole field of human relations as substantively and entirely an aspect of science. This links with a notion of the capability of cumulative and organized knowledge to solve anything and an accompanying view of every problem as something by definition solvable. If not creative scientific thinkers themselves, then certainly popularizers of scientific achievement have nurtured this idea. Whatever the applicability in material relations, the concept is misleading when applied as a universal.

I call to mind a statement of august auspices: "In social science in its broadest sense, which is concerned with the relations of men in society and with the conditions of social order and well being, we have learned only an adumbration of the laws which govern these vastly complex phenomena." That is part of a pronouncement by the American Association of University Professors in 1915 in advocacy of academic freedom. The case for nonrestriction in the study of human affairs here is simply that mankind has not yet done all the homework to be done. The concept of truth implicit here is of something not yet fully mastered rather than something ever unfolding and therefore beyond formulation. . . .

The notion of the power of scientific reason to solve all the problems of our age relates to a habit of mind derived from the study of history. To this I wish to give special emphasis.

The whole continuum of time and space, in all its vastness and variety, far exceeds the compass of any finite mind. Only an infinite consciousness could understand all of it and perceive the lines of relationship among all the entities and all the occurrences within its scope. With his limitations, the individual can work his intelligence only on small portions of it. Within segments comprehensible to him and from his particular standpoint, he observes or construes relationships between one phenomenon and another. In the measure of his understanding he tries to analyze these as lines of cause and effect. From these he seeks to derive principles for comprehending and controlling his environment. This in general is the method of science.

I am concerned here only with its application to history. The historian turns his powers of inquiry and analysis onto some segment of space and some range of past time manageable within his intellectual compass. From what is available to him of the residual record, he infers lines of causation. He distills his knowledge and sorts it into chapters and volumes presenting the essences, as he understands them, of the eras and areas subjected to his analysis.

This is legitimate and necessary intellectual endeavor. To its results, however, one must always take care to apply proper reservations. The past did not actually unfold in chapters and volumes. Its emerging realities were never as compact and crystallized as they are made to appear by the craftsmanship of the historian. The participants in past events never enjoyed those clear vistas marked for us by the historian along the lines of cause and effect. To the contemporaries the proportions in any epoch were very different from what they appear to us in long retrospection.

Besides this tendency to confuse the history with the reality of the past—besides the notion that the residue we retain is the whole and the essence of any departed epoch—let us take note of the notion that history unfolds according to some logical scheme, the whole of which is inferable from any of its parts, much as an archaeologist contrives to reconstruct an entire skeleton from a few stray bones. This is the notion that from history we can derive the key to the future. This is the notion that by sufficient diligence we can lay down the lines of what is to come as neatly and definitively as the systematic historian seems to plot out the lines of what has gone before.

It is only a step from this concept to the idea of manipulating the future. If the pattern of the future is ascertainable by human intelligence, then its determinative elements must be discoverable by human intelligence also, and by pre-empting control of these and working them according to its own will, a human agency can take charge of destiny. So the idea goes.

This notion of finding and working the push-buttons and levers controlling the future involves a great contradiction between two concepts —on the one hand, the deterministic idea of an ascertainable pattern of the future and on the other the concept of the possibility of perfect freedom of will involved in the assumption that a mortal entity can gain ascendancy over the future and make it responsive to its desires as a machine responds to a guiding hand. This notion makes man and his mind, his will, and his institutions on the one hand the puppets of a foreclosed destiny. On the other hand it presumes to place the controlling cords in the hands of human agency.

George Santayana's words caution us against reliance on any special school of thought "which squints and overlooks half the facts and half the difficulties in its eagerness to find in some detail the key to the whole." This fallacy resides in every undertaking to formulate a system about the past and then to apply it to gain mastery over the future. It inheres in every notion of an exclusive formula for being right in human affairs and in every overweening claim to the possession of that formula. It is implicit in every exhortation for us to meet the Communist threat by adopting a system matching that of the adversary in its pretensions to universality and to possession of the keys to the future.

Anyone who has dealt responsibly with foreign policy must have felt the meaning of Whitman's lines:

How can I pierce the impenetrable blank of the future?
I feel thy ominous greatness, evil as well as good;
I watch thee, advancing, absorbing the present, transcending the past;
I see thy light lighting and thy shadows shadowing, as if the entire globe;
But I do not undertake to define thee—hardly to comprehend thee . . .

To perceive the great extent to which a foreign policy, attempting to cope with the future, must be speculative and chancy is not a source of weakness. To the contrary, in Edmund Burke's phrase, "We can never walk surely but by being sensible of our blindness." The gravest errors are consequent from deceiving oneself that it is possible by some prodigy of planning to overcome this inherent circumstance.

Something of this fallacy is basic to every proposition for a perfect, all-embracing solution of our problems in foreign relations. The young Gladstone's mentor advised him that politics was an unsatisfactory business and that he would have to learn to put up with imperfect results. That advice has wisdom akin to the lessons of *Faust* and *Paradise Lost:* that grace derives from a sense of one's limitations and that tragedy is the wage of losing that sense.

Not perfection but utility is the test of planning in a foreign policy, and utility is a modest virtue. Perhaps an illustration from another field, military operations, properly applies here. The Duke of Wellington once referred to the differences in concept and planning between his adversary and himself in the Peninsular Campaign. The French plans, he said, were made with logical perfection and completeness. He likened them to a fine leather harness—admirable and useful until some part broke, whereupon the whole was useless. His own plans, he said, were made on the principle of rope, and as portions broke under the stress of circumstance, he would just tie knots and go on. A foreign policy should be planned on that principle.

Foresight in foreign policy—the planning function, I might call it—is best if seasoned with contingency and a recognition of human limitation. To set proper perspectives, let us take account not only of the finiteness of the state and of the point that the areas concerned in foreign policy lie beyond the span of national jurisdiction, but also of another point implicit in the definition of foreign policy which I gave at the outset. I refer to the essential relationship between foreign policy and action.

At the risk of sounding very academic, I shall labor this with some more definitions. I do not claim exclusive correctness for them. I set them forth only to insure understanding of my use of the terms.

The situation of the state—substitute the term *government* or *nation* if you will—is that of having some, but only some, capability. That is the situation of responsibility. It lies between the extremes of omnipotence and powerlessness. Each of these extremes alike carries no responsibility.

The situation of responsibility involves the necessity of choice. Choice is simply the selection of one possibility to the exclusion of others when no more than one is feasible. Choice inevitably involves renunciation. In the view of the scholastic philosophers, even an infinite being is compelled to make choices because of being unable to will into existence simultaneously inherently contradictory things. Finite entities have to make choices not only as between inherently contradictory possibilities but also as between things which together are practicably unfeasible within the means at hand.

One knows this from the daily circumstances of his own life—the continuing necessity of allocating one's time and rationing one's money, one's inability to spend the same two hours in both studying and going to the movies, and the incapacity to obtain together the rewards of diligence and the comforts of indolence. One must repeatedly put aside one desirable thing in preference for another thing also desirable. This circumstance distinguishes the real life from the myths treasured in childhood with their seven-league boots, lamps of Aladdin, magic carpets, and open sesames.

The situation of the state in its external responsibilities is that of the limits of adult reality, notwithstanding that many Americans persist in talking of foreign policy in a frame of reference akin to the wishful tales of childhood. Let us apply then to the state in its external relations the simple concepts about will applicable to other human endeavors.

Will is the faculty for making choices. The difference between a weak and a determined will is simply a difference in steadfastness in carrying through with the renunciations inescapably involved in making choices. This is as true in the frame of the state as it is in other human affairs.

An exercise of will is a volition. A volition unfolds at three levels. The first of these concerns motives. By that term I mean those impulses rising from some inner need or desire and spurring the mind to volition. The second level involves ends. By an end I mean that which the mind conceives as representing the satisfaction of the need or desire identified as the source of motivation. The third level involves intentions. At this level the mind adds to the conception of ends the projection of action in pursuit of them.

Note that I say pursuit, not attainment. The capacity of the mind to conceive ends is limitless. The means at hand are invariably limited. The level of intention involves above all the establishment of a balance between ends and means—that is, if one is responsible in his undertakings. Balancing ends and means requires at any juncture the selection of some feasible fraction of one's ends to be acted upon and the deferment of the rest. The portions of one's ends selected for action let us call purposes.

All this applies to foreign policy.

The formulation of foreign policy, if done responsibly, must be regarded as the forming of our intentions—as distinguished from our ends—regarding the world external to our national jurisdiction. The distinction makes a difference. The sum of the foreign policy is the sum not of things we should like to achieve but of the things we do or are going to set about doing in the world. Foreign policy is not the business, in words of Kipling, of

> Thinking of beautiful things we know,
> Dreaming of deeds that we mean to do,
> All complete, in a minute or two—
> Something noble, and grand and good,
> Done by merely wishing we could.

Many—one finds them in government as well as out of it—regard foreign policy as a set of good wishes and high aspirations about the world, as that and nothing more. That sort of thinking relates to foreign policy as cheer-leading to quarterbacking or as the sum of a man's New Year's resolutions to his biography.

I do not mean to decry the essentiality of a set of goals in foreign policy. Ultimate purposes have a value in serving as a standard for knowing how to proceed, problem by problem, in this field. Moreover, the good is not always beyond reach, though the way to it is arduous, long, and charged with paradoxes.

A few years ago one of our most distinguished military leaders, one typifying in the best sense the combination of soldiery and statesmanship, made a speech about the criteria for our relationships with the rest of the world. His peroration was a plea for the nation to guide by the

eternal stars instead of steering by the lights of each passing ship. The
sweep and grandeur of his metaphor impressed me. I said so in a conversation with a seafaring friend. "Obviously you don't know much
about the sea," he told me. "One of the easiest parts of seamanship is
celestial navigation. That never keeps you awake on the bridge all night.
The test of seamanship is the shoals, the fogs, the storms that blow and
yet you can't do anything to stop them, and the passing ships. Just try
to imagine sailing under a skipper who thinks the big part of his job is
star-gazing."

That anecdote makes my point. The goal aspect of foreign policy is
essential. It is also easy. It is the easiest part of the business. The difficult part comes not in figuring out what one would do if one could do
everything one may wish to do. It comes in deciding what to do in the
circumstances of being able to do only part of what one may wish to
do. That is the task of handling dilemmas and of rationing means. Here
the making of foreign policy reaches the vital level. Here success is
courted. Here failure is risked.

From this concept of the making of foreign policy as essentially involving not the mere conceiving of ends but the establishment of purposes of action and the allocation of means comes a recognition of the
determinative importance of means. We know this well in the frame
of individual lives. Probably not one of all the men in Sing Sing set Sing
Sing as his goal in life. They all arrived there because of grievous errors
in the calculations of means.

Let us then apply to foreign policy a few simple ideas relating to the
economy of means.

The nation's ends, as I have used the term here, in their whole range
inevitably exceed the means. It is important—nay, necessary—to maintain balance between those portions of ends chosen as purposes for action and the means available. The necessary balance between purposes
and means is not solely a quantitative matter. The means must be not
only sufficient to the purpose. They must also be qualitatively appropriate to the purpose.

Regard for this necessity of balance between means and purposes is
the heart of foreign policy. Let me reinforce the point by quoting from
the Gospel according to St. Luke:

> For which of you, intending to build a tower, sitteth not down first,
> and counteth the cost, whether he have sufficient to finish it? . . . Or
> what king, going to make war against another king, sitteth not down first,

and consulteth whether he be able with ten thousand to meet him that cometh against him with twenty thousand? Or else, while the other is yet a great way off, he sendeth an ambassage, and desireth conditions of peace.

To approach policy without regard to the necessity of bringing purposes and means into balance courts not merely futility but the danger also of violence and tragedy. . . . History is replete with instances of governments which committed themselves overtly to undertakings which they could not fulfill but from which they could not back away and in consequence incurred war.

Once begun, the process of inflating the purposes is most difficult to stop. A government proclaims aims in excess of its means to effect them. Becoming anxious over the disparity between what it can do and what it has proclaimed, it seeks to redress the disparity by even wider assertions of aims still more stridently proclaimed. Eventually the range of assertions and the range of achievements are so obviously and widely disparate that the nation's policy faces imminent disintegration. Here the temptation to resort to coercion by threat and display of force rises, bringing on the danger of counterthreat and counterdisplay, and finally the plunge into general violence. Thus the course of proclaiming goals beyond the margins of capability provided by calculable means tends toward war. This course no nation can afford to begin. We must not presume for our nation any exemption from the penalties imposed for mistaking pronouncement for policy.

Having in mind that a purpose achieved in foreign policy may become the means for achieving a further purpose, let me state as a further point that the economy of means requires that the ends selected as purposes for action be such as, if achieved, will provide the best feasible basis in means for going on to achieve further purposes. That is to say, as far as possible a government disposing great power in the world must project its purposes so as best to progress toward its whole range of ends or, if it cannot progress, at least to minimize the setbacks.

These things can be figured only in a rough sort of calculus. No prodigious formulas are at hand—no easy or perfect ways, no free rides.

My last point relates to the costs.

The use of means involves cost. The achievement of purposes represents gain. It is easy to wish a gain. The difficult part is the envisaging of the cost. The cost aspects of a foreign policy are the aspects despite which a course of action is undertaken. The gain aspects are those because of which a course of action is undertaken.

In the balancing between these two aspects every important policy issue officially familiar to me has been also a close one. The merits in argument for and against an acceptable line of action never occur in ratios of 100 to 0 or even of 80 to 20. They tend rather to occur in the order of 55 to 45 or even 51 to 49. Even at best, the arguments against a line of action in foreign policy tend to be almost as weighty as the considerations in favor. Yet these small margins of difference constitute the distinction between success and failure and are all-important.

I did not find the issues so closely balanced in a former time when I used to write newspaper editorials about foreign policy. Then I could arrive at solutions plain as day and overwhelmingly cogent for even the most serious issues. The process usually took only about forty-five minutes. I did almost equally well with solving the great problems of policy in teaching international relations. In the line of responsibility, however, things look quite different.

Whatever his shortcomings as a philosopher, Jeremy Bentham was surely right in this: the forming of an intention includes the acceptance of the cost as well as the entertaining of the gain. One has truly resolved his will in favor of a course of action only in bringing his mind to the acceptance of those aspects despite which as well as those aspects because of which he acts.

This too applies to affairs of state in world relations.

The limits of our foreign policy are determined not alone by our inherent finiteness and not alone by our extrinsic capability but also by the degree of our steadfastness in shouldering the burdens. That, rather than the righteousness of unexecuted wishes, will be the test of us as a great nation. To forget this would be to say a long farewell to all our greatness.

FOR FURTHER READING:

Dean Acheson, "Morality, Moralism, and Diplomacy," *The Yale Review*, Vol. XLVII, No. 4 (Summer, 1958), pp. 481-493.

Louis J. Halle, *Civilization and Foreign Policy* (New York: Harper and Brothers, 1955).

John H. Herz, *Political Realism and Political Idealism* (Chicago: University of Chicago Press, 1951).

George F. Kennan, *The Realities of American Foreign Policy* (Princeton: Princeton University Press, 1955).

Ernest W. LeFever, *Ethics and United States Foreign Policy* (New York: Meriden Books, 1957).

William Lee Miller, "The 'Moral Force' Behind Dulles's Diplomacy," *The Reporter*, Vol. XV, No. 2 (August 9, 1956), pp. 17-20.

Reinhold Niebuhr, *The Children of Light and the Children of Darkness* (New York: Charles Scribner's Sons, 1944).

Reinhold Niebuhr, *Christian Realism and Political Problems* (New York: Charles Scribner's Sons, 1953).

Kenneth W. Thompson, "The Limits of Principle in International Politics: Necessity and the New Balance of Power," *Journal of Politics*, Vol. XX, No. 3 (August, 1958), pp. 437-468.

Chapter IV

THE NATIONAL INTEREST

The criteria which should be used to select and evaluate foreign policy have been the subject of an intensive and occasionally passionate discussion in the United States in recent years. This controversy began with the publication of two books, George F. Kennan's *American Diplomacy, 1900-1950* and Hans J. Morgenthau's *In Defence of the National Interest*. Both criticized former United States policies and advocated new courses of action. Both maintained that "moralism" and "legalism" had played too great a role in the formulation of past policies and argued that in considering future actions America should primarily be guided by its own security needs or, to use Mr. Morgenthau's term, its national interest. This position found several supporters but also numerous opponents, and a vigorous debate ensued. This chapter examines some of the principal aspects of this controversy.

The first two selections are representative of the two main positions in the controversy. In the first article Mr. Morgenthau, Professor of Political Science and Director of the Center for the Study of American Foreign and Military Policy at the University of Chicago, defends what has come to be known as the "realist" position. He argues that the national interest is a meaningful concept which should be regarded as the touchstone for foreign policy. The second article, by two professors of political science at Johns Hopkins University, Thomas I. Cook and Malcolm Moos, argues what might best be called the "idealist" position. This position, which owes many of its theories to Woodrow Wilson, holds that more positive objectives than security are needed in foreign policy. It also differs from that of the "realists" on the best method of obtaining security, placing less emphasis on military power. The final selection by Arnold Wolfers cannot accurately be placed on either side of the controversy. Phrased primarily in terms of a critique of the "realist" position, it brings out the complexity of foreign policy, the nature of the value judgments involved, and the tentativeness of our knowledge about the effects of alternative policies. It can be used to interpret and evaluate both the "realist" and "idealist" schools of thought.

While the controversy between "realists" and "idealists" centers on basic philosophical perspectives, it also has important and immediate policy implications. However, the two sides defy classification by political party; members of both parties can be found on each side. The participants in this controversy have drawn heavily on Charles A. Beard's pioneering study, *The Idea of National Interest*. Although the focus of foreign policy was considerably different in 1934 when this book was published, the framework of analysis Mr. Beard developed and many of his concepts are still useful. As in many debates, the participants in this controversy frequently talk in different terms. The different definitions of the two schools of thought contained in the first two selections are an example. Both are colored to create the most favorable possible picture of the case being presented. But more than semantic differences are at stake. Both sides present different interpretations of American history and have different and conflicting estimates of the opportunities provided by present world politics. At the root of these differences are differences concerning values and man's basic characteristics. In general terms, the "realist's" basic values—those he desires most to implement and protect—are somewhat narrower than the "idealist's": the "realist" primarily looks toward the nation-state while the "idealist" tends to have a broader orientation, even though he may frequently rationalize his proposals in terms of the nation-state's enlightened self-interest. The "realist" is also more pessimistic about man's capacity for good than the "idealist" and consequently less optimistic about the opportunities provided by foreign policy.

Part of Mr. Morgenthau's article is a refutation of the arguments of one of his most severe critics, Frank Tannenbaum, Professor of History at Columbia University. Mr. Tannenbaum maintained that the United States has always and should continue to base its foreign policy on the concept of the "coördinate state" rather than that of the national interest. His definition of the "coördinate state" centers on concern for the equal sovereignty and dignity of states and rejection of what he calls power politics. Mr. Morgenthau denies the validity and utility of this concept and defends that of the national interest. The core of Mr. Morgenthau's national interest is the integrity of the territory, political institutions, and culture of the nation-state; beyond that its components are variable albeit not unlimited. His arguments are heavily weighted toward security considerations, which he feels have not sufficiently been emphasized. Readers should analyze Mr. Morgenthau's views concerning the role of science in the process of formulating foreign policy and compare them with those of the authors of the other two selections. They should also examine his treatment of the implications for international stability of steadfast pursuit of the national interest.

Messrs. Cook and Moos accept the legitimacy of the national interest as the touchstone of foreign policy, but their definition differs so greatly from Mr. Morgenthau's that the term hardly seems applicable. Mr. Morgenthau would find it difficult to agree that America's ultimate national interest is "the spreading and sharing, with due adaptation and without intolerance, of its societal blessings." Messrs. Cook and Moos would also differ with Mr. Morgenthau on how best to insure United States security: they place more faith in international coöperation and organization. In the final selection, Mr. Wolfers points out the problems involved in attempts to use any simple scheme to select and evaluate foreign policy. He shows how several value and factual judgments are subsumed under seemingly meaningful slogans. He would prefer a case by case approach to foreign policy problems.

The controversy between "realists" and "idealists" has not been and cannot easily be resolved. Those interested in the public debate on foreign policy can perhaps profit most from considering it by using it to clarify their own basic positions, their values and predispositions.

Another "Great Debate": The National Interest of the United States*

by Hans J. Morgenthau

The controversy which has arisen on the occasion of Ambassador Kennan's and my recent publications differs from the great historical debates on American foreign policy in two significant respects. It raises an issue more fundamental to the understanding of American foreign policy and of all politics than those with which the previous "great debates" were concerned, and it deals with the issue largely in terms which are not conducive to understanding.

The great debates of the past, such as the one over intervention vs. neutrality in 1793, expansion vs. the status quo before the Mexican and after the Spanish-American War, international cooperation vs. isolation in the 'twenties, intervention vs. abstention in the late 'thirties—all evolved around clear-cut issues of foreign policy. In 1793 you were in favor of going to war on the side of France or of remaining neutral. In the 1840's you approved of the annexation of Texas or you did not. At the turn of the century you supported overseas expansion or you were against it. In the 'twenties you advocated joining the League of Nations or staying out of it. In the late 'thirties you wanted to oppose the Axis Powers by all means short of war or you wanted to abstain from intervening. What separates the "utopian" from the "realist" position cannot be so sharply expressed in terms of alternative foreign policies. The very same policies can be and are being supported by both schools of thought. What sets them apart is not necessarily a matter of practical judgment, but of philosophies and standards of thought.

The issue which the present debate raises concerns the nature of all politics and, more particularly, of the American tradition in foreign policy. The history of modern political thought is the story of a contest between two schools which differ fundamentally in their conception of the nature of man, society, and politics. One believes that a rational and moral political order, derived from universally valid abstract principles, can be achieved here and now. It assumes the essential goodness and infinite malleability of human nature and attributes the failure of

* From *The American Political Science Review*, Vol. XLVI, No. 4 (December 1952), pp. 961-988. Reprinted by permission of the American Political Science Association.

the social order to measure up to the rational standards to lack of knowledge and understanding, obsolescent social institutions, or the depravity of certain isolated individuals or groups. It trusts in education, reform, and the sporadic use of force to remedy these deficiencies.[1]

The other school believes that the world, imperfect as it is from the rational point of view, is the result of forces which are inherent in human nature. To improve the world one must work with those forces, not against them. This being inherently a world of opposing interests and of conflict among them, moral principles can never be fully realized, but at best approximated through the ever temporary balancing of interests and the ever precarious settlement of conflicts. This school, then, sees in a system of checks and balances a universal principle for all pluralist societies.[2] It appeals to historic precedent rather than to abstract principles, and aims at achievement of the lesser evil rather than of the absolute good.

This conflict between two basic conceptions of man and politics is at the bottom of the present controversy. It is the same conflict which found its classic expression in the polemic of Burke against the philosophy of the French Revolution. Given the sad state of political thought in our time, it would be vain to expect the spokesman of political realism to speak with the voice of Burke and the defenders of political utopianism to measure up to the standards of Condorcet and Rousseau. Yet one has a right to expect that scholars discuss the issue without resort to invective and with proper regard for established facts.[3]

---

[1] This is the ideal type of the utopian position rather than the empirical description of any particular historic type. In actuality, and this is true particularly of the present, the utopian position in international affairs is not always consistent with its philosophic premises.

[2] It ought not to need special emphasis that a principle of social conduct, in contrast to a law of nature, allows of, and even presupposes, conduct in violation of the principle. Robert W. Tucker, in "Professor Morgenthau's Theory of Political 'Realism'" in this Review, Vol. 46, pp. 214-224 (March, 1952), has missed this and many other points in his zeal to find contradictions where there are none.

[3] "This [the realist] doctrine," writes one historian—Frank Tannenbaum, "The Balance of Power versus the Coördinate State," Political Science Quarterly, Vol. 67, p. 173 (June, 1952)—"is confessedly, nay gleefully, amoral. It prides itself upon being realistic and takes Machiavelli as its great teacher. It is contemptuous of the simple beliefs of honest men, jeers at the sentimentalism of those who believe that men may strive for peace among nations, and looks upon democracy as a hindrance to skilled diplomacy. It looks with a certain derisive superiority upon the great leaders of this nation from Jefferson and John Quincy Adams to Woodrow Wilson and Franklin Delano Roosevelt and describes them as moralistic and sentimental, and suggests that our models ought to be Richelieu, Clemenceau and Bismarck. Its adherents believe that international wars instead of being made by men and sup-

[i]

In order to refute a theory which pretends to be scientific, it is first necessary to understand what a scientific theory is. A scientific theory is an attempt to bring order and meaning to a mass of phenomena which without it would remain disconnected and unintelligible. Anyone who disputes the scientific character of such a theory either must produce a theory superior in these scientific functions to the one attacked or must, at the very least, demonstrate that the facts as they actually are do not lend themselves to the interpretation which the theory has put upon them. When a historian tells us that the balance of power is not a universal principle of politics, domestic and international, that it was practiced in Europe only for a limited period and never by the United States, that it ruined the states that practiced it,[4] it is incumbent upon him to tell us how we can dispose by means of theory of the historic data by which, for instance, David Hume demonstrated the universality of the balance of power and Paul Scott Mowrer[5] and Alfred Vagts[6] its practice by the United States; what Kautilya was writing about in the fourth century B.C. when he summarized the theoretical and practical tradition of Indian statecraft in terms of the balance of power; what the

---

ported by institutions humanly contrived have their origin in the nature of man himself and are inevitable."

Another historian, Arthur Schlesinger, Jr., in "Policy and National Interest," *Partisan Review*, Vol. 18, p. 709 (Nov.-Dec., 1951), however, gives Ambassador Kennan a clean bill of moral health. "But what differentiates," he writes, "the Kennan approach from that of, for example, the followers of Professor Hans J. Morgenthau is that he takes the revelations of international amorality in his stride; more than that, he comprehends them in his understanding of the tragedy of history. Mr. Kennan, in other words, is deeply moral, rather than moralistic, like Judge Hull, or immoral, like the boys who have just discovered that politics involve power."

"This dreadful doctrine," we are told (by Tannenbaum, pp. 173-174), "has now won wide acceptance by teachers and scholars in the field of international relations and has, in fact, become the leading theme in such circles in many of our largest universities. It has become the *science* of international relations—and who would quarrel with science, especially when it comes packaged in good clear English and from high sources? But it is not science. It is, in fact, only poor logic based upon false premises, and its claim to be a science is only a bit of unholy conceit."

It may be remarked in passing that to dispose of a scientific theory as "fashionable" or a "fad," as some do with regard to political realism, may reveal something about the state of mind of the writer, but reveals nothing at all about the scientific value of the theory.

[4] Tannenbaum, in the article cited above, and in "The American Tradition in Foreign Relations," *Foreign Affairs*, Vol. 30, pp. 31-50 (Oct., 1951).

[5] *Our Foreign Affairs* (New York, 1924), pp. 246 ff.

[6] "The United States and the Balance of Power," *The Journal of Politics*, Vol. 3, pp. 401-449 (Nov., 1941).

Greek city states, the Roman republic, and the medieval emperors and popes were doing if they did not apply the principles of the balance of power; and how the nations which either neglected these principles or applied them wrongly suffered political and military defeat and even extinction, while the nation which applied these principles most consistently and consciously, that is, Great Britain, enjoyed unrivalled power for an unparalleled length of time.

The historian who wishes to replace the balance of power as the guiding principle of American foreign policy with the "humanitarian and pacific traditions" of the "coördinate state"[7] must first of all explain how it has come about that the thirteen original states expanded into the full breadth and a good deal of the length of a continent, until today the strategic frontiers of the United States run parallel to the coastline of Asia and along the River Elbe. If such are the results of policies based upon "humanitarian and pacific traditions," never in the history of the world has virtue been more bountifully rewarded! Yet our historian must explain not only the great sweep of American expansion, but also the specific foreign policies which in their historic succession make up that sweep. Is it easier to explain the successive shifts of American support from Great Britain to France and back again from the beginning of King George's War in 1744 to the War of 1812 in terms of the "coördinate state" than in terms of the balance of power? The same question might be asked about the postponement of the recognition of the independence of the Spanish colonies until 1822, when the Floridas had been acquired from Spain and Spain had thereby been deprived of the ability to challenge the United States from within the hemisphere. The same question might be asked about the Monroe Doctrine itself, about Lincoln's policies toward Great Britain and France, and about our successive policies with regard to Mexico and the Caribbean. One could go on and pick out at random any foreign policy pursued by the United States from the beginning to 1919 and one would hardly find a policy, with the exception perhaps of the War of 1812, which could not be made intelligible by reference to the national interest defined in terms of power—political, military, and economic— rather than by reference to the principle of the "coördinate state." This inevitable outcome of such an inquiry is well summarized in these words:

---

[7] Tannenbaum, "The Balance of Power versus the Coördinate State" (cited above, note 3), p. 173.

Ease and prosperity have made us wish the whole world to be as happy and well to do as ourselves; and we have supposed that institutions and principles like our own were the simple prescription for making them so. And yet, when issues of our own interest arose, we have not been unselfish. We have shown ourselves kin to all the world, when it came to pushing an advantage. Our action against Spain in the Floridas, and against Mexico on the coasts of the Pacific; our attitude toward first the Spaniards, and then the French, with regard to the control of the Mississippi; the unpitying force with which we thrust the Indians to the wall wherever they stood in our way, have suited our professions of peacefulness and justice and liberality no better than the aggressions of other nations that were strong and not to be gainsaid. Even Mr. Jefferson, philanthropist and champion of peaceable and modest government though he was, exemplified this double temper of the people he ruled. "Peace is our passion," he had declared; but the passion abated when he saw the mouth of the Mississippi about to pass into the hands of France. Though he had loved France and hated England, he did not hesitate then what language to hold. "There is on the globe," he wrote to Mr. Livingston at Paris, "one single spot the possessor of which is our natural and habitual enemy. The day that France takes possession of New Orleans seals the union of two nations, who, in conjunction, can maintain exclusive possession of the sea. From that moment we must marry ourselves to the British fleet and nation." Our interests must march forward, altruists though we are; other nations must see to it that they stand off, and do not seek to stay us.

This realist appraisal of the American tradition in foreign policy was published in 1901 in the *Atlantic Monthly*. Its author was a professor of jurisprudence and political economy at Princeton by the name of Woodrow Wilson.[8]

Nothing more needs to be said to demonstrate that facts do not support a revision of American diplomatic history which tries to substitute "humanitarian and pacifist traditions" and the "coördinate state" for power politics and the balance of power as the guiding principle of American foreign policy. What, then, does support it? Three things: the way American statesmen have spoken about American foreign policy; the legal fiction of the "coördinate state"; finally, and foremost, an emotional urge to justify American foreign policy in humanitarian, pacifist terms.

It is elementary that the character of a foreign policy can be ascertained only through the examination of the political acts performed

---

[8] "Democracy and Efficiency," *Atlantic Monthly*, Vol. 87, pp. 293-294 (March, 1901).

and of the foreseeable consequences of these acts. Thus we can find out what statesmen have actually done, and from the foreseeable consequences of their acts we can surmise what their objectives might have been. Yet examination of the facts is not enough. To give meaning to the factual raw material of history, we must approach historical reality with a kind of rational outline, a map which suggests to us the possible meanings of history. In other words, we put ourselves in the position of a statesman who must meet a certain problem of foreign policy under certain circumstances and ask ourselves, what are the rational alternatives from which a statesman may choose who must meet this problem under these circumstances, presuming always that he acts in a rational manner, and which of these rational alternatives was this particular statesman, acting under these circumstances, likely to choose? It is the testing of this rational hypothesis against the actual facts and their consequences which gives meaning to the facts of history and makes the scientific writing of political history possible.

In the process of writing the history of foreign policy the interpretations by statesmen of their own acts, especially if they are made for public consumption, must needs have a strictly subsidiary place. The public self-interpretation by actors on the political scene is itself, of course, a political act which seeks to present a certain policy to its presumed supporters in terms of their moral and political folklore and to those against which it is directed in terms which intend to embarrass and deceive. Such declarations may indeed shed light upon the character and objectives of the policy pursued if they are considered in conjunction with, and in subordination to, rational hypotheses, actions, and likely consequences. Yet it is quite a different matter to interpret the American tradition of foreign policy in the light of a collection of official statements which, like most such statements, present humanitarian and pacifist justifications for the policies pursued. If anybody should be bold enough to write a history of world politics with so uncritical a method he would easily and well-nigh inevitably be driven to the conclusion that from Timur to Hitler and Stalin the foreign policies of all nations were inspired by the ideals of humanitarianism and pacifism. The absurdity of the result is commensurate with the defects of the method.

It is only from a method which accepts the declarations of statesmen as evidence of the character of the policies pursued, that the principle of the "coördinate state" receives a semblance of plausibility. Statesmen and international lawyers have been wont to speak of the "equal dignity" of all states, regardless of "wealth, power, size, population or culture," [9] which I take the principle of the "coördinate state" to mean. It is also referred to as the principle of "federalism in international relations." [10] As its prime examples are cited the relations amongst the states of the Union, the states of the American system, the members of the Commonwealth of Nations, and the members of the Swiss Confederation. If the whole world were organized in accordance with this principle, as are already these four political entities, it is assumed that the freedom, dignity, and peace of all nations would then be assured.

There is no need to examine the theoretical and practical merits of the principle of the "coördinate state," because for none of the four political entities mentioned does the idea of the "coördinate state" provide the principle of political organization. The equality of the states as the political foundation of the United States became obsolescent when Chief Justice Marshall's Supreme Court resolved the ambiguity of the Constitution in favor of the federal government, and it became obsolete when the Civil War proved Chief Justice Marshall's point. The equality of the states survives today only in the shadow and by virtue of the federal government's political supremacy, and without the cohesive force of that supremacy there would be no union of equal states to begin with. That these powers of the federal government are limited and qualified by the principle of federalism, that is, by the constitutionally granted powers of the states, is quite a different matter; it concerns the distribution of powers between federal government and states within a general system of checks and balances, but has nothing to do with the equality of the states as the alleged political foundation of the American system of government. With the exception of the equality of senatorial representation, the principle of the equality of the states is today as it has been for almost a century, devoid of political content. It survives only as a principle of regional organization, of administrative decentralization, and, above all, of constitutional rhetoric. What it really signifies was pointed out more than fifty years ago by W. A. Dunning when he summarized his answer to the question "Are the states equal under the Constitution?" by saying that "the theory of equal states falls to the ground." [11]

[9] Tannenbaum, p. 177.
[10] *Ibid.*
[11] William Archibald Dunning, *Essays on the Civil War and Reconstruction and Related Topics* (New York, 1931), p. 351.

Similarly, the federalism of Switzerland is the result of a long series of civil wars, the last one fought a little more than a century ago, which established the predominance of the German-speaking cantons within the confederation. Here too, it is the existence of predominant power, located in one segment of the federal system, which makes federalism possible in the first place.

By the same token, the unchallengeable supremacy of the United States within the Western Hemisphere has throughout been the backbone of the system of American states. As long as this supremacy is secure, there is, on the one hand, no need for the United States to assert it in the political and military sphere, and, taking it for granted, the United States can well afford to pursue a policy of the Good Neighbor; and there is, on the other hand, no opportunity for the other members of the system to challenge that supremacy effectively. This is what the principle of the "coördinate state" amounts to in the Western Hemisphere. Consequently, whenever there was even a remote possibility that the supremacy of the United States might be challenged, generally through instigation from outside the hemisphere, the United States asserted its superior power within the hemisphere and acted as all states must act under similar conditions.

Whatever possibility for common political action there remains among the members of the Commonwealth of Nations is the result of the interests which these members may have in common. In other words, the member states may work together or each of them may work with other nations, as their interests dictate. Their membership in the Commonwealth, as the examples of India, South Africa, Australia, and New Zealand clearly show, has no influence upon this decision; that membership is but a faint remembrance of the times when Great Britain could secure cooperation among the member states on its terms by virtue of its superior power.

What, then, have these four examples of the "coördinate state" in common which would establish them as a distinct type of interstate relationship, and what conclusions can be drawn from them for the organization of the world? The only thing that these four examples seem to have really in common is the legal stipulation of the equality of the members of the respective systems and this characteristic is not peculiar to them, but a general principle of international law applicable to all sovereign states. In the political sphere they seem to have nothing in common at all. What they tend to show, however, is the decisive importance of the distribution of political power for the operation of federal and egalitarian relations among states. The political cohesion of a federal system is the result of superior power located in some part of it. It is by virtue of its superior power that the predominant part can afford to grant the other members of the federal system a measure of equality in the non-political sphere. These observations bring us back to power politics and the balance of power to which the principle of the "coördinate state" was supposed to be the alternative.

In truth, it is not the disinterested consideration of facts which has given birth to the theory of the "coördinate state." That theory is rather the response to an emotional urge, and since this emotion is not peculiar to a particular author but typical of a popular reaction to the new role which the United States must play in world affairs, it deserves a brief analysis.

One of the great experiences of our time which have impressed themselves upon the American mind is the emergence of the United States as a nation among other nations, exposed to the same opportunities, temptations, risks, and liabilities to which other nations have been traditionally exposed. This experience becomes the more shocking if it is compared with the expectation with which we fought the Second World War. We expected from that war a reaffirmation of the secure, detached, and independent position in world affairs which we had inherited from the Founding Fathers and which we had been successful in preserving at least to the First World War. By avoiding what we thought had been Wilson's mistakes, we expected to emerge from that war if not more independent, certainly more secure than we were when we entered it. In fact, probably not even in the early days of the Republic were we more exposed to danger from abroad than we are today, and never had we less freedom of action in taking care of our interests than we have today.

It is naturally shocking to recognize that a happy chapter in the history of the nation and in one's own way of life has come to an end. There are those who reconcile themselves to the inevitable, albeit with sorrow rather than with glee, and try to apply the lessons of the past to the tasks at hand. There are others who try to escape from a disappointing and threatening reality into the realm of fantasy. Three such escapist fantasies have arisen in our midst in response to the challenge of American world leadership and power: the fantasy of needless American participation in war, the fantasy of American treason, and the fantasy of American innocence.

The first of these fantasies presumes that the present predicament is a result not of necessity but of folly, the folly of American statesmen who needlessly intervened in two world wars. The second of these fantasies attributes the present predicament to treason in high places whereby the fruits of victory were handed to the enemy. The third of these fantasies denies that the predicament is real and prefers to think of it as an intellectual fraud perpetrated upon the American people. To support this fictional denial of the actualities of the present, it draws upon a fictional account of the past. The United States does not need to bear at present the intellectual, moral, and political burdens which go with involvement in power politics and the maintenance of the balance of power; for it has never borne them in the past, never having been thus involved. The golden age of past political innocence sheds its glow upon a but seemingly less innocent present and promises a future in which all the world will follow the example of America, forswear politics and the balance of power, and accept the principle of the "coördinate state." Our rearmament program, as exemplified in the Atlantic Security Pact, we are told, has nothing to do with the balance of power but aims at the "organization of as much of the world as we can upon the basis of the coördinate state. . . . It may prove impossible under present conditions to build such a system without having to fight a war with Russia, but then at least we will be fighting, as we did before, for the thing we consider worth defending with our lives and treasure." [12] Thus a fictional account of the American past, begun as an act of uncalled-for patriotic piety, issues in an ideology for a third world war. Escape we must from the unfamiliar, unpleasant, and dangerous present, first into the political innocence of the past and from there into the immediate future of a third world war, beyond which the revived and universalized innocence of the more distant future will surely lie.

We have said that to present the American tradition in foreign policy as having been free from concern with power politics and the balance of power is not warranted by the facts of American history. Yet it might still be argued, and it is actually being argued, that, regardless of the evidence of history, the American people will not be reconciled to power

---

[12] Tannenbaum, pp. 195-196.

politics and the balance of power and will support only policies based upon abstract moral principles. While in the past the United States might have pursued balance of power policies and while it might be a good thing if it did do so again, the American people will not stand for it. Here the emotional appeal to patriotic piety is joined by calculations of political expediency. Yet the case for misrepresenting American history has nothing to gain from either.

There is a strong tendency in all historiography to glorify the national past, and in popular presentations that tendency takes on the aspects of the jingoist whitewash. Even so penetrating a mind as John Stuart Mill's could deliver himself of an essay in which he proved, no doubt to the satisfaction of many of his English readers but certainly of few others, that Great Britain had never interfered in the affairs of European nations and had interfered in those of the Indian states only for their own good.[13] Yet it is the measure of a nation's maturity to be able to recognize its past for what it actually is. Why should we not admit that American foreign policy has been generally hardheaded and practical and at times ruthless? Why should we deny Jefferson's cunning, say, in the Puget Sound affair, the cruelty with which the Indians were treated, and the faithlessness with which the treaties with the Indians were cast aside? We know that this is the way all nations are when their interests are at stake—so cruel, so faithless, so cunning. We know that the United States has refrained from seeking dominions beyond the seas not because it is more virtuous than other nations, but because it had the better part of a continent to colonize.

As has been pointed out elsewhere at greater length, the man in the street, unsophisticated as he is and uninformed as he may be, has a surer grasp of the essentials of foreign policy and a more mature judgment of its basic issues than many of the intellectuals and politicians who pretend to speak for him and cater to what they imagine his prejudices to be. During the recent war the ideologues of the Atlantic Charter, the Four Freedoms, and the United Nations were constantly complaining that the American soldier did not know what he was fighting for. Indeed, if he was fighting for some utopian ideal, divorced from the concrete experiences and interests of the country, then the complaint was well grounded. However, if he was fighting for the territorial integrity of the nation and for its survival as a free country where he could

[13] "A Few Words on Non-Intervention," *Dissertations and Discussions: Political, Philosophical, and Historical* (London, 1875), pp. 153-178.

live, think, and act as he pleased, then he had never any doubt about what he was fighting for. Ideological rationalizations and justifications are indeed the indispensable concomitants of all political action. Yet there is something unhealthy in a craving for ideological intoxication and in the inability to act and to see merit in action except under the stimulant of grandiose ideas and far-fetched schemes. Have our intellectuals become, like Hamlet, too much beset by doubt to act and, unlike Hamlet, compelled to still their doubts by renouncing their sense of what is real? The man in the street has no such doubts. It is true that ideologues and demagogues can sway him by appealing to his emotions. But it is also true, as American history shows in abundance and as the popular success of Ambassador Kennan's book demonstrates, that responsible statesmen can guide him by awakening his latent understanding of the national interest.

[II]

Yet what is the national interest? How can we define it and give it the content which will make it a guide for action? This is one of the relevant questions to which the current debate has given rise.

It has been frequently argued against the realist conception of foreign policy that its key concept, the national interest, does not provide an acceptable standard for political action. This argument is in the main based upon two grounds: the elusiveness of the concept and its susceptibility to interpretations, such as limitless imperialism and narrow nationalism, which are not in keeping with the American tradition in foreign policy. The argument has substance as far as it goes, but it does not invalidate the usefulness of the concept.

The concept of the national interest is similar in two respects to the "great generalities" of the Constitution, such as the general welfare and due process. It contains a residual meaning which is inherent in the concept itself, but beyond these minimum requirements its content can run the whole gamut of meanings which are logically compatible with it. That content is determined by the political traditions and the total cultural context within which a nation formulates its foreign policy. The concept of the national interest, then, contains two elements, one that is logically required and in that sense necessary, and one that is variable and determined by circumstances.

Any foreign policy which operates under the standard of the national interest must obviously have some reference to the physical, political, and cultural entity which we call a nation. In a world where a number of sovereign nations compete with and oppose each other for power, the foreign policies of all nations must necessarily refer to their survival as their minimum requirements. Thus all nations do what they cannot help but do: protect their physical, political, and cultural identity against encroachments by other nations.

It has been suggested that this reasoning erects the national state into the last word in politics and the national interest into an absolute standard for political action. This, however, is not quite the case. The idea of interest is indeed of the essence of politics and, as such, unaffected by the circumstances of time and place. Thucydides' statement, born of the experiences of ancient Greece, that "identity of interest is the surest of bonds whether between states or individuals" was taken up in the nineteenth century by Lord Salisbury's remark that "the only bond of union that endures" among nations is "the absence of all clashing interests." The perennial issue between the realist and utopian schools of thought over the nature of politics, to which we have referred before, might well be formulated in terms of concrete interests vs. abstract principles. Yet while the concern of politics with interest is perennial, the connection between interest and the national state is a product of history.

The national state itself is obviously a product of history and as such destined to yield in time to different modes of political organization. As long as the world is politically organized into nations, the national interest is indeed the last word in world politics. When the national state will have been replaced by another mode of organization, foreign policy must then protect the interest in survival of that new organization. For the benefit of those who insist upon discarding the national state and constructing supranational organizations by constitutional fiat, it must be pointed out that these new organizational forms will either come into being through conquest or else through consent based upon the mutual recognition of the national interests of the nations concerned; for no nation will forego its freedom of action if it has no reason to expect proportionate benefits in compensation for that loss. This is true of treaties concerning commerce or fisheries as it is true of the great compacts, such as the European Coal and Steel Community, through which nations try to create supranational forms of organization.

Thus, by an apparent paradox, what is historically relative in the idea of the national interest can be overcome only through the promotion in concert of the national interest of a number of nations.

The survival of a political unit, such as a nation, in its identity is the irreducible minimum, the necessary element of its interests vis-à-vis other units. Taken in isolation, the determination of its content in a concrete situation is relatively simple; for it encompasses the integrity of the nation's territory, of its political institutions, and of its culture. Thus bipartisanship in foreign policy, especially in times of war, has been most easily achieved in the promotion of these minimum requirements of the national interest. The situation is different with respect to the variable elements of the national interest. All the cross currents of personalities, public opinion, sectional interests, partisan politics, and political and moral folkways are brought to bear upon their determination. In consequence, the contribution which science can make to this field, as to all fields of policy formation, is limited. It can identify the different agencies of the government which contribute to the determination of the variable elements of the national interest and assess their relative weight. It can separate the long-range objectives of foreign policy from the short-term ones which are the means for the achievement of the former and can tentatively establish their rational relations. Finally, it can analyze the variable elements of the national interest in terms of their legitimacy and their compatibility with other national values and with the national interest of other nations. We shall address ourselves briefly to the typical problems with which this analysis must deal.

The legitimacy of the national interest must be determined in the face of possible usurpation by subnational, other-national, and supranational interests. On the subnational level we find group interests, represented particularly by ethnic and economic groups, who tend to identify themselves with the national interest. Charles A. Beard has emphasized, however one-sidedly, the extent to which the economic interests of certain groups have been presented as those of the United States.[14] Group interests exert, of course, constant pressure upon the conduct of our foreign policy, claiming their identity with the national interest. It is, however, doubtful that, with the exception of a few spectacular cases, they have been successful in determining the course

---

[14] *The Idea of National Interest: An Analytical Study in American Foreign Policy* (New York, 1934).

of American foreign policy. It is much more likely, given the nature of American domestic politics, that American foreign policy, insofar as it is the object of pressures by sectional interests, will normally be a compromise between divergent sectional interests. The concept of the national interest, as it emerges from this contest as the actual guide for foreign policy, may well fall short of what would be rationally required by the overall interests of the United States. Yet the concept of the national interest which emerges from this contest of conflicting sectional interests is also more than any particular sectional interest or their sum total. It is, as it were, the lowest common denominator where sectional interests and the national interest meet in an uneasy compromise which may leave much to be desired in view of all the interests concerned.

The national interest can be usurped by other-national interests in two typical ways. The case of treason by individuals, either out of conviction or for pay, needs only to be mentioned here; for insofar as treason is committed on behalf of a foreign government rather than a supranational principle, it is significant for psychology, sociology, and criminology, but not for the theory of politics. The other case, however, is important not only for the theory of politics but also for its practice, especially in the United States.

National minorities in European countries, ethnic groups in the United States, ideological minorities anywhere may identify themselves, either spontaneously or under the direction of the agents of a foreign government, with the interests of that foreign government and may promote these interests under the guise of the national interest of the country whose citizens they happen to be. The activities of the German-American Bund in the United States in the 'thirties and of Communists everywhere are cases in point. Yet the issue of the national interest vs. other-national interests masquerading as the national interest has arisen constantly in the United States in a less clear-cut fashion.

A country which had been settled by consecutive waves of "foreigners" was bound to find it particularly difficult to identify its own national interest against alleged, seeming, or actual other-national interests represented by certain groups among its own citizens. Since virtually all citizens of the United States are, as it were, "more or less" foreign-born, those who were "less" so have frequently not resisted the temptation to use this distinction as a polemic weapon against latecomers who happened to differ from them in their conception of the national interest of the United States. Frequently, this rationalization has been dispensed with and a conception of foreign policy with which a writer happened to disagree has been attributed outright to foreign sympathy or influence or worse. British influence and interests have served as standard arguments in debates on American foreign policy. Madison, in his polemic against Hamilton on the occasion of Washington's Neutrality Proclamation of 1793, identified the Federalist position with that of "the foreigners and degenerate citizens among us, who hate our republican government, and the French revolution," [15] and the accusation met with a favorable response in a majority of Congress and of public opinion. However, these traditional attempts to discredit dissenting opinion as being influenced by foreign interests should not obscure the real issue, which is the peculiar vulnerability of the national interest of the United States to usurpation by the interests of other nations.

The usurpation of the national interest by supranational interests can derive in our time from two sources: religious bodies and international organizations. The competition between church and state for determination of certain interests and policies, domestic and international, has been an intermittent issue throughout the history of the national state. Here, too, the legitimate defense of the national interest against usurpation has frequently, especially in the United States, degenerated into the demagogic stigmatization of dissenting views as being inspired by Rome and, hence, being incompatible with the national interest. Yet here, too, the misuse of the issue for demagogic purposes must be considered apart from the legitimacy of the issue itself.

The more acute problem arises at the present time from the importance which the public and government officials, at least in their public utterances, attribute to the values represented and the policies pursued by international organizations either as alternative or supplements to the values and policies for which the national government stands. It is frequently asserted that the foreign policy of the United States pursues no objectives apart from those of the United Nations, that, in other words, the foreign policy of the United States is actually identical with the policy of the United Nations. This assertion cannot refer to anything real in actual politics to support it. For the constitutional structure of international organizations, such as the United Nations, and

---

[15] "Helvidius, in Answer to Pacificus, on President Washington's Proclamation of Neutrality," in *Letters and Other Writings of James Madison* (Philadelphia, 1867), Vol. 1, p. 611.

their procedural practices make it impossible for them to pursue interests apart from those of the member-states which dominate their policy-forming bodies. The identity between the interests of the United Nations and the United States can only refer to the successful policies of the United States within the United Nations through which the support of the United Nations is being secured for the policies of the United States.[16] The assertion, then, is mere polemic, different from the one discussed previously in that the identification of a certain policy with a supranational interest does not seek to reflect discredit upon the former, but to bestow upon it a dignity which the national interest pure and simple is supposed to lack.

The real issue in view of the problem that concerns us here is not whether the so-called interests of the United Nations, which do not exist apart from the interests of its most influential members, have superseded the national interest of the United States, but for what kind of interests the United States has secured United Nations support. While these interests cannot be United Nations interests, they do not need to be national interests either. Here we are in the presence of that modern phenomenon which has been variously described as "utopianism," "sentimentalism," "moralism," the "legalistic-moralistic approach." The common denominator of all these tendencies in modern political thought is the substitution for the national interest of a supranational standard of action which is generally identified with an international organization, such as the United Nations. The national interest is here not being usurped by sub- or supranational interests which, however inferior in worth to the national interest, are nevertheless real and worthy of consideration within their proper sphere. What challenges the national interest here is a mere figment of the imagination, a product of wishful thinking, which is postulated as a valid norm for international conduct, without being valid either there or anywhere else. At this point we touch the core of the present controversy between utopianism and realism in international affairs; we shall return to it later in this paper.

The national interest as such must be defended against usurpation by non-national interests. Yet once that task is accomplished, a rational

---

[16] See, on this point, Hans J. Morgenthau, "International Organizations and Foreign Policy," in *Foundations of World Organization: A Political and Cultural Appraisal*, Eleventh Symposium of the Conference on Science, Philosophy and Religion, edited by Lyman Bryson, Louis Finkelstein, Harold D. Lasswell, R. M. MacIver (New York, 1952), pp. 377-383.

order must be established among the values which make up the national interest and among the resources to be committed to them. While the interests which a nation may pursue in its relation with other nations are of infinite variety and magnitude, the resources which are available for the pursuit of such interests are necessarily limited in quantity and kind. No nation has the resources to promote all desirable objectives with equal vigor; all nations must therefore allocate their scarce resources as rationally as possible. The indispensable precondition of such rational allocation is a clear understanding of the distinction between the necessary and variable elements of the national interest. Given the contentious manner in which in democracies the variable elements of the national interest are generally determined, the advocates of an extensive conception of the national interest will inevitably present certain variable elements of the national interest as though their attainment were necessary for the nation's survival. In other words, the necessary elements of the national interest have a tendency to swallow up the variable elements so that in the end all kinds of objectives, actual or potential, are justified in terms of national survival. Such arguments have been advanced, for instance, in support of the rearmament of Western Germany and of the defense of Formosa. They must be subjected to rational scrutiny which will determine, however tentatively, their approximate place in the scale of national values.

The same problem presents itself in its extreme form when a nation pursues, or is asked to pursue, objectives which are not only unnecessary for its survival but tend to jeopardize it. Second-rate nations which dream of playing the role of great powers, such as Italy and Poland in the interwar period, illustrate this point. So do great powers which dream of remaking the world in their own image and embark upon world-wide crusades, thus straining their resources to exhaustion. Here scientific analysis has the urgent task of pruning down national objectives to the measure of available resources in order to make their pursuit compatible with national survival.

Finally, the national interest of a nation which is conscious not only of its own interests but also of that of other nations must be defined in terms compatible with the latter. In a multinational world this is a requirement of political morality; in an age of total war it is also one of the conditions for survival.

In connection with this problem two mutually exclusive arguments have been advanced. On the one hand, it has been argued against the theory of international politics here presented that the concept of the national interest revives the eighteenth-century concept of enlightened self-interest, presuming that the uniformly enlightened pursuit of their self-interest by all individuals, as by all nations, will of itself be conducive to a peaceful and harmonious society. On the other hand, the point has been made that the pursuit of their national interest by all nations makes war the permanent arbiter of conflicts among them. Neither argument is well taken.

The concept of the national interest presupposes neither a naturally harmonious, peaceful world nor the inevitability of war as a consequence of the pursuit by all nations of their national interest. Quite to the contrary, it assumes continuous conflict and threat of war, to be minimized through the continuous adjustment of conflicting interests by diplomatic action. No such assumption would be warranted if all nations at all times conceived of their national interest only in terms of their survival and, in turn, defined their interest in survival in restrictive and rational terms. As it is, their conception of the national interest is subject to all the hazards of misinterpretation, usurpation, and misjudgment to which reference has been made above. To minimize these hazards is the first task of a foreign policy which seeks the defense of the national interest by peaceful means. Its second task is the defense of the national interest, restrictively and rationally defined, against the national interests of other nations which may or may not be thus defined. If they are not, it becomes the task of armed diplomacy to convince the nations concerned that their legitimate interests have nothing to fear from a restrictive and rational foreign policy and that their illegitimate interests have nothing to gain in the face of armed might rationally employed.

[III]

We have said before that the utopian and realist positions in international affairs do not necessarily differ in the policies they advocate, but that they part company over their general philosophies of politics and their way of thinking about matters political. It does not follow that the present debate is only of academic interest and without practical significance. Both camps, it is true, may support the same policy for different reasons. Yet if the reasons are unsound, the soundness of the policies supported by them is a mere coincidence, and these very same reasons may be, and inevitably are, invoked on other occasions in support of unsound policies. The nefarious consequences of false philosophies and wrong ways of thinking may for the time being be concealed by the apparent success of policies derived from them. You may go to war, justified by your nation's interests, for a moral purpose and in disregard of considerations of power; and military victory seems to satisfy both your moral aspirations and your nation's interests. Yet the manner in which you waged the war, achieved victory, and settled the peace cannot help reflecting your philosophy of politics and your way of thinking about political problems. If these are in error, you may win victory on the field of battle and still assist in the defeat of both your moral principles and the national interest of your country.

Any number of examples could illustrate the real yet subtle practical consequences which follow from the different positions taken. We have chosen two: collective security in Korea and the liberation of the nations that are captives of Communism. A case for both policies can be made from both the utopian and realist positions, but with significant differences in the emphasis and substance of the policies pursued.

Collective security as an abstract principle of utopian politics requires that all nations come to the aid of a victim of aggression by resisting the aggressor with all means necessary to frustrate his aims. Once the case of aggression is established, the duty to act is unequivocal. Its extent may be affected by concern for the nation's survival; obviously no nation will commit outright suicide in the service of collective security. But beyond that elemental limitation no consideration of interest or power, either with regard to the aggressor or his victim or the nation acting in the latter's defense, can qualify the obligation to act under the principle of collective security. Thus high officials of our government have declared that we intervened in Korea not for any narrow interest of ours but in support of the moral principle of collective security.

Collective security as a concrete principle of realist policy is the age-old maxim, "Hang together or hang separately," in modern dress. It recognizes the need for nation A under certain circumstances to defend nation B against attack by nation C. That need is determined, first, by the interest which A has in the territorial integrity of B and by the relation of that interest to all the other interests of A as well as to the resources available for the support of all those interests. Furthermore, A must take into account the power which is at the disposal of aggressor C for fighting A and B as over against the power available to A and B for fighting C. The same calculation must be carried on concerning the

power of the likely allies of C as over against those of A and B. Before
going to war for the defense of South Korea in the name of collective
security, an American adherent of political realism would have demanded an answer to the following four questions: First, what is our
interest in the preservation of the independence of South Korea; second,
what is our power to defend that independence against North Korea;
third, what is our power to defend that independence against China and
the Soviet Union; and fourth, what are the chances for preventing
China and the Soviet Union from entering the Korean War?

In view of the principle of collective security, interpreted in utopian
terms, our intervention in Korea was a foregone conclusion. The interpretation of this principle in realist terms might or might not, depending upon the concrete circumstances of interest and power, have led us
to the same conclusion. In the execution of the policy of collective security the utopian had to be indifferent to the possibility of Chinese and
Russian intervention, except for his resolution to apply the principle of
collective security to anybody who would intervene on the side of the
aggressor. The realist could not help weighing the possibility of the
intervention of a great power on the side of the aggressor in terms of
the interests engaged and the power available on the other side.[17]

The Truman administration could not bring itself to taking resolutely
the utopian or the realist position. It resolved to intervene in good
measure on utopian grounds and in spite of military advice to the contrary; it allowed the military commander to advance to the Yalu River
in disregard of the risk of the intervention of a great power against
which collective security could be carried out only by means of a general
war, and then refused to pursue the war with full effectiveness on the
realist grounds of the risk of a third world war. Thus Mr. Truman
in 1952 is caught in the same dilemma from which Mr. Baldwin could
extricate himself in 1936 on the occasion of the League of Nations
sanctions against Italy's attack upon Ethiopia only at an enormous loss
to British prestige. Collective security as a defense of the status quo
short of a general war can be effective only against second-rate powers.
Applied against a major power, it is a contradiction in terms, for it
means necessarily a major war. Of this self-defeating contradiction Mr.

---

[17] The difference in these two attitudes is well illustrated by the following passage
from a recent Moon Mullins cartoon. An elderly representative of the utopian school
asks little Kayo: "Remember the golden rule. Now, supposing that boy slapped you
on the right cheek, what would you do?" Whereupon Kayo replies realistically: "Jest
how big a boy are you supposin'?"

Baldwin was as unaware in the 'thirties as Mr. Truman seems to be in 1952. Mr. Churchill put Mr. Baldwin's dilemma in these cogent terms: "First, the Prime Minister had declared that sanctions meant war; secondly, he was resolved that there must be no war; and thirdly, he decided upon sanctions. It was evidently impossible to comply with these three conditions." Similarly Mr. Truman had declared that the effective prosecution of the Korean War meant the possibility of a third world war; he resolved that there must be no third world war; and he decided upon intervention in the Korean War. Here, too, it is impossible to comply with these three conditions.

Similar contradictions are inherent in the proposals which would substitute for the current policy of containment one of the liberation of the nations presently the captives of Russian Communism. This objective can be compatible with the utopian or realist position, but the policies designed to secure it will be fundamentally different according to whether they are based upon one or the other position. The clearest case to date for the utopian justification of such policies has been made by Representative Charles J. Kersten of Wisconsin who pointed to these four "basic defects" of the "negative policy of containment and negotiated coexistence":

> It would be immoral and unchristian to negotiate a permanent agreement with forces which by every religious creed and moral precept are evil. It abandons nearly one-half of humanity and the once free nations of Poland, Czechoslovakia, Hungary, Rumania, Bulgaria, Albania, Lithuania, Latvia, Esthonia and China to enslavement of the Communist police state.
>
> It is un-American because it violates the principle of the American Declaration of Independence, which proclaims the rights of all people to freedom and their right and duty to throw off tyranny.
>
> It will lead to all-out World War III because it aligns all the forces of the non-Communist world in military opposition to and against all the forces of the Communist world, including the 800,000,000 people behind the Iron Curtain.
>
> The policy of mere containment is uneconomic and will lead to national bankruptcy.[18]

This statement is interesting for its straightforwardness and because it combines in a rather typical fashion considerations of abstract morality and of expediency. The captive nations must be liberated not only because their captivity is immoral, unchristian, and un-American,

---

[18] *New York Times*, August 14, 1952, p. 1.

but also because its continuation will lead to a third world war and to national bankruptcy. To what extent, however, these considerations of expediency are invalidated by their utopian setting will become obvious from a comparison between the utopian and the realist positions.

From the utopian point of view there can be no difference between the liberation of Esthonia or Czechoslovakia, of Poland or China; the captivity of any nation, large or small, close or far away, is a moral outrage which cannot be tolerated. The realist, too, seeks the liberation of all captive nations because he realizes that the presence of the Russian armies in the heart of Europe and their cooperation with the Chinese armies constitute the two main sources of the imbalance of power which threatens our security. Yet before he formulates a program of liberation, he will seek answers to a number of questions such as these: While the United States has a general interest in the liberation of all captive nations, what is the hierarchy of interests it has in the liberation, say, of China, Esthonia, and Hungary? And while the Soviet Union has a general interest in keeping all captive nations in that state, what is the hierarchy of its interests in keeping, say, Poland, Eastern Germany, and Bulgaria captive? If we assume, as we must on the historic evidence of two centuries, that Russia would never give up control over Poland without being compelled by force of arms, would the objective of the liberation of Poland justify the ruin of western civilization, that of Poland included, which would be the certain result of a third world war? What resources does the United States have at its disposal for the liberation of all captive nations or some of them? What resources does the Soviet Union have at its disposal to keep in captivity all captive nations or some of them? Are we more likely to avoid national bankruptcy by embarking upon a policy of indiscriminate liberation with the concomitant certainty of war or by continuing the present policy of containment?

It might be that in a particular instance the policies suggested by the answers to these questions will coincide with Representative Kersten's proposals, but there can be no doubt that in its overall character, substance, emphasis, and likely consequences a utopian policy of liberation differs fundamentally from a realist one.

The issue between liberation as a utopian principle of abstract morality vs. the realist evaluation of the consequences which a policy of liberation would have for the survival of the nation has arisen before in American history. Abraham Lincoln was faced with a dilemma simi-

lar to that which confronts us today. Should he make the liberation of
the slaves the ultimate standard of his policy even at the risk of destroying the Union, as many urged him to do, or should he subordinate the
moral principle of universal freedom to considerations of the national
interest? The answer Lincoln gave to Horace Greeley, a spokesman for
the utopian moralists, is timeless in its eloquent wisdom. "If there be
those," he wrote on August 22, 1862,

> who would not save the Union unless they could at the same time save
> slavery, I do not agree with them. If there be those who would not save
> the Union unless they could at the same time destroy slavery, I do not
> agree with them. My paramount object in this struggle *is* to save the
> Union, and is *not* either to save or to destroy slavery. If I could save the
> Union without freeing *any* slave I would do it, and if I could save it by
> freeing *all* the slaves, I would do it; and if I could save it by freeing some
> and leaving others alone I would also do that. What I do about slavery,
> and the colored race, I do because I believe it helps to save the Union;
> and what I forbear, I forbear because I do *not* believe it would help to
> save the Union. I shall do *less* whenever I shall believe what I am doing
> hurts the cause, and I shall do *more* whenever I shall believe doing more
> will help the cause. I shall try to correct errors when shown to be errors;
> and I shall adopt new views so fast as they shall appear to be true views.
>   I have here stated my purpose according to my view of *official* duty;
> and I intend no modification of my oft-expressed *personal* wish that all
> men everywhere could be free.

[IV]

The foregoing discussion ought to shed additional light, if this is still
needed, upon the moral merits of the utopian and realist positions. This
question, more than any other, seems to have agitated the critics of
realism in international affairs. Disregarding the voluminous evidence,
some of them have picked a few words out of their context to prove
that realism in international affairs is unprincipled and contemptuous
of morality. To mention but one example, one eminent critic sum-
marizes my position, which he supposes to deny the possibility of judging the conduct of states by moral criteria, in these words: "And one
spokesman finds 'a profound and neglected truth,' to use his words, in
the dictum of Hobbes that 'there is neither morality nor law outside the
state.' "[19] These are indeed my words, but not all of them. What I
actually said was this:

---

[19] A. H. Feller, "In Defense of International Law and Morality," *The Annals of
the American Academy of Political and Social Science*, Vol. 282, p. 80 (July, 1952).

There is a profound and neglected truth hidden in Hobbes's extreme dictum that the state creates morality as well as law and that there is neither morality nor law outside the state. Universal moral principles, such as justice or equality, are capable of guiding political action only to the extent that they have been given concrete content and have been related to political situations by society.[20]

It must be obvious from this passage and from all my other writings on the subject[21] that my position is the exact opposite from what this critic makes it out to be. I have always maintained that the actions of states are subject to universal moral principles and I have been careful to differentiate my position in this respect from that of Hobbes. Five points basic to my position may need to be emphasized again.

The first point is what one might call the requirement of cosmic humility with regard to the moral evaluation of the actions of states. To know that states are subject to the moral law is one thing; to pretend to know what is morally required of states in a particular situation is quite another. The human mind tends naturally to identify the particular interests of states, as of individuals, with the moral purposes of the universe. The statesman in the defense of the nation's interests may, and at times even must, yield to that tendency; the scholar must resist it at every turn. For the light-hearted assumption that what one's own nation aims at and does is morally good and that those who oppose that nation's policies are evil is morally indefensible and intellectually untenable and leads in practice to that distortion of judgment, born of the blindness of crusading frenzy, which has been the curse of nations from the beginning of time.

---

[20] In *Defense of the National Interest: A Critical Examination of American Foreign Policy* (New York, 1951), p. 34.

[21] See, for instance, "The Machiavellian Utopia," *Ethics*, Vol. 55, pp. 145-147 (Jan., 1945); "Ethics and Politics," in *Approaches to Group Understanding*, Sixth Symposium of the Conference on Science, Philosophy and Religion, edited by Bryson, Finkelstein, and MacIver (New York, 1947), pp. 319-341; "The Escape from Power in the Western World," in *Conflicts of Power in Modern Culture*, Seventh Symposium of the Conference on Science, Philosophy and Religion, edited by Bryson, Finkelstein, and MacIver, pp. 1-12; *Scientific Man vs. Power Politics* (Chicago, 1946), Chaps. 7, 8; "Views of Nuremberg: Further Analysis of the Trial and Its Importance," *America*, Vol. 76, pp. 266-267 (Dec. 7, 1946): "The Twilight of International Morality," *Ethics*, Vol. 58, pp. 79-99 (Jan., 1948); "The Political Science of E. H. Carr," *World Politics*, Vol. 1, pp. 127-134 (Oct., 1948); *Politics Among Nations* (New York, 1948), Ch. 14; "National Interest and Moral Principles in Foreign Policy: The Primacy of the National Interest," *The American Scholar*, Vol. 18, pp. 207-212 (Spring, 1949); "The Pathology of Power," *American Perspective*, Vol. 4, pp. 6-10 (Winter, 1950); "The Moral Dilemma in Foreign Policy," in *The Year Book of World Affairs*, 1951 (London, 1951), pp. 12-36.

The second point which obviously needs to be made again concerns the effectiveness of the restraints which morality imposes upon the actions of states.

A discussion of international morality must guard against the two extremes either of overrating the influence of ethics upon international politics or else of denying that statesmen and diplomats are moved by anything else but considerations of material power.

On the one hand, there is the dual error of confounding the moral rules which people actually observe with those they pretend to observe as well as with those which writers declare they ought to observe. . . .

On the other hand, there is the misconception, usually associated with the general depreciation and moral condemnation of power politics, discussed above, that international politics is so thoroughly evil that it is no use looking for ethical limitations of the aspirations for power on the international scene. Yet, if we ask ourselves what statesmen and diplomats are capable of doing to further the power objectives of their respective nations and what they actually do, we realize that they do less than they probably could and less than they actually did in other periods of history. They refuse to consider certain ends and to use certain means, either altogether or under certain conditions, not because in the light of expediency they appear impractical or unwise, but because certain moral rules interpose an absolute barrier. Moral rules do not permit certain policies to be considered at all from the point of view of expediency. Such ethical inhibitions operate in our time on different levels with different effectiveness. Their restraining function is most obvious and most effective in affirming the sacredness of human life in times of peace.[22]

In connection with this passage we have given a number of historic examples showing the influence of moral principles upon the conduct of foreign policy. An example taken from contemporary history will illustrate the same point. There can be little doubt that the Soviet Union could have achieved the objectives of its foreign policy at the end of the Second World War without antagonizing the nations of the West into that encircling coalition which has been the nightmare of Bolshevist foreign policy since 1917. It could have mitigated cunning for its own sake and the use of force with persuasion, conciliation, and a trust derived from the awareness of a partial community of interests and would thereby have minimized the dangers to itself and the rest of the world which are inherent in the objectives of its policies. Yet the Soviet Union was precluded from relying upon these traditional methods of diplomacy by its general conception of human nature, politics, and morality.

---

[22] Morgenthau, *Politics Among Nations*, pp. 174-175.

In the general philosophy of Bolshevism there is no room for honest dissent, the recognition of the intrinsic worth of divergent interests, and genuine conciliation between such interests. On all levels of social inter-action opposition must be destroyed by cunning and violence, since it has no right to exist, rather than be met halfway in view of its intrinsic legitimacy. This being the general conception of the political morality of Bolshevism, the foreign policy of the Soviet Union is limited to a much more narrow choice of means than the foreign policies of other nations.

The United States, for instance, has been able, in its relations with the nations of Latin America, to replace military intervention and dollar diplomacy with the policy of the Good Neighbor. That drastic change was made possible by the general conception of political morality which has been prevalent in the United States from its very inception. The United States is a pluralist society which presupposes the continuing existence and legitimacy of divergent interests. These interests are locked in a continuing struggle for supremacy to be decided by force only as a last resort, but normally through a multitude of institutional agencies which are so devised as to allow one or the other interest a temporary advantage but none a permanent supremacy at the price of the destruction of the others. This morality of pluralism allows the United States, once it is secure in that minimum of vital interests to which we have referred above, to transfer those principles of political morality to the international scene and to deal with divergent interests there with the same methods of genuine compromise and conciliation which are a permanent element of its domestic political life.

The third point concerns the relations between universal moral prin-ciples and political action. I have always maintained that these universal moral principles cannot be applied to the actions of states in their ab-stract universal formulation, but that they must be, as it were, filtered through the concrete circumstances of time and place. The individual may say for himself: *"Fiat justitia, pereat mundus"*; the state has no right to say so in the name of those who are in its care. Both individual and state must judge political action by universal moral principles, such as that of liberty. Yet while the individual has a moral right to sacrifice himself in defense of such a moral principle, the state has no moral right to let its moral disapprobation of the infringement of liberty get in the way of successful political action, itself inspired by the moral principle of national survival. There can be no political morality without prudence, that is, without consideration of the political consequences of seemingly moral action. Classical and medieval philosophy knew this and so did Lincoln when he said: "I do the very best I know how, the very best I can, and I mean to keep doing so until the end. If the end brings me out all right, what is said against me won't amount to anything. If the end brings me out wrong, ten angels swearing I was right would make no difference." The issue between utopianism and realism, as it bears on this point, has been put most succinctly by Edmund Burke, and what he has to say in the following passage about revolution, that is, civil war, may well be applied *mutatis mutandis* to all war.

Nothing universal can be rationally affirmed on any moral or any political subject. Pure metaphysical abstraction does not belong to these matters. The lines of morality are not like the ideal lines of mathematics. They are broad and deep as well as long. They admit of exceptions; they demand modifications. These exceptions and modifications are not made by the process of logic, but by the rules of prudence. Prudence is not only the first in rank of the virtues political and moral, but she is the director, the regulator, the standard of them all. Metaphysics cannot live without definition; but Prudence is cautious how she defines. Our courts cannot be more fearful in suffering fictitious cases to be brought before them for eliciting their determination on a point of law than prudent moralists are in putting extreme and hazardous cases of conscience upon emergencies not existing. Without attempting, therefore, to define, what never can be defined, the case of a revolution in government, this, I think, may be safely affirmed—that a sore and pressing evil is to be removed, and that a good, great in its amount and unequivocal in its nature, must be probable almost to a certainty, before the inestimable price of our own morals and the well-being of a number of our fellow-citizens is paid for a revolution. If ever we ought to be economists even to parsimony, it is in the voluntary production of evil. Every revolution contains in it something of evil.[23]

Fourth, the realist recognizes that a moral decision, especially in the political sphere, does not imply a simple choice between a moral principle and a standard of action which is morally irrelevant or even out-

    [23] *The Works of The Right Honorable Edmund Burke,* 4th ed. (Boston, 1871), Vol. 4, pp. 80-81. Cf. also Burke, "Speech on a Bill for Shortening the Duration of Parliaments," May 8, 1780, in *Works,* Vol. 7, p. 73: "I must see, to satisfy me, the remedies; I must see, from their operation in the cure of the old evil, and in the cure of those new evils which are inseparable from all remedies, how they balance each other, and what is the total result. The excellence of mathematics and metaphysics is, to have but one thing before you; but he forms the best judgment in all moral disquisitions who has the greatest number and variety of considerations in one view before him, and can take them in with the best possible consideration of the middle results of all."

right immoral. A moral decision implies always a choice among different moral principles, one of which is given precedence over others. To say that a political action has no moral purpose is absurd; for political action can be defined as an attempt to realize moral values through the medium of politics, that is, power. The relevant moral question concerns the choice among different moral values, and it is at this point that the realist and the utopian part company again. If an American statesman must choose between the promotion of universal liberty, which is a moral good, at the risk of American security and, hence, of liberty in the United States, and the promotion of American security and of liberty in the United States, which is another moral good, to the detriment of the promotion of universal liberty, which choice ought he to make? The utopian will not face the issue squarely and will deceive himself into believing that he can achieve both goods at the same time. The realist will choose the national interest on both moral and pragmatic grounds; for if he does not take care of the national interest nobody else will, and if he puts American security and liberty in jeopardy the cause of liberty everywhere will be impaired.

Finally, the political realist distinguishes between his moral sympathies and the political interests which he must defend. He will distinguish with Lincoln between his *"official* duty" which is to protect the national interest and his *"personal* wish" which is to see universal moral values realized throughout the world.

The issue has been admirably put by Father Wilfred Parsons of Catholic University in defending Ambassador Kennan's position:

> Mr. Kennan did not say state behavior is not a fit subject for moral judgment, but only that it should not sway our realization of the realities with which we have to deal. Msgr. Koenig continues: "Should we accept power realities and aspirations without feeling the obligation of moral judgment?" And he appeals to the present writer and other political scientists to say whether this doctrine agrees with Pope Pius XII's messages on peace.
>
> I am sure that most political scientists, and also Mr. Kennan, would agree with the Monsignor that we should not accept those realities "without feeling the obligation of moral judgment." But there is a difference between *feeling* this obligation (and even expressing it) and allowing this feeling to sway our actions in concrete negotiations that deal with the national or world common good. We can still feel and yet deal.
>
> To make my meaning clearer, I understood Mr. Kennan to hold that we went off the beam with Woodrow Wilson, when we began to make our moral disapprobation an *essential part* of our foreign relations, even

sometimes at the expense of our own and the world's common good. Logically, such an attitude would inhibit our dealing with Britain, France and a host of countries. Pius XI, speaking of Mussolini after the Lateran Treaty, said he would deal with the devil himself if he must. Here was moral disapprobation, but it was not "carried over into the affairs of states."

This relative position, and not the absolute one of Msgr. Koenig (with which in itself I agree), is, I think, the issue raised by Mr. Kennan, and it is worth debating on that basis.[24]

The contest between utopianism and realism is not tantamount to a contest between principle and expediency, morality and immorality, although some spokesmen for the former would like to have it that way. The contest is rather between one type of political morality and another type of political morality, one taking as its standard universal moral principles abstractly formulated, the other weighing these principles against the moral requirements of concrete political action, their relative merits to be decided by a prudent evaluation of the political consequences to which they are likely to lead.[25]

These points are re-emphasized by the foregoing discussion. Which attitude with regard to collective security and to the liberation of the captive nations, the utopian or the realist, is more likely to safeguard the survival of the United States in its territorial, political, and cultural identity and at the same time to contribute the most to the security and liberty of other nations? This is the ultimate test—political and moral— by which utopianism and realism must be judged.

---

[24] *America*, Vol. 86, p. 700 (March 29, 1952). See also Algernon Cecil, "The Foreign Office," in *The Cambridge History of British Foreign Policy, 1783-1919* (New York, 1923), Vol. 3, p. 605, concerning Lord Salisbury: "Always, however, the motive of his policy was to be found in the political interests as opposed to the political sympathies of Great Britain; and in this way his treatment of Foreign Affairs is at the opposite policy from that of Palmerston or Gladstone." Cf. also the general remarks in Alexander H. Leighton, *Human Relations in a Changing World* (New York, 1949), pp. 155 ff.

[25] See, on this point, Shirley R. Letwin, "Rationalism, Principles, and Politics," *The Review of Politics*, Vol. 14, pp. 367-393 (July, 1952); L. Susan Stebbing, *Ideals and Illusions* (London, 1941); Vernon H. Holloway, *Religious Ethics and the Politics of Power* (New York, 1951); and Dorothy Fosdick, "Ethical Standards and Political Strategies," *Political Science Quarterly*, Vol. 57, pp. 214 ff. (1942).

The American Idea of International Interest*

by Thomas I. Cook and Malcolm Moos

[1]

Disenchantment with moral abstractions as the hallmarks of enlightened foreign policy has recently revived infatuation with the slogans of
"national interest," "power politics," and "balance of power." Until the
eve of World War II, these ideas had been recessive—at times mori-
bund—for at least half a generation. Naive belief in the efficacy of professions of good will, reliance on weak instruments for effectuating
simply noble intentions in the complex realms of policy and practice,
and contentment with lofty exhortations, had too often become the
directives of policy unconcerned with the harshness of politics or the
intricate give-and-take of sustained diplomacy.

Since the Republic's inception, statesmen have proclaimed national
interest as the firmament on which our foreign policy rests. To that
concept they have repeatedly referred as a guide and rationale for action
in foreign affairs. Over the years the concept of national interest has
been endowed with a varied and changing content. Therefore, interpretation has been a matter of historical, rather than etymological,
enquiry. Certainly, a single dictionary definition will not do. Nevertheless, while dominant meanings at different moments and a long-term
trend in the development of meaning are alike discoverable, or imputa-
ble, the actual meaning in our own day rests largely on the setting of
current controversies. A particular concept of the national interest,
therefore, is not "automatically" warranted and acceptable by appeal to
tradition and great names, any more than by formal definition.

That national interest is a necessary criterion of policy is obvious and
unilluminating. No statesman, no publicist, no scholar would seriously
argue that foreign policy ought to be conducted in opposition to, or in
disregard of, the national interest. To do so would reveal at once internal contradiction, logically and psychologically.

The problem, therefore, is to discover what, at the given moment or
through a meaningful period of time, the national interest is. Indeed, a

* From *The American Political Science Review*, Vol. XLVII, No. 1 (March
1953), pp. 28-44. Reprinted by permission of the American Political Science Association.

major difficulty is to define the relevant time-span in the life of the nation whose interest is to be assessed, and to decide on appropriate policy accordingly.

At the one extreme, the advocate of case-by-case decision, emphatic that the hands of the policy-maker and the negotiator must not be tied by specific but lasting commitments or by long-term policies, will argue that flexibility also best serves the long-range national interest. To him, that interest, first defined by an enlightened judgment of what will in each case profit the collective whole, is the product of a series of such decisions made on the basis of information at the moment available or attainable. Insurance of continuity and needful consistency in policy come from the partial identification with the national life and the inherent participation and sharing in it, by those who in each case do the assessing. To define a national interest beyond the ever-operative processes of politics and policy is to limit effectiveness in the pronouncement and pursuit of objectives. It is therefore deleterious to the real national interest.

On the other side stand those who, however much they agree on the need for accommodation and on the importance of utilizing perceived opportunity, still feel that coherence in foreign policy is the prime requisite. In their view, policy must be the consequence of a principled formulation of national interest. For such defined principle, though it often appears as a self-denying ordinance of dubious value, in truth furthers the sustained national interest. On the one hand it provides anchorage and creates confidence at home; on the other it ensures predictability abroad, and gives clear warning to other powers as to what this nation regards as vital.

These two concepts of national interest in relation to time, the one stressing immediate expediency and flexibility, the other a defining of principle based on long-term trend and desired projection, are exclusive when taken as absolutes. But they are not beyond reconciliation when themselves viewed as factors and perceptions to be weighted by statesmen in their endeavor to assess the nation's interest.

Yet behind these concepts lurk more profound divergencies. One extreme viewpoint regards the nation as a real being with an independent life of its own. Its development and full realization are held to be the generic purpose of history, and the imposed and necessary duty of the true statesman. The nation, according to this thesis, is an organic being, engaged in a struggle for life, for strength, for the conquest of hampering limitations, for predominance. Its objectives are first to endure and then to expand. The position takes many forms, is expressed in varied terminology, and has different implications as to inclusiveness or exclusiveness. Yet it results, almost of necessity, in the conviction that there is a real and lasting national interest independent of and apart from the interests of the persons who at any moment constitute the nation. To that interest they must, where necessary, be sacrificed. Indeed, their real obligation is to sacrifice themselves voluntarily; or to conceive the whole purpose of their existence as service to, and absorption in, the greater being, the nation, which alone is properly the bearer of interests.

On this view, the nation's interest is survival and strength. Its chief and primary instrument is force. It is independent, self-centered, and concerned with other nations only externally, in the sense that they are regrettable, yet inescapable, constraints on its pursuit of that interest. There is no community of nations, and there cannot be. Yet, because other nations exist, there are international relations, as there must be foreign policy, which indeed on this definition of national interest becomes the highest concern of the statesman. His objects are to ensure the permanence and maximize the power of the nation. That principle makes any action which supports it, whether by the seizure of immediate advantage or the adoption of coherent and predictable policy, equally correct.

In such a setting the national interest is a clear datum. It is not something springing from institutions and interests within the nation, whose relative importance and value is to be assessed and re-assessed, and whose concerns may transcend purely national considerations and cross national boundaries. Yet, manifestly, a nation is not a talking organism; and in practice such viewpoints tend to the identification of nation with state, and state with rulers or government. Hence the national interest becomes defined as what those in power declare it to be; just as their efficacy in gaining and retaining power rests upon their skill in overcoming or reconciling particular and assessable interests by the use and sale of the very myth of a transcendent national interest.

Reaction against this position, among peoples where tradition has intimately related nation and state, has often followed in the wake of democratization. In such instances the tendency has been to regard the state as instrumental and to insist that the national interest which it serves must proceed out of the conscious interests and the free loyalties of its citizens. Yet the centrality of the state, so general a fact of European life, has meant that though the state may be reduced to instrumentality in doctrine and constitutional law, it has remained the locus and expression of a national interest under which specific interests are to be subsumed and subordinated.

On this thesis, national interest was, and is, an affair of statesmanship, to be defined and implemented by statesmen, and to be discovered and given a simple and unified content by purely political arts and processes. The formulation of such interest, and the statesman's task, were no doubt helped by an inheritance of traditional policies, not to mention stereotypes for their popularization and continuance. Politics might be constitutionalized and concepts of a superior national being or of the national interest as the will of rulers rejected. But national interest involved a continuity of principles, relationships, and objectives. That very continuity at once permitted needful flexibility in short-term operations and prevented incoherence through mere opportunism. Men were no doubt persons and the pluralism of group life was a reality. But centralization and citizenship were primary. And, by being largely unquestioned conditions of self and of associations, they jointly encouraged harsh definition of national interest and an acceptance of its paramountcy, just as they limited and directed debate over its content and established beyond dispute the proper organs and persons for its implementation.

[II]

The American experience has been very different. From the colonial beginnings, and certainly long before the Revolution, many of our leaders were critical of monarchy. Indeed, by Puritan doctrine itself they were antimonarchical, whatever their dependence on the throne for the very bases of their legal existence and their territorial rights. The experience of colonial life in thirteen colonies carved from a wilderness was inimical to centralization, as to a dominantly political loyalty to the state; and later colonial experience with the mother country reenforced these tendencies. The Revolution itself completed the work and fixed an underlying pattern. Henceforth the defining of national interest in terms of the state, whether monarchical or the heir of monarchy, was made lastingly difficult.

Yet, as noted above, the idea of national interest was developed early in these United States, and has remained a touchstone for the measuring of policy. The reasons are easy to divine. The Founding Fathers

were both revolutionaries and self-made heirs of the doctrine that statesmanship was the highest, and appropriate, calling of the natural or aris-
tocratic leaders of society. That view had developed out of the Whig
Revolution, in which landed and commercial leaders inherited, by
default and as the culmination of a revolutionary movement, the major
and essential functions once the prerogatives of Divine Right monarchy.
As successful revolutionaries, our Founding Fathers were driven to
organize public power as they sought lasting safety for their creation.
Separating themselves from the country whose legal possession they had
been, they were forced to proclaim that, whatever the peculiarities of
this country, it was a nation-state belonging to the system of states developed by and in Europe from the Peace of Westphalia on. The new
nation so conceived had a claim to status, interests, and policies which
it was the task of its statesmen to implement and define. Moreover,
as revolutionaries and republicans welding a whole out of separate colonies, they were driven to use the concepts of a nation, a national people,
and a national interest for organizing purposes, internal not less than
international. It is well to remember that the United States, prior to
the French Revolution, was the first country to stress the modern concepts of nationality and national independence, though it happily and
long avoided the European corollary, nationalism.

The social and geographical facts of American life, coupled with distrust of distant political authority and function, did not prevent our
early statesmen from developing a concept of national interest interpreted by a government endowed with exclusive authority in foreign
affairs. But these facts did inhibit any tendency on the part of ordinary
men to esteem their loyalty and nationality as primarily political and
oriented towards the federal government. Men as citizens might meet
their legal obligations thereto, and might bear arms in furtherance of
the nation's policies, though until after the Civil War they performed
the latter duty with little enthusiasm. Even in our own day military
service remains for most a regrettable, though real, necessity which, in
the name of national interest, interferes with the normal pursuit of individual interests, ideally held to constitute in their sum the more appropriate long-term interest of the nation. We also note that the now almost irrelevant right of the citizen to bear arms, though conceived as
being in the national interest because it provided a reservoir of men
trained in the use of arms, was in truth doubly anti-statist. It rested on
fear of professional armies, as well as unwillingness to rely on them. For

they were usually the instruments of governments which identified national interest with their own conceptions of public power and prestige. It rested, secondly, on a popular sense that a citizen body accustomed to use arms was a wholesome check on a possible official temptation to act oppressively, and to equate official ambitions and convictions with the interests of the people constituting the nation.

In general, Americans have rejected the idea of a nation as a real super-being, endowed with independent life and interests, as they have escaped the European concept of the state. Certainly the view that men should be sacrificed to the one or the other, or to the two in combination, is repulsive to Americans; as is the conviction that public authorities are the primary factors in the formulation of concepts of national interest. There have, it is true, been nationalistic movements in the United States. But, apart from their striking differences from European movements, due in part to the absence of equally powerful neighbors, they have generally been short-lived, and have seldom aroused widespread enthusiasm. Thus the first major movement of this sort after the Constitutional period, severely criticized by transcendentalists and by interests differently oriented in geography and commerce, ended with the deepening of sectional conflict and the defection of Calhoun. The nationalism of the Civil War period and after, though it made a genuine impress on constitutional concepts of the nature of the Union, failed to popularize alien ideas of sovereignty and nation-state. In part this was true because the very forces supporting the Union were anti-statist, individualistic, and voluntaristic. Even the later impact of German ideas in the creation of American academic political and social science failed utterly to convert us to the European doctrines of state and nation, since their proponents were driven by outer circumstances and inner conviction to a defense of liberty, of property, and of enterprise beyond the purview of government or state.

The American regards his government as instrumental. But he does not, like the European who shares this view, propound a simple monistic view of national interest by making the state his central symbol of loyalty and identification. Like Europeans he reverences the symbols of the collective public order, such as the flag. Yet loyalty to his nation, though real and deep, is little related to the panoplies of public life. And the occasions when he does thrill to the acts of statesmen, because they embody the sense and reveal the majesty of his nation, are rare.

Rather, American loyalty tends to center around institutions, from the family outward; around sections and scenery and ways of life; around personal freedom and enterprise; and around neighborliness. These interests may be loosely summed up as the much-vaunted American way of life which, for all its varieties of connotation and despite all abuses committed and selfish interests defended in its name, symbolizes a central core of experience, emotion, and attachment. It is not a statist concept; it is not identified with government; and, though it includes our political mores, it is not, in feeling, political. Yet it indicates the fundamental concerns which it is the national interest to protect and promote.

Foreign policies proclaimed or pursued by statesmen are judged to be in the national interest when devoted to such protection and further-ance. Hence, glory and aggrandizement of the nation-state are not, for Americans, synonymous with national interest. Moreover, because that interest is societal, not political, it is possible to conceive of the state purely instrumentally and, simultaneously, to admit that final, as well as instrumental, satisfactions can come from identification with and shar-ing in the national interest. This sharing in the national interest may be enjoyed without men being driven to glorify a super-being whose claim is sacrifice, whose usual ultimate instrument is force, and whose chief impact upon its own members is external and impersonal. The point may be made negatively by noting the relative difficulty in this country (as against England and parts of Europe) of associating the basic emo-tional elements of local attachment—the particular sights and sounds and smells so dear to the poet—with a devotion to political institutions and to sacrifice in furtherance of national policies, whether achieved by means of propaganda or by free and unconscious linkage on the part of individuals.

This peculiar conception of the American self is a product of a long-lived individualism, of local community, of the open horizons associated with the frontier, of the vast range in place and in ways of living of the American adventure. Such pluralistic diversity renders old-world con-cepts of national interest, with their stress upon power politics and bal-ance of power, meaningless and inapplicable to the American situation.

Admittedly the American concept is more imprecise than these, and it therefore necessitates continuous redefinition and re-compounding. This fact, when combined with the inherent unpredictabilities of our political-governmental system, especially as it relates to foreign affairs, creates difficulties for our own and for foreign statesmen, as well as for the analyst who looks for patterns and formulas. Yet, in the modern world of conscious, awakened and aspiring peoples it has one great potential advantage: the tying of national interest to a fluid way of life. True, it may result in exclusive selfishness from an endeavor to preserve the privileges of that life, products of a combination of favorable circumstances and creative energies. But it offers some hope that America's root concern, its ultimate concept of the national interest, may be the spreading and sharing, with due adaptation and without intolerance, of its societal blessings. We may thereby avoid a narrow and resented search for the magnificence of imperial power, always at last a snare, a delusion, and a pointless sacrifice of persons.

In any event, this American idea, which provides a basis for avoiding a naive utopianism unrelated to the particularities of interest and attachment and a power politics whose course is lasting statism on the one hand and tensions beyond peaceful solution on the other, seems to hold superior promise in a world where world conquest and serene isolation are equally delusive aspirations. Thus in the present bi-polar world, the alternatives offered to lesser powers are acceptance of a totalitarian statism or alliance with a coherent yet pluralistic societalism.

[III]

In the realm of international economic relations, however, it is signally difficult to obtain coherence in national policy without lapsing into statism, and while avoiding the dangers of commitment through irresponsible individual venturings. American governmental responsibility for the defense of the nation's interest without means to control the conditions which shaped its contours was the central problem to which Charles A. Beard addressed himself in his *The Idea of National Interest.* Indeed, the difficulty of achieving a satisfactory solution may have been one of the reasons for his ultimate and peculiar brand of isolationism. He sought, but did not find, a modern equivalent of the earlier Hamiltonian realistic concern with national interest. In Hamilton's day, that interest was to be secured by the protection of American industries, at the time infant, or barely conceived. But the long-term consequence of the Hamiltonian system, combined with the impact of the teachings of Adam Smith and his heirs, has conspired to bring about a purely selfish and isolationist economic individualism internally, and support of a free trade competitive individualism externally, as the development of the Open Door policy attested. In combination, the two created the bases of material prosperity, promoted a release of American energies in enterprise, and provided an extraordinary industrial (as well as agricultural) foundation for American world power.

But the accompanying evils created Beard's prime problem, still far from solved. It was necessary to find an equivalent for Hamiltonianism in the realm of exports, as against imports. Such an accomplishment required governmental interference in a field where the tradition of national interest was one of free enterprising, by individual or corporation, regardless of state considerations. Earlier, such activity had profited the nation. But under the new circumstances, as Beard perceived, some exports might not do so, since they could radically change the power relations of other nations to the United States, as well as kill American foreign markets for consumer goods. Thereby they would both decrease our own internal consumption and lessen the volume of employment. In general terms, Beard's solution was a moral equivalent to Hamiltonianism in the export field. Its essence was to be a governmentally-directed and even governmentally-planned system of exporting goods and capital, carefully devised to protect economic welfare at home. Simultaneously, it was designed to encourage, discourage, and direct, insofar as the United States was able, the economic development of other countries to the extent that they depended on us for capital, for consumer goods, or for markets. The object was to further our own national interest, conceived as stable and secure power.

That teaching, again, was a radical revamping, tailored to suit the conditions of the modern world, of Fichte's doctrine of *The Closed Trade State*. Fichte had recognized the difficulty of promoting the material and cultural well-being of a people when the productive and distributive bases of their economy were subject to random and unpredictable calculations. Aware of these uncertainties, which were increased by the whims of traders and enterprisers and by the actions and reactions of foreign citizens and governments, Fichte had argued the need for a completely enclosed system of national economic life under state control. The benefits of trade must be exchanged for the blessings of planning, stability, and security. The objective of his design was long-term individual welfare even more than national power. Economic isolationism was the one sure means to prosperity and peace, and so to the real conditions for the development of persons. His was a system of avoiding shocks by minimizing variables.

Such a project, though it would have involved some immediate self-sacrifice, might conceivably have been practicable at the dawn of industrialism; while gains in social justice and in avoidance of mass misery might well have compensated for losses of wealth or of power. Even so, unless the scheme had become the common policy of nations, the one adopting it would in all probability have suffered from insecurity by generating inadequate power, in the sense of potentially available force, as compared to other nations. When Beard wrote, in any event, industrialism was well developed, world trade a long-standing fact. His search therefore aspired to a nationally controlled trade in a world of international economic relations. Dependence on others for various materials, as well as some dependence on foreign markets, made an absolute economic isolationism undesirable, if not impossible. Thus national calculations aimed at adjusting variations in the economic conditions and policies of other peoples became an inevitable factor in policy. The essence of such policy was predictive planning of foreign trade and investment for the protection and furtherance of national economic and political power. It was the latter that was proclaimed as the national interest, defined as exclusive and over-riding, but also by its very statement not truly isolationist.

Beard's formulation of the problem showed a profound insight. Actually the inter-war years revealed a radical contradiction. Economists and economic conferences professedly sought decreased national restrictions on multilateral trade. But tariffs and other forms of state interference with free international enterprise continuously increased. The free trade ideal, to be achieved by the mere abdication of governments in that sphere, was an irrelevance and an impossibility in a world organized under national sovereignties, however interdependent. It was doubly so, given the general development of state social welfare policies and the restoration (and exaggeration) of the primacy of the political. National interests, not less than international interest, did dictate planning and control, under the auspices of major collective units of international economic relations. It was impossible politically to leave their protection and advancement to free, yet national and politically-minded, legal persons, on the supposition of an unaided hidden hand and the doctrine of comparative advantage.

Nevertheless, Beard's solution was a hazardous one from the viewpoint of internal institutions. As subsequent events increasingly proved, it was an impractical solution. For America had to promote its interest in a world where it possessed leadership and the obligations of leadership. Yet it had to compete with a vastly different, and highly aggressive, ideology under conditions where its professed policy, as implemented in practice, became an article for export, and not for home consumption only.

As a Republican devoted to the early American conviction of the importance of statesmanship and the centrality of statecraft, Beard was in no sense alarmed at the necessity, implicit in his doctrine, of a large area of control over the direction of enterprise, where such enterprise might affect the national destiny. Certainly he was not to be numbered amongst those members of the party who defend as primary the right to absence of governmental intervention in their quest for profit and power. He had a profound sense of the American ethical tradition, as he had a yet more profound American national pride. These rendered the aspirations of acquisitiveness secondary and subordinate. Yet he did not squarely confront the statist implications of the course which he advocated. Rather, he accepted, too readily, the view that political and governmental control or limitation of selfish interests would give proper primacy to the national interest (defined as national power) without destroying that liberty of personal and community life which he likewise held dear.

[IV]

Unfortunately, however, prevalent definitions of national interest, though they combine the insights of Beard and Hans Morgenthau, are in their realism less than realistic. The search for power, and for escape from the delusions of moralizers who believe that the enunciation of fine universal principles is enough, is an insufficient basis for foreign policy in the contemporary world. No matter what the particularities of peoples, there is a shared desire for economic betterment, just as there is a shared aspiration towards increased opportunities for persons to develop and fulfill themselves, however great is the current willingness to forego, or the current incapacity to enjoy, Western freedom. The practicable alternative means to such material betterment are freedom within the constitutional social welfare state or planned industrial development under dictatorship inspired by communist ideology. For better or worse, the United States and Russia are the respective symbols, and the effective leaders and sources, of these ways of social organization; as they are the alternate roads to achievement of the desired objective. Under such circumstances, the consequence of realistic national interest is failure abroad; while at home it leads to the ultimate enthronement of the organic nation-state, with statism as its present-day corollary.

Yet the supreme difficulty Beard confronted, the impossibility of adequate national statesmanship for America as a world power under conditions of private judgment and action in the international economic realm, is not met by noting the inadequacies of his own solution or the related, and greater, inadequacies of a more narrowly political and statist realism. Nor is a neatly compacted answer available. It may be in order, however, to suggest the context for an answer, and thereby to help direct attention to the need for further enquiry and for institutional innovation and development.

The major new perspective on international relations and foreign policy during the last twenty years—a perspective which Beard himself helped to create—is the recognition of the essential unity or wholeness of politics. Foreign affairs have ceased to be exclusively or dominantly a matter of formal political diplomacy, as they have ceased to be shrouded from the eyes of the vulgar. Strictly speaking, there are no longer foreign affairs, wrote Salvador de Madariaga in a discerning tract of 1937, there are only "world affairs." [1] For the relations between nations have become a central concern, and a dominating condition, in men's planning of their lives and the conduct of their business. Again, this development was a necessary consequence of modern intercommunication and of contemporary technology. It was pushed farther by the conflicts of ideology of the period, and the aspirations they betokened. It has been accelerated by wars and threats of wars; though the recent atom and hydrogen bombs have created an over-emphasis on international relations as the first, and often unique, criterion of a nation's conduct of life.

The consequence of this trend has been an unfortunate drive, of which this country now feels the full impact, towards nation-statism: constitutional democracy tends to abandon its own vision, and to become a totalitarianism without dictatorship. It does so, moreover, under conditions where the survival and minimal security of citizens, of cities, of the earth and what men have created thereon, is the over-riding consideration. Thus other nations, rather than pests or human waste of resources, comprise the immediate danger. Having moved from a condition where others were external and often unimportant, we have gone to the opposite extreme, where involvement with others and the hostile

---

[1] *Theory and Practice in International Relations* (Philadelphia, 1937), p. 105.

policies of others become the highest, and highly resented, determinant of our own doings and way of life. In some sense, indeed, the extremes meet: foreign affairs as national policy divorced from daily life, and foreign affairs as the essence of daily life, alike tend towards a statist conception of national interest, and a power realism unrelated to moral considerations and to a genuine doctrine of a nation's international interest. But in the United States, unlike Europe, owing to the chance of geography and the need and opportunity for internal development, the involvement of citizens through foreign policy was formerly casual and occasional: in the main, the concept of national interest was internal and societal, and demands of the state through government rare. Today, on the other hand, such involvement is continuous, nerve-racking, and destructive of the societal nation. The American enterprise is forced, despite resistance and resentment, towards the integral unity of the nation-state under conditions where war is total, and the outbreak of hostilities is always just around the corner.

Nevertheless, the conception of policy and politics, international and national, as one whole of interdependent parts offers a theoretical framework whereby to escape extremisms which lead to glorification of power, governmental power politics, and the imposition of the myth of the nation-state in the name of realism. Conceptualized broadly, it promises a basis for preserving and refining the essential concept of societal nationality to fit modern conditions, with the state as the instrumentality, an approach bedded in the American tradition. Additionally it offers an operational technique for furthering American interests and ideas as world power consonantly with that tradition, with the wider Western and Christian tradition, and with the over-riding criterion of universal ethical principle. At the same time it provides grounds for the avoidance of utopian doctrines of absolute and, of necessity, content-less moralities. Such doctrines offer no substitute for policy, yet create the delusion that they are themselves by mere enunciation adequate policy. Hence they beget the reaction to hard-boiled realism, which we have shown to be contemporaneously unrealistic.

[v]

Clues to the philosophical principles which insist that the state is purely instrumental, yet inevitably positive and concerned with the protection and preservation of social welfare in its whole unified range of activities, are not hard to discover within the course of American

democratic thought. The individualism which leads to release and effective utilization of men's energies and the institutional pluralism which
is so vital a core of American life are hymned in the poetry and prose of
Walt Whitman, who intuits their ethical laws and their grounding in
native mores, as in the folkways later dear to Sumner. Their philosophical underpinning is to be found in Peirce's and in James' Pragmatism,
as these are developed by John Dewey, whose Instrumentalism insists
on the diverse democratic public as the ultimate source, and the proper
beneficiary, of the nation's interest. Long before these men, however,
Tocqueville, in what remains the greatest analysis of the American way
of life, stressed its fundamentally societal and sociological character, as
against the European state.

Nevertheless, these emphases do not provide adequate grounds for
compounding in proper relation the social, political, and governmental,
which must be done if public authority is to properly serve the nation's
total, and internationally-oriented, interest, as formulated by and for
the going American social order. Here the clues, in philosophy and
political philosophy, are to be found especially in the teachings of three
men: Josiah Royce and, among contemporaries, W. Y. Elliott and
Robert MacIver. The first provided an Idealism related to the pluralism
and energy of American life, in his doctrine of loyalties which, expanded, permitted a political expression of the people and a statesmanship consequent thereon, yet which avoided, by reason of the overriding
and unifying doctrine of loyalty to loyalty, at once the compromises of
narrow expediency and the threats of monistic statism. For that doctrine
transcended, yet embraced, the purely *political* concept of allegiance and
obligation.

Elliott, in attacking the modern teaching of political pluralism as at
once socially disruptive and to some degree intellectually irrationalist,
was quite aware of the dangers and difficulties of the orthodox doctrine
of the sovereign state, and even more aware of the anti-intellectualism
and inhumanity of organismic corporative concepts of nation and national destiny. Consequently he tried, under the rubric of co-organism,
at once to acknowledge the necessity of final political decision as basis
for action and to insist on the reality of vital and participating groups
and interests in the society, whose diverse drives must be included and
harmonized as far as possible in the process of statecraft. He desired to
avoid a mere tug of forces without clear outcome in policy or practice.

He desired not less to avoid the evils of statism, and the sacrifice of men to the myth of the state.

MacIver is an ardent defender of human liberty and foe of totalitarianism. He is aware of the omnipresence and the necessity of government, and of its inevitable wide range of functions if it is to serve our needs today. Yet, aware of the dangers of abuse of power and of indignities done to men in the name of the state, he has defended the state's high claim and function even as he has insisted that it be an instrument of a more ultimate, more vital, though less precisely definable, social whole.

These ideas, germane to American experience, inspired by the more generic traditions of Western thought, and relevant to the great problems which have confronted men in modern industrial society, clearly provide the bases for a hitherto undeveloped synthesis which will reveal the creative leadership in the American conception and practice of man in society. At home, such a synthesis will provide an adequate rationale for the avoidance of statism and narrowed national interest as a basis for foreign policy, will allow the adequate and appropriate synthesis of governmental integrative function with societal national interest; and additionally will further and underwrite the unification of politics internal and external. Such an outlook will result in a national concept of American international interest which can further and protect the American way of life. Likewise, by its appeal to universal principles of human dignity, embodied in its own practice, it can make an appeal to others. Thereby it may promote real American interest by its manifest relation to their needs and aspirations. Specifically, such a theory will provide grounds on which to combat narrowing and ungenerous isolationism and the isolationist imperialism (if we may dare the paradox) which is so ready an outcome of those so-called realistic teachings of national interest designed to avoid the supposed pitfalls of moral principle as a basis of policy. For it is our contention that the extremes which meet, and have a common root, are not, as Professor Morgenthau would persuade us, isolationism and utopianism, but isolationism and that doctrine of national interest rooted in power politics as selfish national calculation and balance of power, of which he is the most forceful contemporary exponent in this country. At the same time, such a theory avoids also the dangers of that moralistic utopianism which Morgenthau and others rightfully condemn. For it stresses the life of American society, still particular though deeply rich and varied. It accepts man's limitation by time and place. It refuses to accept the monistic ultimates which, when they do not glorify the state, yet promise perfectibility of men on earth.

[VI]

The issue of institutional implementation remains. That issue is how to get expression of, and consideration for, the insights and interests at large in American society at the points of governmental policy-making and specific decision. Stated otherwise, it is how to get formulated as a coherent whole the societal concept of the nation's generalized interest. No less compelling in importance is how to avoid a purely government-inspired formulation, executive and administrative—a concept put forth as the United States' national interest, and in due course turned into a statist line in the name of unity, effectiveness, prestige, and power.

At the outset, it is important to emphasize here, more than elsewhere, that perpetual vigilance remains the price of liberty. But the pre-condition of vigilance is the clear perception of the tradition, of its vitalizing force, and of its usefulness. Thereby we may combat in ourselves, in our politics, and in our government, that lack of confidence which goes ill together with American power. Americans can escape the degradation consequent on cynical or hard-boiled realism, which is in truth the degradation of democratic dogma, only by perception of their larger heritage and aspiration. They must reject in the name of their living past an attitude of cowed timidity which in its blustering poorly simulates national strength.

At the political level of party politics and the legislative way of life, Americans should therefore reject the dogma and unwisely self-imposed constraint of the touted bipartisan foreign policy, sometimes questioned as to its reality, occasionally indicated on grounds of partisan expediency, but too little challenged as to its ethical goodness. Such a policy is no doubt requisite in times of collective emergency, of clear and present danger to the national whole. It is also appropriate, if defined as intelligent and enlightened abstention from irresponsible partisanship, as loyal support of necessary financial and material means to implement particular policies at the moment in effect, and not in the short run to be changed. The concomitant of such support, however, does not involve abandoning criticism of those policies or unwillingness to suggest and struggle for the adoption of constructive alternatives. Beyond emergency and magnanimous loyalty, bipartisanship becomes a failure to transmit and transform into dynamically fluctuating policy the major elements which collectively constitute the societal national interest; and so it is abdication of a major brokerage function of the party system. For, whatever the ceremonials of formal partisan voting, the total processes of legislation and of executive-legislative relations are not such as to have as their normal end-products laws or policies which represent a strict majority view and majoritarian attitude, with the minority utterly at loggerheads, excluded from consideration, and outragedly rejecting *in toto* the actual decisions made. Fortunately, American constitutionalism goes deeper than formal checks and balances, judicial review, or guaranteed rights. To abandon party planks, party alignments, and party debate in the realm of foreign affairs is in truth to lose the advantage of dynamic and organic continuity in policy, to achieve at best a static and uncreative unity, to forego the confidence which comes from vital debate, and to sacrifice the enlightened national feeling to what is at root a statist line. For the vital center is only vital when it is emergent from the interplay of diverse interests which voluntarily, and perhaps unconsciously, share an over-riding common concern. Imposed as political duty, and by the eschewing of free debate, that center is in fact devitalized, as it is in its consequences deleterious. Moreover, on the thesis here proclaimed that foreign and domestic policy are facets of one whole, partisanship in the one and bipartisanship in the other constitute on their face a ludicrous position, impossible to maintain for long. If it could be maintained, moreover, it could be executed only at the price of a pointless and harmful incoherence in total policy.

Bipartisanship constitutes in essence an internal appeasement which, in its lack of courage and conviction, can be more harmful than external appeasement. It does so whether it involves the following of administration policies by the minority party or that curious developing brand of "me too ism" on the part of the majority, of the executive, or of the relevant administrative departments under the executive, evidenced in the endorsing and proclaiming of allegiance to opposition doctrines of national interest and preachments of policy. In the realm of policy, moreover, it begets an extreme oscillation between appeasement and aggressiveness in our dealings with other nations. Nor is this result accidental. For bipartisanship, which developed out of crisis and constitutes a superb democratic equivalent to emergency power and to dictatorship, has encouraged emergency thinking and the conviction of insecurity, and has helped to make them a constant in our lives. In consequence it has contributed to the prolongation of emergency and to the failure to diminish international tensions. For its artificial consensus has, in the name of realism and loyalty, prevented that healthful enquiry and that ability to dissent without becoming suspect.

Bipartisanship helps to create and to strengthen stereotypes which inhibit thought and breed violent emotion. Inevitably it becomes the handmaid of a dogma of utopian catastrophism. Such catastrophism is inimical to effective policy. Moreover, as a substitute for the proper conduct of diplomacy, it is as unsatisfactory as the utopianism of pure and practically undefiled moral aspiration. A return to the normalcy of partisanship in all spheres of politics is a basic need, then, for the effective pursuit of America's international interest. Such a return might also decrease the excessive compensatory strafing over domestic policy and so, by moderation, aid the creation of a real vital center.

At the level of execution and administration, where functional representation and group consultation so peculiarly belong, institutional innovation is especially requisite to avoid the statist concept of national interest. The objective must be to render viable and to harmonize, in a coherent and dynamic pattern of policy, the diverse elements which in their sum comprise the national interest of the American social order. Roughly, what is needed is an equivalent to Calhoun's doctrine of the concurrent majority, divorced from the sectional basis and the narrowed concept of interests of that suggestive teaching. Essentially, the task is to bring into the formulation and execution of day-by-day policy, with due regard to security considerations, the economic, social, and cultural interests first clearly seen as parts of our political order by A. F. Bentley. In this context certain existing organizations which function in our domestic affairs, largely as a result of our present world position and our defense activities, may be relevant by loose, but suggestive, analogy. As an example, local draft boards operating our selective service system might be cited. Local agencies not composed of experts, these bodies of volunteers express the sense and judgment of their communities in the light of determined national needs and under general instructions and specific restraints. Different again, but also loosely relevant, are the War Labor Boards, national and regional, of the Second World War, and the recent Wage Stabilization Boards, with their tri-partite memberships. These brought into decision-making and policy discussion representatives of the two interests, labor and industry, most specifically affected, and of the public-at-large.

Elsewhere, but directly related to foreign policy, the State Department has a special section whose function it is to encourage and inform private organizations devoted to the better understanding of UNESCO and of the American role therein. Here, indeed, the relationship is different, and in form one-way, while the function itself is promotional and informational, not policy-making or administrative. Yet in practice such interchange tends to become one of mutual influence. Even where the intent may be to popularize official attitudes, the outcome is to aid expression of citizen views and to further the conscious spread of concepts of the international interest of the national society. Again, while the widespread practice of using private experts as consultants on policy is very different in intention and impact from functional participation in administration, it tends towards similar consequences. The same applies to the use of qualified private persons on the Voice of America program. In truth, we already possess, however rudimentary in form and inadequate in quantity, some of the practices and operational techniques most suited to attain the dominance of a societal, rather than a statist, concept of national interest.

The remaining problems are, therefore, to broaden and systematize consultation and participation and to create a recognized and institutionalized share in responsibility on the part of the citizen and his representatives. Curiously enough, a return to partisanship in our own international politics and a systematic development of consultation and participation in the development and execution of policy by those affected can actually aid the solution of one set of real problems. Thus some moderates in the name of effective diplomacy seek a return to the realism of the old European balance of power system, even though they are in no way enamored of the doctrine of amoral national interest. These critics have seen a connection between a moralizing utopianism which has often degenerated in practice into a "holier than thou" attitude on the part of America, and the false democratization of politics through the appeal and organization of mass media. Such media, dependent on lowest common denominator appeals, enthrone the simplest moralities and indignations. And in the sphere of foreign relations they induce pressure on diplomats and diplomatic conferences, to the frequent detriment of the nation's international interest.

The indictment is largely warranted; and it is psychologically easy, especially for those who have a decent awareness of history, to contrast the present with the past. By a simple, yet logically not necessary association, they relate secret diplomacy by trained diplomats, the balance of power system, and fairly stable peace achieved through unexciting adjustments made without publicity, and consequently without hurt prestige and lost face. They contrast such a climate of action with the present-day conduct of international relations, whether between individual nations or in the collective conferences of the U.N., under klieg lights; and the constant tension, indignation, crisis, and conflict which are consequent on a necessity to be absolutely right. Too readily forgotten is the fact that, though the techniques of an earlier diplomacy had much to commend them, the search for open covenants rested precisely on the ground that commitments made in secret by an élite affected the fortunes and the future of citizens whose felt interests as the nation were unconsulted. The system was in truth conducive to the political idea of national interest, and is peculiarly antithetical to the societal concept of international interest, the new and slowly evolved American contribution by example to a better world order. What is more, as politics became democratized, while policy remained untouched by the peoples' hands, there developed a dichotomy between internal and international affairs. For the sake both of internal and international well-being, it is today vital to bring about a new integration, whereby policy becomes one whole.

[VII]

A return to times past is no solution. The problem is to determine the areas, and define the techniques, for the conduct of calm and unobserved diplomacy by responsible statesmen. In this setting the primary area for open debate and for the general formation and expression of public opinion is the sphere of principle and overall policy. The dominant mass opinion, it should be noted, is not an expression of a societal national interest, but tends towards a power and statist line, at least under conditions of bipartisan policy. The result is a democratic totalitarian dogma rather than a genuine vital center. Yet the danger involved in secrecy, in absence of publicity, is precisely a statist concept of national interest made and defined by the élites responsible for the day-by-day conduct of affairs. Whether despite or because of intelligent understanding of other peoples, and skill in dealing with them, such élites, unless properly checked, may develop a professional interest which they identify with the national interest on the basis of their rectitude and expertness in its service. It is at this very point that the idea of relating the layman to the processes of policy administration is so significant. For in that role he becomes an informed critic of the unpublicized conduct of detailed negotiations and an insurance against abuse or confusion of different concepts of interest. Simultaneously, he becomes a broker between government and public, and a source of enlightenment which can help diminish the facile dogmas induced and sustained by mass media. Finally the alert layman aids the politician in bridging the gap and diminishing the tension between misguided yet—to the political leader—imperative mass demands and responses and the difficult requirements of our international interest.

Looking at its main contours, American leadership from Bretton Woods to the Korean crisis has at root embodied a recognition that the interests of these United States are essentially international or corporate, not exclusive and nationalistic. It has revealed a consonance between the American antistatist tradition of freedom and statesmanship on behalf of the societal nation, and the aspirations of other peoples to overcome want and to gain political security as conditions for the release of human energies and the enjoyment of human culture. It has demonstrated that today a realistic concept of national interest must rest upon a genuine morality, in theory and practice, of respect for the finite particularity of peoples. It has perceived that peoples share a common humanity. In a transitional stage from old nationalism to new world order, they strive uncertainly, tentatively, adaptively, and yet determinedly, to create institutions and mechanisms for the furtherance within diversity of that humanity. It has proclaimed, however uncertainly, that in such a world the United States, creator of new patterns for the more effective realization of ancient human insights, and possessor of power for leadership, must interpret its national interest as international interest, in a situation where practical success and moral obligation are consonant and interdependent.

This article is dedicated to the more effective pursuit of such objectives. Whether it is better to abandon the concept of national interest because of its unfortunate connotations of exclusiveness, and its availability as a rationalization to forces of timidity which look backwards and oppose interest to morality; or whether it is possible to win the symbol and transform its connotations is, perhaps, uncertain. To believe, however, that, as a strategy, it is desirable to identify the term "national interest," as its leading proponents tend to do, with a search for power and security divorced from moral considerations is, we submit, an unacceptable premise for an enlightened, successful American policy. To reverse this trend, and to orient the concept of national interest toward a genuine morality seems, indeed, a matter of transcendent importance. American national interest must be re-defined as its international interest, under which are compounded the particular and the universal, power and ethics, the realism of idealism. For today security and sharing are interdependent, and the freedom and fulfillment of persons, the central promise of industrial civilization, depends on both.

"National Security" as an Ambiguous Symbol*

by Arnold Wolfers

Statesmen, publicists and scholars who wish to be considered realists, as many do today, are inclined to insist that the foreign policy they advocate is dictated by the national interest, more specifically by the national security interest. It is not surprising that this should be so. Today any reference to the pursuit of security is likely to ring a sympathetic chord.

However, when political formulas such as "national interest" or "national security" gain popularity they need to be scrutinized with particular care. They may not mean the same thing to different people. They may not have any precise meaning at all. Thus, while appearing to offer guidance and a basis for broad consensus they may be permitting everyone to label whatever policy he favors with an attractive and possibly deceptive name.

In a very vague and general way "national interest" does suggest a direction of policy which can be distinguished from several others which may present themselves as alternatives. It indicates that the policy is designed to promote demands which are ascribed to the nation rather than to individuals, sub-national groups or mankind as a whole. It em-

* From the *Political Science Quarterly*, Vol. LXVII, No. 4 (December 1952), pp. 481-502. Copyright by the Editors of the *Quarterly*, and reprinted with their permission and Arnold Wolfers'.

phasizes that the policy subordinates other interests to those of the nation. But beyond this, it has very little meaning.

When Charles Beard's study of *The Idea of National Interest* was published in the early years of the New Deal and under the impact of the Great Depression, the lines were drawn differently than they are today. The question at that time was whether American foreign policy, then largely economic in scope and motivation, was aimed not at promoting the welfare interests of the nation as a whole but instead at satisfying the material interests of powerful sub-national interest or pressure groups. While it was found hard to define what was in the interest of national welfare or to discover standards by which to measure it, there could be no doubt as to what people had in mind: they desired to see national policy makers rise above the narrow and special economic interests of parts of the nation to focus their attention on the more inclusive interests of the whole.

Today, the alternative to a policy of the national interest to which people refer is of a different character. They fear policy makers may be unduly concerned with the "interests of all of mankind." They see them sacrificing the less inclusive national community to the wider but in their opinion chimeric world community. The issue, then, is not one of transcending narrow group selfishness, as it was at the time of Beard's discussion, but rather one of according more exclusive devotion to the narrower cause of the national self.

There is another difference between the current and the earlier debate. While it would be wrong to say that the economic interest has ceased to attract attention, it is overshadowed today by the national security interest. Even in the recent debates on the St. Lawrence Seaway, clearly in the first instance an economic enterprise, the defenders of the project, when seeking to impress their listeners with the "national interest" involved, spoke mainly of the value of the Seaway for military defense in wartime while some opponents stressed its vulnerability to attack.

The change from a welfare to a security interpretation of the symbol "national interest" is understandable. Today we are living under the impact of cold war and threats of external aggression rather than of depression and social reform. As a result, the formula of the national interest has come to be practically synonymous with the formula of national security. Unless explicitly denied, spokesmen for a policy which would take the national interest as its guide can be assumed to mean that priority shall be given to measures of security, a term to be analyzed.[1] The question is raised, therefore, whether this seemingly more precise formula of national security offers statesmen a meaningful guide for action. Can they be expected to know what it means? Can policies be distinguished and judged on the ground that they do or do not serve this interest?

The term national security, like national interest, is well enough established in the political discourse of international relations to designate an objective of policy distinguishable from others. We know roughly what people have in mind if they complain that their government is neglecting national security or demanding excessive sacrifices for the sake of enhancing it. Usually those who raise the cry for a policy oriented exclusively toward this interest are afraid their country underestimates the external dangers facing it or is being diverted into idealistic channels unmindful of these dangers. Moreover, the symbol suggests protection through power and therefore figures more frequently in the speech of those who believe in reliance on national power than of those who place their confidence in model behavior, international coöperation, or the United Nations to carry their country safely through the tempests of international conflict. For these reasons it would be an exaggeration to claim that the symbol of national security is nothing but a stimulus to semantic confusion, though closer analysis will show that if used without specifications it leaves room for more confusion than sound political counsel or scientific usage can afford.

The demand for a policy of national security is primarily normative in character. It is supposed to indicate what the policy of a nation should be in order to be either expedient—a rational means toward an accepted end—or moral, the best or least evil course of action. The value judgments implicit in these normative exhortations will be discussed.

---

[1] Hans Morgenthau's *In Defense of the National Interest* (New York, 1951) is the most explicit and impassioned recent plea for an American foreign policy which shall follow "but one guiding star—the National Interest." While Morgenthau is not equally explicit in regard to the meaning he attaches to the symbol "national interest," it becomes clear in the few pages devoted to an exposition of this "perennial" interest that the author is thinking in terms of the national security interest, and specifically of security based on power. The United States, he says, is interested in three things: a unique position as a predominant Power without rival in the Western Hemisphere and the maintenance of the balance of power in Europe as well as in Asia, demands which make sense only in the context of a quest for security through power.

Before doing so, attention should be drawn to an assertion of fact which is implicit if not explicit in most appeals for a policy guided by national security. Such appeals usually assume that nations in fact have made security their goal except when idealism or utopianism of their leaders has led them to stray from the traditional path. If such conformity of behavior actually existed, it would be proper to infer that a country deviating from the established pattern of conduct would risk being penalized. This would greatly strengthen the normative arguments. The trouble with the contention of fact, however, is that the term "security" covers a range of goals so wide that highly divergent policies can be interpreted as policies of security.

Security points to some degree of protection of values previously acquired. In Walter Lippmann's words, a nation is secure to the extent to which it is not in danger of having to sacrifice core values, if it wishes to avoid war, and is able, if challenged, to maintain them by victory in such a war.[2] What this definition implies is that security rises and falls with the ability of a nation to deter an attack, or to defeat it. This is in accord with common usage of the term.

Security is a value, then, of which a nation can have more or less and which it can aspire to have in greater or lesser measure.[3] It has much in common, in this respect, with power or wealth, two other values of great importance in international affairs. But while wealth measures the amount of a nation's material possessions, and power its ability to control the actions of others, security, in an objective sense, measures the absence of threats to acquired values, in a subjective sense, the absence of fear that such values will be attacked. In both respects a nation's security can run a wide gamut from almost complete insecurity or sense of insecurity at one pole, to almost complete security or absence of fear at the other.[4]

---

[2] Walter Lippmann, *U.S. Foreign Policy* (Boston, 1943), p. 51.

[3] This explains why some nations which would seem to fall into the category of *status quo* Powers *par excellence* may nevertheless be dissatisfied and act very much like "imperialist" Powers, as Morgenthau calls nations with acquisitive goals. They are dissatisfied with the degree of security which they enjoy under the *status quo* and are out to enhance it. France's occupation of the Ruhr in 1923 illustrates this type of behavior. Because the demand for more security may induce a *status quo* Power even to resort to the use of violence as a means of attaining more security, there is reason to beware of the easy and often self-righteous assumption that nations which desire to preserve the *status quo* are necessarily "peace-loving."

[4] Security and power would be synonymous terms if security could be attained only through the accumulation of power, which will be shown not to be the case. The fear of attack—security in the subjective sense—is also not proportionate to the

The possible discrepancy between the objective and subjective connotation of the term is significant in international relations despite the fact that the chance of future attack never can be measured "objectively"; it must always remain a matter of subjective evaluation and speculation. However, when the French after World War I insisted that they were entitled to additional guarantees of security because of the exceptionally dangerous situation which France was said to be facing, other Powers in the League expressed the view that rather than to submit to what might be French hysterical apprehension the relative security of France should be objectively evaluated. It is a well-known fact that nations, and groups within nations, differ widely in their reaction to one and the same external situation. Some tend to exaggerate the danger while others underestimate it. With hindsight it is sometimes possible to tell exactly how far they deviated from a rational reaction to the actual or objective state of danger existing at the time. Even if for no other reasons, this difference in the reaction to similar threats suffices to make it probable that nations will differ in their efforts to obtain more security. Some may find the danger to which they are exposed entirely normal and in line with their modest security expectations while others consider it unbearable to live with these same dangers. Although this is not the place to set up hypotheses on the factors which account for one or the other attitude, investigation might confirm the hunch that those nations tend to be most sensitive to threats which have either experienced attacks in the recent past or, having passed through a prolonged period of an exceptionally high degree of security, suddenly find themselves thrust into a situation of danger.[5] Probably national efforts to

---

relative power position of a nation. Why, otherwise, would some weak and exposed nations consider themselves more secure today than does the United States?

Harold D. Lasswell and Abraham Kaplan, *Power and Society* (New Haven, 1950), defining security as "high value expectancy" stress the subjective and speculative character of security by using the term "expectancy"; the use of the term "high," while indicating no definite level, would seem to imply that the security-seeker aims at a position in which the events he expects—here the continued unmolested enjoyment of his possessions—have considerably more than an even chance of materializing.

[5] The United States offers a good illustration and may be typical in this respect. For a long time this country was beyond the reach of any enemy attack that could be considered probable. During that period, then, it could afford to dismiss any serious preoccupation with security. Events proved that it was no worse off for having done so. However, after this happy condition had ceased to exist, government and people alike showed a lag in their awareness of the change. When Nicholas J. Spykman raised his voice in the years before World War II to advocate a broader security outlook than was indicated by the symbol "Western Hemisphere Defense"

achieve greater security would also prove, in part at least, to be a function of the power and opportunity which nations possess of reducing danger by their own efforts.[6]

Another and even stronger reason why nations must be expected not to act uniformly is that they are not all or constantly faced with the same degree of danger. For purposes of a working hypothesis, theorists may find it useful at times to postulate conditions wherein all states are enemies—provided they are not allied against others—and wherein all, therefore, are equally in danger of attack.[7] But, while it may be true in the living world, too, that no sovereign nation can be absolutely safe from future attack, nobody can reasonably contend that Canada, for example, is threatened today to the same extent as countries like Iran or Yugoslavia, or that the British had as much reason to be concerned about the French air force in the twenties as about Hitler's *Luftwaffe* in the thirties.

This point, however, should not be overstressed. There can be no quarrel with the generalization that most nations, most of the time—the great Powers particularly—have shown, and had reason to show, an active concern about some lack of security and have been prepared to make sacrifices for its enhancement. Danger and the awareness of it have been, and continue to be, sufficiently widespread to guarantee some uniformity in this respect. But a generalization which leaves room both for the frantic kind of struggle for more security which characterized French policy at times and for the neglect of security apparent in American foreign policy after the close of both World Wars throws

---

and a greater appreciation of the rôle of defensive military power, he was dealing with this lag and with the dangers implied in it. If Hans Morgenthau and others raise their warning voices today, seemingly treading in Spykman's footsteps, they are addressing a nation which after a new relapse into wishful thinking in 1945 has been radically disillusioned and may now be swinging toward excessive security apprehensions.

[6] Terms such as "degree" or "level" of security are not intended to indicate merely quantitative differences. Nations may also differ in respect to the breadth of their security perspective as when American leaders at Yalta were so preoccupied with security against the then enemy countries of the United States that they failed or refused to consider future American security vis-à-vis the Soviet Union. The differences may apply, instead, to the time range for which security is sought as when the British at Versailles were ready to offer France short-run security guarantees while the French with more foresight insisted that the "German danger" would not become acute for some ten years.

[7] For a discussion of this working hypothesis—as part of the "pure power" hypothesis—see my article on "The Pole of Power and the Pole of Indifference" in *World Politics*, vol. IV, No. 1, October 1951.

little light on the behavior of nations. The demand for conformity would have meaning only if it could be said—as it could under the conditions postulated in the working hypothesis of pure power politics—that nations normally subordinate all other values to the maximization of their security, which, however, is obviously not the case.

There have been many instances of struggles for more security taking the form of an unrestrained race for armaments, alliances, strategic boundaries and the like; but one need only recall the many heated parliamentary debates on arms appropriations to realize how uncertain has been the extent to which people will consent to sacrifice for additional increments of security. Even when there has been no question that armaments would mean more security, the cost in taxes, the reduction in social benefits or the sheer discomfort involved has militated effectively against further effort. It may be worth noting in this connection that there seems to be no case in history in which a country started a preventive war on the grounds of security—unless Hitler's wanton attack on his neighbors be allowed to qualify as such—although there must have been circumstances where additional security could have been obtained by war and although so many wars have been launched for the enhancement of other values. Of course, where security serves only as a cloak for other more enticing demands, nations or ambitious leaders may consider no price for it too high. This is one of the reasons why very high security aspirations tend to make a nation suspect of hiding more aggressive aims.

Instead of expecting a uniform drive for enhanced or maximum security, a different hypothesis may offer a more promising lead. Efforts for security are bound to be experienced as a burden; security after all is nothing but the absence of the evil of insecurity, a negative value so to speak. As a consequence, nations will be inclined to minimize these efforts, keeping them at the lowest level which will provide them with what they consider adequate protection. This level will often be lower than what statesmen, military leaders or other particularly security-minded participants in the decision-making process believe it should be. In any case, together with the extent of the external threats, numerous domestic factors such as national character, tradition, preferences and prejudices will influence the level of security which a nation chooses to make its target.

It might be objected that in the long run nations are not so free to choose the amount of effort they will put into security. Are they not under a kind of compulsion to spare no effort provided they wish to survive? This objection again would make sense only if the hypothesis of pure power politics were a realistic image of actual world affairs. In fact, however, a glance at history will suffice to show that survival has only exceptionally been at stake, particularly for the major Powers. If nations were not concerned with the protection of values other than their survival as independent states, most of them, most of the time, would not have had to be seriously worried about their security, despite what manipulators of public opinion engaged in mustering greater security efforts may have said to the contrary. What "compulsion" there is, then, is a function not merely of the will of others, real or imagined, to destroy the nation's independence but of national desires and ambitions to retain a wealth of other values such as rank, respect, material possessions and special privileges. It would seem to be a fair guess that the efforts for security by a particular nation will tend to vary, other things being equal, with the range of values tor which protection is being sought.

In respect to this range there may seem to exist a considerable degree of uniformity. All over the world today peoples are making sacrifices to protect and preserve what to them appear as the minimum national core values, national independence and territorial integrity. But there is deviation in two directions. Some nations seek protection for more marginal values as well. There was a time when United States policy could afford to be concerned mainly with the protection of the foreign investments or markets of its nationals, its "core values" being out of danger, or when Britain was extending its national self to include large and only vaguely circumscribed "regions of special interest." It is a well-known and portentous phenomenon that bases, security zones and the like may be demanded and acquired for the purpose of protecting values acquired earlier; and they then become new national values requiring protection themselves. Pushed to its logical conclusion, such spatial extension of the range of values does not stop short of world domination.

A deviation in the opposite direction of a compression of the range of core values is hardly exceptional in our days either. There is little indication that Britain is bolstering the security of Hong Kong although colonies were once considered part of the national territory. The Czechs lifted no finger to protect their independence against the Soviet Union and many West Europeans are arguing today that rearmament has become too destructive of values they cherish to be justified even when national independence is obviously at stake.

The lack of uniformity does not end here. A policy is not characterized by its goal, in this case security, alone. In order to become imitable, the means by which the goal is pursued must be taken into account as well. Thus, if two nations were both endeavoring to maximize their security but one were placing all its reliance on armaments and alliances, the other on meticulous neutrality, a policy maker seeking to emulate their behavior would be at a loss where to turn. Those who call for a policy guided by national security are not likely to be unaware of this fact, but they take for granted that they will be understood to mean a security policy based on power, and on military power at that. Were it not so, they would be hard put to prove that their government was not already doing its best for security, though it was seeking to enhance it by such means as international coöperation or by the negotiation of compromise agreements—means which in one instance may be totally ineffective or utopian but which in others may have considerable protective value.

It is understandable why it should so readily be assumed that a quest for security must necessarily translate itself into a quest for coercive power. In view of the fact that security is being sought against external violence—coupled perhaps with internal subversive violence—it seems plausible at first sight that the response should consist in an accumulation of the same kind of force for the purpose of resisting an attack or of deterring a would-be attacker. The most casual reading of history and of contemporary experience, moreover, suffices to confirm the view that such resort to "power of resistance" has been the rule with nations grappling with serious threats to their security, however much the specific form of this power and its extent may differ. Why otherwise would so many nations which have no acquisitive designs maintain costly armaments? Why did Denmark with her state of complete disarmament remain an exception even among the small Powers?

But again, the generalization that nations seeking security usually place great reliance on coercive power does not carry one far. The issue is not whether there is regularly some such reliance but whether there are no significant differences between nations concerning their over-all choice of the means upon which they place their trust. The controversies concerning the best road to future security that are so typical of coalition partners at the close of victorious wars throw light on this question. France in 1919 and all the Allies in 1945 believed that protection against another German attack could be gained only by means of continued military superiority based on German military impotence. President Wilson in 1919 and many observers in 1945 were equally convinced, however, that more hope for security lay in a conciliatory and fair treatment of the defeated enemy, which would rob him of future incentives to renew his attack. While this is not the place to decide which side was right, one cannot help drawing the conclusion that, in the matter of means, the roads which are open may lead in diametrically opposed directions.[8] The choice in every instance will depend on a multitude of variables, including ideological and moral convictions, expectations concerning the psychological and political developments in the camp of the opponent, and inclinations of individual policy makers.[9]

After all that has been said little is left of the sweeping generalization that in actual practice nations, guided by their national security interest, tend to pursue a uniform and therefore imitable policy of security. Instead, there are numerous reasons why they should differ widely in this respect, with some standing close to the pole of complete indifference to security or complete reliance on nonmilitary means, others close to the pole of insistence on absolute security or of complete reliance on coercive power. It should be added that there exists still another category of nations which cannot be placed within the continuum connecting these poles because they regard security of any degree as an insufficient goal; instead they seek to acquire new values even at the price of greater insecurity. In this category must be placed not only the "mad Caesars," who are out for conquest and glory at any price, but also

---

[8] Myres S. McDougal ("Law and Peace" in the *American Journal of International Law*, vol. 46, No. 1, January 1952, pp. 102 *et seq.*) rightly criticizes Hans Morgenthau (and George Kennan for what Kennan himself wrongly believes to be his own point of view in the matter; see fn. 15 *infra*) for his failure to appreciate the rôle which non-power methods, such as legal procedures and moral appeals, may at times successfully play in the pursuit of security. But it is surprising how little aware McDougal appears to be of the disappointing modesty of the contributions which these "other means" have actually made to the enhancement of security and the quite insignificant contributions they have made to the promotion of changes of the *status quo*. This latter failure signifies that they have been unable to remove the main causes of the attacks which security-minded peoples rightly fear.

[9] On the problem of security policy (*Sicherheitspolitik*) with special reference to "collective security" see the comprehensive and illuminating study of Heinrich Rogge, "Kollektivsicherheit Buendnispolitik Voelkerbund," *Theorie der nationalen und internationalen Sicherheit* (Berlin, 1937), which deserves attention despite the fact that it was written and published in Nazi Germany and bears a distinctly "revisionist" slant.

idealistic statesmen who would plunge their country into war for the sake of spreading the benefits of their ideology, for example, of liberating enslaved peoples.

The actual behavior of nations, past and present, does not affect the normative proposition, to which we shall now turn our attention. According to this proposition nations are called upon to give priority to national security and thus to consent to any sacrifice of value which will provide an additional increment of security. It may be expedient, moral or both for nations to do so even if they should have failed to heed such advice in the past and for the most part are not living up to it today.

The first question, then, is whether some definable security policy can be said to be generally expedient. Because the choice of goals is not a matter of expediency, it would seem to make no sense to ask whether it is expedient for nations to be concerned with the goal of security itself; only the means used to this end, so it would seem, can be judged as to their fitness—their instrumental rationality—to promote security. Yet, this is not so. Security, like other aims, may be an intermediate rather than an ultimate goal, in which case it can be judged as a means to these more ultimate ends.

Traditionally, the protection and preservation of national core values have been considered ends in themselves, at least by those who followed in the footsteps of Machiavelli or, for other reasons of political philosophy, placed the prince, state or nation at the pinnacle of their hierarchy of values. Those who do so today will be shocked at the mere suggestion that national security should have to be justified in terms of higher values which it is expected to serve. But there is a large and perhaps growing current of opinion—as a matter of fact influential in this country for a long time—which adheres to this idea. We condemn Nazis and Communists for defending their own totalitarian countries instead of helping to free their people from tyranny; we enlist support for armaments, here and in Allied countries, not so much on the grounds that they will protect national security but that by enhancing such security they will serve to protect ultimate human values like individual liberty. Again, opposition in Europe and Asia to military security measures is based in part on the contention that it would help little to make national core values secure, if in the process the liberties and the social welfare of the people had to be sacrificed; the prevention of Russian conquest, some insist, is useless, if in the course of a war of defense a large part of the people were to be exterminated and most cities destroyed.[10]

While excellent arguments can be made to support the thesis that the preservation of the national independence of this country is worth almost any price as long as no alternative community is available which could assure the same degree of order, justice, peace or individual liberty, it becomes necessary to provide such arguments whenever national security as a value in itself is being questioned. The answer cannot be taken for granted.

But turning away now from the expediency of security as an intermediate goal we must ask whether, aside from any moral considerations which will be discussed later, a specific level of security and specific means of attaining it can claim to be generally expedient.

When one sets out to define in terms of expediency the level of security to which a nation should aspire, one might be tempted to assume that the sky is the limit. Is not insecurity of any kind an evil from which any rational policy maker would want to rescue his country? Yet, there are obvious reasons why this is not so.

In the first place, every increment of security must be paid by additional sacrifices of other values usually of a kind more exacting than the mere expenditure of precious time on the part of policy makers. At a certain point, then, by something like the economic law of diminishing returns, the gain in security no longer compensates for the added costs of attaining it. As in the case of economic value comparisons and preferences, there is frequently disagreement among different layers of policy makers as to where the line should be drawn. This is true particularly because absolute security is out of the question unless a country is capable of world domination, in which case, however, the insecurities and fears would be "internalized" and probably magnified. Because nations must "live dangerously," then, to some extent, whatever they consent to do about it, a modicum of additional but only relative security may easily become unattractive to those who have to bear the chief

---

[10] Raymond Dennett goes further in making the generalization that, "if economic pressures become great enough, almost any government, when put to the final test, will moderate or abandon a political association" (such as the alliance system of the United States with its usefulness to national security) "if only an alteration of policy seems to offer the possibility of maintaining or achieving living standards adequate enough to permit the regime to survive." "Danger Spots in the Pattern of American Security," in *World Politics*, vol. IV, No. 4, July 1952, p. 449.

burden. Nothing renders the task of statesmen in a democracy more difficult than the reluctance of the people to follow them very far along the road to high and costly security levels.

In the second place, national security policies when based on the accumulation of power have a way of defeating themselves if the target level is set too high. This is due to the fact that "power of resistance" cannot be unmistakably distinguished from "power of aggression." What a country does to bolster its own security through power can be interpreted by others, therefore, as a threat to their security. If this occurs, the vicious circle of what John Herz has described as the "security dilemma" sets in: the efforts of one side provoke countermeasures by the other which in turn tend to wipe out the gains of the first. Theoretically there seems to be no escape from this frustrating consequence; in practice, however, there are ways to convince those who might feel threatened that the accumulation of power is not intended and will never be used for attack.[11] The chief way is that of keeping the target level within moderate bounds and of avoiding placing oneself in a position where it has to be raised suddenly and drastically. The desire to escape from this vicious circle presupposes a security policy of much self-restraint and moderation, especially in the choice of the target level.[12] It can never be expedient to pursue a security policy which by the fact of provocation or incentive to others fails to increase the nation's relative power position and capability of resistance.

The question of what means are expedient for the purpose of enhancing security raises even more thorny problems. Policy makers must decide how to distribute their reliance on whatever means are available to them and, particularly, how far to push the accumulation of coercive power. No attempt can be made here to decide what the choice should be in order to be expedient. Obviously, there can be no general answer which would meet the requirements of every case. The answer depends on the circumstances. A weak country may have no better means at its

---

[11] Not everyone agrees that this can be done. Jeremy Bentham wrote that "measures of mere self defense are naturally taken for projects of aggression" with the result that "each makes haste to begin for fear of being forestalled." *Principles of International Law*, Essay IV.

[12] The Quakers, in a book on *The United States and the Soviet Union: Some Quaker Proposals for Peace* (New Haven, 1949), p. 14, state that "it is highly questionable whether security can be achieved in the modern world through an attempt to establish an overwhelming preponderance of military power." This can be read to mean that a less ambitious military target than overwhelming preponderance might be a means of achieving security.

disposal than to prove to stronger neighbors that its strict neutrality can be trusted. Potentially strong countries may have a chance to deter an aggressor by creating "positions of strength." In some instances they may have no other way of saving themselves; while in others even they may find it more expedient to supplement such a policy, if not to replace it, by a policy intended to negotiate their opponent out of his aggressive designs.

The reason why "power of resistance" is not the general panacea which some believe it to be lies in the nature of security itself. If security, in the objective sense of the term at least, rises and falls with the presence or absence of aggressive intentions on the part of others, the attitude and behavior of those from whom the threat emanates are of prime importance. Such attitude and behavior need not be beyond the realm of influence by the country seeking to bolster its security. Whenever they do not lie beyond this realm the most effective and least costly security policy consists in inducing the opponent to give up his aggressive intentions.

While there is no easy way to determine when means can and should be used which are directed not at resistance but at the prevention of the desire of others to attack, it will clarify the issue to sketch the type of hypotheses which would link specific security policies, as expedient, to some of the most typical political constellations.

One can think of nations lined up between the two poles of maximum and minimum "attack propensity," with those unalterably committed to attack, provided it promises success, at one pole and those whom no amount of opportunity for successful attack could induce to undertake it at the other. While security in respect to the first group can come exclusively as a result of "positions of strength" sufficient to deter or defeat attack, nothing could do more to undermine security in respect to the second group than to start accumulating power of a kind which would provoke fear and countermoves.

Unfortunately it can never be known with certainty, in practice, what position within the continuum one's opponent actually occupies. Statesmen cannot be blamed, moreover, if caution and suspicion lead them to assume a closer proximity to the first pole than hindsight proves to have been justified. We believe we have ample proof that the Soviet Union today is at or very close to the first pole, while Canadian policy makers probably place the United States in its intentions toward Canada at the second pole.

It is fair to assume that, wherever the issue of security becomes a matter of serious concern, statesmen will usually be dealing with potential opponents who occupy a position somewhere between but much closer to the first of the two poles. This means, then, that an attack must be feared as a possibility, even though the intention to launch it cannot be considered to have crystallized to the point where nothing could change it. If this be true, a security policy in order to be expedient cannot avoid accumulating power of resistance and yet cannot let it go at that. Efforts have to be made simultaneously toward the goal of removing the incentives to attack. This is only another way of saying that security policy must seek to bring opponents to occupy a position as close to the second pole as conditions and capabilities permit.

Such a twofold policy presents the greatest dilemmas because efforts to change the intentions of an opponent may run counter to the efforts to build up strength against him. The dangers of any policy of concessions, symbolized by "Munich," cannot be underestimated. The paradox of this situation must be faced, however, if security policy is to be expedient. It implies that national security policy, except when directed against a country unalterably committed to attack, is the more rational the more it succeeds in taking the interests, including the security interests, of the other side into consideration. Only in doing so can it hope to minimize the willingness of the other to resort to violence. Rather than to insist, then, that under all conditions security be sought by reliance on nothing but defensive power and be pushed in a spirit of national selfishness toward the highest targets, it should be stressed that in most instances efforts to satisfy legitimate demands of others are likely to promise better results in terms of security.[13] That is probably what George Kennan had in mind when he advised policy makers to use self-restraint in the pursuit of the national interest. While in the face of a would-be world conqueror who is beyond the pale of external influence it is dangerous to be diverted from the accumulation of sheer defensive power, any mistake about his true state of mind or any neglect of opportunities to influence his designs, where it has a chance of being successful, violates the rules of expediency. It should always be kept in mind that the ideal security policy is one which would lead to a distribution of values so satisfactory to all nations that the intention to attack and

---

[13] As A. D. Lindsay puts it, "The search for perfect security . . . defeats its own ends. Playing for safety is the most dangerous way to live." Introduction to Thomas Hobbes, *Leviathan*, p. xxii.

with it the problem of security would be minimized. While this is a utopian goal, policy makers and particularly peacemakers would do well to remember that there are occasions when greater approximation to such a goal can be effected.

We can now focus our attention on the moral issue, if such there be.[14] Those who advocate a policy devoted to national security are not always aware of the fact—if they do not explicitly deny it—that they are passing moral judgment when they advise a nation to pursue the goal of national security or when they insist that such means as the accumulation of coercive power—or its use—should be employed for this purpose.[15]

Nations like individuals or other groups may value things not because they consider them good or less evil than their alternative; they may value them because they satisfy their pride, heighten their sense of self-esteem or reduce their fears. However, no policy, or human act in general, can escape becoming a subject for moral judgment—whether by the conscience of the actor himself or by others—which calls for the sacrifice of other values, as any security policy is bound to do. Here it becomes a matter of comparing and weighing values in order to decide which of them are deemed sufficiently good to justify the evil of sacrificing others. If someone insists that his country should do more to build up its strength, he is implying, knowingly or not, that more security is sufficiently desirable to warrant such evils as the cut in much-needed social welfare benefits or as the extension of the period of military service.[16]

---

[14] On the moral problem in international relations see my article on "Statesmanship and Moral Choice," in *World Politics*, vol. I, No. 2, January 1949, pp. 176 et seq., especially p. 185. In one of his most recent statements on the subject, Reinhold Niebuhr, *The Irony of American History* (New York, 1954), points specifically to the moral problem involved in security policy—"no imperiled nation," he writes, "is morally able to dispense with weapons which might insure its survival" (p. 39).

[15] It is not without irony that of the two authors who have recently come out for a policy of the national interest, the one, George F. Kennan, who calls for a policy of national self-restraint and humility, usually identified with morality, should deny "that state behavior is a fit subject for moral judgment" (*American Diplomacy, 1900-1950*, Chicago, 1952, p. 100), while the other, Hans Morgenthau (*op. cit.*), calling for a policy of unadulterated national egotism, claims to speak in the name of morality.

[16] It would be unrealistic to assume that policy makers divide their attention strictly between ends and means and only after having chosen a specific target level as being morally justified decide whether the means by which it can be attained are morally acceptable. Moral judgment is more likely to be passed on the totality of a course of action which embraces both the desired end and the means which lead to it.

Many vivid examples of the moral dilemma are being supplied by current controversies concerning American security policy. Is a "deal with fascist Spain" morally justified, provided it added an increment to our security, though principles valued highly by some were being sacrificed? Should we engage in subversive activities and risk the lives of our agents if additional security can be attained thereby? Should we perhaps go so far as to start a preventive war, when ready, with the enormous evils it would carry with it, if we should become convinced that no adequate security can be obtained except by the defeat of the Soviet Union? In this last case, would not the exponents of amoralism have some moral qualms, at least to the point of rationalizing a decision favoring such a war by claiming that it would serve to satisfy not primarily an egotistical national demand for security but an altruistic desire to liberate enslaved peoples? It is easier to argue for the amorality of politics if one does not have to bear the responsibility of choice and decision!

Far be it from a political scientist to claim any particular competence in deciding what efforts for national security are or are not morally justified. What he can contribute here is to point to the ambiguities of any general normative demand that security be bought at whatever price it may cost. He may also be able to make it more difficult for advisers or executors of policy to hide from themselves or others the moral value judgments and preferences which underlie whatever security policy they choose to recommend or conduct.

The moral issue will be resolved in one of several ways depending on the ethical code upon which the decision is based. From one extreme point of view it is argued that every sacrifice, especially if imposed on other nations, is justified provided it contributes in any way to national security. Clearly this implies a position that places national security at the apex of the value pyramid and assumes it to constitute an absolute good to which all other values must be subordinated. Few will be found to take this position because if they subscribed to a nationalistic ethics of this extreme type they would probably go beyond security—the mere preservation of values—and insist that the nation is justified in conquering whatever it can use as *Lebensraum* or otherwise. At the opposite extreme are the absolute pacifists who consider the use of coercive power an absolute evil and condemn any security policy, therefore, which places reliance on such power.

For anyone who does not share these extreme views the moral issue raised by the quest for national security is anything but clear-cut and simple. He should have no doubts about the right of a nation to protect and preserve values to which it has a legitimate title or even about its moral duty to pursue a policy meant to serve such preservation. But he cannot consider security the supreme law as Machiavelli would have the statesman regard the *ragione di stato*. Somewhere a line is drawn, which in every instance he must seek to discover, that divides the realm of neglect, the "too-little," from the realm of excess, the "too-much." Even Hans Morgenthau who extols the moral duty of self-preservation seems to take it for granted that naked force shall be used for security in reaction only to violent attack, not for preventive war.

Decision makers are faced with the moral problem, then, of choosing first the values which deserve protection, with national independence ranking high not merely for its own sake but for the guarantee it may offer to values like liberty, justice and peace. He must further decide which level of security to make his target. This will frequently be his most difficult moral task though terms such as adequacy or fair share indicate the kind of standards that may guide him. Finally, he must choose the means and thus by scrupulous computation of values compare the sacrifices, which his choice of means implies, with the security they promise to provide.

It follows that policies of national security, far from being all good or all evil, may be morally praiseworthy or condemnable depending on their specific character and the particular circumstances of the case. They may be praised for their self-restraint and the consideration which this implies for values other than security; they may instead be condemned for being inadequate to protect national values. Again, they may be praised in one instance for the consideration given to the interests of others, particularly of weaker nations, or condemned in another because of the recklessness with which national values are risked on the altar of some chimera. The target level falls under moral judgment for being too ambitious, egotistical and provocative or for being inadequate; the means employed for being unnecessarily costly in other values or for being ineffective. This wide range of variety which arises out of the multitude of variables affecting the value computation would make it impossible, and in fact meaningless, to pass moral judgment, positive or negative, on "national security policy in general."

It is this lack of moral homogeneity which in matters of security policy justifies attacks on so-called moralism, though not on moral evaluation. The "moralistic approach" is taken to mean a wholesale condemnation either of any concern with national security—as being an expression of national egotism—or of a security policy relying on coercive and therefore evil power. The exponent of such "moralism" is assumed to believe that security for all peoples can be had today by the exclusive use of such "good" and altruistic means as model behavior and persuasion, a spirit of conciliation, international organization or world government. If there are any utopians who cling to this notion, and have influence on policy, it makes sense to continue to disabuse them of what can surely be proved to be dangerous illusions.

It is worth emphasizing, however, that the opposite line of argument, which without regard for the special circumstances would praise everything done for national security or more particularly everything done for the enhancement of national power of resistance, is no less guilty of applying simple and abstract moral principles and of failing to judge each case realistically on its merits.

In conclusion, it can be said, then, that normative admonitions to conduct a foreign policy guided by the national security interest are no less ambiguous and misleading than the statement of fact concerning past behavior which was discussed earlier. In order to be meaningful such admonitions would have to specify the degree of security which a nation shall aspire to attain and the means by which it is to be attained in a given situation. It may be good advice in one instance to appeal for greater effort and more armaments; it may be no less expedient and morally advisable in another instance to call for moderation and for greater reliance on means other than coercive power. Because the pendulum of public opinion swings so easily from extreme complacency to extreme apprehension, from utopian reliance on "good will" to disillusioned faith in naked force only, it is particularly important to be wary of any simple panacea, even of one that parades in the realist garb of a policy guided solely by the national security interest.

FOR FURTHER READING:

Charles A. Beard with the collaboration of G. H. E. Smith, *The Idea of National Interest: An Analytical Study in American Foreign Policy* (New York: The Macmillan Company, 1934).

Thomas I. Cook and Malcolm Moos, *Power through Purpose: The Realism of Idealism as a Basis for Foreign Policy* (Baltimore: The Johns Hopkins Press, 1954).

Percy E. Corbett, *Morals, Law and Power in International Relations* (Los Angeles: John Randolph Haynes and Dora Haynes Foundation, 1956).

George F. Kennan, *American Diplomacy, 1900-1950* (Chicago: University of Chicago Press, 1951).

Hans J. Morgenthau, *In Defence of the National Interest: A Critical Examination of American Foreign Policy* (New York: Alfred A. Knopf, 1951).

Reinhold Niebuhr, *The Irony of American History* (New York: Charles Scribner's Sons, 1954).

Robert Endicott Osgood, *Ideals and Self Interest in American Foreign Policy The Great Transformation of the Twentieth Century* (Chicago: University of Chicago Press, 1953).

Dexter Perkins, *The American Approach to Foreign Policy* (Cambridge: Harvard University Press, 1952).

Dexter Perkins (edited by Glyndon G. Van Deusen and Richard C. Wade), *Foreign Policy and the American Spirit* (Ithaca: Cornell University Press, 1957).

Frank Tannenbaum, *The American Tradition in Foreign Policy* (Norman: University of Oklahoma Press, 1955).

Arnold Wolfers, "The Pole of Power and the Pole of Indifference," *World Politics*, Vol. IV, No. 1 (October, 1951), pp. 39-63.

Chapter V

THE WORLD ENVIRONMENT

Before considering specific foreign policy problems—
the central feature of the public debate—it is necessary to examine in
greater detail the environment of contemporary world politics. This environment limits the courses of action open to the United States and in
general terms is ultimately responsible for some of the most acute
foreign policy problems currently facing this country. This chapter
analyzes some of the principal aspects of the contemporary world environment, the arena within which United States foreign policy must be
conducted. Some of the elements of the world environment are stable
—the multi-state system for example, which has been the basic framework of world politics for over three centuries—others are distinctive
features of the mid-twentieth century.

The first selection by Boyd C. Shafer, Executive Secretary of the
American Historical Association and Managing Editor of the *American
Historical Review*, deals with nationalism, one of the most important
elements of contemporary world politics and one which, although it
has been present for some time, has recently assumed significantly new
proportions. Because of nationalism the nation-state is, and will continue to be, the basic unit in world politics. In the present period men
owe their primary allegiance to their nation-states. Mr. Shafer analyzes
this complex phenomenon, dispels many of the myths which have
come to surround it, and explains the process by which nationalism is
developed and maintained. Nationalism, in addition to being the basic
factor explaining our present multi-state system, is also an important

176

motive force in contemporary world politics. Nationalism causes peoples to seek independence and statehood and thus is responsible for the large number of states which have recently gained self-government; it also occasionally leads states to adopt expansionist policies. It is impossible to understand the Suez and Hungarian crises of 1956 and the Algerian crisis, to list only a few, without understanding nationalism. In terms of national self-determination—peoples gaining independence and statehood—nationalism has achieved its goal almost everywhere except in Africa. It is on this continent that whatever future crises of independence there may be will occur. The extent to which nationalism will lead to expansionist policies, as it has often in the past, is not clear. Certainly this possibility cannot be ruled out given the fervent nationalism prevalent in many parts of the world. Mr. Shafer correctly points out that nationalism in its origins, if not in its contemporary manifestations, is a product of the highly developed states of Western Europe; ideas which originated there have been transmitted throughout the globe with frequently explosive and unpredictable consequences. It is one of the paradoxes of the present epoch that as nationalism appears to be weakening in Western Europe with the growth of supra-national institutions, it is gaining strength in other areas of the world, most notably in Asia and Africa.

The tendency toward national exclusiveness caused by nationalism is given further impetus in the twentieth century by economic factors. Gunnar Myrdal, an eminent Swedish economist and former Executive Secretary of the United Nations Economic Commission for Europe, examines these factors and their effects in the second selection; he explores the tendency of states to attempt to isolate themselves from outside economic influences and to attain autarky—national economic self-sufficiency. In the twentieth century new pressures in this direction have been added to the traditional demands of national defense and the protection of business interests. Economic isolationism has been found a concomitant of welfare-state policies and programs of rapid economic growth. We have witnessed a vast increase in governments' role in economic affairs in states all over the world which, although it has no doubt led to markedly increased standards of living, has also led to the erection of unprecedented barriers to international trade. Mr. Myrdal analyzes this phenomenon, which he calls national integration, and its international effects.

While the first two selections deal with intra-state developments and their implications, the last two are concerned with problems of inter-state relations. The third, by Hajo Holborn, Townsend Professor of History at Yale University, examines the final collapse of the European political system which governed world politics and provided a measure of stability during the nineteenth century. His analysis of the political events from 1919 till 1945 contributes to an understanding of what the old order was, how it finally ended, and its legacy for the present. Such understanding is obviously necessary to properly understand the present system, and it is vital for those who hope to create a new and in their view better order. Beyond this, understanding the events of this period is a necessary prerequisite to understanding contemporary world politics, for memories of these events are important to today's diplomatists and color their views of the present. These men were in their formative years during this period, and many of the theories they apply to world politics are derived from interpretations they developed then.

The final selection, by Bernard Brodie, Senior Staff Member of the Rand Corporation and one of this country's foremost military analysts, deals with the most dramatic change in the world environment—the revolution in military technology caused by the introduction of nuclear and thermonuclear weapons and new delivery systems. Most of us frequently verbally acknowledge this revolution, but few—if any—have thought through its consequences. Mr. Brodie points out the difficult problems involved in adjusting our ideas about war—its relationship to policy and its strategy and tactics—caused by these new developments and sketches in broad outline the direction the adjustment should follow. With the Soviet Union's rapid increase in nuclear striking power, this rethinking of our basic concepts is all the more urgent.

Full grasp of the meaning of the revolution in military technology, or of any of the other equally important changes in the contemporary environment of world politics, will probably only be achieved, if ever, by future historians. Yet, however imperfect its understanding, the United States must pursue its goals within this framework. The public must therefore attempt to comprehend the contemporary world environment.

Nationalism—Some Myths and Realities*[1]

by Boyd C. Shafer

Nations today are the chief groups into which people politically, economically, and socially divide. The nation today is a major object of men's devotion and loyalty, the one object for which they will commonly fight and die. It is in national groupings that men have fought the great modern wars, been vanquished or victorious—at any rate, in our times, have died in millions. The powerful political units today are the national governments. These tax, administer justice, provide social security, protect and control business and agriculture, spend vast funds, enter into the lives of every citizen; in sum, determine in large part what every man thinks and does. And in turn, good citizens seek their welfare within the nation, demand that their fellow citizens conform to its ideals, protect it, and seek fulfillment of their aspirations within it. The general welfare today is not the general welfare of mankind but of nations of men. Liberties are not universal but national. Mankind exists in imagination, but men are Englishmen, Egyptians, Russians, Chinese, Brazilians, and Americans.

This is true everywhere on our shrinking globe, in Europe where nations are old, in the Near and Far East where old peoples comprise new

* From the *Journal of International Affairs*, Vol. XII, No. 2 (1958), pp. 173-181. Copyright 1958 by the Board of Editors of the *Journal of International Affairs*. Reprinted by permission.

[1] Among the many books on nationalism are: Sir Ernest Barker, ed., *The Character of England*, Oxford, 1947; Merle E. Curti, *The Roots of American Loyalty*, New York, 1946; Francis Delaisi, *Political Myths and Economic Realities*, New York, 1927; Carlton J. H. Hayes, *Essays on Nationalism*, New York, 1926, and *The Historical Evolution of Nationalism*, New York, 1931; Friedrich O. Hertz, *Nationality in History and Politics, A Study of the Psychology and Sociology of National Sentiment and Character*, Oxford, 1944; René Johannet, *Le principe des nationalités*, Paris, new ed., 1923; Otto Klineberg, *Tensions Affecting International Understanding*, New York, 1950; Hans Kohn, *The Idea of Nationalism. A Study of Its Origin and Background*, New York, 1943; Friedrich Meinecke, *Weltbürgertum und Nationalstaat: Studien zur Genesis des deutschen Nationalstaat*, Munich, 1928; Royal Institute of International Affairs, *Nationalism: A Report by a Study Group of Members of the Royal Institute of International Affairs*, London, 1939; Boyd C. Shafer, *Nationalism, Myth and Reality*, New York, 1955; Georges Weill, *L'Europe du XIX siècle et l'idée de nationalité*, Paris, 1938; Albert K. Weinberg, *Manifest Destiny: A Study of Nationalist Expansionism in American History*, 1935; Florjan Znaniecki, *Modern Nationalities: A Sociological Study*, Urbana, 1952. Two bibliographies are Karl Deutsch, *Interdisciplinary Bibliography on Nationalism*, Cambridge, Massachusetts, 1956; and Koppel Pinson, *A Bibliographical Introduction to Nationalism*, New York, 1935.

nations. At bottom, the trouble over the Suez was a conflict among old
and new nationalism: British, French, Egyptian, and Israeli. In Asia,
the nations of India and Pakistan dispute the Kashmir, and the Chinese
and the Indonesians violently rise to throw off what they call "the yoke
of Western Imperialism," the domination of older Western nations. In
South America, "Yankee Imperialism" has long been anathema. Everywhere men seek realization of their dearest dreams, whatever they may
be, within their nations. Everywhere they erect their nations into bulwarks, no matter how shaky, against adversity. This devotion to their
nation we call "nationalism." Men give this devotion, however, for many
different reasons, and their devotion is of many different qualities and
intensities. French nationalism is not the same as English, the Chinese
not the same as the Japanese, the Brazilian not the same as the Argen-
tinean. We shall have to define our terms more fully and precisely.

What is it that men think of the nation? Generally the concept
means at least some unit of teritory, a people with a common past and
some common cultural characteristics as a common language, and an
independent government (actual or hoped for). Men are devoted to
this territory, these characteristics, this history, this government, and this
is what we call nationalism.[2] They love their native land; they hold
their fellow nationals in high esteem while disliking foreigners; they
find pride in the national achievements and sorrow in the national
tragedies; they admire their own real or imagined history; they hope that
their nation will have a glorious future. And so they will fight and, if
need be, die for their nation. The tragedy of the Hungarians is but one
late example. Hundreds of others could be picked from the world's
history of the last two centuries.

When men love their nations, they do so for a variety of reasons,
some of them without foundation in fact. Now patriotism is a glorious
emotion. If men possess it, they ought not base it on myths. Perhaps,
too, if men based their nationalism on realities, their nationalism might
not be so belligerent. It is this belligerency which bothers so many
students and, in an atomic world, makes unbridled nationalism so
potentially dangerous.

Historical myths which people believe are often more real than hard

---

[2] The definitions are many. See Shafer, *op. cit.*, pp. 3-11. The "classic" definition
is that of Renan, "Qu'est-ce qu'une nation?" *Discours et conférences*, Paris, 1887.
See also Guido Zernatto, "Nation: The History of a World," *Review of Politics*,
Vol. VI, 1944, pp. 351-66.

facts which they may ignore. Here, to call a belief a myth is not to deny that in the process of history myths have not had tremendous import, consequences at times transcending even those arising out of actual experienced truth. Quite the contrary. Perhaps most of the time most of us act on beliefs which have little or no concrete facts behind them. But, as students of nationalism, we ought to be exact, sort out the knowable from the unknowable, the fact from fancy.

Men have indulged in a good many fancies about the origin and development of their nations. When they have not found sufficient material explanation, they have, for example, fallen back upon God or divine forces, imagining, as have the Jews and English and French and Germans and Americans, that God singled them out as a chosen people. John Quincy Adams wrote to his famous father: "The whole continent of North America appears to be destined by *Divine Providence* to be peopled by one nation." [3] In England in the nineteenth century an Anglo-Israel Identity Society declared that the English descended from the Lost Tribes.

We cannot here wrestle with the monumental question of God's will in regard to nations. All we can say on this point is that God's will concerning the nations is thus far unfathomable to man.

When, in the eighteenth century, philosophers turned from divine to what they thought more rational interpretations of man, natural law became an explanation for the nation. In simplified form, this meant that men, as Adam Smith and Rousseau wrote, naturally turned to the nation as the chief object of their affections. But here the social philosophers were guessing. Influenced by the new Newtonian science, they thought they could, like the physicists working on natural phenomena, find the natural laws concerning human behavior. They then found that men's love of nation was natural. The ways of nature in this case, however, are as unfathomable as the ways of God. There was and is no evidence that nature intended men to live in nations or that they should be devoted to them. Rousseau quite unconsciously proved this when he had to advise the King of Poland to provide a patriotic education for his subjects.

When conservative political philosophers like Edmund Burke and Georg Wilhelm Friedrich Hegel spurned natural explanations of this kind, they did not reject the nation. They turned to mystical forces

---

[3] Quoted by Samuel Flagg Bemis, *John Quincy Adams and the Foundations of American Foreign Policy*, New York, 1949, p. 182.

arising out of history. To Burke, the nation was an inspired union of
the historical, the present, and the unborn generations, an organic
personality embodying the "moral essences" of the ages.[4] This, of
course, is a kind of mysticism which soars higher than evidence. That
nations evolved in history is a truism, but that is as far as evidence or
logic will go.

There are all sorts of other mystical explanations, or rather, justifications for the nations. Nations are supposed to be determined by the
climate and by natural boundaries. Physical environment turns out to be
no explanation at all. Not only England is another Eden, a demi-
paradise, a blessed plot—at least in other people's minds. The fact is
other people think their lands Edens. The facts are that the climates
of several nations are similar—Russia and the United States, Germany
and France, Japan and England, and each of the major nations possesses
within itself a variety of climates. Nor is the argument about natural
boundaries any more tenable.

Natural boundaries, on examination, turn out to be the boundaries
out to which national groups have reached by chance, diplomatic victories, and national warfare, or they do not exist at all. For France, the
so-called "natural" boundaries, the Rhine, the Alps, the Pyrenees, were
established not by nature, but by the able military exploits of Philip the
Fair, Louis XIV, Joan of Arc, and Carnot.[5] Where are the "natural"
boundaries of eastern Germany, or most any central European nation,
of northwest India, of northwestern United States, of western Russia?
Finally, what about all the natural obstacles, the Mississippi, the Volga,
the Amazon, the Urals, the Rockies, which do not divide? National
boundaries are not natural but national, and national boundaries, unlike
natural, have shifted constantly as nations have been weak or powerful.

More fiercely held than the fantasy about natural boundaries is that
concerning the racial basis of nations, the myth arising out of the bril-
liant rhetoric and factual emptiness of the writings of the Frenchman
Count Gobineau, the Englishman Houston Stewart Chamberlain, and
many a popular neurotic of the nineteenth and twentieth centuries.
Race as an explanation of human behavior has been fairly well de-

---

[4] See particularly his *Reflections on the French Revolution* (many editions) and
his *Reform of Representation in the House of Commons*, Works, Bohn, Ed., London, 1861, Vol. IV, pp. 146 ff.
[5] Cf. Albert Sorel, *L'Europe et la Révolution française*, Paris, 1946.

bunked in our time in well-merited attacks on Hitler's nonsense.[6] The facts are that nobody knows what a race is, or whether, if such a grouping as a race exists, it determines anything about men except some physical characteristics. Historically, men have endlessly mixed. As the anthropologist Ralph Linton told us, there has never been a tribe whose women have been so hideous they have not attracted men of other tribes, and there has never been a tribe whose men were so cowardly that they would not steal women of other tribes. All the nations are mixed—the United States is an outstanding example. Race, then, turns out to be no explanation at all for nations and nationalism, though the belief of people in racial ideas certainly has led them to become nationalistic.

About the same time as the racial myth was arising, about a century ago, Karl Marx and Friedrich Engels were building another one, that the bourgeoisie created nations in order to develop markets for its goods and, thereby, profit.[7] There may be some truth in this: Alexander Hamilton thought of the national government as the agency to develop manufactures, trade, and finance. The trouble with the materialist explanation is that it is too simple, overlooking, by way of illustration, the role of the monarchs and nobility in building nations as well as the loyalty modern workers have given to their nations. Modern nations have long been growing—probably their origins are to be found in the eleventh century; the bourgeoisie was not a decisive force until the eighteenth century. And in the nineteenth and twentieth centuries, workers have usually been as nationalistic as any group.

Most scholars, in trying to find a logical basis for nations and nationalism, have turned to language.[8] Language differences, they say,

---

[6] Among the studies see Jacques Barzun, *The French Race: Theories of Its Origin and Their Social and Political Implications Prior to the Revolution*, New York, 1932; Ruth Benedict, *Race: Science and Politics*, New York, 1940; Franz Boas, *Anthropology and Modern Life*, New York, 1932; William C. Boyd, *Genetics and the Races of Man: An Introduction to Modern Physical Anthropology*, Boston, 1950; Otto Klineberg, *Race Differences*, New York, 1935; Alfred L. Kroeber, *Anthropology: Race, Language, Culture, Psychology, Prehistory*, New York, 1948; Ralph Linton, *The Study of Man: An Introduction*, New York, 1936; UNESCO, *The Race Concept, Results of an Inquiry*, Paris, 1952.

[7] Basic statements on the theory are Vladimir Lenin, *Critical Remarks on the National Question*, Moscow, 1951; Joseph Stalin, *Marxism and the National and Colonial Question: A Collection of Articles and Speeches*, New York, n.d.

[8] There are many studies. The best is Otto Jespersen's *Mankind, Nation and Individual from a Linguistic Point of View*, Oslo, 1925, but Ferdinand Brunot's *Histoire de langue française*, Paris, 1904-47, is a monument of patriotic erudition.

provide the best explanation. Here again there is some truth. After all, languages do differ, do divide. An American in Paris feels strange, partly because *"Il ne parle pas." "Il ne comprend."* An American schoolmarm in Paris when she orders a thirst quencher, may not get orange juice but wine, and when she orders a meal, she may, according to the old cliché, get peas five times. Language differences are hardly the reason for nations, however. Englishmen and Americans speak a common language, or at least they did at the time of the War of Independence. Peoples, even the French, have had to be forced by governmental edict to speak a common language. All languages are medleys of other languages and of foreign words, forever growing forever changing. Language may or may not be a distinguishing national factor.

But enough of myths, though there are others which we might profitably discuss; for instance, the eager zeal of historians to find national origins long before the evidence permits. How did nations and nationalism come into existence? There are many books written on the subject, a few of them good. Here we must be brief and we shall, of course, skim the surface and run the ever present danger of oversimplification.

Nationalism is a product of history, of nurture not nature. Nations were not born full grown, nor are men born with love of nation inherent in them.[9] Nations and nationalism originated and developed in late medieval and modern history, out of the institutions, the ideas, the conditions of the past seven-to-eight hundred years. All I can do here, of course, is to show in outline how institutions and ideas combined to produce them. This is a staggering enough task. You will bear with me as I zoom through history.

From about 1100 to 1600 in western Europe, the monarchs of the middle and late medieval period built, largely by war and diplomacy, large territorial domains. Over these they ruled—established common laws and courts, collected taxes, and raised troops. In short, they imposed a common national authority over a territory and the people or peoples inhabiting it. Through hundreds of years there arose among the inhabitants, say the French or English, a feeling of common history, of common tragedies and glories, a consciousness of common needs of trade and defense, and often the reality of a common language. Here, then, was a basis for a nation.

---

[9] J. Piaget, "The Development in Children of the Idea of the Homeland and of Relations with Other Countries," *International Social Science Bulletin*, Vol. III, 1951.

Sometime around the eighteenth century, we cannot pinpoint a date, the middle classes began to feel that the nation belonged to all the property owners.[10] This was not a new phenomenon, rather it rooted deep in the past; nor was the feeling restricted to the middle classes— a good many nobles and clergymen felt the same way. Now when the nation belonged not only to the king but also to the property-owning people, these people had an interest in the national welfare and thought they should have a voice in national affairs. "When," Voltaire wrote, "those who possess like myself, fields and houses, assemble for their common interests, I have a voice in this assembly. I am a part of the whole, a part of the community. A part of the sovereign. Here is my fatherland." [11] When men possessed a fatherland, they became citizens, not just subjects, and being citizens they could demand or give to themselves rights and privileges. This, in part, was what happened in 1688, 1776, and 1789. There were, then, new reasons for many to be devoted to the nation. Popular nationalism in contradistinction to dynastic nationalism was beginning. Soon all inhabitants, at least all native inhabitants of a nation, were considering themselves citizens entitled to national rights such as those guaranteed by the English unwritten and the American and French written constitutions. And, in turn, as the nation afforded rights and benefits, the citizens were patriotic, that is, nationalistic, national-minded.

The great wars of the French Revolutionary and Napoleonic era accelerated the process. Englishmen, Frenchmen, Germans, Spaniards, Italians all believed themselves threatened or oppressed, feared the foreigners, warred with national armies against each other. Fear led to intensifying national hatreds, greater reliance upon the national governments; and these national governments in consequence acquired more and more power, more and more prestige. The nation became the vehicle of men's hopes and their fortresses against fear, the symbol of better times to come, a refuge in time of trouble.

The governments of the nation-states, to satisfy the most ardent patriots, began consciously to make good citizens, to force all citizens into the national molds. The more they acted, the more nationalist their citizens became, and the more these citizens demanded national institu-

---

[10] See, for example, Robert Palmer, "The National Idea in France before the Revolution," *Journal of Modern History*, Vol. X, 1938, and Boyd C. Shafer, "Bourgeois Nationalism in the Pamphlets on the Eve of the Revolution," Vol. X, 1938.

[11] *Oeuvres complètes de Voltaire*, 1785, Vol. XLII, pp. 263-4.

tions, national ways of living. National governments made the churches and even religion national. By conscription and *levées en masse* they created national armies. Through the establishment of national school systems they fostered national patriotism. Laws, courts, taxes all became increasingly national rather than local or provincial. The citizens thus were conditioned to be interested in, involved in their nation, their nation-state, their common needs and aspirations. On national holidays, on Fourth's or Fourteenth's of July, they celebrated the winning of national independence or national freedoms. And they sang the praises of their nations in *Rule Britannia*, a *Star-Spangled Banner*, a *Marseillaise*, or a *Deutschland über Alles*.

During the nineteenth century the nationalism we have seen beginning in western Europe spread over the world, deepened and intensified everywhere. Europeans not only carried their trade, their diseases, and their guns to Africa, Asia, and the Americas; they carried the spirit of nationalism. The Asian, African, and American nationalisms developed in most respects like those of Europe, but perhaps because they were sparked by hatred and fear of the foreign oppression more than hope for the achievement of liberties, they contained perhaps less fervid love of country and more hatred of the oppressors. In any case, the peoples of the whole world all came to be divided into nations, each people thinking of itself as being different, disliking and fearing other peoples, being devoted almost exclusively to its own national interests.

Almost every activity and idea seemed to conspire to promote nationalism. Ideas re-enforced national institutions. These institutions fostered national ideas. How could men enlarge their freedoms, obtain protection against the vicissitudes of everyday life or foreign enemies? Through unity of thought and action within their own nations. What once king, noble, and priest provided for them in the way of protection, the independent national state could do and do more completely and efficiently. Outside the state, though increasingly brought within it, economic forces and cultural influences worked toward the same national ends. Railroads stitched the Italian boot, made possible the economic cohesiveness upon which Mazzini, Garibaldi, and Cavour could politically unify Italy. In the United States, Henry Clay's "American System," and similar schemes brought the sections together. Everywhere tariffs protected national economic interests. Banking systems became national and, later, great industries became national industries with plants and sales covering the nation. All these chiefly protected and aided business. But workers and farmers became involved, as well, as they demanded, and over the years usually obtained, protection against foreign labor or crops, as they received social security insurance or crop loans, as they were guaranteed minimum wages or parity prices.

Men do not necessarily love the hand that feeds them or worship their benefactors. Indeed some men have fought against the pervading patriotism and resisted the power of the Leviathan national states. The fact remains that over the world men have become increasingly national-minded. When the Negro in the United States wants equality, he asks action by the national government because he thinks that he cannot get this equality through any other agency. When the Hungarians want rights today, they believe that they must throw off Russian domination and obtain Hungarian independence. They know no other way. For the achievement of needs and desires, for order and safety, the nation seems to be the modern means.

Everything the citizen hears and sees seems to re-enforce this observation. The radio is national, television is national. The schools teach national citizenship. The historians chiefly teach and write national histories. Literature and cooking and sports are judged on national criteria. Even science and music, written in international notation and symbol, becomes Russian, German, French, or American rather than just science and music. To make certain that national values rather than others prevail, patriotic societies in every country demand with some success that foreign influences be rooted out, that only good national or "one hundred per cent" ideas be encouraged. A man does not necessarily love his benefactor, but in this case he has not much opportunity to do otherwise.

The nation-state has hence often become an end in itself, the one end, indeed, socially approved for the supreme sacrifice. It can and often does in our contemporary world, control everything a man does or thinks, especially in times of national emergencies. The most extreme nationalisms of our time, those of Hitler and Mussolini, grew out of war, lived on war or probability of war, and themselves made war. Here we see nationalism self-perpetuating, each nationalism living and growing in imitation and in fear of other nationalisms. To beat Naziism and Fascism, as Goebbels and the Nazis predicted, other nations unfortunately had to become somewhat like them. "The true nationalist," the French newspaper *L'Action Française* once declared, "places the fatherland above everything." Not all men in the twentieth century were "true nationalists" in this ultimate sense, but the pressures which conditioned them were relentlessly pushing them in that direction.

Is there no way out of this never-ending circle, whether it is vicious or not? I am a historian. I cannot predict. If we are to have, at any future time, a truly international order above the nations, or if we are to have a world state, the international or world government will have to grow as national governments did, and if it is to have substance and viability, if indeed it is to exist, it will have to touch the vital interests of each world citizen. It, too, will have to grow, as nationalism did, out of the concrete fears and hopes, desires and actions of people who are passionately interested in its maintenance for their own freedom and safety. It will, too, have to afford the promise of a better life and, at the same time, protect man in the ways national governments have. But whether this can or will happen, whether or not we have time in this age of national hydrogen bombs, I do not know.

The reality of nationalism is the feeling of people, a feeling based upon each people's historical myths and realities. The reality of the nation lies in the hope and freedom, the protection and security it affords. If nationalism today is suicidal for the human race, some other realities, some new myths will have to provide as much and touch the citizens of the nations as deeply.

National versus International Integration*

by Gunnar Myrdal

THE GROWTH OF ECONOMIC NATIONALISM

Prior to the First World War, and in the partial world which was the center of attention in that period, there was little apparent conflict between the two lines of development: towards national and towards international integration.

The rapid economic growth in all the countries in this partial world was both a condition and an effect, actually an essential phase, of their development towards national integration. To a considerable extent,

---

* From *An International Economy* by Gunnar Myrdal, pp. 32-53. Copyright 1956 by Harper and Brothers. Reprinted by permission.

this economic growth was made possible only because of the relatively unhampered movement of labor, capital, goods, and services between these countries; these movements signified a high level of, and a continuous development towards, international economic integration. International trade was increasing, not only absolutely but—unlike towards the end of the nineteenth century—also in comparison with total production; rather high—and in some cases rising—tariff walls could not stop but only slow down this development. And the trend of international capital movements and labor migration also pointed upwards, at least in absolute terms.

Beginning with the First World War, however, when an uninterrupted sequence of international political and economic crises gradually removed even the expectancy of a return to normalcy, a discord between the two lines of integration became increasingly visible. Gradually, all these countries built up an armory of national policies to defend their economic welfare and stability from the adverse influences of outside events.

In the course of this development—and more definitely after the onset of the Great Depression—all international movements were securely curtailed by national policies. Movements of labor over national boundaries were restricted to localized and tiny streams, and the international capital market ceased to function after the financial crisis of 1931. At about the same time international trade became tied up in national regulations that in their general effects were restrictive and discriminatory, exchange rates became nationally managed prices, often unrelated to market values, and general convertibility was finally abandoned. The Second World War saw a new upsurge of national regulations and the postwar years were so filled by international crises, partly due to structural maladjustments, that a return to anything like the pre-1914 situation was impossible.

It is tempting to consider this trend towards international economic disintegration as simply the result of "bad" national policies. That would be an overoptimistic view; for a corollary would be that the development could be turned back equally simply by a reversal of these policies, thus instigating a return to free entrance and exit of labor and capital and to free trade. But in the sequence of emergencies we have passed through the individual states had for the most part no alternative to taking these measures.

Furthermore, there are deeper causes for these national policies. They have become so entrenched and so solidly supported by all political parties because they represent in many ways essential elements in the welfare state of mutual solidarity and economic stability. The succession of international crises during the past forty years has had such lasting effects on national policies simply because these crises have been pushing in the direction of national economic consolidation—a trend that, however, had its own independent causes which were merely strengthened by the repeated economic crises and the emergency policies adopted to meet them.[1] Particularly in the field of trade, the later development towards autarky had, in fact, its forebodings in the rise of protectionism from the eighties and nineties onwards.

By this I do not imply the existence of logical elements of conflict between the ideals of national and international integration. I am more convinced than ever that, on the contrary, national economic progress and integration can only reach the highest possible levels in a well-integrated world. But in the severely disintegrated world in which we actually live, there is an obvious lack of institutional balance that works forcefully against international solutions that would satisfy people's cravings for economic progress, equality, and security.

National political machinery is strong and effective and has a firm basis in people's attitudes of allegiance and solidarity; this machinery is getting stronger and its psychological basis firmer every year. It is used in the service of interests that are felt to be commonly shared within the nation. Machinery for international cooperation is, by contrast, weak and ineffective, and it lacks a solid basis in people's valuations and expectations. Even without any real inherent conflict between the two goals, this tremendous and steadily increasing preponderance of national political machinery has deflected—and, if a radical change of the trend is not induced, will continue to deflect—the development of practical policy towards economic nationalism.

Under these circumstances, internationalism tends more and more to be relegated to abstract utopianism. There is in the world of today so little possibility of giving reality to such strivings that they appear unrealistic and impractical; they are dreams and theories, while economic nationalism is realistic and practical. The only effective counterforce I can think of would be the knowledge, if it could be widely spread, of the

---

[1] I have developed this argument more fully in "The Trend Towards Economic Planning," *The Manchester School of Economic and Social Studies*, January, 1951.

very great gains that would accrue to all countries from every step, however modest, towards international cooperation; and the great dangers inherent in the present development.

NATIONAL INTEREST CONSOLIDATION

Meanwhile, the national integration processes are proceeding in all the advanced countries to ever higher levels and, generally speaking, national integration is apt to hamper international integration by directing the individual's interests ever more exclusively to the national state.

Undoubtedly, there exists an emotional basis for this. A state boundary, almost independently of its origin and location, satisfies directly an urge, felt by most people, to be set apart from other people. The studied mutual uncooperativeness which, for instance, the English and the Scots would have been able to develop, had they been divided by a state boundary invested with the awe of some centuries' existence, can easily be imagined. Psychologists might find the explanation of this strange negative attitude in those elements of frustration in our education and in all our daily lives that seek an outlet in aggression. To draw distinctions is always a temptation; it is generally easier to divide than to unite. But as the modern national welfare state develops, existing emotional nationalism will be forcefully strengthened by motives which are, indeed, rational to the individual.

One result of national integration is that decisions of the national legislatures and operations of all other public and quasi-public institutions and of organized interest groups, functioning within the national framework, come to have a greater and greater bearing upon the life and welfare of every citizen. Even individual professional careers become predetermined according to closed systems of merit and seniority, built up as national standards and defended by national organizations. Neither the doctor nor the teacher, nor the postman, the policeman, nor the building worker, can leave the nationally paved road without economic loss, often amounting to total exclusion from his means of livelihood. The national boundary thus takes on increasing practical importance for everyone. Undoubtedly this tends by itself progressively to lessen the experience, and weaken the feeling, of international solidarity.

The modern welfare state is also not inexpensive; even people in the lower and middle income brackets carry comparatively heavy burdens of taxes, insurance premiums, and membership fees. It is natural that they are bent upon getting the maximum benefits for themselves out of the national welfare state which they very intensely feel has been built for them and is being paid for by them. We can witness in all advanced countries how people's interests become more and more focused upon salary scales and other material rewards—a very remarkable effect of the higher levels of income and of the intensified democratic participation in determining the course of economic process.

Organizations become increasingly directed towards winning material advances for their members; when the advances are procured, these are felt to have been earned by group solidarity. As they all operate within the national framework, this whole trend tends to turn people's interests inwards, towards the situations and problems at home, and to spread a defensive ideology of national group protectionism. In these relatively rich countries and in the mental climate of the protective welfare state, international issues other than those related to national defense become embarrassing. For, at least in the short view, which is also the common man's view, international interests, if they aspire to the more than platonic, would imply willingness to carry sacrifices for others, who are outside the comprehensive national security system the citizens have provided for themselves by their mutual solidarity and are paying for out of their own earnings.

Cultural differences between populations on different sides of state boundaries, which were originally minor, are steadily accentuated as interests are focused on national issues and increasingly institutionalized within the state framework. The improved schools and the press have a similar influence, as have the radio and television. It is also unwise to assume that, under these circumstances, technical developments in transport and other means of communication, which are now forcibly bringing even distant peoples into more frequent contact with each other, automatically create a basis for greater international solidarity. Popular awareness of cultural dissimilarities and conflicts of interests may, at least in the short run, have strong effects in the opposite direction.

By the mere fact of its existence and its functioning the modern welfare state is thus continuously strengthening its own psychological foundation in people's valuations and expectations. . . .

THE FALTERING STRENGTH OF INTERNATIONALISM

It is interesting to note how in this development popular movements which fifty years ago were imbued with internationalism have now become narrowly nationalistic. This is true of the Socialist Labor movement. An operative cause of this defection to nationalism was the severe disillusionment brought about by the First World War, when the Second International split wide open and its members joined the national camps, whereas the plan—and, with many, the hopeful expectation— had been that the workers' noncooperation would stop the war. The more important and permanent cause, however, was the fact that the Labor parties in many countries became a power in internal politics and thereby responsible for the active pursuit of national policies.

Labor was often the main architect of, and always a driving force towards, the modern welfare state, the nationalistic features of which I discuss. The international ideals were long preserved in verbal formulas. Slogans, flags, and songs expressing allegiance to these ideals were a revered heritage from the pioneers of the movement, though gradually fading out as new generations succeeded the old ones. Meanwhile, practical work absorbed more and more of the party member's energy and was focused on the national and local issues where concrete results could be reaped. Per Albin Hanson, the late Swedish Socialist leader and Premier in a government which has now been directed by the Labor Party for more than twenty years, found an entirely adequate expression for Labor's aspiration in the new age when he described it as that of making the country "the people's home" (*folkhemmet*).

It is indicative of this trend that in the many countries where the Labor parties have come to power and been confronted with the task of forming cabinets, they have always had an abundance of competent candidates for their ministers of social and economic affairs but have usually had great difficulty in manning the post of foreign minister. In the last British Labour Government Bevin and Morrison had to be drafted for the job of Secretary of Foreign Affairs from lifelong political pursuits of very different interests. Foreign policy was no longer a central issue for the Labor parties.

Another indication is that there has been so little practical cooperation between the national Labor parties since they acquired political influence. Labor economists have usually carried out their practical studies under more narrow national premises than their colleagues to the right. And labor ministers have taken what amounts almost to pride in showing their senior civil servants that they could be just as nationalistic as the members of any Conservative government—in fact considerably more so—and that they had no inclination to let Labor "comradeship" soften their hearts. I am, of course, thinking of Great Britain in particular but the phenomenon is more common. The history of the Labor movement in several countries might well have been different if more of the internationalistic spirit of bygone times had been preserved.

Many other popular strivings besides the political Labor movement before the First World War and even somewhat later had strong international allegiances. All the movements for liberty, equality, and welfare for the masses—the movements for universal suffrage, for women's equal rights and opportunities, against alcoholism, for consumers' co-operation, for trade unionism, etc.—that later, in the progress towards national integration, saw their ideals gradually realized, started off as internationally inspired efforts. The pre-1914 movement for peace and international arbitration belonged to this same group.

Various professional groups kept close international contacts, particularly in Europe, which was at that time a much larger part of the world. National integration was then only in its beginning and class differences were often rather sharp; in the upper classes the social distance from foreign aristocracy was often shorter than from the lower classes at home; greater equality and closer ties within the nations, when they were achieved, have undoubtedly been won at the cost of losing some of the earlier international social integration on the upper-class level. Even in the crafts, however, there had been, before the First World War, close international ties, supported both by the movements referred to above and by free migration of labor.

A study of a half-century's contents of professional journals and journals of organizations for various political, cultural and social causes, from the point of view of the kind and degree of interest they showed in people and events in other countries, would . . . reveal, I believe, the strong inward turn of sympathies. Some time ago I had occasion to glance through some such publications from various countries for the years 1914 to 1918, and I was struck by their reserved friendliness—indeed, guarded solidarity—towards persons, organizations, and accomplishments in enemy countries; I found even appreciative obituaries.

This caused me to reflect how much less civilized in this particular respect of international understanding the world has become in the course of little more than one generation—in spite of all our tourist travel and the increased volume of other secondary contacts resulting from rapidly improved means of communication, and in spite of the growing number of international conferences of all kinds.

THE TREND TO NATIONAL AUTARKY

Apart from the effects of national integration on the all-important factor of psychological identification and solidarity, the modern integrated welfare state is likely to enlarge vastly the scope of public or quasi-public responsibility for the economic development of the country. The limits within which the state can freely dispose and organize in accordance with directives emanating from the national political process are fixed by its territorial boundaries. The state is in a position to control capital exports; usually there are reasons to preserve capital within the country in order to push ahead with national economic development. The state is also in the position to keep out foreign labor; it will find the means to discourage immigration if it is commonly felt to be harmful or even if this is demanded by powerful pressure groups that take advantage of public apathy.

To all economic planning—whether done by the state, by organized interest groups, or by private enterprise—investment in the country itself, internal production and consumption, and internal supply and demand are factors which are more or less calculable and which can even be influenced in accordance with national, group, or individual interests. The international markets, on the other hand, are independent variables, that is, they represent an economic risk that purely national planning cannot control.

National economies simply have to adjust themselves as best they can to external market conditions. Among these exogenous and nationally uncontrollable conditions to be found in the international markets are not only ordinary business fluctuations but also the interventions of other governments in their own economy and, in particular, in their imports and exports. When the economies and the policies of other countries follow the same course, these outside interferences can, as seen from the viewpoint of every single government, be expected to multiply and grow in magnitude, thus increasing the general riskiness of foreign markets.

While foreign markets, determined by the actions of other governments and groups, thus increasingly involve economic risks, one of the surest and simplest means of stabilizing the conditions for production and employment at home consists in regulating imports. Such public controls usually have the political advantage—at least immediately—of shifting the effects of adverse developments on to the foreigner, while helping domestic industries or leaving them undisturbed.

For four decades this secular trend towards national autarky has been spurred on in each of the highly integrated countries by the risk, or actual fact, of war and involuntary isolation, and also, of course, in most of these countries for most of the time, by foreign exchange considerations. More recently the cold war and the dollar shortage have again intensified these drives towards autarky.

In this way international disintegration feeds national autarky, which in turn tends to further intensify international disintegration. The process is cumulative; and every new policy step along the autarkic line is followed by a redirection of national investment of capital and employment of labor to fill the protected space created; the new situation is thus consolidated by vested interests.

"World trade is directed by a monstrously complex network of trade and payments arrangements which has minimized the role of market forces in determining what nations will produce and what they will sell to one another"—this is the conclusion Dr. Raymond F. Mikesell reaches from his comprehensive study of present trade and payments relations.[2]

THE ROLE OF THE LARGE COUNTRIES

The decisive and leading role in this development towards national autarky played by the great industrial powers has usually not been sufficiently stressed. One of the interesting parts of Professor Ingvar Svennilson's recently published investigation of European economy between the two world wars is the analysis he devotes to this problem.[3]

Svennilson finds it a striking feature of the development of world

---

[2] Raymond F. Mikesell, *Foreign Exchange in the Post-War World*, The Twentieth Century Fund, 1954, p. 523.

[3] United Nations, Economic Commission for Europe, *Growth and Stagnation in the European Economy*, Geneva, 1954, pp. 170 ff.

trade since the First World War that the manufacturing industries of the United States, Great Britain, Germany, and France have become national autarkic units:

The Soviet Union completes, in an excellent way, this picture of a world economy where a few countries, which together dominate world industrial output, provide markets for each other's industrial output only to a very small extent. . . . The five largest industrial countries in the world have almost completely isolated their industrial systems from each other. In this respect, the division of the world into a number of isolated economic blocks is almost a reality. Work on a unified world market is useless if these large countries are not prepared to open up their frontiers to imports of manufactured products.[4] . . . It is to the economic relations between these large countries that the world disintegration can most properly be applied. The smaller industrial countries, on the other hand, are not only highly dependent on the supply of industrial goods from the larger countries but also maintain a comparatively intensive trade between themselves.[5]

Because of its position as the main creditor country in the world, the extreme protectionism of the United States, effected by high tariffs and many other devices, is of importance in this context. In the United States there are, of course, local and special interests behind every protective measure. The collusion of these interests and the appeal to nationalist sentiments have ensured their application, and it has proved impossible for successive administrations, though all with good intentions, to do anything substantial about it. Professor Jacob Viner, who recently has again surveyed the situation, reaches the conclusion that "the duties of our tariff which have survived the trade agreements negotiations probably account for almost all of the restrictive effect on imports of the tariff as it was before 1934";[6] the other devices of national protectionism have been still better preserved and even strengthened.

---

[4] I am here quoting from an unpublished paper which Professor Svennilson has kindly available to me; for further substantiation I refer to the main work mentioned above.

[5] "Five smaller countries, Italy, Belgium, the Netherlands, Sweden and Switzerland, represent together a market which—measured by their income—is less than one-third of the joint market of Britain, France and Western Germany. *Ceteris paribus*, one would therefore expect the trade between the three bigger countries to be more than twice as large as their exports to the group of five smaller countries. The relative order of magnitude of these two currents of international trade is, however, just the opposite: the latter is twice as big for textiles, two and a half times as big for chemicals, three times as big for machinery, and six times as big for motorcars and other transport equipment" (*ibid.*).

[6] "The Role of the United States in the World Economy," paper prepared for Columbia University's *Conference on National Policy for Economic Welfare at Home and Abroad*, New York, 1954; to be published.

The United States, with a gross national product now exceeding 350 billion dollars a year, proud of the great resilience of its economy, accustomed by now to absorbing one violent shock to its economy after another, prepared for a continuous economic growth of truly startling dimensions,[7] and having since Cordell Hull's time assumed the leadership in a virtual world crusade to break down the barriers to international trade, does not see its way to permit the few hundred million —or, at most, a few billion—dollars a year of additional imports of various commodities that would follow a lowering of its own trade barriers. The content of the Randall Report,[8] the discussion around it, and the reception by the United States Congress of its rather timid suggestions, have made it clear that the whole movement towards trade liberalization in America—urged by a unanimous world, dramatically and movingly staged by American administrations of both political parties in repeated prologues, and widely publicized as the main American contribution to international economic integration—is in great danger of becoming an anticlimax with worldwide repercussions on all our strivings towards internationalism. . . .

Undoubtedly, Svennilson is right in pointing out that the big countries played the leading role in the development towards world disintegration in the field of trade; undoubtedly, also, the United States has been in a particularly strategic position in this context, both because of the height of its trade barriers and because of its size and its dominant position as the main creditor country. But in this general climate, the smaller countries are following the same course, even if they have not yet moved so far towards effective autarky.

The above analysis has been focused on the industrially advanced countries; it is, however, also fully relevant to the underdeveloped countries. They are now emerging from the lethargy of foreign political and economic domination and internal stagnation, and are attempting, against heavy odds, to press on with their economic development; but they do not adopt the relatively liberal policies in their foreign economic relations that were followed by the developed countries in their early stages of development. Indeed, they cannot do so, as the world

---

[7] Cf. Joseph S. Davis, "The Economic Potentialities of the United States," paper prepared for Columbia University's Conference on National Policy for Economic Welfare at Home and Abroad, New York, 1954; to be published.

[8] United States, Commission on Foreign Economic Policy, Report to the President and the Congress, January 1954.

environment into which they have to fit themselves is no longer what it was for those other countries in the nineteenth century.

They are, therefore, bound to equip themselves with the nationalistic economic policies that were forged by the advanced countries after 1914. As a matter of fact, they are compelled to give these policies an even more radical shape, as their national development needs are so much more urgent and as all their margins are narrower and their resources scantier.

In their struggle for national independence and economic development strong forces of nationalism are released which give emotional force to these policies. Even in this respect the underdeveloped countries are not out of tune with what has been happening in recent decades in the advanced countries.

THE DETERIORATION OF INTERNATIONAL LAW

This play of forces has resulted in the gradual paralysis of the inherited quasi-automatic system of national adjustments to the exigencies of international trade. On a deeper level of policy attitudes, the norms and mores of a previously more integrated—partial—world economy which, as always, derived their social reality from being unquestioned and obeyed, were permanently destroyed as they were repeatedly disobeyed. An example of these fallen idols is the whole complex of functionally purposive behavior patterns and taboos upholding the gold standard.

Related to this has been the gradual deterioration of international law as we knew it prior to the First World War. The closely knit international community of economically progressive countries, which I have referred to as the partial world of the period before 1914, had seen the development of an ever-more-diversified body of commonly respected rules for correct behavior in public and private international relations. These rules had their origin partly in regular intergovernmental treaties and conventions, but they also grew out of a gradually established common law practice. Increasingly they were reflected in domestic laws and their administration and execution; as a matter of fact these national streams of legislation and precedents were a main source of international law. All this was then systematized—and so strengthened and made still more specific—into a consolidated doctrine of international jurisprudence, which also drew on the ancient inheritance of a *jus gentium*.

The true nature of this international law as it existed in the era before 1914 and, particularly, the crucial question of its sanctions, was widely disputed; but meanwhile it functioned with considerable efficiency and resulted in a high degree of security in international business. Obligations stretching over national boundaries were honored, and the foreigner's rights were respected. We may recall that before the First World War alien property rights were protected even during war and even when the property owner belonged to an enemy state.

Under the pressure of the sequence of wars and international crises and the growth of the new nationalism since 1914, this situation has changed fundamentally. The precedents in interstate relations set during this period, beginning with the German invasion of neutral Belgium in spite of solemn written commitments, have everywhere and continuously been breaches of the agreed rules. By a mutual process of competition in ruthlessly exploiting strategic interests, the whole body of international law governing the conduct of warfare—built upon the distinction between the soldier and the civilian and incorporated in the Hague and Geneva Conventions—is thus in almost complete ruin, as we all know too well. Conventional war has changed to total war, bound by no limitations other than those imposed by military expediency; with the enormous destructive power of the new, unconventional weapons there seems to be no way back.

Even in the economic and financial sphere the rule of international law has been severely weakened. As the volume of state interference has increased the very concept of property has gradually changed in all countries. The now accepted practice that belligerent states can do as they please with enemy property—which is only an application of the new doctrine of total war—has naturally dealt a severe blow to the basic principle of the old international law that foreign property is inviolable. A principle is, so to speak, indivisible and must be universally applicable; failure to apply it in one field tends to undermine its general validity.

For a time—and particularly in countries under economic and political domination—this principle of the inviolability of foreign property frequently resulted in preferential treatment of the foreigner. It was, for example, often accepted, or still is accepted, that foreigners have a right to compensation for nationalization measures, even when such an obligation is not recognized for citizens.

In the modern state nationalization is, however, only one among a large number of state interferences with property rights, many of these implying financial burdens on the property owner. With the present increase of state activity in the economic field, it becomes practically and politically impossible to preserve a sanctuary for foreign property. In fact, the old principle was related to quite a different kind of state and in the new state now coming into being it loses its original meaning. The effect is, however, a lowered degree of security throughout the whole field of international business.

The evolution of international law in the economic and financial field, like that of all other law, is, of course, only one element in the totality of changes in the national economies and their interrelations, and it is hardly one of the basic elements. A reconstruction of international law aimed at recreating a measure of security in international business will naturally and to a large extent have to be in the nature of an adjustment to new circumstances.

It will, in fact, concern the same problems and meet the same difficulties as generally do the efforts to coordinate national economic policies, about which I have some comments later in this chapter. As a matter of fact, the reconstruction of international law is part and parcel of this more general problem; law has no independent existence outside its social context. Law must be operational; it can be established neither by pronouncements, nor by majority votes in international organizations, nor by writing constitutions for "superstates" which have as yet no basis in international solidarity.

For the time being, what we have seen is the breakdown of international law as inherited from the nineteenth century, without its replacement by a body of rules better adjusted to the rapidly changing world and, therefore, accepted as part of social reality with standards that are actually being applied. The present state of legal anarchy is a significant element in the process of international economic disintegration which we are here studying. It hardly needs mentioning that in this sphere, too, it has been the bigger of the industrially advanced countries that have taken the lead in gradually destroying a functioning international system, while for natural reasons the smaller ones in this group have had a greater interest in attempting to preserve and uphold the crumbling international law.

INTERNATIONAL DISINTEGRATION FROM
A NATIONAL POINT OF VIEW

Ordinary citizens in our advanced countries are usually only mildly disturbed when confronted with this grim diagnosis of the world's economic disintegration; they are naturally more concerned with problems nearer home. Paradoxically, on this closer national scene there has meanwhile been progress and integration.

In spite of world wars and depressions, we have seen in each of our advanced countries a tremendous rise in productivity, security of employment, and standards of living, and also greater equality of opportunity for the individual citizens and a general equalization of incomes and wealth. In the last forty years, with all their international turmoils, these countries have witnessed a more rapid national integration than ever before in history. The ordinary citizen is apt to believe—and very largely with good reason—that the national policies by which this has been brought about are good, even if they are exactly those which are here pictured as the causes of international disintegration.

I believe we may completely misinterpret the whole problem of how the development to international disintegration may be reversed if we do not try to go deeper in our understanding of the purposes of the national policies we are bound to criticize when we apply the value premise of international integration. These policies are, indeed, mostly —by no means always—motivated by good reasons, and nationally they have on the whole been successful.

If we want to avoid their resulting in increasing international disintegration, our duty is to propose such adjustments to them as will be favorable to international integration, while at the same time taking care to protect equally well or even better the national interests that they serve. That this should theoretically be possible is implied in the faith I have expressed, that national economic progress and integration can only reach the highest possible levels in a well-integrated world.

We might first observe that the interest in stable markets—which also implies stable employment and continuous high utilization of plant and machinery, as well as of the distribution apparatus—is naturally a very legitimate one. If we wish to prevent this interest from expressing itself in national policies implying discrimination against foreign markets, we must find the means of giving increased stability to the international economy. This special reason for a nationalistic economic policy is bound to become ever more urgent; for the importance to individual enterprises and to the national economies of stable markets—and hence the economic disadvantage of unstable markets—has been steadily increasing, and will continue to do so, as modern industry progresses towards a higher level of mechanization and capital intensity.

More particularly, full employment is a legitimate national interest, not only socially but also economically. Full employment largely explains why investment and production have been held on such very high and generally rising levels after the Second World War in most industrial countries and why productivity has been making such strides. At the high level of capital costs, typical of modern industry, enormous productivity gains follow from a high and stable level of employment. A high level of output permits higher savings, investment risks are at the same time reduced, and the more capital-intensive methods, resulting from the higher savings and investments, induce a further rise in total output.

The experience of the Great Depression and the popular appeal of the type of thinking we have become accustomed to associate with the name of Keynes have been epoch-making in our countries. No well-integrated nation will now hesitate to assert its control over exports, imports, and foreign exchange, if it is a question of maintaining the level of employment. Once more, to avert national discrimination against foreign trade and restrictive controls of foreign payments, invoked to defend full employment in the individual countries, we must organize the whole world economy by concerted international action in such a way that depressing effects on national welfare from events outside a country's national boundaries are less likely to arise.

The conflict between the aims and policies of the national welfare state and the ideal of international integration becomes intense when we consider the redistributional aspects of national economic policy. All the advanced countries have embarked in recent decades upon a comprehensive complex of fiscal and social policies aimed at a fairer sharing between their citizens of the exigencies of economic fortune; but this ever more intensified solidarity stops at the national boundary.

However, the main reason why these national welfare systems tend to disintegrate the world economy is that the redistributional intentions are not limited to a direct transfer of income via the collectors of taxes and insurance contributions, but invade the whole field of national economic policy, changing the basic conditions for the operation of the price system.

Workers in the United States have a long-standing tradition of regarding protective tariffs over practically the whole industrial field as a justifiable defense of their own living standards—which they know are high—since they prevent the products of cheap foreign labor from intruding upon the American market. The fact that this argument has logical flaws, and yet, in spite of all the orthodox teachings of the theory of comparative costs by generations of professors of economics, is nevertheless so tenaciously upheld, demonstrates how solidarity is limited to the nation. Nationalism is stronger than reason.

When the redistributional policies come to be applied in the broader field of economics, this is usually, however, not the result of an intellectual mistake but, in the given setting of international relations, quite a rational approach. In almost all the advanced countries farmers have needed state assistance to preserve their living standards on more or less the same level as other social groups and, following the principle of solidarity, the nonagricultural majority of citizens has everywhere been prepared to accept very far-reaching modifications of the price system in order to ensure some degree of "price parity" for farm production.

Such agicultural price policies have everywhere become important cornerstones in the construction of the modern welfare state, but it has never seriously occurred to any influential and politically responsible group in any country that this expression of solidarity should expand beyond the state boundary. Instead, the international market has been freely used as a dumping ground, hurting particularly those exporting countries that have narrow margins and have to count their foreign exchange carefully.

In this connection it is interesting and illustrative to compare, on the one hand, the universal acceptance by a national political majority of the obligation to support economically the farming minority at home—almost as if it were self-evident—and, on the other hand, the cold-hearted disinclination in the industrial countries to do anything at all in order to stabilize the prices of raw materials and staple agricultural commodities of the underdeveloped and very poor countries, whose whole economic and political existence is continuously in jeopardy because of their unstable export markets. We are faced here, not only with an unwillingness to accept a real redistribution of incomes, like the one that has been accepted within their own countries, but also with a reluctance even to consider schemes that would merely stabilize the markets over a period of years, without any international redistribution.

Agricultural policy is only one example, but an outstanding one, because of the large number of beneficiaries and the large aggregate amount of income redistribution involved. The same principle of national solidarity and almost total disregard of the interests of the foreigner operates over the whole field of economic policy. Everywhere there is demonstrated a readiness to improve the economic basis of national production; at bottom, a social equality and welfare interest is often the driving force. This is true of the coal policy in Britain, of the regulation of the fishing industry in Norway, and of wine production in France, to mention only a few examples.

The fixing of differential tariffs by the publicly owned and publicly managed railroads offers a flexible means in most countries of reallocating the relative advantage of national industries—and of discriminating against the foreigner. The same often goes for other means of communication, like ports and airlines. The whole body of regulations in the shipping industry follows the same pattern; a Norwegian is apt to point out that the high subsidies paid to the American shipping industry and the protection given it by other means in the postwar period may have cost the Norwegian economy more than all it received in the way of Marshall aid. As the state and local authorities handle ever larger budgets and so become increasingly important as buyers in many markets, their orders for goods and services are, by law or custom, directed so as to encourage so far as possible domestic industry. In all cases the purely national interest is emphasized and the principle of national solidarity followed.

Measures against restrictive business practices are a good illustration of the nationalistic direction of economic policy. While most governments have introduced legislation against internal cartels, in order to protect the consumers from exploitation, few responsible politicians would be prepared to extend this kindly interest to the protection of the foreign buyer, and in the international markets cartels have so far been given free play. In most parliaments it would, indeed, be looked upon as a strange and almost subversive thought if somebody were to suggest that sometimes the foreigner's interests in paying less for exports from the country than he is at present obliged to might need protection. Directed towards the outside, monopolistic exploitation becomes a patriotic virtue.

To except the international cartels from control is, incidentally, often a mistake from a national point of view. In many cases the international cartels are in reality collusions of industries in different countries, agreeing to leave each other undisturbed by competition from taking what the traffic will bear in their established markets. The powerful Scandinavian pulp and paper cartel has many purposes, but one is to permit the paper industry to charge higher prices at home; for decades stationery, produced from Scandinavian raw materials and often exported in the form of paper, could be bought cheaper in London than in Stockholm.

Apart from this and other self-deceptions—and economic policy is, relatively speaking, less influenced by ignorance and emotional irrationality than foreign policy in general [9]—the nationalistic economic policies of the modern welfare state are rationally suited to their purposes: to create more stable markets and to bring about a redistribution of incomes within the nation. The greater capital intensity of modern industry tends continuously to magnify the first interest. The progressing national integration is partly a result of the pursuit of the second interest, but is at the same time continuously strengthening its driving force.

This process, by which national integration induces international disintegration, is thus cumulative. International disintegration in its turn implies that foreign markets become even more unstable, which again strengthens the rational urge to concentrate on the home market and give it better protection, for the sake of internal stability. Progressive international disintegration makes it likewise ever more difficult to visualize clearly, and to urge effectively, a policy of international, instead of national, solidarity.

The international payments problem has naturally taken its present aggravated form as a result of the international crises, with their major disturbances of the trading and payments positions. A deeper and more permanent cause, however, is the unwillingness of the national welfare states to accept the infringements on their policies of economic stability and economic equality that an automatic trade and payments system would imply if it were to bring about changes in the national economies

---

[9] Cf. my article, "Psychological Impediments to Effective International Co-operation," *The Journal of Social Issues*, Supplement Series, No. 6, 1952, pp. 12 ff.

corresponding to changes in international economic relations. The whole complex of national policies, to which I have referred above, introduces rigidities—from an international point of view—that limit the possibilities of adjustments to ensure balance of payments equilibrium without short-term controls over international trade and payments.

To restore convertibility and eliminate trade discriminations that are caused by payments difficulties and that do not, per se, represent national interests, would seem to be a first step in preventing further international disintegration. The problem is, however, whether even this very modest goal can be reached in a world where the more basic national interventions have gone so far and are backed by such strong national interests.

INTERNATIONALIZATION OF NATIONAL POLICIES

This general world conflict between national and international integration obviously cannot be resolved in the interest of the latter ideal simply by preaching internationalism and denouncing nationalism. No advanced country is prepared to give up, or even to risk slightly, the fruits of national integration, which remains a supreme value to its citizens. And the goal for underdeveloped countries must be to start their own processes towards national integration, their success in doing so is also a first pre-condition for their incorporation in a better integrated world. To deprive nations of their right to organize their own affairs and, in particular, to control and steer their internal economic development, is out of the question.

It is wrong to believe that the volume of national interventions that could be abolished in a process of simple "international economic disarmament" is large. It is true that some of them stem from misunderstandings of reality; even more of them have been instigated by special interest groups without ever having been intellectually tested by having their consequences thoroughly explained to and understood by the people. It is my view, for instance, that the strict control over international migration largely belongs to this category of measures, which it was possible to push through only because of ignorance, apathy, or nationalistic emotionalism among the general public, as does also the high protectionism of the United States, whose economy stands for various reasons in a special position.

More generally, we should note that some smaller and highly developed national welfare states, such as the Scandinavian ones, have traditionally followed a much less autarkic economic policy than the bigger ones and have nevertheless succeeded in reaching an exceptionally high level of national economic integration and in maintaining a rate of economic progress and a standard of living as high as or higher than the bigger, more autarkic countries. This should serve as an indication that there is room for reconsidering many of the present national economic policies.

We should only be deceiving ourselves, however, if we did not recognize the fact that in most cases there are valid national reasons for these policies. In many cases there exists also an interrelationship between different types of national policies which makes it difficult or impossible to abolish even those that are not strongly backed by national interests for their own sake. Most industrially advanced countries may sincerely want to abolish, if they could, those trade and payments regulations that are directly caused by payments difficulties. However, the lack of international balance revealed by the payments difficulties is itself the result not only of the changes caused by wars and the like, but also of the trend to national integration and the national policies, inherent in this trend, aimed at stability and equality. These policies the governments are not in a position to renounce. They have mostly very important national purposes, even if their total effects—direct and indirect—are disastrous for international integration.

"The fact is that we have moved far form a world in which complete international specialization of labor is possible. Some of the rigidities . . . are here to stay. . . . This means that completely free trade is not feasible." Behind this statement of a commonly accepted negative fact, which I have chosen to cite from the Randall Report,[10] is the more important and positive fact that national integration, though it has its essence in equalization of opportunity for people in all social groups and geographical areas, has not been achieved simply by the abolition of barriers within the country, but rather by a process of social organization.

If, therefore, we realize that it is a misdirected and, in any event, hopeless attempt to try to reach international integration unless it be as a concomitant and, indeed, as a further development of national integration, we have to draw the further conclusion that international integration in this age has similarly to imply more than a breaking

---

[10] *Op. cit.*

down of national barriers; it has to attempt reunification and harmonization of the national policies of cooperating states.[11]

The task for international integration becomes, then, a matter of coordination. International labor and capital movements or freer trade cannot be expected to re-emerge simply as a result of agreements to undo national policies. On both sides of every boundary practically all "markets" are now highly organized by the state and by interest groups. What is needed is *an internationalization of these national policy structures themselves, preserving the essential values they represent to the several nations.*

If governments came together intent upon a more ambitious cooperation of this kind, some of the present policies would clearly be seen to be misdirected and irrational. In many other cases it would become apparent that national protective measures served interests which, even when not unimportant viewed unilaterally, are minor compared with the major common gains that could be realized by mutual agreement to abstain from them. This is all in the realm of what I called "international economic disarmament."

There are, though, other policies—for example, agricultural protection or other intentional support of industries as part of a national development program—that are indispensable from the national point of view. If, however, these policies were worked out on the basis of international solidarity, they could be framed so as not to lead to a competition between the countries to shift their burdens onto each other.

A primary object of cooperation would naturally be to create stable international markets and, in particular, to guarantee a stable world trend of business and production. To the extent that stability was achieved, a great number of existing national policies would prove unnecessary and, in the first instance, the quantitative trade and payments restrictions, unpopular with all governments, could be abolished.

In this new type of international relations, founded upon a widening

---

[11] In his recent book, *L'Europe sans Rivages* (Presses Universitaires de France, 1954), Professor François Perroux—though working in a conceptual framework, following lines of reasoning, and having his main interest in problems very different from the present author's—arrives at certain general conclusions parallel to those developed in this text: that in the present world the nation-states constitute the main and almost exclusive agencies for policy, that the practical problems, therefore, cannot be to abolish frontiers or create superstates but to reach intergovernmental agreements on the coordination of national policies, and that a primary condition for such an internationalization of national policies is a climate of worldwide economic expansion.

of economic solidarity, freer movement of labor and capital would play a natural role, as also would, in some measure, the sharing of burdens for common objectives, and even the giving of economic aid.

As was the case in the advanced nation-states, which offer a prototype for our model of international economic integration, this whole process would need the impetus and momentum of economic progress. Only in an expanding world economy will there exist the conditions for mutual generosity without which the integration process would not get far.

The whole movement towards international integration along these lines will have to be argued in positive terms of the wider community of interests and aspirations, not the negative ones of wanting to break up the defenses of national integration. Indeed, the stepping stone will have to be the recognition of the great accomplishment that national integration really is in a few advanced countries. The goal has to be one of transforming this national integration into a more inclusive international solidarity. It must meet the request of actually strengthening the values of national integration—and it will have to be realized that a great hindrance to international integration is the fact that so many countries are still badly integrated nationally.

This is a technically much more difficult task than the old internationalists, who saw the problem only in terms of tearing down barriers, have ever grasped. Yet this task of coordinating national policies is the one we are actually attempting to grapple with in the international organizations when, on occasion, we succeed in proceeding one step beyond the delivery by delegates of propaganda speeches and the voting of pious resolutions. Even though our attempts so far are feeble and the results small and insecure, this is the task and there is no way around it.

THE NEED FOR INTERNATIONAL SOLIDARITY

Too often, when the internationalist denounces nationalistic economic policies, he finds himself in the company of the reactionaries, who in all our countries are waging a rearguard battle against the developing welfare state. And so he becomes allied with—and, with him, unfortunately, his ideal of international integration—historical forces which in the long run are bound to lose out.

There is to my mind no doubt that, basically, the reason why efforts towards international integration in Western Europe have achieved so little is that the deeper questions have not been faced honestly and courageously. It was assumed that international integration could be attained without the basis of solidarity that national integration required, and without accepting the consequences of such widened solidarity. Under these circumstances the common man in Europe remained cold and suspicious. He felt that this was perhaps a new way of raising obstacles to national welfare policies.

There is no retreat from the welfare state, and its further growth is intimately bound up with further progress in national integration. The events of the last years in America under a Republican regime, where the main social advances made under the Democratic New Deal and in the entire field of economic policy have been preserved or extended,[12] and similar features of Conservative rule in Britain, Australia, and New Zealand after an era of Labor governments, seem amply to illustrate this point. The biggest break we can expect in the trend towards the welfare state is the flatness of an individual step in a staircase.

A social trend is never an entirely straight line but moves by fits and starts. In addition to a natural tendency for a certain slowing down after a prolonged and rapid upward movement, we have had in recent years the complicated reactions to the cold war and the heavy burden of defense expenditure. These changing historical circumstances, and the counterbalancing main trend towards the welfare state, firmly backed by the interests and valuations of a democracy, have such an overwhelming preponderance that the fluctuations of political parties and personalities in power are almost without influence, if we take the broad and long view. As a matter of fact, the break in the upward movement has not been very much larger in the United States and Britain than in those Scandinavian countries which have been continuously governed by the Labor parties, as a matter of tradition.

From an international point of view, national economic policy is not to blame for seeking stability and equalization. Its failing is that it re-

---

[12] With understandable glee, but at bottom deeply satisfied, as an American citizen, with the basic unity and steadfastness of his nation's internal policy, Mr. Adlai E. Stevenson, the defeated Democratic candidate for the Presidency in the 1952 election, spoke one and a half years later at Harvard University: "Not very long ago there was a lot of 'radical' agitation, so-called in this country. What did the 'radicals' want? They wanted social security, old-age pensions, regulation of utilities and securities, government aid for housing and education, a nine-hour-day and collective bargaining. Those were heresies not long ago, but in 1953 a Republican President raises the welfare state to Cabinet status and asks for an extension of social security" (*Call to Greatness,* Harper, 1954, p. 102).

stricts solidarity to the individual nations. We have to attempt to build a better integrated world upon states that are all, and for the most excellent reasons, continuously seeking better integration nationally. To face this issue clearly is the first requirement when attempting to tackle the problem of international integration.

I have criticized traditional internationalism—that seeks a short cut to international integration by the simple and wholesale abolition of national economic policies—as not only reactionary but also as ineffective, since it goes against an immutable historical trend, determined by people's interests and valuations in a democracy. I do not pretend that my proposed substitution—a policy of international coordination of national policies based upon a widened international solidarity—is an easy road. I do, however, believe that while the other solution is not practical—and, in addition, would harm values that are dear to us and destroy accomplishments that are the pride of our generation—this one is, at least, a sensible goal, however difficult to reach, and one that good and well-informed people would wish to strive for.

The Collapse of the European Political System, 1914-45 *

by Hajo Holborn

Any attempt at the formulation or critical review of American policies in Europe is conditioned by our historical conceptions. . . . We are consciously or unconsciously influenced by what we consider to be the "normal" organization of Europe, and are thereby led to direct our political actions as much as possible toward the restoration of the traditional order. There exists, on the other hand, a general awareness of radical changes in world politics and especially European affairs, and our practical political experiences demonstrate that we are constantly driven to adopt unprecedented measures which run counter to what we still envisage as the historical pattern of Europe.

During the last ten years, in which the United States was suddenly forced to assume a leading role in Europe, American policy-makers have committed some serious mistakes owing to the belief that a return was possible to a Europe in many respects similar to that of the nineteenth

* From World Politics, Vol. I, No. 4 (July 1949), pp. 442-466. Reprinted by permission of World Politics.

century. We have also stumbled in inferring from the novelty of the European situation that we could dispose of an analysis of historical factors altogether. A constructive treatment of European problems calls, indeed, for historical thinking. But historical knowledge, and even more the mere memory of a past age, are quite different from historical thinking. The foremost task of historical analysis is to establish a clear distinction between the forces and ideas of past ages which continue to have a bearing on our present-day problems, and those which have ceased to be live issues for our times or, perhaps, forever.

Historians seem to be habitually inclined to overrate the lasting quality of historical factors and to underestimate the ruptures in the process of history. But every page of history records not only survival but also death. Therefore, it should be stated clearly and emphatically that what is commonly called the "historic" Europe is dead and beyond resurrection. What we still have to gain is a critical insight into the events which destroyed the props of the old European system and the causes which made it an illusion to hope for the reconstruction of an autonomous Europe. The European political system collapsed during World War I, and since the statesmen at the Peace Conference of Paris and in the interwar period failed to revive it on a stable foundation it was swept away by World War II. Without an understanding of the general character of this revolutionary event in twentieth century history we cannot hope to make intelligent decisions with regard to our future course of action.

[I]

For practically a thousand years Europe meant the community of western peoples who lived, broadly speaking, between Scandinavia and Sicily, the British Isles and the Pripet marshes. These European nations were not politically unified, even in the middle ages, but were bound together chiefly by religious and cultural ties. In early modern times the balance of power system was the expression of whatever political integration they had achieved. But even in this period, the balance of power system was not an exclusively European system. Individual members of the European family have always been tempted to increase their weight by alliances with non-European powers. During the sixteenth and seventeenth centuries the Franco-Turkish alliance was the classic example of this tendency, while in the eighteenth century Russian influence began to be felt. By the end of the century Russia had acquired the Baltic provinces and large parts of Poland, countries which had formed the eastern outposts of the western world. In 1760 a Russian army occupied Berlin, and in 1799 Russian troops fought in Holland and Italy. It is interesting that Suvorov, who led Russian troops to victory in North Italy, has been built up in the Russia of Stalin as one of the great heroes of the Soviet Union.

Napoleon's conquest of Europe to the Vistula in the years 1805-1809 left England and Russia as the only powers capable of resistance. Though both England and Russia proved unconquerable, the two powers were not strong enough in 1813 to dislodge Napoleon from Central Europe without the assistance of the nations and states of Central Europe itself. A Russian army could never have reached Paris in 1814 if Prussia and Austria had not joined forces with Czar Alexander I. As a result, Europe during the nineteenth century was not dominated by two super-powers, but by five great powers. Metternich took great care to avoid any action that would have made Alexander I the virtual ruler of the Continent, and in cooperation with England and even France he limited the expansion of Russia into Europe. As a result, though Metternich was not strong enough to keep Russia from taking central Poland, Russia's westward march was halted there for more than a century. Only in the Balkans did the disintegration of the Turkish empire allow further Russian advances in this period. British counteraction succeeded in thwarting Russian attempts at the full control of the Near East.

Czar Alexander's decision to carry on the war of 1812 beyond the frontiers of Russia and Poland to the complete defeat of Napoleon was sharply criticized by the Soviet historian Eugene Tarlé in his notable book on the war of 1812, written during the heyday of Soviet isolationism.[1] Tarlé expressed the opinion that Russian blood and strength were spent gratuitously, and that the policy of Alexander I only paved the way for the British hegemony of the nineteenth century. Unquestionably Britain was the chief winner in 1815, but Tarlé failed to discuss the great advantages which Russia gained from her participation in the European wars of 1813-15. Metternich, in spite of his anxious search for the establishment of a European system that would prevent a Russian invasion of Central Europe, realized at the same time that Central Europe had to be organized in such a way as to offer Russia the assur-

---

[1] Eugene Tarlé, *Napoleon's Invasion of Russia, 1812*, New York, Oxford University Press, 1942 (first Russian edition, Moscow, 1938).

ance of peace along her major frontier. He also wanted to use Czarist Russia to bolster the autocratic regimes of Central Europe. But the objective of the Holy Alliance, and of subsequent agreements between Russia, Austria, and Prussia, though grounded in common ideological partisanship, was largely found in the desire to assure Russia of the friendship of the powers along her western borders.

Metternich's policy satisfied Russia's demand for national security and for influence in the affairs of her western neighbors. When the revolutions of 1848-49 threatened to wreck the system of Metternich, Czar Nicolai I actively intervened to restore the old Central European regimes and did not demand any *quid pro quo* for dispatching Russian troops into Hungary. Russia contributed substantially to the defeat of liberalism in Central Europe—a defeat from which Central European liberalism never fully recovered.

The shift of power from Vienna to Berlin in the 1860's did not seriously affect Russia's position or attitude. Bismarck was as much concerned as Metternich had been with impressing upon the Czar the harmony of Russian and German political interests as well as their common faith in monarchy. The Germany of William II, by turning from continental to world policy, antagonized not only Russia but also Britain, and these two powers, which had been farthest apart in every respect during the nineteenth century, united together with France in order to contain Central Europe.

[π]

The political system of Europe as created in 1815 broke down in World War I. German military victories drove Russia out of the provinces and states which the Czars had acquired since the early eighteenth century. If Russia had survived the German blows and had still been an Allied power in the fall of 1918, she probably could not have been denied control of the Turkish Straits, which the western powers promised her in 1915. In addition she would, of course, have retained her Baltic provinces and, in all likelihood, have annexed East Prussia. Poland would probably have been restored, though only as an autonomous state under the Russian crown. In this position Russia would have exercised great power in Europe, particularly in the succession states and in Germany.

The Bolshevist revolution, made possible by the chaos engendered by Germany's military triumphs in the East, induced the western powers not only to withhold all these potential gains from their wartime ally, but also to confirm the territorial losses which Russia had suffered by the treaty of Brest-Litowsk. If German policies during World War I had not been marred by unnecessary brutality and outright stupidity, Germany might have earned considerable gratitude in some of the new states which she had first brought to life. As it was, the states along the northeastern fringe of Europe as well as the succession states in the Danubian area looked toward the West for protection both against Russia and Germany.

For the first time since the early eighteenth century, all the peoples of the western Christian creed were free from Russian domination. Moreover, even some Russian territories, like parts of Byelo-Russia and the Ukraine, together with the strategic approaches to Russia, remained in western hands. But there was another side to the picture. To be sure, during the nineteenth century Russia held important non-Russian territories and wielded great influence in general European affairs. Yet at the same time Europe was not lacking in some power over Russia. As has been seen, Russian outward expansion was kept within certain bounds, and she was compelled to respect international treaties. Her internal development was heavily dependent upon foreign capital and technological advice. European ideas had a deeply stirring effect upon Russian intellectual life. Even a doctrine with the special overtones of the slavophile movement cannot be fully understood without some consideration of the impact of western thought.

Russia was being "westernized" in many respects and in this process displayed an unusual capacity for blending her own cultural heritage with modern western ideas. In the second half of the nineteenth century the great Russian novel and music became in their turn a leaven in western European thinking. This political and cultural *rapprochement* between Europe and Russia came to an end with World War I. It should be remembered, however, that Marxism is not a native Russian doctrine, though in the hands of Lenin, and even more so of Stalin, it has been adapted to the circumstances and needs of a Russia plunged into chaos and misery by military defeat. The philosophy of Karl Marx is an arsenal from which many political schools can draw arms. Bolshevist theory itself has undergone considerable change since 1917 in response to new political developments. In the early years after the October revolution, the western powers might well have moulded the circumstances which conditioned the evolution of that theory. In addition, the western powers could have overthrown the Bolshevist government itself.

In his recent speech in Boston, Winston Churchill characterized the "failure to strangle Bolshevism at its birth and to bring Russia . . . by one means or another into the general democratic system" as one of the major mistakes of the peacemakers of 1919.[2] This seems historically correct, and Mr. Churchill also deserves credit for having seen in 1919 the loss and danger to Europe involved in the separation and hostility of a Bolshevist Russia. It still remains doubtful, however, whether the policies in support of the white Russian interventionists, whom Mr. Churchill, as the British secretary of war, backed in the years after 1918, were wisely chosen. To give assistance to groups which were largely dominated by reactionary elements was not likely to win the confidence of the Russian masses. Russian interventionists, who enjoyed the support of the western powers, were also suspected of being collaborators in the despoilment of Russia, who had just been deprived of many of her western provinces with the approval of the western powers.

The attempt at intervention in Russia after World War I gave the Communist rulers in Moscow the chance to pose as the true defenders of the national interests of the country. They have derived great strength from this role ever since. It is revealing that the Soviet government appealed again mainly to Russian national sentiment when it officially named the Russo-German war of 1941-45 the "great patriotic war." The Allied interventions in Russia after World War I, undertaken without realistic plan and clear determination, greatly helped such an identification of the Bolshevist program with the historic Russian state.

The policy of half-hearted intervention was followed by the lukewarm policy of the *cordon sanitaire*. It represented the open admission of the inability of the western powers to influence the course of Russian domestic affairs except by increasing the difficulties, first of the stabilization, and then of the forced expansion of the Russian economy. It must be admitted, however, that the policy of the *cordon sanitaire* contributed to the defeat of early Soviet attempts to turn the Russian revolution into a world revolution, although events like the German recovery in the mid-twenties and the anti-Communist turn of the Chinese revolution were undoubtedly more important than the negative policy of abstention.

---

[2] The *New York Times*, April 1, 1949.

[III]

It was dubious from the beginning whether the new eastern states would be able to live between Russia and Germany, if Russia was not integrated in some fashion into a European system. Yet many people tended to forget Russia altogether. To them Poland seemed to have taken the place that Russia occupied in Europe before 1914, and the Little Entente that of the former Austro-Hungarian empire. But neither one could fill the role of the former Romanov and Habsburg empires. It must suffice here to mention only a few of the major weaknesses of the new eastern states. Since they looked in many different directions, toward the Baltic, the Adriatic, Aegean, and Black Seas, they had not much unity among themselves. While the Habsburg empire, in spite of its pernicious internal controversies, had formed a viable economic entity, the new states were confronted with unsolvable economic problems in addition to their formidable political difficulties.

Among all these states Czechoslovakia was the most democratic and prosperous one. Practically none of the other states ever acquired an economic or political equilibrium. They were driven to adopt governmental methods which had only a superficial resemblance to democracy, while their living standards remained far below the European average. The ensuing social crises, brought to a head by the depression of the late twenties, inflamed again the conflict of nationalities. Not only did states like Poland and Czechoslovakia continue to be at loggerheads, but issues of nationality also undermined the internal cohesion of such states as Yugoslavia and Czechoslovakia. Hungary, smarting under her defeat, kept revisionist forces alive with the support of Italy.

It was an illusion to conceive of the Little Entente and Poland as substitutes for the empires of the Romanovs and Habsburgs. Between 1887 and 1917 France had spent about sixteen billions of francs in loans and investments in order to build up her Russian ally.[3] If she could have employed similar amounts of money to set the new eastern states on the road toward prosperity, the system of French eastern alliances might have become a strong underpinning of the European status quo. But the French depositor, having lost more than a quarter of all his foreign investments as a result of the World War, was not inclined to permit his government to conduct a bold foreign economic policy. Since the

---

[3] Cf. Herbert Feis, *Europe the World's Banker, 1870-1914*, New Haven, Yale, 1930, p. 51; and Harold G. Moulton and Leo Pasvolsky, *War Debts and World Prosperity*, Washington, The Brookings Institution, 1932, p. 426.

new states remained economically weak, the foremost potential cus-
tomer, Germany, continued to hold considerable power in the southeastern European states.

Naturally, the military agreements between France and the eastern
states were practical only as long as France was physically capable of
cooperating with her eastern allies and making a substantial contribution to their defense both against Germany and the Soviet Union. This
required the disarmament of Germany, at least to the extent that French
troops could force a junction with the Czechoslovak army along a line
from Metz-Diedenhofen to Eger-Pilsen. It also called for a French army
capable of strategic maneuver and not one almost exclusively designed
for defensive operations along the frontiers of France.

The responsibility for maintaining the Paris settlement, however, lay
as much with Britain as with France. From the outset there was a great
deal of skepticism in Britain regarding all the new eastern states. During
World War I the champions of the partition of the Habsburg empire
had gained only a slight superiority over the forces which insisted on the
preservation of a reorganized Habsburg empire, or at least the establishment of some Danubian federation.[4] In any event, after 1919 British
diplomacy tried to keep the Polish state within certain bounds, in order
to mollify Russian and German animosity against the revived Poland.
The Curzon line on the one side, and the acceptance of plebiscites in
Upper Silesia, East- and West-Prussia and the drafting of the Danzig
statute on the other, were illustrations of this British policy.

No doubt, it would have been possible and perhaps even wise to
correct the Versailles treaty in Germany's favor as long as such changes
could be achieved by procedures of international law and multilateral
agreement, and not by unilateral *faits accomplis*. But British diplomacy
failed conspicuously to discourage the latter methods. The most important event in this connection was the decision by the Conservative
British cabinet in 1924 to reject the Geneva Protocol and to negotiate
instead the Locarno Treaty. Britain thereby drew a definite distinction
between the western and eastern parts of the Paris settlement. She declared her reluctance to participate in the active support of the new
order in eastern Europe, and her determination to limit her commitments to the protection of the Rhine.

The historical adviser to the British Foreign Office, Sir James Head-

---

[4] Cf., for example, David Lloyd George, *Memoirs of the Peace Conference*, 2 vols.,
New Haven, Yale, 1939, vol. I, pp. 17 ff.

lam-Morley, in a remarkable and prophetic memorandum, warned the British cabinet in February, 1925, that "the danger point in Europe" was not the Rhine, but the Vistula, and he went on to inquire:

> Has anyone attempted to realize what would happen if there were to be a new partition of Poland, or if the Czechoslovak state were to be so curtailed and dismembered that in fact it disappeared from the map of Europe? The whole of Europe would at once be in chaos. There would no longer be any principle, meaning, or sense in the territorial arrangements of the continent. Imagine, for instance, that under some improbable condition, Austria rejoined Germany; that Germany using the discontented minority in Bohemia, demanded a new frontier far over the mountains, including Carlsbad and Pilsen, and that at the same time, in alliance with Germany, the Hungarians recovered the southern slope of the Carpathians. This would be catastrophic, and, even if we neglected to interfere in time to prevent it, we should afterwards be driven to interfere, probably too late.[5]

Headlam-Morley argued that Great Britain could only be defended on the European continent, irrespective of the fact that she formed at the same time the center of a world-wide empire. England had always been a part of the European political system, and most certainly so in the days of Elizabeth, Cromwell, Marlborough, Chatham, Pitt, Castlereagh, Canning, Palmerston, Salisbury, Lansdowne, and Grey.[6] The British historian was also right when he called it the supreme achievement of statesmanship in the first half of the nineteenth century that France was brought back to the councils of the great European powers without ever being allowed to upset the order of Europe which the Congress of Vienna had established. He recommended analogous concessions to Germany, particularly by a revision of reparations, but warned British statesmen not to give Germany the chance to wreck the basic arrangements of the Paris Conference. This would be possible, he correctly predicted, if the new eastern European states were left without general protection, and if Germany were permitted to cooperate with Russia against them.

But British diplomacy, in line with the prevailing public opinion in England, chose a different course. Sir Austen Chamberlain, in spite of his strong personal sympathies for France and his suspicions of Germany, was swayed by the general sentiment that Britain could avoid

---

[5] Sir James Headlam-Morley, *Studies in Diplomatic History*, New York, A. H. King, 1930, pp. 182-84.
[6] *Ibid.*, p. 176.

continental entanglements except for limited commitments made for the immediate security of the English Channel. By confining the British guarantee to western Europe, Britain gave the impression that she was willing to tolerate changes in eastern Europe, in contrast to the declared French policy.

If Stresemann found a majority in support of his Locarno policy among the Germans, it was largely due to the hope that the treaty seemed to open the gates for a revision of Versailles in the East. To be sure, Germany had to sign arbitration treaties with Poland and Czecho-slovakia, and France strengthened her ties with the two states simultaneously with the signing of the Locarno treaty. But the eastern peace settlement was not reinforced by a British guarantee. Moreover, Germany, in a special protocol, was assured by the other Locarno powers that her cooperation in the defense of the League Covenant against a Russian infraction would take into account her "military situation" as well as "geographical situation." [7] This actually meant that Germany was given great latitude to determine her relations with Russia without much reference to her League obligations. When in April, 1926, Germany concluded the Treaty of Berlin with the U.S.S.R., Stresemann could tell the Soviet government that the question of whether or not the U.S.S.R. would be judged an aggressor by the League in the event of a conflict with a third state "could only be determined with binding force for Germany with her own consent." [8]

The Locarno treaties and Germany's entrance into the League of Nations have often been described as the apogee of the international system of 1919. In reality Locarno failed to create a European peace. It covered up certain cracks, which had appeared in the building, but allowed others to continue unchecked. It would have been unobjectionable to make concessions to Germany between 1924 and 1930 in such matters as the occupation of the Rhineland and reparations. Probably much more should have been done to enable German democracy to develop under normal conditions. But it was a tragic fallacy to believe that eastern Europe could be neglected economically and politically without courting the gravest dangers.

We have seen already that the new eastern states did not possess

[7] Arthur Berriedale Keith, ed., *Speeches and Documents on International Affairs, 1918-1937*, 2 vols., London, Oxford University Press, 1938, vol. I, p. 124.

[8] Note by the German Foreign Minister, Stresemann, to the Soviet Ambassador, Krestinski, April 24, 1926; *ibid.*, pp. 128 ff.

sufficient unity among themselves. Nor was this lack of unity among them surprising, since they had developed in different directions as borderlands of the historic European community. For a time the Habsburg monarchy had tied the nationalities of the Danubian basin together, and Austria in turn had been a major force in the maintenance of the European continent. But once the Turkish pressure subsided and democratic national movements raised their heads, the Habsburg empire was lost. No doubt, the establishment of some sort of Danubian federation after 1919 would have been desirable for a good many reasons, but it would not have solved the major problems of security of the new eastern states. They could have found a solution only within a closely integrated European system, which the League of Nations and the European diplomacy of the interwar period failed to provide.

[IV]

Winston Churchill has called World War II the "unnecessary war." [9] Of course, Mr. Churchill probably would not deny that there is an overriding necessity in the course of history, grounded not so much in political events, as in the moral and intellectual fiber of nations and men. But in the more narrowly defined "political" sense, in which this article is conceived, we must assume with Mr. Churchill that statesmen have a choice not only of objectives but of methods to achieve them. It is doubtful whether after World War I the victorious European powers had it in their hands to restore the continent to full prosperity without active American cooperation, but it is much less doubtful that Britain and France together could have built and upheld a European political system in spite of the withdrawal of the United States from Europe after 1920. The opportunity for rebuilding an integrated political system in Europe had already been missed by the time Hitler came to power.

The reaction of the western states to the rise of National Socialism was only another manifestation of their lack of awareness of the general problems of Europe. In 1935 Hitler succeeded in restoring the German *Wehrmacht* (which included imposing air forces), and thereby became an immediate threat to Britain as well as France. By the remilitarization of the Rhineland in 1936 he made effective military cooperation between France and her eastern allies impossible. Two years later Hitler could force England and France to collaborate in undoing

---

[9] Winston S. Churchill, *The Gathering Storm*, Boston, Houghton Mifflin, 1948, p. iv.

the European order of 1919 by becoming accomplices in the dissection of Czechoslovakia, the most strategically placed and strongest of the new European states.

The Munich treaty gave Germany undisputed control over southeastern Europe on the condition that Hitler would not go to war against the East and that he would respect certain rules of international law. If Hitler had been satisfied with the annexation of Austria and the Sudetenland, he could have gained ever increasing control over southeastern Europe through economic penetration. It was unlikely that the western powers would have had either the minds or the means to challenge such a German policy, which could have led to a German-dominated federation of *Mitteleuropa*. On the other side, Russia would have grown uneasy over an eastward expansion of Germany, but could hardly have interfered without the active support of the western powers. As a matter of fact, Britain and France, in excluding the Soviet Union from the Munich settlement, had seemed to turn the pressure of German power deliberately away from the West and toward Russia.

Yet it is idle to speculate on the course that history might have taken if Hitler had concentrated on the peaceful exploitation of his vast gains after 1938. He had geared the German economy to war and had prepared the German people for tribal conquest. Indeed, he had been pouting already when Chamberlain, at Munich, deprived him of "his" war.[10] Thus the march into Prague, and, shortly thereafter, the struggle for Poland followed. British diplomats suddenly realized that the Vistula was as important as the Rhine, but their attempt in 1939 at building up an eastern "cordon" against Germany with Rumania, Hungary, and Poland, was more an act of faith than a political performance. In any event, the decisive question was the future attitude of the Soviet Union, and this diplomatic problem was tackled last.

In the summer of 1939 it had become clear that effective military cooperation between Russia and the new Anglo-French entente would be even more difficult than it had been during World War I. The Russians undoubtedly knew that the western powers had decided, at least for the initial phase of the imminent war, upon a defensive strategy in the West, which meant that the Russians would have to

---

[10] The best historical treatment so far of the events leading up to Munich and the Polish crisis is to be found in two English books: John Wheeler-Bennett, *Munich: Prologue to Tragedy*, New York, Duell, Sloan, and Pearce, 1948; and Lewis B. Namier, *Diplomatic Prelude, 1938-39*, London, Macmillan, 1948.

carry the burden of the fight. Possibly the western armies would not go beyond what came to be known as a *Sitzkrieg*, and Chamberlain might conclude a new compromise at the expense of Russia. It is at least understandable that the Soviet government entertained grave suspicions in view of both the events prior to 1939 and of the realities of the moment.

It cannot be denied that the Soviet rulers were asked to assume awful risks when they were invited to join in the resistance against Hitler. In these circumstances it was natural that they requested permission to occupy the natural ramparts in the Baltic that had protected Russia in the eighteenth and nineteenth centuries, and that they inquired what forms Russian-Polish military cooperation could take. The answers were disconcerting. Poland refused to admit Russian troops, and the western powers maintained that the integrity of the Baltic states was protected by the Covenant. It is difficult to see how the western powers could have acted differently, though in the Czechoslovak crisis they had hardly even paid lip-service to their League obligations. The Molotov-Ribbentrop pact of August 23, 1939, was the result of this unexampled breakdown of every concerted action. Under the terms of the treaty the Soviets could occupy most of the Baltic states, Bessarabia, and one third of Poland. Their western defenses were greatly improved and, for the time being at least, Russia was relieved of the threat of a German attack. Germany was turned against the West.

It would be difficult to find in international history a comparable moment of general confusion. Every major actor in the events of 1939 was sooner or later to discover his lack of foresight. The final result of the war should, one may hope, convince the Germans of the criminal folly which Hitler committed not only in unleashing a general war, but also in removing the buffers between Russia and Germany which had largely been created by German military efforts in World War I. The blind contempt which the Germans had always felt for the Poles played an important part in these events.

Stalin himself soon had reason to rethink the practicability of the Soviet-German pact. The consequences of this eastern "Munich" were as catastrophic as those of the Munich treaty of 1938 had been. The pact was concluded in the hope that a struggle between Germany and the West would ensue, and that it would last some time and weaken Germany as well. Stalin's general judgment—that France and Britain were weak, despite Germany's inclination to underrate British skill and determination[11]—proved correct, but the Nazi conquest of the continent was faster and more thorough than the Russian leaders had expected. There is a bitter note in all subsequent reported statements by Stalin on France, which "opened the gates to the fascist enemy," contributed less to the final victory than the Poles, and should not be readmitted to the councils of the great powers.[12] Once Russia was attacked by Hitler's armies, the Soviet Union realized the need for cooperation with the West and began to clamor for the "second front," which she herself had helped to undermine by her assistance to Hitler and the propaganda of the Comintern, which had been particularly effective in France.

But it should not be overlooked that Russia, even at the height of German power in the fall and winter of 1940, did not give up certain interests, even beyond the line of demarcation which the pact of 1939 seemed to have drawn between Germany and Russia. In his talks with Hitler and Ribbentrop in November, 1940, Molotov firmly insisted upon Russia's rights with regard to the Straits and adjacent Balkan areas.[13] He was not cajoled by Ribbentrop into accepting an outlet to the Persian Gulf instead. It should also be noted that Molotov was not impressed by Ribbentrop's glib sales talk about the defeat of England, which the German minister asserted had actually already been accomplished. Molotov's shrewd and cagey statements in Berlin were an indication that the Russians derived some comfort and courage from Britain's continued resistance after the battle of France and western Europe had been lost. On the basis of the available documents no one can say whether Molotov and other Russian leaders considered in this connection the interest that the United States took in the independence of the British Isles and of the British Commonwealth. But we may surmise that the expressions of American sentiment and official policy were carefully analyzed in the Kremlin.

[v]

With the conquest of Norway, Denmark, the Netherlands, Belgium, and France, soon to be rounded off by the occupation of southeastern Europe and the Balkans, the continent was virtually in Hitler's hands.

[11] Raymond James Sontag and James Stuart Beddie, eds., *Nazi-Soviet Relations, 1939-1941*, Washington, Department of State, 1948, p. 74.
[12] James F. Byrnes, *Speaking Frankly*, New York, Harper, 1947, pp. 25, 28.
[13] *Nazi-Soviet Relations, op. cit.*, pp. 217-54.

The defeated nations were deeply shaken in their traditional beliefs, and if Hitler had offered them a dignified role in a reorganized Europe he might have been able to consolidate his conquests, and might even have received considerable support for his war against Russia. But his "new order" of Europe was only a device for the rule of a master race over subjugated peoples, and Hitler's "crusade" to protect European civilization against the Russian menace was an equally false label. Inevitably resistance to German military government grew, particularly after the German war machine stalled in Russia and the Allies could begin to extend active support to the national undergrounds.

Nevertheless, the nations of the European continent ceased after 1940-41 to be a major element in deciding the fate of Europe, and the circumstances of their defeat and their subsequent Nazi bondage made it extremely doubtful that they could easily recover something approximating their former political stature after liberation. As in the years after 1809, only Russia and Britain seemed to count, but the differences in the historical ages were great. Napoleon's European regime did not have the methods of the twentieth century police state at its disposal nor the planned war economy, in which millions of vanquished people could be exploited for the industrial production of the victorious state. Early nineteenth century warfare and resistance depended on arms which could be supplied with relatively small effort, while in the modern age highly technical weapons were required. The speedy rearming of Prussia after 1812, largely accomplished with British assistance, could not be repeated with France or Belgium in 1944.

There were other differences between 1810 and 1940. Britain fought her continental wars with small armies augmented by allied and auxiliary forces. During World War I Britain was compelled to mobilize a large national service army. But even then she had achieved only a stabilization of the western front in France, and without American assistance the western powers could not have turned the balance against Germany in 1918, particularly in view of the breakdown of Czarist Russia. The battle of France in 1940 left Britain without any continental allies, and an invasion of the continent by the British and British Commonwealth forces after 1940 could not have broken Hitler's iron grip on the continent. Even the mere defense of the British Isles and the empire required at least the financial and industrial support of the United States.

Hitler's invasion of Russia in June, 1941 and his declaration of war

on the United States after Pearl Harbor made it possible to plan realistically the full destruction of the Nazi domination of Europe. Without the gallant and prodigious war effort of Britain, American power
could never have been brought to bear upon Germany, as Americans
well know. Incidentally, even the Russians should ponder what might
have happened to them if the British had not fought on after Dunkirk.
But it is true that from 1941 until 1944 the Russians had to carry the
main burden of the German war, with losses of life and devastation of
land such as no people has suffered in modern history. They cannot
claim that they won the war by themselves, but it is correct to say that
they broke the *offensive* power of the German army, particularly in the
gigantic struggle in the plains of southern Russia during the winter of
1942-43. The isolation of the Sixth German army around Stalingrad
took place at the same time that Anglo-American forces landed in
North Africa. After the fall of Stalingrad the Russians began their advances to the West, tying down the bulk of the German armies in the
process, and deflecting to the East most of Germany's war production,
which continued to rise until early 1944.

Undoubtedly, American and British lend-lease deliveries contributed
to the Russian successes, but how much it is impossible to say. The
official Russian contention today is that they constituted six percent of
the Russian war production, which is probably too low a figure. More
over, at the critical turning point of the war, before the transplanted
Russian factories were fully operating, even a smaller percentage of the
overall production, if delivered in time, could have been decisive. On
the other hand, could the western powers have afforded to see the Soviet
Union knocked out? The Russians, on their part, did not complain so
much about western niggardliness with regard to lend-lease as they did
about the lack of a second front, which seemed to indicate a hesitation
on the part of the western powers to commit their major military forces
to an invasion of the Continent. The United Nations Declaration of
January 1, 1942, pledged all signatories to support each other by employing their "full resources, military or economic, against those members of the Tripartite Pact and its adherents with which such government is at war." [14] But until June, 1944, the western Allies could not
use their full military resources.

A good case can be made out to prove that a cross-channel operation

---

[14] Leland M. Goodrich, ed., *Documents on American Foreign Relations*, Boston,
World Peace Foundation, 1942, vol. IV, p. 203.

in 1942 or early 1943 would have brought little relief to the Russians. General Marshall, however, urged such an operation in the event that the Russian front should be seriously disrupted by the Germans.[15] But he was overruled in the combined Anglo-American councils, and Churchill's strategy of limited investments and peripheral approaches prevailed for the time being. The Anglo-American armies invaded North Africa and Sicily, but proceeded, even after the Mediterranean had been made safe and their numerical strength had grown, to divert some of their power to the Italian peninsula. Only thereafter did General Marshall's conception of a massed invasion of northwestern Europe become the central theme of western strategy.

There has been a great deal of idle talk in the American press about Mr. Churchill's superior strategic judgment. It has been argued that his idea of defeating Hitler by attacking the "soft underbelly" of Europe would have left the West in control of the major part of southeastern Europe. To such a thesis the answer can only be that such an attack might have brought western armies to Salonika, Sofia, Valona, possibly even Budapest, but also Russian armies to Hamburg, Bremen, and the Ruhr. It is hard to think of a worse misnomer for the southern part of Europe than the one coined by Mr. Churchill. Indeed, nowhere is Europe protected by harder shells than along the Alps and the Balkan mountains, and no soldier who fought in southern and central Italy will be inclined to agree with Mr. Churchill.

The major objection to Mr. Churchill's plan of pressing the Italian campaign and following it up with an invasion of the Balkans is found in the limitations which terrain and lines of communications would have placed on any such operation. The Balkan peninsula would not have permitted the deployment of more than a part of the Anglo-American forces, partly on account of the nature of the country involved, partly because the supply lines were far longer than those of a cross-channel operation. Consequently, only relatively small German forces could have been brought to bay in the Mediterranean.

The strategy proposed by the American chiefs-of-staff under General Marshall's leadership was based on the consideration that, according to

---

[15] Cf., Henry L. Stimson and McGeorge Bundy, *On Active Service in Peace and War*, New York, Harper, 1948, pp. 413 ff.; Robert E. Sherwood, *Roosevelt and Hopkins, an Intimate History*, New York, Harper, 1948, pp. 560 ff. Cf., also, General Marshall's report, *The Winning of the War in Europe and the Pacific*, Washington, Simon and Schuster, 1945, pp. 8 ff.; Dwight David Eisenhower, *Crusade in Europe*, Garden City, Doubleday, 1948, pp. 44 ff., 66 ff., 138 f., 167.

Clausewitz's dictum, the supreme strategic objective is the annihilation of the enemy's army, and that such an end can be attained only by the use of the maximum of one's available forces. In World War II this could be achieved only in the northwestern European theater. Nowhere else could the western powers have deployed all their divisions, and deployed them so effectively, in a war of maneuver likely to lead finally to the capture of the main arsenal of the enemy, the Ruhr. But even this campaign depended heavily on Russian military cooperation, since it could succeed in achieving its major objectives only if the Red Army continued to hold down the bulk of the German forces.

[VI]

This was the setting in which American statesmen, in the years from 1942 to 1945, had to formulate a program for the reconstitution of Europe after the War. Would the intervention of the United States in Europe again be as temporary as it had been after 1917? Very grave doubts existed about the willingness of the American people to assume long-range commitments in Europe. It was assumed that America would not withdraw from a new League of Nations, and the response which the idea of a permanent United Nations organization found in both American parties gave an early assurance that the United States would not become as isolationist a power as she had been in the interwar period. But special commitments in Europe beyond a participation in the Allied occupation of Germany and possibly Austria seemed not within the realm of possibility. Furthermore, with another war in the Far East still to be fought and won, once the war in Europe had come to an end, there was an imperative need for the speedy transfer of American divisions to the Pacific and a natural tendency not to be involved too deeply in European matters. Finally, there was the desire to win Russian cooperation in the war against Japan.

Moreover, the thinking of American policy-makers was still dominated by the vague notion that somehow the old Europe would ultimately reemerge. It was a foregone conclusion that Russia would extend her influence beyond her pre-World War II frontiers and, perhaps, even beyond her 1914 frontiers in certain cases. Prussia-Germany would be wiped out as a great power, and an equivalent to the Habsburg empire in the form of a Danubian federation was not likely to be restored. At the end of the war only Britain would be able to counterbalance Russian power to some extent. She was expected to rule the Mediterranean.

United States military government of Italy was, at least in its early phase, run with the idea that the British should be given every opportunity to reestablish their old economic and political ties with Italy. In the case of Greece the American military chiefs refused to have U.S. troops participate in the landings. After a great deal of argument a small group of American officers was allowed to direct the administration of civilian relief goods.

The Italian and Greek as well as other cases made it clear that for the time being, and probably for some time to come, the United States would have to provide Britain with the means to implement her policies.[16] It was realized, too, that the British economy itself would have to be bolstered after the War. But the prevailing opinion was that Britain would get back on her feet and be capable of exercising a powerful influence in western and southern Europe. There was also the hope that France, after a more prolonged period of recuperation, would ultimately regain her prewar position, as would the Benelux and the three Scandinavian countries. The finality of the breakdown of Europe as a political system, balanced within itself, was at best sensed, but hardly recognized.

In the economic field the total impact of the interwar period and of World War II was not fully grasped either. No doubt the American government, backed by a substantial body of enlightened public opinion, had taken certain lessons of recent history to heart. The disastrous consequences of the treatment of reparations and war debts in the international affairs of the interwar period were not forgotten. Lend-lease avoided the pitfalls of inter-Allied financial relations which had been experienced after World War I, and in the discussion of future reparations large money payments were excluded. It was also understood that recovery had to be approached on a worldwide scale and organization. There was general agreement, too, that it was undesirable to have a repetition of the sudden discontinuation of the inter-Allied economic agencies at the time of the armistice, as had occurred in 1918 with the result that certain *ad hoc* councils had had to be improvised after a short, but costly interval. During World War II the International Monetary Fund and the International Bank for Reconstruction and Development were set up to act as central international agencies in the rebuilding of world economy in the postwar era.

---

[16] Sherwood, *op. cit.*, prints on pp. 748 f. a document, presumably representing the opinion of the Joint Chiefs of Staff and expressing very succinctly the prevalent opinion of the future roles of Russia and Britain in Europe.

Nevertheless, the size of the problem involved in the reconstruction of Europe was grievously underestimated. The United Nations Relief and Rehabilitation Administration was confined to relief operations in liberated areas during the immediate post-hostilities period. The second "R" in UNRRA was never pronounced. Lend-lease came to an end as soon as hostilities ceased, while the Monetary Fund and the International Bank were given very limited means and functions. Today . . . one may well wonder whether American policy could not have achieved a much higher degree of political stability, if it could have begun to employ the financial and economic resources of the United States in a systematic plan for the rehabilitation of Europe . . . years earlier.

But even if the United States Government in the years between 1943 and 1945 had diagnosed the weakness of western Europe correctly and had been in a position to assume as onerous a role as it has taken, it could not have revived a European political system standing on its own feet, as the concert of European powers had done during the nineteenth century. With the great powers in Central Europe destroyed, and with western Europe weakened, there was no power in Europe which by its own strength or in alliance with all the other western European states could have blocked Russian progress into Europe. For that matter, even the United States would have been hardly strong enough to oppose the immediate demands of the Soviet Union. The decisions of the Moscow, Teheran, Yalta, and Potsdam conferences were on the whole the logical and inevitable outcome of this situation. If one wants to criticize them, one should direct criticism not so much against the actual results of the wartime conferences, which after all laid the foundations for the military defeat of the enemy countries and for the building of the United Nations, as against the expectations entertained at the time by western statesmen with regard to the future of Western-Russian relations. The whole wartime policy of the Soviet Union, not to mention her prewar policy, demonstrated that the Soviet leaders never were ready to abandon the sovereignty of Russian policy and were determined to push Russian interests wherever they did not meet with opposition, though they were ready to keep the weapons of the Communist International in reserve.

It remains a problem whether or not it would have been more practical to negotiate with Russia a clear division of spheres of interest, as the British proposed and proceeded to do in the case of Greece against the warning of the American government, which considered such

spheres as incompatible with the contemplated United Nations organization.[17] But the practice of United States foreign policy turned out to
be less rigid. The United States never considered associating Russia with
Britain and herself on equal terms in the military government of Sicily
and Italy, though this meant that the western powers would be represented only weakly in the Soviet military government of southeastern
Europe. Czechoslovakia was informed that she was not on the list of
European states to be liberated by western armies. Thus Beneš had no
other choice but to conclude, on May 8, 1944, a bilateral agrement with
the Soviet Union regarding the administration of civil affairs in Czechoslovakia after the arrival of the Russian armies.[18]

In such actions the Soviet Union could find her view confirmed that
the West would ultimately be willing to tolerate the creation of a Russian orbit along the western frontiers of the Soviet Union. And there
would have been relatively little resentment in the West to such a
policy, if the Soviet Union had shown and maintained a minimum
respect for the democratic rights and processes of the liberated eastern
states. But one of the major factors that was bound to make the years
between 1945 and 1947 barren years in the progress of a European peace
settlement was probably the expectation of the Kremlin that, in the
absence of a constructive program of stabilization for western Europe,
time was on the Russian side, and that social disintegration would open
new opportunities for Russian influence, and perhaps full control over
the rest of the continent.

The Marshall Plan speeded the recovery of western Europe and made
possible a much higher degree of self-help and mutual assistance among
the western European nations. In the political field the Western Union
has made a beginning toward overcoming national divisions and pooling
the military resources for the common defense of western Europe. But
even a closely allied western Europe, if it could be created in the near

---

[17] Cordell Hull, *The Memoirs of Cordell Hull*, 2 vols., New York, Macmillan,
1948, vol. II, pp. 1451 ff.

[18] See text in Louise W. Holborn, ed., *War and Peace Aims of the United Nations*, 2 vols., Boston, World Peace Foundation, 1943-48, vol. II (1943-45), pp.
767 ff. The Department of State released for publication an exchange of correspondence between SHAEF and the Soviet High Command concerning Allied military
operations in Czechoslovakia during April and May, 1945, which does not affect
the statement in the text. The Department of State confirms that "no prior political
agreements or commitments had been made with respect to Czechoslovakia," and
apparently does not believe that this correspondence constituted a step in this
direction. The *New York Times*, May 10, 1949.

future, would not be a match for the power of the Soviet Union. Western Europe can survive only if the United States is ready to defend the integrity of the western European states, as she has promised in the North Atlantic Pact. The Pact merely proves that no European political system is left—that it has been superseded by a Russian and Atlantic system.

This conclusion, of course, does not mean that Europe has ceased to exist and that her general history has become nothing but the memory of a dead past. The historic bonds which traditionally linked the Czech, Polish, and Hungarian nations with the West seem completely broken at this moment. But even if we are unable at present to see how these historic links can be used to narrow the gulf that separates East and West, we should not lose sight of such possibilities. We would also be ill-advised if we were to forget the strong economic ties which existed between eastern and western Europe and were to underrate their importance in the future.

Strategy Hits a Dead End *

by Bernard Brodie

One of the commonest slogans in strategic literature is the one inherited from Jomini, that "methods change but principles are unchanging." Until yesterday that thesis had much to justify it, since methods changed on the whole not too abruptly and always within definite limits. Among the most important limits was the fact that the costs of a war, even a lost one, were somehow supportable. At worst only a minor portion, literally speaking, of a nation's population and wealth would be destroyed. Even the two world wars did not go beyond this limit, despite their horrendous magnitude.

There could therefore be a reasonable choice between war and peace. There could also be a reasonable choice among methods of fighting a war, or "strategies." However unrestricted they were intended to be, wars were inevitably limited by the limited capabilities (as we now see it) of each belligerent for heaping destruction on the other. Indeed,

---

* From *Harper's Magazine*, Vol. CCXI, No. 1 (October 1955), pp. 33-37. © 1955 by Harper and Brothers. Reprinted by permission of Bernard Brodie.

there were even slogans insisting that the application of force in war *must* be unrestricted.

If the time has not already arrived for saying good-by to all that, it will inevitably come soon—depending only on when the Soviets achieve an air-atomic capability comparable to the one we already have. For unless we can really count on using ours first and, what is more, count on our prior use eliminating the enemy's ability to retaliate in kind—and surely the combination would deserve long betting odds—we can be quite certain that a major unrestricted war would begin with a disaster for us, as well as for them, of absolutely unprecedented and therefore un-imaginable proportions.

There are impelling psychological reasons why strategists have in the past found it almost impossibly difficult to adjust their war plans to the possibility of national disaster at the outset. If not now, then soon, no other assumption for an unlimited major war will be realistically pos-sible. Because we face a situation unique in history, most of our descrip-tions of it are understatements. For example, people speak bravely of atomic explosives being the most portentous military invention "since gunpowder." In doing so they only prove how hard it is to believe that something which has happened in one's own day—before one's very eyes, as it were—makes every other comparable development of the entire five or six thousand years of recorded time pale in importance.

Since we have recently passed the end of the first atomic decade, this is an appropriate time to observe how much has changed in these ten years. Though it was immediately apparent in 1945 that something of tremendous military importance had happened, we can see now how many of the interpretations then offered were too conservative. In retrospect it is clear that many of them were wedded to presumptions soon to be disproved—for example, that the bomb was fated to remain scarce, extremely costly, bulky and therefore difficult to deliver, and limited to about the same power and spatial effective as the Nagasaki bomb.

The first decade of the atomic age has seen the collapse of the Ameri-can monopoly, of the myth of inevitable scarcity, and of reasonable hopes for international atomic disarmament; it has seen also the devel-opment in both major camps of a thermonuclear weapon of vastly greater destructiveness. Since we have been living with the fission type of atomic bomb for a decade, it might appear to some that the fusion type introduces nothing essentially new other than a greater economy of force. That unfortunately is not the case.

No doubt the implications of the first atomic bombs were radical in the extreme, and it was right at the time they appeared to stress the drastic nature of the change. The utility of strategic bombing could no longer be questioned. At once it became incontrovertibly the dominant form of war, especially since it could be entirely carried through with air forces existing at the onset of war and at speeds which were phenomenally fast by any previous standard. Also, it could be carried out successfully over any distances that might separate the various great powers on this globe. This was change enough from the conditions of World War II.

Nevertheless, the bomb yields were still sufficiently limited to make the delivery of a substantial number of bombs necessary in order to achieve decisive results. That in turn made it possible to visualize a meaningful air defense, even if not a satisfactory one. It was therefore still necessary to think in terms of a real struggle for "command of the air." It was also still necessary to apply, though in much modified form, the lore so painfully acquired in World War II concerning "target selection" for a strategic bombing campaign. And the functions of ground and naval forces, though clearly affected by the new weapons, still appeared vital even in the "all-out" type of war.

These ties with the past, tenuous enough at best, were immediately threatened by the appearance of the modern type of thermonuclear bomb. Among the questions that thereupon became obsolete were most of those concerning the selection of strategic targets. Since a thermonuclear bomb could not be used on an industrial concentration in or near a city without destroying that city—and since one such bomb will effectively eliminate all the industry associated with that city—there is not much point in asking which industries should be hit or in what order. Whether we like or not, the thermonuclear bomb used strategically is a "city-buster."

The same is of course true if we hit air fields near cities. We cannot talk about strategies being aimed against the enemy air force as distinct from the enemy economy or population, unless we actually intend taking deliberate measures to refrain from hitting cities. It cannot matter greatly whether the destruction of cities is a by-product of the destruction of air fields or vice versa.

The number of cities that account for the bulk of the so-called economic war potential of either the U.S. or the U.S.S.R. is small—possibly fifty or less, and certainly not over two hundred (the range depends on the weighting one gives to certain factors, such as industrial interdependence). Most of these cities, moreover, are concentrated in the eastern part of the United States, and especially the northeastern part, where urban and nonurban populations alike are subject to overlapping patterns of radioactive fallout. The concentration of industry in Russian cities, and the concentration of cities and populations in the western part of the country, makes the Soviet Union comparable as a target to the United States.

It seems likely, in the event of an all-out thermonuclear war, that the survival of people and industries will be far more important in determining the recovery of the nation following hostilities than in controlling the subsequent course of those hostilities. The reason for this is simply that the minimum of destruction one can reasonably expect from any *unrestricted* strategic attack will inevitably be too high to permit further meaningful mobilization of resources, perhaps too high even to permit the effective use of surviving military units.

So far as the population is concerned, the uninjured survivors may be many, though it is also conceivable that they may be relatively few— that is, down to a quarter or less of the original figure. In either case they are unlikely to be much concerned with the further pursuit of political-military objectives. We learned something about that from the apathy of the German and Japanese peoples in the latter stages of World War II.

The idea that prolonged hostilities might be carried on with conventional weapons following the initial massive exchange of nuclear ones has fortunately been abandoned, at least on the level of official pronouncement, both by us and by the British (as their *Defense White Paper for 1955* makes clear). Everything is now stacked on deterrence, and on the measures and attitudes that will make deterrence work.

Sir Winston Churchill has even derived some comfort from the phenomenon of fallout, because (he said) it tends to equalize in degree of vulnerability a small country like Britain with a large one like the Soviet Union. And in a sense he is right, because the difference is only one of numbers of bombs required to achieve comparable results, and whatever the larger number may be it will very likely be within easily deliverable limits.

Most of what I have so far said implies the judgment that the prospects for significant improvement of defenses against strategic bombing in the next decade or so are not bright. There are several reasons for this assumption. First, since the coming of the A-bomb, and largely as a result of a steady increase in the bomb's power, developments in the strategic bombing offense have outpaced to a fantastic degree those of the defense—and this movement has by no means run its course. (Sir Winston, among many others, tells us that the intercontinental ballistic missile is somewhere in the offing.) Second, the growth of national nuclear stockpiles is irrepressible, and while delivery capabilities do not normally expand with the same exuberance, it is nevertheless likely to be far easier and less costly for one side to double the number of bombs on targets than for the other to double, by dispersing them, the number of targets that the enemy must hit.

Finally let us note the fact that there are enormous impediments—psychological, political, economic and, let us admit it, doctrinal—to the adoption of really drastic measures for defense. The proof of that lies in all we have conspicuously failed to do after ten years of living with the atomic bomb, especially in the field of "passive" defense. Our industry is not noticeably less concentrated than before, and existing measures of civil defense are almost universally regarded as ludicrous. New and effective stimuli to action may yet turn up, but some exceedingly powerful ones have so far failed to move us.

From all this it would seem that at least one conclusion can be drawn: barring revolutionary advances in air defense, an unrestricted strategic air campaign in a war in which the U.S. is engaged is bound to be decisive. On the other hand, when I say "decisive," I am not using the term in its traditional sense—that is, in the sense that implies a clear victory for one side or the other. I mean instead that if strategic bombing occurs on the grand scale, other kinds of military operations will prove either unfeasible or superfluous and most likely both.

I have thus far been discussing nuclear weapons strictly in terms of what is usually called strategic use—that is, against the enemy homeland. There also must be considered a prospective tactical use—that is, on the battlefield.

Whether or not we can relinquish strategic bombing as a way of war, it appears that we cannot afford to abjure the tactical use of nuclear weapons without dooming ourselves and allies to a permanent inferiority to the Soviet and satellite armies, at least in Europe. But the problems involved in the tactical use of atomic weapons seem to have peculiarly forbidding difficulties. It is all very well to say that the general development of troops must combine low spatial density with the capacity for instantaneous concentration, but how to accomplish it is another story. The few who are attempting to grapple with the problem in published books and articles seem always to assume—tacitly and perhaps also unconsciously—various restraints or restrictions on the size and availability of tactical nuclear weapons. And they also show a general predilection for small bombs.

In fact, one sees an increasing tendency to distinguish between tactical and strategic nuclear weapons according to size of weapons, the big ones being reserved strictly for the strategic function. Before this particular habit becomes too firmly established, we might ask whether there is any basis for it other than the obvious one—that it is easier to imagine ground forces operating in not too unaccustomed a fashion if the nuclear weapons they use and contend with are small and relatively few in number. But the enemy may not be so accommodating.

A justification one sometimes hears for using the smaller bomb is that one must be able to exploit through immediate advance of one's own troops the advantage gained. Here again we discern tacit assumptions—this time from thinking only in terms of the offensive. But if the French high command had possessed the thermonuclear weapon when the German forces were pouring through the Ardennes gap in May of 1940, they would surely not have withheld it because of a craze for exploitation.

The growing abundance of nuclear weapons on both sides may, however, force us to the ultimate conclusion that under their unrestricted use tactically no substantial forces will be able to live in the field at all. If organized bodies of troops cannot exist above ground in the field—or at any rate, cannot operate effectively there—it would seem that they must be either under ground or in the air. In either case we must think in terms of greatly reduced numbers; and, as for airborne forces, we must remember that in nuclear war usable air fields will become quickly scarce, and that small combat aircraft competing for the use of surviving fields can carry nuclear bombs.

Thus we tend in the end to get the same result in considering unrestricted tactical war in the future that we get in unrestricted strategic war. In each case the conclusion tends toward the nihilistic. The only distinction would seem to be that the strategic interchange must have prior consideration in our thoughts, because whatever else it is that an army is fighting for, it must be fighting for a nation that is healthy enough to have national interests.

If what I have said thus far makes any sense at all, it means at the very least that for any war among the major powers we cannot henceforward consider air strategy, naval strategy, and land strategy (or the political objectives they are supposed to secure) in separate categories— *unless* there is some form of deliberate restriction on the use of nuclear weapons.

There is a stark simplicity about an unrestricted nuclear war that almost enables it to be summed up in one short statement: be quick on the draw and the trigger squeeze, and aim for the heart. One then has to add: but even if you shoot first, you will probably die too! This brings us a long way from the subtleties of a Clausewitz, a Jomini, or a Mahan. It brings us even a long way from Douhet, the prophetic theorist of strategic air power. It brings us, in short, to the end of strategy as we have known it.

And it requires us also to face one of the most disturbing of all the implications of nuclear weapons. With the speed and magnitude of destruction available through their use, any unrestricted war between the major powers must have a character and a conclusion that are fully predetermined at the outset. That is not to say that the relevant war plans will, in complete contrast to those of the past, prove themselves wholly "realistic"; it is only to say that they will govern the commitments made at the outset, and the results of those commitments will prevent any recovery from the errors exposed in the process of executing them.

A refusal to look plain facts in the face, on the grounds that to do so leads one to be too pessimistic, leads straight to dangerous nonsense. On the other hand, the fact that an inherited strategy tends toward the nihilistic, which is to say suicidal, indicates that it is wrong—that it reflects a tragically mistaken national policy. Let us be careful to distinguish between what is impossible and what is merely wrong. A future war resulting in mutual annihilation is far from being impossible. But surely it needs no argument to say that a policy that has such an end is a mistaken one.

There are those who believe they have found the answer in deterrence, which is hardly a new conception; but even the British in their *Defense White Paper* make allowance for peripheral challenges which do not call for total reactions. So far they seem to be stanchly refusing to consider the many conceivable borderline cases, but soon they will have to. Do not let me imply that we as a nation are in advance of them in this respect. Their planners have merely exposed their ideas in organized fashion in an official paper, while we leave that sort of communication to the conflicting, off-the-cuff remarks of high officialdom.

The key to the dilemma, if there is one, must be found in discovering the true sense for modern times of the old axiom of Clausewitz that "war is a continuation of policy." War is rational, he argued, only insofar as it safeguards or carries forward the political interests of the state. Certainly no one can dispute that, but it also seems at times that no idea could be further from the minds of people who presume to discuss national policy and strategy. One trouble is that even ordinary politicians and journalists feel impelled to utter resounding though meaningless platitudes when the phrase "national objectives" is mentioned, so that almost everything said on the subject is likely to be unrepresentative of what really lies in the minds and hearts of the people at large.

An unrestricted thermonuclear war is to the national interest of no nation. In view of the direction in which we are moving and the speed at which we are going, it seems absolutely beyond dispute that we and our opponents will have to adapt ourselves mutually to ways of using military power which are not orgiastic. The Great Deterrent will have to remain as the Constant Monitor, and its efficiency in that role should never be subject to doubt. But to argue that its efficiency requires it always to be straining at the leash is to uphold an argument today which —if we are actually intent on preserving the peace—we are bound to abandon tomorrow.

At a time when the opponent will be able to do to our cities and countryside whatever we might threaten to do to his, the whole concept of "massive retaliation"—and all that it stands for in both military and political behavior—will have to be openly recognized as obsolete. It is not enough to let a strategic idea die a lingering death from occasional verbal rebukes, leaving behind only confusion in public and professional opinion—including confusion about whether or not it is really dead. It is not enough to say that an unrestricted thermonuclear war cannot happen anyway because both sides will recognize its folly. There are various positive steps we must take to prevent its occurring even when military force is resorted to in disputes between nations.

In a world still unprepared to relinquish the use of military power, we must learn to effect that use through methods that are something other than self-destroying. The task will be bafflingly difficult at best, but it can only begin with the clear recognition that most of the military ideas and axioms of the past are now or soon will be inapplicable. The old concepts of strategy, including those of Douhet and of World War II, have come to a dead end. What we now must initiate is the comprehensive pursuit of the new ideas and procedures necessary to carry us through the next two or three dangerous decades.

FOR FURTHER READING:

Max Beloff, *The Great Powers: Essays in Twentieth Century Politics* (New York: The Macmillan Company, 1959).

Bernard Brodie, *Strategy in the Missile Age* (Princeton: Princeton University Press, 1959).

Samuel Glasstone (ed.), *The Effects of Nuclear Weapons* (Washington, D.C.: Government Printing Office—prepared by the Armed Forces Special Weapons Project and published by the Atomic Energy Commission— 1957).

John H. Herz, *International Politics in the Atomic Age* (New York: Columbia University Press, 1959).

Hajo Holborn, *The Political Collapse of Europe* (New York: Alfred A. Knopf, 1951).

Morton A. Kaplan, *System and Process in International Politics* (New York: John Wiley and Sons, 1957).

Grayson L. Kirk and others, *The Changing Environment of International Relations* (Washington, D.C.: The Brookings Institution, 1956).

James E. Meade, *The Theory of International Economic Policy* (London: Oxford University Press, 1951 and 1955), 2 vols.

Raymond F. Mikesell, *Foreign Exchange in the Postwar World* (New York: The Twentieth Century Fund, 1954).

Reinhold Niebuhr, *The Structure of Nations and Empires* (New York: Charles Scribner's Sons, 1959).

Barbara Ward, *Five Ideas That Changed the World* (New York: W. W. Norton, 1959).

Chapter VI

THE CHALLENGE OF SOVIET
COMMUNISM

O ne final yet necessary preliminary analysis remains
before proceeding to the substance of the public debate on foreign
policy; that is an examination of the nature of the challenge to the
United States posed by Soviet communism. Although there is grave
danger in viewing contemporary world politics too exclusively in terms
of Soviet-American tensions, and forgetting that there would be serious
problems even if the Bolshevik revolution had never occurred, no one
can doubt the central role of the Soviet Union in United States foreign
policy. The Soviet challenge is one of the most difficult ever faced by
this country. Since the conclusion of the Second World War the principal aspects of America's foreign policy have largely been responses to
this challenge, and this will probably continue to be the case in the
immediate future. Assumptions about the Soviet challenge are vital
features in the consideration of almost any foreign policy proposal: thus
it is most important to fully understand the nature of this challenge.

Fully understanding the Soviet challenge, however, is difficult. First,
although the data available for studying the Soviet Union have significantly increased in recent years, there are still important gaps in our
knowledge. Some of the most important figures—for example, those
concerning military capabilities and even gross national product, the
total of goods and services produced during a given period—are still only
well-informed guesses. The U.S.S.R. does not publish data equivalent to

that of highly developed Western states. And we know very little about basic aspects of decision-making in the Soviet Union. The veil of secrecy, although raised somewhat, still covers much of the governmental process. Secondly, the Soviet challenge is subtle and complex. While the U.S.S.R. has maintained huge armed forces since the end of the Second World War and presently devotes a considerable portion of its resources to military efforts, it does not seem disposed to strike an immediate blow; yet this might change if we were to relax our own military posture. The Soviet Union actively engages in subversion, but only a small portion of Soviet activities abroad can correctly be viewed in conspiratorial terms, and the U.S.S.R.'s basic gains in world politics are not the result of such activities. The pronouncements of Soviet diplomatists sound so strange in Western terms that they are often dismissed as mere propaganda, yet given the background and training of these men, their pronouncements may well represent their view of the world. The Soviet way of life appears repulsive when measured by our standards, but features of it—particularly its ability to produce rapid economic growth—have considerable appeal for those in underdeveloped countries. To fully comprehend the nature of the challenge Soviet communism poses we must use a broader perspective than that of our own cultural context.

It is appropriate to begin an analysis of the Soviet challenge by considering a speech of Nikita S. Khrushchev, First Secretary of the Central Committee of the Communist Party and Chairman of the Council of Ministers of the Soviet Union. The selection reproduced here is taken from his major policy pronouncement to the Twentieth Congress of the Communist Party of the Soviet Union in February, 1956. He outlined then what have since become the cardinal features of Soviet foreign policy. His speech is notable for its self-confidence, an attitude markedly different from that of earlier Soviet leaders. His assurance reflects the increased size of the Soviet bloc and the growth of Soviet military and economic power. The peaceful coexistence theme—so prominent in present Soviet foreign policy—is also clearly evident. But at the same time the speech contains no renunciation of the struggle to achieve the "victory of communism" nor of belief in the validity of this goal. And no Soviet pronouncement since then, either by Mr. Khrushchev or by any other official, would indicate that the long-held goals of Soviet communism have been abandoned. Even during his famous trip to the United States, Mr. Khrushchev took great pain to point out his belief in the ultimate triumph of the Soviet system. Therefore his peaceful coexistence does not in any way imply a cessation of the struggle between communism and capitalism, it concerns rather the means by which this struggle will be pursued. Even here caution is necessary. Mr. Khrushchev's speech was widely heralded as signifying the abandonment of the Leninist concept concerning the inevitableness of a violent clash between communist and capitalist states. A careful reading of this portion of the speech, as well as that concerning the accession to power of communist regimes, will reveal that Mr. Khrushchev does not rule out the use of force, but rather advances the opinion that communist victories may be possible without it. The willingness, indicated in the speech, to accept the possibility of various forms of socialism probably represents a more significant change in Soviet doctrine. However, Soviet actions in the Hungarian crisis indicate that there are distinct limits of tolerance and that neutralism would not be an acceptable policy for a Soviet satellite. Mr. Khrushchev's address foreshadowed many specific aspects of recent Soviet foreign policy, for instance the growing emphasis on foreign trade and the increased attention devoted to the newly independent and economically underdeveloped states of Asia and Africa. Although given several years ago, this speech still represents the best guide to current Soviet policies.

The other two selections in this chapter are Western analyses of Soviet strength. The first is a comprehensive and sobering examination of Soviet power by Allen W. Dulles, Director of the United States Central Intelligence Agency. While Mr. Dulles shows the redoubtable qualities of Soviet military strength, he does not think that the U.S.S.R. is presently superior to the United States in this sphere, nor does he think that a Soviet attack is imminent. His analysis of Soviet subversion and the U.S.S.R.'s economic strength are equally well balanced. He clearly indicates the challenge of the Soviet trade-and-aid offensive. The second selection, by Herbert S. Levine of Harvard University's Russian Research Center, considers the Soviet Union's present seven-year economic plan. Earth satellites and lunar probes have given wide publicity to Soviet military capabilities; there have been no similarly startling events to draw the American public's attention to the U.S.S.R.'s equally important economic capabilities. More attention needs to be focused here. Indeed, if peaceful—or perhaps more aptly competitive—coexistence is the mode for the next few years, economic capabilities may well be the determining factor in world politics. Mr. Levine indicates how strong the Soviet Union is economically and the dimensions of its future potentialities.

The challenge of Soviet communism is formidable and will be persistent. Successfully meeting it will require the United States' best and most carefully considered efforts.

International Situation of the Soviet Union*

by Nikita S. Khrushchev

The period that separates us from the nineteenth party congress is not a very long one—three years and four months. But on account of the volume of work done by the party, on account of the importance of events that happened in that period in our country and beyond its frontiers, this is one of the important periods in the history of the Communist party of the Soviet Union, in the history of its struggle for the consolidation of the might of our country, for the building of Communist society, and for peace in the whole world.

It is now clear to all that the measures taken by the party were correct and well timed. They have insured the steady growth of the Socialist economy and the further rise of the material well being and cultural level of the Soviet people.

Important events in foreign policy occurred in the period under review.

Thanks to the consistent peaceable foreign policy of the countries of the Socialist camp, the tension in international relations, the tension fraught with great perils, yielded to a certain detente [since the last party congress in 1952].

Real prospects for the better opened out on the international scene.

The principal feature of our epoch is the emergence of socialism from the confines of one country and in its transformation into a world system. Capitalism has proved impotent to hinder this world-historic process.

The simultaneous existence of two opposed and world economic systems of capitalism and socialism, developing according to different laws in the opposite direction, has become an irrefutable fact.

In accordance with concluded treaties, the Soviet Union is today helping the peoples democracies to build 391 enterprises and more than ninety separate shops and installations. We have granted to the peoples democracies long-term guarantees totalling 21,000,000,000 rubles at most favorable conditions.

---

* Excerpts from the official Soviet Information Bureau and *Tass* translation of the report of the First Secretary of the Central Committee of the Communist Party of the Soviet Union to the Twentieth Party Congress. As printed in the New York *Times*, February 15, 1956, p. 10.

The Soviet Union is also helping friendly countries and organizing production and the peaceful use of atomic energy.

Our country is helping the Peoples Republic of China to build in one five-year period alone 156 enterprises and twenty-one separate shops, supplying it with about 5,600,000,000 rubles worth of equipment.

The economy of world capitalism is developing in an exceedingly irregular manner and is becoming still more unstable.

We should closely follow the economies of capitalism, not accept Lenin's thesis of the decay of imperialism in a simplified fashion, but study all the best that sciences and techniques yield in the world of capitalism, in order to use the achievements of world technical progress in the interests of socialism.

On the basis of the present situation, talk about "prosperity" has been renewed in certain circles in the West. Efforts are made to prove that allegedly the Marxist theory of crises is "outmoded."

Bourgeois economists are silent about the fact that only a timely confluence of circumstances of a favorable nature in capitalism retarded the growth of economic crises.

Even so, at the period of a brisker situation, even crisis phenomena are showing themselves.

The commodity stock and also consumer credits have reached dangerous proportions in the U.S.A.

Britain is displeased with the growing activity of West Germany and Japan. Western Germany and Japan are displeased with Britain barring them from its markets.

Altogether, they have more than enough grounds to be displeased with the United States, which is disorganizing the world market by carrying on unilateral trade, fencing off its markets from foreign imports, banning trade with the East, and resorting to dumping of agricultural produce and other measures hitting hard at other countries.

The economic struggle between the capitalist countries is flaring up with ever-growing force. As hitherto, the main contradiction is between the United States and Great Britain.

Anglo-American antagonism embraces a wide range of matters. Under the banner of "Atlantic commonwealth" the transoceanic rivals are laying their hands on the key strategic and economic positions of the British Empire, are trying to straddle imperial communications, shatter the system of preferred tariffs, and subjugate to themselves the sterling area.

The revival of Western Germany's economic might particularly aggravates the situation on the world market. The lessons of the two world wars show that, in their struggle for world markets, the German monopolies stop short of nothing.

In this connection, the situation in Western Europe is also becoming worse, as the emergence of a rapidly growing German rival harbors no good for France and Britain, the more so if it is to be pushed further along the road of militarization.

The situation is also getting worse inside Western Germany itself, and the re-establishment of the might of the concerns and the monopolies intensifies the peril of the revival of the forces that in their day brought fascism to power.

Soon after the end of the second World War, the influence of the reactionary, military circles began increasingly to tell on the policy of the United States of America, Great Britain and France.

The international atmosphere became poisoned by war psychosis. The arms drive began to assume ever more monstrous proportions.

On the territories of states situated thousands of kilometers away from the boundaries of the United States, many large American military bases were set up spearheaded against the Soviet Union and the peoples democracies.

The sponsors of the cold war took the path of creating military blocs.

Many countries, against the wills of their people, found themselves drawn into close aggressive alignment—the North Atlantic bloc, the Western European Union, SEATO, the Baghdad Pact.

The organizers of the military blocs allege that they united for protection against the "Communist menace." This is utter hypocrisy.

The new feature here is that by creating all kinds of blocs and pacts the United States wants to secure the dominating position in the capitalist world and reduce all its bloc partners to the position of docile executors of its will.

The sponsors of the "from positions of strength" policy allege that this policy makes a new war impossible, as it insures "an equilibrium of forces on the world arena."

The arms drive, "from positions of strength," the whipping together of aggressive blocs, the cold war—all this could not but aggravate and actually did aggravate international tension.

The forces of peace have grown considerably with the appearance in the world arena of the group of peace-loving states in Europe and Asia, which have proclaimed nonparticipation in blocs to be the principle of their foreign policy.

As a result, an extensive "zone of peace," including both Socialist and non-Socialist peace-loving states of Europe and Asia, has appeared on the world arena.

This zone extends over a vast area of the globe, inhabited by nearly 1,500,000,000 people, or the majority of the population of our planet.

No little unhappiness in the world today stems from the fact that in many countries the working class remained split for many years and its different detachments do not act in a united front, a situation that plays only into the hands of the forces of reaction. But now, in our opinion, the prospects of changing the situation is opening up.

Here cooperation also with sections of the Socialist movement adhering to other views than ours in the question of the transition to socialism is possible and necessary.

Today many Social Democrats are for an active struggle against the war danger and militarism, for closer relations with Socialist countries, and for unity of the labor movement. We sincerely welcomed the Social Democrats, and are ready to do everything possible to unite our efforts in a fight for the noble cause of the defense of peace and the interests of the working people.

For the first time since the war a certain detente has set in international tension. In this atmosphere the Geneva four-power heads of government conference became possible.

The conference demonstrated the viability and correctness of the methods of negotiations between countries. It confirmed the Soviet Union's viewpoint that by negotiations the most complex of international problems can be solved, given mutual desire for cooperation and agreement.

Now some people are trying to bury the spirit of Geneva. As the facts show, certain Western circles have still not abandoned the hope of exerting pressure on the Soviet Union and wresting unilateral concessions from it.

It is, however, high time to realize that such calculations are unrealistic. The Soviet Union has done a lot to bring closer the positions of the great powers.

It is now up to the United States, Great Britain and France. This, of course, does not mean that the Soviet Union will refuse further efforts for easing international tension and strengthening peace.

On the contrary, since there has appeared a possibility of bringing closer together the positions of the powers on a number of major international problems, the Soviet Union will with still greater persistence strive to establish mutual confidence and cooperation between all countries, and between the great powers first and foremost.

And in this, absolutely necessary requisites in relations between great powers are equal efforts and mutual concessions. The method of negotiation must become the only method of resolving international issues.

Collective security in Europe, collective security in Asia, and disarmament—these are the three major problems, whose solution can create a basis for a stable and lasting peace.

The creation of a collective security in Europe would conform to the vital interests of the countries of Europe, big and small, and would simultaneously be a firm guarantee of world peace.

This would at the same time make it possible to solve the German problem. The present state of this problem cannot but cause uneasiness.

Germany still remains split; Western Germany is being speedily rearmed. It is no secret that by restoring German militarism, each of the three Western powers pursues its own ends.

But who will gain from this short-sighted policy? First of all, the imperialist forces of Western Germany. First among the losers will be France, which by such a policy is being reduced to the position of a third-rate power.

There is emerging ever more clearly a new Washington-Bonn axis that is increasing the dangers of war.

Under the present situation there is a real possibility of solving the German problem in a new way, in the interests of peace and security of the peoples, including the German people.

The creation of a system of collective security in Europe, rejection of the Paris agreements, rapprochement and cooperation between the two German states—such is the sure way of solving the German problem.

As regards disarmament, we shall spare no effort to solve this all-important problem.

Pending agreement on the major questions of disarmament, we express readiness to agree to certain partial measures in this sphere, such as the cessation of tests of thermo-nuclear weapons, not to permit troops on the territory of Germany to have atomic weapons, and the reduction of military budgets.

Implementation of the states of these measures would clear the road to agreement on other, more complex questions of disarmament.

For the strengthening of world peace, it would be of tremendous importance to establish firm, friendly relations between the two biggest powers of the world, the Soviet Union and the United States.

We believe that if the famous five principles of peaceful coexistence were made the basis of relations between the U.S.S.R. and the United States, this would be of truly outstanding significance for all mankind and would, of course, be no less beneficial to the people of the United States than to the peoples of the U.S.S.R. and all other nations.

We have lately undertaken new important steps aimed at securing a fundamental improvement of Soviet-American relations.

We refer to the proposal for the conclusion of a treaty of friendship and cooperation between the U.S.S.R. and the United States contained in the message of Comrade N. A. Bulganin to President D. Eisenhower.

We want to be friends and to cooperate with the United States in the effort for peace and security of the peoples as well as in the economic and cultural fields.

We pursue this with good intention, without holding a stone behind our back.

We have made a proposal for a treaty with the United States because the conclusion of such a treaty would accord with the deepest desires of the peoples of both countries to live in peace and friendship.

If good relations are not established between the Soviet Union and the United States, and mutual distrust exists, this will lead to an arms race on a still greater scale and to a still more dangerous growth of the forces on both sides.

We intend to continue to work for the further improvement of our relations with Great Britain and France.

We welcome the desire of the people of the Arab countries to uphold their national independence. Likewise the belief that also in Iran, Turkey and Pakistan it will be understood that normal relations with the U.S.S.R. are in the vital interests of those countries.

It is necessary to emphasize the importance of non-aggression of friendship treaties, the conclusion of which will help to remove existing suspicion and mistrust in relations between the states and to improve the international situation.

For its part, the Soviet Union is prepared to conclude such treaties with the respective states.

Trade, too, should play a great part in expanding the basis for businesslike cooperation between the countries.

Counterposing the slogan of the North Atlantic pact: "Let us arm," we advise the slogan: "Let us trade."

The Leninist principle of the peaceful coexistence of states with differing social systems was, and remains, the general line of our country's foreign policy.

It is alleged that the Soviet Union advocates the principle of peaceful coexistence exclusively from tactical considerations of the moment.

However, it is well known that we have advocated peaceful coexistence just as persuasively from the very inception of Soviet power. Hence, this is not a tactical stratagem but a fundamental principle of Soviet foreign policy.

The focs of peace still allege that the Soviet Union intends to overthrow capitalism in other countries by "exporting" revolution. It goes without saying that there are no adherents of capitalism among Communists.

But this does not at all signify that we have interfered or intend to interfere in the internal affairs of countries where a capitalist system exists.

It is ridiculous to think that revolutions are made to order.

When we say that in the competition between the two systems of capitalism and socialism, socialism will triumph, this by no means implies that the victory will be reached by armed intervention on the part of the Socialist countries in the internal affairs of the capitalist countries.

We believe that after seeing for themselves the advantages that communism holds out, all working men and women on earth will sooner or later take to the road of the struggle to build a Socialist society.

We have always asserted and continue to assert that the establishment of a new social order in any country is the internal affair of its people.

Such are our positions, based on the great teachings of Marxism-Leninism.

The principle of peaceful co-existence is gaining increasingly wider international recognition.

And this is logical, since there is no other way out in the present situation. Indeed, there are only two ways: either peaceful coexistence, or the most devastating war in history. There is no third alternative.

We presume that countries with differing social systems cannot just simply exist side by side. There must be progress to better relations, to stronger confidence among them, to co-operation.

As will be recalled, there is a Marxist-Leninist premise which says that while imperialism exists wars are inevitable.

While capitalism remains on earth the reactionary forces representing the interests of the capitalist monopolies will continue to strive for war gambles and aggression, and may try to let loose war.

There is no fatal inevitability of war.

Now there are powerful social and political forces, commanding serious means capable of preventing the unleashing of war by the imperialists, and—should they try to start it—of delivering a smashing rebuff to the aggressors and thwarting their adventuristic plans.

To this end it is necessary for all the forces opposing war to be vigilant and mobilized. It is necessary for them to act in a united front and not to slacken their efforts in the fight to preserve peace.

In view of the fundamental changes that have taken place in the world arena, new prospects have also opened up with regard to the transition of countries and nations to socialism.

It is quite likely that the forms of the transition to socialism will become more and more variegated. Moreover, it is not obligatory for the implementation of those forms to be connected with civil war in all circumstances.

The enemies are fond of depicting us, Leninists, as supporters of violence always and in all circumstances. It is true that we recognize the necessity for the revolutionary transformation of capitalist society into Socialist society.

This is what distinguishes revolutionary Marxists from reformists and opportunists. There is not a shadow of doubt that for a number of capitalist countries the overthrow of the bourgeois dictatorship by force and the connected sharp aggravation of the class struggle is inevitable.

But there are different forms of social revolution and the allegation that we recognize force and civil war as the only way of transforming society does not correspond to reality.

Leninism teaches us that the ruling classes will not relinquish power of their own free will.

However, the greater or lesser degree of acuteness in the struggle, the use or not of force in the transition to socialism, depend not so much on the proletariat as on the extent of the resistance put up by the exploiters, and on the employment of violence by the exploiting class itself.

In this connection the question arises of the possibility of employing the parliamentary form for the transition to socialism. For the Russian Bolsheviks, who were the first to accomplish the transition to socialism, this way was excluded.

However, since then radical changes have taken place in the historical situation that allows an approach to this question from another angle.

Socialism has become a great magnetizing force for the workers, peasants and intelligentsia in all lands. The ideas of socialism are really conquering the minds of all toiling mankind.

At the same time, in a number of capitalist countries, the working class possesses in the present situation realistic opportunities of welding under its leadership the overwhelming majority of the people and of insuring its transition of the principal means of production into the hands of the people.

The right-wing bourgeois parties and the Governments they form are becoming bankrupt more and more often.

In these conditions, by rallying around itself a toiling peasantry, the intelligentsia and all the patriotic forces, and by meting out a determined rebuff to opportunistic elements incapable of abandoning a policy of conciliation with the capitalists and landlords, the working class has the possibility of inflicting a defeat on the reactionary anti-popular forces and of gaining a firm majority in parliament, and converting it from an organ of bourgeois democracy into an instrument of genuinely popular will.

In such an event, this institution, traditional for many highly developed capitalist countries, may become an organ of genuine democracy, of democracy for the working people.

The winning of a stable parliamentary majority, based on the mass revolutionary movement of the proletariat and the working people, would bring about for the working class of a number of capitalists and former colonial countries, conditions insuring the implementation of fundamental social transformations.

Of course in countries where capitalism is still strong and where it controls an enormous military and police machine, the serious resistance of the reactionary forces is inevitable.

There the transition to socialism will proceed amid conditions of an acute class revolutionary struggle.

The political leadership of the working class, headed by its advance detachment, is the indispensable and decisive factor for all the forms of the transition to socialism. Without this, the transition to socialism is impossible.

Such are the considerations the Central Committee of the party deems necessary to set forth with regard to the questions of the forms for the transition to socialism in present day conditions.

What are the further tasks of the party in the sphere of foreign policy?

1. Undeviatingly to follow the Leninist policy of peaceful coexistence among different states, irrespective of their social order. To fight actively for peace and the security of nations, and for confidence among states, by seeking the conversion of the relaxation achieved in international tension into lasting peace.

2. To strengthen by all means the fraternal relations with the Peoples Republic of China, Poland, Czechoslovakia, Bulgaria, Hungary, Rumania, Albania, the [East] German Democratic Republic, the Peoples Democratic Republic of [North] Korea, the Democratic Republic of [North] Vietnam and the Mongolian Peoples Republic, remembering that the greater the unity and might of the Socialist countries the more secure is the cause of peace. To strengthen by all means friendship and cooperate with the fraternal people of the Federal Peoples Republic of Yugoslavia.

3. To reinforce indefatigably the bond of friendship and cooperation with the republic of India, Burma, Afghanistan, Egypt, Syria, and other states that stand for peace. To support countries that refuse to be involved in military blocs; to cooperate with all forces seeking to preserve peace. To develop and strengthen friendly relations with Finland, Austria and other neutral countries.

4. To conduct an active policy of further improving relations with the United States of America, Britain, France, Western Germany, Japan, Italy, Turkey, Iran and other countries, with a view to strengthening mutual confidence, extending trade, and expanding contacts and cooperation in the sphere of cultural science.

5. To follow vigilantly the intrigues of circles not interested in the relaxing of international tension, and to expose in good time the subversive activities of the enemies of peace and security of the nations; to take the necessary steps to strengthen further the defense capacity of our Socialist state; to maintain our defenses at the level demanded by modern armament and science and to insure the security of our socialist state.

The Challenge of Soviet Power*

by Allen W. Dulles

The challenge of Soviet power presents today a triple threat: first, military; second, economic; and third, subversive.

This challenge is a global one. As long as the principles of international communism motivate the regimes in Moscow and Peiping, we must expect that their single purpose will be the liquidation of our form of free society and the emergence of a Sovietized, communized world order.

They change their techniques as circumstances dictate. They have never given us the slightest reason to hope that they are abandoning their overall objective.

We sometimes like to delude ourselves into thinking that we are faced with another nationalistic power struggle, of which the world has seen so many. The fact is that the aims of the Communist International with its headquarters in Moscow are not nationalistic; their objectives are not limited. They firmly believe and eloquently preach that communism is the system which will eventually rule the world, and each move they make is directed to this end. Communism, like electricity, seeks to be an all-pervasive and revolutionary force.

To promote their objectives they have determined—cost what it may —to develop a military establishment and a strong national economy which will provide a secure home base from which to deploy their destructive foreign activities.

---

* From the *Department of State Bulletin*, Vol. XL, No. 1035 (April 27, 1959), pp. 583-589.

SOVIET MILITARY ESTABLISHMENT

To achieve this objective they are devoting about twice as much of their gross national product to military ends as we do. The U.S.S.R. military effort as a proportion of GNP is greater than that of any other nation in the world. Their continuous diversion of economic resources to military support is without any parallel in peacetime history.

We estimate that the total value of their current annual military effort is roughly equivalent to our own. They accomplish this with a GNP which is now less than half of our own.

Here are some of the major elements which go into their military establishment. The Soviet Union maintains an army of 2½ million men, and the tradition of universal military training is being continued. The Soviet Army today has been fully reequipped with a post-World War II arsenal of guns, tanks, and artillery. We have reason to believe the army has already been trained in the use of tactical nuclear weapons.

They have the most modern types of aircraft for defense: night and day fighters, a very large medium-bomber force, and some long-range bombers. They have built less of these long-range bombers than we had expected several years ago and have diverted a major effort to the perfection of ballistic missiles.

Their submarine strength today is many times that with which Germany entered World War II. They have over 200 long-range, modernized submarines and a like number of less modern craft. They have made no boasts about nuclear powered submarines, and on all the evidence we are justified in concluding that we are ahead of them in this field. We must assume, however, that they have the capability to produce such submarines and will probably unveil some in the near future.

BALLISTIC MISSILE SITUATION

I would add a word on the ballistic missile situation.

When World War II ended the Soviet acquired much of the German hardware in the missile field—V-1 and V-2—and with them many German technicians. From that base, over the past 10 years, they have been continuously developing their missile capability, starting with short-range and intermediate-range missiles. These they have tested by the hundreds and have been in production of certain models for some time.

They also early foresaw that, in their particular geographical position, the long-range ballistic missile would become their best instrument in the power struggle with their great rival, the United States. As the size and weight of powerful nuclear weapons decreased with the improvement of the art, they became more and more persuaded of this. Hence they have concentrated on these weapons, have tested some, and assert that they now have ICBM's in serial production.

They hope in this way eventually to be able to hold the U.S. under the threat of nuclear attack by ICBM's while they consolidate their position in the fragile parts of the non-communistic world.

Before leaving the military phase of the Soviet threat, I want to dispel any possible misinterpretations. First, I do *not* believe that the Soviet now have military superiority over us; and second, I do *not* believe that they desire deliberately to provoke hostilities with the U.S. or the Western World at this time. They are well aware of our deterrent force. They probably believe that the risks to them, even if they resorted to surprise attack, would be unacceptable.

Taking into account our overall military strength and our strategic position vis-à-vis the Soviet Union, I consider that our military posture is stronger and our ability to inflict damage is today greater than that of the Soviet Union.

Furthermore, we have allies. The strength, the dependability, and the dedication of our allies put them in a very different category than the unwilling and undependable allies of Moscow, even including the Chinese Communists.

But as the Soviet military capabilities and their nuclear power grow, they will feel that their foreign policy can be somewhat more assertive. In 1956, during the Suez crisis, we had the first Soviet missile-rattling as a new tactic of Moscow diplomacy. Since then there have been the Taiwan Straits and Berlin crises and today the aggressive Communist pentration of Iraq. Hence we must assume that they will continue to probe and to test us, and they may even support other countries in aggression by proxy. They will put us to the test.

There are two points to keep in mind as we view the military future. Firstly, with a much lower industrial base than we, they are producing a military effort which is roughly equivalent to our own; and secondly, they have conditioned their people to accept very real sacrifices and a low standard of living to permit the massive military buildup to continue. If the Soviet should decide to alter their policy so as to give their own people a break in the consumer field with anything like the share in their gross national product which we, as a people, enjoy, the prospects of real peace in our time would be far greater.

SOVIET "ECONOMIC ORDER OF BATTLE"

I will turn now to some of the highlights of the economic aspect of the Soviet challenge.

The new confidence of Khrushchev, the shrewd and vocal leader of the Soviet Communist Party and incidentally Head of Government, does not rest solely on his conviction that he, too, possesses a military deterrent. He is convinced that the final victory of communism can be achieved mainly by nonmilitary means. Here the Soviet economic offensive looms large.

The proceedings of the recent 21st Party Congress laid out what we might call the Soviet economic order of battle.

Khrushchev explained it in these words, to summarize the 10 hours of his opening and closing remarks:

> The economic might of the Soviet Union is based on the priority growth of heavy industry; this should insure the Soviet victory in peaceful economic competition with the capitalist countries; development of the Soviet economic might will give communism the decisive edge in the international balance of power.

In the short space of 30 years the Soviet Union has grown from a relatively backward position into being the second largest industrialized economy in the world. While their headlong pace of industrialization has slowed down moderately in the past few years, it still continues to be more rapid than our own. During the past 7 years, through 1958, Soviet industry has grown at the annual rate of 9½ per cent. This is not the officially announced rate, which is somewhat larger. It is our reconstruction and deflation of Soviet data.

Our own industrial growth has been at the annual rate of 3.6 per cent for the 7 years through 1957. If one included 1958, the comparison with the rate of Soviet growth would be even less favorable.

INVESTMENT FOR NATIONAL POLICY PURPOSES

I do not conclude from this analysis that the secret of Soviet success lies in greater efficiency. On the contrary. In comparison with the leading free-enterprise economies of the West the Communist state-controlled system is relatively inefficient.

The secret of Soviet progress is simple. It lies in the fact that the Kremlin leaders direct a far higher proportion of total resources to national policy purposes than does the United States. I define national policy purposes to include, among other things, defense and investment in heavy industry.

With their lower living standards and much lower production of consumer goods, they are in effect plowing back into investment a large section of their production—30 per cent—while we in the United States are content with 17 to 20 per cent. Soviet investment in industry as planned for 1959 is about the same as U.S. investment in industry during 1957, which so far was our best year.

Although the Soviets in recent years have been continually upping the production of consumer goods, their consuming public fares badly in comparison with ours. Last year, for example, Soviet citizens had available for purchase barely one-third the total goods and services available to Americans. Furthermore, most of the U.S. output of durable consumer goods is for replacement, while that of the U.S.S.R. is for first-time users. In summary, the Soviet economy is geared largely to economic growth and for military purposes; ours is geared largely to increasing consumer satisfactions and building a higher standard of living.

Here are some examples:

While the Soviets last year were producing only 1 automobile for every 50 we produced, they were turning out 4 machine tools to our 1.

This contrast in emphasis carries through in many other fields. Our capital expenditure for transportation and communications is more than double the comparable Soviet expenditure. Yet this is largely accounted for by our massive highway building program, which has been running 15 to 20 times the U.S.S.R. spending, whereas their annual investment in railroad rolling stock and fixed assets substantially exceeds ours.

At the moment they do not feel much incentive in the roadbuilding field. They have no interest in having their people travel around on a massive scale. Also this would put pressure on the Kremlin to give the people more automobiles.

Commercial investment, which includes stores, shopping centers, drive-in movies, and office buildings, has been absorbing over $6 billion a year in the U.S., and only $2 billion in the U.S.S.R.

Our housing investment is roughly twice that of the Soviet, even though living space per capita in the U.S. is already four times that of the U.S.S.R.

INDUSTRIAL PRODUCTION TRENDS

What of the future? In Khrushchev's words, "The Soviet Union intends to outstrip the United States economically. . . . To surpass the level of production in the United States means to exceed the highest indexes of capitalism."

Khrushchev's ambitious 7-year plan establishes the formidable task of increasing industrial production about 80 per cent by 1965.

Steel production, according to the plan, is to be pushed close to 100 million net tons. Cement output is set at a level somewhat higher than industry forecasts place United States production in 1965.

The energy base is to be revolutionized. Crude oil and natural gas will constitute more than one-half of the total energy supply, and relatively high-cost coal will be far less important than now.

By 1965 the U.S.S.R. plans to produce about 480 billion kilowatt hours of electricity. As a study comparing U.S. and U.S.S.R. electric power production prepared by a leading industrial research group pointed out, this means that the absolute gap between the U.S. and U.S.S.R. in the quantities of electricity generated will increase somewhat in our favor over the next 7 years.

This interesting study received a considerable amount of deserved publicity. We agree with its conclusion. However, what is true about electric power is not true across the board, as some commentators concluded.

For example, compare primary energy production trends in the two countries. Soviet production of coal, petroleum, natural gas, and hydroelectric power, expressed in standard fuel units, amounted to 45 per cent of the U.S. production in 1958. By 1965 it will be close to 60 per cent. The absolute gap in primary energy has been closing since 1950. At the present pace it will continue to narrow over the next 7 years.

Similarly, the absolute gap in steel *production* has been shrinking over the past 5 years. The maximum gap in steel *capacity* apparently was reached in 1958.

The comforting illusion spread by the "disciples of the absolute gap" should not serve as a false tranquilizer.

SOVIET EXAGGERATION

At the same time it is important not to exaggerate Soviet prospects in the economic race. In the propaganda surrounding the launching of the 7-year plan, Khrushchev made a number of statements about Soviet economic power which were nothing more than wishful thinking. Specifically he stated that "after the completion of the 7-year plan, we will probably need about 5 more years to catch up with and outstrip the United States in industrial output." "Thus," he added, "by that time [1970], or perhaps even sooner, the Soviet Union will advance to first place in the world both in absolute volume of production and in per capita production."

First of all, to reach such improbable conclusions the Kremlin leaders overstate the present comparative position. They claim U.S.S.R. industrial output to be 50 per cent of that of the U.S. Our own analyses of Soviet industrial output last year concluded that it was not more than 40 per cent of our own.

Secondly, Khrushchev forecasts that our future industrial growth will be only 2 per cent a year. If this is true, the United States will be virtually committing economic suicide. This prediction I regard as unrealistic.

A saner projection would place 1965 Soviet industrial production at about 55 per cent of our own. By 1970, assuming the same relative rates of growth, U.S.S.R. industrial output as a whole would be about 60 per cent of that in the United States.

Further, when Khrushchev promises his people the world's highest standard of living by 1970, this is patently nonsense. It is as though the shrimp had learned to whistle, to use one of his colorful comments.

IMPLICATIONS OF SOVIET ECONOMIC PROGRESS

These Soviet exaggerations are a standard tool of Communist propaganda. Such propaganda, however, should not blind us to the sobering implications of their expected economic progress.

First of all, rapid economic growth will provide the Kremlin leaders with additional resources with which to intensify the arms race. If recent trends and present Soviet policies continue, Soviet military spending could increase by over 50 per cent in the next 7 years without increasing the relative burden on their economy.

Secondly, some additional improvement can be made in the standards of living of the Russian people, even with continued emphasis on heavy industry and armaments. It is only since the death of Stalin in 1953 that serious attention has been given to improving living standards. The moderate slowdown in the headlong growth of heavy industry which then ensued has been caused in large part by the diversion of more resources to housing, to agriculture, and to consumer goods.

Living standards, based on present Soviet plans, are expected to increase about one-third over the next 7 years. This level, if achieved, will still be far below that which our own citizens are now enjoying, but it will look good to people who for long have been compelled to accept very low standards.

Finally, the Soviet 7-year plan, even if not fully achieved, will provide the wherewithal to push the expansion of trade and aid with the uncommitted and underdeveloped nations of the free world. By 1965 Soviet output of some basic raw materials and some industrial products will be approaching, and in a few cases exceeding, that of the United States. Most prominently, these products will be the kind that are needed for industrialization in the less developed countries.

The outcome of this contest—the Communist challenge in underdeveloped areas—is crucial to the survival of the free world.

COMMUNIST TRADE-AND-AID PROGRAMS

This is an unprecedented epoch of change. Within little more than 10 years, over three-quarters of a billion people in 21 nations have become independent of colonial rule. In all of these newly emergent countries there is intense nationalism coupled with the determination to achieve a better way of life, which they believe industrialization will bring them.

The leaders of world communism are alert to the opportunity which this great transformation provides them. They realize the future of communism can be insured only by expansion and that the best hope of such expansion lies in Asia and Africa. While they are attempting to focus all our concern on Berlin, they are moving into Iraq with arms, economic aid, and subversion and giving added attention to Africa.

The Communist bloc trade-and-aid programs in undeveloped countries moved into high gear during 1958. The equivalent of over $1 billion in new credits was extended to underdeveloped countries by the bloc in this year. In the 4-year period ending 1958 the total of grants and credits totaled $2.5 billion, of which $1.6 billion came from the U.S.S.R. and the balance from the satellites and China. Three-fifths of the total delivered to date has been in the form of arms to the U.A.R. —Egypt and Syria—Yemen, Iraq, Afghanistan, and Indonesia. These same countries, plus India, Argentina, Ceylon, Burma, and Cambodia, have received the bulk of the economic aid.

Over 4,000 bloc technicians have been sent to assist the development of nations in the free world. About 70 per cent of these technicians are engaged in economic activities. Others are reorganizing local military establishments and teaching bloc military doctrine to indigenous personnel.

The bloc also has a well-developed program for training students from underdeveloped countries. About 3,200 students, technicians, and military specialists have now received such training behind the Iron Curtain.

While these figures are still well below the total of our own aid, loan, and training programs, this massive economic and military aid program is concentrated in a few critical countries, and of course these figures do not include Soviet aid and trade with the East European satellites and Communist China.

India, which has received over $325 million of bloc grants and credits, is a primary recipient. The Soviet economic showplace here is the Bhilai steel mill, being built by the Russians. The U.A.R. over the past 4 years received over $900 million in aid and credits. This investment today does not seem quite as profitable to the Soviet as it did last year.

Iraq provides a prime example of the opportunistic nature of the bloc's aid program. Prior to the coup d'etat on July 14th last year, Iraq's economic involvement with Communist nations had been negligible. In the past few months the U.S.S.R. has provided over $250 million in military and economic development credits. The Iraq Development Board has dropped its two Western advisers. Western technicians are also being dismissed and contracts with many Western firms canceled. Increasingly, Moscow is pressuring the Iraq Government to accept dependence on Communist support, and the number of fellow travelers in high government posts is growing.

COMMUNIST CAMPAIGN OF SUBVERSION

The Soviet policy of economic penetration fits like a glove into their worldwide campaign of subversion, which is the third main element of the triple Soviet challenge: military, economic, and subversive.

International communism has not changed its operating procedure since the days of the Comintern and the Cominform. The Communist Party of the U.S.S.R., of which Khrushchev is the leader, is the spearhead of the movement. It has a worldwide mission, formulated by Lenin and Stalin and now promoted by Khrushchev but with more subtle techniques than those of Stalin. This mission continues to be the subversion of the entire free world, starting of course with those countries which are most vulnerable.

Its arsenal of attack is based, first of all, on the Communist Parties of the Soviet Union and Communist China. These in turn direct the hard-core Communist organizations which exist in practically every country of the world. Every Communist Party maintains its secret connections with Moscow or, in case of certain of the Communist parties in the Far East, with Peiping.

These parties also have an entirely overt association with the international Communist movement. At the 21st meeting of the Soviet Party Congress there were present representatives of some 60 Communist parties throughout the world, including two representatives of the U.S. Communist Party. The single theme of these Communist leaders was their confidence in the eventual worldwide triumph of the Communist movement.

From time to time Moscow has made agreements, such as the Litvinov pact in 1933, not to interfere in the internal affairs of other countries. On the strength of this we resumed relations with the Soviet. They are eager to conclude like agreements of "friendship and nonaggression" with all countries of the world. These are not worth the paper they are written on. During World War II Moscow abolished the international Comintern to propitiate the United States, its then wartime ally. Its functions have, however, been carried on continuously under other forms.

In addition to its worldwide penetration through Communist Party organizations, the Communists in Moscow and Peiping have set up a whole series of front organizations to penetrate all segments of life in the free countries of the world. These include the World Federation of

Trade Unions, which claims some 90 million members throughout the world. International organizations of youth and students stage great festivals at frequent intervals.

They have the Women's International Democratic Federation, the World Federation of Teachers Unions, the International Association of Democratic Lawyers, and Communist journalists and medical organizations. Then cutting across professional and social lines, and designed to appeal to intellectuals, the Communists have created the World Peace Council, which maintains so-called peace committees in 47 countries, gaining adherents by trading on the magic word of "peace."

To back up this massive apparatus the Soviet has the largest number of trained agents for espionage and secret political action that any country has ever assembled. In Moscow, Prague, and Peiping, and other Communist centers, they are training agents recruited from scores of other countries to go out as missionaries of communism into the troubled areas of the world. Much of the Middle East and Southeast Asia, and particularly black Africa, are high on their target list. They do not neglect this hemisphere, as recent disclosures of Communist plotting in Mexico show us. Their basic purpose is to destroy all existing systems of free and democratic government and disrupt the economic and political organizations on which these are based. Behind their Iron Curtain they ruthlessly suppress all attempts to achieve more freedom—witness Hungary and now Tibet.

The task of destruction is always easier than that of construction. The Communist world, in dealing with the former colonial areas and the newly emerging nations of the world, has appealing slogans to export and vulnerable economic conditions to exploit. The fragile parliamentary systems of new and emerging countries are fertile ground for these agitators.

Also under the heading of subversion we must not overlook the fact that the Communist leaders have sought to advance their cause by local wars by proxy—Korea, Viet-Nam, Malaya are typical examples.

In conclusion I wish to emphasize again the pressing need for a clearer understanding of the real purpose of the Sino-Soviet program. There is no evidence that the present leaders of the Communist world have the slightest idea of abandoning their goal or of changing the general tactics of achieving them.

Those who feel we can buy peace by compromise with Khrushchev are sadly deluded. Each concession we give him merely strengthens his position and prestige and the ability of the Soviet regime to continue its domination of the Russian people, whose friendship we seek.

Our defense lies not in compromise but in understanding and firmness, in a strong and ready deterrent military power, in the marshaling of our economic assets with those of the other free countries of the world to meet their methods of economic penetration, and finally in the unmasking of their subversive techniques.

The overall power of the free world is still vastly superior to that under the control of the leaders of international communism. If they succeed and we fail, it will only be because of our complacency and because they have devoted a far greater share of their power, skill, and resources to our destruction than we have been willing to dedicate to our own preservation.

They are not supermen. Recently they have made a series of blunders which have done what words could not do to help us unmask their true intentions. These very days Communist actions in Iraq and Tibet have particularly aroused Muslims and Buddhists against international communism. The institution of the so-called commune system on the China mainland has shocked the free world, and even the Soviet leaders apologetically refuse to endorse it.

Despite the problems surrounding the Berlin issue, Western Europe is stronger than it ever has been since World War II. Much of free Asia and the Middle East is becoming alerted to the true significance of communism.

The outcome of the struggle against international communism depends in great measure upon the steadfastness of the United States and its willingness to accept sacrifices in meeting its responsibility to help maintain freedom in the world.

The New Seven-Year Plan*

by Herbert S. Levine

[i]

At the recent 21st Soviet Communist party Congress, a set of economic targets was proclaimed, which, if fulfilled, will bring the Soviet

* From The New Leader, Vol. XLII, No. 21 (May 25, 1959), pp. 12-17, and No. 22 (June 1, 1959), pp. 10-13. Reprinted by permission from The New Leader.

Union by 1965 ever closer to its goal of surpassing the United States as the world's leading economic power. Though these targets, officially termed "Control Figures," are merely summary statements which serve as the basis upon which a detailed plan will be constructed, I shall refer to them here as the Seven-Year Plan (SYP).

This plan is unique. It is the first *seven*-year plan. And it comes on the heels of the first peacetime abandonment of an economic plan in Soviet history. On September 26, 1957, it was announced that the sixth Five-Year Plan (FYP), which was to have run from 1956 through 1960, was to be abandoned and replaced by an SYP. The resolution published in *Pravda* stated that the sixth FYP had been scrapped for two reasons. First, the reorganization of industry (which began in July 1957) had changed the entire focus of economic administration from the centralized ministries of the republics and the 105 economic regions, thus necessitating basic changes in the method of planning. Second, discoveries of new resources in the eastern regions called for a reworking of the plan to make use of these resources in production. The three years which were left in the sixth FYP were not enough time in which to accomplish these tasks, and so it was decided to embark on a new long-term plan—a seven-year plan.

One is not wholly convinced that these reasons were sufficient to call for the drastic move of abandoning a five-year plan. It is quite interesting that in the recently released fourth volume of the "Directives of the CPSU and the Soviet Government on Economic Questions," the resolution on the SYP has undergone some significant changes, which shed light on the reasons for abandoning the FYP. An entire paragraph which did not appear in the original resolution as published in *Pravda* has been added. It states that the draft of the sixth FYP submitted by the former Gosplan (State Economic Commission) on April 9, 1957, has a number of fundamental deficiencies. (The December 1956 *plenum* of the Party Central Committee had ordered a reworking of the Control Figures of the sixth FYP. This presumably is the "draft" mentioned here.) For example, the draft does not propose adequate measures for the most rapid eradication of the disproportions in the national economy; it still does not secure the necessary concentration of capital construction; and it does not sufficiently develop measures to employ the natural wealth of the eastern regions.

[As an aside on Kremlinology, I think it is interesting that in this added paragraph the Gosplan, as it existed before Soviet Premier Nikita

Khrushchev reorganized it, is attacked. Later in the resolution, in another added paragraph, it states that the Government has decided to accept Gosplan's suggestion for a draft of an SYP. Here it is the present Gosplan, Khrushchev's Gosplan, which received credit.]

The reasons stated in the inserted paragraph for rejecting the revised draft of the sixth FYP are probably the major reasons for the decision to abandon the plan entirely and shift to the SYP. The sixth FYP was unrealizable—the supply of raw and other materials was not sufficient for the planned output targets ("disproportions"), and the planned outlays on capital investment were too high and were dispersed among too many projects. This, coupled with the necessity of adapting the plan to the new organizational structures resulting from the reorganization of industry, led to the abandonment of the plan. To this can be added the failures of intra-bloc planning. . . .

It was expected, therefore, that when the SYP came out, it would contain planned rates of growth lower than those in the sixth FYP. Some concrete evidence to support this expectation was given by Khrushchev in his address to the 40th Anniversary session of the Supreme Soviet (November 6, 1957). He announced a number of superficially impressive 15-year targets, for such products as steel, oil, electricity and some consumer goods, which Soviet industry was to achieve by 1972. Even though the targets represented doublings and triplings, the average annual rates of growth implied were between one-half and one-third less than those in the sixth FYP.

Thus the machinery for constructing the plan was set in motion, and some indication was available as to the direction the plan would take. The preliminary draft of the plan itself appeared, somewhat behind schedule, in November 1958, when Khrushchev's theses on the "Control Figures for the Economic Development of the USSR, 1959-1965" were published. These were to be discussed by the entire nation and then submitted for ratification to a Party Congress in January 1959.

[Another aside to Kremlinologists: In the past, Party Congresses ratified "Directives" which were then built up into Control Figures by Gosplan, and which in turn were used as the basis for a detailed plan. But here Khrushchev and the 21st Congress are dealing directly with Control Figures. It almost seems they want to give the impression that these targets are more precise, more scientific than the "Directives" of some previous Congresses, with special intention, perhaps, to differentiate them from the ill-fated "Directives on the Sixth FYP" of the 20th Party Congress.]

Before going on to the plan itself, we might ask—what is a Soviet economic plan? First of all, it is more than just an economic plan. It describes in general terms what lies ahead in the planned period for the Russian people in matters concerned not only with the output of economic goods, but also education, science, culture, international developments and the Communist party. Secondly, it is more than just a technical document; it is also a sociological instrument used to rally the people behind the leadership and aims of the state. The nationwide "discussion" of the coming plan is a process of reinvigoration and dedication. The "discussion" both before and at the 21st Congress was studded with pledges to fulfill and overfulfill the plan.

It is noteworthy that this "discussion" was also full of laudatory tributes to Comrade Khrushchev, reminiscent of days supposedly gone by. There are, to be sure, certain differences from the past. In at least two notable instances, well-known economists took issue directly and indirectly with Khrushchev on certain points (showing that though the "thaw" may have ended in other fields, it still remains in economics). Yet Khrushchev dominated the scene—the original Control Figures came out under his name, he gave the opening speech at the Congress and in this speech covered all the major economic, political, social and ideological questions. There were no signs of collective leadership at the 21st Party Congress. Khrushchev stood alone. Therein lies one of the meanings of the SYP.

The Control Figures on the SYP comprise a document which in length ran to about nine regular-size newspaper pages. The first chapter covers some results of economic and cultural developments in Russia since 1917. The second chapter, the key chapter, covers the principal economic targets for the years of the SYP, 1959-1965. Included are: industry (heavy and light), agriculture, transportation, communications and capital investment. The third chapter discusses the location of economic activity. The fourth—national income and standard of living; the fifth—education, science and culture; the sixth—international significance of the SYP; and the seventh—the role and task of the Communist party.

This discussion will cover only the main economic elements of the plan, the chances of its fulfillment and its meaning for us.

Industry The aggregate gross industrial output is to grow at an average rate of 8.6 per cent per year, which means about 80 per cent in seven years and 100 per cent in about eight and a half years. The principle of the priority of heavy industry over light industry is repeatedly reaffirmed and manifests itself in the fact that the industrial output of producer goods is to grow at a higher rate than that of consumer goods.

As will be clear from the following short descriptions of the plans for individual industries, there is a consistent drive to conserve resources, to gain more output through technological change, through the extended use of cost-saving products and processes. This principle is also to be seen in the non-industrial sections of the plan.

Metals: The output of metals is to grow at rates below those achieved in the past, but still at a quite high rate. For example, at the planned rate, the output of steel will double in about 10 years. Aluminum will be stressed—its output is to triple by 1965 and its use in machines, vehicles, construction and consumer goods will be increased.

Fuels: The output of fuel energy will rise 70 per cent by 1965. But the striking thing is the drastic shift away from coal. In 1965, oil and gas will account for 51 per cent of fuel energy produced, as against the present 31 per cent. Great cost savings in production, transportation and use are envisaged—enough, it is claimed, to build all the power stations contemplated in the SYP.

Electricity: The output of electric power will more than double. The big news, however, is the announced priority for construction of thermal-power stations instead of hydro-power stations. This will be done to get the new capacity into operation faster.

Chemicals: Chemicals are one of the high-priority items—a tripling in output is planned. Synthetics and fertilizers are to be stressed. Expansion will be based on raw materials from the expanding oil and gas industry.

Machinery: Output is to double and more use is to be made of aluminum and plastics. There is a call for more specialization and subcontracting in the supply of parts (perennial problems) and more automation.

Consumer Goods: The output of fabrics and clothing is to increase about 50 per cent, processed foods, 70 per cent and household appliances, 100 per cent.

Soviet planners may have had a change of heart after preparing the 15-year targets, or there may exist a tendency to underestimate production possibilities when planning for periods as long as 15 years (as was the case with Stalin's postwar 15-year plan), for the average annual rates of industrial growth in the SYP are consistently above those implied in the 15-year targets. At the same time, they are, as expected, below those planned in the sixth FYP. The figures in the table below will help illustrate the comparative tempos of these plans. The last column of the table shows how much of the 15-year targets will be achieved by 1965. These figures, consistently above 50 per cent, demonstrate the effect of the faster pace envisaged in the SYP than in the 15-Year Plan. They also result from the high rates of growth achieved in 1958.

Comparison of SYP with Other Plans

PRODUCTS	APPROXIMATE[1] PERCENTAGES OF AVERAGE ANNUAL RATES OF GROWTH				APPROXIMATE PERCENTAGES OF 1972 GOALS TO BE ACHIEVED BY 1965
	SIXTH FYP (1956-60)		15-YEAR TARGETS (1958-72)	SYP (1959-65)	
	PLANNED	ACHIEVED (1956-58)			
Iron Ore	9.7	7.3	8.2	8.3	56
Steel	8.6	6.6	5.3	7.1	80
Coal	8.7	8.2	2.8	2.9	87
Oil	13.8	10.9	9.3	11.0	63
Electric Power	13.5	11.0	9.8	11.8	60
Cement	19.6	14.0	8.6	12.9	78
Woolen Fabrics	7.6	6.3	5.2	7.4	83
Leather Footwear	8.8	9.1	4.9	5.4	79
Sugar (granulated)	13.8	16.4	5.1	8.6	100

[1] These figures are approximations, even though presented to one decimal place. They are often mid-points of ranges.

Several other interesting points are illustrated in this table: (1) the sixth FYP was, in general, not being fulfilled; (2) the rate of growth of iron ore falls least of all from the sixth FYP to the 15-Year Plan, illustrating that the need to overcome the presumably sharp deficit in this vital raw material was recognized in the 15-Year Plan; (3) the shift away from coal to oil began in the 15-Year Plan; (4) the three consumer goods included are at the upper end of the figures on the percentages of 1972 goals to be achieved by 1965. This may just be fortuitous, or it may mean there was a slight change in attitude between November 1957 and November 1958 toward the heavy industry-light industry relationship, in favor of the latter. The recent appointment of Alexei N. Kosygin as chairman of Gosplan at least does not discourage one from thinking along these lines.

Agriculture   The agricultural section of the SYP clearly bears Khrushchev's stamp. Agriculture is the field he seems to know best and in which he has shown a great deal of interest. He has not been afraid to make changes, where he thought they were needed. In the last five years, truly revolutionary moves have been made: the virgin lands program, the corn campaign, the agricultural price reform, the abolition of the machine-tractor stations and the sale of the machinery to the farms themselves. So far these reforms have borne fruit—agricultural indicators have been on the way up since 1953. (These indicators are affected by the end years chosen; 1953 was a bad crop year and 1958 was a good one, but even when averages for 1949-53 are compared with averages of 1954-58, the latter show significant increases.)

Furthermore, Khrushchev appears to have a much more realistic attitude toward past accomplishments and future possibilities. For example, he has exposed and abandoned the bogus grain output statistic called the "biological yield" ("You can't bake bread with the 'biological yield'! Bread is made from the grain that reaches the barns."). And the planned average annual rates of growth of the major agricultural commodities in the SYP are roughly 50 per cent lower than those in the sixth FYP and in fact are, with certain exceptions, quite close to the average rates achieved since 1953.

The SYP calls for an average annual rate of growth of about 8 per cent in the aggregate gross volume of agricultural products. This is just what was achieved in the last five years. Yet it is interesting to note that in the 1954-58 period, crops were above this average, while animal products were on the whole below it, and that in the SYP the situation is more or less the reverse. This reflects the fact that in the past five years much of the increase in the output of crops resulted from a vast increase in the cultivated area, a situation that will not recur in the SYP. Thus in the SYP, the greater burden of the aggregate increase in agricultural products will be borne by animal products.

In the case of both crops and animal products, much is expected from increased output per unit of input. The 1965 grain target of almost 180 million tons (the 1960 target of the sixth FYP), is predicated on a

30-40 per cent increase in grain yields, to be achieved through improved scheduling of operations, better crop rotation, the sowing of selected seed and the use of more fertilizer. Also, output per worker is to be raised. In animal husbandry the main emphasis is on increased labor productivity. There is no lack of proposed measures. They range from significant increases in mechanization, and further growth in the fodder base, which has already increased greatly since 1953, primarily due to Khrushchev's corn campaign, to further decentralization in planning and improvement in incentives.

In recent years there has been a relative growth in state farms at the expense of collective farms (state farms are like state-owned factories in the countryside, whereas collective farms are, in form, collectively owned and operated by the peasants who work them). It is not clear whether this trend will continue in the SYP, but a number of arguments can be raised to support the contention that it will. The state farm is ideologically more acceptable. It produces more cheaply (especially now that higher prices are being paid the collectives), and Khrushchev has stated that in the future the state will buy only from the least expensive sources. Also, the practice, which has just begun, of establishing large state farms on the outskirts of big cities to supply the cities with vegetables and potatoes ("truck farms") will certainly continue in the SYP.

Capital Investment   If we recall that overextension of capital investment was one of the major reasons for abandoning the sixth FYP, it is not surprising to find that the rate of growth of state-fixed investment in the SYP is significantly below that planned in the sixth FYP. The statistics here are a bit difficult to deal with; but it can reasonably be inferred that whereas the average rate of growth of state-fixed investment in the sixth FYP was about 11 per cent per year, it is only 6-7 per cent in the SYP. These calculations imply that state-fixed investment in 1965 will be 50-60 per cent greater than it was in 1958. It should be kept in mind, however, that what is planned by the state does not cover all the fixed investment in the Soviet economy. In addition, there is unplanned and decentralized fixed investment, and fixed investment by collective farms. The latter is to increase sharply during the SYP.

The need to concentrate resources on projects already begun is stressed repeatedly. One of the problems in the past was that though aggregate investment plans may have been fulfilled or almost fulfilled, the plans for the actual utilization of new capacity were not. There is also, in the SYP, heavy emphasis on renewal and modernization of existing plants in preference to the construction of new ones. The reason given for these policies is that the increase in industrial output will be speeded up.

The distribution of investment is about the same as in the previous period, with heavy industry getting about 40 per cent, light and food industry about 5 per cent, and agriculture (including investment by collective farms) a little more than 20 per cent.

Finally, the SYP envisages significant increases in the output of building materials; for example, cement production is to increase almost two and one-half times. And it calls for modernization of techniques within the construction industry itself: prefabrication, use of precast, reinforced concrete, and so forth.

Location of Industry There is a great deal of talk in the SYP and in Khrushchev's speeches about the industrial development of the eastern regions: 40 per cent of total state investment will go to these areas; a new metallurgical center, which in 1965 will produce 7.5 million tons of pig iron, will be erected in Siberia; and by 1965 over 70 per cent of the aluminum produced in the Soviet Union will be produced in the east. The east's share in the output of electric power, coal, lumber and cement will also increase. Yet some indicators will show little change. For example, the share of the east in the total output of ferrous metals will be almost the same in 1965 as it was in 1958.

Transportation Railroad freight turnover is to increase only about 40 per cent while industrial output is to increase 80 per cent. Since most of the freight in the Soviet Union is carried by rail, how is it possible for the disparity between freight turnover and output to be so large? There are perhaps two possible explanations: (1) the long struggle to cut the length of hauls will be helped by the recent reorganization of industry, with its pressures to use local resources, and by the aforementioned development of industry in the east, which will bring producers closer to users; (2) the shift in the fuel balance from coal to oil and gas will result in tremendous savings in railroad transportation.

The SYP envisages a sharp increase in the use of diesel and electric locomotives: In 1965 they will haul 85 per cent of the total freight, compared with about 25 per cent in 1958.

Labor There are some new developments in the field of wages and hours. Wages of the lowest paid are to rise substantially, thus bringing them much closer to the average wage. (Interestingly enough, there is in Khrushchev's speech a strong defense of wage inequality and an attack on the egalitarians.) The working day will be reduced to seven hours by 1960. In 1962, it is planned to introduce a 40-hour week, and by 1966-68 a 35-hour week.

The size of the labor force (not including collective farmers) is to increase by 12 million and reach 66.5 million in 1965. This is surprisingly large since the period of the SYP encompasses the years when those who were not born during and immediately after the War will not be entering the labor force. According to some Western specialists, during the nine years, 1957-1965, the population in the prime working age group (males 15-59, females 15-54) is expected to show an absolute increase only about 60 per cent as large as that shown in the six years, 1950-56. Yet the absolute increase in the labor force planned for 1959-65 is to be greater than the absolute increase in the labor force achieved in 1950-56. How is this to be accomplished? If the same rate of absorption of the prime working-age-group increase into the labor force were applied in the SYP as took place in 1950-56, the Russians would fall about 10 million short of the 66.5 million target. These 10 million workers will come mainly from three sources: agriculture, women and teenagers.

In 1956 the non-agricultural labor force in the USSR was about the same as that in the United States, but its agricultural labor force was seven times as great. Much emphasis is being put, in the SYP, on increasing agricultural labor productivity, so as to free workers for work in the cities. Comparing the planned increase in agricultural output with that of agricultural labor productivity, it can be said that in rough order of magnitude the Russians are hoping to release about 4 million agricultural workers.

The substitution of state farms for collective farms would also lead to an increase in labor productivity and thus the possibility of the release of workers to the cities. [It would also, however, have a purely statistical effect, in that members of state farms are included in the labor force ("workers and employees") while members of collectives are not.]

In his speech to the 21st Congress, Khrushchev disclosed the aim of creating conditions "to draw fresh millions of women into the active building of Communism. . . . By extending the network of boarding schools, kindergartens, nurseries, public catering establishments and public services we are creating these conditions for all women." Sprinkled throughout the speeches and discussions of the SYP are references to the need to ease the housewife's work, in order to free her for "more productive" labor. The proposed increases in wages of the lowest paid will also have the effect of attracting more women into the labor force.

The education reform will release many young people for production work—estimates range up to four million for the entire SYP period. It is not clear, however, how and to what extent they will be included in the labor force.

Consumption   The Soviet definitions of national income and consumption (basically material goods only) are to increase about 65 and 63 per cent respectively. The major part of consumption is accounted for by retail trade. This is to increase by 62 per cent whereas in the previous seven years, retail trade more than doubled. Thus the SYP envisages a slackening in the rate of increase of retail trade, but still a highly respectable average rate of growth of about 7 per cent per year (implying a doubling in 10 years).

There are some changes contemplated in the composition of retail trade as the Soviet standard of living rises. The relative importance of non-food items is to be increased slightly, and within the food category, animal products, vegetables and fruits are to increase and bread products decrease. Sugar sales have been increasing rapidly and the 1972 target has been moved down to 1965. (The influence of American methods is to be seen in Khrushchev's remark: "Consumer goods must be of good quality, attractive and they must be neatly packaged." . . .

In order to lighten the housewife's work, it is planned to increase the supply of household appliances. Sales of washing machines are to be about nine times greater in the coming seven years, and sales of refrigerators almost six times greater.

One of the worst shortages plaguing the Russian consumer is the shortage of housing. In his November 1957 speech, Khrushchev announced a plan to end the shortage in 10-12 years. And now in the SYP, 15 million apartments are to be built in urban areas (more than twice what was built in the previous seven years) and seven million dwellings in rural areas.

Stage of Development In his speech to the Congress, Khrushchev spent a fair amount of time on ideology and on the "stage of development" in which he claimed the Soviet Union now finds itself. This is the period of the gradual transition from Socialism to Communism, and he stated that they were now entering the stage of building the material base of Communism. He spoke of the period of full Communism as being in the "not too distant future"—a period "when we shall have provided an abundance of everything needed to satisfy the requirements of all our people." It is interesting that he was careful later to define these requirements—food, housing and clothing "commensurate with the normal needs of a cultured person." One thinks of how the general "normal needs of a cultured person" have changed since 1848 and how they will change in the future; and one wonders whether this stage of full Communism will, for a good many years if not always, be in the "not too distant future."

In one of the most unusual articles in the entire discussion of the SYP, a prominent Soviet economist, Academician Vasili S. Nemchinov, acts the part of national spoil-sport. The general attitude, stirred vigorously by the ever-ebullient Khrushchev, is one of euphoria. Nemchinov attempts to puncture this rosy bubble with some sobering statistics. By using per capita output data, he shows that the Soviet Union is far down the list in comparison with Western nations in the production of such key industrial goods as steel and energy; he points out that even in 1965 the Soviet Union will be behind the current levels of per capita output in the leading Western nations.

Nemchinov notes that the housing shortage is colossal and that since more than half of the yearly housing construction will be absorbed by the yearly growth in population, the eradication of the problem will be a long way off even at the end of the SYP. Finally, he claims that Russian passenger-car production is far too low. If the people are to have more leisure, they should have cars in which to travel. Mobility is an important element of a high standard of living. The essence of his entire argument is that the glorious period of full Communism is indeed in the *very* distant future. (To complete his iconoclasm, he does not once laud or even mention Khrushchev.)

[II]

Can the Russians fulfill their new Seven-Year Plan (SYP)? They themselves believe this Plan has a great deal of slack. For the first time they seem to be talking in terms of minimum plans instead of maximum ones. Here is an extremely illuminating passage from Soviet Premier Nikita Khrushchev's speech to the 21st Congress of the Soviet Communist party:

"The SYP is being drawn up in such a way that it can be carried out without overstrain. Why has this been done? Because, if we have a very strained plan, there is always the chance that some of its targets may not be reached, that some branches of the economy may not get all they require in the way of raw materials, supplies and equipment. This may cause interruptions in the work and, consequently, under-capacity operation of plants and factories, idle working time and all attendant consequences. This is what economists call disproportions. The SYP is being drawn up in such a way as to rule this out. Over-fulfillment of the Plan will give us a chance to create additional reserves and obtain additional accumulations."

It is interesting to note that Academician Stanislav G. Strumilin, the "dean" of Soviet economists, attacked the Plan for being too slack: Much more can be accomplished in the next seven years, he said, and the Plan should provide for it.

The Russians also claim that more care was taken in the preparation of this Plan than in the past. I. I. Kuzmin, the former director of Gosplan (State Planning Commission), stated that many well known scientists and specialists took part in working out the Plan. Professor A. Efimov, director of Gosplan's Economic Research Institute, wrote that more than 200 research institutes worked on the single problem of specialization and subcontracting; never before in the history of the Soviet Union was this done, he said. It is clear, therefore, that at least the Russians consider this to be a fairly slack, well constructed, consistent plan and confidently expect it to be not only fulfilled but over-fulfilled.

Over-fulfillment of the yearly industrial plans has been the rule since 1950. In the past two years, the plans have been over-fulfilled by 2.7 per cent and 2.2 per cent respectively. This compares with an average over-fulfillment since 1950 of about 2 per cent. If this practice were carried over into the SYP, the average annual rate of industrial growth would be more than 10.5 per cent instead of the planned 8.6 per cent. Soviet economic statistics are often difficult to deal with and the more aggregative the statistics (e.g., gross output) the more difficult the problem. But most specialists agree that Russian statistics have improved since 1950.

Two independent calculations by Westerners of the rate of industrial growth between 1950 and 1956 give average annual rates of about 10 per cent (official Soviet statistics give an average rate of about 12.5 per cent for 1950-56 and a rate of 10 per cent for 1957 and 1958). In comparison with the performance achieved since 1950, the planned average rate of 8.6 per cent does not appear to be out of line.

Another way of looking at the possibilities of fulfilling the industrial plan is to look at the figures for increase in the industrial labor force (20 per cent) and increase in output per industrial worker (50 per cent). Together, they are responsible for the increase in industrial output (80 per cent).

If one projects past relationships, one gets a "non-agricultural" labor force figure for 1965 roughly 10 million less than the plan calls for. The question is—can this deficit be made up by new recruits from the ranks of agricultural workers, women and juveniles?

There has been a tendency among Western specialists to argue that even though the ratio of agricultural labor to industrial labor in the Soviet Union is much greater than in the West, Soviet agricultural productivity is so low and the needs so high that the flow of workers to the cities has probably stopped. However, in the last few years Khrushchev has made a great many changes in the organizational structure of agriculture, and these, coupled with the stress in the SYP on increased labor productivity through increased and especially better-balanced mechanization, may give new impetus to the flow of labor from country to city. Whether it will reach the approximately 4 million apparently planned for is hard to say.

It is also hard to say how many women can be attracted into the labor force. The ratio of women in the labor force to women in the prime working age group has risen from about 20 per cent in 1940 to about 30 per cent in 1950 and 35 per cent in 1956. If this were to rise to 40 per cent by 1965, then an additional 3 million women would be added to the labor force. Furthermore, the estimated additions to the labor force resulting from the school reform range around 4 million. (How useful these teen-agers will be is another question.)

Thus in a very rough and incomplete way, it can be seen that it will be difficult, but not completely impossible, for the labor force as a whole to increase as planned and therefore for the industrial labor force to increase the planned 20 per cent. The biggest problem is whether the flow from the countryside will be as heavy as contemplated. In the Fifth

Five-Year Plan (FYP), even though the industrial output plan was over-fulfilled, the industrial labor productivity plan was under-fulfilled. The over-fulfillment of the output plan was achieved by means of increasing the labor force 10 per cent more than planned.

This safety factor of over-plan increase in the labor force probably does not exist in the SYP, and therefore the critical question is whether industrial output per worker can be raised the 50 per cent (or 6 per cent per year) envisaged in the SYP. The average rate of 6 per cent is below what was achieved in the Fifth FYP (7.6 per cent) and is also slightly below what has been achieved in the last three years. On the other hand, it may be argued that if the rate of capital investment growth is really to diminish then the increase in labor productivity should also diminish. This may be true, but it need not be.

To begin with, there is to be a concentration of resources on projects already begun. Thus the ratio of the introduction of new capacity to total investment will increase. But perhaps even more important, the increase in output per worker is related not only to the increase in capital per worker, but also to a residual factor usually called technology. This includes, in addition to changes in technology itself, changes in the skill, intensity and stability of labor, management and organizational efficiency, and other elements. It has been shown by Western economists that this "residual factor" has been of predominant importance in the increase of output per worker in the West. And it is the elements of this factor which are being stressed in the SYP. One is impressed by the new, more rational approach the Russians are now taking toward prices, investment decisions and other economic questions. They may, indeed, reap significant returns from increases in the "residual factor."

As for the agricultural plan, many Western analysts feel there is less likelihood of fulfilling these targets than of fulfilling the industrial targets. Yet here, too, one should be careful before pronouncing failure in advance. Khrushchev has claimed that the grain targets could be achieved if yields per acre were to be raised 30-40 per cent. Up to 1953, the Soviet record of raising yields was not too impressive: The average yield in 1949-53 was only 10 per cent greater than in 1910-14! But since 1953, progress has been made. The average grain yield in 1954-58, according to official Soviet data, was about 20 per cent greater than in 1949-53.

At least two major ways of raising yields, discussed by Khrushchev, have bright prospects for success in the period of the SYP. One is the use of fertilizer and pesticides—the supply of fertilizer to the farms is to triple. The other is the scheduling of work on the farms. With the farms owning their own machinery and with more decentralization in planning, this will most likely show much improvement. Beside grain, the other major part of the agricultural plan concerns animal husbandry. The planned average annual rates of growth are not too different from those achieved since 1953, except for meat, and here much is expected from increased technology, mechanization, incentives and fodder production.

All in all, perhaps the best answer to the question—can the SYP be fulfilled?—is to say that it would be imprudent to bet against it.

What, then, can be said of the meaning of the SYP for us? Khrushchev sees the Soviet Union in an economic race with the capitalist world, specifically the United States. He stresses the need for speed—he builds thermal stations instead of hydro-power stations, he concentrates capital investment on projects already begun and he renovates and modernizes existing plants instead of constructing new ones. His time horizon is a short one. He is interested in the outcome of this "race" in the next 7 to 15 years, not in the distant future. To get some idea of how close he is to his objective, it will be necessary to look, if only briefly and impressionistically, at some comparative statistics.

Some of the figures on heavy industrial products do not present too reassuring a picture for us. True, if per capita figures are cited, the Soviet Union does not come out too well. But it is questionable whether, when dealing with heavy industry, it is the per capita figures which are the most pertinent. For purposes of national power, propaganda and military capability, figures for the state as an entity are perhaps more important. By 1965, the Soviet Union will be producing 85-90 per cent of the U.S. 1957 output of steel, about 70 per cent of U.S. 1957 output of electric power and fuel energy, and about 150 per cent of U.S. 1957 cement. In addition, according to Western experts, Russian machine tool production already matched ours in 1956 and by 1965 they plan to double their present levels.

In most consumer goods, the U.S. lead will remain substantial, although the well-publicized Russian campaign to overtake the U.S. in per capita output of milk, butter and meat will in part be successful. That is, by 1965 the Russians will probably surpass us in per capita output of milk and butter, but only approach us in per capita output of meat.

Inter-country comparisons of aggregate industrial output are treacherous, but perhaps some very rough idea about the comparative levels of aggregate industrial output can be derived from the accompanying table. Most Western specialists estimate that Soviet industrial output is currently 40-50 per cent of ours. Let us assume it is 45 per cent. Then for the various annual rates of growth listed (these are the rates most expected), the intersecting box gives the number of years it will take Soviet industry to catch up to ours. For example, if Soviet industry grows at an average annual rate of 9 per cent and that of the U.S. at 3 per cent (a very likely situation), then Soviet industrial output will equal ours in 14 years.

		U.S. RATES OF INDUSTRIAL GROWTH		
		2%	3%	4%
	7%	17 yrs.	21 yrs.	28 yrs.
USSR RATES	8%	14 "	17 "	21 "
OF INDUSTRIAL	9%	12 "	14 "	17 "
GROWTH	10%	11 "	12 "	14 "

Again the caveat: These figures are only impressionistic. However, the impression they give is somewhat startling. A continuation of present and planned Russian rates of growth (9-10 per cent) and a continuation of present U.S. rates of growth (3-4 per cent), will result in the Russians catching up to us in industrial output in the next 10-20 years.

Russian success in catching up is a result of both the natural advantages accruing to the latecomer in the industrialization process (an instructive example is provided by the relative positions of Germany and the U.S. in the 19th century) and Soviet centralized economic institutions. The plan as a channel for commands to production units is, on the whole, a better instrument for growth than is the market-price and profit-motive system. In the Soviet system, those giving the commands are the central leaders and growth is one of their prime objectives. And those receiving the commands, the managers of Soviet firms, never need ask whether they will be able to sell all their output. Virtually their sole objective is to fulfill the established targets. This factor, a guaranteed market, provides obvious advantages for growth through continuously expanding, large-scale production and planned advances in technology.

In a profit system, commands are given both by the people and the government, and manifest themselves in the form of profit opportunities to which managers of firms respond. Those who give the commands are not primarily concerned with growth, but with current wants. Thus the pattern of commands may better serve those wants, but will not necessarily ensure the highest level of growth. In addition, in a mature economy without a great reserve of unemployed resources, a swell of commands (demand) leads to high profit opportunities and through them to inflationary pressures. The decentralized methods of coping with inflation act to reduce this demand, thus depressing the level of output and the rate of growth.

Economists, drawing on historical examples, speak of diminishing rates of growth. The rate of growth in the Soviet Union has been diminishing, but this does not necessarily mean it will diminish, in the near future, to rates comparable to our own. Diminishing rates of growth result perhaps as much from demand factors as from production factors. And in the Soviet system, the demand factors and the mechanism for transmitting these demands are essentially different from ours.

Thus we find ourselves at a disadvantage in the production "race." And to this observer, at least, our chances of winning this "race," short of a drastic reorganization in our institutions, are dim. The question, however, is how much do we want to win this "race." Is a race in which the goal appears almost to be production for production's sake worth our becoming a mobilized state (for it might be argued that this is the only way we will win it)? This is not to say that there is nothing we should do to better our institutions and to improve our rate of economic growth. There is much to do, both in increasing our output and in changing its composition, but it should be done to satisfy our needs as we ourselves define them, not merely to match the Russians.

However, the fact that the Russians are catching up will doubtless present a serious challenge to our foreign policy aims. Both successful Soviet economic development and increased Soviet economic aid will make adherence to Communist principles more attractive to underdeveloped nations. To combat this (and also, of course, on its own humanitarian merits), we will need a substantial expansion in our foreign aid, perhaps in concert with other nations of the free world, thus helping the underdeveloped nations through the critical period of initial capital formation; and we will need a more sympathetic understanding of the economic, political and social problems involved in the process of their industrialization.

We will also need something else—both for our foreign policy and for ourselves at home. Russia's catching up in the economic sphere will administer greater shocks to the American people than those administered by the launching of the Russian earth satellite. It is self-defeating to consider ourselves superior in every aspect of life, for we then become dismayed and unsure of ourselves as the Russians begin to match our accomplishments. It is necessary for us to determine what is important and what is not. The current rethinking and analysis of our values and institutions should be pursued with vigor. We should clearly define, both for ourselves and for the world, what we believe in and what our aspirations are. And it should be done soon. This ought to be the meaning for us of the new Soviet Seven-Year Plan.

FOR FURTHER READING:

Gabriel A. Almond, *The Appeals of Communism* (Princeton: Princeton University Press, 1954).

Joseph S. Berliner, *Soviet Economic Aid: The New Aid and Trade Policy in Underdeveloped Countries* (New York: Frederick A. Praeger, 1958).

Raymond Dennett and Joseph E. Johnson (eds.), *Negotiating with the Russians* (Boston: World Peace Foundation, 1951).

Raymond L. Garthoff, *Soviet Strategy in the Nuclear Age* (New York: Frederick A. Praeger, 1958).

C. Grove Haines, *The Threat of Soviet Imperialism* (Baltimore: The Johns Hopkins Press, 1954).

Oleg Hoeffding, "Substance and Shadow in the Soviet Seven Year Plan," *Foreign Affairs*, Vol. XXXVII, No. 3 (April, 1959), pp. 394-406.

Nikita S. Khrushchev, "On Peaceful Coexistence," *Foreign Affairs*, Vol. XXXVIII, No. 1 (October, 1959), pp. 1-18.

Evron M. Kirkpatrick (ed.), *Year of Crisis: Communist Propaganda Activities in 1956* (New York: The Macmillan Company, 1957).

Alexander G. Korol, *Soviet Education for Science and Technology* (New York. The Technology Press of Massachusetts Institute of Technology and John Wiley and Sons, 1957).

Nathan C. Leites, *A Study of Bolshevism* (Glencoe: The Free Press, 1953).

Walter Lippmann, *The Communist World and Ours* (Boston: Little, Brown and Company, 1959).

Gerhart Niemeyer with the assistance of John S. Reshetar, Jr., *An Inquiry into Soviet Mentality* (New York: Frederick A. Praeger, 1956).

Henry L. Roberts, *Russia and America: Dangers and Prospects* (New York: Harper and Brothers, 1956).

Chapter VII

THE AMERICAN RESPONSE

At the heart of the public debate on foreign policy is the question of the most appropriate American response to the challenge of Soviet communism—what general posture should the United States adopt to counter Soviet pressures? Positions on specific foreign policy issues flow from the answer given to this basic question. In the years immediately after the Second World War this topic was broadly debated; the entire range of possible alternatives was explored. America was forced in these years to abandon its hopes of relying on the United Nations collective security machinery to insure peace and stability, and to reëxamine its entire outlook toward world affairs. Since 1947, however, the range of debate has been considerably narrowed. Consensus has been reached on the necessity of containing Soviet expansionism through economic assistance, collective defense agreements or alliances, and when necessary military force. Thus a number of alternatives, notably those relying on moral suasion to protect American interests, have been ruled out. At the same time we have also ruled out alternatives at the other end of the continuum by repeatedly refusing to use military force to attempt to roll back the Iron Curtain and reduce the territory under Soviet control. But even within these limits, several alternatives remain: these are the subject of the present public debate.

The best statement of the rationale for present United States policy remains George F. Kennan's now classic article, "The Sources of Soviet Conduct," reproduced as the first selection in this chapter. Published in 1947, when Mr. Kennan was head of the Department of State's Policy

Planning Staff, under the pseudonym "X," it provided the intellectual
base for the containment policy which was put into effect then and
which continues to be the keystone of United States foreign policy. In
the article Mr. Kennan gives his (and the official) interpretation of the
Soviet threat. He shows how Russian history and national character have
been combined with communist ideology to produce its peculiar nature,
and he indicates clearly the gap between Soviet patterns of thought and
our own. On the basis of his analysis he concludes that the only way
to stop Soviet expansionism is by "the adroit and vigilant application
of counter-force at a series of constantly shifting geographical and political points, corresponding to the shifts and manoeuvers of Soviet policy. . . ." Since 1947 the United States has attempted to apply this
prescription.

The question inevitably arises of whether this analysis remains valid.
Viewing it himself over a decade later, Mr. Kennan found little need
for revision.* He recognized that the U.S.S.R.'s economy had recovered
from the war and had grown much more rapidly than he had anticipated, and he also saw new political difficulties in Mr. Khrushchev's
relationship with his associates at the highest level of government and
in the regime's relationship with its subjects, but he appeared content
with the basic elements of his analysis and concluded that the gap between Soviet thinking and our own had not been bridged.

That Mr. Kennan's analysis continues to be the basis for official policy
can be seen in the second selection, a major policy statement by the late
John Foster Dulles, Secretary of State for over six years in the Eisenhower Administration and long an active participant in foreign policy.
Mr. Dulles, working from the premises elaborated in the "X" article,
shows how the containment policy had been carried out. He briefly
describes the United States major economic assistance programs and
the network of alliances resulting from our collective defense agreements (see Map I, pp. 292-293). To the commitments he lists should
be added the executive agreements of March, 1959 with Turkey, Iran,
and Pakistan which brought the United States into a still closer association with the Baghdad Pact, or the Central Treaty Organization as
it came to be called after the withdrawal of Iraq.† He also describes the

---

* See his *Russia, the Atom and the West* (New York: Harper and Brothers,
1958).

† The Baghdad Pact, an alliance including Iran, Iraq, Pakistan, Turkey, and the
United Kingdom, was signed in 1955. Although the United States was instrumental
in its formation, and has always been closely associated with the work of the Pact's

role that our own economic and defense policies play in foreign affairs. Although the specific focus of various United States policies has changed since the adoption of Mr. Kennan's prescription, shifting from reconstruction to economic development and from rapid military build-up designed to meet a presumed immediate threat of all-out war to preparations for the "long haul," the basic theme has remained constant. This is true despite the 1952 change in administration. Both major political parties accept Mr. Kennan's premises; the differences between them are in matters of application.

In a sense, both Mr. Kennan and Mr. Dulles were optimistic in their expectations. In the "X" article some hope for different and less menacing Soviet policies was held out if the United States could contain the U.S.S.R. for a period of from ten to fifteen years. That period has almost elapsed, the United States has steadfastly and successfully—except in the case of China—pursued the containment policy, but the challenge of Soviet communism remains unabated. Mr. Stalin passed, but his death did not bring the expected crisis in Soviet government; it brought a new, more skillful and subtle leader, Nikita S. Khrushchev. Mr. Dulles voiced confidence in the world-wide triumph of Christian and democratic values even though the record of events since the Second World War reveals few indications of the immediacy of this victory. But the policies these men advocate do not necessarily depend on their optimistic assumptions; they can be defended without them.

Taken together the first two selections provide a basic exposition of present United States policy—Mr. Kennan presents the intellectual rationale and Mr. Dulles, the concrete applications of these premises. The last two selections are critiques of the official position. Using almost the same premises concerning the nature of the Soviet threat, they present alternative conclusions and policy proposals. A wider range of differences could be found if one were willing to accept radically different premises. In the third selection Hans J. Morgenthau analyzes the United States network of alliances. He first creates a theoretical framework for the consideration of alliances and then uses this to examine those of the Western world and the communist bloc. He indicates that alliances bring costs as well as gains and points out some of the dilemmas inherent in present United States policy.

---

principal committees, it never actually joined the alliance. After the overthrow of the Iraqi monarchy in July 1958, that country's participation ceased, and it formally announced its withdrawal on March 24, 1959.

The final selection, by Senator John F. Kennedy, a member of the powerful Senate Committee on Foreign Relations and one often mentioned for higher office, provides a broader review including most aspects of foreign affairs. He is critical of both the mode and substance of present United States policy. Broadly speaking, Mr. Kennedy advocates greater economic efforts to exploit centrifugal forces in the Soviet bloc, more flexibility concerning European and Far Eastern problems, greater sympathy for colonial peoples and states, and increased programs of economic assistance. These selections at least introduce the public debate on the appropriate American response to the challenge of Soviet communism.

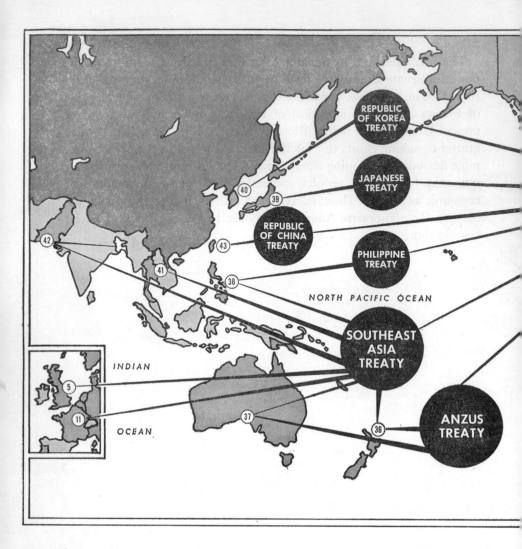

I. The Basic Security Treaties of the United States

NORTH ATLANTIC TREATY (15 NATIONS)

A treaty signed April 4, 1949, by which "the parties agree that an armed attack against one or more of them in Europe or North America shall be considered an attack against them all; and . . . each of them . . . will assist the . . . attacked by taking forthwith, individually and in concert with the other Parties, such action as it deems necessary including the use of armed force . . ."

1 United States	7 Denmark	13 Greece
2 Canada	8 Belgium	14 Turkey
3 Iceland	9 Luxemburg	15 Federal Repub-
4 Norway	10 Portugal	lic of Germany
5 United Kingdom	11 France	
6 Netherlands	12 Italy	

RIO TREATY (21 NATIONS)

A treaty signed September 2, 1947, which provides that an armed attack against any American State "shall be considered as an attack against all the American States and . . . each one . . . undertakes to assist in meeting the attack . . ."

1 United States	22 El Salvador	29 Peru
16 Mexico	23 Nicaragua	30 Brazil
17 Cuba	24 Costa Rica	31 Bolivia
18 Haiti	25 Panama	32 Paraguay
19 Dominican Republic	26 Colombia	33 Chile
20 Honduras	27 Venezuela	34 Argentina
21 Guatemala	28 Ecuador	35 Uruguay

ANZUS (Australia—New Zealand—United States) TREATY (3 NATIONS)

A treaty signed September 1, 1951, whereby each of the parties "recognizes that an armed attack in the Pacific Area on any of the Parties would be dangerous to its own peace and safety and declares that it would act to meet the common danger in accordance with its constitutional processes."

1 United States	36 New Zealand	37 Australia

PHILIPPINE TREATY (BILATERAL)

A treaty signed August 30, 1951, by which the parties recognize "that an armed attack in the Pacific Area on either of the Parties would be dangerous to its own peace and safety and each party agrees that it will act "to meet the common dangers in accordance with its constitutional processes."

1 United States	38 Philippines

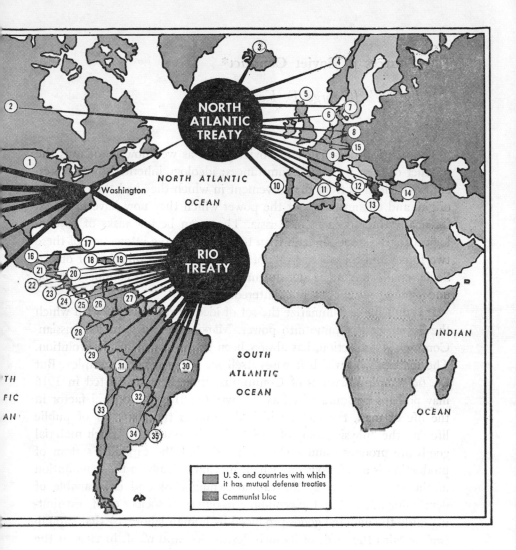

Labels on map: NORTH ATLANTIC TREATY, RIO TREATY, NORTH ATLANTIC OCEAN, Washington, SOUTH ATLANTIC OCEAN, INDIAN OCEAN, numbered circles 1–35.

Legend:
- U. S. and countries with which it has mutual defense treaties
- Communist bloc

Source: U.S. Department of State, *American Foreign Policy, 1950-1955* (Washington, 1957), pp. 788-789.

JAPANESE TREATY (BILATERAL)

treaty signed September 8, 1951, whereby Japan on a pro-
sional basis requests, and the United States agrees, to "main-
n certain of its armed forces in and about Japan . . . so
to deter armed attack upon Japan."

    1 United States   **39 Japan**

**EPUBLIC OF KOREA (South Korea)
REATY (BILATERAL)**

treaty signed October 1, 1953, whereby each party "recog-
es that an armed attack in the Pacific area on either of
e Parties . . . would be dangerous to its own peace and
ety" and that each Party "would act to meet the common
nger in accordance with its constitutional processes."

    1 United States   **40 Republic of Korea**

OUTHEAST ASIA TREATY (8 NATIONS)

treaty signed September 8, 1954, whereby each Party "rec-
nizes that aggression by means of armed attack in the
eaty area against any of the Parties . . . would endanger

its own peace and safety" and each will "in that event act
to meet the common danger in accordance with its constitutional processes."

1 United States	**36 New Zealand**	**41 Thailand**
5 United Kingdom	**37 Australia**	**42 Pakistan**
11 France	**38 Philippines**	

**REPUBLIC OF CHINA (Formosa) TREATY
(BILATERAL)**

A treaty signed December 2, 1954, whereby each of the parties
"recognizes that an armed attack in the West Pacific Area
directed against the territories of either of the Parties would
be dangerous to its own peace and safety," and that each
"would act to meet the common danger in accordance with
its constitutional processes." The territory of the Republic
of China is defined as "Taiwan (Formosa) and the Pescadores."

    1 United States   **43 Republic of China (Formosa)**

The Sources of Soviet Conduct*

by "X" (George F. Kennan)

[1]

The political personality of Soviet power as we know it today is the product of ideology and circumstances: ideology inherited by the present Soviet leaders from the movement in which they had their political origin, and circumstances of the power which they now have exercised for nearly three decades in Russia. There can be few tasks of psychological analysis more difficult than to try to trace the interaction of these two forces and the relative rôle of each in the determination of official Soviet conduct. Yet the attempt must be made if that conduct is to be understood and effectively countered.

It is difficult to summarize the set of ideological concepts with which the Soviet leaders came into power. Marxian ideology, in its Russian-Communist projection, has always been in process of subtle evolution. The materials on which it bases itself are extensive and complex. But the outstanding features of Communist thought as it existed in 1916 may perhaps be summarized as follows: (a) that the central factor in the life of man, the factor which determines the character of public life and the "physiognomy of society," is the system by which material goods are produced and exchanged; (b) that the capitalist system of production is a nefarious one which inevitably leads to the exploitation of the working class by the capital-owning class and is incapable of developing adequately the economic resources of society or of distributing fairly the material goods produced by human labor; (c) that capitalism contains the seeds of its own destruction and must, in view of the inability of the capital-owning class to adjust itself to economic change, result eventually and inescapably in a revolutionary transfer of power to the working class; and (d) that imperialism, the final phase of capitalism, leads directly to war and revolution.

The rest may be outlined in Lenin's own words: "Unevenness of economic and political development is the inflexible law of capitalism. It follows from this that the victory of Socialism may come originally

* From Foreign Affairs, Vol. XXIV, No. 4 (July 1947), pp. 566-582. Copyright 1947 by the Council on Foreign Relations, Inc., New York. Reprinted by special permission from Foreign Affairs.

in a few capitalist countries or even in a single capitalist country. The victorious proletariat of that country, having expropriated the capitalists and having organized Socialist production at home, would rise against the remaining capitalist world, drawing to itself in the process the oppressed classes of other countries." [1] It must be noted that there was no assumption that capitalism would perish without proletarian revolution. A final push was needed from a revolutionary proletariat movement in order to tip over the tottering structure. But it was regarded as inevitable that sooner or later that push be given.

For 50 years prior to the outbreak of the Revolution, this pattern of thought had exercised great fascination for the members of the Russian revolutionary movement. Frustrated, discontented, hopeless of finding self-expression—or too impatient to seek it—in the confining limits of the Tsarist political system, yet lacking wide popular support for their choice of bloody revolution as a means of social betterment, these revolutionists found in Marxist theory a highly convenient rationalization for their own instinctive desires. It afforded pseudo-scientific justification for their impatience, for their categoric denial of all value in the Tsarist system, for their yearning for power and revenge and for their inclination to cut corners in the pursuit of it. It is therefore no wonder that they had come to believe implicitly in the truth and soundness of the Marxian-Leninist teachings, so congenial to their own impulses and emotions. Their sincerity need not be impugned. This is a phenomenon as old as human nature itself. It has never been more aptly described than by Edward Gibbon, who wrote in "The Decline and Fall of the Roman Empire": "From enthusiasm to imposture the step is perilous and slippery; the demon of Socrates affords a memorable instance how a wise man may deceive himself, how a good man may deceive others, how the conscience may slumber in a mixed and middle state between self-illusion and voluntary fraud." And it was with this set of conceptions that the members of the Bolshevik Party entered into power.

Now it must be noted that through all the years of preparation for revolution, the attention of these men, as indeed of Marx himself, had been centered less on the future form which Socialism[2] would take than on the necessary overthrow of rival power which, in their view, had to

---

[1] "Concerning the Slogans of the United States of Europe," August 1915. Official Soviet edition of Lenin's works.

[2] Here and elsewhere in this paper "Socialism" refers to Marxist or Leninist Communism, not to liberal Socialism of the Second International variety.

precede the introduction of Socialism. Their views, therefore, on the positive program to be put into effect, once power was attained, were for the most part nebulous, visionary and impractical. Beyond the nationalization of industry and the expropriation of large private capital holdings there was no agreed program. The treatment of the peasantry, which according to the Marxist formulation was not of the proletariat, had always been a vague spot in the pattern of Communist thought; and it remained an object of controversy and vacillation for the first ten years of Communist power.

The circumstances of the immediate post-revolution period—the existence in Russia of civil war and foreign intervention, together with the obvious fact that the Communists represented only a tiny minority of the Russian people—made the establishment of dictatorial power a necessity. The experiment with "war Communism" and the abrupt attempt to eliminate private production and trade had unfortunate economic consequences and caused further bitterness against the new revolutionary régime. While the temporary relaxation of the effort to communize Russia, represented by the New Economic Policy, alleviated some of this economic distress and thereby served its purpose, it also made it evident that the "capitalistic sector of society" was still prepared to profit at once from any relaxation of governmental pressure, and would, if permitted to continue to exist, always constitute a powerful opposing element to the Soviet régime and a serious rival for influence in the country. Somewhat the same situation prevailed with respect to the individual peasant who, in his own small way, was also a private producer.

Lenin, had he lived, might have proved a great enough man to reconcile these conflicting forces to the ultimate benefit of Russian society, though this is questionable. But be that as it may, Stalin, and those whom he led in the struggle for succession to Lenin's position of leadership, were not the men to tolerate rival political forces in the sphere of power which they coveted. Their sense of insecurity was too great. Their particular brand of fanaticism, unmodified by any of the Anglo-Saxon traditions of compromise, was too fierce and too jealous to envisage any permanent sharing of power. From the Russian-Asiatic world out of which they had emerged they carried with them a skepticism as to the possibilities of permanent and peaceful coexistence of rival forces. Easily persuaded of their own doctrinaire "rightness," they insisted on the submission or destruction of all competing power. Outside of the Communist Party, Russian society was to have no rigidity. There were to be no forms of collective human activity or association which would not be dominated by the Party. No other force in Russian society was to be permitted to achieve vitality or integrity. Only the Party was to have structure. All else was to be an amorphous mass.

And within the Party the same principle was to apply. The mass of Party members might go through the motions of election, deliberation, decision and action; but in these motions they were to be animated not by their own individual wills but by the awesome breath of the Party leadership and the overbrooding presence of "the word."

Let it be stressed again that subjectively these men probably did not seek absolutism for its own sake. They doubtless believed—and found it easy to believe—that they alone knew what was good for society and that they would accomplish that good once their power was secure and unchallengeable. But in seeking that security of their own rule they were prepared to recognize no restrictions, either of God or man, on the character of their methods. And until such time as that security might be achieved, they placed far down on their scale of operational priorities the comforts and happiness of the peoples entrusted to their care.

Now the outstanding circumstance concerning the Soviet régime is that down to the present day this process of political consolidation has never been completed and the men in the Kremlin have continued to be predominantly absorbed with the struggle to secure and make absolute the power which they seized in November 1917. They have endeavored to secure it primarily against forces at home, within Soviet society itself. But they have also endeavored to secure it against the outside world. For ideology, as we have seen, taught them that the outside world was hostile and that it was their duty eventually to overthrow the political forces beyond their borders. The powerful hands of Russian history and tradition reached up to sustain them in this feeling. Finally, their own aggressive intransigence with respect to the outside world began to find its own reaction; and they were soon forced, to use another Gibbon-esque phrase, "to chastise the contumacy" which they themselves had provoked. It is an undeniable privilege of every man to prove himself right in the thesis that the world is his enemy; for if he reiterates it frequently enough and makes it the background of his conduct he is bound eventually to be right.

Now it lies in the nature of the mental world of the Soviet leaders, as well as in the character of their ideology, that no opposition to them can be officially recognized as having any merit or justification whatsoever. Such opposition can flow, in theory, only from the hostile and incorrigible forces of dying capitalism. As long as remnants of capitalism were officially recognized as existing in Russia, it was possible to place on them, as an internal element, part of the blame for the maintenance of a dictatorial form of society. But as these remnants were liquidated, little by little, this justification fell away; and when it was indicated officially that they had been finally destroyed, it disappeared altogether. And this fact created one of the most basic of the compulsions which came to act upon the Soviet régime: since capitalism no longer existed in Russia and since it could not be admitted that there could be serious or widespread opposition to the Kremlin springing spontaneously from the liberated masses under its authority, it became necessary to justify the retention of the dictatorship by stressing the menace of capitalism abroad.

This began at an early date. In 1924 Stalin specifically defended the retention of the "organs of suppression," meaning, among others, the army and the secret police, on the ground that "as long as there is a capitalist encirclement there will be danger of intervention with all the consequences that flow from that danger." In accordance with that theory, and from that time on, all internal opposition forces in Russia have consistently been portrayed as the agents of foreign forces of reaction antagonistic to Soviet power.

By the same token, tremendous emphasis has been placed on the original Communist thesis of a basic antagonism between the capitalist and Socialist worlds. It is clear, from many indications, that this emphasis is not founded in reality. The real facts concerning it have been confused by the existence abroad of genuine resentment provoked by Soviet philosophy and tactics and occasionally by the existence of great centers of military power, notably the Nazi régime in Germany and the Japanese Government of the late 1930's, which did indeed have aggressive designs against the Soviet Union. But there is ample evidence that the stress laid in Moscow on the menace confronting Soviet society from the world outside its borders is founded not in the realities of foreign antagonism but in the necessity of explaining away the maintenance of dictatorial authority at home.

Now the maintenance of this pattern of Soviet power, namely, the pursuit of unlimited authority domestically, accompanied by the cultivation of the semi-myth of implacable foreign hostility, has gone far to shape the actual machinery of Soviet power as we know it today. Internal organs of administration which did not serve this purpose withered on the vine. Organs which did serve this purpose became vastly swollen. The security of Soviet power came to rest on the iron discipline of the Party, on the severity and ubiquity of the secret police, and on the uncompromising economic monopolism of the state. The "organs of suppression," in which the Soviet leaders had sought security from rival forces, became in large measure the masters of those whom they were designed to serve. Today the major part of the structure of Soviet power is committed to the perfection of the dictatorship and to the maintenance of the concept of Russia as in a state of siege, with the enemy lowering beyond the walls. And the millions of human beings who form that part of the structure of power must defend at all costs this concept of Russia's position, for without it they are themselves superfluous.

As things stand today, the rulers can no longer dream of parting with these organs of suppression. The quest for absolute power, pursued now for nearly three decades with a ruthlessness unparalleled (in scope at least) in modern times, has again produced internally, as it did externally, its own reaction. The excesses of the police apparatus have fanned the potential opposition to the régime into something far greater and more dangerous than it could have been before those excesses began.

But least of all can the rulers dispense with the fiction by which the maintenance of dictatorial power has been defended. For this fiction has been canonized in Soviet philosophy by the excesses already committed in its name; and it is now anchored in the Soviet structure of thought by bonds far greater than those of mere ideology.

[II]

So much for the historical background. What does it spell in terms of the political personality of Soviet power as we know it today?

Of the original ideology, nothing has been officially junked. Belief is maintained in the basic badness of capitalism, in the inevitability of its destruction, in the obligation of the proletariat to assist in that destruction and to take power into its own hands. But stress has come to be laid primarily on those concepts which relate most specifically to the Soviet régime itself: to its position as the sole truly Socialist régime in a dark and misguided world, and to the relationships of power within it.

The first of these concepts is that of the innate antagonism between capitalism and Socialism. We have seen how deeply that concept has become imbedded in foundations of Soviet power. It has profound implications for Russia's conduct as a member of international society. It means that there can never be on Moscow's side any sincere assumption of a community of aims between the Soviet Union and powers which are regarded as capitalist. It must invariably be assumed in Moscow that the aims of the capitalist world are antagonistic to the Soviet régime, and therefore to the interests of the peoples it controls. If the Soviet Government occasionally sets its signature to documents which would indicate the contrary, this is to be regarded as a tactical manoeuvre permissible in dealing with the enemy (who is without honor) and should be taken in the spirit of *caveat emptor*. Basically, the antagonism remains. It is postulated. And from it flow many of the phenomena which we find disturbing in the Kremlin's conduct of foreign policy: the secretiveness, the lack of frankness, the duplicity, the wary suspiciousness, and the basic unfriendliness of purpose. These phenomena are there to stay, for the foreseeable future. There can be variations of degree and of emphasis. When there is something the Russians want from us, one or the other of these features of their policy may be thrust temporarily into the background; and when that happens there will always be Americans who will leap forward with gleeful announcements that "the Russians have changed," and some who will even try to take credit for having brought about such "changes." But we should not be misled by tactical manoeuvres. These characteristics of Soviet policy, like the postulate from which they flow, are basic to the internal nature of Soviet power, and will be with us, whether in the foreground or the background, until the internal nature of Soviet power is changed.

This means that we are going to continue for a long time to find the Russians difficult to deal with. It does not mean that they should be considered as embarked upon a do-or-die program to overthrow our society by a given date. The theory of the inevitability of the eventual fall of capitalism has the fortunate connotation that there is no hurry about it. The forces of progress can take their time in preparing the final *coup de grâce*. Meanwhile, what is vital is that the "Socialist fatherland" —that oasis of power which has been already won for Socialism in the person of the Soviet Union—should be cherished and defended by all good Communists at home and abroad, its fortunes promoted, its enemies badgered and confounded. The promotion of premature, "adventuristic" revolutionary projects abroad which might embarrass Soviet power in any way would be an inexcusable, even a counter-revolutionary act. The cause of Socialism is the support and promotion of Soviet power, as defined in Moscow.

This brings us to the second of the concepts important to contemporary Soviet outlook. That is the infallibility of the Kremlin. The Soviet concept of power, which permits no focal points of organization outside the Party itself, requires that the Party leadership remain in theory the sole repository of truth. For if truth were to be found elsewhere, there would be justification for its expression in organized activity. But it is precisely that which the Kremlin cannot and will not permit.

The leadership of the Communist Party is therefore always right, and has been always right ever since in 1929 Stalin formalized his personal power by announcing that decisions of the Politburo were being taken unanimously.

On the principle of infallibility there rests the iron discipline of the Communist Party. In fact, the two concepts are mutually self-supporting. Perfect discipline requires recognition of infallibility. Infallibility requires the observance of discipline. And the two together go far to determine the behaviorism of the entire Soviet apparatus of power. But their effect cannot be understood unless a third factor be taken into account: namely, the fact that the leadership is at liberty to put forward for tactical purposes any particular thesis which it finds useful to the cause at any particular moment and to require the faithful and unquestioning acceptance of that thesis by the members of the movement as a whole. This means that truth is not a constant but is actually created, for all intents and purposes, by the Soviet leaders themselves. It may vary from week to week, from month to month. It is nothing absolute and immutable—nothing which flows from objective reality. It is only the most recent manifestation of the wisdom of those in whom the ultimate wisdom is supposed to reside, because they represent the logic of history. The accumulative effect of these factors is to give to the whole subordinate apparatus of Soviet power an unshakable stubbornness and steadfastness in its orientation. This orientation can be changed at will by the Kremlin but by no other power. Once a given party line has been laid down on a given issue of current policy, the whole Soviet governmental machine, including the mechanism of diplomacy, moves inexorably along the prescribed path, like a persistent toy automobile wound up and headed in a given direction, stopping only when it meets with some unanswerable force. The individuals who are the components of this machine are unamenable to argument or reason which comes to them from outside sources. Their whole training has taught them to mistrust and discount the glib persuasiveness of the outside world. Like the white dog before the phonograph, they hear only the "master's voice." And if they are to be called off from the purposes last dictated to them, it is the master who must call them off. Thus the foreign representative cannot hope that his words will make any impression on them. The most that he can hope is that they will be transmitted to those at the top, who are capable of changing the party line. But even those are not likely to be swayed by any normal logic in the words of the bourgeois representative. Since there can be no appeal to common purposes, there can be no appeal to common mental approaches. For this reason, facts speak louder than words to the ears of the Kremlin; and words carry the greatest weight when they have the ring of reflecting, or being backed up by, facts of unchallengeable validity.

But we have seen that the Kremlin is under no ideological compulsion to accomplish its purposes in a hurry. Like the Church, it is dealing in ideological concepts which are of long-term validity, and it can afford to be patient. It has no right to risk the existing achievements of the revolution for the sake of vain baubles of the future. The very teachings of Lenin himself require great caution and flexibility in the pursuit of Communist purposes. Again, these precepts are fortified by the lessons of Russian history: of centuries of obscure battles between nomadic forces over the stretches of a vast unfortified plain. Here caution, circumspection, flexibility and deception are the valuable qualities; and their value finds natural appreciation in the Russian or the oriental mind. Thus the Kremlin has no compunction about retreating in the face of superior force. And being under the compulsion of no timetable, it does not get panicky under the necessity for such retreat. Its political action is a fluid stream which moves constantly, wherever it is permitted to move, toward a given goal. Its main concern is to make sure that it has filled every nook and cranny available to it in the basin of world power. But if it finds unassailable barriers in its path, it accepts these philosophically and accommodates itself to them. The main thing is that there should always be pressure, unceasing constant pressure, toward the desired goal. There is no trace of any feeling in Soviet psychology that that goal must be reached at any given time.

These considerations make Soviet diplomacy at once easier and more difficult to deal with than the diplomacy of individual aggressive leaders like Napoleon and Hitler. On the one hand it is more sensitive to contrary force, more ready to yield on individual sectors of the diplomatic front when that force is felt to be too strong, and thus more rational in the logic and rhetoric of power. On the other hand it cannot be easily defeated or discouraged by a single victory on the part of its opponents. And the patient persistence by which it is animated means that it can be effectively countered not by sporadic acts which represent the momentary whims of democratic opinion but only by intelligent long-range policies on the part of Russia's adversaries—policies no less steady in their purpose, and no less variegated and resourceful in their application, than those of the Soviet Union itself.

In these circumstances it is clear that the main element of any United States policy toward the Soviet Union must be that of a long-term, patient but firm and vigilant containment of Russian expansive tendencies. It is important to note, however, that such a policy has nothing to do with outward histrionics: with threats or blustering or superfluous gestures of outward "toughness." While the Kremlin is basically flexible in its reaction to political realities, it is by no means unamenable to considerations of prestige. Like almost any other government, it can be placed by tactless and threatening gestures in a position where it cannot afford to yield even though this might be dictated by its sense of realism. The Russian leaders are keen judges of human psychology, and as such they are highly conscious that loss of temper and of self-control is never a source of strength in political affairs. They are quick to exploit such evidences of weakness. For these reasons, it is a *sine qua non* of successful dealing with Russia that the foreign government in question should remain at all times cool and collected and that its demands on Russian policy should be put forward in such a manner as to leave the way open for a compliance not too detrimental to Russian prestige.

[III]

In the light of the above, it will be clearly seen that the Soviet pressure against the free institutions of the western world is something that can be contained by the adroit and vigilant application of counter-force at a series of constantly shifting geographical and political points, corresponding to the shifts and manoeuvres of Soviet policy, but which cannot be charmed or talked out of existence. The Russians look forward to a duel of infinite duration, and they see that already they have scored great successes. It must be borne in mind that there was a time when the Communist Party represented far more of a minority in the sphere of Russian national life than Soviet power today represents in the world community.

But if ideology convinces the rulers of Russia that truth is on their side and that they can therefore afford to wait, those of us on whom that ideology has no claim are free to examine objectively the validity of that premise. The Soviet thesis not only implies complete lack of control by the west over its own economic destiny, it likewise assumes Russian unity, discipline and patience over an infinite period. Let us bring this apocalyptic vision down to earth, and suppose that the western world finds the strength and resourcefulness to contain Soviet power over a period of ten to fifteen years. What does that spell for Russia itself?

The Soviet leaders, taking advantage of the contributions of modern technique to the arts of despotism, have solved the question of obedience within the confines of their power. Few challenge their authority; and even those who do are unable to make that challenge valid as against the organs of suppression of the state.

The Kremlin has also proved able to accomplish its purpose of building up in Russia, regardless of the interests of the inhabitants, an industrial foundation of heavy metallurgy, which is, to be sure, not yet complete but which is nevertheless continuing to grow and is approaching those of the other major industrial countries. All of this, however, both the maintenance of internal political security and the building of heavy industry, has been carried out at a terrible cost in human life and in human hopes and energies. It has necessitated the use of forced labor on a scale unprecedented in modern times under conditions of peace. It has involved the neglect or abuse of other phases of Soviet economic life, particularly agriculture, consumers' goods production, housing and transportation.

To all that, the war has added its tremendous toll of destruction, death and human exhaustion. In consequence of this, we have in Russia today a population which is physically and spiritually tired. The mass of the people arc disillusioned, skeptical and no longer as accessible as they once were to the magical attraction which Soviet power still radiates to its followers abroad. The avidity with which people seized upon the slight respite accorded to the Church for tactical reasons during the war was eloquent testimony to the fact that their capacity for faith and devotion found little expression in the purposes of the régime.

In these circumstances, there are limits to the physical and nervous strength of people themselves. These limits are absolute ones, and are binding even for the cruelest dictatorship, because beyond them people cannot be driven. The forced labor camps and the other agencies of constraint provide temporary means of compelling people to work longer hours than their own volition or mere economic pressure would dictate; but if people survive them at all they become old before their time and must be considered as human casualties to the demands of dictatorship. In either case their best powers are no longer available to society and can no longer be enlisted in the service of the state.

Here only the younger generation can help. The younger generation, despite all vicissitudes and sufferings, is numerous and vigorous; and the Russians are a talented people. But it still remains to be seen what will be the effects on mature performance of the abnormal emotional strains of childhood which Soviet dictatorship created and which were enormously increased by the war. Such things as normal security and placidity of home environment have practically ceased to exist in the Soviet Union outside of the most remote farms and villages. And observers are not yet sure whether that is not going to leave its mark on the over-all capacity of the generation now coming into maturity.

In addition to this, we have the fact that Soviet economic development, while it can list certain formidable achievements, has been precariously spotty and uneven. Russian Communists who speak of the "uneven development of capitalism" should blush at the contemplation of their own national economy. Here certain branches of economic life, such as the metallurgical and machine industries, have been pushed out of all proportion to other sectors of economy. Here is a nation striving to become in a short period one of the great industrial nations of the world while it still has no highway network worthy of the name and only a relatively primitive network of railways. Much has been done to increase efficiency of labor and to teach primitive peasants something about the operation of machines. But maintenance is still a crying deficiency of all Soviet economy. Construction is hasty and poor in quality. Depreciation must be enormous. And in vast sectors of economic life it has not yet been possible to instill into labor anything like that general culture of production and technical self-respect which characterizes the skilled worker of the west.

It is difficult to see how these deficiencies can be corrected at an early date by a tired and dispirited population working largely under the shadow of fear and compulsion. And as long as they are not overcome, Russia will remain economically a vulnerable, and in a certain sense an impotent, nation, capable of exporting its enthusiasms and of radiating the strange charm of its primitive political vitality but unable to back up those articles of export by the real evidences of material power and prosperity.

Meanwhile, a great uncertainty hangs over the political life of the Soviet Union. That is the uncertainty involved in the transfer of power from one individual or group of individuals to others.

This is, of course, outstandingly the problem of the personal position of Stalin. We must remember that his succession to Lenin's pinnacle of preëminence in the Communist movement was the only such transfer of individual authority which the Soviet Union has experienced. That transfer took 12 years to consolidate. It cost the lives of millions of people and shook the state to its foundations. The attendant tremors were felt all through the international revolutionary movement, to the disadvantage of the Kremlin itself.

It is always possible that another transfer of preëminent power may take place quietly and inconspicuously, with no repercussions anywhere. But again, it is possible that the questions involved may unleash, to use some of Lenin's words, one of those "incredibly swift transitions" from "delicate deceit" to "wild violence" which characterize Russian history, and may shake Soviet power to its foundations.

But this is not only a question of Stalin himself. There has been, since 1938, a dangerous congealment of political life in the higher circles of Soviet power. The All-Union Congress of Soviets, in theory the supreme body of the Party, is supposed to meet not less often than once in three years. It will soon be eight full years since its last meeting. During this period membership in the Party has numerically doubled. Party mortality during the war was enormous; and today well over half of the Party members are persons who have entered since the last Party congress was held. Meanwhile, the same small group of men has carried on at the top through an amazing series of national vicissitudes. Surely there is some reason why the experiences of the war brought basic political changes to every one of the great governments of the west. Surely the causes of that phenomenon are basic enough to be present somewhere in the obscurity of Soviet political life, as well. And yet no recognition has been given to these causes in Russia.

It must be surmised from this that even within so highly disciplined an organization as the Communist Party there must be a growing divergence in age, outlook and interest between the great mass of Party members, only so recently recruited into the movement, and the little self-perpetuating clique of men at the top, whom most of these Party members have never met, with whom they have never conversed, and with whom they can have no political intimacy.

Who can say whether, in these circumstances, the eventual rejuvenation of the higher spheres of authority (which can only be a matter of time) can take place smoothly and peacefully, or whether rivals in the quest for higher power will not eventually reach down into these politically immature and inexperienced masses in order to find support for their respective claims? If this were ever to happen, strange consequences could flow for the Communist Party: for the membership at large has been exercised only in the practices of iron discipline and obedience and not in the arts of compromise and accommodation. And if disunity were ever to seize and paralyze the Party, the chaos and weakness of Russian society would be revealed in forms beyond description. For we have seen that Soviet power is only a crust concealing an amorphous mass of human beings among whom no independent organizational structure is tolerated. In Russia there is not even such a thing as local government. The present generation of Russians have never known spontaneity of collective action. If, consequently, anything were ever to occur to disrupt the unity and efficacy of the Party as a political instrument, Soviet Russia might be changed overnight from one of the strongest to one of the weakest and most pitiable of national societies.

Thus the future of Soviet power may not be by any means as secure as Russian capacity for self-delusion would make it appear to the men in the Kremlin. That they can keep power themselves, they have demonstrated. That they can quietly and easily turn it over to others remains to be proved. Meanwhile, the hardships of their rule and the vicissitudes of international life have taken a heavy toll of the strength and hopes of the great people on whom their power rests. It is curious to note that the ideological power of Soviet authority is strongest today in areas beyond the frontiers of Russia, beyond the reach of its police power. This phenomenon brings to mind a comparison used by Thomas

Mann in his great novel "Buddenbrooks." Observing that human institutions often show the greatest outward brilliance at a moment when inner decay is in reality farthest advanced, he compared the Buddenbrook family, in the days of its greatest glamour, to one of those stars whose light shines most brightly on this world when in reality it has long since ceased to exist. And who can say with assurance that the strong light still cast by the Kremlin on the dissatisfied peoples of the western world is not the powerful afterglow of a constellation which is in actuality on the wane? This cannot be proved. And it cannot be disproved. But the possibility remains (and in the opinion of this writer it is a strong one) that Soviet power, like the capitalist world of its conception, bears within it the seeds of its own decay, and that the sprouting of these seeds is well advanced.

[IV]

It is clear that the United States cannot expect in the foreseeable future to enjoy political intimacy with the Soviet régime. It must continue to regard the Soviet Union as a rival, not a partner, in the political arena. It must continue to expect that Soviet policies will reflect no abstract love of peace and stability, no real faith in the possibility of a permanent happy coexistence of the Socialist and capitalist worlds, but rather a cautious, persistent pressure toward the disruption and weakening of all rival influence and rival power.

Balanced against this are the facts that Russia, as opposed to the western world in general, is still by far the weaker party, that Soviet policy is highly flexible, and that Soviet society may well contain deficiencies which will eventually weaken its own total potential. This would of itself warrant the United States entering with reasonable confidence upon a policy of firm containment, designed to confront the Russians with unalterable counter-force at every point where they show signs of encroaching upon the interests of a peaceful and stable world.

But in actuality the possibilities for American policy are by no means limited to holding the line and hoping for the best. It is entirely possible for the United States to influence by its actions the internal developments, both within Russia and throughout the international Communist movement, by which Russian policy is largely determined. This is not only a question of the modest measure of informational activity which this government can conduct in the Soviet Union and elsewhere, although that, too, is important. It is rather a question of the degree to which the United States can create among the peoples of the world generally the impression of a country which knows what it wants, which is coping successfully with the problems of its internal life and with the responsibilities of a World Power, and which has a spiritual vitality capable of holding its own among the major ideological currents of the time. To the extent that such an impression can be created and maintained, the aims of Russian Communism must appear sterile and quixotic, the hopes and enthusiasm of Moscow's supporters must wane, and added strain must be imposed on the Kremlin's foreign policies. For the palsied decrepitude of the capitalist world is the keystone of Communist philosophy. Even the failure of the United States to experience the early economic depression which the ravens of the Red Square have been predicting with such complacent confidence since hostilities ceased would have deep and important repercussions throughout the Communist world.

By the same token, exhibitions of indecision, disunity and internal disintegration within this country have an exhilarating effect on the whole Communist movement. At each evidence of these tendencies, a thrill of hope and excitement goes through the Communist world; a new jauntiness can be noted in the Moscow tread; new groups of foreign supporters climb on to what they can only view as the band wagon of international politics; and Russian pressure increases all along the line in international affairs.

It would be an exaggeration to say that American behavior unassisted and alone could exercise a power of life and death over the Communist movement and bring about the early fall of Soviet power in Russia. But the United States has it in its power to increase enormously the strains under which Soviet policy must operate, to force upon the Kremlin a far greater degree of moderation and circumspection than it has had to observe in recent years, and in this way to promote tendencies which must eventually find their outlet in either the break-up or the gradual mellowing of Soviet power. For no mystical, Messianic movement—and particularly not that of the Kremlin—can face frustration indefinitely without eventually adjusting itself in one way or another to the logic of that state of affairs.

Thus the decision will really fall in large measure in this country itself. The issue of Soviet-American relations is in essence a test of the over-all worth of the United States as a nation among nations. To avoid destruction the United States need only measure up to its own best traditions and prove itself worthy of preservation as a great nation.

Surely, there was never a fairer test of national quality than this. In the light of these circumstances, the thoughtful observer of Russian-American relations will find no cause for complaint in the Kremlin's challenge to American society. He will rather experience a certain gratitude to a Providence which, by providing the American people with this implacable challenge, has made their entire security as a nation dependent on their pulling themselves together and accepting the responsibilities of moral and political leadership that history plainly intended them to bear.

Challenge and Response in United States Policy*

by John Foster Dulles

[1]

The 35th anniversary of the founding of *Foreign Affairs* is a suitable occasion for comment on the evolution of United States foreign policy and the role we can play today in accord with our enduring national principles.[1] During this third of a century, the American people have altered their conception as to the proper part which their Government should take in world affairs.

Since the founding of this nation, the American people have believed that it had a mission in the world. They have believed that "their conduct and example" ("The Federalist," No. 1) would influence events throughout the world and promote the spread of free institutions. But they have traditionally felt that it would be better for their Government to avoid involvement in international issues. So, with rare exceptions, the United States left the field of international politics to the governments of the "great powers" of the 19th century.

It took the First World War to bring us into major involvement in

---

* From the *Department of State Bulletin*, Vol. XXXVII, No. 954 (October 7, 1957), pp. 569-579.
[1] Article prepared for publication in the October issue of *Foreign Affairs* (press release 528 dated Sept. 18).

world crises and conflicts. Then in the decade of the thirties a series of critical events culminated in the greatest of all wars. By its end, a transformation had been effected. It had become obvious that the conduct and example of our people no longer, alone, sufficed to prevent recurrent challenges to our security and our way of life. It was also apparent that only in association with others could we repel such challenges. Furthermore, our national power had grown to be so impressive as to preclude its being merely a reserved, negative force.

Thus, since 1945, our Government has played a leading role in a coalition of free nations dedicated to the principles of international order to which our people have long subscribed.

There still remains a nostalgia for the "good old days." This is reinforced by recurrent demonstrations that, great as is our strength, we are not omnipotent. We cannot, by fiat, produce the kind of a world we want. Even nations which depend greatly upon us do not always follow what we believe to be the right course. For they are independent nations and not our satellites. Our power and policy are but one significant factor in the world in which we live. In combination with other factors we are able to influence importantly the course of events. But we cannot deal in absolutes. This, to many Americans, is a source of worriment.

The American people may not yet have completely accepted the role that history has made inevitable. But at least a good beginning has been made. It is unlikely that there could now be a successful effort to withdraw the United States Government from official and active participation in international affairs. But in order that such participation should command popular support, our foreign policies should be more than politics. They must evidently reflect the traditional aspirations of our people.

II. COMMUNIST HOSTILITY

United States foreign policy since 1945 has been forced to concern itself primarily with one major threat to the peaceful and orderly development of the kind of international community the American people desire. This is the threat posed by those who direct the totalitarian system of international communism. Because orthodox communism represents a materialistic and atheistic creed, it inevitably is repugnant to those who believe in the supremacy of the spirit. Because it seeks world rule through the domination of all governments by the international Communist Party, it is repugnant to all who understand its purposes and, as patriots, cherish national independence. And because it employs fraud and violence to achieve its ends, it is repugnant to all who seek a world society of decency and order.

The United States, as the strongest nation of the non-Communist world, has had the major responsibility for meeting this challenge which, since 1950, has been able to exploit the resources of most of the Eurasian land mass and one-third of the world's population.

Since the death of Stalin in March 1953, there has been a Soviet disavowal of the ruthlessness of the Stalinist period. Internally, that disavowal has found some practical expression. Externally, Soviet policy has been marked by a more diversified range of political, diplomatic, and economic tactics vis-à-vis the non-Communist world. This became especially pronounced in 1955. There were such gestures as the sudden consent to a long-overdue Austrian treaty and the overtures to Yugoslavia. At the "summit" conference at Geneva there were professions of peaceful intent and an agreement to reunify Germany by free elections. There were profuse offers of "assistance" to many nations and a plea for "cultural relations."

But nowhere, except perhaps in Austria, did the Soviets yield anything of substance or enter into genuine negotiations on basic issues. Economic and military "assistance" was a Trojan horse whereby influence could be gained to promote political subversion. There was no honest acceptance of Yugoslavia's right to have a national Communist government not dominated by international communism. And in November 1955 at Geneva the Soviet Government flatly repudiated the July "summit" agreement for German reunification.

The year 1956 gave further evidence that the new rulers in Moscow were not essentially changed. Enticements were mingled with threats. When "de-Stalinization," proclaimed by the 20th Party Congress in February 1956, was interpreted in the satellites as justifying more freedom and independence, there were fierce reactions first at Poznan, Poland, and then in Hungary. Obviously, those who presently dictate the doctrines of international communism are not in fact prepared to accept the consequences of their professed liberalization.

In all the 40 years of Bolshevik rule there is no episode more brutal than the Red Army suppression of the Hungarian people's 1956 uprising against intolerable oppression. And recent Soviet policies in the Near East are inexcusably mischievous.

That area, rich in cultural and religious tradition, yet stricken with historic dissensions and tragic poverty, was chosen in 1955 to be the scene of a new Communist hunt for power. Communist propaganda studiously sought to inflame animosities. The Soviet Government, drawing upon its semiobsolete war equipment, stimulated an arms race. As a direct or indirect result, violence and bitterness were increased and abject poverty was riveted more firmly as some governments mortgaged the future economic productivity of the people in order to buy Soviet arms. It has indeed been a cynical performance by those who profess to love peace and to desire to uplift the masses.

More than a decade of cold-war experience has confirmed our earlier judgments of international communism. It and the governments it controls are deeply hostile to us and to all free and independent governments. Its basic doctrine precludes its changing of its own accord. Self-advertised changes must be considered as mere stratagems.

We need not, however, despair. International communism is subject to change even against its will. It is not impervious to the erosion of time and circumstance. Khrushchev's speech of February 1956, the July 1957 shakeup in the ruling clique at Moscow, and Mao's speech of February 27, 1957, indicate that, even in Russia and the China mainland, Soviet and Chinese Communist regimes are confronted with great internal pressures and dilemmas. The yeast of change is at work, despite all the efforts of "democratic centralism" to keep matters moving in a strictly Leninist pattern. The rulers in Russia do not find it possible to combine industrial and military modernization with the personal repressions of the Middle Ages; and the rulers in China will not find it possible to fit the richly diversified culture of the Chinese into a Communist mold of conformity.

The time may come, indeed we can be confident that it will come, when the nations now ruled by international communism will have governments which, whatever their label, in fact serve their own nations and their own peoples rather than the insatiable worldwide ambitions of an international party. There will be broadening participation in government. There will be increasing personal security under law. There will be a significant degree of freedom of thought and expression. And the workers will be permitted to have some choice of the work that they do and to enjoy more of the fruits of their labor. Under those conditions, the people, if not the masters of their government, will at least not be its abject slaves. Vast military power will no longer be completely at the disposal of those who accept no restraints either of a governmental or moral character and whose goal is worldwide rule. When that day comes, we can rejoice. Until that day comes, we shall need to remain on our guard.

III. COLLECTIVE SECURITY

During the last two decades, the United States has found it necessary to recast its ideas and policies regarding national security. The course of our thinking and planning has been in the direction of collective security. In our modern world no nation, however powerful, can find safety in isolation, and security for one is only to be achieved through cooperation with other like-minded nations.

The society of nations is undergoing the transformation that occurs whenever primitive societies develop. There is a gradual evolution from conditions where security is a matter of each for himself and the Devil take the hindmost, to a condition where security is a collective effort to which each contributes and from which each benefits. In that way there is greater security at less cost. The society of nations is gradually and painfully evolving from a primitive condition to one where security is a matter of collective effort and where defense is a common defense.

It is not easy to realize these principles in a world where people have long thought of sovereignty as a status unqualified by interdependence. Yet after a second generation of bitter experience, the United States, with many others, sees the indispensability of interdependence. Today we seek security through the strengthening of universal institutions, by regional arrangements, by maintaining military capabilities in conjunction with our allies, and by determined efforts to diminish the risk of surprise attack and to limit and control armaments.

In 1945 the United States took the lead in organizing the United Nations. We hoped that it would become an effective instrument of collective security. But it still falls short of being that. United Nations action in a divided world has often been paralyzed. For example, the U.S.S.R. has exercised the veto in the Security Council about 80 times. No joint U.N. military force has been set up as contemplated in the charter, although Korea and Suez point to possible progress in this direction. Also, the Assembly, in the Suez and the Hungarian crises of last fall, displayed surprising determination and virtual unanimity.

It is sometimes said by way of reproach that in these matters the

United Nations applied a "double standard"—severity toward Israel, France, and the United Kingdom, and leniency toward the Soviet Union. This charge has no basis in fact. The Assembly resolutions directed against the use of force in Egypt and in Hungary were equally peremptory.

The double standard was not in the United Nations but in the nations. There was the moral sensitivity of the Western nations, and their decent respect for the opinions of mankind. There was the immorality of Soviet communism, and its contempt for the opinions of mankind. We can rejoice that, among the nations, there are governments having standards higher than those of the Government of Soviet Russia. That is not a matter of reproach to them, or to the United Nations.

Despite hopeful indications of progress in the United Nations, the nations of the free world which felt endangered have, for the most part, felt it necessary to resort to collective, and usually regional, arrangements to safeguard their security. This has been in entire accord with the charter. In this development the United States has assumed a major role and responsibility. Since 1945 we have entered into collective security treaties with 42 other nations, and we have less formal arrangements with several more.

The first such treaty, the Rio Pact, was with our own neighbors of this hemisphere. We went on to broaden the base of collective security through a series of multilateral and bilateral pacts which now encompass much of the free world. The forces of NATO, now including the Federal Republic of Germany, stand guard over the treaty-defined North Atlantic region, which includes the vital area of Western Europe. In the West Pacific and Far East, the SEATO and ANZUS pacts and four bilateral treaties establish the principle that a threat to one is the concern of all. In the Middle East, the Baghdad Pact and the Eisenhower Doctrine assure collective response to Communist aggression at points of special danger or weakness. This nearly worldwide system of regional collective security has served all the participants well. It has deterred aggression and given much needed assurance to peoples who are especially exposed to attack.

We must, in candor, admit that all of the participants do not look upon these arrangements alike. Some consider them broad political alliances, binding the parties, at least morally, to support each other generally. But the net result has been to further the application of the principle of collective security within the society of nations.

IV. THE STRATEGY OF COLLECTIVE SELF-DEFENSE

Collective security must, of course, be buttressed by military capabilities to deter armed aggression and to cope with it if it should occur. In December 1950, in an address before the American Association for the United Nations, I spoke to this problem, pointing out that, "With more than 20 nations strung along the 20,000 miles of Iron Curtain, it is not possible to build up static defensive forces which could make each nation impregnable to such a major and unpredictable assault as Russia could launch. To attempt this would be to have strength nowhere and bankruptcy everywhere." I went on to say, "Against such military power as the Soviet Union can marshal, collective security depends on capacity to counterattack against the aggressor," and I pointed to our Strategic Air Force and our stock of weapons as constituting an arsenal of retaliation.

During the ensuing years the military strategy of the free-world allies has been largely based upon our great capacity to retaliate should the Soviet Union launch a war of aggression. It is widely accepted that this strategy of deterrence has, during this period, contributed decisively to the security of the free world.

However, the United States has not been content to rely upon a peace which could be preserved only by a capacity to destroy vast segments of the human race. Such a concept is acceptable only as a last alternative. In recent years there has been no other. But the resourcefulness of those who serve our nation in the field of science and weapon engineering now shows that it is possible to alter the character of nuclear weapons. It seems now that their use need not involve vast destruction and widespread harm to humanity. Recent tests point to the possibility of possessing nuclear weapons the destructiveness and radiation effects of which can be confined substantially to predetermined targets.

In the future it may thus be feasible to place less reliance upon deterrence of vast retaliatory power. It may be possible to defend countries by nuclear weapons so mobile, or so placed, as to make military invasion with conventional forces a hazardous attempt. For example, terrain is often such that invasion routes can be decisively dominated by nuclear artillery. Thus, in contrast to the 1950 decade, it may be that by the 1960 decade the nations which are around the Sino-Soviet perimeter can possess an effective defense against full-scale conventional attack and thus confront any aggressor with the choice between failing or himself initiating nuclear war against the defending country. Thus the tables may be turned, in the sense that, instead of those who are non-aggressive having to rely upon all-out nuclear retaliatory power for their protection, would-be aggressors will be unable to count on a successful conventional aggression but must themselves weigh the consequences of invoking nuclear war.

It is precisely this evolution that Soviet diplomacy and propaganda strive most vigorously to prevent. They oppose all such experimental testing of nuclear devices as is necessary to find ways to reduce fallout and to reduce size. They seem to prefer that nuclear weapons be only the "horror" type of weapons. They apparently calculate that humanitarian instincts will prevent us from using such weapons. They know that, if Soviet conventional forces were operating in Europe, the megaton-type weapon with large fission fallout could not be used by Western forces without endangering the friendly peoples of the area. Under these conditions Sino-Soviet manpower and its conventional weapons would become the dominant military force in Eurasia. Such considerations make it important to combine the suspension of testing with other measures which will limit armament and the possibilities of surprise attack.

The Soviet Union, in its May 10, 1955, disarmament proposals, said:

> There are possibilities beyond the reach of international control for evading this control and for organizing the clandestine manufacture of atomic and hydrogen weapons, even if there is a formal agreement on international control. In such a situation the security of the States signatory to the international convention can not be guaranteed, since the possibility would be open to a potential aggressor to accumulate stocks of atomic and hydrogen weapons for a surprise atomic attack on peace-loving states.

The foregoing is certainly true, at least as regards the use of existing stocks of fissionable material. That is why we do not seek to control existing stocks. We accept their inevitability, limiting our control proposals to newly created fissionable material that can be controlled.

The Soviet statement continued:

> Until an atmosphere of trust has been created in relations between States, any agreement on the institution of international control can only serve to lull the vigilance of the peoples. It will create a false sense of security, while in reality there will be a danger of the production of atomic and hydrogen weapons and hence the threat of surprise attack and the

unleashing of an atomic war with all its appalling consequences for the people.

This, again, is a true statement. Unless there are effective measures to reduce "the threat of surprise attack," whether nuclear or otherwise, it would be imprudent to interrupt the safeguarded search for methods to apply nuclear power to weapons in a manner to enlarge the possibilities of defense greatly and at the same time greatly reduce the lethal fallout factor inherent in weapons which are still in a relatively early stage of development.

As nuclear weapons come to provide greater possibilities for defense, this will require changes in military and related political strategy. So long as collective security depends almost wholly upon the deterrent of retaliatory power and the ability to wreak great destruction upon an aggressor nation, there has to be almost sole dependence upon the United States. No other nation can afford the cost of maintaining adequate deterrent power. This requires a vast arsenal of planes, weapons, and perhaps long-range missiles. These must be constantly renewed to overcome increasing defensive capabilities. This, in turn, requires vast outlay for experimentation.

However, as nuclear weapons become more tactical in character and thus more adaptable to area defense, there will inevitably be a desire on the part of those allies which are technically qualified to participate more directly in this defense and to have a greater assurance that this defensive power will in fact be used. Such factors are already leading to study of a so-called atomic weapons stockpile which could be established by the United States in the European NATO area and, as becomes appropriate, made available to NATO.

A concomitant of this problem is how to prevent the promiscuous spread of nuclear weapons throughout the world. Without safeguards, such weapons might in the future get into the hands of irresponsible dictators and be used as a form of international blackmail. The world would indeed become an unhappy place to live in if humanity had to accept an ever-present threat of this character.

We are only beginning to envisage the drastic changes in political-military relations which will be consequent upon the rapid growth of scientific knowledge and operating experience in the nuclear field. New weapons possibilities are opening up in rapid succession. Political thinking finds it difficult to keep up with that pace. And, of course, there is inevitably some interval between the thinking and the institutionalizing of the results of thinking.

The development of a common defense has meant, and will continue to mean, heavy outlays for an effective and modern United States military establishment. It has also required, and will continue to require, the United States to give military assistance and support to the military forces of those nations associated with us in collective arrangements or in special need or danger. Such assistance is in no sense to be viewed as charity. It is based on a hardheaded appraisal of our own defense needs. Without it, our own defense costs would be far greater and our security far less. The aggregate military and economic resources of the free world coalition represent the greatest and least costly insurance against war.

v. "DISARMAMENT"

The United States recognizes that armaments alone are no lasting guaranty of peace. We are, therefore, pursuing a policy designed to set up safeguards against surprise attack and to bring national armaments, both nuclear and conventional, under effective international limitation and supervision. It is true that so-called "disarmament" efforts in the past have proved futile. The Hague peace conferences, the Versailles treaty, the Washington Naval Limitation Agreement, the League of Nations disarmament conferences, are recent conspicuous examples of failure. But there are important differences today.

Past efforts have usually proceeded from the assumption that it is possible to establish and maintain certain defined levels of military strength and to equate these dependably as between the nations. Actually, military potentials are so imponderable that this always has been and always will be a futile pursuit. Today there is a new approach. It is proposed to establish a system of international supervision which will make massive surprise attack unlikely. If this happens, then general war becomes less likely and the level of armaments will almost automatically go down.

Today the great military establishments derive largely from one of two calculations. A potential attacker calculates that he may be able to accumulate the power to gain a decisive initial advantage by surprise attack. Those who feel that they may be attacked calculate that the only effective deterrent to attack is to possess, collectively, power so great and so decentralized that it cannot be rendered nugatory by a massive surprise attack.

New discoveries and their application lead to constantly mounting exertions to develop means of attack and of retaliation and of means of survival. The only effective way to stop the cycle is to establish such international supervision of the great sources of military power that it becomes unlikely that there can be undetected preparation for an attack massive enough to destroy the opposing source of power. That was President Eisenhower's "open skies" concept, first put forward at the Geneva "summit" conference of 1955.

A potential aggressor, subject to inspection from the air, supplemented by a ground component, will know that he probably cannot use vast armament to advantage. And nations exposed to aggression will know that they probably cannot be wiped out at a single blow and that therefore they can rely more than now upon potential military strength rather than strength actually in being. Thus there will be no stimulation, as at present, for an arms race. This will not solve all the problems of armament, or guarantee peace. But the new approach could create an atmosphere in which other measures, now impossible, would become possible.

The most important difference from the past is, of course, the fact that never before has there been such need to reduce the risk of war. Today a general war between the great military powers could destroy almost all human life, certainly in the northern latitudes. Our working hypothesis must be that what is necessary is possible. We assume that the forces which man has created man can, by wisdom, resourcefulness, and discipline, harness and control. We persevere in common efforts to free the world from the continuing threat of destruction by the weapons that its civilization has produced.

VI. FREE-WORLD HEALTH AND VITALITY

Nations, like individuals, cannot live to themselves alone. Realizing this, the American people have always given generously of their substance to victims of disaster in many parts of the world and have engaged in innumerable programs of humanitarian assistance. These, until recently, have been the outcome mainly of philanthropic motives. During the past decade they have reflected enlightened national self-interest.

We now see that the world has become so much a unit that, wherever the body politic is afflicted, the whole is endangered. We realize that peace and prosperity for one requires, in the long run, that all should have the opportunity to pursue happiness. We see the need for more vital domestic forces in all free lands, to resist Communist subversion or attack.

Since 1945 our nation has granted, outright, nearly $50 billion in aid, military and economic. That has evidenced an enlightened conception of our own national interest. It is significant that, despite this assistance to others at the rate of about $5 billion a year, our own economy has developed in a healthy manner. This has been a decade of rising prosperity. In 1946 our national income was approximately $180 billion. In 1951 it was approximately $277 billion. In 1956 it was approximately $344 billion.

The Marshall plan was the most dramatic of our economic assistance efforts. It provided Western Europe with some of the means, and with the time and opportunity, to save itself. Now we see in Western Europe the development of a degree of unity which had been the vision of enlightened statesmen for many years. There has been, first, the Coal and Steel Community, then the Brussels treaty for European union, and now the treaties for a common market and EURATOM. These developments are momentous in terms of developing unity, strength, and well-being in an area which for centuries has been the seat of recurrent wars threatening the very existence of Western civilization.

In recent years, as the Western European economy has been reestablished, the United States has placed increasing emphasis on economic and technical assistance to the newly awakened and needy peoples of Asia and Africa. As upwards of 800 million people, representing 20 new nations, have won political liberty, one of the momentous issues of our time has been whether this political liberty would also mean the liberation of the people from a quagmire of economic misery and hopelessness. If not, present political liberty may prove a mere transition from one form of colonial rule to another far worse.

All of our aid programs, whether military, economic, or technical, are rightly viewed as ventures in mutual security. If we have given more than others, this reflects our greater ability to give. An important question now raised about our mutual security policies is, will there be an early end to them? Recent studies by expert commissions all attest to their continuing necessity.

The time to end such assistance will be when it no longer serves the enlightened self-interest of the United States. Military assistance and defense support represent about 70 per cent of the entire program. That is part of our own defense. As regards economic assistance, we can expect private capital gradually to assume increasing responsibility for promoting the development of less well-developed areas, provided there is political stability. It is to be noted that, while the dollar value of our mutual security spending has not greatly declined in recent years, an increasing amount of this is in terms of loans rather than of grants. Also, the total of public loans and grants now represents only about 1 per cent of our national income, whereas a few years ago grants alone represented about 3 per cent.

A cessation of our mutual security programs would, under present conditions, be disastrous. What is needed is to put necessary aid programs on a more long-term, businesslike basis, reducing grant aid to a minimum and applying our assistance in ways that will best help needy peoples to help themselves. As a result of intensive studies independently initiated by the Executive and the Congress, one new instrumentality is now being inaugurated, the Development Loan Fund. This, when adequately capitalized, will place major responsibility on the receiving countries and stimulate self-help and private investment.

United States foreign economic policy has been vigorous in fields other than aid. President Eisenhower's speech to the United Nations in December 1953 dramatized the possible peaceful uses of atomic energy. Much has been accomplished to realize these possibilities through bilateral agreements. Recently the United States ratified the statute for the International Atomic Energy Agency, which should be a milestone in the general application of this marvelous new resource for the benefit and not for the destruction of mankind.

We recognize that governmental restrictions on trade have in the past throttled world commerce to the detriment of every nation. We have entered into international undertakings, notably the General Agreement on Tariffs and Trade, to prevent this and to promote the interchange of goods and services. This expansion materially benefits the United States and friendly nations. Measures which might adversely affect a nation are avoided. Economic growth is stimulated throughout the world. The benefits of advances in one country are readily diffused to others.

We do not forget that every government has a primary duty to serve its own people. But usually that service can be best rendered by finding ways which help others also, or which at least do not hurt others. Occasionally, and happily only rarely, situations arise which cannot be resolved by this formula. But in general we seek an international society in which men, goods, and ideas flow freely and without obstruction throughout a wide area and in which the opportunity to pursue happiness is open to every man and woman. The United States market, which dependably offers so much that others want and which dependably buys so much that others would sell, is the great economic stabilizer of the free world. It helps to combat communism and the self-centered nationalisms which are alike in rejecting the concept of interdependence.

Few economic theories are today as obsolete as those of Marx. They were propagated nearly a century ago in relation to a society which since then has rapidly transformed itself through the force of its own dynamic qualities.

The social and economic basis of democracy has been widened throughout the Western World, and the same process is beginning and accelerating in other free-world areas. International communism is a reactionary movement. Its "planning" makes slaves of the producers and creates a new exploiting and ruling class. It is replete with contradictions which, in free countries, have been resolved by a peaceful, yet dynamic, evolution.

We cannot, of course, claim perfection. The dramatic and peaceful development of the social and economic structure of our free societies must and will go forward. But even though we do not claim perfection, we can claim that the social goals which communism pretends to seek are in fact achieved to a far greater extent within our free society than they are achieved in Soviet Russia or Communist China.

VII. PEACEFUL CHANGE

As our country has been swept more fully into the broad currents of human affairs, we have been made more and more conscious of those rapid world movements of our century which seem incessantly to transform the international landscape. Change is the law of life, and that includes international life. Our common problem, in a world of rapid and often momentous change, is to insure that necessary changes occur in peaceful fashion without upheaval or war. Violent change is never selective change. It destroys the good as well as the bad. Change is beneficent when it is selective, continuing and developing the good while shedding that which is evil, outmoded, or inadequate.

We have already alluded to some of the areas where change is most conspicuous. There is first of all the change which will inevitably result from the splitting of the atom. A vast new source of power is available to man, and we can be sure that it will be used to effect momentous changes. It can destroy man, or it can enrich him. The choice is up to man himself. The United States first had the power of fission and used it in war to defend freedom. We feel a special responsibility to help to assure that man's momentous choice shall be "atoms for peace."

Another vast force for change is political nationalism. This is operating strongly in Asia and Africa. Since 1945 it has resulted in the creation of a score of new nations. Other peoples are well on their way to political independence.

But the mere act of granting political independence does not of itself assure that the newly independent peoples will in fact have governments of their own choosing or governments able and willing to serve the governed. It does not of itself mean that the society of nations is enriched by new recruits dedicated to principles of interdependence and an international order of law and justice. It is going to be necessary to find policies to cope with new demands of colonial peoples, with strident and embittered nationalisms, and with social unrest among those who tend to feel that political liberty automatically should provide them with new economic opportunity.

The United States, once itself a colony, shares and sympathizes with the aspirations of peoples for political independence. Also, we know the extent to which liberty, for its own self-preservation, requires the self-restraint of moral law and the education to make sound judgments. We can and should play an important part in finding the policies to cope with the political and social ferment of much of the human race.

We recognize, as does the United Nations Charter in article 14, that there will be constantly arising particular situations likely to impair the general welfare or friendly relations among nations and calling for peaceful adjustment. We have noted in recent years the emergence of such situations, for example, the disputes over Cyprus, Kashmir, and West Irian; between Arabs and Israelis; and over Suez. These not only disrupt world peace and comity. They provide fertile soil for Communist propaganda and penetration.

The United States recognizes that, in the case of such disputes, all of the merits are not on one side. Therefore we do not identify ourselves with any purely partisan approach. The Soviet rulers, unconcerned with the merits and eager only to extend their power, are prepared to back one side against the other if, in return, they obtain political advantages. Because they sometimes gain advantages out of such disputes, their interest lies in creating and exacerbating disputes and preventing their settlement.

This illustrates how important it is for the free world to establish regular procedures for the settlement of disputes between its members. This has already been done in the Western Hemisphere through the Organization of American States. Within the past few years several serious disputes between American states have been successfully dealt with by the procedures of this organization. Its members deserve the highest praise for their loyalty to the peaceful processes of law and justice which they have established. They have set a notable example which ought to be followed more generally.

Largely as a result of United States initiation, the North Atlantic Treaty Organization is now developing processes for the settlement of disputes between its members. Last year the Secretary-General of NATO was given new responsibilities in this respect.

There are, in the long run, great potentialities in article 11 of the United Nations Charter, which authorizes the Assembly to recommend change in the status quo. The exercise of this delicate function requires knowledge, wisdom, and self-restraint. It becomes particularly difficult for the Assembly to exercise this function when a powerful minority of members seeks not fair and just settlements but unsettlements which lend themselves to the use by international communism of its revolutionary tactics.

Sometimes it is felt that the United States ought more often to use its power to effectuate settlements. The United States can and does exert an influence in quiet and inconspicuous ways as a friend of all the parties. We stand ready to exercise our good offices if and when invited to do so under adequate terms of reference. But we do not assume the right to meddle or be the arbiter of other peoples' affairs.

The most dangerous of all unresolved disputes are those within the areas now under the rule of international communism. The pattern here is classic. There is the inevitability of change, but the situation is dominated by those who do not believe in peaceful change at the expense of their power. Such a state of affairs has historically produced violent eruptions. Some of the areas in question are especially explosive as they involve the artificial division of historic nations—Germany, Korea, and Viet-Nam. Others, as lately demonstrated in Hungary and Poland, contain resentments so bitter that many patriots would die in revolt against hopeless odds rather than continue to suffer in silence.

United States policy, as proclaimed repeatedly, will never sanction these injustices nor accept them as permanent. But we strive only by peaceful means to achieve justice. It would not be in the general interest, nor in the interest of the peoples directly concerned, for events to shape up into war. We shall continue to employ all the resources of the United Nations and all diplomatic means and moral pressures to alleviate the injustices and oppressions suffered by these peoples and to make their plight known to world opinion. We have faith in their ultimate freedom and independence. When the Russian leaders decide to serve the interests of Russia and cease to be the agents of international communism, they will act in the knowledge that Russia's long-term interests require the reunification of Germany in freedom and the liberation of the satellites. Only thus can Russia achieve its proper desire to be surrounded by friendly peoples. The martyrs of Hungary have not died in vain if they have advanced the coming of that day.

Even such a brief survey of the forces working for change cannot but leave us with a sense of their immensity and the relative paucity of political means for keeping them within peaceful channels. Peace and justice are surely in jeopardy.

Within a stable individual society there are institutions to effectuate and legalize change—usually parliamentary bodies which make and remake laws so that political, economic, and social changes occur peacefully and with legitimacy. In the international field concepts of sovereignty which have become obsolete lead nations to feel that they can put what they deem to be their own national rights and interests above the need of the whole society of nations—the need for peaceful settlement. It will probably be a long time before there is any universal mandatory process for effectuating international change. But there can and should be a far greater willingness than there now is to subordinate national interests to the interest of the world community, to use existing agencies such as the Court of International Justice, and to develop and accept a body of written or unwritten international law.

VIII. CONCLUSION

Two significant facts stand out respecting United States foreign policy. The first is that our policies have developed as a reflection of deeply ingrained national characteristics. The second is that our policies have been influenced and modified by changing world conditions in the effort to apply our basic concepts to actual conditions and to the challenges they have presented.

These two features of our policy are by no means incompatible. To hold to national judgments of right and wrong does not mean that we are so closely wedded to doctrinaire concepts that we cannot adjust our policies to the demands of the hour. To think of our policies as shifting and changing in order to cope with varying situations need not be to infer that no central and governing core of principle gives them continuity.

In this article we have dwelt mainly on the manner in which policy has adapted itself to new and challenging problems; but the manner and conduct have been guided throughout by certain principles.

These principles were unforgettably formulated by George Washington in his Farewell Address. He there points out that "of all the dispositions and habits which lead to political prosperity, religion and morality are indispensable supports." And he went on to emphasize the primary importance of a general diffusion of knowledge. "In proportion as the structure of a government gives force to public opinion, it is essential that public opinion should be enlightened."

Because of our religious beliefs we attach exceptional importance to freedom. We believe in the sanctity of the human personality, in the inalienable rights with which men are endowed by their Creator, and in their right to have governments of their own choosing. But we also believe that individuals as well as governments are subject to moral law. We recognize that liberty, whether it be individual or national, can be dangerous license unless it is exercised under the disciplines of moral law and with adequate knowledge and education to assure that moral judgments in fact take all relevant factors into account.

We are as a nation unsympathetic to systems and governments that deny human freedom and seek to mold all men to a preconceived pattern and to use them as tools to aggrandize the state. We are also unsympathetic to assertions of sovereignty which do not accept the concept of social interdependence. As Americans we have built our nation on the federal principle, drawing together what were sovereign states into a cooperative community. We thus naturally invoke the idea of cooperation between nations in the pursuit of ends which correspond with the aspirations of all people.

Despite a certain superficial indifference to the niceties of law observance, Americans have developed a profound respect for law as the basis of social and civic life. We conceive of manmade law as an effort to apply the moral law to the conditions of time and place. Our Constitution is the oldest basic written law in the world today. This concept of law permeates our entire political system and gives it a stability and moderation rarely matched among contemporary governments. We yearn to see the behavior of nations in their relations with one another rest upon the foundation of agreed legal principles derived from moral concepts. We abhor arbitrary government which reflects only the caprice of a tyrant.

These concepts, taken together, constitute our American way of life. They represent, for us, the idea and reality of freedom under law—of which the most authoritative is moral law. It is inevitable that they should influence our foreign policy. For, under a representative form of government, foreign policy is valid only as an expression and a projection of national character and national convictions. Whoever would understand our policy should try to comprehend us as a nation.

The constancy of our national character is what, even in such a swiftly changing era, gives stability and continuity to our foreign policy. It is well that this is so, for it enables those who understand the United States to comprehend also the mainsprings of its action and thus estimate, in their own interest, what the response of the United States to any situation is likely to be.

The fact has an important bearing on our alliances. As leader of a great coalition, we can never hope to please all countries. But we can win respect if it is felt that we are acting in true character.

It is important also in relation to those who are hostile to us. Potential enemies will be less inclined to gamble on our behavior—with all the risks of miscalculation—if they can count with a reasonable degree of certainty upon our national conduct.

So toward all, whether friendly or not, we should act as a people proud of our heritage, assured in our convictions, and confident in our destiny. We have no desire to impose upon others the pattern of our thought and our institutions. Yet we may take pride in the fact that our principles are drawn from the great thinkers of the 18th-century "age of enlightenment" who impressed their ideas deeply upon modern Western culture as a whole. These principles are not narrowly parochial but universal in their application. In America they were the inspiration of the greatest democratic experiment in history. Insofar as our national behavior reflects these principles, it is certain to meet, in the long run, with understanding and respect.

Alliances*

by Hans J. Morgenthau

[I]

Alliances are a necessary function of the balance of power operating within a multiple state system. Nations A and B, competing with each other, have three choices in maintaining and improving their relative power positions. They can increase their own power, they can add to their own power the power of other nations, or they can withhold the power of other nations from the adversary. When they make the first choice they embark upon an armaments race. When they choose the second and third alternatives, they pursue a policy of alliances.

Whether or not a nation shall pursue a policy of alliances is, then, not a matter of principle but of expediency. A nation will shun alliances if it believes that it is strong enough to hold its own unaided or that the burden of the commitments resulting from the alliance is likely to outweigh the advantages to be expected. It is for one or the other or both of these reasons that, throughout the better part of their history, Great Britain and the United States have refrained from entering into peace-time alliances with other nations.

Yet Great Britain and the United States have also refrained from concluding an alliance with each other even though, from the proclamation of the Monroe Doctrine in 1823 to the attack on Pearl Harbor in 1941, they have acted, at least in relation to the other European nations, as if they were allied. Their relationship during that period

* From *Confluence: An International Forum*, Vol. VI, No. 4 (1957-1958), pp. 311-334. Reprinted by permission. This article is a modified version of a paper presented in September 1957 at the annual meeting of the American Political Science Association.

provides another instance of a situation in which nations dispense with
an alliance. It occurs when their interests so obviously call for concerted
policies and actions that an explicit formulation of these interests, policies and actions in the form of a treaty of alliance appears to be redundant.

Both Great Britain and the United States have had with regard to
the continent of Europe one interest in common: the preservation
of the European balance of power. Thus when Great Britain went to
war in 1914 and 1939 in order to protect the European balance of
power, the United States first supported Great Britain with a conspicuous lack of that impartiality befitting a neutral, and then joined
her on the battlefield. Had the United States been tied to Great Britain
by a formal treaty of alliance in 1914 and 1939, it might have declared
war earlier, but its general policies and concrete actions would not have
been materially different than they actually were.

Not every community of interests, calling for common policies and
actions, also calls for legal codification in an explicit alliance. Yet, on
the other hand, an alliance requires a community of interests for its
foundation. Under what conditions, then, does an existing community
of interests require the explicit formulation of an alliance? What is it
that an alliance adds to the existing community of interests?

An alliance adds precision, especially in the form of limitation, to an
existing community of interests and to the general policies and concrete
measures serving them.[1] The interests nations have in common are not
typically so precise and limited as to geographic region, objective, and
appropriate policies as has been the American and British interest in
the preservation of the European balance of power. Nor are they so
incapable of precision and limitation as concerns the prospective common enemy. For while a typical alliance is directed against a specific
nation or group of nations, the enemy of the Anglo-American community of interests could in the nature of things not be specified beforehand. As Jefferson shifted his sympathies back and forth between
Napoleon and Great Britain according to who seemed to threaten the
balance of power at the time, so during the century following the
Napoleonic Wars Great Britain and the United States had to decide in
the light of circumstances ever liable to change who posed at the mo-

---

[1] Glancing through the treaties of alliance of the seventeenth and eighteenth centuries, one is struck by the meticulous precision with which obligations to furnish
troops, equipment, logistic support, food, money and the like were defined.

ment the greatest threat. This blanket character of the enemy, determined not individually but by the function he performs, brings to mind a similar characteristic of collective security, which is directed against the abstractly designed aggressor, whoever he may be.

The typical interests which unite two nations against a third are both more definite as concerns the determination of the enemy and less precise as concerns the objectives to be sought and the policies to be pursued. In the last decades of the nineteenth century, France was opposed to Germany and Russia was opposed to Austria, while Austria was allied with Germany against France and Russia. How could the interests of France and Russia be brought to a common denominator, determining policy and guiding action? How could, in other words, the *casus foederis* be defined so that both friend and foe would know what to expect in certain contingencies affecting their respective interests? It was for the treaty of alliances of 1894 to perform these functions. Had the objectives and policies of the Franco-Russian alliance of 1894 been as clear as are the objectives and policies of Anglo-American cooperation in Europe, no alliance treaty would have been necessary. Had the enemy been as indeterminate, no alliance treaty would have been feasible.

Not every community of interests calling for cooperation between two or more nations, then, requires that the terms of this cooperation be specified through the legal stipulations of a treaty of alliance. It is only when the common interests are inchoate in terms of policy and action that a treaty of alliance is required to make them explicit and operative. These interests, as well as the alliances expressing them and the policies serving them, can be distinguished in five different ways: according to their intrinsic nature and relationship, the distribution of benefits and power, their coverage in relation to the total interests of the nations concerned, their coverage in terms of time and their effectiveness in terms of common policies and actions. In consequence, we can distinguish alliances serving identical, complementary and ideological interests and policies. We can further distinguish mutual and one-sided, general and limited, temporary and permanent, operative and inoperative alliances.[2]

The Anglo-American alliance with regard to Europe provides the classic example of an alliance serving identical interests. The alliance between the United States and Pakistan is one of many contemporary

---

[2] Sanskrit has sixteen words for different types of alliances.

instances of an alliance serving complementary interests. For the United States it serves the primary purpose of expanding the scope of the policy of containment; for Pakistan it serves primarily the purpose of increasing her political, military and economic potential vis-à-vis her neighbors.

The pure type of an ideological alliance is presented by the Treaty of the Holy Alliance of 1815 and the Atlantic Charter of 1941. Both documents laid down general moral principles to which the signatories pledged their adherence and general objectives whose realization they pledged themselves to seek. Much more typical is the addition of ideological commitments to material ones in one and the same treaty of alliance.[3] Thus the Three Emperors League of 1873 provided for military assistance among Austria, Germany and Russia in case of attack on any of the three and at the same time emphasized the solidarity of the three monarchies against republican subversion. In our times, the ideological commitment against Communist subversion, inserted in treaties of alliance, performs a similar function. The ideological factor also manifests itself in the official interpretation of an alliance, in terms of an ideological solidarity transcending the limitations of material interests. The conception of the Anglo-American alliance, common before the British invasion of Egypt in 1956, as all-inclusive and world-embracing, based upon common culture, political institutions and ideals, is a case in point.

As concerns the political effect of this ideological factor upon an alliance, three possibilities must be distinguished. A purely ideological alliance, unrelated to material interests, cannot but be stillborn; it is unable to determine policies or guide actions and misleads by giving the appearance of political solidarity where there is none. The ideological factor, when it is superimposed upon an actual community of interests, can lend strength to the alliance by marshalling moral convictions and emotional preferences to its support. It can also weaken it by obscuring the nature and limits of the common interests which the alliance was supposed to make precise and by raising expectations, bound to be disappointed, concerning the extent of concerted policies and actions. For both these last possibilities, the Anglo-American alliance can again serve as an example.

Ideally, the distribution of benefits within an alliance should be one of complete mutuality. This ideal is most likely to be approximated in

---

[3] It ought to be pointed out that both the Holy Alliance and the Atlantic Charter actually supplement material commitments contained in separate legal instruments.

an alliance concluded among equals in power and serving identical interests; here the equal resources of all, responding to equal incentives, serve one single interest. The other extreme in the distribution of benefits is one-sidedness, in which one party receives the lion's share of benefits while the other bears the main bulk of burdens. Insofar as the object of such an alliance is the preservation of the territorial and political integrity of the receiving party, such an alliance is indistinguishable from a treaty of guarantee. Complementary interests lend themselves most easily to this kind of disproportion since they are by definition different in substance and their comparative assessment is likely to be distorted by subjective interpretation.

The distribution of benefits and determination of policies is thus likely to reflect the distribution of power within an alliance. It is for this reason that Machiavelli warned weak nations against making alliances with strong ones except by necessity.[4] However, this correlation between benefits, policies and power is by no means inevitable. A weak nation may well possess an asset which is of such great value for its strong ally as to be irreplaceable. Here the unique benefit the former is able to grant or withhold may give it a status within the alliance completely out of keeping with the actual distribution of material power. The relationships between the United States and Iceland with regard to bases and between Great Britain and Iraq with regard to oil can serve as examples.

The misinterpretation of the Anglo-American alliance, mentioned before, is also a case in point for the confusion between limited and general alliances. In the age of total war, wartime alliances tend to be general in that they comprise the total interests of the contracting parties both with regard to the waging of the war and the peace settlement. On the other hand, peace-time alliances tend to be limited to a fraction of the total interests and objectives of the signatories. A nation will conclude a multitude of alliances with different nations which may overlap and contradict each other on specific points.

A typical alliance attempts to transform a small fraction of the total interests of the contracting parties into common policies and measures. Some of these interests are irrelevant to the purposes of the alliance, others support them, others diverge from them and others still are incompatible with them. Whether and for how long an alliance will remain operative depends upon the strength of the interests underlying

---

[4] *The Prince,* Chapter 21.

it as over against the strength of the other interests of the nations concerned. The value and the chances of an alliance, however limited in scope, must be considered within the context of the over-all policies within which it is expected to operate.

General alliances are usually of temporary duration and most prevalent in wartime. The overriding common interest in winning the war and securing through the peace settlement the interests for which the war was waged is bound to yield, once victory is won and the peace treaties are signed, to the traditionally separate and frequently incompatible interests of the individual nations. On the other hand, there exists a correlation between the permanency of an alliance and the limited character of the interests it serves; for only such a specific, limited interest is likely to last long enough to provide the foundation for a durable alliance. The alliance between Great Britain and Portugal, concluded in 1703, has survived the centuries because Portugal's interest in the protection of her ports by the British fleet and the British interest in the control of the Atlantic approaches to Portugal has endured. Yet it can be stated as a general historical observation that while alliance treaties have frequently assumed permanent validity by being concluded "in perpetuity" or for periods of ten or twenty years, they could not have been more durable than the generally precarious and fleeting configurations of common interests which they were intended to serve.

The dependence of alliances upon the underlying community of interests also accounts for the distinction between operative and inoperative alliances. For an alliance to be operative, its members must agree not only on general objectives but on policies and measures as well. Many alliances have remained scraps of paper because no such agreement was forthcoming, and it was not forthcoming because the community of interests did not extend beyond general objectives to concrete policies and measures. The Franco-Russian alliances of 1935 and 1944 and the Anglo-Russian alliance of 1942 are cases in point.

The examination of contemporary alliances in the light of these categories will be divided under three headings: the Atlantic Alliance, the Western alliances outside Europe, the Communist alliances.

[II]

The vital interest of the United States in the protection of the nations of Western Europe against Russian domination is identical with the interest of these nations in preserving their national independence.

Yet this foundation of the Atlantic Alliance has undergone a change both subtle and drastic. The Atlantic Alliance is beset by a crisis which the events of November 1956 made obvious but did not create.

Seen from the perspective of the nations of Western Europe, three factors sustained the Atlantic Alliance in the decade following the Second World War: the atomic monopoly of the United States, the economic weakness of the nations of Western Europe and the intransigence of Stalinist policies. The conjunction of these factors confronted the nations of Western Europe with the choice between suicide and the acceptance of the political, economic and military support of the United States. In other words, the Atlantic Alliance was for the nations of Western Europe a prerequisite for national survival.

This connection between national survival and the Atlantic Alliance is no longer as close nor as obvious as it used to be. The atomic monopoly of the United States provided the nations of Western Europe with absolute protection against Russian conquest. With the Soviet Union having become an atomic power equal, if not superior, to the United States, the Atlantic Alliance is no longer for the nations of Western Europe solely a protection, but has become also a liability. The atomic stalemate threatens not only the two super-powers but also their allies with total destruction. Paradoxical as it may seem, the drastically increased threat of Soviet power has drastically weakened the Western alliance. The Soviet Union has not been slow to point out, and the man in the street in Western Europe has not been slow to understand, that if there is a chance for the nations of Western Europe to survive in an atomic war it may lie in not being too closely identified, or perhaps not being identified at all, with the United States. Thus a latent neutralism has had a slowly corrosive influence upon the Atlantic Alliance. The rise of this neutralism in Western Europe as a popular mass movement is not primarily the result of Communist propaganda, or of faintness of heart, but of the new objective conditions under which the nations of Western Europe must live in the age of the atomic stalemate.

Secondly, the economic recovery of the nations of Western Europe has greatly diminished their dependence upon the United States. The Coal and Steel Community, Euratom, the Common Market and the development of East-West trade are likely to decrease it still more. Thus while the nations of Western Europe are still in need of American economic aid, that aid is no longer a question of life and death, as it was ten years ago. Today they have, or at least have evidence that they soon will have, an alternative. They can stand on their own feet again and look beyond the wall of containment for new outlets for their energies and products.

These factors affect West Germany's attitude toward the Atlantic Alliance with particular intensity. Their effect is strengthened by the political issue which has the widest, and is likely to have an ever deepening, emotional appeal: unification. The Western alliance has been presented to West Germany, both by American and German official spokesmen, as the instrument through which unification would be achieved. While this view was from the outset open to serious doubts, the historic experience of its failure has lead to a crisis of confidence which is likely to deepen as time goes on. The Atlantic Alliance, far from being supported as the instrument of unification, is ever more loudly and widely blamed as the main obstacle to it.

The Soviet Union has been eager to use these new political, military and economic conditions under which the nations of Western Europe live for the purpose of weakening and ultimately destroying the Atlantic Alliance. What has been called the "new look" of Soviet foreign policy is essentially a new flexibility which has taken the place of the monotony of the Stalinist threats. In the face of these threats, no nation which wanted to survive as a nation had any choice; thus Stalin was really the architect of the Atlantic Alliance. The new Soviet foreign policy alternately threatens and tempts, as the occasion seems to require, but always seeks to hold before the eyes of Western Europe an acceptable or even preferable alternative to the Atlantic Alliance. In consequence, the Atlantic Alliance has lost much of its urgency and vitality. Great Britain and France, for instance, no longer feel that they have to subordinate their separate national interests to the common defense against the Soviet Union; and they have begun, in different degrees, to pursue those interests regardless, and sometimes at the expense, of the common interests of the alliance. They have also begun to vent openly their resentment at their lack of great-power status and to allow their policies to be influenced by it. The rise of Germany to a position of political, military and economic eminence cannot but add to the opportunities of the new Soviet foreign policy.

As viewed from the vantage point of the United States, the Atlantic Alliance is also in the process of undergoing a subtle change, which in the end is bound to be drastic. For the United States, the Atlantic Alliance is the political and military implementation of its perennial interest in the maintenance of the European balance of power. However, the military implementation of this interest is likely to change under the impact of a new technology of warfare. As long as the main deterrent to Russian aggression remains the atomic bomb delivered by plane, the military strategy of the United States requires military installations in Western Europe; and the nations of Western Europe have a corresponding interest in providing them. To the extent that the intercontinental guided missile will replace airplanes as a means of delivering atomic attack, the interest in American military installations in Western Europe will diminish on both sides of the Atlantic. This interest will decrease still further when some of the nations of Western Europe have atomic installations of their own. When this day comes, the Atlantic Alliance will take on a new complexion, probably losing some of its specific military aspects and tending to revert to an implicit community of interests like that which tied the United States to Great Britain from 1823 to 1941.

However, the interests of the United States and the nations of Western Europe are not limited to that continent. Those of the United States and Great Britain are world-wide, and France is engaged in Africa. And whatever the community interests within the Atlantic Alliance in Europe, these interests do not necessarily coincide elsewhere. The coincidence or divergence of these non-European interests has had, as the case might be, a strengthening or debilitating effect upon the Atlantic Alliance itself; and the vital interest of all members of the alliance has, in turn, limited their freedom of action outside Europe.

The United States in particular, in dealing with the colonial revolutions which are directed primarily against Great Britain and France, has been continuously confronted with a painful and inherently insoluble dilemma. The horns of that dilemma are the interest of the United States in the continuing strength of Great Britain and France as her principal allies and the American interest in preventing the colonial revolutions from falling under the sway of communism. If the United States underwrites the colonial position of Great Britain or France, as it did in Indochina, it may strengthen its principal European allies, but will impair its standing with the anticolonial peoples of Asia and Africa. If the United States sides unreservedly with the Afro-Asian bloc, as it did in the United Nations on the occasion of the Suez Canal crisis of autumn 1956, it weakens Great Britain and France and, in consequence, the Atlantic Alliance.

Faced with this dilemma which can only be solved at the price of impairing the vital interests of the United States in one or the other respect, the United States has inevitably been reduced to straddling the fence by halfheartedly supporting one side on one occasion and the other side on another, or else keeping hands off altogether. Algeria and Cyprus exemplify at present the dilemma and its evasion. In such situations, then, the Atlantic Alliance does not operate at all; for there are no common interests which could support its operation.

That such divergencies of interest and policy have not imposed greater stresses upon the Atlantic Alliance and have left it essentially unimpaired testifies to its inherent strength. But that strength cannot be taken for granted. The common interests underlying the Atlantic Alliance have thus far prevailed over the divergent ones only because of the conviction of the members of the alliance that they have a greater stake in their common than in their divergent interests. But in recent years the latter have grown stronger and the former, weaker. If this trend should continue unchecked it would indeed put in jeopardy the very survival of the Atlantic Alliance.

Common interests are the rock on which all alliances are built. Yet upon this rock all kinds of structures may be erected, some solid and spacious, others crumbling and confining. In other words, there are good and bad alliances: some work smoothly and are enthusiastically supported, others are cumbersome and are grudgingly accepted as a lesser evil. While the existence of the alliance depends upon a community of interests, the quality of the alliance is determined by the manner in which common interests are translated into concrete policies and day-by-day measures.

It is in this latter respect that there is cause for concern about the Atlantic Alliance. Here, too, the crisis of November 1956 has made obvious defects which antedate that crisis. Three such defects have, continuously and to an ever-increasing degree, impaired the operation of the Atlantic Alliance: its organizational structure; the policies, domestic and international, of its leading members; and the prestige enjoyed by some of its leading statesmen.

The common interest of the members of the Atlantic Alliance in the military protection of their independence has found its organizational expression in the North Atlantic Treaty Organization. The strategic conception which underlies NATO is the assumption that the European members of the Atlantic Alliance are able to defend themselves through a cooperative effort against a military attack by the Soviet Union. But NATO has never developed a convincing philosophy of purpose. All members of NATO are agreed upon one objective: to defend their independence without having to fight for it. But how is this purpose to be achieved? Is primary reliance to be placed upon atomic retaliation with the local forces of NATO performing the function of the "plate glass" or "trip wire," or is a prospective aggressor to be deterred by the inherent military strength of local forces? The members of NATO have not seen eye to eye on this fundamental question, and NATO itself, in its official proclamations and policies, has not seemed to be of one mind either.

More particularly, the declared purposes of NATO have been consistently at variance with the measures requested of its members for implementation of these purposes; and the measures requested, in turn, have been invariably at variance with the measures actually taken. Furthermore, declared purposes, requested measures and the measures actually taken have been subjected to a number of drastic and confusing changes which cannot be explained exclusively by the revolutionary transformation which military technology is in the process of undergoing.

This confusion in policy, itself conducive to political disunity and friction in day-by-day operations, has been magnified by the elaborate organizational superstructure which is intended to put the policies of NATO into practice. This superstructure, which encompasses a plethora of committees charged with coordinating a variety of political, military and economic policies of the member states, must make for friction and inefficiency, even under the best of circumstances. It magnifies defects because it is much too ambitious in purpose and elaborate in operation for the agreed purpose of NATO. In the absence of agreement on philosophy and basic policy, an elaborate organizational superstructure can be a source of weakness rather than of strength.

Since an alliance, in its day-by-day operations, rests in good measure upon mutual confidence, the character and ability of its leading statesmen and the policies they pursue become of critical concern. In both respects, the Atlantic Alliance has shown itself deficient.

There can be no doubt that the prestige of the United States as leader of the Atlantic Alliance has drastically declined. Rightly or wrongly, the United States is no longer looked upon by its allies, as it was during the period immediately following World War II, as the leader whose strength and resolution can be relied upon to keep the Atlantic Alliance on an even course. Three factors are in the main responsible for this crisis of confidence.

In foreign policy it is sometimes useful to keep the enemy guessing. But to keep allies guessing is bound to erode the foundations of confidence upon which an alliance must rest. The allies of the United States have noted discrepancies between the policy pronouncements of our leaders and the actual policies pursued, which appear to them to have evolved into a consistent pattern of unreliability.

This slow accumulation of loss of confidence reached a critical stage in the Suez Canal crisis; for here unreliability in policy appeared to be joined by indifference, if not hostility, to the vital interests of America's principal allies. For the vital interests of the United States and her allies to coincide in Europe and diverge elsewhere is one thing; but for the vital interests of her principal allies elsewhere to be actively opposed by the United States is quite another. To the former, the allies of the United States could reconcile themselves with relative equanimity; the latter could not help but raise for our allies the crucial question as to whether the Atlantic Alliance was worth so high a price. That they answered the question in the affirmative testifies to the vitality of the alliance. Their resentment was kindled by the demonstration of their inability to pursue active foreign policies of their own without the support and against the opposition of one or the other of the superpowers. Thus, under the dramatic impact of the experience which saw their interests and power destroyed in a region vital to themselves, with the approval and active participation of the United States, the Atlantic Alliance has tended to transform itself for our allies from an association of like-minded nations into a burden grudgingly borne.

As far as long-range policies are concerned, the relations among nations must be conceived in terms of interests. As concerns their day-by-day relations, we must also think in terms of personalities. We say that the United States and Great Britain have agreed on a certain policy, but tend to forget that Great Britain and the United States are abstractions and that in actuality the President and Secretary of State of the United States and the Prime Minister and Secretary for Foreign Affairs of Great Britain, speaking in the name of their respective nations, have agreed with each other. The smooth and effective operation of an alliance, then, depends in good measure upon the maintenance of trust and respect among its principal statesmen. There is no gainsaying the fact that the absence of such relations has become a great handicap in the day-by-day operations of the Atlantic Alliance. Regardless of the objective merits of the case, there can be no doubt that the leaders of our European allies have no longer the same confidence in the judgment and the authority of the President of the United States they had in times past, and that they dislike and mistrust the Secretary of State with varying degrees of intensity but with virtual unanimity. These reactions have increased the strains under which the Atlantic Alliance operates at present.

Our reactions, similarly negative, cannot help but add to the strain. The instability of French governments, the collapse of the Eden cabinet, the seeming futility of British and French policies in Cyprus and Algeria, the failure of their intervention in Egypt, all have produced some doubt regarding both the power of our principal allies and the wisdom of their leadership.

The traditional political rhetoric on both sides of the Atlantic has tended to gloss over all these stresses and strains and has made it appear as though the Atlantic Alliance were something broader and smoother and also something more diffuse than it actually is. It is indeed built upon a rock of common interests, but the rock is of limited dimensions and its surfaces are sometimes rough. In spite of the great damage which the crisis of November 1956 has done to the Atlantic Alliance, it has been useful in circumscribing more closely its limits and demonstrating, for all to see, its still considerable strength.

[III]

While the Atlantic Alliance reposes upon the firm foundation of identical interests, no such general and reassuring statement can be made about the Western alliances outside Europe. Considering Asia and the Middle East, it can be said that of the American alliances only those with Formosa, South Korea, South Vietnam and Japan are based upon identical interests. These nations, with the exception of Japan, owe their very existence as nations to the interests and power of the United States. Yet only their complete dependence upon the United States has prevented some, if not all, of these nations from pursuing policies at variance with those of the United States. Thus the stability of these alliances rests both upon identical interests and extreme discrepancy of power.

Our alliance with Japan, like that with Germany, was, during the first decade following the Second World War, likewise based upon the dual foundation of identical interests and overwhelming American power. Yet neither foundation can be any longer taken for granted. Three factors have combined to restore Japan's freedom of choice. First, Japan has again become the strongest power in Asia, leaving even China a considerable distance behind. If the wartime memories of Japan's imperialism were not still alive in the rest of Asia, Japan would be the favorite candidate for taking over the economic and political leadership of Asia. Second, the atomic stalemate has had the same psychological effect on Japan as on Western Europe; the American alliance has become for Japan a mixed blessing if not a liability. Finally, to the degree that the aggressiveness of Stalinist and Chinese Korean War policies is replaced by a new flexibility which stresses the complementary character of Russian, Chinese and Japanese interests, Japan may find a practical alternative to its identification with the United States.

The other Asian alliances, of which SEATO and the Baghdad Pact provide the outstanding examples, are of an entirely different type. They have three characteristics in common: complementary interests tending toward transformation into incompatible ones, a radically unequal distribution of benefits and an ideological emphasis.

These alliances, on the face of them, were conceived in terms of common action on behalf of common interests. However, in view of the remoteness of the apparent *casus foederis*, that is, Communist attack upon a member, and of the virtual impossibility in case of such an attack for most members to act in common, commitment to common action has receded into the background and been distilled into an anti-Communist ideological commitment. Of the Asian members, this commitment requires nothing more than membership in the alliance; it requires no common objective, policy and action—beyond anti-communism at home and abroad. Yet of the Western members, especially the United States, it requires specific policies and actions on behalf of the Asian members.

The Asian members are interested in these alliances primarily because of the economic, military and political support they receive from the United States. Many of them consider their membership in the alliance to constitute a special claim upon the American Treasury, American weapons and American political support for their special national aspirations. However valuable the United States judges this membership to be, in terms of actual policies and measures it bears a unilateral burden. The United States is under continuous pressure to act as an ally while the Asian allies, once they have signed the treaty of alliance, preserve virtually complete freedom of action. Their foreign policies, for instance vis-à-vis China, could hardly be more different if they were not members of the alliance. In order to show the irrelevance of the alliance in terms of common objectives, policies and actions, the Prime Minister of one Asian nation has gone so far as to equate his country's membership in SEATO with membership in the United Nations.

Insofar as the West wants the maximum number of Asian allies and the Asian allies want the maximum amount of Western support, the interests of the two parties can be said to complement each other. This compatibility is bound to disintegrate whenever a latent conflict of interests between two allies or an ally and another nation becomes acute. The conflicts between Pakistan and India over Kashmir, between Great Britain and Greece, and Turkey and Greece, over Cyprus, between Iraq and Israel are cases in point. It is only because these alliances limit a commitment to common action to the very unlikely event of Communist aggression that they have survived such incompatibilities. The United States, in particular, is frequently forced into the uncomfortable position of having either to straddle the fence, as between Great Britain and Greece, or else to sacrifice its interests to its alliance, as between India and Pakistan.

Thus, by virtue of its alliance, the United States increases the armed strength of Pakistan and thereby forces India to increase its expenditures for armaments from thirty million pounds in 1955 to ninety million pounds in 1957. This diversion of scarce funds from economic development to armaments threatens India with economic and political disaster, which the United States has a vital interest in staving off through financial aid. In consequence, the United States engages, as it were, in an armaments race with itself by proxy, its left hand supporting Pakistan by virtue of the alliance, its right hand aiding India by virtue of its vital interests.

As for the alliance among the nations of the Western hemisphere, appearances are deceptive. As long as the supremacy of the United States within the Western hemisphere provided unchallengeable protection for the independence of the American nations, these alliances could indeed be taken for granted. For the United States, these alliances provided complete safety since, in view of its unchallengeable supremacy within the hemisphere and of the protection of two oceans, its security could be endangered only by a non-American nation acting in concert with an American one. For the other American nations, these alliances provided complete security from great-power domination since the United States would use its superior power only for the protection and not for the subversion of their national independence.

This identity of interests and the ability of the United States to implement it has provided the rationale and life-blood of the American state system from the proclamation of the Monroe Doctrine to this day. The intercontinental guided missile confronts this system with a challenge never before experienced. For the supremacy of the United States within the Western hemisphere, as unchallengeable as ever from within, is of no avail as protection against these novel weapons of tomorrow. The United States can no more protect its American allies against these weapons than it can protect itself. The American allies of the United States will come to view the alliance with the same misgivings with which the European allies and Japan view it already. They may no longer regard their interests as identical with those of the United States and may conclude that safety lies not in closeness to, but rather in distance from, the United States.

While these considerations are admittedly speculative from the vantage point of 1957, they may well reflect the actuality of 1960.

[IV]

The Communist alliances present three different types which must be sharply distinguished: the alliances of the Soviet Union and China, on the one hand, with North Korea and North Vietnam, on the other; the alliances between the Soviet Union and the nations of Eastern Europe; the alliances of the Soviet Union, on the one hand, with China, Egypt, Syria and probably Yemen, on the other.

The position of North Korea and North Vietnam within the Communist alliances is identical—in the particulars which interest us here —with the position of South Korea and South Vietnam within their alliances with the United States. There is complete identity of interests and extreme disparity of power.

The alliances between the Soviet Union and the nations of Eastern Europe, codified in the Warsaw Pact of 1955, are in a class by themselves. They are not true alliances in that they do not transform a preexisting community of interests into legal obligations. It is their distinctive quality that a community of interests is irrelevant for their existence and operation and that they are founded on nothing but unchallengeable superiority of power. Power is here not superimposed upon common interests but becomes a substitute for them. Such so-called treaties of alliance are in truth in the nature of treaties establishing a modern version of protectorates, and the nations subjected to them are correctly called satellites rather than allies.

The nature of this relationship has not been affected, although it might well be in the future, by the development of a community of interests between the Soviet Union and certain satellites, such as Poland and Czechoslovakia, resulting from the emergence of Germany as the predominant power in Europe. Poland and Czechoslovakia, situated as they are between two nations of superior strength, have had to seek protection either from one neighbor against the other or from Western Europe against both. Their present relationship to the Soviet Union provides this protection. Given a change in both Russian and German policies, this protective function might well form the basis for a future genuine alliance.

While this development is purely speculative, the relations between the Soviet Union and the satellites have in recent years undergone an actual transformation similar to that which has affected the Atlantic Alliance, and for similar reasons. The emergence of an atomic stalemate between the United States and the Soviet Union has loosened the ties of the satellite relationship. The threat of mutual atomic destruction has stimulated both the desire for self-preservation in the form of neutralism and the aspirations for national independence which had lain dormant under the yoke of the Red Army.

These latent tendencies were brought to the fore by the "new look" in Russian policy following the death of Stalin. In response to it, the spirit of national independence started to push against the lid of Russian oppression, and the Russian pro-consuls yielded to the pressure. They rehabilitated most of the national leaders who had tried to combine communism and at least a measure of national independence and relaxed the authoritarian controls over the economic and intellectual life of the satellite. Yet popular reaction went beyond domestic reforms to a striving for national independence, that is, the end of the satellite relationship itself. At this point, the Soviet Union called a halt, reasserting the paramountcy of its interests by the supremacy of its power.

The exact nature of the community of interests between the Soviet Union and China is a matter for speculation. Russian and Chinese interests appear to be identical insofar as their common objective is the strengthening and expansion of the Communist and the weakening and retraction of the anti-Communist camp. They appear to be complementary insofar as the alliance serves the Chinese interest in economic and military development and the Russian interest in keeping the United States militarily engaged and politically handicapped in the Far East.

The alliances between the Soviet Union and the Middle Eastern nations clearly serve complementary interests. The Middle Eastern nations allied with the Soviet Union are enabled by the military support they receive to pursue actively their specific interests, all with regard to Israel, some with regard to Jordan, Saudi Arabia, Turkey and the remaining British possessions and spheres of influence. The Soviet Union, on the other hand, has no stake in these specific interests except insofar as their active pursuit serves to maintain a state of tension which keeps the Western nations engaged and handicapped in still another region and threatens them with economic distress.

[v]

Considering the overall picture of the alliances as it emerges from the foregoing analysis, one is impressed by the similarity of the changes which have occurred in the structure of the European alliances on both sides of the Iron Curtain. The seemingly irreversible trend toward a two-bloc system which marked the immediate postwar era has been arrested, if not reversed. The uncommitted nations not only want to remain uncommitted but also have, with a few exceptions, shown the ability to do so. On the other hand, many of the European nations which are committed as allies of one or the other of the superpowers would like to join the ranks of the uncommitted nations but have, with the exception of Yugoslavia, been unable to do so. They have at best been able to move to the outer confines of the blocs to which they belong. In consequence, the two-bloc system is in the process of loosening but not of breaking up.

The satellites may become even more unwilling and unreliable partners of the Soviet Union than they are already. Short of outside intervention, which is unlikely, they cannot move out of the Soviet orbit as long as Russian interest—backed by Russian power—requires their submission. And the interest of Russia in the domination of Eastern Europe has been perennial, despite drastic changes in the personnel, philosophy and structure of government. The weakening of that interest cannot be foreseen short of a revolution in military technology which would make the control of outlying territory irrelevant.

The fate that may be in store for the Atlantic Alliance is similarly not its formal dissolution but rather its slow erosion to the point of becoming inoperative. The common fear of communism, either as a subversive force from within or an aggressive one from without, and the common dedication to the values of Western civilization are likely to remain stronger than the disruptive tendencies of divergent and incompatible interests and thus to keep the common framework of the Atlantic Alliance intact. The demonstrated inability of even Great Britain and France to pursue positive foreign policies against the opposition of the United States adds to this outward stability of the Atlantic Alliance. The real danger lies in this common framework becoming an empty shell, drained of its vitality. History abounds with legal compacts, constitutional devices and institutional forms which have, sometimes—as in the case of the Holy Roman Empire—for centuries, survived as ritualistic observances or, in the words of Chief Justice Marshall, "a solemn mockery," without any longer being capable of directing the interests of men into the channels of common policies and actions.

The danger with which the German situation threatens the Atlantic Alliance is, however, far more serious. The tension between the German commitment to the Atlantic Alliance and the national goal of unification, which can be achieved only on Russian terms, inevitably raises in German minds the question of whether that commitment and this objective are truly compatible and whether the former must not be sacrificed in order to achieve the latter. This conclusion can be prevented from being translated into actual policy only by the intransigence of Russian and the wisdom of American policies. The danger of German defection from the Atlantic Alliance, then, raises in specific terms the general issue of the merits of our alliance policy and of our response to the structural changes which the alliances have undergone in recent times.

Our alliance policy partakes of the doctrinaire, legalistic and mechanical character of much of American foreign policy. These perennial vices reappear in it in a new form. Instead of recognizing that alliances can be useful, harmful or superfluous depending on the circumstances and therefore discriminating among them in view of the interests to be served and the policies to be pursued, we have followed what might be called the collector's approach to alliances: the more nations sign a legal document declaring their support for our policies, the better. While once we were, on principle, against all "entangling alliances," now we are, again on principle, in favor of all alliances.

This emphasis upon the quantity of alliances and, more particularly, upon their military advantages—actual or illusory—has tended to jeopardize our political interests. Frequently our allies have turned our interest in the alliance *per se* to their political advantage, without any corresponding political advantage accruing to us or, at worst, at the expense of our political interests. In consequence, the weak members of the alliance, knowing what they want to get out of it, have tended to convert the alliance into an instrument of their policies with the United States paying the political and economic cost.

This tendency to see intrinsic merit in any alliance has been most pronounced in Asia. SEATO, originating in an indiscriminate invitation by the United States to join, is the classic example. Its membership was determined not by the United States in view of its interests but by the other members in view of theirs. Nor has the issue of the mutuality of benefits and liabilities been correlated to our overall Asian interests which—except for Formosa, South Korea and South Vietnam—are political rather than military.

SEATO is for the United States a useless alliance from the military point of view and a harmful one politically and economically in that it alienates the broad masses of Asians. NATO, on the other hand, especially in view of its elaborate organizational superstructure, may well prove to be a superfluous alliance—a view held by a minority within and outside the government when NATO was created in 1949. It may well be asked again—as it was then—whether the obvious identity of interests between the United States and the nations of Western Europe could not have been adequately served by a unilateral guarantee on the part of the United States, fashioned after the model of the Monroe Doctrine. While the very existence of NATO has made this question obviously academic, the rationale underlying it could still be put into practice by dismantling what is useless and harmful in NATO and strengthening what is useful, essential and lasting.

These speculations culminate in the observation that the problem of alliances must be considered in the context of the overall character of world politics. If the task facing a nation is primarily military, not to be mastered by its isolated strength alone, a policy of alliances is the answer; and this answer is still the correct one in Europe and in certain exposed regions of Asia. Insofar as the task is political, requiring a variety of means to be applied with subtlety, discrimination and imagination, a policy of alliances will be useless, if not harmful; and this is indeed the situation which confronts the United States in most of the world today where the issue is political allegiance and not military defense. A policy of alliances, in its doctrinaire insistence upon joining the club, in its legalistic concern with signatures and stipulations, in its mechanical counting of heads, serves but as a substitute for political creativeness, the lack of which it may temporarily conceal. What it can neither conceal nor stave off is the failure which attends upon wrong policies as punishment follows the crime.

A Democrat Looks at Foreign Policy*

by John F. Kennedy

[I]

The past months have set before our policy-makers a map whose essential features are not unfamiliar to those who have studied or been a part of the events of the past decade, but it is also crowded with new silhouettes. There are new projections, contours and dimensions. International events in recent months have accelerated in pace and have been in a flux not yet comprehended by the leadership of our nation or taken account of in adjustments in the machinery of our foreign policy. To an observer in the opposition party there appear two central weaknesses in our current foreign policy: first, a failure to appreciate how the forces of nationalism are rewriting the geopolitical map of the world—especially in North Africa, southeastern Europe and the Middle East; and second, a lack of decision and conviction in our leadership, which has recoiled from clearly informing both the people and Congress, which seeks too often to substitute slogans for solutions, which at times has even taken pride in the timidity of its ideas.

* From *Foreign Affairs*, Vol. XXXVI, No. 1 (October 1957), pp. 44-59. Copyright 1957 by the Council on Foreign Relations, Inc., New York. Reprinted by special permission from *Foreign Affairs*.

[II]

International events today are subject to a double pull—a search for political *identity* by the new states and the search for *unity* among the established states of the world. As Europe draws in upon itself toward a Common Market and greater political integration, Africa, its former colonial estate, is breaking apart into new and emergent states. Through the world today there runs both a tide toward and away from sovereignty. Many Americans view these tendencies with equal favor, reading into the one our own Declaration of Independence and Revolution, into the other the work of our Constitutional builders of a federal state. In fact, of course, we dangerously misread the movements of our time if we set them only in the prisms of our own historic experience. It is easy by a false parallelism to mistake nationalism itself for national salvation, to mistake the assertion of broad unity for its healthy substance.

Modern nationalism, too, has a twin heritage. In one of its aspects it reflects a positive search for political freedom and self-development, in another it is the residue of disintegration and the destruction of the old moorings. The cardinal result of the First World War was the political collapse of the old continental Europe; the most apparent outcome of the Second World War was the erosion of Europe overseas. It is a temptation to write the history of the last 40 years in terms of the symmetric rise of two giant states, the U.S.S.R. and the U.S.A. But it is quite as important to see this period in terms of the decline of other states and the substitution for them of new combinations and clusters of power. In this perspective we see that the United States and the Soviet Union are not only magnets which attract power; they are also, by their overarching influence, repellent forces. This has become especially clear in the events of the last year.

Whereas the coming of the nuclear age reinforced the bipolar structure of world power, its secondary effects now stimulate a dispersion of strength and influence. Great Britain has felt the need to chart an independent course in nuclear development; France is preparing to cut a separate path; China, Germany and India and several smaller nations may soon possess nuclear tools of destruction. In the period of NATO build-up the Western nations had a rough strategic agreement; today even the essential purposes of NATO have come into dispute, and on disarmament even close allies have shown a diversity of aims.

A generation ago the British Commonwealth was a bedrock fact of world politics. Today the Commonwealth has not simply widened in conception with the inclusion of new nations such as India, Pakistan and Ceylon; even among the core members the events of last fall produced a cleavage, when Canada seized the initiative in applying a brake against the British and French adventure in Egypt. India, which itself represents a pole within the Commonwealth, is the leading claimant for the rôle of a "broker" middle state in the larger bipolar struggle; she is also a centerpiece in a "middle zone" of uncommitted nations extending from Casablanca to Djakarta. These nations have gained an effective voice in the United Nations, especially in the General Assembly whose prestige we ourselves helped to enhance by Secretary Acheson's "Uniting for Peace Resolution" of 1950. Today the Arab states alone have as many Assembly seats as all the countries of Western Europe, and the steady increase in the number of U.N. members and the expanded authority of the General Assembly have more and more diluted the commanding positions of the "big" states that have permanent seats in the Security Council. Indeed, to set the constellation of power in the U.N. today against the pattern envisaged at Dumbarton Oaks and San Francisco a little more than a decade ago is to appreciate the scope and rapidity of the change which has taken place. In diplomacy as in military command there is a temptation to fight today's battles with the pattern books and position papers of yesterday's successes.

The task is to strike a realistic balance between the legitimate appeals to national self-determination which pulsate through the uncommitted world and the gravitational pulls toward unity which grow from the technological and economic interdependence of modern states. This is a very difficult exercise in political ballistics. Different parts of the world are at divergent points along the trajectory of political independence. Both democratic self-government and large supra-national mergers have preconditions—a capacity to govern and a communality of interest which cannot be created only out of military fear or idealistic impulse. Americans have always displayed a faith in self-enforcing moral principles and have hankered for apocalyptic solutions and fixed patterns; they must learn that most current issues in international politics do not encourage such unrealistic hopes. Many of the old conceptions of war and peace, friend and foe, victory and defeat, must be reshaped in the light of new realities.

[III]

We usually attribute to the enemy camp a rigidity of outlook and method; and certainly Russian thinking is hard in texture, its message unrelenting, its outward cast unchanging. We deceive ourselves, however, if we believe that on this account we are the more manœuvrable and flexible in our actions. At times in recent years it has been hard to distinguish Secretary Dulles' emphatic reaffirmations of the imminent collapse of Soviet totalitarianism from the wooden Marxist-Stalinist view of the essential fragility of the capitalist order. While retaining faith in our forms of government and economy, we should not underestimate the Russian capacity for feint and adjustment. While the United States was going through the giddy months after the empty triumphs of Geneva, the Russian leaders, noting the climate of Bandung and the restlessness of the "middle belt," set in motion new forces of ruble diplomacy, economic penetration and political manœuvre. Our only response to these series of actions was to continue to rely unsuccessfully on the paper defenses of the Baghdad Pact, which rested on the false assumption that there was an identity of interest among all the states of the Middle East. This period ended with Mr. Dulles' unhappy efforts to call the Russian bluff over the Aswan Dam.

In other ways, too, we have underestimated as a nation the capacity of the Russians to compete with us militarily and economically. After the war we greatly misjudged their ability to build the atomic bomb and the hydrogen bomb; we underestimated their technological manpower in numbers and quality; we had an easy confidence that we could outdo them in producing planes, missiles and heavy weapons; and we miscalculated the rate of basic economic growth and its rate of acceleration in the U.S.S.R. and China.

While underestimating the potentialities of Russian developments we held exaggerated hopes as to how Western influences could flow into cracks occurring in the Soviet and satellite structure. Hardly had we announced the intention to "liberate" the satellite states of Europe before the Berlin riots occurred. After we found ourselves unable to turn this uprising to more than slight propaganda advantage, we tended to switch to the view that the states of East Europe were closed cells. The Administration saw little hope that new generations could wrench themselves free from the Soviet spell; yet it was precisely university youth and labor unionists, both peculiarly exposed to Soviet indoctrination, who led the rebellions against domination from Moscow. Once again the United States was able to offer little assistance during the ordeal. It has been slow to exploit the possibilities opened up by the gradual detachment of Poland from Russian rule; it was hesitant on granting economic aid and cut the amount to but a fraction of need.

It is in this sort of situation that American thinking, conditioned to the notion of two world camps, most needs reorientation—to accept partial gains in order to undercut slowly the foundations of the Soviet order. For it is most unlikely that any Iron Curtain country will defect simply from East to West. The movement will be gradual, along a spectrum. It would be a kindly recognition of the changing conditions behind the curtain if the Battle Act, Surplus Disposal Act and Mutual Security Act were amended so that economic and financial assistance might be given to countries existing in a kind of Communist limbo. These legislative Acts were drawn for different conditions, in days when there was only one "flower" in the Communist garden—Stalin.

The fragmentation of authority within the Soviet orbit has been one of the main gains of the post-Stalinist era. The totalitarian succession has not passed easily from Stalin to Khrushchev. There are other Communists—Mao, Tito, Gomulka—who claim to speak with Communism's authentic voice. Nationalism is a force cutting into the Soviet world as well as the Western. What will be the full effect of the growth of these centripetal currents remains to be seen, but Mao is surely right in the belief that Moscow's once total monopoly of the gardener's craft has gone.

[IV]

What Walter Millis has called "the hypertrophy of war" has helped to create the loose-jointed nature of current world politics. The need to face the prospect of having to wage a limited war while holding the levers of unlimited destruction, the need to discriminate between pressures and the appropriate responses in different parts of the world, the need to keep strategy flexible without letting it become formless—these are challenges which Americans with their inclination to problem-solving and passkey formulas are not well equipped to meet. As the threat of total war has seemed to decline and as the danger we faced in 1947-48 has become less clear, the more traditional forms of diplomacy have resumed their old importance and we have again become concerned with the interstitial problems of the world community. The new situation has also brought about the reëmergence of small and middle states as important international factors and has set up a more complicated and fluid balance of power. Various states gain strength because they provide concessions for military bases or contain special resources; others such as Germany and Sweden have an industrial vigor which gives them levers of influence, not only because they can contribute to one or another power bloc but also because they can be leading exporters of both goods and expertise to the underdeveloped nations.

In Europe itself there is alike a new crystallization and a new diffusion of power. The unnecessarily forced pace of German rearmament and the cross-pressures of French politics and commitments aborted the hopes for establishing the European Defense Community. Painful as the French parliament's burial of this scheme was for much European and American opinion, the defeat for American diplomacy may have been salutary in that it destroyed false images. The countries of Europe are now more aware of the practical obstacles to integration, better appreciate the price of unity, more fully understand that concrete if gradual achievements are better than indulgence in great dreams that do not come true. The United States, too, is more aware that the drive for European integration does not represent any European fancy for imitating or being absorbed into American patterns, but in part, at least, a way to win detachment from the United States. Such revolutionary developments as the Common Market and Euratom offer two possibilities—either that the ending of old rifts will release new energies, or that the continental states will become locked in a closed system. It is time for the United States as well as Great Britain to realize that activation of the European Common Market and its companion agreements may well set in motion forces running counter to our present pattern of alliances and relationships with Europe.

Clearly one of the great successes of postwar policy has been the economic revival of Germany in a political framework with a democratic cast considerably stronger and therefore more hopeful than that of the twenties. However, partly out of appreciation and admiration for this outstanding reinvigoration of German politics, American policy has let itself be lashed too tightly to a single German government and party. Whatever elections show, the age of Adenauer is over. The biggest question in any government must now be the identity of Adenauer's eventual successor. The present Administration, like its Democratic predecessor, has riveted its policy and favor exclusively on one leader and party and made pariahs of the opposition, who will inevitably be a part of some future German government. The fidelity to the West of the Socialist opposition is unquestionable, and yet sometimes our statements and actions seem almost to equate them with the puppet régime in East Germany. In all Europe a new generation is coming to power, and it is dangerous to become alienated from them. The giants of the postwar period—Churchill, Adenauer, DeGasperi—have left their imprint. But in the last two years the French Socialist and Radical parties, British Labor, the Italian Christian Democrats, have all been experiencing the transfer of power to new leaders for whom many of the old distinctions between "Left" and "Right" have lost validity. The United States is ill-advised to chase the shadows of the past and ignore the political leadership and thinking of the generation which is now coming of age.

[v]

Our response to the Soviet challenge in Asia and the Middle East has been exaggeratedly military. However, in Asia our policy has been probably too rigid, in the Middle East too soft. In Asia we have shifted from a hyperbolic image of a free China to the brittle conception of a shiftless totalitarian China. Objectives have become so distorted that our State Department first adamantly opposed even the dispatch to China of newsmen whose reports might allow us to test the validity of our policy; and then set extraordinary conditions with regard to an agreement for their admission. Information and independent judgment about China are so hard to secure that it is very difficult to make an estimate of developments there. There have been—and still are—compelling reasons for the non-recognition of China; but we must be very careful not to strait-jacket our policy as a result of ignorance and fail to detect a change in the objective situation when it comes. If a low ceiling is placed on criticism, policy tends to rigidity and vested interests harden to the point where established viewpoints cannot be modified.

At the moment there is a "deëmphasis" in our Far Eastern concerns, but the presence of important new problems is only thinly concealed. Not only is there the need to reëxamine our military and political position in Korea, but the place of Japan in the Far East deserves special attention. Though many observers have assumed that the military build-up of Japan is of supreme importance, the first need is in fact to find the roads by which Japan may stage an enduring economic revival. Dependent on trade for survival, Japan must find new markets in Asia, and particularly in China. Whether or not Western countries relax their own trade barriers, the issue has important political consequences for Japan.

In the Middle East, since the war, there has been no clear overall conception of American policy. We were right to support the establishment of the state of Israel, whose democratic stamina and military effectiveness have withstood the hard tests of outside challenge and aggression. But in dealing with the other nations of the area we have wavered. In Iran we built up Mossadegh and then scaled him down. In Egypt we encouraged the formation of a revolutionary régime and belatedly restrained its excesses. We helped to make the Aswan Dam an imposing symbol of Western economic leadership and then foreclosed it. Periodically after the war we tinkered with notions of a Middle Eastern defense pact, but never were able to decide who would be defended and against whom. Toward both the Arabs and Israelis we have had an on-and-off policy. Some economic aid was provided for the Arab states, but almost half of the funds appropriated between 1951-1956 were unexpended because of the seeming scarcity of suitable projects.

In this period Middle Eastern political development has generally speaking been in mid-passage between feudal colonialism and semi-feudal independence. British economic interest and political guidance were considered predominant there and we preferred to leave the area under the umbrella of British influence and protection. Events, however, conspired to bring the influence of the United States into play. Our services were often more remedial than preventive. More than in any other area of the world, our policy in the Middle East has been a creature of crisis, jagged in its ups and downs and ambiguous in its direction. The Persian oil crisis, the Israeli war for independence, the British evacuation from the Suez area—these and other events marked a recession of British influence from the Middle East and a sudden pressure for American intervention. On each occasion the United States helped with the immediate problem but without being able to do much toward healing the underlying organic maladies. In the end, it took the British and French invasion of Suez to jolt the United States into recognizing the need for a broader-gauge and more sustained policy. There had been no lack of pointers toward what that policy might include—a multilateral regional development fund, the Jordan River scheme, a food pool making imaginative use of our agricultural surpluses, a program for

Arab refugees. What was missing was active political leadership to break the paralysis of purpose.

Occurrences in the Middle East and Asia now cast their shadow over Africa. Here again a sudden inflammation of tension is to be noted, a drive to cut the cords of colonial rule and at the same time to meet the need for economic development and growth. All over the continent several revolutions are occurring at once and many ideas and influences are in collision. The rapidity of the changes makes the formulation of policy both difficult and the more necessary. Here more than almost anywhere else the modern era of communications, with its rapid cross-fertilization of ideas and the reaction of social pressures, makes attempts to segment and isolate individual political conflicts entirely futile. Americans are perhaps too inclined to take at face value cheap caricatures of British and French colonial rule in Africa. The past achievements and current progress of those nations, however, especially in Central Africa, do not make new adjustments unnecessary. When Morocco and Tunisia are free states, Algeria cannot be kept an armed camp.

There are important and subtle political and cultural differences, of course, between different parts of Africa, but the complexity of problems thereby created does not absolve the United States of the duty of interesting itself in them. The temptation is to accept the idea that since our coalition allies have a primary interest there, the United States, like it or not, had best take an enforced diplomatic holiday. In an impasse such as that created by the Algerian rebellion we are told that an American declaration of interest would be illegitimate, a rash provocation of a major ally and a gross departure from accepted standards of international conduct—this in spite of the fact that the influences of the crisis spill over into the rest of free Africa, eat into the fabric of NATO and contaminate our relationships in the United Nations.

We face here one of the harshest perplexities of our policy. The resolution of it would greatly enhance the whole position of the West in Asia and Africa. There obviously is danger in making international policy on the basis of popularity polls; some of the liberal critics of American policy toward neutrals fail to see the risks of setting policy courses by volatile barometric readings. The United States should maintain a priority among its interests and not exchange an ally for a relationship based on a fleeting friendship or a quixotic flirtation. This does not argue, however, for letting slip a main chance to win the world of uncommitted nations. A pose of benign "neutrality" or "non-interven-tion" will not help us to advance the cause of our NATO allies or the Western position in general. Washing one's hands of responsibility, like plans for "sanitary war" and "clean bombs," induces an illusion of antisepsis and tidy order, but it is only an illusion. The consequences of abstention can be quite as positive as those of direct action. Our policies in Indochina and North Africa since the Second World War indicate that the forces of nationalism cannot be reversed in an effort to cushion their results for an ally.

From now on, our policy in Africa must not be hinged only on metro-politan Europe. In charting it, we must not seek to use it only as a tool of anti-Communism. Neither should we seek to displace European rule where it is making visible and sustained progress in establishing the bases for political independence. And we must show special care not to give grounds for an accusation that we helped to create a free Africa merely as a new arena for economic exploitation. There is no question, for example, that the countries of North Af̄r̄c̄ should enjoy a special interdependent economic relationship with France. Independence does not require a total severance of old relations, as the newest British dominions well illustrate; what it does require is the substance and not the mere shadow of self-government.

[vi]

In the years immediately ahead we face a challenge in how to help the new and underdeveloped nations bear their economic burdens. Again we must strike a balance between what Denis Brogan has labelled "the illusion of American omnipotence" and a somber contemplation of the impossibility of absolute solutions.

It is sobering to realize that population curves turn steeply upwards in underdeveloped lands, that as a result the economic backwardness of much of the world is increasing, and that the process of social disintegra-tion intensifies with the rising curve of expectations among many peo-ples. Old liberal bromides have no appeal to nations which seek a quick transition to industrialization and who admire the disciplined attack which Communism seems to make upon the problems of economic modernization and redistribution. The more immediately persuasive ex-periences of China and Russia probably approximate what lies ahead for states such as Indonesia or Egypt, suffering from deteriorating economic standards and steeply rising populations.

The United States is economically capable of increasing aid for development purposes, but it cannot scatter its assistance on each parched patch of misery and need. The first step would seem to be to make a small number of investments through aid and loans, selected with an eye to their likelihood for success. There is no need for us to be neutral as to the objectives which it should serve. Successful foreign aid must be selective; otherwise a large amount of aid goes into projects designed to enhance the prestige of the receiving government and into military panoply which may only perpetuate feudalism. The general approach furnished in the Millikan-Rostow proposals (though too much patterned on the Indian economy and perhaps too sanguine about the possibility of freeing economic assistance from political objectives) furnishes some useful guideposts, particularly in stressing the need for more durable aid commitments and for finding methods which minimize political blackmail and indiscriminate handouts. In this regard the Senate has made beginnings this year in providing a long-term basis for assistance, which has the advantages not only of permitting better planning and a more rational evaluation of the political and psychological effects of aid, but also will tend to avoid the disadvantages of making annual aid appropriations which cannot be spent effectively.

In future years, other nations can probably make larger contributions in skills and money to world-wide economic development. Germany already is a sizable foreign investor and lender, and other nations will grow in such capacity. The development of atomic power has given Great Britain the prospect of becoming a prime exporter of atomic reactors. Chances for developing oil await the French in the Sahara if they can establish a political settlement in North Africa. With opportunities like these opening up, a wider system of multi-national aid, pioneered in Asia by the Colombo Plan, can become a reality.

[VII]

The new dynamics in foreign relations make it all the more important to consider afresh the methods by which foreign policy is formulated and applied. In this realm there is a special danger that a received body of doctrine will continue to be accepted when it no longer retains its original meaning and validity. The phrase "bipartisanship" in particular is abused and stretched beyond logical limits. It reflects the fact that most of the great departures in American policy since the Lend-Lease Act of 1941 have had substantial support from the opposition party. It recognizes that the opposition party of today may become the governing party tomorrow and that the broad stream of national purpose should not be thrust out of its main channel for fleeting partisan advantage which will later demand payment not only in trouble for the party but damage to the country.

Bipartisanship also designates the method which enables the Government to enlist the active coöperation of the leadership of both parties and of distinguished individuals in them. Under Mr. Truman a large number of Republicans—Paul Hoffman, John Foster Dulles, John J. McCloy, John Sherman Cooper, Robert Lovett and many others—were given important foreign policy responsibilities. In Congress, too, there was shared responsibility and leadership. Yet Mr. Vandenberg himself was the first to suggest that bipartisanship was not a blanket under which to smother dissent and genuine difference. China was never "bipartisan," nor was Point Four, nor were some extensions of the aid program. European assistance and United Nations policy generally were. Today, however, there is a prevailing view in Washington that to criticize the Administration on any foreign policy count exposes at worst a moral flaw, at best political irresponsibility. The Secretary of State and the President both have fobbed off responsible critics of specific phases of our policy as being captious or ignorant. Few Democrats have served in responsible administrative posts despite the fact that the party controls Congress.

Bipartisanship cannot be permitted to be an excuse for burying dissent. Especially at a time as fluid as the present it must not become a restraining wall against the flow of fresh ideas and the expression of honest doubts. Doubtless a Congressional opposition such as the Democratic majority forms today is not wholly consistent within itself and does not provide a completely adequate set of alternatives. Thus it regrettably has suffered severe fissions in the current year in the support which it has given to the traditional policy of strong mutual security measures. Significant Democratic groups have supported excessive cuts in foreign aid, have backed restrictive trade policies and, after five years of fighting for stronger national defense policies for both ground and air, have assented to excessive reductions in our defense appropriation. Some of this backsliding has come from weariness and discontent with the results achieved by similar measures in the past, some is consequent on important changes in the American economy, some is due to political reasons—"the duty of the opposition party is to oppose." Whatever the reason for the aberrations, they do furnish ground for concern as to whether our position as a responsible Democratic opposition in the field of foreign policy may not become blurred.

Against this, however, the Democrats can place a record which refutes the conception that foreign policy is too sensitive and that its many gears are too finely meshed to make constructive initiative or criticism in Congress possible. Our current and increasingly successful policy in Indochina (never a strong feature of the State Department under either Republican or Democratic control) has its origins within Congress. The Middle Eastern Resolution was not only refined and clarified in Congressional review and debate; its meaning was for the first time made clear to its authors, who had argued that prompt and automatic passage of the original text was essential if it was to have any effective impact. A workable concept of long-range economic development grew out of the study organized by the Senate into the foreign assistance program.

There are other illustrations. But the central point is that Congress not only can enrich the content of our policy but also make more certain that responsibility in the Executive is placed where it belongs—in the White House and State Department. President Eisenhower has been in the habit of holding a light rein on the conduct of policy and of parcelling responsibility out to many officials. Because of the President's confidence in the integrity of his associates, because of the elaborate mosaic of command and review within the Executive, and because he has the assured affection of the American people, the President in some instances has tended to mistake form for performance.

The National Security Council and its companion bodies have improved the continuity and coördination of policy-making, but at a price. The massive paper work and the clearance procedure, the compulsion to achieve agreement among departments and agencies, often produce policy statements which are only a mongrelization of clashing views. Sparks of dissent and a clear confrontation of alternatives may sometimes be more useful as guides to action than an amalgam on paper of conflicting judgments. We like to believe that the National Security Council previews all likely crises and has on file studies that set forth the right responses. In reality, the anthology of decisions which the N.S.C. compiles has only contingent reliability. Despite its elegant lacework of committees and boards of review, such major crises as Dien Bien Phu and Suez do not appear to have been forecast very accurately and seem to have surprised and divided leaders of government. It is also evident that on major questions such as H-bomb testing, disarmament and even the allocation of functions to the military services for varying types of warfare the N.S.C. has failed to write the score for a united chorus of Administration officials. Indeed, there have been times in recent months when the conflict of wills and policies has been almost as apparent as in the days of F.D.R.—without the drive and direction which then came from the White House itself.

We would lose much if we scrapped the major administrative changes which have been made both under the National Security Act and by executive reorganizations.[1] But a capacity for leadership and a clear articulation of policy at the pinnacle remain an essential dynamic of our system of government. The administrative structure, however constructed or refurbished, supplies only an environment for the making of decisions. It cannot itself produce a wise decision. There is a dangerous tendency today both within our Government and in the United Nations to take too mechanistic a view of the tasks to be accomplished. Sometimes a ferment of ideas is to be preferred above fabricated harmony. It would be unfortunate if our central policy-making bodies became mere vendors of compromise.

To criticize the style of operation of this Administration raises dilemmas which are a continuing feature of our foreign policy. The technological and scientific evaluations which have become so important an ingredient of major decisions mean that the inherent difficulties of the decisions themselves have never been greater. Matters such as our draft and conscription policy, our weapons system, disarmament, East-West trade, all require a knowledge in depth of scientific gains made and scientific potentialities ahead which few informed persons in any branch of government can fully grasp. Even the President himself is torn in many directions, just as the scientists are sharply divided on many of the effects of their researches and discoveries. Yet decisions must be made today and cannot await the compilation of clinical records, based on experience, regarding all the social, political and cultural by-products of our aid and the infusion of new techniques. If Don Quixote is a poor inspiration for the makers of our foreign policy, so, too, is Hamlet.

Now that the smoke surrounding "l'affaire Gluck" has cleared, it

---

[1] These developments have been elaborated and defended by Robert Cutler in "The Development of the National Security Council," *Foreign Affairs*, April 1956, pp. 441-458.

would seem appropriate for the State Department and the Congress to consider effective steps for improving our representational responsibilities abroad. Can the United States have a really first-class career service if the most prominent posts are reserved for the politically faithful and the economically successful? And can we have an effective foreign policy if our agents are selected for qualities other than experience, judgment and responsibility? There is a definite rôle for non-career men in Foreign Service; certainly the successes of Chester Bowles and John Sherman Cooper in India and the services of David Bruce and Clare Boothe Luce in Europe indicate that on many occasions ambassadors with special skills of personality or experience or with close ties with the President may play very useful rôles, sometimes influencing events in a way that a career man might not. But it should become a maxim that no Foreign Service post should be beyond the reach of any man, career or non-career, because of inadequate allowances, and that ambassadorships should not be among the loaves and fishes customarily handed out to the party stalwarts.

Finally we return always to the growing inter-connectedness of policy. Perhaps the most dramatic illustration of this is Germany. Again and again we have seen that the discussion of any plan for German reunification involves not only the terms of such a merger, but that the achievement of it would immediately call into question the structure and strategic basis of NATO, the status of the satellite states of Europe and German rearmament. During recent months there have been influential voices arguing that the occasion was ripe for an omnibus settlement of all these points on the basis of a reunified but militarily neutral Germany. It is unlikely that the Russians are in fact willing now to make such a settlement, but it is most difficult to think what should be our attitude toward such a scheme when there is so little agreement within our Government on each of the constituent features of such a plan and its probable results.

We have been fortunate as a nation that our successes in foreign policy have been shared and are not exclusively to the credit of any one party. Likewise our failures and flaws have been shared and are not to be attributed solely to a party or administration. In the tests which lie ahead the problems once again are national ones and the necessary adaptations to new circumstances as they arise will not come easily for a person of any tight party persuasion. The veil of illusions hangs over each of us to some degree. The fundamental task for both parties and for all branches of Government is to understand the forces which move the future. Extended autopsies of past failures tend only to add one more layer of unreality to the basis on which we must build—the belief that China was lost because of the action of a few diplomats, for instance, rather than because of underlying revolutionary forces; or the misunderstanding of the rise of Asian or African nationalism as either a Communist or a United States conspiracy; or the idea that there are not social forces running through all the world which have a validity apart from the bipolar struggle.

Recent years have witnessed still another wholly unforeseen phenomenon in parts of India, Indonesia and other sections of Southeast Asia and Latin America—the success of Communists and their associates at the polls and through other ordinary political processes. Western policies have long been predicated upon the assumption that Communist gains would be manifested through either external military threat or intervention, or internal supervision or violence. Consequently, reassessment is urgently required for those American aid programs which have reflected an ill-conceived and ill-concealed disdain for the "neutralists" and "socialists" who—in a nation such as India—represent the free world's strongest bulwarks to the seductive appeal of Peking and Moscow.

The agenda of tasks is large. Our chief concern should be major items. We must see that our actions stimulate the healthy development of the new states even if they are neutral; that we do not encourage the prolongation of Western colonialism where it is stagnant; that the position we take against Soviet imperialism in Eastern Europe is not weakened by Western "imperialism" in Africa or Asia. This is not a sentimental attitude, but one which tries to take measure of the inevitable and come to terms with it. It is futile to think that we can purge our foreign policy of all ambiguities—perfectionism is an empty standard for policy when effectiveness must depend not on abstract principles alone but also on estimates of power and national interest. But with respect to some of the major challenges in the world at the present moment there is an opportunity for the idealistic initiative of our people and the self-interest of the nation to intersect. I am certain that a sufficient clarity of will and purpose within the Administration can gain the support of both parties and of the broad public to meet these challenges in unity.

FOR FURTHER READING:

Dean G. Acheson, *Power and Diplomacy* (Cambridge: Harvard University Press, 1958).

American Friends Service Committee, *The United States and the Soviet Union: Some Quaker Proposals for Peace* (New Haven: Yale University Press, 1949).

Chester Bowles, *Ideas, People and Peace* (New York: Harper and Brothers, 1958).

James Burnham, *Containment or Liberation: An Inquiry into the Aims of United States Foreign Policy* (New York: John Day, 1952).

John Foster Dulles, *War or Peace* (New York: Macmillan, 1957).

Thomas K. Finletter, *Foreign Policy: The Next Phase* (New York: Harper and Brothers, 1958).

Walter Lippmann, *The Cold War: A Study in U.S. Foreign Policy* (New York: Harper and Brothers, 1947).

John J. McCloy, *The Challenge to American Foreign Policy* (Cambridge: Harvard University Press, 1953).

Adlai E. Stevenson, *Friends and Enemies: What I Learned in Russia* (New York: Harper and Brothers, 1959).

Robert Strausz-Hupé and others, *Protracted Conflict* (New York: Frederick A. Praeger, 1959).

Cyrus L. Sulzberger, *What's Wrong with U.S. Foreign Policy* (New York: Harcourt, Brace and Company, 1959).

James P. Warburg, *The United States in a Changing World* (New York: Putnam, 1954).

William Appleman Williams, *The Tragedy of American Diplomacy* (Cleveland and New York: The World Publishing Company, 1959).

Arnold Wolfers (ed.), *Alliance Policy in the Cold War* (Baltimore: The Johns Hopkins Press, 1959).

Chapter VIII

MILITARY POLICY

In the public debate on American foreign relations few questions are more basic and central than those concerning military policy. That this is true indicates the tremendous change of the past two decades both in the United States world position and in American thinking. The harsh military realities of a great power's responsibilities and problems in the multi-state world, obscured for so many years by our geographical position and good fortune, are now painfully apparent. And Americans have become increasingly aware of the close connection between military and foreign policy. The alliance structure described in the last chapter provides a framework for the containment of Soviet expansionism, but without an appropriate and credible military policy to fill in this framework, we will have nothing but paper guarantees. Military policy also indirectly affects foreign affairs through its economic impact here and abroad. Further, military policy is an important determinant of the world's image of America. Whether other countries view the United States as a bellicose menace to peace or as a benign state albeit determined to safeguard its legitimate interests depends in no small measure upon our military policy. And the conduct of many in world politics, not only the most opportunistic, will be partly determined by their perception of United States strength and our ability to protect and defend them. Thus military policy, fundamentally important in itself, also has crucial implications for several other foreign policy issues.

The first selection in this chapter, by John Foster Dulles, presents the rationale for present United States military policy. During its first year in office the Eisenhower administration conducted a far-reaching review which provided the basis for its long-range policies. Mr. Dulles somewhat baldly announced the results of this examination with reference to military affairs in a speech in New York before the Council on Foreign Relations. He stated then that the United States would rely "upon a great capacity to retaliate, instantly, by means and at places of our own choosing" to deter the Soviet bloc from future aggression. This was widely interpreted as indicating that the United States would respond to local attacks by nuclear strikes against the heart of Soviet power. The fear that this might provoke all-out nuclear war, plus doubts about its efficacy in view of growing Soviet nuclear capabilities—they too could soon (if not then) retaliate massively—brought forth immediate and voluminous criticism. The article reproduced here is Mr. Dulles' attempt to clarify his speech and meet this criticism. Although he qualifies the emphasis on massive retaliation, he adheres to the position that deterrence must be gained primarily through reliance upon high-yield nuclear weapons. This is the core of the Eisenhower administration's military policy. In budgetary terms it has meant that the Air Force has received the largest share of military appropriations (over 40 percent in the 1960 fiscal year) and that the greatest portion of this has gone to the Strategic Air Command, whose *forte* is intercontinental strategic bombing. This policy is similar in many ways to that which the Truman administration pursued prior to the outbreak of the Korean War. The rationale Mr. Dulles gave for the adoption of this policy is that because of the Soviet bloc's greater population and interior position, attempting to erect an adequate defense without reliance on high-yield nuclear weapons would impose intolerable economic and social burdens on the West. He also assumes that these weapons favor the West.

Mr. Dulles' critics, however, were not silenced; the controversy begun then still flames. Current United States military policy continues to be opposed by several congressmen, officers of the armed services, scholars, and journalists who doubt that primary reliance on high-yield nuclear weapons is the best way to deter Soviet aggression. These critics would prefer that the United States have a greater capacity to meet varied threats, particularly to meet local aggressions at their place of origin. They do not deny the necessity of maintaining the Strategic Air Command at a high level of readiness, but in addition they would like to develop and expand other forces and thereby increase United States tactical capabilities. Although they would not attempt to match Soviet bloc tactical forces, they would lessen the present disparity. They criticize the Eisenhower administration's "actual policy," either arguing that current military appropriations should be apportioned differently, or that these appropriations should be increased and that the new funds should be devoted to tactical forces. They also criticize its "declaratory policy," arguing that the threat of massive retaliation creates unnecessary dilemmas and that it is not credible either to the Soviet bloc or the West. One of the first fully developed critiques of present United States military policy, an article written by Rear Admiral Sir Anthony W. Buzzard, is reprinted as the second selection in this chapter. His arguments may also be used against his own country, the United Kingdom of Great Britain and Northern Ireland; for its military policy perhaps emphasizes high-yield nuclear weapons even more than the United States. Although not all critics of the present policy would accept Admiral Buzzard's recommendations concerning the use of tactical nuclear weapons, all would agree with his plea for more diversified capabilities and most would subscribe to the arguments he uses to reach this conclusion.

Even within the framework of Mr. Dulles' premises and conclusions there is room for controversy, as the recent discussion of the "missile gap" indicates. This debate centers around the question of what constitutes adequate deterrent power. Is it necessary to have more missiles and greater nuclear stockpiles than the U.S.S.R. (or at least equal amounts), or is there a finite strategic capability which, regardless of the other side's strength, will serve to deter it from aggressive action? The answer would be extremely difficult even if we had full information concerning Soviet military capabilities.

As so much of the controversy concerning military policy hinges on estimates of the effects of military spending on the United States economy, the third selection was chosen to illuminate this question. It is taken from a report of the Committee for Economic Development, a group of business leaders who from time to time convene study groups and issue statements on matters of national policy. It clarifies the value choices involved and identifies the places where controversy is legitimate and should be focused. Even if one does not agree with the report's conclusions, its method of analysis must be accepted.

Officers of the armed forces have inevitably become engaged in the public debate on foreign policy. Their professional competence is applicable to many of the issues and their own and their service's interests are intimately involved. When they are vocal, Army officers, and to a lesser extent Naval officers, generally oppose present policies. Their arguments are similar to those presented by Admiral Buzzard. Most Air Force officers support the current conception. The final selection by Colonel Ephraim M. Hampton, a member of the Staff of the Air War College, provides a sample of Air Force opinion. The crux of his argument is that it is difficult if not impossible to distinguish between limited and total war and that there is no assurance that war once started will remain limited. He concludes that total war presents the greatest danger to the United States and that the greatest share of available resources should be devoted to preparations for it; it is hoped that this will prevent its occurrence. Together with the previous selections this article spreads to full range the outline of issues involved in the public debate on military policy.

Policy for Security and Peace*

by John Foster Dulles[1]

Since World War II, the United States has faced the difficult task of finding policies which would be adequate for security and peace and at the same time compatible with its traditions. Never before has a great nation been called upon to adjust its thinking and its action so radically in so short a period.

During the 19th century the maintenance of peace and order depended largely on Great Britain, with its Navy and the system of naval bases which enabled it to operate with mobility and flexibility throughout the world. By suitable commercial, investment, and monetary policies, Great Britain and other nations with surplus capital stimulated economic growth in underdeveloped areas. The French Revolution had aroused men to respect and promote human rights and fundamental freedoms. The United States also made its contribution. Our people devoted their energies largely to domestic matters, not because they lacked concern for others but believing that what our founders called "the conduct and example" of freedom would exert a liberating influence everywhere. In fact, it did so. The "great American experiment" was a source of hope and inspiration to men everywhere, and especially to those living under despotism. Our dynamic example of freedom drew many to our shores and inspired others, in the Old World and the New, to emulate our course.

All of these influences contributed to giving the world relative peace and security for the 100 years between the ending of the Napoleonic wars and the beginning of the First World War. During this period there were many advances in the practice of political liberty, and generally throughout the world there was a great advance in material and social well-being.

The events of the 20th century, and especially the two World Wars and their aftermaths, have created an entirely new situation. In large measure the United States has inherited a responsibility for leadership which, in the past, has been shared by several nations. Today there rests

* From the *Department of State Bulletin*, Vol. XXX, No. 770 (March 29, 1954), pp. 459-464.
[1] Article prepared for publication in the April issue of *Foreign Affairs* (press release 139 dated Mar. 16).

upon us, to a unique degree, the threefold task of providing insurance against another world war; of demonstrating the good fruits of freedom which undermine the rule of despots by contrast; and of providing a major part of the effort required for the healthy growth of under-developed areas.

The Eisenhower administration inherited security policies that had much worth. Many of these policies were bipartisan in character. They reflected a national recognition of the peril facing the civilized world, a united determination to meet it, and an acceptance of the role of lead-ership thrust on us by events. We had helped to reestablish the econ-omies of other countries shattered by the war. We had taken a major part in resisting the aggression in Korea. In the face of the Soviet threat we were engaged in rebuilding our military strength and that of other free countries.

These and like measures were costly. But they were necessary to our security. However, they partook much of an emergency character. By 1953 there was need to review our security planning and to adjust our continuing military effort to the other requirements of a well-rounded, permanent policy.

Under the conditions in which we live, it is not easy to strike a perfect balance between military and nonmilitary efforts and to choose the type of military effort which serves us best. The essential is to recognize that there is an imperative need for a balance which holds military expendi-tures to a minimum consistent with safety, so that a maximum of liberty may operate as a dynamic force against despotism. That is the goal of our policy.

THE NATURE OF THE THREAT

The threat we face is not one that can be adequately dealt with on an emergency basis. It is a threat that may long persist. Our policies must be adapted to this basic fact.

The Soviet menace does not reflect the ambitions of a single ruler and cannot be measured by his life expectancy. There is no evidence that basic Soviet policies have been changed with the passing of Stalin. . . . The Soviet Communists have always professed that they are planning for what they call "an entire historical era."

The assets behind this threat are vast. The Soviet bloc of Communist-controlled countries—a new form of imperialist colonialism—represents a vast central land mass with a population of 800 million. About 10 million men are regularly under arms, with many more trained millions in reserve. This land force occupies a central position which permits of striking at any one of about 20 countries along a perimeter of some 20 thousand miles. It is supplemented by increasing air power, equipped with atomic weapons, able to strike through northern Arctic routes which bring our industrial areas in range of quick attack.

The threat is not merely military. The Soviet rulers dispose throughout the world of the apparatus of international communism. It operates with trained agitators and a powerful propaganda organization. It exploits every area of discontent, whether it be political discontent against "colonialism" or social discontent against economic conditions. It seeks to harass the existing order and pave the way for political coups which will install Communist-controlled regimes.

By the use of many types of maneuvers and threats, military and political, the Soviet rulers seek gradually to divide and weaken the free nations and to make their policies appear as bankrupt by overextending them in efforts which, as Lenin put it, are "beyond their strength." Then, said Lenin, "our victory is assured." Then, said Stalin, will be the "moment for the decisive blow."

It is not easy to devise policies which will counter a danger so centralized and so vast, so varied and so sustained. It is no answer to substitute the glitter of steel for the torch of freedom.

An answer can be found by drawing on those basic concepts which have come to be regularly practiced within our civic communities. There we have almost wholly given up the idea of relying primarily on house-by-house defense. Instead, primarily reliance is placed upon the combining of two concepts, namely, the creation of power on a community basis and the use of that power so as to deter aggression by making it costly to an aggressor. The free nations must apply these same principles in the international sphere.

COMMUNITY DEFENSE

The cornerstone of security for the free nations must be a collective system of defense. They clearly cannot achieve security separately. No single nation can develop for itself defensive power of adequate scope and flexibility. In seeking to do so, each would become a garrison state and none would achieve security.

This is true of the United States. Without the cooperation of allies, we would not even be in a position to retaliate massively against the war industries of an attacking nation. That requires international facilities. Without them, our air striking power loses much of its deterrent power. With them, strategic air power becomes what Sir Winston Churchill called the "supreme deterrent." He credited to it the safety of Europe during recent years. But such power, while now a dominant factor, may not have the same significance forever. Furthermore, massive atomic and thermonuclear retaliation is not the kind of power which could most usefully be evoked under all circumstances.

Security for the free world depends, therefore, upon the development of collective security and community power rather than upon purely national potentials. Each nation which shares the security should contribute in accordance with its capabilities and facilities. The Inter-American Treaty of Reciprocal Assistance (Rio Pact) of 1947 set a postwar example in establishing the principle that an armed attack against one would be considered as an attack against all. The North Atlantic Treaty is based on the same principle. Its members have gone much further in organizing joint forces and facilities as a part of the integrated security system. NATO provides essential air and naval bases, to which its various members can contribute—each according to its means and capabilities. It provides the planes and ships and weapons which can use these bases. It provides so many points from which an aggressor could be harassed, in so many different ways, that he cannot prudently concentrate his forces for offense against a single victim.

While NATO best exemplifies this collective security concept, there are other areas where the same concept is evolving, although as yet in a more rudimentary form. An example is the Western Pacific, where the United States has a series of collective security treaties which now embrace Australia, New Zealand, the Philippines, Japan, and Korea. Collective arrangements are now in the making in the Middle East, with Turkey-Pakistan as the nucleus. These developments show the growing acceptance of the collective security concept we describe.

The United Nations is striving to make collective security effective on a basis broader than regionalism. The central principle of the charter is that any armed attack is of universal concern and calls for collective measures of resistance. The Soviet Union, by its veto power, has made it impractical, as yet, to make available to the Security Council the "armed forces, assistance, and facilities" contemplated by article 43 of the charter. When aggression occurred in Korea, however, the principle of collective action was invoked by the United Nations and acted on by more than a majority of the members, including 16 which sent armed forces to Korea to repel the aggression. The "Uniting for Peace" Resolution, adopted by the General Assembly in November 1950, grew out of that experience. That resolution will enable members of the United Nations to join in carrying out similar collective measures against any future aggression without being blocked by a Soviet veto.

The free world system of bases is an integral part of its collective security. At the recent Four Power Conference in Berlin, Mr. Molotov repeatedly attacked these bases as evidence of aggressive purpose. Actually these bases on the territory of other sovereign countries are merely a physical expression of the collective security system. They were constructed only at the request of the host nation and their availability depends upon its consent, usually as a legal condition and always as a practical one. The requisite consent to the use of these bases would never be accorded unless it was clear that their use was in response to open aggression, and reasonably related to its scope and nature. This gives assurance of their community function.

Thus the free world has practical means for achieving collective security both through the United Nations and the various regional arrangements already referred to.

THE STRATEGY TO DETER AGGRESSION

The question remains: How should collective defense be organized by the free world for maximum protection at minimum cost? The heart of the problem is how to deter attack. This, we believe, requires that a potential aggressor be left in no doubt that he would be certain to suffer damage outweighing any possible gains from aggression.

This result would not be assured, even by collective measures, if the free world sought to match the potential Communist forces, man for man and tank for tank, at every point where they might attack. The Soviet-Chinese bloc does not lack manpower and spends it as something that is cheap. If an aggressor knew he could always prescribe the battle conditions that suited him and engage us in struggles mainly involving manpower, aggression might be encouraged. He would be tempted to attack in places and by means where his manpower superiority was decisive and where at little cost he could impose upon us great burdens.

If the free world adopted that strategy, it could bankrupt itself and not achieve security over a sustained period.

The free world must devise a better strategy for its defense, based on its own special assets. Its assets include, especially, air and naval power and atomic weapons which are now available in a wide range, suitable not only for strategic bombing but also for extensive tactical use. The free world must make imaginative use of the deterrent capabilities of these new weapons and mobilities and exploit the full potential of collective security. Properly used, they can produce defensive power able to retaliate at once and effectively against any aggression.

To deter aggression, it is important to have the flexibility and the facilities which make various responses available. In many cases, any open assault by Communist forces could only result in starting a general war. But the free world must have the means for responding effectively on a selective basis when it chooses. It must not put itself in the position where the only response open to it is general war. The essential thing is that a potential aggressor should know in advance that he can and will be made to suffer for his aggression more than he can possibly gain by it. This calls for a system in which local defensive strength is reinforced by more mobile deterrent power. The method of doing so will vary according to the character of the various areas.

Some areas are so vital that a special guard should and can be put around them. Western Europe is such an area. Its industrial plant represents so nearly the balance of industrial power in the world that an aggressor might feel that it was a good gamble to seize it, even at the risk of considerable hurt to himself. In this respect, Western Europe is exceptional. Fortunately, the West European countries have both a military tradition and a large military potential, so that through a European Defense Community, and with support by the United States and Britain, they can create an adequate defense of the Continent.

Most areas within the reach of an aggressor offer less value to him than the loss he would suffer from well-conceived retaliatory measures. Even in such areas, however, local defense will always be important. In every endangered area there should be a sufficient military establishment to maintain order against subversion and to resist other forms of indirect aggression and minor satellite aggressions. This serves the indispensable need to demonstrate a purpose to resist, and to compel any aggressor to expose his real intent by such serious fighting as will brand him before all the world and promptly bring collective measures into operation. Potential aggressors have little respect for peoples who have no will to fight for their own protection or to make the sacrifices needed to make that fighting significant. Also, they know that such peoples do not attract allies to fight for their cause. For all of these reasons, local defense is important. But in such areas the main reliance must be on the power of the free community to retaliate with great force by mobile means at places of its own choice.

A would-be aggressor will hesitate to commit aggression if he knows in advance that he thereby not only exposes those particular forces which he chooses to use for his aggression, but also deprives his other assets of "sanctuary" status. That does not mean turning every local war into a world war. It does not mean that, if there is a Communist attack somewhere in Asia, atom or hydrogen bombs will necessarily be dropped on the great industrial centers of China or Russia. It does mean that the free world must maintain the collective means and be willing to use them in the way which most effectively makes aggression too risky and expensive to be tempting.

It is sometimes said that this system is inadequate because it assures an invaded country only that it will eventually be liberated and the invader punished. That observation misses the point. The point is that a prospective attacker is not likely to invade if he believes the probable hurt will outbalance the probable gain. A system which compels potential aggressors to face up to that fact indispensably supplements a local defensive system.

PRACTICAL APPLICATIONS

We can already begin to see applications of these policies.

In Korea the forces fighting aggression had been so closely limited that they were forbidden even to apply the doctrine of "hot pursuit" in relation to enemy planes that were based across the Yalu. The airfields from which attacks were mounted were immune, as were the lines and sources of their supply. The fighting there was finally stopped last July on terms which had been proposed many months before. That result was achieved, at least in part, because the aggressor, already denied territorial gains, was faced with the possibility that the fighting might, to his own great peril, soon spread beyond the limits and methods which he had selected, to areas and methods that we would select. In other words, the principle of using methods of our choice was ready to be invoked, and it helped to stop the war which the enemy had begun and had pursued on the theory that it would be a limited war, at places and by means of its choosing.

The 16 members of the United Nations who fought in Korea have invoked the same principle. They have given public notice that if the Communists were to violate the armistice and renew the aggression, the response of the United Nations Command would not necessarily be confined to Korea.[2] Today, if aggression were resumed, the United Nations Command would certainly feel free to inflict heavy damage upon the aggressor beyond the immediate area which he chose for his aggression. That need not mean indulging in atomic warfare throughout Asia. It should not be stated in advance precisely what would be the scope of military action if new aggression occurred. That is a matter as to which the aggressor had best remain ignorant. But he can know and does know, in the light of present policies, that the choice in this respect is ours and not his.

In relation to Indochina, the United States has publicly stated that if there were open Red Chinese Army aggression there, that would have "grave consequences which might not be confined to Indochina." [3]

On December 26, 1953, President Eisenhower made an important statement which clearly reflected our present policy as applied to Asia.[4] He announced a progressive reduction of United States ground forces in Korea. However, he went on to point out that United States military forces in the Far East will now feature "highly mobile naval, air, and amphibious units"; and he added that in this way, despite some withdrawal of land forces, the United States will have a capacity to oppose aggression "with even greater effect than heretofore." In the same month the United States reaffirmed its intent to maintain in Okinawa the rights made available to us by the Japanese peace treaty. This location is needed to insure striking power to implement the collective security concept.

In Europe, our intentions are primarily expressed by the North Atlantic Treaty. Following the aggression in Korea of June 1950, the treaty members proceeded to an emergency buildup of military strength

---

[2] *Department of State Bulletin* of Aug. 24, 1953, p. 247.
[3] *Ibid.*, Sept. 14, 1953, p. 342.
[4] *Ibid.*, Jan. 4, 1954, p. 14.

in Western Europe. The strength built between 1950 and 1953 has served well the cause of peace. But by 1953, it did not seem necessary to go on at the original pace.

At the April 1953 meeting of the NATO Council, the United States put forward a new concept, now known as that of the "long haul." It meant a steady development of defensive strength at a rate which would preserve and not exhaust the economic strength of our allies and ourselves. This would be reinforced by the availability of new weapons of vastly increased destructive power and by the striking power of an air force based on internationally agreed positions. President Eisenhower is now seeking an amendment of the present law to permit a freer exchange of atomic information with our NATO allies.

When we went back to the NATO Council meeting of last December, we found that there was general acceptance of the "long haul" concept. The result is that most of our NATO allies are now able to achieve budgetary and economic stability, without large dependence on our economic aid.

The growing free-world defensive system, supported by community facilities and coupled with adequate policies for their use, reflects the nearest approach that the world has yet made to a means to achieve effective defense at minimum cost.

THE CURRENT MILITARY PROGRAM

One of the basic tasks of the new administration has been to review our military program in the light of the foregoing policies.

In the years 1945-53, our military programs went through wide fluctuations which hindered orderly and efficient administration. During the first part of this period, the policy was to reduce the military establishment drastically. During the latter part of the period, the policy was to increase the military establishment rapidly. During both the decrease and the increase the military budget reflected the so-called "balance of forces" concept. In practical terms, this meant splitting the available funds into three roughly equal slices for the Army, Navy, and Air Force.

When the Eisenhower administration took office, our national security programs, at home and abroad, were costing over $50 billion a year, and were planned at about $55 billion for the next year. Budgetary deficits were of the order of $10 billion, despite taxes comparable to wartime taxes. Inflation was depreciating the purchasing power of the dollar. Our allies were similarly burdened.

The American people have repeatedly shown that they are prepared to make whatever sacrifices are really necessary to insure our national safety. They would no doubt support military expenses at the levels which their government told them were required for security, even at the cost of budget deficits, resultant inflationary pressures, and tax levels which would impair incentives. But the patriotic will to sacrifice is not something to be drawn upon needlessly. Government has the high duty to seek resourcefully and inventively the ways which will provide security without sacrificing economic and social welfare. The security policies we here describe make possible more selective and more efficient programs in terms of the composition of forces and of procurement.

The new administration has sought to readjust, in an orderly way, the program for the military forces. Before this could be done, it was necessary to clarify the extent of our reliance on collective security; to define more clearly our basic strategy both in Europe and the Far East; to reassert our freedom of action in repelling future aggression; to assess the impact of newer types of weapons; and to relate the composition and size of our ready and potential forces to all these factors.

Inevitably this has taken time. It has required a series of difficult basic decisions by the President with the advice of the National Security Council and with supporting decisions by the Department of State, the Department of Defense, and the Treasury Department. It has been necessary to exchange views with congressional leaders and our principal allies and to inform world opinion so that neither our friends nor our enemies abroad would misinterpret what we were doing. By now, however, the new course is charted and is guiding our military planning. As a result, it is now possible to get, and share, more basic security at less cost. That is reflected in the budget which the President has submitted for the 1955 fiscal year. In this budget, national security expenditures for fiscal year 1955 will amount to $45 billion as compared with $50 billion for 1953 and $49 billion for 1954.

Initially this reshaping of the military program was misconstrued in various respects. Some suggested that the United States intended to rely wholly on large-scale strategic bombing as the sole means to deter and counter aggression. What has already been said should dispose of this erroneous idea. The potential of massive attack will always be kept in a state of instant readiness, and our program will retain a wide variety in the means and scope for responding to aggression. Others interpreted the program as a move away from collective security. The exact opposite is the case, as has been shown. Our policies are based squarely on a collective security system and depend for their success on its continuing vitality. Still others feared that we intended to withdraw our forces from abroad in the interest of mobility. Now that the fighting is ended in Korea, our forces in the Far East will be reduced in numbers, as has previously been announced, but the kind of force that remains will have great striking power. Moreover, the program does not mean that we intend to pull our forces out of Europe. It is, of course, essential that the continental nations themselves provide a harmonious nucleus of integrated defense. If they do so, the United States would expect to maintain substantial forces of its own in Europe, both in support of the forward strategy of defense and for political reasons.

Another consequence of our new policies is that it has become practicable to reduce our economic aid to our allies. The technical assistance program will go on and economic aid is not wholly excluded. There are still some places near the Soviet orbit where the national governments cannot maintain adequate armed forces without help from us. That is notably so in the Middle and Far East. We have contributed largely ungrudgingly, and I hope constructively, to end aggression and advance freedom in Indochina. The stakes there are so high that it would be culpable not to contribute to the forces struggling to resist Communist oppression.

But broadly speaking, economic aid in the form of grants is on its way out as a major element of our foreign policy. This is highly desirable from many standpoints. It helps to make our own budget more manageable and it promotes more self-respecting international relationships. That is what our allies want. Trade, broader markets, and a flow of investment are far more healthy than intergovernmental grants-in-aid. It is, of course, important that we do actually develop these mutually advantageous substitutes for "aid." To do so is one of the major objectives of the Eisenhower administration. It is an essential component of the overall policies already described.

In the ways outlined, the United States and its allies gather strength for the long-term defense of freedom.

OUR NATIONAL PURPOSE

We do not, of course, claim to have found some magic formula that insures against all forms of Communist successes. Despotism is entrenched as never before. It remains aggressive, particularly in Asia. In Europe, its purposes remain expansive, as shown by Mr. Molotov's plans at the Berlin conference for Germany, Austria, and all Europe. However, time and fundamentals will work for us, if only we will let them.

The dictators face an impossible task when they set themselves to suppress, over a vast area and for a long time, the opportunities which flow from freedom. We can be sure that there is going on, even within the Soviet Empire, a silent test of strength between the powerful rulers and the multitudes of human beings. Each individual seems by himself to be helpless in this struggle. But their aspirations in the aggregate make up a mighty force. There are some signs that the Soviet rulers are, in terms of domestic policy, bending to some of the human desires of their people. There are promises of more food, more household goods, more economic freedom. This does not prove that the dictators have themselves been converted. It is rather that they may be dimly perceiving that there are limits to their power indefinitely to suppress the human spirit.

That is a truth which should not be lost sight of as we determine our own policies. Our national purpose is not merely to survive in a world fraught with appalling danger. We want to end this era of danger. We shall not achieve that result merely by developing a vast military establishment. That serves indispensably to defend us and to deter attack. But the sword of Damocles remains suspended. The way to end the peril peacefully is to demonstrate that freedom produces not merely guns, but the spiritual, intellectual, and material richness that all men want.

Such are the guiding principles we invoke. We have confidence that if our Nation perseveres in applying them, freedom will again win the upper hand in its age-long struggle with despotism, and that the danger of war will steadily recede.

Massive Retaliation and Graduated Deterrence*

by Rear Admiral Sir Anthony W. Buzzard
ROYAL NAVY (RETIRED)

Reliable disarmament, particularly of nuclear weapons, requires inspection and control, which in turn require much mutual trust. None of this is yet in sight. Disarmament of nuclear weapons is therefore still a long way off, although a measure of conventional disarmament may be nearer.

Meanwhile, as we try to nourish the necessary mutual trust and negotiate the many issues between East and West, the main menace to peace surely is Communist subversion. But that is not all. Behind the forces of subversion stand strong local armies, designed to support the subversive elements, to negotiate from strength further Communist advances, and to engage in local aggression, if opportunity offers, on a minor or even quite large scale, probably with conventional weapons.

Still another menace is that of minor wars arising from local nationalistic quarrels, and caused more by third parties than by the main rivals in the East-West struggle. Deliberate, premeditated aggression on a world-wide, or even a continental, scale by the Communists is seemingly out of the question. World war is therefore likely to result only from these local Communist or nationalist menaces, aggravated by pride and miscalculation. If these conflicts should lead to a deadlock between East and West, a world war might then ensue, and might well be started by a surprise Communist attack on the style of Pearl Harbor.

The foreign policy of the West seems therefore to require a defense policy which, while continuing to maintain the deterrent against deliberate world war, can also provide the local tactical strength necessary to negotiate from local strength, to deter limited Communist aggression, and to deal with the local nationalistic quarrels of third parties. Yet our present policy of massive retaliation hardly seems to meet these requirements, for, in effect, it threatens to destroy civilization as a result of any aggression too powerful for our small conventional forces to handle. Thus, NATO states that it intends to use nuclear weapons in the event of an attack from the East; and at the same time we are

* From *World Politics*, Vol. VIII, No. 2 (January 1956), pp. 228-237. Reprinted by permission of *World Politics*.

told that there is no distinction between the tactical and strategic use of such weapons.

That we should, in fact, try to establish distinctions between the strategic and tactical use of nuclear weapons is the proposition which this article attempts to develop. The suggestion is that we work out and declare, without waiting for Communist agreement, distinctions of the following order. The *tactical* use of nuclear weapons, we might say, is to be confined to atomic weapons, and is to exclude even these from use against towns and cities. Their *strategic* use, we might further declare, is to include hydrogen weapons and the mass destruction of targets in towns and cities. We might also state generally that, in order to pursue the moral principle of never using more force than necessary, we would not resort to the strategic use of nuclear weapons unless their employment proved absolutely essential. Thus, without committing ourselves unalterably in advance, or showing our hand too clearly, we would have the option, when threatened with a limited aggression too great for our conventional forces to cope with, of saying to the prospective aggressor: "If you do attack, we will, if necessary, use atomic and perhaps chemical weapons against your armed forces. But we will not, on this issue, use hydrogen or bacteriological weapons at all, unless you do, and we will not use any mass destruction weapons against centers of population, unless you do deliberately." To this statement we might append certain exceptions, such as cities in the front line of the land fighting and those with airfields alongside.

By an announcement of this character we would be modifying our present policy of massive retaliation to one aptly named "graduated deterrence." The obvious practical difficulties of such a policy may be dealt with later. Assuming practicability for the moment, let us consider the moral, political, military, and economic merits of graduated deterrence.

[1]

Moral Considerations Morally the issue is, surely, quite clear. We should not cause, or threaten to cause, more destruction than is necessary. By this criterion, all our fighting should be limited (in weapons, targets, area, and time) to the minimum force necessary to deter and repel aggression, prevent any unnecessary extension of the conflict, and permit a return to negotiation at the earliest opportunity—without seeking total victory or unconditional surrender. The moral standards which we profess to defend, demand not only this action in the event of aggression, but the pursuance of long-term policies directed toward this end.

Political Considerations So far, massive retaliation, despite its shortcomings and failure to halt aggression in Korea and Indo-China, has been a fairly effective deterrent because the Russians have been incapable of striking back massively, particularly at the United States. With this situation changing, massive retaliation, although still an effective deterrent against an all-out attack by the Communists, is no longer effective against the much more likely threat of local aggression by Soviet and satellite armies, because the Communists might well expect the United States to refrain from action which is becoming akin to suicide. Increasingly, therefore, our present policy is in danger of being interpreted as bluff—if indeed it does not prove to be one—for any aggression between an all-out war and a very minor one; and it leaves much room for misunderstanding and Communist exploitation.

Graduated deterrence, by providing an intermediate deterrent, guards against these dangers, and gives more latitude for our diplomacy, without reducing our deterrent against all-out attack. This option of intermediate action, together with the removal of the element of bluff, would not only improve our capacity to deter; it would also enhance our ability to negotiate from local tactical strength, an ability which becomes increasingly important as the strategic hydrogen stalemate approaches.

Graduated deterrence, by being at the same time less drastic than massive retaliation, would also help to reduce tension and build up trust. For example, in the disarmament discussions, an announcement of this new policy would constitute an assurance of our sincerity, since it would show that we genuinely wish to limit all possible use of nuclear weapons until their disarmament can be arranged. Conversely, such an announcement would be a test of the Communists' sincerity in these negotiations, for their denunciation of it would demonstrate the intention to continue exploiting our present tactical weakness.

Further, by blocking Communist pressure politics and every form of aggression, we might get the Soviets to see that their vast armaments are useless. Indeed, experience in the limited *use* of armaments would also nourish the trust essential for limiting their *possession*. Finally, by relying more on tactical strength with which to match Communist tactical strength, we would convert our security requirements into terms more comparable to those of the Communists, and therefore more easily balanced and reduced, stage by stage. Thus, the surest road to ultimate disarmament probably leads through graduated deterrence.

Military Considerations Graduated deterrence certainly complies with the basic military principle of first concentrating on the enemy's armed forces, as opposed to his people. But would the proposal to bar hydrogen weapons and the mass destruction of cities pay the West or the Communists more? On the one hand, if we decided to adhere to such a policy, we should be unable to attack with any mass destruction weapons key points like headquarter cities, Russian industries, submarine bases, and communication centers. On the other hand, the Russians would be unable to use these weapons against similar targets, including the many ports on which the development and supply of so much of the Allied potential depend.

Thus, both sides would gain enormously on an *absolute* basis, and this would heavily outweigh the *relative* considerations. But, insofar as the relative considerations counted, the Western allies would surely gain in view of their great dependence on ports, which form such bottlenecks and such ideal targets for nuclear and chemical weapons. This advantage would be particularly important in the crucial early stages of a war, because the mobilization and deployment of the Allied forces are always likely to be much less advanced at the start than those of the Communists. Moreover, since targets in towns and cities could still be attacked with high-explosive weapons, the Allied superiority in technique and precision attack would represent an added advantage for the West. Submarine bases could still be effectively mined, and key industrial targets and bridges attacked efficiently with high-explosive guided missiles.

We would also gain in three other respects. First, the advantage to our morale of not having to initiate the strategic use of nuclear weapons would be great. Secondly, by making possible the limited employment of these weapons against local aggression, we could if necessary exploit our great atomic superiority, not only directly against the Communist armies, but also against their supporting airfields and ships. Thirdly, in trying to halt the Communist armies, we could also exploit the great defensive properties of atomic and chemical weapons (both of which are so much more effective in defense than on the attack) without provoking their use against our vulnerable ports.

Thus it seems that, militarily, the ability to impose the suggested limitations would be to our advantage *relative* to the Communists, as well as of tremendous *absolute* advantage to both sides. Such a policy would help particularly to redress the tactical balance of power and improve our ability to hold territory.

Economic Considerations   At first sight, massive retaliation might seem to be the cheapest way of keeping the peace. But now that the Russians, too, are becoming able to retaliate massively, this policy by itself will not be an effective deterrent to limited aggression. Strong tactical land, sea, and air forces are therefore necessary in any case for deterring and repelling limited aggression. In providing this kind of strength, within the framework of a policy of graduated deterrence, the economies that we achieve by using tactical atomic weapons to help match the vast Communist conventional forces will be of real value. With our present policy, according to which an attack of any magnitude immediately provokes all-out hydrogen war, many of our tactical atomic preparations are a waste of money.

Moreover, with massive retaliation, a full scale of air and civil defense for our cities against every possible form of mass destruction is essential if our deterrent is to be convincing to the Communists. But this is becoming increasingly impracticable economically (except perhaps for the United States), and it is already quite beyond the means of the more exposed and less prosperous NATO countries. The meager air and civil defense measures which these countries can afford for their cities would be much more justifiable as part of a policy of graduated deterrence, both as an insurance against our deterrents failing to stop the Communists from initiating city destruction and as a reasonable defense against conventional weapons. Thus, although there would be no relief from our present defense expenditures, graduated deterrence would give us better security for our money. In sum, then, these moral, political, military, and economic considerations make graduated deterrence seem in principle far preferable to massive retaliation.

[II]

Objections to the practicability of such a policy seem formidable at first. But, when scrutinized, are they any worse than the many dangers and shortcomings of massive retaliation? Let us look at the three main objections to graduated deterrence.

(1) *That it would reduce our deterrent and thus increase the chances of war.* This, as we have seen, is becoming a fallacy now that Russia, too, is increasingly capable of retaliating massively. Indeed, graduated deterrence will decrease the chances of war, provided that we pay reasonable attention to our tactical strength, and do not renounce generally, and in advance, the initiation of strategic bombing with nuclear weapons, regardless of the scale or theater of aggression. In other words, against the unlikely eventuality of deliberate all-out aggression, our deterrent would be unchanged. Against the eventuality of a deadlock arising on some crucial issue, city destruction no longer being inevitable, we would have reduced the temptation for the Communists to attempt a "Pearl Harbor" against us.

Against major aggression by the Red armies, the Communists would know that our deterrent—not necessarily being suicidal—would be less likely to be bluff, and that we would be more united in our determination to retaliate. They would know that if we imposed the limitations of graduated deterrence, conditions would favor our great tactical atomic superiority, our atomic and chemical weapons used in defense, and our precision with high explosives. They would know, too, that there would still be a risk of hydrogen bombs being used, and of the mass destruction of cities.

Against minor aggression, our deterrent would be increased by the possibility of our using atomic and chemical weapons. We would be less likely to shrink from the prompt action required to prevent small wars from spreading; thus, we would be less likely to get into a position where a series of Communist nibbles forced us to take action leading to a major war. Finally, against the danger of war by mistake, or one brought on by a third party, there would be less scope for such misunderstandings as an intended minor aggression being taken for, and treated as, a major aggression.

(2) *That the Communists would not agree to our limitations in peace, or conform to them in war, if we elected to try and impose them.* It is true that, in peace, they probably would refuse to agree to our distinctions at first, arguing, as they do now, that the use of nuclear weapons must be abolished altogether, and knowing that this would leave the Red armies supreme. But, in war, it seems almost certain that the Communists would do their utmost to conform. They must appreciate

the vast superiority of the United States in nuclear weapons, her skill in delivering them, and her advantage in having air bases, on land and sea, so much closer to Russia and China than the Communist bases are to America.

In weighing the *relative* advantages, the Communists might well conclude, as we have, that the limitations would often favor us in our efforts to hold territory. But the *absolute* disadvantage of having their cities pounded by hydrogen weapons would far outweigh such relative considerations. As hydrogen weapons become more plentiful, this absolute consideration will surely weigh more heavily with the Communists.

But even if this estimate should prove wrong in war, we would have gained immeasurably in the unity and morale of the Allied nations by having placed the onus for initiating the mass slaughter of people on the enemy. Moreover, we would risk little, since to be a few hours after the enemy in the destruction of cities would not matter. It is true that the enemy could, if he dared to disregard our limitations, forestall us by a short time with hydrogen bombs against, say, our airfields while we were still attacking his with atomic weapons. But, if he did, we would probably be no worse off than with a policy of massive retaliation, where the enemy would have every incentive thus to forestall us with hydrogen weapons.

(3) *That distinctions in the use of nuclear weapons are impracticable, that the tactical use of them would spread to unlimited use, and that any such distinctions would therefore prove illusory.* The problems of making useful distinctions between hydrogen and atomic weapons, and of defining centers of population and their geographic limits, are certainly difficult ones. But provided they are thoroughly studied beforehand, there is no reason to suppose that they are insuperable. The weapons to be classed as strategic, instead of being defined as hydrogen, might be more appropriately characterized as those with major fall-out effects, or those exceeding in power a certain number of kilotons. Similarly, centers of population could be defined in a number of ways; but there is much to be said, where tactical operations are concerned, for excluding mass destruction of all towns and cities over a certain size, except those actually in the front line of the land fighting not declared and proved "open." The front line, in turn, might be defined as extending so many miles beyond the most advanced land units of each side. Such a definition could then be adhered to regardless of

the targets that the towns and cities contained, unless perhaps offensive missiles were launched from them, or offensive aircraft took off from airfields close alongside.

With some such distinctions established well in advance, the problem of limitations seems far from hopeless. For the difference between a bombing policy intentionally designed to strike the middle of cities with hydrogen bombs, and one designed to strike other targets with atomic bombs, but occasionally near-missing a city by mistake, would be obvious. Moreover, the Communists, like us, would be desperately anxious for cities to be spared from mass destruction. Thus, both sides would be eager—not reluctant—to overlook an occasional accidental breach of the rules; and both sides would want to avoid doing anything that would give the other an opportunity to put the worst interpretation on its actions.

In sum, it is far from certain that we would not succeed in maintaining these limitations during at least the early stages of any nuclear war, which is really what matters. Moreover, once our distinctions were established, and thus could grow in the minds and plans of both sides, the risks of the limitations breaking down in war would gradually diminish as the years went by. Finally, even if our limitations should break down in war, would anything have been lost by making the attempt to uphold them? Little or nothing, surely, provided only that we never lose sight of the risk of this happening, and avoid becoming "trigger happy" with our tactical atomic weapons.

This risk, if not sufficiently clear for both sides to see, could easily be advertised, and if any atomic weapons ever were used tactically, the spectacle would serve as a potent reminder of the consequences of employing them against cities, or of using hydrogen weapons thousands of times more powerful. Thus, the argument that it would be a dangerous illusion to toy with limitations cannot be sustained; and to deny ourselves a policy based on sound principles all around, because we fear we shall be blind to its shortcomings, would be defeatist in the extreme.

[III]

The conclusion surely is that graduated deterrence, providing us with the option of imposing limitations on the use of nuclear weapons, is in *principle* fundamentally right from the moral point of view, and advantageous politically, militarily, and economically. In *practice* there is a major difficulty, that of establishing and imposing distinctions in nuclear weapons, and the targets attacked by them, which stand a good enough chance of being maintained in war.

Before coming to a final decision about the merits of graduated deterrence, one may wonder whether it is better to introduce such distinctions immediately, or withhold an announcement until the eleventh hour before the outbreak of certain forms of war. Surely the latter would be most unwise, for the Communists might become so committed in their plans and weapons to fighting us on the basis of massive retaliation that they would be incapable of conforming to the limitations that we attempted to impose. A delay, in fact, would increase the general risk of the limitation breaking down in war; it would also increase the chances of an all-out war resulting from some misunderstanding. Indeed, by foregoing a peacetime declaration of our distinctions, we would also be denying ourselves the contribution that such a declaration would make toward redressing the tactical balance of power, helping our negotiations on disarmament and other issues, and strengthening the Western moral position both in our own eyes and in those of the uncommitted countries. What is more, an issue of this magnitude must surely be treated in the democracies as a national matter if it is to be properly prepared for in peace and acted upon with unity and restraint in war. In particular, it is only by showing the need for tactical strength that the effort will be made to provide it.

If the distinctions of graduated deterrence are not to be made at the eleventh hour, when then should they be established? Clearly, our tactical strength cannot at least for some time be such that we can afford to promise in advance never to initiate the strategic use of nuclear weapons in any circumstances. But there is every reason for establishing the necessary distinctions as soon as they can be worked out and agreed upon by the Western allies. For it will take some time thereafter for both sides to adjust to the idea of limited nuclear war. Indeed, the longer the delay, the more difficult these adjustments will become, and the longer we shall have to suffer from the shortcomings and dangers of our present policy.

The present circumstances seem particularly appropriate for introducing graduated deterrence on other grounds as well. It is becoming increasingly difficult to convince the peoples of the Allied nations that there is any point in continuing to build NATO and other forces with real tactical strength when our policy is to blow the world up in retaliation for any substantial aggression. Moreover, Western opinion seems to be under the delusion that a *general* stalemate is the military factor responsible for bringing the Russians hurrying to Geneva, and that we can therefore now afford to relax our defense preparations. In fact, only a *strategic* stalemate is about to be reached, and that thanks more to recent Russian progress than to ours. The *tactical* situation still remains substantially in the Communists' favor.

The establishment of the distinctions of graduated deterrence would both help to dispel these two doubts and, at the same time, indicate the need to enhance greatly our present tactical strength. In particular, it would convince the Germans, who are becoming increasingly impatient for reunification, of the need to press on with their contribution to NATO of twelve divisions, wherein lies the best hope of the Russians agreeing to withdraw from East Germany. It might also encourage the United States, who alone can afford substantially increased defense expenditures, to continue building tactical strength.

In our dealings with the Communists, this juncture also seems appropriate, because they (unlike our public) labor under no delusions. Quickly, while we are still only able to negotiate from strategic strength, they hurry to Geneva to try and prevent us from gaining the tactical prizes in Germany which could redress our tactical inferiority, knowing that these become decisive once the impending strategic stalemate arrives. Graduated deterrence, by showing our determination to produce a tactical balance of power, might help to convince them that there will be no alternative but to negotiate settlements with us on Germany, disarmament, and other outstanding issues.

Finally, graduated deterrence would provide a complementary corollary to our recent proposals for ground and air inspection, which in themselves are also measures for limiting the use of armaments rather than for disarmament. If we should get the Communists to agree to these measures, the moment would then be ripe for exploiting such success with graduated deterrence. If they should refuse, or procrastinate, graduated deterrence would enable us to retain the initiative with further positive action in our continuing efforts to face the Communists with the "necessity for virtue."

Surely, then, there is much to be said on the side of graduated deterrence. Let us therefore fully investigate this proposal, and weigh it carefully against the shortcomings of our present policy. For if, in the years to come, the help of German forces, a measure of conventional

disarmament, and improved relations with the Communists should ever
enable us to feel we could keep the peace without the strategic use of
nuclear weapons, we might even renounce in advance initiation of their
use. Thus might graduated deterrence gradually lead toward the elimination of the hydrogen bomb's threat to civilization.

How Much Defense Can the Economy Stand? *

by the Committee for Economic Development

In each of the periods of contraction of defense spending, civilian officials and military leaders, as we have seen, stressed their belief that the
American way of life is threatened by economic deterioration from
within as well as by aggression from without, and that a "sound economy" is, in the long run, the first mainstay of defense. This concern
with the American economy and way of life undoubtedly raises a question of the first importance. However, there is reason to suspect that this
sharply felt but vague apprehension has acted and may still be acting as
an impediment to rational decision by the nation and its leaders. For
we usually do not try to explore the effects of alternative levels of defense outlays on the economy as deeply and rationally as we are inclined
to examine their effects on our military preparedness. To do so is,
admittedly, by no means easy. Indeed, the strong conviction with which
many of us anticipate debilitating effects of large defense expenditures
on the economy stands in striking contrast to the paucity of our empirical knowledge about such effects.

Even if exaggerated weight were to be attached to the adverse economic effects of high military spending, the result might still, of course,
be a level of defense spending in excess of reasonable defense needs.
Overestimation of the costs might be more than counter-balanced by
overestimation of the needs.

Furthermore, with national security making huge claims on the
nation's resources, it is indisputably more essential to minimize waste
in the use of public funds in both defense and non-defense programs,
and to retrench public expenditures that are luxuries we can no longer
afford. There must be a new look at non-defense expenditure programs

---

* From *The Problem of National Security*, Research and Policy Committee, Committee for Economic Development (July 1958), pp. 20-28.

of government. Since we are facing a protracted period of large defense requirements, what is called for is close examination of the size and character of continuing programs, not temporary deferral of necessary expenditures.

We warn against interpreting our recommendation for realistic assessment of the economic costs as in itself a recommendation for higher military spending than is contained in the current budget proposals. We do not know whether better analysis of both military needs and economic costs would lead to more military spending. However, this Committee is better equipped to judge the cost side of the problem, and it is convinced that this needs looking into if policy is not to be guided by glib assumptions of fact. Preconceptions about the expenditures we can afford, the taxes we can stand or the debt we can bear should not be allowed to interfere with informed and rational balancing of the gains and losses from enlarged national security programs.

IMPAIRMENT OF LIVING STANDARDS DISTINGUISHED
FROM DAMAGE TO THE ECONOMY

We must distinguish two major aspects of the cost problem if we are to grapple with it. There is first the matter of public acceptance of a high rate of defense expenditures and corresponding taxation in order to provide for national security, even if spending and taxing at so high a level leaves the nation's economy fully intact. This turns upon public appraisal of the contribution defense expenditures actually make to our security, and of the sacrifice involved in high taxes. Secondly, there is the question: Will high spending and taxing undermine the soundness of the economy even though we are individually willing to assume our share in the tax burden? The two questions are altogether different. If the public is not convinced that it should spend a proposed portion of its income on national security, this does not necessarily mean that the proposed level of spending would be harmful to the economy.

The question of agreeing to personal sacrifice is, in principle, clear enough. The security benefits that various levels of defense expenditures can buy take the place of personal benefits from private expenditures or other public expenditures that could have been made instead. It is for the American citizen to weigh and compare these sets of benefits in the light of information available to him and to record his choice through the political process. However, assuring the public sufficient information about defense needs, costs, and capabilities to decide rationally poses a difficult problem. Except in wartime, there is no direct and observable test of our military strength. Clearly, the greatest possible frankness and clarity in public statements by high government officials is a requisite. Congressional and private investigations and studies are invaluable. The budget can be made a more effective informational document. However, no full solution is in sight, and additional ways for the public to become adequately informed must be sought.

But the second question is even more in need of careful examination. If high Federal expenditures on defense sap the strength of the economy, we must take heed. For the economy is a major base for the American defense effort, which as we have seen will probably have to be long continued, and for the American way of life that is to be defended.

CHARACTERISTICS OF A HEALTHY ECONOMY

The first steps in any orderly inquiry are obviously to define what we mean by a healthy economy and to specify the harm possibly resulting from huge outlays on national security. At present, there should be general agreement on the proposition that a soundly functioning American economy would exhibit the following three characteristics: (1) saving, investment and innovation sufficient to keep the economy growing in productive power at least as much as in the past, so that, in view of current population growth, the real gross national product will rise by an average of 3 to 4 per cent a year; (2) reasonably full employment, major inflationary as well as deflationary bouts being avoided; and (3) maintenance of something like the present balance between private and public economic decisions, with no further serious extension of government control over private decisions.

All of these are of prime importance, but there is one reason why the prerequisites of economic growth should be stressed in a statement dealing with national security. The best prospect that we can now plan on is that we may maintain the present uneasy peace by accepting the cost of maintaining a high level of military preparedness for decades. As time goes on, the Soviet system, growing in economic and technological capacity, will in all likelihood increase the pressure on our defense capacity unless profound changes in the political structure of Soviet society should make for dependably less aggressive behavior in foreign affairs.

Clearly, whatever security burdens are imposed on the American economy, they can be borne more easily if the GNP keeps rising rapidly and without serious interruption. A $600 billion economy will be better, from this point of view, than a $500 billion economy. The United States can maintain a higher defense capability as a regular feature and will be better able to cope with the variety of contingencies that may suddenly arise. Above all, we will be safer if in planning for American survival our leaders are less restrained by lack of resources than they now are.

RELATION OF DEFENSE SPENDING TO ECONOMIC GROWTH

Other statements by CED's Research and Policy Committee have urged a variety of positive measures to foster economic growth in ways consistent with the preservation of our liberties. But whatever constructive action is taken, it is also necessary to spot, assess, and counteract any developments that threaten to clog the sources of economic growth. And it is precisely this concern which leads us to inquire into the effects of a large peacetime burden of defense on the nation's economy.

Inflation is one possible source of interference with all of the objectives that we have specified—growth, stability, and preservation of a free, basically private enterprise, economy. And high defense outlays could contribute to inflation. The likelihood of this is reduced in periods, such as the present, when the economy is operating below capacity. Even in periods of generally full employment, however, a high level of defense expenditures over the long run will not cause inflationary pressures if the American public is willing to let itself be taxed sufficiently. If the economy is to function productively and the going American economic system is to be preserved, prolonged defense expenditures at a high level must be put on a pay-as-you-go basis.[1] If the taxes that

---

[1] This does not imply that the total Federal budget should be balanced annually at all times. Previous statements by the Research and Policy Committee have recommended that tax rates be set at levels that would provide a moderate surplus under conditions of high employment and stable prices. If tax receipts fall because of lowered incomes in periods of recession, the budget should be permitted to exercise its normal, stabilizing effect on the economy; we should not try to make up the deficiency in Federal receipts by raising taxes or by lowering expenditures. In severe recessions tax cuts should be considered. See especially *Taxes and the Budget: A Program for Prosperity in a Free Economy*, and *Defense Against Recession: Policy for Greater Economic Stability*.

the public is ready to tolerate fall short of the rate of expenditures that is urgently required, it is for the nation's leadership to explain to the public why larger security outlays are called for.

If defense expenditures are not financed by inflationary methods, national security measures will not, short of a war emergency, require the introduction of direct government controls over the economy to stabilize prices. Neither are they likely to be needed to obtain materials required for the defense program. Both persistent inflation and an extensive spread of government control over private business are in conflict with America's major economic objectives, but neither is a necessary accompaniment of a large and continuing national security program.

The diversion of scarce skills, materials and other resources from the civilian sector to defense may impede economic growth. But if, as we should, we plan in terms of defense requirements remaining high over a long period, we may also think in terms of increasing the total supply of individuals with scarce skills and of scarce materials. And this particular ill effect should be balanced against an important beneficial by-product of a large defense effort—the channeling of more money, energy and ingenuity into research, much of which has broad civilian applications, than would be forthcoming in its absence. There is no doubt that this extra spur to science and technological advance has yielded vast benefits in terms of increased productivity, new techniques, and new products, and hence furthered economic growth.

THE LEVEL AND STRUCTURE OF TAXATION

While inflation occasioned by large defense expenditures, and widespread government controls occasioned by persistent inflation, can be avoided by sufficient taxation, a large tax burden, in turn, is also widely suspected of being subversive of economic progress. A large tax load will harm the productive growth of the economy if it discourages work effort, enterprise, investment, and the capacity as well as the incentive to save. It is essentially these indirect and insidious costs of high defense spending which are feared as a potential cause of deterioration of the American economy and the American way of life.

Revenues of all levels of government equaled over one-fourth of the gross national product of this country in 1956. These revenues were allocated as follows: national security expenditures, 39 per cent; other government purchases of goods and services, 35 per cent; income returned to the private sectors of the economy without absorbing current output (interest, transfer payments such as social insurance benefits or veterans pensions, and subsidies), 22 per cent; and surplus of governments, 4 per cent.[2] National security expenditures thus occasion a large part—almost two-fifths—of the total tax burden. Unlike most other government expenditures, they absorb current output of the nation without, for the most part, providing services that directly enhance consumer welfare or add to the nation's capital stock.

The tax problem has two closely related aspects. There is the problem of the total tax burden in relation to the national income, and there is the problem presented by the particular structure of taxation by which government revenues are extracted. Even a large total burden of national defense might, if financed by taxes that are carefully levied, leave the American people enough income to provide for a high and rising standard of living, essential civilian government services, the saving and investment needed for rapid economic growth, and strong incentives to work and be enterprising. But the same total revenue might also be extracted by a system of taxes that, while raising the necessary revenue, would have serious effects on economic efficiency and growth.

There is no way to measure at all precisely the effect of high taxes on growth. We do not, for example, know what would have happened since the start of the Korean War—when defense expenditures and taxes for military security were lifted to very high levels—had these expenditures been smaller. But we do know that the growth of our productive capacity and the rate of saving, investment and innovation in this period of large outlays have not been below our average past experience.

The effect of higher taxes on the amount of work people do is, in fact, not certain. Higher tax rates mean that the net income reward for additional work is smaller, and this may discourage effort. But they also mean that more effort is required to achieve or maintain any given standard of living. Individuals react differently to these counter-influences. While there is much grumbling about high taxes, it is not clear whether, on balance, there has been any appreciable slackening of work effort in this country as a result of high taxes.

High tax rates also impair the incentive to save and invest, and espe-

---

[2] These percentages are based on the national income accounts of the Department of Commerce. Other classifications would yield results only slightly different.

cially to undertake the risk of investments in new products, processes, and businesses, the type of investment that is particularly important to growth.[3]

But we are convinced, and this is crucial, that there is no sharp breaking point—a specific percentage of the national product—at which the retarding effects of high taxes would become suddenly important. Once these effects are generated, we believe, they are at first marginal and then increase gradually if the tax burden is raised progressively. We are also convinced that the total amount of taxes now collected is one which, though presumably having some retarding effect, the American economy can stand without becoming debilitated; and we believe that a somewhat larger burden is fairly safe from this point of view.

However, the structure of the tax system is an independent factor in the equation. As this Committee has pointed out in numerous statements, there are important deficiencies in the present Federal tax system. Given the total amount of revenue to be raised, we believe that the American economy would be more productive and grow more rapidly if we reduced the extremely high marginal rates now built into our income tax structure and if in other ways the tax system were made less burdensome on saving and on incentives to take economic risks. The case against this tax structure is not that it prevents growth but that it probably retards growth below the rate of which our economy is capable and thus increases the indirect cost of national security expenditures by comparison with an ideal tax system. This consideration must be taken into account in deciding on the level of defense expenditures and on the structure of Federal taxation.

OUR ECONOMY CAN SUPPORT ADEQUATE DEFENSE

The general reappraisal of defense requirements that has been taking place has brought fairly general agreement that national security expenditures should be lifted above their previous rate. The Committee wishes to stress that we are not recommending that the size of defense programs now contemplated should or should not be expanded, since we

---

[3] *Footnote by Allan Sproul:* "High tax rates are suspected of impairing incentives and are feared for that reason, among others, but we do not know nor can we measure their effect on incentives. There is some reason to believe that incentives have been preserved, in part, at the expense of broad equity, by the variety of loopholes in the present tax laws. These have added or enlarged one of the incentives of economic life—the incentive of tax avoidance."

have not made any independent appraisal of military needs. The expansion of our defense programs, or even maintenance of their present levels, imposes real costs of many kinds on the American people. We should be no more profligate with defense outlays than with any other kind of public expenditure. We realize, however, that the nation's security requires military programs at the levels proposed in the 1959 budget and very possibly higher.

We see no need to be apprehensive about whether or not the American economy can stand the strain of this or even a considerably larger budget. The risk that defense spending of from 10 to 15 per cent of the gross national product, or if necessary even more, will ruin the American way of life is slight indeed. It is even less likely that there is some magic number for defense expenditures that, if exceeded, would bring economic disaster; rather, the impairment of growth caused by increasing taxes is a gradually rising one. We have not reached a point at which anxiety over the healthy functioning of the economy demands that defense expenditures be slashed regardless of the dictates of military prudence. We can afford what we have to afford. But we are also convinced that the economic costs of national security can be held down by a system of taxation more conducive to economic growth.

LARGE DEFENSE EXPENDITURES NOT NEEDED FOR PROSPERITY

The chance is slight that we shall be in a position any time soon sharply to reduce national security expenditures with safety. But if changes in the world situation should create the opportunity of doing so, we should not fear that contraction of defense markets would cause a depression. Lower defense expenditures would permit a commensurate reduction in taxes. This would mean an increase in private disposable income, and a consequent expansion of private purchasing to offset the decline in defense spending. If desired, some portion of defense outlays could be diverted to useful government programs of a civilian character, such as large-scale urban redevelopment or improved education. We might also, as offered by the President, use some of the savings from disarmament for expanded developmental assistance abroad. There is, in fact, no end of desirable uses to which the resources freed by a reduced armament burden could be applied.

Such an adjustment cannot be carried out without some temporary unemployment and disruption of production. But twice within the past

15 years—after World War II and after the Korean armistice—it has been shown that the readjustment period need not be long. Such transitional difficulties would be a small price to pay for the permanent increase in living standards that a substantial reduction in the defense burden would make possible.

Unlimited Confusion over Limited War*

by Colonel Ephraim M. Hampton

Statements frequently emanate from high military and civilian sources in the national government to the effect that the likelihood of total war in the foreseeable future is rather remote and, therefore, the prospect of limited war is more likely. These statements have indicated the necessity of exploring just what is meant by the term "limited war," what is the likelihood of a limited war that will involve U.S. forces in active combat, and what the role of the Air Force should be in such a conflict.

Although the prospects of a World War III appear to be receding, existing world tensions and conflicts are opening the way for other forces to come into play. It appears therefore that the world is most likely to be confronted with a period of revolts, civil wars, guerrilla wars, wars between smaller nations, and wars between big nations and little nations. It has become fashionable to label all such wars as limited wars, and to attempt to arrive at some sort of magic formula for coping with them. There are many who hold the view that it is most unrealistic and dangerous to attempt to categorize and cope with war on such a basis. The arguments they offer in substantiation of such a view are pertinent to the subject of this article and will now be presented in detail.

THE ARGUMENT AGAINST CATEGORIZING WAR

If war is viewed in its broadest context, there is no such thing as limited war. It does not exist in fact; it is at best a hope and not a reality. In actual fact there is only one condition of war, which is—war. War is war: a condition of combat, and it is potentially total at all

---

* From the *Air University Quarterly Review*, Vol. IX, No. 2 (Spring 1957), pp. 28-47. Reprinted by permission of the *Air University Quarterly Review*.

times. There is no assured method of keeping it limited. Armed conflicts between modern nations inevitably involve the risk of mutual annihilation. Perhaps war's potential of totality is not crystal clear in all circumstances, but the fact of this potential will become increasingly clear with each new advance in weapons and technology. This is so because whenever a nation resorts to war as the "other means" that Clausewitz speaks of, it is inherent in the term "war" that military forces, without specific definition as to degree or intensity, will be used. There is always a possibility that all available forces (total force) will be brought to bear.

Despite the ineluctable facts of the nature of war, we have fallen into the habit within the last few years of talking about war as "total" or war as "limited," much as though it is possible to control the intensity of war like water at a faucet, turning it off and on and otherwise regulating it at will. There is much evidence to indicate that this habit may be an escapist device—a case of candy-coating the bitter truth.

Is it logical to proceed on the assumption that any major nation in the nuclear age could be assured of conducting or sponsoring a war with enough control to exercise absolute restrictions? The answer must be a categorical "no." There are some very sound reasons for this emphatic negative.

Consider for instance how unrealistic it is to attempt to predetermine the degree or intensity of force that is to be applied in war, when it is not possible to predict the precise form, scope, location, significance, and scale of the combat actions that will be involved. One very cogent reason for the unpredictableness of warfare is the possibility that a combatant confronted by the prospect of a tactical disaster, or a complete defeat, may take actions that increase the intensity of combat or broaden its scope far beyond any limits thought of in the beginning as enduring restrictions.

This being so, is it not realistic to ask, Who *is it that can invariably limit a war?* Because if war can be limited only occasionally, or only when some special set of circumstances prevails, then there is, in fact, no such thing as a general category of "limited war." There are only specific instances when, for reasons that may be different in each case, military force was not utilized as fully as it could have been. As long as it is possible for antagonists to expand a limited war, how can we have a satisfactory degree of control? How can we, by predetermined military means, actually limit what may happen? . . .

Consideration keeps coming back to the fact that war is always potentially total. Some may hold the view that this position is rendered invalid by the fact that low-intensity or small-scope combat may occur from time to time. But this basis for its validity or invalidity is not necessarily sound. It is correct that there may be recurring instances of less than total war, but it is also a fact, as most of the experts agree, that continued intermittent aggression against the free world could in time be as destructive as massive attack. If in practice we, as a nation, could be disposed of by war conducted at a lesser intensity than "total," then differences in method are of no particular consequence. The end result is the same. If this is so, then it is possible to ask, *What is the precise designation of the point at which the war of lesser intensity would stop being "limited" and become "total"?*

Where exactly to draw the line between "limited" and "total" war is a key difficulty. It must be solved in specific terms if the limited-total categorizing of war is to have any real meaning in the programing of forces, the planning of strategies, and the formulation of national policies.

What then *is* the answer? The answer is that in all the widespread use of the term "limited war" and discussions of what it constitutes there is to be found no completely satisfactory answer. The question cannot be answered satisfactorily. Every situation is different. There can be an infinite number of combinations of circumstances. The purely military aspects of limited war cannot be realistically blueprinted in advance. They can only be generalized, and it is this generalization that complicates in the extreme the job of military planners, because they, in order to do their work, must deal in specifics.

CONSIDERATIONS INVOLVED IN CATEGORIZING WAR

Having presented the thoughts of those who view the question of war in its broadest context and who believe it unrealistic and dangerous to categorize "war" on the basis of "total" and "limited," let us now turn to a more specific consideration of what is involved when war is so categorized. To do this, it is essential that we examine the predominant factors which generate limitations on full utilization of existing capabilities of forces engaged in war. However, before proceeding with this examination, since public thinking and usage have now firmly established the term "limited war" in the lexicon of the military, it is essential to define the two categories of war—total and limited.

Anyone who has given any thought whatsoever to the problem of defining these terms is immediately aware of the difficulty and danger of the attempt. Nevertheless, no meaningful conclusions are likely to be reached unless there is some common agreement as to what these terms mean. Modern instruments of power provide such great destructive force that national extinction is a very great possibility in an international conflict. In view of this we may, I think, define "total war" as conflict in which the national survival of the U.S. and U.S.S.R. as sovereign nations is the issue of the war.

When we come to defining "limited war" the task is more complex and difficult. Today the term has come to mean many different things to different individuals, ranging across the whole belligerency spectrum from a major war with the U.S.S.R., but not involving nuclear weapons, down to minor police actions against small nations. For the present and the immediate future we will live in a bipolar world of power blocs in which the U.S. and U.S.S.R. are the leaders. As long as this international situation obtains I think we can for all practical purposes define "limited war" as any war however large or small, regardless of the geography, objectives, weaponry, or strategy, in which the national survival of the U.S. and the U.S.S.R. is not at issue. The term "total war" as defined is intended to include such terms as general war, unrestricted war, all-out war, etc. The term "limited war" as defined is intended to include such terms as local war, small war, brush war, etc.

What are the predominant factors of limited war? They are the objectives for which the war is fought, the nations engaged, the geography involved, and the weaponry used, i.e., type of weapons, yields, and force pattern.

Objectives The objectives for which the war is fought, and here we open Pandora's box, are first and foremost of these factors. Are the objectives of the war limited primarily because of political considerations? It is argued that it is impossible to make a distinction between political and military considerations as related to the objectives of the war. This view is based on the contention that these considerations are too closely meshed to admit of a clear-cut distinction between them. It is believed that the acceptance of such a view has in the past complicated the task of the military in waging limited wars and will continue to do so in the future if its validity is not contested. Since the objectives for which a war is fought set the pattern for everything that is done in the war, it is essential that the *political* objectives be clearly set forth and understood by both the political and military leadership of the government prior to the time decision is made to wage a specific limited war. However, the futility of attempting to be specific concerning the *military* objectives for which limited wars may be fought, in advance of any knowledge concerning what the specific political objectives are to be in the war, is obvious.

Wars of the past have been fought with the attainment of at least one or more of the following general objectives in mind:

a. To attain specific economic or political goals.

b. To cause a hostile force to cease and desist from military action in which it is engaged.

c. To restore the status quo that existed prior to the outbreak of hostilities.

d. To bring about complete and unconditional capitulation of enemy military forces in the field.

Within the framework of any of these four objectives, one can visualize an infinite variety of combinations and circumstances that would result in the establishment of specific and lesser included objectives. The establishment of the first three of these generalized categories or their combinations as objectives of a war serves to generate limitations on the full utilization of existing capabilities of the forces engaged in the war. Only where the objective is to bring about the complete and unconditional capitulation of enemy military forces in the field does the existing potential and capability of the military really become the determining factor. In all other cases the objectives themselves establish the limitations on the forces engaged, and very definitely circumscribe the extent to which the military is free to capitalize on existing military capabilities and potentialities. For this reason the policy maker and the military planner are severely handicapped in their efforts to assess in advance the impact that limitations arising from objectives may have upon the course of a war, the strategy being employed, and the forces to be used in such a war. It is almost trite to say that the advent of nuclear weapons has changed the whole complexion of war. Having stated this change, however, the question still must be answered as to exactly how the manner in which war is waged has been changed. One thing is certain: whereas in the past peoples and nations could wage wars of extermination, the means available to them for such action were, relatively speaking, primitive and time-consuming when compared with the means afforded by nuclear weapons. The nuclear weapon has placed in the hands of mankind the capability of exterminating his fellow man in a minimum of time. *But the existence of such a capability does not presuppose that it will be exercised in full measure on all occasions or that restrictions which have been tacitly accepted and followed in wars of the past will necessarily be abrogated in wars waged during the nuclear age.* It is this thought more than any other that makes the current talk of limited war so worthy of examination by the politician, the diplomat, and the military man.

A limited war involving the overt participation of United States forces would probably involve Soviet support of our enemy in the form of weapons and materiel. Such a war would involve the struggle for the attainment of certain objectives that each side considers of sufficient importance to warrant engaging in the adventure. How vital one side, U.S. or U.S.S.R., considers these objectives to be will determine the self-imposed limitations in waging a restricted war. It seems inevitable that if these objectives are of *transcendent importance* to one side or the other, a situation would ultimately be reached when that side must decide to utilize whatever military effort it considers necessary to achieve its objectives, and total war is likely to follow. If the objectives are not considered vital, then either side or both sides may decide to stop short of all-out effort and, accordingly, sacrifice the attainment of the initial objectives. If this line of thinking is valid, then all limited wars involving U.S. and U.S.S.R. resources must end either in what amounts to preservation of the status quo or must expand into total war. It therefore follows that we could only "win" a limited war if our objective is the maintenance of the status quo. Or said another way, I think we must consider that all limited wars will have to end in what amounts to a rather limited victory or limited defeat for one side or the other or in a stalemate, or else expand into total war.

Earlier I defined limited war as war in which the national survival of the U.S. and the U.S.S.R. is not at issue. This definition deliberately ignores what will happen when the possession of nuclear weapons ceases to be in effect a monopoly of the U.S. and U.S.S.R. When this situation obtains, I believe the definition will still hold. As long as the U.S. —U.S.S.R. have in effect a monopoly of nuclear weapons they, by virtue of this fact, are in the position of being the arbiters or umpires, if you will, of any hostility less than total. In other words, as long as this monopoly situation exists, no nation in the world, however great or small it may be, can engage in war except by consent of the U.S. and U.S.S.R. The truth of the foregoing was amply demonstrated in the recent Suez crisis.

Once nuclear weapons become available to nations not now possessing them, the picture will change. Then the ability to absorb all a potential antagonist can deliver and still survive will become the determining factor. The degree to which the belligerents are willing to risk putting to the ultimate test of total war their assessment of their ability to survive while pursuing the attainment of their objectives, will in the final analysis determine the scope of limited war. The physical size and power of the U.S. and U.S.S.R. will continue to give them the edge in this matter, even though their nuclear monopoly ceases to exist. Accordingly, not until a nation or coalition of nations approximating their size and power appears on the scene to oppose either of these great powers will they lose their ability to umpire a limited-war situation. Once the world is confronted with this tripolar situation, it may reasonably be asked who then becomes the umpire? Who then is in a position to determine and enforce limitations on the scope and weaponry of a so-called limited war? I think the answer is obvious. There will be no one. And when that time comes mankind will indeed be in a much more precarious situation, if such is possible, than it is today.

The Nations Engaged Let us now examine the second big factor that must be considered in any discussion of limited war—the nations engaged. Earlier it was mentioned that a continuation of a limited war was only possible at the sufferance of the U.S. and U.S.S.R. If this is a valid statement, and I think it is, we can dismiss the unilateral war actions of all other nations as being controllable to the extent the U.S. and U.S.S.R. consider it expedient to control them. The main considerations in limited-war actions then revolve around the actions and intentions of either the U.S. or the U.S.S.R., or both.

An examination of U.S. treaty commitments around the globe reveals the U.S. is obligated to intervene in cases of overt Communist aggression against any nation on the periphery of the Communist bloc, except Afghanistan, India, Burma, Sweden, and Switzerland. Similarly Soviet Russia has mutual defense pacts with all her satellite nations and Red

China. If the United States and Soviet Russia see fit actually to discharge in full their treaty obligations, it appears unlikely that limited war in these periphery areas could long remain limited. Thus the same factors that tend to deter total war also have a profound effect in deterring limited war. It would therefore appear more likely that both the United States and the Soviets would recognize the danger of the conflict expanding to proportions of total war, possibly with disastrous consequences to both, and that each would propose alternative solutions rather than engage in military actions which could lead to this eventuality.

The world has become so polarized between the Communist bloc and the U.S., with the balance of power between the two blocs becoming so fine, that the loss of even a small nation or geographical area could have significant impact on this balance. Each side is so enmeshed in a tangle of treaty obligations that any realignment in orientation of the nations involved is likely to precipitate a chain reaction. Just where such a reaction is likely to start or end is impossible to predict. If this analysis of the existence of a polarized condition is valid, any action in these periphery areas that threatens to upset the balance and precipitate the chain reaction might constitute a threat and probably would be construed as a threat to the national survival of either the U.S. or the U.S.S.R. Total war would be more likely to be the result in such a situation than limited war.

One exception to the foregoing analysis could occur. There is a rather remote possibility of a limited war with Red China should she embark on armed aggression on her own or with only the tacit approval of the Kremlin. In such a situation it is conceivable that the Soviets might deem it to their advantage not to intervene with their armed forces in the event the U.S. reacted strongly. The Soviet objective in this case might be to cause the U.S. and China to expend significant resources in a war, which expenditure could have great long-range strategic significance if the participants, as a consequence, suffered an appreciable degradation of military strength.

Such a conflict would fit the definition given for a limited war. However it would appear much more likely that Soviet Russia would do everything in her power to prevent China from embarking on a venture of this nature unless it fitted the Communist time schedule for an attack on the United States.

Our national policy requires our military planners to concede to the

U.S.S.R. the initiative of striking the first blow in a total war. Such initiative should be and probably is considered as a priceless jewel by the Soviet military, and it is not likely to be jeopardized or thrown away via the medium of a limited war that involves their forces and ours directly or indirectly and that gradually expands into a total war. If one is willing to discount completely the possible occurrence of the exception discussed, then the foregoing, I believe, adds weight to the premise that general war (total) is a greater threat than limited war. However, the value of this "priceless jewel" will decrease in almost direct proportion to the security of our total-war deterrent force, that is, to our ability to decrease its vulnerability to surprise attack. Its value is practically nil when a condition of invulnerability is attained for our retaliatory force and the foregoing premise is correspondingly compromised.

The United States is less likely than the U.S.S.R. to act swiftly in the umpire role in limited-war situations by direct action on a unilateral basis. The Soviets never exhibited much concern for the attitudes and views of their satellites. The United States contrasts sharply with its greater desire to give due consideration to the views of its allies and its desire to strengthen and enhance the prestige of the United Nations Organization by acting through it rather than outside of it. At present the United Nations is little more than a forum for international debate. Until it attains a basic strength for decision and action, which it does not now possess, the influence that we permit it to exert upon our capability to take swift and direct action is significant and dangerous. The restraint our allies are able to bring to bear on our acting unilaterally is of equal import. Here our widespread system of alliances, embodying as it does nations of many gradations of economic, political, and military strength, makes it almost axiomatic that our actions will always reflect the views of our allies. The views, in the main, will reflect the lowest common denominator.

Geography Let us now turn to the third predominant factor that must be considered in any discussion of limited war: the geography of the war. This factor includes consideration of such subjects as "sanctuaries," nature of the terrain, physical size of the area of conflict, and the presence or absence in the area of the facilities that can be used for the conduct of limited-war operations. Such aspects of the problem confront the military planner and complicate his generally already complicated job of planning limited-war operations.

Political rather than military objectives will exercise the greatest influence on the determination of those areas that antagonists will seek to establish and have honored as sanctuaries. I think this was true in the Korean situation and will be equally true in the future. The area that offers the greatest geographical opportunity for successful results from military operations may well be the one that is denied to the tactician or strategist by the political element of the government. This points up the mandatory requirement, previously mentioned, that the political elements of the government establish and clearly state to the military, *in advance* of the initiation of hostilities, the political objectives for which a limited war is to be fought. Unless this is done, the military will be unable to ensure, commensurate with these political objectives, the most efficient and effective utilization of their forces and the geography available to them for the conduct of operations.

Certainly the physical size of the area of conflict will have an increasing impact on air power operations. Advances in modern technology, which continue to result in ever-greater speeds in air vehicles, complicate in the extreme such problems as those associated with the honoring of sanctuaries under "hot pursuit" conditions, where the area of operations is relatively small in relation to the speed of weapons operating in it.

Of no less significance is the ability to support logistically with the greatest efficiency and least cost a force equipped with modern and complex weapons. This ability varies inversely with the size of modern forces engaged and the distance of the area from the source of modern logistical support. The larger the size of the modern forces engaged and the more primitive and rugged the area of operations, both as to terrain and available resources for logistical support, obviously the greater the problem of logistically supporting such forces and operations and the cost associated with them.

The Weaponry The fourth and last predominant factor that requires attention in any examination of the subject of limited war is the weaponry. I shall use this term as embracing such considerations as the possible use or nonuse of conventional or nonconventional weapons, the force pattern, and the size of the forces required.

Everyone is familiar with the controversy that continues to swirl around the question of when and where to use conventional and nonconventional weapons. The mere fact that so much has been written and said on the subject is indicative of its highly political nature.

That nuclear weapons will be used in total war I think goes without saying. With the power that nuclear weapons place at their disposal the United States and the Soviet Union have a relatively simple task of blueprinting strategy and doctrine for such a war. In fact the type of forces and the strategy each will employ become almost self-evident.

The war in its most fundamental aspects becomes one of national survival with no holds barred and the utilization of the most powerful weapons against the enemy, with the sole objective of threatening his national existence to the extent necessary to cause him to lose the will and capacity to wage war or offer effective opposition. Our NATO allies have accepted the use of nuclear weapons as vital for the defense of West Europe in the event of total war. What the attitude of our allies is likely to be concerning their use in limited-war situations is far less clear.

There are those who strongly contend that any use of nuclear weapons in limited war will "inevitably" expand the war to total proportions. Since war is potentially *total* at all times, there is certainly great cause for concern, and such a premise is worthy of the closest examination. Whether the element of "inevitability" is an ever-present ingredient I doubt. The conditions that could generate a limited war in this nuclear age will in the majority of cases be far too complex to permit such a positive view.

The factors bearing on the problem of limited war which have already been discussed serve to emphasize the foregoing statement. Such a premise has implicit in it the view that all that is required is the decision not to use nuclear weapons and all will be well. Could we be sure that, under all conditions that are likely to arise, agreement could be obtained by *all* belligerents to follow such a course of action, then and only then would we be safe in planning to wage limited war by conventional means only. To state the proposition is to deny its possibility. How could we ever be sure an enemy possessing nuclear weapons would keep his agreement not to use them? Were he to break his agreement, how could we punish him except by resort to the use of nuclear weapons ourselves? To believe or to assume that belligerents possessing nuclear weapons will not use them in limited war, should such use appear to be to their advantage, is, to say the least, dangerous and foolhardy.

Common sense dictates that we *must* assume that nuclear weapons will be used in limited war if those nations possessing them consider it *expedient* to do so. It certainly would seem advantageous from the Communists' point of view to be able to continue to wage limited wars in which nuclear weapons are not used—enjoying as they do a tremendous superiority in manpower and probably a like superiority in conventional weapons. The course of events in Korea and in Indo-China emphasizes the advantages that accrue to them under such terms. The Communist propaganda against the use of nuclear weapons undoubtedly has as its aim the retention of this advantage. Irrespective of the foregoing there will undoubtedly be situations where the characteristics of the nuclear weapon are such as to make it the least desirable and effective weapon for the task at hand. In my view the key determinant will be the extent to which a belligerent possessing nuclears considers that its vital interests may or may not be affected by the use or nonuse of nuclears. What his antagonist may or may not do in this regard will certainly enter into his considerations, but it will not be the final determinant.

Any discussion of using nuclear weapons raises the issue of the morality of their use in war. The whole history of weaponry has been one of ever-increasing efficiency and destructiveness. History is replete with examples of newly developed weapons whose use was deplored as being uncivilized and inhuman; yet without exception, if they proved efficacious in furthering victory in war, they inevitably became a part of the arsenals of military forces the world over, replacing completely less efficient weaponry. (Some will cite the nonuse of gas in World War II as an exception to the foregoing. I think it is generally conceded that gas was not used in World War II simply because it was not to the advantage of either side to use it—it simply was not the most suitable or best available weapon.) There are many, both in and out of the military, who feel that history will repeat itself in this regard as concerns nuclear weapons—that far from remaining "unconventional" they will become the "conventional" weapons of the future. Perhaps this "future" is already with us.

From the standpoint of absolute morality, killing is immoral and the means by which killing is accomplished must also be immoral. Human nature being what it is, it seems unlikely that humanity will reach the millennium of nonviolence during the nuclear era. This being so, it is more rational to say that the morality or immorality lies *in the manner in which weapons of destruction are used rather than the weapons themselves.*

Only conventional weapons were used in Korea, yet the destruction wrought could hardly have been greater had nuclear weapons been used, and certainly the misery and suffering sustained by troops and the Korean people were dragged out over a period of years. If the use of nuclear weapons can bring a quick decision in war and thereby shorten it, even though initial destruction and casualties may be high, who can argue that such usage is more inhuman and immoral than a war of conventional weapons that drags on and on, piling casualties upon casualties, destruction upon destruction, and misery upon misery?

Because of budgetary considerations the British have recently decided to revamp their defense structure—placing major reliance on nuclear-equipped forces. There is evidence that others of our allies are likely to do the same as soon as they are able either to produce or obtain nuclear weapons. The implications, for the U.S. and its allies, of such a revamping of defense forces, on considerations of the morality of using nuclear weapons are most significant. Once this change in their defense structure is accomplished, our allies are less likely to oppose the use of nuclear weapons in limited war than is now the case. Indeed they will hardly have a choice in the matter. Further, the accomplishment of this change by our major allies will suggest, I believe, the desirability of our ultimately reaching an agreement with them whereby they assume the major responsibility for the maintenance of the free world's limited-war type of forces and thereby reduce to a minimum the necessity for the United States to maintain them. Under such an agreement the U.S. could provide the bulk of the free world's total-war deterrent forces, and its allies could provide the bulk of the free world's limited-war forces. The reduction in defense expenditures for all concerned which could result from such an agreement makes its attainment both possible and attractive.

Earlier mention was made of the polarization concept and the possibility of a chain reaction from an upset of the present alignment among nations of the world. It must be assumed that Soviet Russia and Red China have also recognized this concept. The Communists therefore might conceivably attack an unprepared area in such strength and with such speed that their objectives would be gained prior to any attempts to block them. The U.S. would then find itself in the position of declaring war if it wanted to wrest the captured territory from the Communists. Obviously such a situation would be most unsatisfactory for us. Under such conditions neutral nations or those friendly to the

West might feel that the West could not protect them, thus causing a chain reaction to align with the Communists. It therefore appears that reaction time may well play as decisive a role in limited war as in total war. Selective and discriminatory use of nuclear weapons affords the United States the best means of accomplishing decisive results with a minimum of reaction time and, for reasons already mentioned, may well be the "morally right" weapon to use. Contrary to opinion that exists in some civilian circles, the ability to use nuclear weapons on a selective and discriminatory basis, i.e., with correct yield for a particular target, does not present a problem that the military cannot satisfactorily handle.

Before leaving the subject of conventional versus nonconventional weapons it might be well to remember that the advent of atomic weapons seems to have caused the military to focus its attention on the use of nuclear weapons of varying degrees of killing power to the exclusion of weapons that have the capability to neutralize but not to kill. Certainly weapons of neutralization, such as certain chemical and biological measures, have a place in limited war for purposes of neutralization or denial and cannot logically be objected to on moral grounds.

Force Pattern This brings us to a consideration of the force pattern of weaponry. I should like to enter this facet of our subject by posing a question: *Does limited war generate a requirement for specially developed limited-war forces?*

Discussion of this question centers on two divergent viewpoints. It has been postulated that if we prepare adequately for total war, then we can handle limited wars in stride with the forces so created. Opponents to this idea raise certain objections:

(1) Total-war forces cannot efficiently perform limited-war tasks (using a sledge hammer to kill a gnat).

(2) The utilization of total-war forces in a limited-war situation will, because of their massive destructive potential, inevitably and unacceptably increase the risk of enlarging the conflict into a total war.

(3) The utilization of total-war forces in limited-war situations will degrade our total-war capability, thus lessening our power to deter total war and increasing the probability that total war will occur under conditions least favorable to us.

The reconciliation of these arguments seems to lie in policy and doctrine. What the proponents of both viewpoints are really trying to say is that we must always maintain an adequate total-war force in such a state of readiness and security that its availability is ensured under any circumstances. We thus preserve its deterrent effect and its ability to prosecute the total war if this deterrence fails. If we should have forces in excess of this requirement, they can be used in limited-war situations. The extent to which national resources are devoted to the creation and support of these excess forces must not be allowed to influence adversely the amount of national effort required for the support and maintenance of the total-war deterrent force. The use of the total-war deterrent force in limited-war situations must always be such as to permit its rapid reorientation toward total-war tasks in the event this becomes necessary.

Careful consideration of all the aspects of the limited-war problem raised in this article indicates, I believe, the necessity of weaponry that provides for:

1. Maintenance by the free world of a "hard core" total-war deterrent force constituted of secure strategic air power.

2. Maintenance, at least for the present, by the free world of limited-war "cushion" forces. The composition of these "cushion" forces must be such as to prevent the Communists from gaining something for nothing whenever they probe free-world defenses.

Neither the United States nor the remainder of the free world need attempt to match *in the aggregate* the Communists' limited-war strengths in order to obtain a cushion effect sufficient to force the Communists to disclose the extent of their determination in each probing action and/or prevent their obtaining something for free.

In the foregoing we have the crux of what is almost exclusively a military problem that can and must be solved by military men and need not await a clearer delineation by the statesman of the impact of certain political considerations on the conduct of limited wars. Yet there is much lack of agreement as to the answer to this problem and to the question posed among the services and wide divergence of opinion between the military services as to how the United States can and should prosecute a limited war. The Army and Navy appear to believe that U.S. participation in a limited war would be, in general, along the lines of World War II operations on a reduced scale. In the Air Force, on the other hand, there appear to be two schools of thought. One school seems to believe that in limited-war situations air power can establish conditions that would either be decisive in themselves and thus preclude the need for surface operations or that would establish conditions so favorable as to make successful exploitation of results by surface forces a foregone conclusion. Such a premise makes the role of air power forces a decisive one and that of the surface forces a secondary consideration. The other school seems to believe that in limited war the role of air power forces and specifically the Air Force should be one of primarily supporting surface actions and exploiting surface operations. The premise of this school would require that the Air Force give greater consideration to the development of tactical-type forces than we are presently doing. Certainly when one considers the various factors relating to limited war discussed in this article, it is evident that there is no magic formula that can be applied, and the views of the services on this matter cannot be labeled totally right or totally wrong. Determination of the force size and composition is at the heart of the military part of this problem.

Generally speaking, the longer a war lasts the greater the requirement for large numbers of men and materiel and the greater will be the losses in blood and treasure for both sides. The speed and dispatch with which a war is brought to an end may well spell the difference between the winning of a clear-cut victory and the winning of a Pyrrhic victory.

The child who asks a parent how high is up is asking a question no more difficult to answer positively than that confronting the military planner faced with determining what size forces the nation needs for waging limited war. Although the Korean war is classed as a limited war, with the connotation in the minds of many that it was a small-sized war, a study of history will reveal that as far as size of forces engaged, casualties, and destruction and devastation accomplished in the war area are concerned, the war was not small in size by any historical standards. Certainly the prospect of a series of limited wars such as Korea is not only grim but unacceptable. The differences of opinion that exist concerning what yardstick is to be used in determining how much and what kind of forces are essential to meet our requirements for limited war will continue to confuse the picture.

SUMMATION

However confused the situation concerning limited war is or may become, we must not fail to take due cognizance of the following when determining and meeting U.S. force requirements for the nuclear era:

1. The greatest threat to our national existence lies in a sudden and devastating nuclear attack on this country. The strategic air force required to deter such an attack or to defeat the enemy should we fail to deter him is the *sine qua non* of any force structure we have today and must have in the future. This deterrent force must continue in the future to have number-one priority on our resources. We must under no condition diminish the strength of this force below the level required for the destruction of the enemy should total war be forced upon us.

2. Budgetary considerations, if nothing else, make it impossible for the military to have all the forces it would like to have. This being so, the military will always have to settle for less than the military planner would like to have in forces. Compromise and calculated risk will continue to be the order of the day. The ever-increasing complexity and cost of weaponry dictate the urgency and necessity of determining those weapon systems that will give us capabilities commensurate with the risks we are willing to assume. We cannot be strong everywhere, nor can we continue to pour vast sums into every type of weaponry just because someone thinks this weaponry will do this or that, or that it would be desirable to have such a weapon or system. Compromise and calculated risk must be the criteria to be followed in determining the amount and type of forces the nation should have for limited-war purposes over and above the deterrent force.

3. The ever-increasing emphasis on the horror of nuclear war has generated in the United States and elsewhere in the free world an atmosphere of dread and fear—almost a psychosis that peace at any price is preferable to nuclear war. This feeling has given rise to a growing climate of political opinion against any use of nuclear weapons in limited wars, however selective and discriminatory their use might be. Thus the military stands in danger of being confronted with the paradox of possessing a weapon system *designed to give it an advantage* over possible adversaries and yet unable to capitalize on the possession of such an advantage. The Soviets cannot be blind to this situation nor fail to see in it ever-increasing opportunities for the nuclear blackmail of the Western world. The recent threatening statements directed by the Soviets to certain Scandinavian countries concerning Soviet possession and use of nuclear weapons serve to underscore the truth of this statement. As long as this political climate exists in the United States, and in the remainder of the free world, our military forces must possess a

conventional non-atomic capability to wage limited war but should not under any circumstances relinquish or diminish their efforts to develop and maintain a superior nonconventional nuclear capability for waging limited war, for the nonconventional of today is the conventional of the morrow.

FOR FURTHER READING:

Thomas K. Finletter, *Power and Policy: United States Foreign Policy and Military Power in the Hydrogen Age* (New York: Harcourt, Brace and Company, 1954).

Edgar S. Furniss, Jr. (ed.), *American Military Policy* (New York: Rinehart and Company, 1957).

James M. Gavin, *War and Peace in the Space Age* (New York: Harper and Brothers, 1958).

William W. Kaufmann (ed.), *Military Policy and National Security* (Princeton: Princeton University Press, 1956).

Henry A. Kissinger, *Nuclear Weapons and Foreign Policy* (New York: Harper and Brothers, 1957).

Robert Endicott Osgood, *Limited War: Challenge to American Strategy* (Chicago: University of Chicago Press, 1957).

George C. Reinhardt, *American Strategy in the Atomic Age* (Norman: University of Oklahoma Press, 1955).

Rockefeller Brothers Fund, *International Security: The Military Aspect* (Garden City: Doubleday, 1958).

Albert Wohlstetter, "The Delicate Balance of Terror," *Foreign Affairs,* Vol. XXXVII, No. 2 (January, 1959), pp. 211-234.

Chapter IX

EUROPE AND NATO

The close connection between military and foreign policy is seldom so evident as it presently is in the United States relations with Europe. An area of great intellectual and industrial productivity and one which has contributed important segments of our cultural heritage, the fate of Europe will be of fundamental importance in determining the outcome of the struggle between communism and democracy. In recognition of this, and to prevent the U.S.S.R.'s expanding beyond the areas its troops occupied at the close of the Second World War, in 1949 the United States pledged in the North Atlantic Treaty to regard an attack on Western Europe as an attack on itself and in such an event to take all necessary action to restore and maintain security. This commitment forms the core of present United States policy toward Europe. Signing the North Atlantic Treaty marked a sharp break with tradition, for although the United States had signed an equally binding alliance two years earlier—the Inter-American Treaty of Reciprocal Assistance—that commitment concerned an area in which we had long been actively involved, not the one from which we had been counseled to stay aloof. The North Atlantic Treaty assumed even more revolutionary aspects when in peacetime it established a multi-national unified command structure to which troops of the member states were assigned. This military force was essential to make the commitment credible, both to the Soviet Union and to our allies. But it has never been easy to settle on a military doctrine which would at the same time be acceptable to the NATO partners and also promise military effectiveness. This difficult task has been further complicated by new developments in the Soviet scene and in weapons technology, and finding an appropriate military doctrine for NATO is one of the major problems the United States faces in Europe today.

But this is only one of many problems confronting the United States. Indeed, finding an appropriate military doctrine would not be so urgent if it were not for these other problems. They largely result from the fact that now—over a decade and a half after the conclusion of the Second World War—there is still no general peace treaty for Germany. That country unhappily remains divided on what increasingly seems to be a permanent basis. Berlin remains under four-power control and West Berlin forms an enclave of freedom within the communist bloc, an enclave which is as precarious for the West as it is irritating for the East. Europe itself is still split into a Western and an Eastern half, and even though recent years have brought increased contacts between the two, they in no way approximate those of prewar days. For a time after the Second World War the United States attempted to treat Europe as a unit, but after repeated rebuffs, we began to concentrate on the area we could assist and influence. Our assistance to Western Europe began in a major way in 1947 with the inauguration of the Truman Doctrine and the European Recovery Program, or Marshall Plan as it was called. Even at that time we offered to make the Marshall Plan open to all European countries, but the Soviet bloc refused to participate. The North Atlantic Treaty followed these programs. In addition, the United States encouraged the various movements to integrate Western Europe and particularly welcomed such steps as the European Coal and Steel Community which included Western Germany. These various measures have in the main been remarkably successful, and Western Europe today is strong and vital. But it is only a part of Europe; the unsolved problems of peacemaking remain. These are the major problems of Europe. However, one cannot deal with them without considering the military aspects and the contrary is also true.

Until recent years there appeared to be a high degree of consensus concerning United States policies in Europe. But now, perhaps because of growing Soviet nuclear capabilities, perhaps because of real or imagined changes in Soviet policy, or perhaps for other reasons, a number of questions have begun to be raised both here and abroad. Some are broadly oriented, doubting our over-all policies, others are more narrow, dealing with limited aspects such as military doctrine. George

II. NATO and Warsaw Pact
Forces in Europe

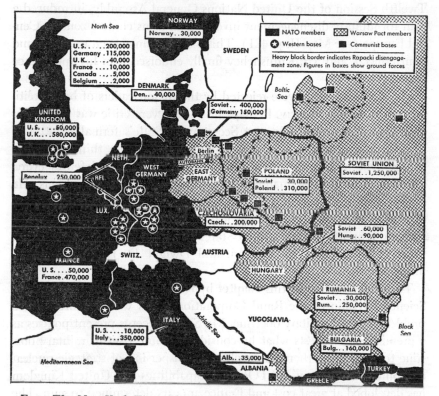

North Sea

NORWAY
Norway . . 30,000

SWEDEN

U.S. 200,000
Germany . 115,000
U.K. 40,000
France 10,000
Canada . . , . 5,000
Belgium 2,000

NATO members Warsaw Pact members
Western bases Communist bases
Heavy black border indicates Rapacki disengage-
ment zone. Figures in boxes show ground forces

DENMARK
Den. . . 40,000

Baltic
Sea

Soviet . . 400,000
Germany 150,000

UNITED
KINGDOM
U.S. . . . 50,000
U.K. . . . 580,000

NETH.

Berlin
AUTOBAHN

SOVIET UNION
Soviet . . 1,250,000

WEST
GERMANY

EAST
GERMANY

POLAND
Soviet 30,000
Poland . . 310,000

Benelux 250,000

BEL.

LUX.

CZECHOSLOVAKIA
Czech . . . 200,000

Soviet . 60,000
Hung . . . 90,000

FRANCE

SWITZ.

AUSTRIA

HUNGARY

U.S. . . . 50,000
France . 470,000

RUMANIA
Soviet . . . 30,000
Rum. . . . 250,000

ITALY

Adriatic Sea

YUGOSLAVIA

Black
Sea

U.S. 10,000
Italy . . . 350,000

BULGARIA
Bulg. . . 160,000

Mediterranean Sea

Alb. . . 35,000
ALBANIA

GREECE

TURKEY

From *The New York Times* News of the Week in Review, March 29, 1959.

F. Kennan, architect of the containment policy, former head of the Department of State's Policy Planning Staff, and later Ambassador to the U.S.S.R., has probably been the most outspoken and articulate critic of general United States policies in Europe. He first voiced his doubts in his Reith Lectures delivered on the BBC in the fall of 1957. These were later published in this country as *Russia, the Atom and the West*. The sections of those lectures which attracted greatest public attention, those dealing with Europe, are reprinted here. In these sections Mr. Kennan argues that a plan for military disengagement would be the most fruitful approach to Europe's problems. He envisages a mutual withdrawal of Soviet and Western forces and the possible neutralization of a unified Germany. This proposed solution found a receptive audience in Western Europe and the British Labour Party later made a similar proposal part of its official program. In addition, also in the fall of 1957, Adam Rapacki, Foreign Minister of Poland, at the Twelfth Session of the United Nations General Assembly, introduced a plan for military disengagement involving an arms control zone in Central Europe (see Map II, p. 421). This plan has since been modified and reintroduced, and Mr. Khrushchev finally endorsed it in his appearance before the U.N.

Mr. Kennan's ideas were rejected by the major leaders of both political parties in this country. Perhaps his most severe critic was his former chief, Dean Acheson. The past Secretary of State's formal rebuttal of Mr. Kennan's theories is reprinted here. Mr. Acheson thinks that disengagement in Europe would most likely weaken our defenses everywhere and would not materially lessen Soviet-American tensions. He doubts that the neutralization of Germany is possible and fears that disengagement might ultimately lead to a German-Soviet accord. He strongly supports present United States policies. On this issue, he, John Foster Dulles, Harry S. Truman, and Dwight D. Eisenhower stood firmly together.

The final selection in this chapter by Hans Speier, head of the Social Science Division of the Rand Corporation, deals with a more limited problem, that of military doctrine. Mr. Speier accepts present policies as a premise and suggests what he considers a more fruitful military doctrine to implement them. It involves the dispersion of strategic nuclear capabilities among our NATO allies, capabilities the United Kingdom has developed at great cost and France appears determined to gain. The grim and awesome nature of this alternative underlines the seriousness of the questions confronting the United States in Europe. The public debate should consider them with the respect and care they deserve.

The Problem of Eastern and Central Europe*

by George F. Kennan

I would know of no basic issues of genuine gravity between Russia and the West other than those arising directly from the manner in which the recent world war was allowed to come to an end. I am referring here particularly to the fact that the authority of a united German government was expunged on the territory of Germany itself and throughout large areas of Eastern Europe, and the armies of the Soviet Union and the Western democracies were permitted to meet in the middle of this territory and to take control of it, before there was any adequate agreement among them as to its future permanent status. This was, of course, the combined result of the unconditional surrender policy, which relieved the Germans of all responsibility for the future status of this area, and the failure of the Allied governments to arrive at any realistic understandings among themselves about it while the war was on. Since it has not been possible to reach such understandings subsequently, except in the case of Austria, the provisorium flowing from these circumstances has endured. It is this that we are faced with today.

There is, of course, a similar problem in the Far East. A precisely analogous situation prevails in the case of Korea and Formosa. The Allies dislodged the Japanese from these areas without having arrived at any proper understanding with the Russians as to their future status. There, too, the question remains open; and it does indeed constitute an issue in the relations between the Soviet Union and a portion of the Western community.

For reasons of time, and of simplicity, I shall restrict myself here to the European theater, though much of what I shall have to say would have its applicability to this situation in the Far East as well. In Europe, the difficulty obviously breaks down into two parts: the satellite area and Germany.

I am sure there is no need for me to go into detail about the situation in the satellite area. Everyone knows what has happened in these past three or four years. The Moscow leaders made an attempt to undo some of the harm that Stalin had done with his policies of ruthless political oppression and economic exploitation. The first effect of this relaxation, as shown in the disorders in Eastern Germany and Poland and later in Hungary, was not to reconcile people to the fact of Soviet rule but rather to reveal the real depths of their restlessness and the extent to which the postwar arrangements had outworn whatever usefulness they might once have had. The Soviet leaders, startled and alarmed by these revelations, have now seen no alternative, in the interests of their own political and military security, but to reimpose sharp limits to the movement for greater independence in these countries, and to rely for the enforcement of these restrictions on the naked use or presence of their own troops.

The result has been, as we all know, the creation of an extremely precarious situation. It is a dangerous and unsatisfactory situation from everyone's standpoint. The state of the satellite area today, and particularly of Poland, is neither fish nor fowl, neither complete Stalinist domination nor real independence. Things cannot be expected to remain this way for long. There must either be further violent efforts by people in that area to take things into their own hands and to achieve independence by their own means, or there must be the beginning of some process of real adjustment to the fact of Soviet domination. In the first of these contingencies, we in the West could easily be placed once more before the dilemma which faced us last year at the time of the Hungarian uprising; and anyone who has the faintest concern for the stability of the world situation must fervently pray that this will not happen.

As for the second alternative, which at this moment seems to be the more likely of the two, it seems no less appalling. If things go on as they are today, there will simply have to be some sort of adjustment on the part of the peoples of Eastern Europe, even if it is one that takes the form of general despair, apathy, demoralization and the deepest sort of disillusionment with the West. The failure of the recent popular uprisings to shake the Soviet military domination has now produced a state of bitter and dangerous despondency throughout large parts of Eastern Europe. If the taste or even the hope for independence once dies out in the hearts of these peoples, then there will be no recovering it; then Moscow's victory will be complete. Eastern Europe will then be permanently lost to Europe proper and to the possibility of any normal participation in international life.

I can conceive of no escape from this dilemma that would not involve the early departure of Soviet troops from the satellite countries. Recent events have made it perfectly clear that it is the presence of these troops, coupled with the general military and political situation in Europe, which lies at the heart of the difficulty. Only when the troops are gone will there be possibilities for the evolution of these nations toward institutions and social systems most suited to their needs; and what these institutions and systems might then be is something about which I think we in the West can afford to be very relaxed. If socialism is what these people want and need, so be it; but let it by all means be their own choice.

Now it is plain that there can be no Soviet military withdrawal from Eastern Europe unless this entire area can in some way be removed as an object in the military rivalry of the Great Powers. But this at once involves the German problem. It involves the German problem not only because it implies the withdrawal of Soviet forces from Eastern Germany, but because so long as American and other Western forces remain in Western Germany it will be impossible for the Russians to view their problem in Eastern Europe otherwise than in direct relation to the over-all military equation between Russia and the West. Any solution of the problem of the satellite area is thus dependent on a solution of the German problem itself. This is one of the reasons why I am inclined to feel that the German question still stands at the center of world tensions; that no greater contribution can be made to world peace than the removal of the present deadlock over Germany, and that if, in fact, it is not removed, the chances for peace are very slender indeed.

This being the case, I think we cannot scrutinize too closely or too frequently, in the light of the developing situation both in Europe and in the world at large, the position our governments have taken in the question of Germany in recent years.

We are all familiar with what that position has been. It is one that has insisted, and with very good reason, that the modalities of German unification, as a domestic program, must flow from the will of the German people, expressed in free elections. But it has gone farther than that. It has also insisted that no restrictions whatsoever must be placed in advance on the freedom of a future all-German government to determine its own international orientation and to incur military obligations to other states. Specifically, the Western governments have insisted that such an all-German government must be entirely free to continue to adhere to the NATO Pact, as the German Federal Republic does today;

and it is taken everywhere as a foregone conclusion that an all-German government would do just that.

Now the question at once arises as to what would happen in such a contingency—in the contingency, that is, that a future united Germany should choose to adhere to NATO. What would happen then with the garrisons of the various Allied powers now stationed on German soil? The Western position says nothing specific about this. But the Soviet Union is, of course, not a member of NATO; and while British, French and American forces would presumably remain in Germany under the framework of the NATO system, one must assume that those of the Soviet Union would be expected to depart. If this is so, then Moscow is really being asked to abandon—as part of an agreement on German unification—the military and political bastion in Central Europe which it won by its military effort from 1941 to 1945, and to do this without any compensatory withdrawal of American armed power from the heart of the Continent.

Now this, in my opinion, is something the Soviet Government is most unlikely to accept, if only for reasons of what it will regard as its own political security at home and abroad. It will be hard enough, even in the best of circumstances, for Moscow ever to extract itself from its present abnormal involvements in Eastern Europe without this having repercussions on its political system generally. It cannot, realistically, be asked—that is, it cannot be asked if agreement is wanted—to take this step in any manner that would seriously jeopardize its prestige. The Soviet leaders are not likely to be impressed with such paper assurance as the Western powers may undertake to give, to the effect that a unilateral withdrawal would not be exploited to Russia's disadvantage. The mere fact of Soviet withdrawal without any compensatory withdrawal on the Western side would create the general impression of a defeat for Soviet policy in Eastern and Central Europe generally.

The Soviet leaders will therefore see in these present Western proposals a demand for something in the nature of an unconditional capitulation of the Soviet interest in the German question generally; and it will surely occur to them that if they ever should be so weak as to have no choice but to quit Germany on these terms, it would scarcely take an agreement with the Western Powers to enable them to do so. So long, therefore, as it remains the Western position that the hands of a future all-German government must not be in any way tied in the matter of Germany's future military engagements, I see little hope for any removal of the division of Germany at all—nor, by the same token, of the removal of the division of Europe.

There are those in our Western camp, I know, who find in this state of affairs no great cause for alarm. A divided Germany seems, for the moment, to be less of a problem to them than was the united Germany of recent memory. They regard the continued presence of American forces in Germany as an indispensable pledge of American military interest in the Continent, and they tremble at the thought that this pledge should ever be absent. It is agreeable to them that America, by assuming this particular burden and bearing it indefinitely, should relieve Western Europe of the necessity of coming to grips itself with the German question.

This view is understandable in its way. There was a time, in the immediate postwar period, when it was largely justified. But there is danger in permitting it to harden into a permanent attitude. It expects too much, and for too long a time, of the United States, which is not a European power. It does less than justice to the strength and the abilities of the Europeans themselves. It leaves unsolved the extremely precarious and unsound arrangements which now govern the status of Berlin the least disturbance of which could easily produce a new world crisis. It takes no account of the present dangerous situation in the satellite area. It renders permanent what was meant to be temporary. It assigns half of Europe, by implication, to the Russians.

Let me stress particularly this question of Berlin. There is a stubborn tendency in our two countries to forget about the Berlin situation so long as it gives us no trouble and to assume that everything will somehow work out for the best. May I point out that the Western position in Berlin is by no means a sound or safe one; and it is being rendered daily more uncertain by the ominous tendency of the Soviet Government to thrust forward the East German regime as its spokesman in these matters. Moscow's purpose in this maneuver is obviously to divest itself of responsibility for the future development of the Berlin situation. It hopes by this means to place itself in a position where it can remain serenely aloof while the East German regime proceeds to make the Western position in the city an impossible one. This is a sure portent of trouble. The future of Berlin is vital to the future of Germany as a whole: the needs of its people and the extreme insecurity of the

Western position there would alone constitute reasons why no one in the West should view the present division of Germany as a satisfactory permanent solution, even if no other factors were involved at all.

It would, of course, be wholly wrong to suggest that it is only the uncertainty of the Western position about the future of the garrisons in Germany that stands in the way of a settlement. I have no doubt that any acceptable arrangement for German unification would be an extremely difficult thing to achieve in any case. Many other obstacles would be bound to arise. It took ten years to negotiate a similar settlement for Austria. I can imagine that the negotiation of a German settlement might also take years, in the best of circumstances. But I think we are justified in assuming that it is this question of the indefinite retention of the American and other Western garrisons on German soil which lies at the heart of the difficulty; and until greater clarity is achieved about this point, there can be no proper beginning.

It will at once be held against what I have said that Moscow itself does not today want German unification on any terms. Perhaps so. Certainly in recent months there have been no signs of enthusiasm in Moscow for any settlement of this sort. But how much of this lack of enthusiasm is resignation in the face of the Western position, we do not know. Until we stop pushing the Kremlin against a closed door, we shall never learn whether it would be prepared to go through an open one. Today, our calculations about Moscow's reaction to proposals for a mutual withdrawal of forces rest exclusively on speculation; for Moscow has been given no reason to suppose that Western forces would under any circumstances be withdrawn from the major portion of Germany.

We must also bear in mind that things change from time to time in Moscow, just as they do here in the West. If the disposition to conclude a German settlement does not exist today in Moscow, our positions should at least be such as to give promise of agreement when and if this attitude changes.

Finally, the question is not just whether Moscow, as people say, "wants" German unification. It is a question of whether Moscow could afford to stand in the way of it if there were a real possibility for a general evacuation of Europe. Gomulka not long ago promised the Polish people that the day the Americans leave Germany, he will take up with the Soviet Government the question of the departure of the Soviet forces from Poland. And it is quite clear that as Poland goes, in this respect, so goes the rest of the satellite area. Khrushchev has not specifically demurred at Gomulka's position; on the contrary, he has, in fact, even murmured things himself, from time to time, about a possible mutual withdrawal of forces, although he has intimated that the price of a Soviet withdrawal might be somewhat higher than what Gomulka implied. In any case, the interest of the satellite governments in a general evacuation of Germany is perfectly clear. If, therefore, a more promising Western position would not assure agreement at this time, it would at least serve to put a greater strain on Moscow's position, and to shift clearly and definitely to the Soviet side the onus of delaying a reasonable European settlement—an onus which in this case would have to be maintained against the feelings of many people in the satellite regimes as well as people elsewhere.

Are there, then, points at which the Western position could safely be improved? It is hard for an outsider to answer such a question in this rapidly moving time. Only governments are privy to all the relevant information. I can only say that there are two features of our present thinking which, in my opinion, might well undergo particular re-examination.

I wonder, in the first place, whether it is actually politic and realistic to insist that a future all-German government must be entirely free to determine Germany's military orientation and obligations, and that the victor powers of the recent war must not in any way prejudice that freedom by any agreement among themselves. This is outwardly a very appealing position. It gratifies the Western attachment to the principle of national self-expression. It is, for obvious reasons, a position no German politician can lightly oppose. We can hardly expect of the Germans that they should take the initiative in questioning it. But is it sound, and is it constructive?

A peace treaty has not yet been concluded. The powers of the victors have not yet formally lapsed in Germany. Might it not just be that the only politically feasible road to unification and independence for Germany should lie precisely through her acceptance of certain restraints on freedom to shape her future military position in Europe? And, if so, is it not just a bit quixotic to cling, in the name of the principle of German freedom and independence, to a position which implies the sacrifice of all freedom and all independence for many millions of Germans, namely the people of Eastern Germany, for an indefinite time to come? No useful purpose is going to be served by the quest for perfect solutions. The unlocking of the European tangle is not to be achieved except at some sort of a price. Is there not, in this insistence that the hands of a future German government must not be in any way tied, an evasion of the real responsibility the victor powers bear for resolving this present dangerous situation in Central Europe? This is, after all, a situation which they, not the Germans, created. Are they now to resign entirely to the Germans the responsibility for resolving it?

The second element of Western thinking about the German problem that might well stand further examination is the common assumption that the Western powers would be placed at a hopeless military disadvantage if there were to be any mutual withdrawal of forces from the heart of Europe.

It is, of course, impossible to discuss this question in specific terms unless one knows just what sort of withdrawal is envisaged—from where and to where, and by whom and when. Here, as is frequently forgotten, there are many possible combinations; and I am not at all sure that all of these have really been seriously explored by our planners.

But beyond this, I have the impression that our calculations in this respect continue to rest on certain questionable assumptions and habits of thought: on an overrating of the likelihood of a Soviet effort to invade Western Europe, on an exaggeration of the value of the satellite armies as possible instruments of a Soviet offensive policy, on a failure to take into account all the implications of the ballistic missile; and on a serious underestimation of the advantages to Western security to be derived from a Soviet military withdrawal from Central and Eastern Europe. I wonder how the military implications of a general withdrawal would appear if these distortions were removed.

People will ask: how do you envisage the future of Germany, if not as a full-fledged member of NATO? Is it neutrality you are recommending, or demilitarization, or a general European security pact?

These again are problems for the planners. The combinations are many; and they must be studied minutely, as alternatives. No outsider can judge which is best. I would only say that it seems to me far more desirable on principle to get the Soviet forces out of Central and Eastern Europe than to cultivate a new German army for the purpose of opposing them while they remain there. And as for a European security pact— well, I am no lover of security pacts and have, as a historian, never understood the great value other people still attach to them; but I cannot see that this sort of thing would necessarily invalidate the essential relationships of NATO. It cannot be stressed too often that NATO's real strength does not lie in the paper undertakings which underpin it; it lies—and will continue in any circumstances to lie—in the appreciation of the member nations for the identity of their real interests, as members of the Western spiritual and cultural community. If this appreciation is there, NATO will not be weaker, as a political reality, just because it may be supplemented or replaced by other arrangements so far as Germany is concerned.

I shall also be asked whether I am suggesting that Bonn should deal with the East German regime, as Mr. Khrushchev says it must if unification is ever to be arranged. This, I think, is very much Western Germany's own business. The German problem is not going to be solved, as things stand today, by Germans alone. Moscow, try as it may, cannot avoid its responsibility in this question; it is with Moscow that we Americans and British, in particular, at any rate, must deal.

The Kremlin would of course like to see the East German regime extort, as a price for unification, some sort of privileged and protected position for itself as a political faction within a future all-German state. This is obviously quite undiscussible. But it would seem to an outsider that people in Western Germany could afford to be very generous in defining the stages by which complete unification should be arrived at. Nothing could be more foolish, on the West German side, than to let vindictiveness, intolerance or political passion block the road. The long period of Communist rule in Eastern Germany will have left strong marks on the structure of life there. There will certainly be a demand on the Communist side that not all these marks should be obliterated. Well, one can have one's own opinion as to whether they are positive or negative, whether they represent scars or achievements. But there is no reason why many of them should not be taken account of as facts, in any future settlement. Whether or not, for example, the industries of that region should remain socialized would seem to me, compared with what else is at stake, one of the least important of the problems in question.

My plea, then, is not that we delude ourselves that we can have a German settlement tomorrow; and it is not that we make frivolous and one-sided concessions to obtain one. My plea is only that we remember that we have a problem here, which must sooner or later be solved, and better sooner than later; and that we do our best to see that the positions we adopt with relation to it are at all times as hopeful and constructive as they can be made.

Now let me just add one last word on the general background of this German problem.

One of the arguments most frequently heard in opposition to the introduction of any greater flexibility into the Western position in Germany is that "you can't trust the Germans." It is therefore better, people say, that Germany should be held divided and in part dependent on the West, than that the Germans should once again be permitted independence of action as a nation. This is a judgment drawn, in the overwhelming majority of cases, from the unhappy experience of the past. Many of those who draw it are not acquainted with contemporary Germany.

I cannot share this opinion. Germany is in a state of great transition, and one can easily find, within its changing scene, anything one seeks. It is true that many of the older generation are not likely ever to recover entirely from the trauma of the past; they tend to be twisted people in one way or another, which does not necessarily mean that they are still Nazis. But I have seen, as an academic lecturer, whose own education took place partly in Germany, a bit of the younger Germany; and I am convinced that these young people, troubled, bewildered, unsupported at this time by any firm tradition from their own national past, will not fail to respond to any Western appeal that carries the ring of real vision, of conviction and of seriousness of purpose. The younger generation of Germans are more threatened today by the inroads of a pervasive cynical materialism than they are by any extreme nationalistic tendencies; and it is precisely here that we in the West have given them, I fear, little help or inspiration. To stake our future on this younger Germany is admittedly to take a chance; but I can think of no greater risk than the trend toward nuclear war on which we are all now being carried.

If Germany cannot be accorded reasonable confidence in these coming years, then I would know of no promising solution to the entire problem of Europe. To assume that such confidence cannot be given is to cut ourselves off in advance from possibilities that may be vital to our very survival. If we are going to make so negative and so hopeless an assumption, let us be terribly, terribly sure that our judgment is drawn not from the memories and emotions of the past but from the soberest sort of attention to present realities.

The Military Problem*

by George F. Kennan

What I have to speak about now is the military aspect of our conflict with Soviet power. It may seem strange, and scarcely fitting, that a civilian and common citizen, and a person not privy to governmental information, should venture to speak of it at all. But whoever thinks seriously about the problem of our relations with Russia cannot avoid doing his best to understand its military aspect, and making certain assumptions with regard to it . . . The so-called tactical atomic weapon is now being introduced into the armed forces of the United States and there is an intention, as I understand it, to introduce it into Great Britain. We must assume that the same thing is occurring in the Soviet Union. While many people in our respective governments have become convinced, I am sure, of the need for being able to fight limited as well as total wars, it is largely by the use of the tactical atomic weapon that they propose to fight them. It appears to be their hope that by cultivation of this tactical weapon we can place ourselves in a position to defend the NATO countries successfully without resorting to the long-range strategic one; that our adversaries can also be brought to refrain from employing the long-range one; that warfare can thus be restricted to whatever the tactical weapon implies; and that in this way the more apocalyptic effects of nuclear warfare may be avoided.

It is this thesis which I cannot accept. That it would prove possible, in the event of an atomic war, to arrive at some tacit and workable understanding with the adversary as to the degree of destructiveness of the weapons that would be used and the sort of target to which they would be directed, seems to me a very slender and wishful hope indeed.

But beyond this, let us bear in mind the probable ulterior effects— the effects, particularly, on the people in whose country such a war

---

* From *Russia, the Atom and the West* by George F. Kennan, pp. 50-65. Copyright © 1957, 1958 by George F. Kennan. Reprinted by permission of Harper and Brothers and the Oxford University Press.

might be waged—of the use of tactical atomic weapons. There seems to
be a cheerful assumption that these weapons are relatively harmless
things, to be used solely against the armed forces of the enemy and
without serious ulterior disadvantages. But surely this is not so! Even
the tactical atomic weapon is destructive to a degree that sickens the
imagination. If the experience of this century has taught us anything, it
is that the long-term effects of modern war are by no means governed
just by the formal outcome of the struggle in terms of victory or defeat.
Modern war is not just an instrument of policy. It is an experience in
itself. It does things to him who practices it, irrespective of whether he
wins or loses. Can we really suppose that poor old Europe, so deeply
and insidiously weakened by the ulterior effects of the two previous
wars of this century, could stand another and even more horrible ordeal
of this nature? Let us by all means think for once not just in the mathematics of destruction—not just in these grisly equations of probable
military casualties—let us rather think of people as they are; of the
limits of their strength, their hope, their capacity for suffering, their
capacity for believing in the future. And let us ask ourselves in all seriousness how much worth saving is going to be saved if war now rages for
the third time in a half-century over the face of Europe, and this time in
a form vastly more destructive than anything ever known before.

Unfortunately, the danger is not even limited to the possible effects
of the use of the tactical atomic weapon by our own English or American forces in time of war. There is a further contingent danger, and a
very imminent one, as things now stand; and this is that atomic weapons, strategic or tactical or both, may be placed in the arsenals of our
continental allies as well.

I cannot overemphasize the fatefulness of such a step. I do not see
how it could fail to produce a serious increase in the existing military
tension in Europe. It would be bound to raise a grave problem for the
Russians in respect of their own military dispositions and their relations
with the other Warsaw Pact countries. It would inevitably bring about
a further complication of the German and satellite problems. Moscow
is not going to be inclined to entrust its satellites with full control over
such weapons. If, therefore, the Western continental countries are to be
armed with them, any Russian withdrawal from Central and Eastern
Europe may become unthinkable once and for all, for reasons of sheer
military prudence regardless of what the major Western Powers might
be prepared to do.

In addition to this, it is perfectly obvious that the larger the number of hands into which the control over atomic weapons is placed, the smaller will be the possibility for their eventual exclusion from national arsenals by international agreement, and the more difficult it will be to preclude complications of all sorts. So long as only three great powers are involved, there is at least a chance that things can be kept under control. To place these weapons in the hands of a number of further countries is practically to assure that there can in future be no minor difficulty in Europe that does not at once develop into a major one.

I am aware that similar warnings against the introduction of the atomic weapon into the armaments of the continental countries have also recently been part of the stock-in-trade of Soviet diplomacy. I cannot know what the motives of the Soviet Government have been in taking this position. I certainly cannot say that they have all been ones we could respect. But I think we must beware of rejecting ideas just because they happen to coincide with ones put forward on the other side. Moscow says many harmful and foolish things; but it would be wrong to assume that its utterances never happen to accord with the dictates of sobriety and good sense. The Russians are not always wrong, any more than we are always right. Our task, in any case, is to make up our minds independently.

Is there, then, any reasonably hopeful alternative to the unpromising path along which we are now advancing? I must confess that I see only one. This is precisely the opposite of the attempt to incorporate the tactical atomic weapon into the defense of Western Europe. It is, again, the possibility of separating geographically the forces of the great nuclear powers, of excluding them as direct factors in the future development of political relationships on the Continent, and of inducing the continental peoples, by the same token, to accept a higher level of responsibility for the defense of the Continent than they have recently borne. This is still a possibility. Close as we are to it, we have not yet taken the fatal step. The continental countries have not yet prejudiced their usefulness for the solution of continental problems, as we have ours, by building their defense establishments around the atomic weapon. If they could be induced to refrain from doing this, and if there could be a general withdrawal of American, British and Russian armed power from the heart of the Continent, there would be at least a chance that Europe's fortunes might be worked out, and the competition between two political philosophies carried forward, in a manner disastrous neither to the respective peoples themselves nor to the cause of world peace. I would not know where else this chance is to be looked for.

I am aware that many people will greet this suggestion with skepticism. On the Continent, in particular, people have become so accustomed to the thought that their danger is a purely military one, and that their salvation can be assured only by others, that they rise in alarm at every suggestion that they should find the necessary powers of resistance within themselves. There is a habitual underestimation among these peoples of the native resources of Europe. The Western Europe of 1957 reminds me of the man who has grown accustomed to swimming with water wings and cannot realize that he is capable of swimming without them.

It is plain that in the event of a mutual withdrawal of forces, the continental NATO countries would still require, in addition to the guarantees embodied in the NATO Pact, some sort of continuing local arrangements for their own defense. I am free to admit that for this purpose their existing conventional forces, based on the World War II pattern, would be generally inadequate. These conventional forces are designed to meet only the least likely of the possible dangers: that of an outright Soviet military attack in Europe, and then to meet it in the most unpromising manner, which is by attempting to hold it along some specific territorial line. All of this is obviously futile. If this were the problem, then of course foreign assistance would be needed, although it is questionable whether it could ever be enough.

But this is not the problem. We must get over this obsession that the Russians are yearning to attack and occupy Western Europe, and that this is the principal danger. The Soviet threat, as I have had occasion to say before, is a combined military and political threat, with the accent on the political. If the armed forces of the United States and Britain were not present on the Continent, the problem of defense for the continental nations would be primarily one of the internal health and discipline of the respective national societies, and of the manner in which they were organized to prevent the conquest and subjugation of their national life by unscrupulous and foreign-inspired minorities in their midst. What they need is a strategic doctrine addressed to this reality. Under such a doctrine, armed forces would indeed be needed; but I would suggest that as a general rule these forces might better be paramilitary ones, of a territorial-militia type, somewhat on the Swiss example, rather than regular military units on the World War II pattern. Their function should be primarily internal rather than external. It is on the front of police realities, not on regular military battlefields, that the threat of Russian Communism must primarily be met. The training of such forces ought to be such as to prepare them not only to offer whatever overt resistance might be possible to a foreign invader but also to constitute the core of a civil resistance movement on any territory that might be overrun by the enemy; and every forethought should be exercised to facilitate their assumption and execution of this role in the case of necessity. For this reason they need not, and should not, be burdened with heavy equipment or elaborate supply requirements, and this means—and it is no small advantage—that they could be maintained at a fraction of the cost per unit of the present conventional establishments. I am inclined to wonder whether this concept could not well find application even as things are today, and in the absence of any Great Power withdrawal.

I would not wish to make a fetish of this or to suggest any sweeping uniform changes. The situations of no two NATO countries are alike. There are some that will continue to require, for various reasons, other kinds of armed forces as well. I mean merely to suggest that if there could be a more realistic concept of the problem and the evolution of a strategic doctrine more directly addressed to the Soviet threat as it really is and not as we have imagined it, the continental countries would not be as lacking in the resources or means for their own defense as is commonly assumed.

Let me reiterate that the primary purpose of the dispositions would be not the defense of the country at the frontier, though naturally one would aim to do whatever could be done in this respect, but rather its defense at every village crossroads. The purpose would be to place the country in a position where it could face the Kremlin and say to it: "Look here, you may be able to overrun us, if you are unwise enough to attempt it, but you will have a small profit from it; we are in a position to assure that not a single Communist or other person likely to perform your political business will be available to you for this purpose; you will find here no adequate nucleus of a puppet regime; on the contrary, you will be faced with the united and organized hostility of an entire nation; your stay among us will not be a happy one; we will make you pay bitterly for every day of it; and it will be without favorable long-term political prospects." I think I can give personal assurance that any country which is in a position to say this to Moscow, not in so many words, but in that language of military posture and political behavior which the Russian Communists understand best of all, will have little need of foreign garrisons to assure its immunity from Soviet attack.

The Illusion of Disengagement*

by Dean Acheson

The other day I was re-reading Clarence Day's wise and delightful book, "This Simian World," and came across the paragraph remarking on what unpromising entrants in the struggle for supremacy on this planet the lemurs might have seemed many millions of years ago. "Those frowzy, unlovely hordes of apes and monkeys," he wrote, "were so completely lacking in signs of kingship; they were so flighty, too, in their ways, and had so little purpose, and so much love for absurd and idle chatter, that they would have struck us . . . as unlikely material. Such traits, we should have reminded ourselves, persist. They are not easily left behind, even after long stages; and they form a terrible obstacle to all high advancement."

It does seem to be true that, in our day, only in a sort of cyclical way do free societies retain an understanding of their own experience, and hold to the purposes which it has inspired. Is this because some echo of those early traits still persists, or because the inevitable hardening of the arteries of each generation brings on some failure of memory, or for still other reasons?

Certainly moods change as memories, once fearful, become dimmed, as new anxieties arise, and as present exertions become increasingly distasteful. The bitter teachings of 1914-1918, and the determination they fired, had quite disappeared by 1938, to be replaced by ideas of neutralism, withdrawal from conflict, "America First." After these, in turn, were swept away by the devastation of another world war and by a display of world leadership entailing vast national effort, another 20 years has ended by bringing back the old yearnings and errors under a new name. "Disengagement," it is called now; but it is the same futile—and

* From *Foreign Affairs*, Vol. XXXVI, No. 3 (April 1958), pp. 371-382. Copyright 1958 by the Council on Foreign Relations, Inc., New York. Reprinted by special permission from *Foreign Affairs*.

lethal—attempt to crawl back into the cocoon of history. For us there is only one disengagement possible—the final one, the disengagement from life, which is death.

Soon after we had awakened from the daze of the Second World War, it became clear to us that our protected adolescence as a great Power was over. The empires which had spawned us, whose capital had developed us, whose balance of power had given us security, either disappeared in the two world wars or passed to more minor rôles. We were face to face with the responsibility of adult national life in the most critical situation imaginable. A world which for a century had had an integral life of sorts was split into three segments. One—the Soviet-Communist segment, militarily unequalled, except in nuclear power in which it was weak, was held together by an ideological and economic system supported by force. Another—containing the vast populations of Asia, the Middle East, and North and West Africa—was left in confusion and turmoil at the end of the war; and, in addition, either had newly gained national independence or was demanding it from rulers gravely weakened. To these people had come also expectations of an improving life to a degree never before imagined and, perhaps, unfulfillable.

The third segment was what was left of the old world order—roughly Europe and the Western Hemisphere. The second and third segments had certain important common characteristics. They were not in the Soviet power system. But various and large parts of them could, under some conditions, be added to it.

In this situation, as it appeared not long after the end of the Second World War, the task of what has since come to be called the Atlantic Community, that is, the states of Western Europe and the Western Hemisphere, was to bring about and maintain with increasing strength and vitality a non-Communist world system. Within this system, not only the states mentioned, but those in the second segment as well, should, if the system was workable and working, be able to pursue their national ends in their own way.

This effort required, at the beginning, a great deal of reconstruction, particularly in Europe. The only state strong enough to furnish the leadership in this effort was the United States. Both its government and its people responded vigorously to the press of necessity. The steps which were taken are well known and need not be recalled here. The important thing is that they were successful in bringing about a common sense of purpose, certainly in Western Europe and the Western Hemisphere, and to a large extent were effective in giving opportunity to those nations in Asia and Africa which were just coming to the point where they were free to pursue their national destinies undirected from the outside.

Since the war, therefore, the foreign policy of the United States has become, by necessity, a positive and activist one. It has been one of attempting to draw together, through various groupings, that Western area which must be the center of a free and open world system, and of taking the leading part in providing it with military security, and with a developing economy in which trade could grow and industrial productivity could be developed, both in areas which were already industrially advanced and those which were at the threshold. At the same time it was an essential part of this policy to produce the maximum degree of cohesion throughout the whole non-Communist area, through political policies which would make for integration and strength rather than for exploitation.

Various aspects of this effort—the military, the economic, the political—I have attempted to describe in some detail elsewhere. I have there pointed out the interdependence of the Western Hemisphere and Western Europe; how the power factors involved make it essential that this part of the world shall stand firmly united; how, without the American connection, it is impossible to maintain independent national life in Western Europe; and how, without Western Europe, the power factors would turn disastrously against the United States.

Broadly speaking, these conceptions have for the past decade or more had wide acceptance both in this country and throughout the Western world. They have been successful beyond the dream of those who first advocated them. They are beginning to bear the most valuable fruit.

Recently, efforts have been relaxed. Our military security and much of our prestige resting upon it have been impaired, though not so far that vigorous action cannot make the necessary repair. But, throughout the world, as I indicated at the beginning of this article, voices are being raised to ask whether it is necessary to continue facing the hazards of the military situation, to continue bearing the expense of making vital and progressive the economic life of the whole free world; whether coexistence with the Communist system cannot be bought at a cheaper price and with less effort. And so, when people are told, as they have been by Mr. George Kennan, a man of the highest character and reputation and justly entitled to a respectful hearing, that this is possible, his words have a powerful impact.

Mr. Kennan's views are not new to him. They do not spring from a fresh analysis of the current situation. He has held and expressed these views for at least a decade. The effect which they have had currently makes us realize anew that the reception given to the expression of ideas depends upon the mood of the hearers. This reception may have little to do with the truth of the ideas expressed; it has a great deal to do with their power. Mr. Kennan has told people what they want to hear, though not because they want to hear it. What is it that he has said?

The ideas are almost as vague as the style is seductive. The thoughts are expressed as musings, wonderings, questionings, suggestions. But what comes out of it is about this: First, there is the idea of disengagement in Europe. By this is meant mutual withdrawal of American, British and Canadian, as well as Russian, forces from somewhere. This somewhere first appears to be East and West Germany; then the "heart of Europe"; again, the Continent; and sometimes, from the general ethos of the discussion, it appears to be all overseas areas.

The second idea is the neutralization of Germany. The third is that there should be no nuclear weapons in Europe. And the fourth is that throughout Asia and Africa, in what are called the "uncommitted areas," there is little "to be done . . . except to relax"; that "It is perfectly natural that Russia . . . should have her place and her voice there too"; that "our generation in the West" has no "obligation vis-à-vis the underdeveloped parts of the world," and, anyway, there is no "absolute value attached to rapid economic development. Why all the urgency?" If any sound schemes for development are presented, we should support them, "when they arise"; but, only on the condition that they tell us first "how you propose to assure that if we give you this aid it will not be interpreted among your people as a sign of weakness and fear on our part, or of a desire to dominate you." If Asian and African states should find in this grudging, meager and humiliating policy no opportunity to push their economic development within the non-Communist system, and should turn to Communist methods and Communist help, we should accept their action without concern and with good nature.

One sees at once that these conceptions are the very opposite of those which the West has been following for the past ten years or more. It is an assertion that the struggle naught availeth; that it is dangerous, unwise and unproductive. It is a withdrawal from positive and active leadership in the creation of a workable system of states. It is a conception, blended of monasticism and the diplomacy of earlier centuries, by which the United States would artfully manœuvre its way between and around forces without attempting to direct or control them.

If we attempt to analyze these suggestions, the problems which they create promptly emerge. First, let us consider the idea that something called disengagement can be brought about by removing American, British, Canadian and Russian troops from some area in Europe. What disengagement does this bring about? Very little, as one sees if one pauses to consider the realities. Compare the confrontation which takes place between the United States and the Soviet Union in Germany with that which occurs along the DEW line—that system of early warning stations which stretches from Alaska, across the Arctic regions and far out into the Atlantic. Here there are daily contacts on a thousand radarscopes, and doubtless the same is true on the other side of the screen. Some of these blips on the radar are actual aircraft; sometimes atmospheric conditions produce them. But they represent a contact which no action in Germany can disengage. There is confrontation in every part of the world where the area of the open and free world system may be reduced by Soviet military, economic or political penetration. No action in Germany will produce disengagement here. The word is a mere conception, which confuses and does not represent any reality.

So, let us turn from it to consider something more capable of delineation. For instance, exactly what is the extent of the mutual withdrawal about which we are asked to negotiate? The answer to this question does not depend upon penetrating the vagueness of Mr. Kennan's language. For there can be little doubt, I believe, that, once a withdrawal begins, it will be complete, so far as United States, British and Canadian troops are concerned. All the forces, foreign and domestic, will combine to bring this about. As the withdrawal makes the military position weaker, our forces will be less desired wherever they may remain. If withdrawal is represented as advantageous for Germans, it would seem equally advantageous to Frenchmen. Icelanders, Moroccans, Saudi Arabians and the rest would quickly follow. And, once the idea caught hold, Americans would, of course, join in the general demand. The New Statesman shows us how the matter is now being presented to a small section of

British opinion and how it could bemuse a still larger one in that country:

> Yet the missile agreement is one of the most extraordinary and com-
> plete surrenders of sovereignty ever to be made by one country for the
> exclusive benefit of another. For the missiles are not intended to defend
> Britain; on the contrary, they decisively increase its vulnerability. Their
> prime purpose is to reduce the likelihood of a Soviet ICBM onslaught on
> America during the crucial three-year period which must elapse before
> America possesses ICBMs herself. The sole beneficiary will be America.[1]

We should not deceive ourselves. After disengagement, we would
soon find ourselves discussing complete withdrawal from all European
areas and, very possibly, from bases in the Far East and Near East as
well. Indeed, Mr. Khrushchev has twice served warning, once in Berlin
in 1957 and again in January of 1958, that the sort of withdrawal which
he is talking about is withdrawal from all overseas bases. This would
cut the striking power of the free world by at least a half, and, perhaps,
until our missile program accelerates, by much more.

We must think of what we purchase for this vast price. What would
Russian withdrawal from Germany or the heart of Europe amount to?
Is it possible to believe that the Soviet Government, whatever it may
say or whatever agreement it may sign, would, or could, contemplate
withdrawing its forces behind, say, the River Bug, and keeping them
there? And, by forces, I mean effective Russian physical power, by whatever name called. It is hard to see, after the events in Poland and
Hungary, whatever the Russian Government might wish, how it could
possibly undertake so hazardous a course. For, if its physical force were
permanently removed from Eastern Europe, who can believe that even
one of the Communist régimes would survive? Therefore, wherever
Soviet forces might be garrisoned, the expectation and threat of their
return must continue to be ever present (at most it would require from
12 to 18 hours) if Russia is to maintain the power which it has insisted
upon as recently as the Hungarian uprising.

At this point in our discussion we must examine the conception of the
neutralization of Germany; and then bring together the consequences
of withdrawal and neutralization. It is necessary, we are told, that Germany should not be allowed to be free to choose its own course after
unification. It must accept limitations upon its military forces and its

---

[1] "Britain's Suicide Pact," *New Statesman: The Week-end Review,* January 4,
1958, p. 1.

military alignment. In other words, its national life will be conducted under far greater limitations than those in which other sovereign people live. The possibility that any such situation could endure seems to me quite fantastic.

Whatever Germans might initially think they would be willing to do, there is no precedent in history for, nor does there seem to me to be any possibility of, the successful insulation of a large and vital country situated, as Germany is, between two power systems and with ambitions and purposes of its own. Constant strain would undermine the sanctions of neutralization. The final result would be determined by the relative strength of the pressures from the two sides. As I have already suggested, the pressure would all be from the Russian side. For, there would be no Power in Europe capable of opposing Russian will after the departure of the United States from the Continent and the acceptance of a broad missile-free area. Then, it would not be long, I fear, before there would be an accommodation of some sort or another between an abandoned Germany and the great Power to the East. Under this accommodation, a sort of new Ribbentrop-Molotov agreement, the rest of the free world would be faced with what has twice been so intolerable as to provoke world war—the unification of the European land mass (this time the Eurasian land mass) under a Power hostile to national independence and individual freedom.

But, without this withdrawal of forces and the neutralization of Germany, Mr. Kennan sees "little hope for any removal of the division of Germany at all—nor, by the same token, of the removal of the division of Europe." Naturally enough, these words have found a strong echo in Germany. But it is a fading one, as Germans ponder the conditions which would flow from unification by withdrawal and neutralization, and see the end of the best hopes of the German people. Two weak states—East and West Germany—jockeying for position in a sort of no-man's land, could raise the East-West "tensions" to a point compared to which anything we have yet experienced would seem mild indeed. In all this West Berlin would, of course, be the first victim. It would be a wholly inadequate judgment upon those whose naïveté and weakness produced this result that they should share the guilt of those Western politicians whose preaching of "liberation" encouraged the uprisings in East Berlin and Hungary, and, like them, should sit in supine impotence while more gallant men suffered. The best hope for German unification I shall mention shortly.

Turning to Eastern Europe, Mr. Kennan sees those countries, without the withdrawal of Russian troops, caught between the dilemma of constant revolutions, bloodily suppressed, and the acknowledgment of Soviet domination. This view seems to me founded on nothing but its assertion. I cannot for the life of me see how the movement toward a greater degree of national identity in Eastern Europe is furthered by removing from the Continent the only Power capable of opposing the Soviet Union.

Nor do I see that the facts bear out Mr. Kennan's gloomy predictions. For instance, if the experience of 1956 had produced only the development in Poland or if the Hungarians had acted with as much restraint, it would have been plain to all that the attraction of the power of the West, of the possibilities which its system opens to all, was proving very strong indeed—stronger even than the secret police and Soviet occupation troops. The fact that in Hungary the reaction was pushed to the point where the Russians felt it necessary to suppress it with force proves only that it was handled unwisely.

So, as we think about the matter, we must wonder whether there is anything we can purchase "one-half so precious as the goods" we sell. We are told not to worry about this; that, even though it seems quite unlikely that the Russians would carry out any withdrawal, nevertheless, it is good propaganda to make the offer and cause them to refuse it. This seems to me profoundly false. In the first place, it treats international negotiations as though all the figures on the chessboard were made of wood or ivory; whereas, in fact, we are dealing with living people, subject to all the emotions of mankind. If I were a European and had to live through two or three years of American negotiations about withdrawing from the Continent, I think that very early in the game I would discount America's remaining and would prepare to face a new situation. Furthermore, to believe that the Russians can be put in the position of refusing to evacuate Europe underrates their skill in negotiation. They would simply, as they have already done, continue to raise the price. And it would be we and not they who would do the refusing.

The evils of a timid and defeatist policy of retreat are far deeper than its ineptness as a move in the propaganda battle. It would abandon the efforts of a decade, which are bringing closer to realization the hopes of Western Europe, of Germany, and of Eastern Europe as well. From the low point of 1946-1947 the economic, social and political health and strength of Western Europe—of which West Germany has become an integral and vital part—have grown greatly. Their pull on Eastern Europe continues to mount. To continue this the American connection is essential. The success of the movement toward unity in the west of Europe is no longer in doubt. Only the rate of progress is undecided. The Coal and Steel Community, Euratom, the Common Market have been accepted. A common currency and political community are on the way.

All of this is threatened by the call to retreat. It will not do to say that a united Germany, made militarily impotent and neutralized, can play an effective part in bringing to fruition a united and vigorous European community. The slightest puff of reality blows this wishful fancy away. The jockeyings and tensions of the two parts of Germany, the un-opposable threat of Russian power, the bribes which can be dangled before Germany by the Soviet Union in the form of boundary rectifications and economic opportunities—these alone are enough to put an end to hope of a united and strong Europe, invigorated by Germany.

For those who believe that Eastern Europe would welcome American and Russian troop withdrawals as the beginning of liberation, I suggest a quiet sampling of candid Polish opinion. I venture to predict that what they would find is a horror at being abandoned by the West and left between the Soviet Union and a Germany similarly abandoned, to which the offer of another partition of Poland might be irresistible.

But, if one looks at the other side of the medal, what a different face it bears! A strong, united Europe could have the men and the resources —along with British and United States contingents—to deal by conventional forces with invasion by conventional forces, particularly as the Eastern European satellites are becoming a danger, and not an asset, to Soviet military power. This, if pressed, gives real mutuality of benefit to a negotiated reduction in forces. It makes possible, too, a time when nuclear forces would no longer have to be relied on as a substitute for conventional forces, and with it a real opportunity to negotiate this threat further and further into the background.

Finally, a thriving Western Europe would continue its irresistible pull upon East Germany and Eastern Europe. This would, in turn, have its effect upon the demands of the Russian people on their government. With a rise in the standards of living in the Soviet Union, and as some broader participation in the direction of affairs was made essential by their very magnitude and complexity, the Russian need for the forced communization and iron control of Eastern Europe would diminish. Then negotiations looking toward a united Germany, under honorable and healing conditions, and toward the return of real national identity to the countries of Eastern Europe, while preserving also the interests of the Russian people in their own security and welfare, could for the first time be meaningful and show the buds of hope. This has been the goal of Western policy for the past decade.

It would be self-delusion to close our eyes to the difficulties which lie before us along this road. Some we have created ourselves. Our military strategy, with its sole reliance on massive retaliation, and a budgetary policy which has neglected even that, have caused us a loss of relative military power and of prestige. Some of our political policies have weakened our alliances. Our allies, too, are having their troubles. In what are perhaps the two closest of them, we could wish (as they undoubtedly do, too) that both the present and the immediate future held greater promise for the development of strength and popular attitudes more attuned to reality. We all share together the common problem of devising a military policy for NATO which will avoid making the proposed defense seem as fearsome as the potential enemy's threat, and which will be a real deterrent because it is a credible one.

I have suggested elsewhere that this is possible. Briefly, the way is to create a situation in fact which equals the political purpose of the North Atlantic Treaty—that is, a situation where in order for the Soviet Union to attack, or coerce, Europe it would have to attack, or coerce, the United States as well. This, if we all use a fair degree of intelligence about our defenses, the Soviet Union could be deterred from doing. What is required is a short-range effort which does not preclude a sustained effort toward a wiser long-range goal. The short-range effort would be to provide NATO with such effective nuclear power that the Soviet Union could not have its way without destroying that power; and an attempt to destroy it would be impractical apart from a simultaneous attempt to disable the United States, which could be made too dangerous. The longer-range purpose would be to develop adequate conventional forces in Europe, with British and American participation, to make mutually desirable a real reduction and equalization of both Soviet and NATO forces and a controlled elimination of nuclear material for military use.

I quite understand that all of this is difficult. But I believe also that "the mode by which the inevitable comes to pass is effort."

Finally, Mr. Kennan's discussion of the uncommitted countries of
Asia and Africa seems to me to disclose a complete lack of understanding of the forces which are at work there. In the first place, he would
like to tell them, as Thoreau would have done, that the whole march
of industrial civilization since the beginning of the nineteenth century
has been a mistake; that they must be patient about increasing their
standard of living; that they must curb the mad rate at which they re-
produce; that we have no sense of guilt or obligation to them because
we are in a position to help their economic development as our own
was helped. But when they have any sound plans, we will consider
them on terms which they cannot accept. This means that we find
nothing to our interest in their industrialization; and that they are in
reality ward heelers who threaten one political side with desertion to
the other unless they receive a handout or a sinecure.

Nothing could be further from the truth. These governments are
faced with a demand, just as are the Government of the United States
and the Government of the Soviet Union, that conditions shall exist
under which a rising standard of living is possible. The conditions in
these countries vary from those which are still deep in an agricultural
stage to those which have begun industrialization and are ready, once
capital is available, to push it speedily forward. Governments cannot
stay in power unless they respond to the demands of those who will
keep them there. Even the oligarchs in the Kremlin are under pressure,
which they cannot altogether refuse, to expand the standard of living
in Russia.

There are two ways in which the governments of the undeveloped
countries can bring about conditions which their peoples demand. Both
of these involve acquiring capital, but under very different conditions.
One involves the adoption of totalitarian authority, a temporary depression of the standard of living, forced savings, and industrial equipment
from Russia, paid for by the export of raw materials. The other involves
the maintenance, and perhaps a steady expansion, of the standard of
living, the maintenance of systems of government in which there is a
considerable area of freedom, the import of capital from Western
Europe and North America, and the repayment of these loans over a
considerable period of time by participation in the expanding trade of
an open economic system. To say that economic development has nothing whatever to do with political alignment is a fallacy of the gravest
sort. It is, of course, true that economic aid cannot force, cannot ensure,

a political alignment from any country. But it is certain that, without it, a different alignment will take place.

May I conclude by repeating that the new isolationism which we have been discussing, and the reception it has received, is gravely disturbing, not only because it is utterly fallacious, but because the harder course which it calls on us to forego has been so successful. If one compares the non-Communist segments of the world today with what they were 12 years ago, one sees enormous progress. If one compares, as we have tried to do here, the pull of a vigorous free system, held together by the joint efforts of at least some of its members to provide military security, economic power and political leadership, one sees how strong it is and what effect it has had. If one considers the changes which have already occurred within the Soviet Union, one can see the time approaching when adjustments in Eastern Europe are possible, when military forces can be reduced, and when the menace of nuclear destruction will be greatly diminished, if not removed. Surely, there are dangers, and great dangers, but with good sense we can live through these. We will not make them less by weakening ourselves, destroying the confidence of our allies, and refusing to help those people who are willing to work to some extent, at least within the system which we and our allies, together, have created and can make ever more vigorous and appealing.

Prospects*

by Hans Speier

The major political and military problems of the North Atlantic alliance stem from two salient features of the prevailing balance of power, the virtual nuclear bipolarity of the world with the United States and the Soviet Union as the two giant powers, and the virtual American monopoly of nuclear power in NATO.

If other members of NATO as well as the United States, and to a considerably lesser extent Great Britain, possessed *strategic* deterrent power, the present bipolarity of the world would diminish. The Euro-

---

* From *German Rearmament and Atomic War* by Hans Speier, pp. 227-234. Copyright 1957 by the Rand corporation. Reprinted by permission.

pean countries would be able to pursue a more independent policy and some measure of the multipolar balance of power that existed in the pre-atomic age would be restored. In such a world, smaller nations that are now atomically destitute would each be able to reap the benefits of peace under the agonizing conditions of multilateral strategic deterrence. A variant of this development would consist in a redistribution of the strategic deterrent capability of the West so as to endow not individual countries but a group or groups of nations with the independent strategic deterrence which at present only the United States and the Soviet Union (and Great Britain) possess. Such redistribution of strategic nuclear power would not fully restore political multipolarity, however, since strategic deterrence would strengthen merely the defensive posture of smaller countries against atomic blackmail and nuclear attack. While it would enable them to withstand pressure both against and within the Western coalition with more equanimity, they would not necessarily be in a position to exert pressure themselves. For that purpose they would still need supplementary conventional power. In fact, if the acquisition of a strategic deterrent capability were to accelerate the present trend toward curtailment of nonatomic armament, the smaller countries would find their political choice further restricted whenever they faced issues unrelated to atomic blackmail or nuclear war.

Nuclear multipolarity will emerge in the course of time, as other nations follow the Soviet Union and Great Britain in breaking the American monopoly in nuclear weapons. And there is no *technological* reason why the development of multipolarity could not be speeded up by the present nuclear powers themselves if they were willing to share nuclear capabilities with some other nations. Loan or sale of arms is no novelty in military history. But the general reluctance of great powers to lend or sell their most advanced means of destruction to others is multiplied in the case of nuclear weapons: these weapons are of unprecedented destructiveness; the nuclear powers derive an increment of security from secret leads in nuclear science and technology; and they are concerned that sharing such weapons with others might entail their use by allied powers in their minor wars.

The doctrine of "the sword and the shield" obscures the political significance of the unequal distribution of nuclear capabilities among the members of NATO. "The sword" stands, by and large, for the nuclear capabilities of the U.S. Strategic Air Command (and the U.S.

Navy), "the shield" for the NATO forces in Europe. But until 1957 both the strategic nuclear capability of the West and the nuclear armament in Europe were largely under American control. None of the atomic weapons in Europe was integrated into the NATO defense system. The American nuclear weapons were either under the authority of the U.S. Air Force (like the B-61 Matadors) or of the Supreme Commander of NATO (like the atomic 280-mm guns, the Honest John rockets, and the Corporal missiles); but he had this authority as commander of the U.S. forces stationed in Europe and not in his role as Supreme Allied Commander, Europe. Furthermore, the atomic firepower of the American ground forces in Europe may be increased in the future while their numbers may be reduced. The American contribution to the common ground defenses in Europe might be confined to atomic support groups.[1] The military posture of NATO might then be stronger than it is today, but the cleavage between the United States and the atomically destitute powers in NATO would be deepened. The United States would be superior to her European allies not merely because she possessed "the sword" in the form of intercontinental striking forces, but also because her ground forces in Europe would be modernly equipped elite units, while those of her allies would be auxiliary forces armed with less advanced weapons.

In order to buttress the defensive strength of the coalition despite its reduced military manpower, the United States decided in April, 1957, to make available to her continental European allies certain advanced weapons that could be used in tactical atomic warfare. This aid will not extend to the atomic warheads themselves. Nor will it affect strategic inequalities within NATO. If anything, the latter have been exacerbated by the new defense policy of the British, who will rely in the future primarily upon a strategic deterrent capability of their own. While the U.S. decision has narrowed somewhat the nuclear weapons gap within NATO, the British decision will create new inequalities and try the political viability of NATO, if not its ability to survive.

Technological differentiation of military capabilities among allies is not new in the history of alliances. A division of military functions and a gradation of military technology among various units of a military

---

[1] The importance of such atomic task forces was recognized in Germany when the neutralization of Austria cut the contiguous contact over land routes through NATO territory between West Germany and northern Italy. For a German discussion of the Southern European Task Force, see Wilhelm Ritter von Schramm, "Atom-Sperrverbände," *Deutsche Soldaten-Zeitung*, October, 1955, p. 3.

establishment has often existed not only in individual nations, but also on an international level, in military alliances. Strictly speaking, there has never been a coalition in which all partners were equally strong and possessed armaments of equally advanced technology. In particular, alliances of the past between sea powers and land powers testify to the fact that viable arrangements for common defense can be made on the basis of functional specialization among the partners. An international division of armament functions among the partners of a coalition, however, is bound to generate certain frictions which in their mildest form may be said to correspond to service rivalries in a national defense establishment and which in their strongest form may sap the strength of the alliance. . . .

American policy cannot entirely remove the fear of nuclear war in Europe, and this has a potentially corrosive effect upon the North Atlantic alliance. As has been shown, this fear provides the Soviet Union with possibilities for atomic threats designed to undermine or destroy the solidarity of NATO. Early in November, 1956, the Soviet Union was quick to exploit the deep rift that had developed between the United States on the one hand and Britain and France on the other over the war in Egypt. In January, 1957, the Soviet press issued new warnings of atomic retaliation against those countries which would tolerate U.S. atomic support groups being stationed on their soil. Tass explained to Western Europe, Iran, Japan, and the island of Okinawa, all of which were mentioned explicitly, that by sending atomic forces to these countries the United States intended, in the event of atomic war, to divert the main Soviet blows from her own territory.[2] The latest Soviet threat, on April 27, 1957, took the form of a diplomatic note in which the federal government was warned that nuclear retaliation could turn Germany into "a veritable graveyard." The note, which made reference to "all kinds of modern weapons, including guided missiles," was delivered on the eve of a *Bundestag* debate on atomic armament. Adenauer spoke of an attempt to exploit internal political controversy in Germany, and the Bonn government said sharply that the Soviet note was "a massive threat and an attempt at intimidation with a view to separating the Federal Republic from her allies." [3]

It can readily be seen that any effective ban on large, "unconventional" nuclear bombs could not reduce the fear of atomic war in

[2] For the text of the Tass statement, see *The New York Times*, January 24, 1957.
[3] See *The New York Times*, April 28 and April 30, 1957.

Europe, where atomic weapons could be used for tactical purposes. A disarmament arrangement that would not cover small "conventional" atomic weapons would not reduce apprehensions among our allies that their territory might become a theater of nuclear warfare; in fact, such an arrangement might have the opposite effect, since it would eliminate the American strategic capability of deterring general war and thereby increase the danger of localized war in areas close to the Soviet empire. For this reason, no Western European power can really afford to make or endorse seriously any differential nuclear disarmament proposal aimed at abolishing large atomic and hydrogen bombs. Such a policy would be reasonable only if Soviet superiority in these weapons was manifestly overwhelming; in that case, however, all disarmament proposals would be without any interest whatever to the Soviet Union.

In two press conferences early in 1957, Adenauer favored a ban on nuclear weapons, but neither he nor any of Germany's military experts seem to have recognized that of all policies concerning nuclear armament, the least reasonable from the viewpoint of Western Europe is acceptance of the "conventionality" of tactical nuclear weapons and the outlawing of strategic, "unconventional" ones.

The United States can best forestall Soviet attempts at intimidating the weaker members of the Western coalition by maintaining superiority in strategic nuclear weapons and long-range delivery capabilities. If such deterrence cannot eliminate the fear of nuclear war in Europe, it can reduce it by preventing the crassest forms of its political exploitation through Soviet threats, and by giving assurances that derive from strength. The balance of nuclear power, however, has shifted in an adverse direction.

A second way in which the United States might deter Soviet attempts to intimidate the smaller powers in NATO would be to help them to acquire a strategic nuclear capability of their own, individually or jointly. The effects of such a policy on international affairs would be momentous, but no less shocking than a bare outline of the present balance of nuclear power would have been ten years ago. Only two possible political implications of an arrangement for the sharing of strategic nuclear weapons need be mentioned. First, to protect their bases from destruction by surprise attack, the participating European powers might have to share their bases as well, and presumably locate a large proportion of them in Africa, Canada, and possibly in the United States. If in the course of time the smaller countries were to develop a strategic capability of their own, it is possible that each of them might strive to render a Soviet attack on its territory as costly as possible but withdraw from any responsibility for the fate of its neighbors. If the United States were to play an active part in the creation of such capabilities, however, she might be able to control any politically disruptive tendencies and use nuclear sharing as an additional spur to unity, if not political union, of the European countries involved. It might also permit the United States to repay the present host countries of U.S. bases in Europe in kind. In any event, by diffusing the capability required for strategic nuclear war more widely, frictions in the alliance generated by the present American monopoly on the West's strategic deterrent power would be reduced.

Second, if smaller countries were given a certain retaliatory strategic capability, they might thereby acquire an unexpectedly great *deterrent* power. An aggressor who dared to defy that power would know that he risked damage to himself so great that even the total destruction of the small country would not be worth that price. The *deterrent* power of small countries with a nuclear capability does not necessarily correspond to the destructive power of their weapons. Correspondingly, the political (deterrent) value of the strategic nuclear capability of a coalition appears under certain conditions to be sensitive to the distribution of that capability among the members of the alliance, although the military worth of that capability may not be affected in the same way.[4] The total deterrent power of the coalition may exceed the military worth of its nuclear capability, if the latter is not monopolized by one nation, but distributed among several. . . .

---

[4] It may indeed be affected adversely.

FOR FURTHER READING:

M. Margaret Ball, *NATO and the European Union Movement* (New York: Frederick A. Praeger, 1959).

H. T. N. Gaitskill, *The Challenge of Coexistence* (Cambridge: Harvard University Press, 1957).

Ernst B. Haas, *The Uniting of Europe: Political, Social and Economic Forces, 1950-1957* (Stanford: Stanford University Press, 1958).

Malcolm W. Hoag, "NATO: Deterrent or Shield?" *Foreign Affairs*, Vol. XXXVI, No. 2 (January, 1958), pp. 278-292.

Michael Howard, *Disengagement in Europe* (Baltimore: Penguin Books, 1958).

Henry A. Kissinger, "Missiles and the Western Alliance," *Foreign Affairs*, Vol. XXXVI, No. 3 (April, 1958), pp. 383-400.

Klaus Knorr (ed.), *NATO and American Security* (Princeton: Princeton University Press, 1959).

Ben T. Moore, *NATO and the Future of Europe* (New York: Harper and Brothers, 1958).

Harry Bayard Price, *The Marshall Plan and Its Meaning* (Ithaca: Cornell University Press, 1955).

Ronald S. Ritchie, *NATO: The Economics of an Alliance* (Toronto: Ryerson Press, 1956).

Arnold Wolfers, "Europe and the NATO Shield," *International Organization*, Vol. XII, No. 4 (Autumn, 1958), pp. 425-439.

Chapter X

THE RECOGNITION OF
COMMUNIST CHINA

In contrast with the complexity of the issues involved in the public debate concerning United States European policy, those featured with regard to American policy in East Asia seem to be simple: essentially, Should we or should we not recognize the Peoples Republic of China? But this simplicity is deceptive, for although the public debate may profitably be focused on this narrow issue, its implications are equally complex. When the communists gained control of mainland China in the winter of 1949-1950, the United States was forced to reëxamine its entire policy toward East Asia. The outbreak of the Korean War the following summer made this even more urgent. At the conclusion of the Second World War we had hoped to rely on China to preserve security and peace in the surrounding area, and we had forced our allies to accept this premise and to grant China the symbols of great-power status, including a permanent seat in the United Nations Security Council. Our hopes proved futile; in 1950 new policies were clearly called for. The process of reformulation begun then still continues. New policies put into effect in the early Fifties have been revised and aspects of them continue to be seriously questioned.

At the heart of the controversy is the question of what the United States relationship with Communist China can and should be: the issue of recognition provides a convenient focal point for the conflicting arguments. The United States' immediate reaction to the communists' assumption of power—a reaction largely forced by communist hostility in Korea and elsewhere—was one of enmity. We refused to recognize the new regime (as we refused to recognize the Bolsheviks when they gained power in 1917), blocked its admission to the United Nations, imposed a trade embargo against it, and attempted to erect a series of barriers to prevent its further expansion, using our Seventh Fleet to protect Taiwan. To buttress our strength in eastern Asia we altered our relationship with Japan (as we did with Germany in Europe), quickly concluding a peace treaty and an alliance in 1951. Alliances with Australia and New Zealand and with the Philippines were necessary concomitants of this policy shift; these states needed assurances before they would acquiesce to Japan's new position. Later, in 1953 and 1954, we added an alliance with the Republic of Korea, the South East Asia Treaty and an alliance with the Republic of China to our commitments in the area. Now the question of recognition involves all these issues as well.

United Nations meetings provide widely publicized occasions for the periodic reopening of the issue of Chinese recognition. The question of admitting the Peoples Republic of China to the U.N. is repeatedly raised by representatives of the uncommitted states and, of course, of the Soviet Union, including Mr. Khrushchev who in his personal appearance before the Fourteenth General Assembly stated that it was time to dispose of "the corpse of reactionary China." Thus far, the United States position has prevailed in the U.N., but by ever-dwindling majorities. Although admission of the Peoples Republic of China to the United Nations would not necessarily imply United States recognition, the two issues are closely linked. It is the United States which has blocked Communist China, and the American policy of non-recognition is an issue in U.N. discussions. If the United States were to recognize Communist China, it is likely that some solution would be found in the United Nations.

Pressures for recognition of the Chinese Peoples Republic and for its admission to the United Nations have increased, particularly since the end of the Korean War. At the same time, events in South and Southeast Asia and Peiping's pronouncements concerning the future of Taiwan indicate that Chinese communist leaders retain expansionist aims. The issues of recognition and admission to the U.N. then pose many difficult questions. What would the effects of an alternative policy be on Communist China itself: would it decrease or increase expansionist pressures? What would the effects be on the relationship between Communist China and the Soviet Union? Would it strengthen or weaken American alliances? What would the reaction of uncommitted countries be? What would be the implications for American policy in the United Nations? Assumptions about these and other problems must be made by those who engage in the public debate on the recognition of Communist China.

Walter S. Robertson, Assistant Secretary of State for Far Eastern Affairs from 1953 until July, 1959 and the individual charged with rebutting Mr. Khrushchev and others on this issue in the Fourteenth General Assembly, defends present United States policy in the first selection in this chapter. He claims non-recognition is necessary to preserve the American alliance structure in East Asia and to preserve the faith of many mainland and overseas Chinese. He also argues that recognition is something a regime must earn—it is not entitled to it by fiat. Implicit in this is the fact that recognition is one of the few negotiable items the United States has for bargaining with Communist China. Something strongly desired by Peiping's leaders, recognition is an instrument the United States can use to gain its ends in East Asia. It is difficult, however, to find an equally self-enforcing Chinese concession which could be given in return; recognition, once conceded, is difficult to retract.

The second selection by Quincy Wright, Professor Emeritus of International Law at the University of Chicago and a leading authority on international affairs, analyzes the domestic political controversy concerning this issue and gives many of the arguments advanced for the recognition of Communist China. Many of these are legal arguments. In addition, he assumes that recognition would be more likely to modify Chinese behavior than non-recognition. Increased trade and contacts, he feels, might diminish Chinese hostility and expansionist urges and loosen the ties with Moscow. He also argues that recognition would strengthen the West.

The final selection by Reinhold Niebuhr, Professor of Applied Christianity and Vice President of Union Theological Seminary, deals solely with the question of admitting Communist China to the United Nations. Although this is inseparably linked with recognition, there are several differences. The most important is that while recognition is something that the United States alone can extend or withhold, admission to the U.N. is inevitably a group decision. Pressures from other states may force a revision of United States policies in the U.N. Communist China's admission to the United Nations is complicated by the permanent position assigned China in the Security Council, the now ironic result of our earlier policy. While Mr. Niebuhr has no illusions concerning Chinese communists, he feels that the net result of the admission of the Peoples Republic of China to the U.N. would be favorable to the United States.

The questions involved in the public debate on the recognition of Communist China are difficult; they involve numerous imponderables and an area concerning which our knowledge has proved fallible in the past. Among the greatest problems the participants in the public debate must face is that the most frequently suggested solution, recognizing two Chinas and admitting them both to the U.N., is one which neither China has as yet been willing to accept.

U.S. China Policy*

by Walter S. Robertson

In the seeming security of our daily routine lives it is difficult to realize that our world is in a state of crisis, that we are indeed engaged in a global struggle for the survival of a free civilization. The Far East is a strategic and critical area in this struggle. It is a vast area: 13 countries, 900 millions of people, approximately one-third of the world's population. It includes: Japan, Korea, China, the Philippines, Viet-Nam, Laos, Cambodia, Burma, Thailand, Indonesia, Malaya, Australia, and New Zealand; 11 Asian countries and 2 Anglo-Saxon countries in an Asian setting.

The 11 Asian countries comprise a region of great diversity, divided by sharp differences in tradition, religion, culture, and circumstances. The economies range from the great industrial, mercantile complex of Japan to the primitive economies of Southeast Asia. Eight out of the 11 of these countries have achieved their independence since 1945.

Taken as a whole, the area is one of great potential wealth in both human and natural resources but, with few exceptions, suffering from mass poverty and ignorance, economic and political instability, shortage of investment capital, shortage of technicians of all kinds, shortage of educational facilities, deep resentments of Western colonialism, deep suspicions of the white man, and fears of a new exploitation. It is an area seething with a new spirit of nationalism, social unrest, and rising aspirations for a place in the sun and a better life for its poverty-stricken millions. And interrelated with and overriding all of its problems are the aggressions, infiltrations, and subversions of the international Communists.

Now it is the policy of the United States to meet this pervasive threat by helping to build up the military, political, and economic strength of our Far Eastern allies and friends as rapidly as possible. This is the sole purpose of our mutual security programs in these countries.

Yet the governments of all of these free countries without exception have a gnawing fear of the growing power and threat of Red China. And because Red China is a major threat to their new-found independence and therefore a major threat to the security of the free world, it

* From the *Department of State Bulletin*, Vol. XL, No. 1032 (April 6, 1959), pp. 472-478.

is essential that China policy be coldly realistic and one that best serves free-world security interests and objectives.

BIPARTISAN SUPPORT

I need not remind you that U.S. China policy has been a subject of bitter controversy. It has disrupted friendships, has lent itself to name calling, to the questioning of motives, and in some tragic instances to the questioning of loyalty itself. But, strange as it may seem, U.S. China policy has probably enjoyed a larger measure of bipartisan support in the United States than any other major policy of our Government.

Since 1950 the difference in basic China policy between former President Truman and President Eisenhower is the difference between Tweedledum and Tweedledee.

In early 1950, following the Communist takeover of the mainland in December 1949 and about the time of British recognition, President Truman vetoed the recommendation made to him that we recognize Red China. The Republican attack on the Democrats in the 1952 election campaign was not on basic China policy as it then was but rather on what was alleged to have been the vacillations and blunders which had helped to create the Frankenstein monster of Red China and enhance its menace to the free world. In 1956, an election year, a Democratic-sponsored resolution, reaffirming support of the Republic of China and opposing the seating of Red China in the United Nations, passed the House by a vote of 391 to 0 and of 86 to 0 in the Senate. Not a single Congressman or Senator of either party was willing to vote against this resolution. This is a phenomenon unprecedented in American political history. When the parties later assembled for their national conventions they adopted almost identical planks in support of this policy. In the recent Taiwan crisis Mr. Truman was among the first to come out in strong support of President Eisenhower's position. To repeat, the differences of opinion about China policy do not represent differences between political parties but rather differences between individuals, irrespective of party lines.

Herbert Feis called his book on the subject *The China Tangle.* It is a good name. The controversy is indeed a tangle, a tangle of truths, untruths, and half-truths. It is entangled by Communist propaganda and distortions. The Communists will always see to it that this is so. It is entangled by the unwitting acceptance by many highly respected and intelligent Americans of the subtle propaganda and misinformation to which they are subjected. It is entangled by our early failures to recognize the origin, nature, direction, and control of the Communist revolution in China. It is entangled by the corruption and ineptness which existed in certain elements of the Kuomintang but which was exploited so as to make it appear that all Chinese Government leaders were corrupt and inept. And, finally, it is entangled by honest differences of opinion among the objective and well-informed—differences of opinion which, thank God, have always existed and always will exist concerning public questions in the kind of free society we are struggling to preserve in the world today.

U.S. POLICY SIMPLE TO STATE

But despite the tangle and however complex it might be in implementation, our policy is simple to state. On the one hand, our policy is to face up to the realities of Chinese Communist objectives, opposing the further spread of Chinese Communist influence and power. On the other hand, as a principal means to this end, our policy is to keep alive, support, and strengthen a non-Communist Chinese Government, firmly oriented to the free world, as a foil and a challenge to the fanatical, aggressive, hostile, and threatening International Communist regime of Peiping, an implacable enemy dedicated to the destruction of all the foundations upon which a free society rests.

It is often charged that our policy is tied to the political fortunes of one man: Chiang Kai-shek. This is a *reductio ad absurdum*. Chiang is in fact a time-tested friend and ally. He has never broken his word to us or an agreement with us. Following Pearl Harbor in 1941 all of the Western powers were soon swept from the Western Pacific. We were swept about as far as we could be swept this side of the South Pole— Melbourne, Australia. When the Japanese had Chiang bottled up in Chungking, having occupied all of his ports of entry and large sections of his country, and Chiang with no ally within thousands of miles, they made him a princely offer to sell out to them. He refused, fighting on against overwhelming odds. This refusal saved thousands of Allied lives. Had he sold out, there would have been released from 1½ to 2 million additional Japanese troops to oppose our advance from the south.

He refused to sell out to the Russians. After the Russians had occupied Manchuria—that great prize which they received for 5 days of nominal participation in the Pacific war and, incidentally, the most strategic base in all of Asia for carrying out their objectives of communizing Asia—they invited Chiang to come into their economic orbit, saying that they would settle his Communist problem for him. He rejected this offer, and they retaliated by refusing to allow the United States to transport troops of the Nationalist Government into Manchuria to take over territory in accordance with solemn agreements to which the Soviets were party. Instead, the Soviets turned over vast areas and Japanese arms and equipment to the Chinese Communists. This despite the fact that on August 14, 1945, the day the Japanese surrendered, the Soviets had signed a treaty with the Republic of China acknowledging its sovereignty over Manchuria and pledging all moral, material, and military support to that Government.

And finally, Chiang has repeatedly refused to sell out to Peiping, which constantly plies him with lavish offers.

Be all this as it may, if Chiang should die tonight, the validity of our policy would in no way be affected. Today, as in the past, there are only two choices available to us: the anti-Communist Republic of China, our friend, or the International Communist regime of Peiping, a deadly enemy dedicated to our destruction.

In Chungking back in 1945, some of my friends and associates thought that the Democratic League offered a third force which we should cultivate and support. It was later recognized as a Communist front organization designed to ensnare the middle-of-the-road intellectuals.

BASIS FOR NONRECOGNITION OF RED CHINA

Our opposition to the Red regime is not, as you are often told, based upon the disapproval of an ideology or an economic system, much as we abhor both. We recognize many totalitarian regimes with varying economic systems, and we have not refused to sit down with them in the world forum of the United Nations. Nor is our policy, as sometimes charged, based upon an emotional reaction to the Korean war. Our policy is a coldly realistic one, based upon three major considerations, all directly related to the overall collective security of the free world.

The first of these considerations is the security interest of the United States. It is often forgotten or ignored that the recognition of Red China would, as a practical matter, mean the liquidation of the Republic of China with all that would mean to our strategic, psychological, and moral position in our opposition to Communist expansion in the Far East. Taiwan is a vital link in our island chain of defenses in the Pacific, all now covered by bilateral defense treaties. The Chinese military forces on Taiwan of some 600,000 are an important factor in the military balance of power in the Pacific and a continuing deterrent to the renewal of Communist aggression in Korea or elsewhere in Asia. If Taiwan should be given over to the Communists, Japan, the Philippines, and all of Southeast Asia would be seriously threatened.

The second basic consideration is our interest in helping other Asian nations maintain their national independence. Our bilateral and multilateral defense treaties, as well as our mutual security programs, are designed to this end. If the United States were to abandon its commitments to the Republic of China in order to appease the threatening Red Chinese, no country in Asia could feel that it could longer rely upon the protection of the United States against the Communist threat. These comparatively weak nations would have no alternative but to come to terms—the best they could get—with the Peiping colossus. Not only could we then expect a rapid expansion of communism throughout Asia, but the moral position of the United States upon which we must rely for much of our strength throughout the world would suffer irreparable damage.

The third major consideration is the long-range interests and future orientation of the Chinese people themselves. The anti-Communist Government of the Republic of China is a symbol of Chinese opposition to communism—the only rallying point in the world for non-Communist Chinese, the only Chinese alternate focus of loyalty for millions of Chinese on the mainland, on Taiwan, and throughout Southeast Asia. If the Republic of China should be liquidated, it would extinguish a beacon of hope for millions of mainland Chinese. Taiwan's 10 million would be delivered to the slavery of the mainland, and the 12 million overseas Chinese would automatically become increasingly dangerous cells of infiltration and subversion in the countries where they reside.

Let no one say that representation is being denied to 600 million mainland Chinese. The fanatical Marxists of Peiping come no closer to representing the will and aspirations of the Chinese people than the puppet regime of Budapest comes to representing the will and aspirations of the Hungarian people or William Z. Foster comes to representing the will and aspirations of the American people. They have given indisputable evidence that they are part and parcel of the apparatus of the international Communist conspiracy to communize the world.

PEIPING'S UNITY WITH MOSCOW

Back in the 1940's, when the Chinese Communists were being reported by some observers as not being real Communists but rather the leaders of a democratic revolution for agrarian reform, Mao Tse-tung was writing of himself, "I am a Marxist dedicated to communizing China and the world under the leadership of Moscow." All of his subsequent actions have borne out his dedication to that goal. Peiping has demonstrated its unity with Moscow by faithfully following the labyrinthine twistings and turnings of Moscow's ideological line on bloc and world affairs. When there were rumblings of revolt in Eastern Europe, Mao sent Chou En-lai to rally the wavering satellites into unity "under the leadership of Moscow." In November 1957, when Mao visited Moscow, he spoke to the students, including many Chinese, of Moscow University: "In the association of Socialist states," he said, "there must be a leader and that leader is Moscow."

Despite the price it had to pay in Asian opinion, Peiping proclaimed vigorous approval of Moscow's bloody suppression of the Hungarian revolt. It publicly applauded the execution of Nagy. Mao's bitter denunciation of Tito was not because Tito was not a Communist but rather because he dared to challenge the leadership of Moscow. Most recently, at the 21st Congress of the Soviet Union in Moscow, Chou En-lai addressed the Communists in these words: "The most sacred international duty of Communists in all countries at any time is to strengthen the unity of the countries in the socialist camp headed by the Soviet Union." Chou En-lai said to me one day in Chungking back in 1945, "Why do Americans come over here and go back and write that we are not Communists, that we are just agrarian reformers?" Then, with a light in his eyes, he said, "We are not agrarian reformers; we are Communists, and we are proud of it!"

The Peiping regime was imposed by force with the volition of only an infinitesimal fraction of the Chinese people. Today, after 9 years, less than 2 per cent belong to the Party. It has kept itself in power by bloody purges and the liquidation of some 18 million of mainland Chinese in 9 years. No regime representative of its people would have to resort to wholesale murder in order to keep itself in power.

AN OUTLAW REGIME

In our view the security interests of ourselves, of Asia, and of the free world as a whole demand that we take no action which would create international prestige for this regime, which would increase its capacity for advancing its objective of communizing all of Asia, or which would betray the hopes of those having the will and the courage to resist it.

Even if no security interests were involved, there is no basis either for the recognition of Peiping by the United States or for admission of that regime to the United Nations. By every standard of national and international conduct, it has proven itself to be an outlaw regime.

Take first the question of recognition by the United States. Since the days of Jefferson, diplomatic recognition of a government by the United States has involved two major tests. The first test is whether the act of recognition would be in the interests of the United States. In our view the diplomatic recognition of Red China would not be in our country's national interests for reasons I have already mentioned. The other test for diplomatic recognition involves not only *de facto* control of territory but also the ability and willingness to live up to international obligations. What is the record of Peiping by this standard?

Gaining control of the mainland in December 1949, it promptly repudiated the international obligations of China. It confiscated without compensation properties of other nationals valued in the hundreds of millions of dollars, something over $1 billion for the United Kingdom alone. It demanded and received as blackmail money hundreds of thousands of dollars additional before it would issue exit visas for the personnel operating these properties. It threw foreign citizens into jail without trial and subjected many of them to the most inhuman tortures. It has flagrantly violated the Korean and Indochina armistice agreements. It has failed to live up to its commitment to us, reached after long negotiation and publicly announced in Geneva on September 10, 1955, to release expeditiously all American citizens imprisoned in China.[1] Five are still being held as political hostages.

If any of you are inclined to say that, if we can tolerate the broken agreements of the Soviets, we should be able to overlook the long record of broken agreements by the Red Chinese, I would remind you that

---

[1] For text of announcement, see the *Department of State Bulletin* of Sept. 19, 1955, p. 456.

Soviet perfidy in breaking international agreements followed rather than preceded recognition by the United States.

The Bolsheviks seized power in 1917. Nevertheless we continued for 16 years to recognize the Kerensky government-in-exile. By 1933 it seemed that the Communist regime in Moscow might indeed be considered a peaceful member of society. It had committed no action of armed aggression for more than a decade. It had accepted the independence of Estonia, Latvia, Lithuania, and Poland—all later betrayed. It pledged itself to cease its subversive activities in the United States, to respect American rights in Russia, and to settle Russia's public and private debts to the United States.

We need not question that action of recognition under the circumstances which prevailed at the time. However, who can now doubt that recognition would not have been accorded even in 1933 had there been clear warning that Soviet promises given in that connection were totally unreliable and that aggressive war would soon become an instrumentality of Soviet policy. In the case of Communist China, we have been clearly and unmistakably forewarned.

QUESTION OF U.N. MEMBERSHIP

Now how does Communist China qualify for membership in the United Nations?

You will remember when the United Nations was organized in 1945 it was exhaustively debated whether membership should be based upon universality or whether there should be qualifications for membership. It was decided that universality was not the test but rather that an applicant must fulfill certain qualifications. The charter finally adopted provides that only peace-loving nations willing to assume and live up to the obligations of the charter are eligible for membership. It further provides for the expulsion of members who violate the charter.

Is Red China a peace-loving nation?

Let us again look at the record. In February, 1950, approximately 2 months after establishing its regime on the mainland, it issued a call to all the peoples of Southeast Asia to overthrow their governments, denouncing their leaders as puppets of the imperialists. Before the year was out, it invaded Tibet, even though the Peiping regime had just promised the Government of India that it "would settle the Tibetan question by peaceful means." Nine years later it is still engaged in fighting the rebellious Tibetans. Also, before the year was out, it invaded Korea. For the Korean aggression it was denounced by United Nations resolution as an aggressor against the peace of the world.[2] That resolution is still outstanding, and Red China is still defying the United Nations, charging that the United Nations are the aggressors in Korea and therefore without moral competence to supervise free elections for the unification of the country. Today Red China is still threatening war in the Taiwan Strait, stubbornly refusing throughout 87 meetings in Geneva and Warsaw to renounce war as an instrument of national policy. Its philosophy was recently expressed by the Peiping Defense Minister in this language: "Ours is a policy of fight-fight, stop-stop— half-fight, half-stop. This is no trick but a normal thing."

By no stretch of interpretation of the United Nations Charter could Red China qualify under that charter as a peace-loving nation eligible for membership. Those advocating membership for Peiping are not demanding that Red China change its ways and conform its policies to United Nations standards but rather are insisting that the United Nations modify its standards to accommodate the lawlessness of Peiping. Those who are opposed to such denigration of the United Nations Charter are charged with being unrealistic and denying the existence of 600 million Chinese.

A MAJORITY POSITION

You might think from much of what you read in the press that the U.S. occupies an isolated position in its refusal to recognize Red China. I would remind you that, of the free countries of the world, 44 recognize the Republic of China, 22 recognize Peiping. Many of the 22 recognized Peiping before it had demonstrated its lawlessness. Of the 13 countries of the Far East, only 3 recognize Red China. Instead of being isolated, we stand with the overwhelming majority of the countries of the free world in this position. It is essential that this majority continue to stand together. Other countries, particularly those most exposed to the immediate menace of Communist power, have been following the lead of such countries as ours. Many of them are watching anxiously to see what we are going to do. If we should begin to break ranks and with-

---

[2] For text of resolution adopted on Feb. 1, 1951, see *ibid.*, Jan. 29, 1951, p. 167.

draw opposition to the reckless course of this aggressor, these countries would have no alternative but to get on the bandwagon so as not to be left out on a limb of opposition, deserted by strong free-world support.

I believe you will agree that the United States is the main military obstacle to Communist overt aggression in Asia. You might be interested in an evaluation of the Asian situation during the time of the Taiwan crisis by the Far East expert of the London *Economist* published October 11, 1958:

> America's underlying dilemma . . . might be summed up in the words: "Little Brother is watching you." Anxious little brothers are indeed watching the United States from all sides, and their anxieties are of excruciatingly contradictory kinds. When Mr. Dulles talks tough about Quemoy, European stomachs flutter; but when he seems to be giving even a mere inch of ground, Far Eastern hearts sink. The Quemoy drama is being played out with the ringside seats occupied by uneasy Japanese, Koreans, Vietnamese, Filipinos, and other Asian peoples who must take into account the possibility that some day American power may withdraw altogether across the wide Pacific, leaving them alone with the newborn Chinese giant. . . . And they recall that for years Peking and Moscow have canvassed twin projects for "mutual security" systems in Asia and in Europe, both of which would exclude the United States, so that China would be the dominant power in one sphere, Russia in the other. It is the complete disappearance of the American "presence" from the scene that the communists are after. And whether anti-western feeling and neutralism are weak or strong in these Asian countries and whatever their public postures, they know well enough that if the eagle once takes flight, the dragon—and perhaps the bear too—will have to be propitiated.
>
> If America really retires, China's immediate neighbors will inevitably again become China's vassals—not necessarily by military conquest, but by the impossibility of their resisting for long the pressure which their huge and dynamic neighbor can put upon them in many forms.

Our view of the China situation is the same as that we hold with respect to the other three divided countries of the world where the Communists now exercise *de facto* control over large areas of territory. We consider it to be in our national interest and in the interest of the free world as well to recognize the Republic of Korea, not the Communist regime of north Korea; to recognize the Republic of Viet-Nam, not the Communist Viet Minh regime of Ho Chi Minh; to recognize the Federal Republic of Germany, not the Communist East German regime. In none of these countries do we advocate the use of force to achieve unification, nor do we advocate the use of force for the unification of China. In fact, the contrary was recently proclaimed in the joint communique of President Chiang Kai-shek and Secretary Dulles in Taiwan in October of last year.[3]

It is now being stated in certain quarters that we are drifting to a two-China policy. We do not have a two-China policy any more than we have a two-Korea policy, a two-Viet-Nam policy, or a two-German policy.

In closing I should like to mention an ancient Chinese proverb. It is in the form of question and answer. "What is the cure for muddy water?" the question goes; "Time" is the answer. In the long rollcall of history, nazism and fascism will be episodes only, dark incidents if you will. So, too, will communism be, although the most evil and pervasive of the three. Man will not permanently endure the cruel enslavement imposed by the ruthless regimes of international communism. But his liberation will be immeasurably delayed by frustrated appeasement of the forces which enslave him. An awful responsibility rests upon us— upon our patience, upon our steadfastness, upon our courage, and, above all, upon our strength. How we counter the menace now posed to our rrecuouwill determine the climate of the world for as far into the future as we can see.

The Status of Communist China*

by Quincy Wright

The United States appears to have been on the verge of recognizing the Communist Government of China in the winter of 1950 after that Government had gained control of the Chinese mainland and had been recognized by twenty-eight states including the United Kingdom, India, Pakistan, Burma, Ceylon, Afghanistan, Indonesia, Israel, the Netherlands, Switzerland, the Scandinavian states and the Communist states. It appears to have been deterred by the popular agitation on domestic communism at the time and took a position, not only against recognition, but also against admission of the Communist delegation to repre-

---

[3] For text, see *ibid.*, Nov. 10, 1958, p. 721.

* From the *Journal of International Affairs* (Columbia University), Vol. XI, No. 2 (1957), pp. 161-186. Copyright 1957 by the Board of Editors of the *Journal of International Affairs*. Reprinted by permission.

sent China in the United Nations. The refusal of United Nations organs to accept the Soviet's demand that the Communist delegation be seated resulted in the Soviet's withdrawal of its own delegations from United Nations organs until August, 1950, and in a memorandum by the Secretary-General of the United Nations on March 8, 1950, suggesting that, irrespective of diplomatic recognition, states should be represented in the United Nations by the government able to fulfill the obligations of membership and that United Nations organs should regulate the acceptance of credentials of rival delegations by this principle. Thus, the Secretary-General implied that the Communist delegation from China should be seated.

In June, 1950, while this opinion was still under discussion, the North Korean invasion of South Korea took place, resulting in the Security Council's assertion that North Korea was guilty of an "armed attack" and "breach of the peace," referred to in a later resolution as "aggression." In the winter of 1951, after the Chinese Communist Government had encouraged "volunteers" to assist North Korea, the General Assembly asserted that that government also was guilty of "aggression." The conclusion of an armistice at Panmunjom in 1953 ending Korean hostilities has been followed by continuous complaints of arms buildup by the Communists in North Korea in violation of the armistice. These events prevented acceptance of the Communist Government to represent China in the United Nations and further recognition of that government by United Nations members until Nepal extended recognition on August 1, 1955, followed by Egypt and Syria on May 16 and July 3, 1956, respectively.

The position of the United States against recognition of Communist China or its representation in United Nations organs hardened as a result of the above narrated events and of the refusal of the Communist Government to release American fliers captured in the Korean hostilities and to renounce the use of force in the Straits of Formosa. This hardening of position was also influenced by extensive domestic propaganda and several Congressional resolutions against recognition or acceptance of the Communist Government in the United Nations. Furthermore, in December, 1954, the United States concluded a defense agreement with the Government of Formosa designating it "the Republic of China." United States initiative has contributed to preventing the acceptance of the Communist Government by United Nations organs and to maintaining an economic embargo against mainland China, although the pressure for modification of both of these positions has increased, especially because of the widespread desire of Great Britain, Japan, and other states to trade with mainland China, and of India, Indonesia, and other Asiatic states to maintain the solidarity of the Bandung group against "imperialism" by either the NATO or the Warsaw alliances.

The issue was emphasized by Prime Minister Nehru's conversation with President Eisenhower in April, 1957, urging United States recognition of Communist China, and by the British Government's plea at the NATO Council in May, 1957, for relaxation of the Chinese embargo. The failure of NATO to act because of United States opposition was followed by Britain's unilateral action in removing the embargo except on strategic materials on May 30, 1957. Both Congress and the President then began to consider American relaxations. The Taipei riots on May 25, 1957, sacking the United States Embassy in Formosa in protest against the release by United States Court Martial of a soldier who had killed a Chinese, may have manifested an underlying frustration and dissatisfaction with the United States by the Formosan Chinese. This also suggested the expediency of reconsidering American Far Eastern policy. Such modifications have indeed been considered, as indicated by President Eisenhower's talk of "two Chinas" in January, 1955, after he had abandoned the policy of "unleashing Chiang" to reconquer the mainland and had concluded a defense treaty with the Chiang Government with the understanding that such an attempt would not be made without American consent. Furthermore, informal negotiation had continued at Geneva between representatives of the United States and Communist China concerning release of imprisoned American fliers and the maintenance of peace in the Straits of Formosa. In spite of these circumstances, the official American position against recognition or representation of Communist China continues.

AMERICAN POSITION SUPPORTED BY FOUR GROUPS

This American position appears to be supported by four groups. (1) The "China Lobby," dominated by a feeling of friendship and loyalty to Chiang Kai-shek and the Nationalist Government;[1] (2) the "Committee of One Million," dominated by a moral disapproval of the

---

[1] This somewhat inchoate group, inspired by a businessman, Alfred Kohlberg, at one time engaged in China trade, was discussed in the *Reporter* of July 12, 1956.

Communist Government because of its ideology, its oppression, its aggression, particularly in Korea, and its assumed similarity to the Governments of Hitler and Mussolini;[2] (3) Republican politicians who think votes have been won by propagating the idea that the triumph of communism in China was due to negligence, stupidity, or treason of the Democratic Administration in not giving more effective support to Chiang, and that votes can continue to be won by asserting that the debacle can be remedied by a stalwart stand behind the Chiang Government;[3] and (4) the Government, influenced by the weight in domestic politics of the first three groups, by fear that the United States would morally compromise itself with its allies if it abandoned or weakened its Formosan ally, and also by calculation that nonrecognition strengthens the West materially in the cold war. Government spokesmen suggest that nonrecognition makes possible the trade embargo, thus withholding war potential from the Communist bloc, and sustains the Formosan Government as a valuable ally. That ally, they point out, has a substantial army deterring Communist expansion in Formosa, Korea, and Vietnam; a strategic territory providing air bases to the West and denying them to the Communists; a Chinese Government attracting overseas Chinese, especially those in Southeast Asia, away from communism and encouraging whatever opposition exists in mainland China; and a membership in the United Nations contributing to the Western majority and preventing another permanent Communist veto in the Security Council.[4]

Opinion in the United States favorable to recognition is supported by no propaganda organizations and by no audible voices in the government. It is represented by some writers on international law and relations and by occasional businessmen and journalists who often advocate the "two China" policy, according to which the Communist Government would be recognized as the Government of China, representing that country in the United Nations, while Formosa (or Taiwan)

---

[2] This group, with Ambassador Warren Austin as Honorary Chairman, Frederick McKee as Treasurer, and such well known opponents of recognition as Senator William F. Knowland of California and Representative Walter Judd of Minnesota, claims to include 24 senators, 97 representatives, 9 governors, 8 former ambassadors, one former Secretary of State and 1,037,000 signatories of a petition.

[3] These themes were emphasized in the campaign of 1952 by Republican orators.

[4] These arguments are presented by Ambassador Stanley K. Hornbeck, "Which Chinese?" *Foreign Affairs*, October, 1955, and by addresses by Assistant Secretary of State Walter S. Robertson and Secretary of State Dulles, *Department of State Bulletin*, Feb. 25, 1957, vol. 36, p. 297; April 1, 1957, vol. 36, pp. 531, 546.

would be recognized as an independent state, if the population so desired, and admitted as such to the United Nations.[5]

Persons with this general opinion often argue against the "China Lobby" that sentimental attachment to obsolete conditions is not a satisfactory basis for foreign policy; against the "Committee of One Million" that they misunderstand principles of international law and morality and that there is no real similarity to the Fascist and Nazi situations; against the politicians that it is not good politics to try to "fool all the people all the time"; and against the official position that it misstates the genuine goals of United States policy and miscalculates the consequences of the alternative policies available. These arguments will be briefly discussed.

THE "CHINA LOBBY"

(1) No one questions that loyalty to alliances is an essential characteristic of sound international relations nor that the Government of China under Chiang Kai-shek, as a party to the Declaration of the United Nations of January 1, 1942, made important contributions to winning World War II. States, however, not individuals, are parties to alliances, as recognized by Washington when he decided that the Alliance of 1778 was made with France, not with Louis XVI. The identification of loyalty to the China alliance of 1942 with present loyalty to the Chiang Kai-shek Government of Formosa assumes that the latter not only was but still is the head of the Government of China.

It is said, however, that the Taipei Government, while not actually administering any part of mainland China, maintains contact with the mainland Chinese people, represents their political aspirations more genuinely than does the Communist Government, and will, when the occasion arises, be welcomed back by the Chinese people. There is little tangible evidence in the . . . years since the Communists took over China to sustain this opinion. On the contrary, the evidence, which will

---

[5] The businessmen at the State Department's Round Table on American Foreign Policy Toward China held in October, 1949, and released in 1951 generally favored recognition, as did those consulted by the New York Council on Foreign Relations in March, 1950. See also articles in the *Annals of the American Academy of Political and Social Science*, vol. 277 (1951), especially articles by Earl H. Pritchard and George E. Taylor; Quincy Wright, "The Chinese Recognition Problem," *American Journal of International Law*, vol. 49 (1955), p. 320; and A. Doak Barnett, "The United States and Communist China," *The American Assembly; The United States and the Far East*, Columbia University, Dec., 1956, p. 106 ff.

be discussed at a later stage, indicates that the Communist Government is the *de facto* Government of China. Chiang Kai-shek is the head of the Government of Formosa, and the limits of the loyalty to him required by the alliance of 1942 is to protect his Government and territory against invasion. This has been done by the treaty of 1954, which includes an understanding that Chiang will not attempt to reconquer the mainland without the consent of the United States. To believe that Chiang can reoccupy the mainland and to insist that loyalty to him prevents recognition of the actual Government of China is sentimentalism similar to that of the Federalists of 1792, who insisted that loyalty to Louis XVI, whose alliance with the United States in 1778 had contributed to winning the revolution, prevented recognition of the Government of the French Republic which had sent him to the guillotine.

THE "COMMITTEE OF ONE MILLION"

(2) Modern international law is based on the principle of territorial sovereignty accepted by European states after a century of ideological war between Catholics and Protestants culminating in the devastating Thirty Years War. The Treaty of Westphalia, which ended that war in 1648, left religious controversy to each territorial sovereignty—*Cuius Regia Eius Religio*. The United Nations Charter is based on the "sovereign equality" of states and forbids intervention by the United Nations in matters essentially within the domestic jurisdiction of a state. Domestic jurisdiction has been held to include all matters concerning which the state is under no obligations of customary international law or treaty. Thus, except insofar as a state has assumed obligations in respect to internal administration, such as to respect human rights, it is free to maintain in its own territory the system of government, economy, or religion which it sees fit. As President Eisenhower said on April 16, 1953:

> Any nation's right to a form of government and an economic system of its own choosing is *inalienable*. Any nation's attempt to dictate to other nations their form of government is *indefensible*.[6]

This principle of international law rests upon the principle of international morality which requires respect by each nation for the independence, self-government, and opportunity for self-development of the

---

[6] *U.S. Department of State Bulletin*, April 27, 1953, vol. 28, p. 599.

national genius of each of the others, with due regard for the equal rights of all. The nonrecognition of a government for the purpose of influencing the form of government, economy, culture, or ideology of another state amounts, therefore, to intervention in the domestic affairs of that state and violates a basic principle of international morality and international law.

It is true that many writers on international law have accorded a wide discretion to states in recognizing or refusing to recognize governments established by revolution, but few have treated this discretion as absolute.[7] Such discretion is accorded because of the frequent uncertainty whether a revolutionary government is actually in control of the territory and administration of a state or is sufficiently supported by its people and sufficiently committed to the observance of international law to give it an expectation of long life; in other words, whether it is the *genuine* government of a state. When sufficient time has passed to give an assurance of affirmative answers to these questions, it has been the usual practice of states to recognize the new government. Some statesmen, such as Mexican Foreign Minister Estrada in 1930, have gone further, asserting that formal recognition should be no more necessary in the case of revolutionary change than of constitutional change and should be assumed as soon as a government is established in fact.[8] Others, while according considerable discretion in recognition, agree with Jefferson:

> We surely cannot deny to any nation that right whereon our own government is founded—that everyone may govern itself according to whatever form it pleases, and change these forms at its own will . . . The will of the nation is the only thing essential to be regarded.[9]

Jefferson thus asserted that nonrecognition should not be used as an instrument of national policy and that recognition should be guided by facts giving evidence that the new government is supported by the national will.

This position was generally supported by the United States Government until 1907 when it subscribed to the "Tobar Doctrine" by supporting the Central American Treaty of that date forbidding the recognition of revolutionary governments in Central America. President

---

[7] See, however, Arthur H. Dean, *Note on Diplomatic Recognition of Governments,* American Assembly, *op. cit.,* p. 208.

[8] Philip Jessup, *American Journal of International Law,* vol. 25, p. 722 (1931).

[9] J. B. Moore, *Digest of International Law,* vol. 1, p. 120.

Wilson followed this policy in 1913 by refusing to recognize the Huerta Government of Mexico, which had come to power through assassination. This policy was for a time pursued in regard to Latin American revolutions but has subsequently been dropped for that area of the world. Recognition was refused to the Soviet Government, at first on the ground that it was unstable and later because of its repudiation of international law. Nevertheless, it was recognized in 1933.[10] In the main the United States has followed the Jeffersonian theory, which differs little from that of Judge Hersh Lauterpacht, who considers recognition a duty when the evidence clearly indicates that the government in power is a *genuine* government, sufficiently supported by its public and sufficiently mindful of international law to make its continuance probable.[11] The arbitral tribunal under Judge William Howard Taft found the Tinoco government of Costa Rica from 1917 to 1921 to be such a government, even though the United States and other important countries had not recognized it for political reasons.[12] Lauterpacht states:

> The emphasis—and that emphasis is a constant feature of diplomatic correspondence—on the principle that the existence of a state (or of a government) is a question of fact signifies that, whenever the necessary factual requirements exist, the granting of recognition is a matter of legal duty.[13]

With this concept, the charge that the Communist Government of China should not be recognized because it is communistic, totalitarian, dictatorial, brutal, and therefore immoral, according to American, democratic, and Christian standards, cannot be sustained. An extension of the standards of a particular nationality, religion, doctrine, or ideology to the society of nations runs counter to the basic principle of national independence.

But it is said that the behavior of the Communist Government has violated not only particular standards but also universal standards of international law and international morality by ignoring the obligation of China to respect human rights, to refrain from aggression, and to observe treaties. There can be no doubt but that international law permits a state to take appropriate measures (not, according to the

---

[10] Green Hackworth, *Digest of International Law*, vol. 1, pp. 174, 180, 186.

[11] Hersh Lauterpacht, *Letter to the London Times*, Jan. 6, 1950; *Recognition in International Law*, Cambridge, 1947, p. 24; 7th ed., Oppenheim, *International Law*, 1948, vol. 1, p. 122.

[12] *American Journal of International Law*, vol. 18, p. 152 (1924).

[13] Lauterpacht, *Recognition*, p. 24.

Charter, involving the use of armed force) to obtain redress for violations of international law by other states or to indicate disapproval of breaches of international morality. But is nonrecognition of a government an appropriate measure for such purposes?

It is said, on the one hand, that recognition implies that the recognized government will conduct relations under international law and that, therefore, it is idle to recognize a government that repudiates international law. But it is said, on the other hand, that states are bound by international law, that their will to observe international law is to be presumed, and that determination of charges by one state that another has violated international law is only possible if each has a government which the other regards as capable of representing the state so that the issue can be settled by negotiation or arbitration. To refuse recognition of its government on the ground that the state has violated international law or international morality is, therefore, to decide an international issue unilaterally. If I refuse to recognize you because I consider your conduct illegal or immoral, I judge you without listening to your defense, certainly a procedure which is neither legal nor moral.

This argument seems convincing. The existence and scope of obligations of international law and morality are not to be finally decided unilaterally, but only by international procedures, and such procedures are impossible between states that do not reciprocally recognize each other's government.

GENEVA NEGOTIATIONS

It is true that negotiations have been conducted between governments that do not recognize each other, as for example the armistice negotiations at Panmunjom and the Geneva negotiations between U. Alexis Johnson and Wang Peng-nan. What, however, is the meaning of such negotiations? It is clearly assumed that if agreement is reached it will bind not merely the individuals that negotiate, but the states they represent. Thus, the initiation of negotiation is often said to imply, at least tentatively, reciprocal recognition of the representative character of the negotiators and of the governments that instruct them. If the United States asserts that the Panmunjom Armistice binds China, it would appear that it has already recognized the Communist Government as the Government of China. If it merely asserts that it binds the

Communist Government, it would seem to have asserted that that Government represents some sort of international personality.

Charges by a generally recognized government that a government which it refuses to recognize has violated international law, or has failed to negotiate in good faith, or has violated accepted principles of international morality, suffer from their implicit assumption that the parties are unequal. Good faith can only be expected in international relations between states that recognize each other as equals. Furthermore, a state cannot deal effectively with an agent unless it is clear who the principal is and what authority he has given the agent. For that reason, diplomatic practice normally requires an exchange of "full powers" by the negotiators before negotiation begins. By this formality each indicates to the other the scope of his authority. Such procedure is not possible when dealing with an agent of an unrecognized government. The proper practice was followed by the United States in negotiating for peace with Great Britain in 1782. The American negotiators, Franklin, Adams, and Jay, refused to deal with a representative of the British Colonial Office and successfully demanded that a properly accredited representative of the British Foreign Office be sent. Thus, the independence of the United States was recognized, and negotiation proceeded between equal states through agents properly accredited by each.

We must conclude that nonrecognition of a government, if used as an instrument of national policy, constitutes intervention whether it seeks to influence the domestic institutions or policy of another state, or to influence the observance of international obligations by, or the settlement of international disputes with, another state. Recognition and nonrecognition of governments have often been used politically or "constitutively" to create or destroy governments but should, according to principles of international law, be used only judicially or "declaratively" to announce whether a claim to be a government is supported by fact.[14]

The alleged analogy between the present Chinese situation and the German situation before World War II breaks down on analysis. Even

---

[14] Quincy Wright, "Some Thoughts about Recognition," *American Journal of International Law*, July, 1950, vol. 44, pp. 548, 556. Stanley K. Hornbeck, however, writes: "Diplomatic recognition is an expression of policy." *Op. cit.*, Note 4, p. 4. E. M. Borchard considered nonrecognition "a form of intervention" without distinguishing between nonrecognition of *de facto* government and of illegal acquisitions. See Q. Wright, *et al.*, *Legal Problems in the Far Eastern Conflict*, Institute of Pacific Relations, 1941, pp. 119, 161, 175.

though communism is, as Nazism was, hostile to liberal democracy, these two totalitarian systems differ so greatly in ideology, policy, and capability that they must be dealt with by different methods. The Nazi concept of inequality was incapable of expanding widely by propaganda because the overwhelming majority of the world's people were publicly proclaimed by the Nazis to be inferior. Consequently conquest by war was inherent in Nazi doctrine. But the Communist doctrine of the equality of peoples, the competitive coexistence of nations, and the elevation of economic standards is attractive especially to the under-developed peoples. Thus expansion by propaganda and internal revolution is not impossible and has been proclaimed as the Communist method. While Communist governments have in fact utilized subversion, infiltration, and nibbling aggression and may be expected to utilize them in the future if conditions are favorable, these methods do not necessarily involve general war. The Nazis hoped for success by developing superior conventional weapons, tactics, and strategies against the more numerous democracies, even if they failed to keep them divided by diplomatic maneuver, but today all leaders in both the Communist and the free world recognize that the possession of stockpiles of hydrogen bombs would make a general war mutually suicidal. Inapplicable as the analogy is to the general problem of "making the world safe for democracy," it is even less applicable to the limited problem of recognizing the Communist Government of China. Recognition of Hitler's Government was never questioned by the United States, the League of Nations, or any government. Hitler's illegal acts were determined by negotiations, recognitions, and League resolutions after Hitler had had ample opportunity to defend himself through official channels. Nonrecognition was not considered a suitable weapon to use against the Axis governments.

THE STIMSON DOCTRINE

The Stimson Doctrine, which sought to discourage aggression by declaring that the fruits of aggression should not be recognized, raised an issue different from that usually raised by the nonrecognition of revolutionary governments. It concerned breaches of international law through the wrongful seizure of territory by a recognized government or its puppet, not breaches of constitutional law by internal revolution.[15]

---

[15] Q. Wright, *Legal Problems, cit.* note 14, p. 118.

Secretary Stimson asserted that the claim of Japan or its puppet Manchukuo to the Chinese territory of Manchuria should not be unilaterally recognized. Subsequently, the United States took the position that the claim of Mussolini's Italy to Ethiopian territory and the claim of Hitler's Germany to Austria should not be recognized because they were based on aggression contrary to the Kellogg-Briand Pact. The Chiang Government of China sought to invoke this doctrine in the United Nations, asserting that the Communist Government of China was a puppet of the Soviet Union and had been able to occupy the Chinese mainland only because of the aggression of the Soviet Union. The United Nations, however, refused to accept this argument. Although it condemned the Soviet Union for violating treaties with China, it implied that the success of the Communist Government in China was due to the self-determination of the Chinese people rather than to Soviet aggression.[16]

It may be argued that international law, based on the sovereign equality of states and the self-determination of nations, is obsolete and that the shrinking world requires universal moral and legal standards similar to those applied to individuals. The most superficial survey of current opinion and practice and of the distribution of military and political power, suggests, however, that it is premature to read national consciousness and the sovereign state out of existence. The generally recognized principles of international law, of international morality, and of the United Nations Charter create a strong presumption in favor of the recognition of governments which govern with the acquiescence of their peoples and a probability of doing so for an indefinite future.

THE POLITICAL OPPONENTS

(3) The issue raised by politicians turns on the facts of history and reasonable prognostications of the future. The political criticism of the motives and wisdom of American policy-makers in respect to China, during World War II and up to the Communist triumph in 1949, is irrelevant to the present problem except insofar as it provides evidence of whether that triumph was the consequence of Chinese self-determination or of Soviet aggression and whether the government resulting from that triumph is likely to continue to govern China.

Information about Communist China is incomplete, in part because

---

[16] Quincy Wright, "The Chinese Recognition Problem," *op. cit.*, p. 327.

of the embargo on news reporting, rather surprisingly imposed by the United States. A great deal of information is available, however, and it generally supports the position that the Communist Government is the Government of China. The Chiang Government is undoubtedly the Government of Formosa and the Pescadores, but these areas have not been part of China since they were ceded to Japan in 1895. In the Cairo Declaration of 1943, Roosevelt, Churchill, and Chiang agreed that these islands should be returned to China, and Chiang's forces occupied them in 1945 while Chiang was still the unquestioned head of the Chinese Government, but formal change of title awaited the Japanese Peace Treaty. By that instrument, not concluded until 1951, Japan renounced title but without specifying the recipient. This seems to mean, as both the United States and the United Kingdom have subsequently affirmed, that the formal transfer of the islands to China has not yet been effected, although both the Chiang and Mao Governments claim that it has. Neither of these governments was party to the peace treaty though the Chiang Government has subsequently concluded a treaty with Japan. The parties to the Cairo Declaration accepted the principle of self-determination by ratifying the United Nations Charter. Subsequently the Government of China was changed. Since it is doubtful that the Formosan Chinese wish to become part of a Communist-governed China, the Cairo Declaration may be no longer applicable, and the status of Formosa may best be settled by the parties to the Japanese Peace Treaty applying the principle of self-determination by a plebiscite in Formosa.[17] The Peiping Government appears to control all of China except a few small coastal islands in the Straits of Formosa still occupied by Chiang's forces. It is, therefore, a general *de facto* government alone capable of binding China under the principles of international law set forth in the Tinoco arbitration.[18]

Information available on the internal situation of China indicates that the Peiping Government enjoys greater political stability, economic efficiency, and popular approval than any government which China has had for centuries in spite of its use of dictatorial and brutal methods applied internally and of aggression, treaty breaches, and violations of international law externally. This evidence indicates also that it is acting

---

[17] Wright, "Chinese Recognition Problem," *cit.*, p. 332.
[18] Above Note 12. Sec. Dulles has asserted that the U.S. is under no commitment to Chiang in respect to these islands, Quemoy and Matsu. See Dept. of State Bull., April 22, 1957, vol. 36, p. 641.

independently in its domestic and foreign policy, not as a Soviet satellite, although it is in considerable measure dependent on Soviet trade and loans for economic development. A summary of the Chinese situation by A. Doak Barnett presented to the meeting of the American Assembly in November, 1956,[19] concludes:

> First of all, the Peking regime does have effective, in fact unprecedented, control over all of China except for Taiwan and other Nationalist held islands off the China coast. The totalitarian methods by which the Chinese Communists have established this control are repugnant to the United States, but there is no basis for disputing the *de facto* control of the Communist regime in China any more than there is for questioning the *de facto* control of the Communists in Russia. Successful internal revolt against Peking or successful reinvasion by the Nationalists of the mainland are both so improbable that they cannot be considered practical possibilities in planning American policy. Communist China is a reality with which we must deal, even though we do not like it. (p. 160)
>
> Secondly, the strength of Communist China is growing, and the present industrialization program will greatly increase China's independent basis for military power within a relatively few years. With Soviet assistance, Communist China's actual military power has already expanded to the point where China is clearly the strongest country in Asia. (p. 161)
>
> In the competition for influence throughout Asia, Peking's prestige has steadily risen . . . Asian leaders are still divided between those who admire and those who fear Communist China, but there are few who are not strongly affected by China's influence. (p. 162)
>
> American policy is based upon a central fiction. The United States refuses officially to recognize the existence of the Peking regime as the *de facto* government of China, and it continues to support the claims of the Nationalist regime to be the government of all of China. (p. 163)
>
> It may be possible to postpone the problem of recognition a short while because the uneasy truce in Korea has not put a permanent end to the war. But any firm, unyielding position on recognition tends to reduce the area for negotiation, compromise, or maneuver. Probably in the long run, it would be highly desirable to avoid this kind of issue and rely almost automatically upon the objective tests. (p. 163)
>
> It would appear that the offshore island region *is one* in which a tactical withdrawal would minimize the risks of major conflict. (p. 166)
>
> It is only realistic, therefore, to accept the proposition that in the China coast area, the most the United States can hope and work for is stabilization of a new *status quo*, with Taiwan and the Pescadores maintaining their independence under an internationally acceptable local regime. (p. 167)

---

[19] *Cit.* Note 5 above.

This report clearly looks toward the "two Chinas" solution as did the able paper presented by Ernest Gross, former United States Ambassador to the United Nations, on the same occasion. He recognized the importance of an independent Taiwan; the value of a continuous diplomatic channel with Red China rather than the "sporadic behind-the-barn type of negotiation" as at Geneva or through self-appointed friends and self-appointed Communist representatives; and the probability that such negotiations would eventually lead to recognition, though he thought that "at the present time recognition would be premature and unwise." [20]

The formal conclusion of the American Assembly was less realistic, emphasizing the "arrogant action" of the Communists and their obduracy in the Korean, Formosan Straits, and American fliers issues.

> Consequently, it is the consensus of the American Assembly that recognition of Communist China by the United States would not be appropriate or timely. Nevertheless, the policy of non-recognition, justified in the light of existing circumstances, must be continuously reappraised in terms of our national interests. Some participants contend that recognition would be taken as a sign of weakness, would demoralize our Asian allies, and would enhance the position of the Communist regime. Others argue that recognition should not be regarded as implying approval, that it would provide useful contact points, and that it would remove a divisive element within the free world. (p. 226)

THE POSITION OF THE GOVERNMENT

(4) The United States has officially justified nonrecognition on the ground that international law places no limitations on the discretion of states in recognizing new governments and that nonrecognition would serve United States national interests better than recognition. The Executive however has been less rigid than the Congress, as indicated by President Eisenhower's reference to a two-China policy and by Secretary Dulles' commitment before he became Secretary of State to the proposition that "if the Communist government of China in fact proves its ability to govern China without serious domestic resistance, then it too

---

[20] Ernest A. Gross, *Illusions of Our Asian Policy*, Nov. 17, 1956 (Mimeographed, p. 5).

should be admitted to the United Nations." As Secretary of State, however, Mr. Dulles expressed the opinion that the National Government "represents the true aspirations and hopes of the Chinese people." [21] The flexibility of the administration's view is also indicated by its refusal to support a Nationalist invasion of the mainland, by its conduct of negotiations with the Communist Government at Panmunjom and Geneva, and by its favorable attitude toward relaxing the trade embargo in June, 1957.

The Government, however, appears to consider nonrecognition politically expedient at the moment because it contributes to Western strength in the cold war by weakening China directly and the Soviet Union indirectly, and by assuring in Formosa an ally and bases for preventing Communist expansion in Asia.

Are these estimates of the situation valid? Recognition might tend to decrease the solidarity of Peking and Moscow, to increase the solidarity of the United States and the United Kingdom, to increase goodwill for the United States in India and Japan, to develop commercial and cultural relations and, if recognition were followed by insistence on Chiang's withdrawal from the coastal islands, to decrease the danger of involvement in war on account of those islands, always recognized as part of the mainland. These advantages might more than compensate for any decrease in the authority of the Chiang Government and any increase in the prestige and attractiveness to overseas Chinese which Communist China might gain through recognition.

However, the political issues should probably be argued on broader grounds than victory in cold war. That conception is in fact self-contradictory. The bi-polarization of the world and the arms race, flowing from the effort of both Moscow and Washington to gain a superior power position which might be called "cold war victory," would probably result in atomic war and mutual destruction. While cold war may have been a suitable policy in the past, the conditions which made it so no longer exist. Both the policy and the capability of the Soviet Union have radically changed since the death of Stalin and the Soviet acquisition of the hydrogen bomb. Today the Soviet Union seems to fear atomic war and to seek competitive coexistence.

---

[21] John Foster Dulles, *War or Peace*, New York, Macmillan, 1950, p. 190; Senate Subcommittee Hearings on *Review of the United Nations Charter*, 83rd Cong., 3rd Sess., Pt. 1, p. 20.

A BETTER WORLD ENVIRONMENT

The United States should formulate its policy in such a way as to promote national security and progress through the development of a suitable world environment. Such an environment requires a more stable balance of power by stopping the tendency toward bi-polarization and establishing a number of major centers of power. This might be accomplished by simultaneous decentralization of the two great power blocs. A trend in this direction has in fact been manifested by the growing influence of national communism in both the European satellites and in China and by the development of policies more independent of Washington by the United Kingdom and the rest of the Commonwealth and by France and other Western European countries. The development of neutralism in India, the Middle East, Austria, and perhaps Germany and Scandinavia is also away from bi-polarity. Thus a system of checks and balances, both within and among the great ideological blocs in the world, seems both possible and desirable and might well be encouraged.

A suitable environment also requires a firmer commitment by all states to international law based on the sovereign equality and peaceful coexistence of states of diverse cultures and conditions, on the self-determination of genuine nationalities capable of self-government, on respect for human rights and fundamental freedoms for all people, on the abandonment of armed intervention as an instrument of national policy, and on mutual respect for the independence of states on matters of domestic jurisdiction. These principles, developed from traditional international law, stated in the United Nations Charter, asserted by the five principles of Bandung, and implicit in the principles accepted by the Summit Conference of 1955, are formally binding on all states but are not yet established in the policy of governments and the cultures of peoples.

A suitable environment also requires a more effective United Nations for preventing aggression, adjusting international conflicts, promoting international cooperation, and affirming international law. To serve this function the United Nations should be universal. China, Germany, Korea, Vietnam, and Switzerland, together constituting a quarter of the world's population, should be represented, and each member should by government policy, national law, and public opinion more clearly identify its national interest with the maintenance of the principles of the Charter.

Recognition of Communist China by the United States and its acceptance as the Government of China by the United Nations would probably contribute to improving the world environment in all of these respects and would, therefore, serve the ultimate goals of United States policy. It would increase China's commercial and cultural relations outside the Soviet orbit and would augment its independent position, making it more capable of checking the Soviet Union. Such recognition would affirm the principles of international law respecting the self-determination of states in form of government, economy, and ideology. It would probably strengthen the United Nations by making it more genuinely representative of world opinion and would open the way to settlement, through bi-lateral negotiations and United Nations mediation, of the problems of Korea, Vietnam, and Formosa, which have kept the Far East on the threshold of war. While none of these salutary results would be certain and would in any case require careful diplomacy and discussion after recognition, it seems likely that stability and peace would be served better by bringing the most populous state of the world and the greatest power of Asia into normal relations with the United States, the United Nations, and the world community than by treating it as an outcast.

China and the United Nations*

by Reinhold Niebuhr

Our opposition to the entrance of China into the United Nations is the consequence of a fiction, of which we have been prisoners as a nation for decades. That fiction is that the Communists conquered in China only because we did not give the Nationalists sufficient support. One of the many illusions of this fiction is that Chiang's army could still conquer China if we gave them full support now. But our military leaders know this to be a fiction, and the Joint Chiefs of Staff under Eisen-

---

* From the *Journal of International Affairs* (Columbia University), Vol. XI, No. 2 (1957), pp. 187-189. Copyright 1957 by the Board of Editors of the *Journal of International Affairs*. Reprinted by permission.

hower, as well as under Truman, have vetoed any such venture. Our treaty with the Nationalists on Formosa provides, in fact, that they cannot invade the mainland without our consent. It is not likely that we will ever give it. Meanwhile, Chiang has resorted to recruiting young conscripts for his aging army from the Formosan population, which means that his army would not even be going "home" but away from home in the event of an invasion. In any case, such an invasion would cost a tremendous price of American treasure and possibly of American blood. As the years slip by, it becomes more and more improbable.

We recognize the improbability as much as the other nations in the United Nations. But we dare not tell our people that they are the victims of a fiction, and the Republican party must deal with men who still believe the fiction. Therefore, we ask each year for a postponement of the issue. We know that we would be defeated if the issue ever came to a vote. Members of the staff of the State Department, who know the truth about these realities, can be confirmed by the Senate only if they do not confess their convictions too openly and if they pretend to have an "open mind" on the question.

Our European allies think that we are slightly daft on this problem, but they also know that we are very powerful. They, therefore, connive in the perpetual postponement of the question. It is a sorry situation for the world's most powerful democracy. Sooner or later we will be forced to accept the Communist conquest of China as an ineluctable fact and admit Communist China to the United Nations. The United Nations is not a club for democratic or for "good" nations. It is supposed to have as many nations in its membership as are willing to join. Nor can we hope to "convert" China by admitting her. The Chinese are probably more fanatic Communists than the Russians. They are "true believers" in the Communist dogma. We cannot hope to wean Communist China from her alliance with Russia though there was a time when that was at least a possibility, though never a probability. There will, of course, be a possibility of exploiting the differences between the two Communist giants if China is admitted. But the hope of doing this could not be the chief reason for her admission. The chief reason is that we must not prolong the fiction that the pathetic government on Formosa is, in fact, the government of the great Chinese nation. It is an utterly discredited outfit which has no chance of gaining either political or military victories.

A DEFIANCE OF OBVIOUS HISTORY

If we really bowed to the inevitable and ceased our defiance of obvious history, our allies would probably help us to make the adjustments in the United Nations Charter, without which the step would be unthinkable. One hazard to the step is the permament seat which China has on the Security Council. This is an arrangement which we optimistically forced on our allies at San Francisco. We thought that China would become a great power center in the postwar world. Ironically enough, Communist China more nearly conforms to this hope than Chiang's China would ever have done. But China must not have a permanent seat on the Security Council. Perhaps it should simply be stipulated that an Asian nation must have such a seat. The obstacle is, in short, not insuperable.

The other difficulty concerns Formosa, or Taiwan, as the Chinese insist upon calling the island, thereby drawing attention to its Chinese character before the long Japanese occupation. For many reasons, some of them having to do with American politics and some with Asian politics, we cannot sacrifice the Formosans to the Communists. This does not mean that the Formosans are enamored of Chiang's Government. After all, it descended upon them. While it has engaged in moderate land reform it has hardly commended itself to the native population as "democratic" or even as a tolerable government. Ideally, the Formosans ought to be free to choose their own government. But in any event, the admission of Communist China would make the recognition of two Chinas inevitable, and one of the prices which we must exact is the promise of Communist China that she will accept the other China's sovereignty. We cannot count on a faithful keeping of covenants from Communist China, but the promise must nevertheless be exacted if only for the record.

Many students have suggested that Formosa be defined as a trusteeship territory under the United Nations. But this solution is unrealistic. It assumes that the United Nations is a kind of supergovernment. It is not that; and we cannot forget that Russia always retains a veto power. The United Nations cannot administer territories impartially. It would be much simpler if we continued our protection of Formosa, as in the past. We might even prompt some wholesome reforms in the government of the island. In any event, the recognition of two Chinas is not a very high hurdle to take in our adjustment to the political realities in Asia. We cannot support the fiction, which even we no longer believe, indefinitely.

The recognition of China presents fewer difficulties than the admission into the U.N. It has been a settled policy of our nation, as well as other nations, to recognize a government which has proved that it is in effective control of its nation. If we were to establish moral and political criteria of recognition, many of the South American governments would certainly not deserve recognition, not to speak of some rather obvious dictatorships in other parts of the world. The only other reason for not recognizing China is that it will interfere with our embargo on trade with China, but I think that Japan ought to be allowed to trade with China because that is her natural market. Nonrecognition will certainly not solve any of the basic problems which we face in such a fanatical movement as Chinese communism.

FOR FURTHER READING:

The American Assembly, *The United States and the Far East* (New York: Graduate School of Business, Columbia University, 1955).

Howard L. Boorman, Alexander Eckstein, Philip E. Mosely, and Benjamin Schwartz, *Moscow-Peking Axis: Strengths and Strains* (New York: Harper and Brothers, 1957).

Benjamin H. Brown and Fred Greene, *Chinese Representation: A Case Study in United Nations Political Affairs* (New York: Woodrow Wilson Foundation, 1955).

John King Fairbank, *The United States and China* (Cambridge: Harvard University Press, 2nd ed., 1958).

Herbert Feis, *The China Tangle: The American Effort in China from Pearl Harbor to the Marshall Mission* (Princeton: Princeton University Press, 1953).

Herrymon Maurer, *Collision of East and West* (Chicago: Henry Regnery, 1951).

Edwin O. Rieschauer, *Wanted: An Asian Policy* (New York: Alfred A. Knopf, 1955).

W. W. Rostow with Richard W. Hatch, *An American Policy in Asia* (Cambridge: Harvard University Press, 1955).

Robert Strausz-Hupé, Alvin J. Cotrell, and James E. Daugherty (eds.), *American-Asian Tensions* (New York: Frederick A. Praeger, 1956).

Li Thian-hok, "The China Impasse: A Formosan View," *Foreign Affairs*, Vol. XXXVI, No. 3 (April, 1958), pp. 437-448.

Richard L. Walker, *The Continuing Struggle: Communist China and the Free World* (New York: Athene Press, 1958).

Chapter XI

COLONIALISM

One of the most contentious issues facing the United States in the geographically and politically in-between Asian-African world is that of colonialism. Although the remaining dependent territories are mainly in Africa, real and imagined colonial issues rouse intense passions in the newly independent states of South and Southeast Asia and of the Middle East as well as in the subject peoples themselves. The newly independent states are constantly suspicious that attempts may be made to reëstablish colonial relationships, and they are firmly convinced, as they announced in the final communique from the Bandung Conference in 1955, "that colonialism in all its manifestations is an evil which should speedily be brought to an end." In their attack on colonialism, the Asian and African states are frequently joined by those of Latin America. Traditionally the United States has shared the emotional bias against colonialism, so much so that our own colonies were never called that, and the imperialists among us could never too openly express their ambitions. American diplomatists have been among the most articulate exponents of national self-determination. Woodrow Wilson, for one, roused strong expectations and gave voice to the ardent hopes of many with his eloquent pleas for self-determination during the First World War. Our record in the Philippines, promising and granting independence, added concrete accomplishment to these pronouncements. Both earned the United States a reservoir of good will among anti-colonialists everywhere. But in recent years colonial problems have confronted the United States with a series of dilemmas

492

which could not easily be resolved. The reservoir of good will has been severely drained, and colonial problems have complicated our relations in other parts of the world.

Anti-colonial pressures have increased since the end of the Second World War. The political collapse of Europe and the growth of nationalism unleashed new forces which sought to hasten the liquidation of colonialism. Communist propaganda gave added impetus to these forces and exploited the inherent conflicts. At the same time the United States itself assumed new colonial commitments in the Strategic Trust Territory of the Pacific Islands. And our alliances brought us into a new, closer relationship with European colonial powers, who, even when they were willing to grant independence to their territories, did not necessarily agree with the pace demanded by the anti colonialists. Supporting the European states in colonial disputes alienates the Asian-African group, something the United States can ill afford—particularly in view of the Soviet attempts to woo these countries. The contrary position alienates the Europeans and risks weakening our alliance structure. For the United States to abstain is obnoxious to both sides. The United Nations has provided a forum for the exponents of national self-determination, and a particularly potent one because of their numerical strength. As United Nations discussions usually conclude with the passage of one or more resolutions, the United States repeatedly has been forced to take clear stands with the inevitable discomforting effects. But the United Nations also provides opportunities for the solution of colonial conflicts, which would exist even without the U.N. United States policy has generally been to assume a middle role with regard to problems of colonialism, abstaining at times and at others favoring one side and then the other. National security considerations have been uppermost, though vestiges of our anti-colonial bias are apparent. Whether other policies would be more successful is an open question.

This chapter explores the dilemmas caused by colonial problems and the major alternative policies available to the United States. The first selection, by Philip C. Jessup, Hamilton Fish Professor of International Law and Diplomacy at Columbia University and sometime United States Representative in the United Nations, describes the evolution of the concept of national self-determination, the dilemmas this doctrine currently poses for the United States, and the role of the United Nations in contemporary colonial disputes. Mr. Jessup's analysis of the implications of national self-determination is helpful: he considers it a doctrine of perfection, to which in the "real world" limits must be set. Despite his full awareness of the many difficulties involved, Mr. Jessup nevertheless argues that the United States should adopt a more forthright anti-colonial position, both inside and outside the United Nations.

Philip W. Bell, a member of the Economics Department at the University of California (Berkeley), develops a contrary position in the second selection. He maintains that the United States should give greater support to the colonial powers. He thinks that the United States interests in political stability, strategic bases, and access to vital raw materials will best be protected if the colonial powers continue to control their dependent territories and if we assist them in this. He points to the interdependence of colonial problems and the consequent need for a consistent policy. His description of the present status of colonialism provides a useful base for any analysis of this problem.

The final selection, by William Henderson, Associate Executive Director of the Council on Foreign Relations, takes an even stronger stand than Mr. Jessup for support of the anti-colonial position. His analysis deals not only with the problems involved in gaining independence, but also with those of the post-colonial era. He indicates the opportunities the United Nations affords for easing colonial tensions and the close connection between colonial problems and those of economic development.

Regardless of the position one adopts, no one can deny the strength of nationalism in the contemporary world. Coming to grips with the concrete manifestations of nationalism in colonial problems is one of the major tasks confronting the United States.

Self-Determination Today in Principle and in Practice*

by Philip C. Jessup

It is sometimes thought that the objective of United States foreign policy is to achieve popularity among all countries of the world—at least those outside the Communist bloc. This is an objective impossible of attainment and it is doubtful if responsible officials have ever thought in those terms. But it may be practicable to have a foreign policy which will ensure that the United States is respected. One of the problems which presents a severe test for such a policy is the so-called "colonial question" and the accompanying doctrine of self-determination.

It is the common assumption that Americans are practical people. De Tocqueville remarked: "Scarcely any one in the United States devotes himself to the essentially theoretical and abstract portion of human knowledge." Although this generalization is not true today, De Tocqueville as usual put his finger on an American characteristic.

Some say this means that we are essentially materialistic. In Latin America our neighbors long thought this was true. It is the same elsewhere. Last May I had the privilege of meeting in Cairo a truly great man, the blind Egyptian scholar, Taha Hussein. "We know your great material progress in America," he said, "but there are few Egyptians who can even name your leading poets, essayists, novelists, or artists, although their French and English counterparts are well known." Only recently have we learned that it is just as important to export our intangibles as our tangibles—our culture as well as our machines.

Our political philosophers are better known abroad. A South Asian is apt to tell you that the only trouble with the political philosophy of Jefferson, Lincoln, Wilson, and Franklin Roosevelt is that the United States no longer adheres to it. He can cite examples to prove his point, but generally speaking he is, I think, mistaken about the general philosophy of contemporary America. He may also forget the problem of the inevitable dilemmas. Lincoln, for instance, believed in freedom for the slaves, but not for the Confederacy.

It is still true that in some American groups a person who attaches more value to ideas than to things is dismissed by a wave of the cigar

* From The Virginia Quarterly Review, Vol. XXXIII, No. 2 (Spring 1957), pp. 174-188. Reprinted by permission of The Virginia Quarterly Review and Philip C. Jessup.

over the whiskey and soda, as a dreamer, an egghead, or just a professor. "Practical" Americans were astonished that Woodrow Wilson, scholar, professor, idealist, could succeed in achieving the governorship of New Jersey and the Presidency of the United States. They were surprised that his Administration could produce such practical measures as the Federal Reserve System, the Federal Trade Commission, and the graduated income tax. The same sort of people took satisfaction in the defeat of what they considered Wilson's impractical program for world peace. They did not deny that peace was desirable and they ignored the fact that no one else had alternative "practical" plans for achieving it.

Both materialists and idealists are still searching for the magic formula for peace. The search will never end because peace is a problem of human nature which is never static. The fallacy is in searching for a *single* formula. As each problem is solved, another arises to plague us, and this must be solved in its turn. The process requires patience, wisdom, courage, ingenuity, and ideals. No solution is sound which is reached in an *ad hoc* vacuum; it must be inspired by a philosophy based on integrity. Yet while it meets each new problem with new solutions, it must also be consistent.

Charles Seymour has written that "The recurrent leitmotif of Wilson's policy lay in his ideal of freedom, whether of the individual or the national group." Wilson said in his "Constitutional Government" that "liberty belongs to the individual or it does not exist." But, as Mr. Seymour also points out, Wilson himself did not find it easy to apply this principle to every factual situation.

In his address before the League to Enforce Peace in May, 1916, President Wilson described as the first of certain fundamental things which we Americans believe, "that every people has a right to choose the sovereignty under which they shall live." This is, in essence, the principle of self-determination. But, notes Seymour, at the Paris Peace Conference this principle was "an untrustworthy guide, incapable of universal application. How was Wilson to decide the validity of conflicting aspirations? Linguistic statistics often proved as unreliable a criterion as the rhetoric of partisan leaders. In various areas he found the principle of self-determination to be in clear conflict with other Wilsonian doctrines. It would seem to justify the separation of the German Sudetenland from Bohemia, an obvious disaster to the Czechoslovak state, itself founded upon the principle of self-determination."

A distinguished British diplomat and felicitous writer, Harold Nicolson, has appraised the pronouncements of Woodrow Wilson in his Fourteen Points and subsequent statements. Nicolson does not agree with many of them as a practical guide for a nation's diplomacy but he concedes that they "constitute a magnificent gospel." "The misfortune was," he writes, "that the public imagined that what was intended as a doctrine of perfectibility was in fact a statement of American intentions."

E. H. Carr has pointed out that Wilson sometimes confused the subjective right of self-determination with the objective fact of nationality; he assumed that "states" and "nations" would coincide, "that states should be constituted on a national basis and that nations ought to form states."

It was the problems of the tangled intermixed peoples of Europe that Wilson had chiefly in mind in advocating self-determination, although the same basic ideal of freedom underlay also his advocacy of the new régime for colonial areas which were to be placed under mandates supervised by the League of Nations. There can be no regional or geographic limits to the ideal of freedom, whatever other boundaries may be fixed by the practical impossibilities of achieving omniscience and omnipotence.

Today, the right of self-determination for the peoples of Eastern Europe is still an issue—a burning issue. The people of Poland have just asserted it with apparently some success. Hungarians are giving their lives for it. The Soviets try to crush it under the treads of tanks. Wilson believed an international organization was needed to transform the doctrine of self-determination into political reality. The United Nations, Woodrow Wilson's grandchild, is trying to play the rôle in which he, in effect, cast it. Like Wilson, the U.N. accepts "the fact of nationalism and the need for internationalism."

What is the situation elsewhere in the world? It is not necessary to go through the whole catalogue of historical events since the end of the war, such as the independence of the Philippines, of Syria and Lebanon, of Libya, Tunis, and Morocco, of India, Burma, and other former parts of the British Empire. Many new states have been born and are now independent members of the United Nations or soon will be. But if we go back to the war days, we will find that Franklin Roosevelt was as enthusiastic about—and as baffled by—the ideal of self-determination as was Woodrow Wilson.

Cordell Hull wrote in his memoirs: "Our prime difficulty generally with regard to Asiatic colonial possessions, of course, was to induce the colonial powers—principally Britain, France and The Netherlands—to adopt our ideas with regard to dependent peoples. . . . But we could not press them too far with regard to the Southwest Pacific in view of the fact that we were seeking the closest possible co-operation with them in Europe. We could not alienate them in the Orient and expect to work with them in Europe."

This is the dilemma which still faces the United States. Not only do we need to work with the Western European countries, but they are old friends of ours with whom we have much in common. On the other hand, we have a deep-rooted feeling of sympathy with any people which is aspiring to freedom. In the 1820's when the Spanish-American colonies revolted, the United States was first to recognize their independence but in those days we were not threatened by a Soviet Union and we stood aloof from European alliances. The problem is easier for a small power, as we then were. Small powers can still enjoy the luxury of a particularistic viewpoint. Now we are a very great power and must take a global view. When two of our friends are at odds, each one expects us to side wholly with him. He cannot see any justice in the other country's point of view and an impartial attitude on our part seems like desertion or active opposition. It is the usual fate of the mediator. We have to face this difficulty constantly in the usual course of diplomatic relations and in the United Nations.

This issue today is sharply drawn. The voice of France and England in denouncing the brutal suppression of self-determination for the Hungarians was not a clarion call but a muted whisper, because their actions in Egypt, Algeria, and Cyprus speak louder than their words. Of course, in the present Egyptian case much more than self-determination is involved, but differing views on self-determination are involved in the problem. The cynical hypocrisy of the Soviets may be taken for granted, but it is a tragedy—for which we also are not without blame—that in the U.N. we must vote one day with the Soviets against France and England and the next day vote with them against the Soviets.

As Dean Herbert Nicholas of New College, Oxford, points out, there are always difficulties in applying the principle of self-determination but the difficulty of application does not still the insistent demand for it. All our experience, he writes, confirms the rightness of Wilson's conviction "that there is no alternative to conceding it." In some cases, if one concedes the principle today, it may be feasible to defer the realization until tomorrow.

Yet the demand for self-determination is often unreasoning and illogical. Tito, speaking as an independent Communist, is reported to have said recently in regard to Hungary: "Look how a people with naked hands, badly armed, shows the strongest resistance if before it there is one goal—to free itself and to be independent. It is no longer interested in what kind of independence this will be, whether there will be a restoration of the bourgeois and a reactionary system in the country or whether it will be truly independent."

In the United Nations the problem of self-determination comes up in two ways. First, there are the cases of clearly identified political communities and, secondly, there are cases of minority groups. In the first category, let us take Indonesia as an example. Indonesia was a Dutch colony. As a result of the war, the rising tide of nationalism, and general historical development, the Indonesians wished to be free. Blood was spilled. The problem came before the United Nations Security Council. The United States finally threw the weight of its influence in favor of the independence of Indonesia. Many of our Dutch friends were very bitter—and indeed still are. They are not bitter because they are bad people but because they think that we were wrong and that their side was just. They felt they had been doing a good conscientious job in Indonesia and should have been allowed to continue without interference, gradually bringing the Indonesians to self-government and independence. I think they were wrong; the tides of history were too strong to swim against. As Wilson said, to try to stop a revolutionary movement by armies in the field is like trying to stop the tides of the sea with a broom. But I respect the sincerity of the position of many Netherlanders.

Take the cases of Tunisia and Morocco in North Africa. When the Moroccan case first came before the United Nations, the United States supported France in keeping this item off the agenda. As the years went by, after 1948, the American position followed generally a middle course. France, from a position of absolute and indeed violent opposition, moved forward with the negotiations which have now led to the inclusion of Tunis and Morocco among the independent states of the world, members of the United Nations. Algeria remains a scene of violence and bloodshed, and the French effort to distinguish the Algerian from the Moroccan and Tunisian cases does not carry conviction, despite the very real historical and factual differences.

The case of the Sudan was interesting. The Sudan was under the condominium of Great Britain and Egypt. The Sudan desired its independence. Undoubtedly some of the old-timers in the British service believed it was in the best interests of the Sudan as well as of Great Britain that British administration should continue. It is equally clear that some Egyptians were eager to incorporate the Sudan in a greater Egypt. In a quiet way, the United States supported the negotiations for Sudanese independence. When the Sudan became free, the United States took the initiative in moving its admission to the United Nations.

In parts of Africa south of the Sahara there is notable progress with the independence of the Gold Coast as the new state of Ghana and the rapid progression in the same direction of Nigeria and British Togoland. For other areas in Africa independence, or even local self-government, seems to lie rather far ahead. There is always the problem of applying the principle, the problem of timing.

It is easy for us to say that any people who want to be free should be free tomorrow. In general this is the position taken by many representatives of countries of Asia, Africa, and the Arab world, and also of Latin America. But it was interesting to see how responsibility tempered this rather exuberant attitude. The responsibility fell alike on the so-called colonial powers and on the new states and other perennial champions of self-determination, when the General Assembly of the United Nations was given the task of deciding on the future of the former Italian colonies in North Africa. The Assembly was given this unique power by the Italian Peace Treaty. There were three former colonies to be disposed of: Libya, Eritrea, and Somaliland. When the General Assembly debates began in 1947, there was an insistent demand that immediate independence be adopted as the solution for all three areas. But discussion under a sense of responsibility produced a different result. In regard to Libya it was agreed that there should be immediate independence (after a two-year interval) and Libya is now a sovereign state. In regard to Eritrea, it was apparent that if you applied the doctrine of self-determination, part of the population which was Coptic Christian would like to join with Ethiopia and another part which was Moslem, would like to join with the Sudan or Egypt. There was at first a tendency in some quarters to insist that all of Eritrea should want to be and therefore must be a new and separate state, on the principle of the nurse in the Punch cartoon who is yanking a wailing child through the park saying "I brought you 'ere to be 'appy and 'appy you'll be." It was eventually agreed that Eritrea should be federated with Ethiopia, and this has been done, and done satisfactorily. In the case of Somaliland, it was agreed that the Somalis were not yet ready for independence and again all agreed that independence should be postponed for ten years and that meanwhile Somaliland should be under a United Nations Trusteeship. Bear in mind that these solutions were not dictated by the Great Powers. They were hammered out in long and generally amicable discussions and debates and were eventually accepted by the whole General Assembly.

In the second group of cases, how can one tell whether a people or minority group which demands independence should be given it and given it now? "*Every people*," said Wilson, "has a right to choose the sovereignty under which they shall live." But how do you identify a "people"? The Nagas are a rather primitive people in Assam. Some of them are pagan headhunters but others are advanced and formed a Federated Naga Government which organized an army of several thousand men fighting for their independence. Indian troops were sent to suppress them in what Indian officials described as "just a police operation against a band of terrorists." Yet no one was more outraged than the Indians when the Dutch resorted to what they called a "police action" against the Indonesians. The Indian Government is clear that the Nagas should not and will not have independence. Quite possibly Mr. Nehru's Government is right. The Khurds in Iraq and Iran have long had an independence movement, sometimes no doubt stimulated by outsiders (as many independence movements are). The Iranian and Iraqui governments, so far as I know, have never given serious thought even to the possibility of granting this Khurdish demand. There is an active group purporting to speak for the South Molluccas, who demand their independence from Indonesia, but the Government of Indonesia dismisses the demand as wholly unreal and unrepresentative.

Surely it is not enough to find that some group wants or clamors for independence. There is more to every case than that. In many instances in Africa it seems to be true that there are wide differences of opinion among various tribal chiefs and indigenous groups about their future. Some may want a separate state, some may want federation with another group, some may want to be part of the British Commonwealth, some may want progressive development with European help. The U.N.

General Assembly at this session considered the case of French Togoland, where a referendum not under U.N. auspices resulted in a majority
vote for the termination of the French trusteeship and membership in
the French Union; the Assembly refused to approve. The Assembly also
dealt with British Togoland where a U.N. supervised plebiscite favored
union with the independent Gold Coast; the Assembly approved.

In the United Nations, as I have suggested, the question of self-
determination comes up in various aspects, again illustrating the difference between situations where a well-identified community demands
independence and where a minority group seeks the same end. The
trouble is that representatives in the United Nations have not always
kept this distinction in mind.

In cases like Indonesia, Tunis, and Morocco, the matter has been
discussed in the Security Council or in the Political Committee of the
General Assembly. Where the issue of self-determination is raised in
regard to non-selfgoverning territories like Puerto Rico or Greenland, it
is debated in the Assembly's Fourth Committee, which also considers
the administration of trust territories. But concurrently self-determination as a general principle is considered by the Human Rights Commission, which has been trying to draft an appropriate statement to include
in a general convention on human rights. It is at this last point that it
seems hard for government representatives to see that if you are talking
about a general problem of human rights you can't distinguish between
the position of people in a colony like the Belgian Congo and, let us
say, the Nagas in India, the Khurds in Iran, or the Indians in the
Amazon valley.

Wilson realistically saw that the right of self-determination is something which people can only be denied if you are going to deny them all
other human rights as well. In the U.N. Human Rights Commission,
the majority has accepted this view and has included self-determination
as a human right. In the last few years the United States, apparently
frightened by the long shadow of the Bricker Amendment, has held
back and argued that self-determination is not a human right but a
political principle. We rely too much on the position of Harold Nicolson that it is a doctrine of perfectibility rather than a statement of
American intentions. In this session of the General Assembly we do not
appear as obviously two-faced as the British and French, but there is no
reason to suppose, as these lines are written, that we shall be wholly
consistent. In the First (Political) Committee, we will be the champion

of self-determination for Hungary. Will we be as forthright when the questions of Cyprus and Algeria are reached? Will our delegate in the Fourth Committee dealing with trusteeships and non-selfgoverning territories be able under his instructions to take an unequivocal position? What stand will the United States delegate take in the Third Committee (Social Questions) when that Committee considers the problem of self-determination as presented in the report of the Economic and Social Council on the proposals of the Human Rights Commission?

There is still another aspect to the problem of self-determination in the world today which is illustrated by the case of Egypt. It is linked to the idea of sovereignty. As often invoked, it means the right to do as one pleases. It refers to freedom from all external influences and pressures after independence has been attained. It is a natural reaction of newly born states, which feel a sense of frustration when they find that they have gained their independence but do not have the means of making it as enjoyable as they had anticipated in their dreams. A people which is neither literate nor politically sophisticated is apt to think of independence as a utopia in which they will be free from all governmental restrictions. When they become independent, they may be outraged at the idea that their own government still insists on collecting taxes, which they had thought of merely as one of the evils of colonial rule. They want help but without any strings attached and are apt to regard a requirement of interest on an international loan as a string or even a slave chain. They find it hard to realize that in the modern world independence and interdependence are inseparable. Woodrow Wilson's inability to take the United States into the League of Nations was in part due to the fact that the American people had not then learned the lesson of interdependence. As Dean Nicholas says, Wilson was both "the apostle of self-determination and the prophet of internationalism."

Interdependence is a political reality. It is also descriptive of the international legal situation. Every state in the world has treaty relations with other states. Every treaty is a limitation on freedom, on sovereignty. The sovereign freedom of the United States to do as it pleases is limited by hundreds of treaties. In the Suez Canal controversy, Egypt insists upon its sovereignty but admits freely that it is bound by the Suez Canal Convention of 1888, which limits its freedom of action in regard to the Canal. We are free men and women but our freedom is regulated and restricted by law because we and our fellow citizens are interdependent. Although our world community is politically under-developed, the United States and every other free state which is a member of that community is under limitations imposed by law. There are law-breaking citizens and law-breaking states but responsible statesmen do not proclaim that their countries are above the law.

Like almost any great concept, the idea of self-determination based on freedom can be abused and distorted. Professor Hans Morgenthau has cited a striking example:

> It was by a stroke of propagandistic genius that Hitler hit upon the principle of national self-determination in order to disguise and justify his policies of territorial expansion. The German minorities of Czechoslovakia and Poland, under the banner of national self-determination, were now to play the same rôle in undermining the national existence of Czech-oslovakia and Poland which the Czech, Slovak, and Polish nationalities, under the same ideological banner, had played in undermining the national existence of the Austrian-Hungarian Empire. With their own ideological weapon turned against them, the benefactors of the status quo of Versailles had no ideology, except the one of law and order, with which to defend that status quo. Thus Austria and Czechoslovakia were surrendered, and Poland was exposed to mortal danger. After the settlement of Munich granted the German demands with regard to Czechoslovakia, the London Times, making the German ideology its own, declared: "Self-determination, the professed principle of the Treaty of Versailles, has been invoked by Herr Hitler against its written text, and his appeal has been allowed."

Arab leaders—and I do not suggest they are comparable to Hitler—have a perfect right to dream of a self-determination of Arab peoples which will unite them all in a great Arab federation stretching from the Atlantic to the Persian Gulf. But in doing so they may deny the right of self-determination to more than a million French residents in Algeria and perhaps to Jewish and Berber minorities in Morocco. If, for purposes of illustration, one were to assume that Libya preferred to remain a separate independent state and not be part of an Arab federation, it would not be without historical precedent if its Arab neighbors forced it to be happy in their way instead of in its own way.

The Greeks on Cyprus invoke the right of self-determination in struggling for union with Greece, but the smaller Turkish population of that island invokes the same right in opposing the Greek proposal.

To an American it seems natural and easy to say that all such problems should be decided by majority vote. We have a representative form

of government and have just passed through one of our periodic sub-
missions to the decision of the majority. It by no means follows that the
system so well adapted to the American scene is equally well adapted to
a country where conditions are very different, for example let us say in
parts of central Africa.

Whether we like it or not, the fact clearly is that self-determination
is still a "doctrine of perfectibility" and cannot function like an IBM
machine which automatically turns out the answers. I think American
Governments (irrespective of the Administration in office) realize this.
I think that representatives of some other governments are not quite
willing to admit it.

There is a story of the janitor of a scientific laboratory who asked
two researchers what they were working on. "We are trying to find a
universal solvent," one of them replied. "What's a universal solvent?"
asked the janitor. "Why," said the scientist, "it is something which will
dissolve everything else." The janitor thought a moment and then
asked: "After you find it, what are you going to keep it in?"

If self-determination is a universal solvent for the world's political ills,
there is only one possible container in which it can be kept. That container is the United Nations. But it must be a United Nations in which
people trust and which is given appropriate powers. The experiment
with the Italian colonies in North Africa was a success. The League of
Nations had considerable success in the administration of some of the
European minorities after World War I. But these are exceptional cases.

We are still on the threshold of international organization. The
European Coal and Steel Community is a brave venture into the further
realm of supernational institutions for which the world as a whole is not
yet ready. But progress is being made. The United Nations Emergency
Force at the Suez Canal marks another milestone.

The General Assembly contains representatives of many new members, some of them new states and some old states. This is a time when
much can be done if ideals are used as ideals and not as slogans, and
if each actual problem is faced with a sense of responsibility. It is
necessary to make a success of the marriage of the practical and the
ideal. Difficult as this may be, it can be done without hypocrisy.

It would be stupid and irresponsible for the United States to try to
curry favor with the Arab-Asian bloc by supporting every demand for
the immediate independence of all peoples who are not now self-
governing. It would be insincere and domestically unacceptable to give

unquestioning support to the resistance to U.N. consideration of the (often understandably) irritated powers now responsible for administering such peoples. In the long run it would be helpful to such peoples and advantageous to ourselves if we would base our policy on these three points:

1. A public declaration describing our adherence to the Wilsonian concept of self-determination but insisting that we will in every specific case reach and explain openly our own conclusion on timing.

2. Advocacy and support of a plan for providing United Nations guidance and support to new nations as they emerge into independence.

3. Unpublicized talks with each of the administering powers on the one hand and with each of the persistent champions of independence on the other, explaining that from time to time, and from case to case we may well disagree, but that we hope our governments can co-operate in cushioning the hostile clamor of public opinion in the interest of long-range cooperation between us.

Such a policy, if consistently pursued, would certainly not make the United States universally popular, but it might well make us respected.

Colonialism as a Problem in American Foreign Policy*

by Philip W. Bell **

[I]

Colonialism has been a sore spot in the handling of American foreign policy in the post-World War II period largely because of ambivalent forces, domestic and foreign, which have been tugging at the United States.[1] At the heart of the colonial problem which has faced this

* From World Politics, Vol. V, No. 1 (October 1952), pp. 86-109. Reprinted by permission of World Politics.

** The author is heavily indebted to George F. Kennan for much stimulation and guidance in the preparation of this paper. The ideas expressed and conclusions reached are, of course, entirely the responsibility of the author. Professors Jacob Viner and Percy Corbett and Mrs. Annette Baker Fox read the manuscript and offered helpful suggestions on the clarification of certain points.

[1] The term "colonialism" in this paper is used to describe the relationship between metropolitan countries and non-contiguous territories which are avowedly dependent politically upon them. It explicitly excludes, therefore, certain types of dependence which might be classified as "colonialism" in a broader use of the term: (1) minority, or even majority, groups under political domination of others within the

country is the central issue of eventual political status for colonial territories. On this question United States policy has traditionally been and
continues to be one of condemnation of colonialism and in favor of
independence for colonial peoples, with certain reservations added in
small print—the grant of independence should not be too hurried and it
should be given only to peoples who desire it and are capable of assuming the responsibilities involved.[2] In earlier years, when American interest and influence in the colonial world were not so great, such a position
could be maintained as a general moral-political attitude, without its
having any extensive practical implications aside from those of the
Monroe Doctrine. Today, in the face of United States membership in
the United Nations and the expanding strategic and economic interest
of this country in colonial territories, this attitude deserves re-examination from the standpoint of its applicability to American purposes and
to external realities.

The American attitude condemning the traditional form of colonial-

---

boundaries of a nation-state; (2) contiguous dependent relationships, as in Tibet or
in the outlying Soviet Republics in fact, if not in theory; and (3) all forms of
"concealed colonialism," both of a purposeful nature as in the Soviet-satellite relationships, and of an accidental nature, brought about, for example, by the preponderance of a small country's exports on a single large-country market, as in the
case of Bolivia and the United States, or New Zealand and Ireland and the United
Kingdom. "Colonialism" frequently connotes a state of mind, either on the part of
peoples in the metropole or in the overseas territories, and is sometimes used in-
terchangeably with "imperialism." Technically, "colonialism" should probably be
used to describe the relationship between a mother country and politically dependent
territories populated by groups transplanted from the mother country, and "imperialism" the dependent relationship between a metropolitan country and subject
territories in which people are of different origin from that of the metropole. In most
existing non-self-governing territories there is a combination of both elements, however, and "colonialism" has now come to mean a politically dependent relationship
without distinction as to how it arose and without connotation of any specific state
of mind on the part of the people in the metropole or in the territory—i.e., it
describes an existing political fact.

[2] Space does not permit detailed documentation of American policy on colonialism.
It is to be found in a great variety of sources, including wartime proclamations (the
Atlantic Charter and statements by Secretary of State Hull), debates and voting on
non-self-governing territorial questions in the United Nations, abstentions from
resolutions of the Organization of American States, and unilateral statements by
high State Department officials. While many of our words, votes, and deeds have
been of the "pinprick" variety, this has been true neither of the example set in our
colonies (which has not been antithetical to our own direct interests but has had
extensive repercussions in the dependencies of other countries), nor of the important role this country played in the establishment of the Indonesian and Libyan
republics. It has been made clear by the State Department that failure to vote with
the anti-colonial bloc in the recent Moroccan and Tunisian cases brought before the
United Nations has been a matter of temporary expediency rather than any basic
change in policy.

ism goes deep into our history and our beliefs, but like so many foreign policy issues which have been put in moral terms, it is an attitude which has been reinforced by economic considerations, with respect both to our own colonies and to those of other countries. The role of economic pressure groups in the grant of Philippine independence is a matter of public record, and the expensiveness of Puerto Rico has frequently led to demands for that island's independence by various groups in this country.[3] Similarly, because of discriminatory trade and investment restrictions in the colonies of European countries, agitation for independence of all colonies has served the economic interests of business and other groups in the United States.

The traditional basis for our attitude toward colonialism has been superseded to some extent since formation of the United Nations by the need for finding some middle ground in the world public opinion battle—ground which would lend itself to our advancement of "every effort to convince the European governments that we are not trying, out of sheer fuzzy-minded liberalism, to aid and abet those who want to give their Empires away," but not put us "in the position of trying to prop up the decaying structures of last-century imperialism." [4] Our basic aims have not been changed, but debates and resolutions on colonial matters in the United Nations have served to smoke us out on a number of issues which we otherwise might have avoided. The assumption that colonial matters of other countries did not materially affect the national interest of the United States, which earlier allowed us the luxury of sticking to what we conceived to be our moral-political ideals

---

[3] The strong influence of farm and dairy groups and the American Federation of Labor in promoting Philippine independence in the early 1930's has been traced in J. W. Pratt, *America's Colonial Experiment*, New York, 1950, pp. 302-3. The Bell Trade Act of 1946 specified that equal rights should be granted United States citizens in the development of Philippine natural resources (necessitating an amendment to the Philippine Constitution) before large-scale payments could be made under the 1946 Rehabilitation Act. This provision was more an injudicious use of dollar diplomacy to further private economic interests than a string attached to the grant of independence, but the timing of the measure leaves this country open to the charge of replacing standard colonialism with a form of concealed colonialism. Cf. Rupert Emerson's review of pamphlets in *Pacific Affairs*, xx (December 1947), p. 451; and E. G. Crossman, "American-Philippine Relations: The Prospect," *Proceedings* of the Academy of Political Science, xxii (January 1948), p. 31. The average annual expenditure of around $150 million in Puerto Rico during the post-World War II period has led to numerous demands by Millard Tydings and others that Puerto Rico be given its independence.

[4] G. Kirk, "Declining Empires and American Interest," *Survey*, lxxxv (May 1949), p. 257.

supported by minor economic interests, has now led us to a role based on making ourselves least antagonistic to the rest of the world. We have generally tried to water down proposals of the anti-colonial bloc in the United Nations and then vote with it against the European colonial powers, thus maintaining our traditional principles, yet not antagonizing European countries as much as we might have.[5]

Such a middle-road policy has been criticized for its "lack of character," its tendency to avoid a strong, principled stand. Abstention from an extreme may well be our best policy, however, if we have no substantial interests involved. Unfortunately this is no longer true. A policy condemning colonialism and favoring independence, with hesitations and reservations, is now an unreal policy, for it is attuned neither to developments in colonial relationships nor to the vast increase in the degree of national interest involved in the problem.

[II]

Analysis of the problem of colonial dependency today leads us to four inferences which are relevant for the formation of United States policy.[6] First, the issue of eventual political status for colonial territories is not *a* problem at all, but a collection of diverse problems, each quite distinct but all nevertheless interdependent. Under such conditions interrelationships must be recognized, yet general principles are difficult to formulate and apply.

This variety is caused by the presence in different degree of a multitude of factors which affect the political relationship between colony and mother country. It was recognized . . . by the Special Committee on non-self-governing territories in the United Nations when it sought to establish certain standards to determine whether or not a territory should be classified as non-self-governing. The Committee's report allowed that no simple tests existed, that the factors entering into the problem of a justifiable final status for a colony were so many and so

---

[5] In a few cases, where a resolution was particularly objectionable to colonial powers, we have sided with them or abstained, and recently we have recognized our own interests involved in North Africa and, temporarily at least, helped to prevent airing of the Moroccan and Tunisian disputes.

[6] There has been no comprehensive study made of colonial problems since that of the Royal Institute of International Affairs in the 1930's. Cf. *The Colonial Problem*, London, 1937. Of the many works published on the topic since then, none has been so exhaustive and only a few, all of British authorship, have indicated a keen insight into the complex of diverse problems involved; for example, J. S. Furnivall, *Colonial Policy and Practice*, Cambridge, 1948.

varied that the best the Committee could do was to list the many con-siderations.[7] Geographic factors, ethnic and cultural bonds between metropolitan country and colony, plural societies within a colony (i.e., extent of cultural homogeneity), the desires of the colonial population, the degree of political, economic, and educational development, the extent of interests of mother country and colony in the political ties— all vary in degree in different colonial relationships. No two colonial situations are identical, although of course distinctions may be carried too far. The hostility between Berbers and Arabs in Morocco, which French colonial authorities have utilized to their advantage, probably does not make the Moroccan problem very different from the Tunisian. But the issue of status in these areas is surely quite different from that of Madagascar because of strategic and geographic considerations, or from that of French Guiana because of the degree of development, the desires of the local inhabitants, the cultural bonds with the mother country, and so forth.

A second conclusion which may be drawn from a survey of existing colonial relationships is that colonies are almost entirely European problems, with the remaining dependencies in the tropics and these mostly in Africa. Ninety-seven per cent of the people in the world living under what has been defined as a colonial relationship are tied to Euro-pean countries. Of these 200 million people, three-quarters are in Africa . . . Ranked in order of the number of people overseas attached to metropolitan countries, the colonial powers of the world are: (1) France, (2) United Kingdom, (3) Belgium, (4) Portugal, (5) United States, (6) Spain, (7) Australia, (8) Netherlands, (9) New Zealand, and (10) Denmark.[8] If land area is considered the relevant factor, the ten powers would be ranked the same, except that Denmark, with the large, underpopulated land mass of Greenland, is in fourth place, with Portugal and those following on the list each moved down a notch. Colonial problems enter into our foreign policy in both the Far East and Latin American areas, but for the most part the issues bear upon our relations with European countries and their dependencies in Africa.

Thirdly, almost all colonial relationships are in a state of transition, evolving into something new all the time. This is one of the fundamen-

---

[7] United Nations, *Report of the Special Committee on Information Transmitted under Article 73(e) of the Charter*, 1950, pp. 41-43.

[8] Italy, which has a temporary ten-year trusteeship over Italian Somaliland under United Nations auspices, is not here included.

tal aspects of colonial dependency. There are exceptions, some temporary, a few not. Stagnation in the political development of Portuguese and Spanish territories is probably temporary; with economic development and outside pressures, political subjection of indigenous inhabitants will probably evolve into new relationships between mother country and colony. The political situation in most territories is one of constant change, moving toward a status which may or may not be clearly defined.

Our fourth inference from analysis of existing colonial relationships concerns this "final" status into which the various colonial arrangements are being resolved but which few have yet reached. The political objectives for about 80 per cent of the world's colonial peoples are known, having been expressed on paper or in practice by the colonial powers. The aims are varied and for the most part involve a middle ground between the extremes of subjection and full independent sovereignty. The four powers whose colonial aims are fairly well established are France, Great Britain, the Netherlands, and the United States.

The road ahead for the French Union, comprising Title VIII of the 1946 constitution, will be bumpy, but the blueprint is clear in establishing objectives for French overseas territories. The basic conflict of loose federation vs full assimilation, reflected both in domestic French politics and in the desires of people in the territories, is compromised by granting local autonomy to the Associated States(Laos, Cambodia, and Viet Nam in Indochina and presumably Morocco and Tunisia) and assimilation into the "one and indivisible" French Republic for all overseas departments and territories. The practical application of this blueprint is proving to be extremely difficult, however, because metropolitan France is a minority in the Union with the result that essentially undemocratic means must be employed to ensure French control, because of the lack of consideration of the desires of the inhabitants of overseas territories, and because of the centralized nature of the French administrative structure, which even in France tends to restrict the expression of local interests and freedoms.[9] The concept of the French

---

[9] The undemocratic nature of the French Union is to be found both in the organization of the legislative superstructure, which thus far has hardly functioned and even on paper affords the Associated States only an advisory voice in foreign affairs and security matters of the Union, and in the legislature of the Republic, which, because of dual electoral colleges in overseas territories heavily populated by non-European inhabitants, results in these regions averaging "only one deputy for 800,000 inhabitants, the metropolitan French one for 75,000 inhabitants" (F.

Union will probably have to be modified considerably, especially to provide for greater decentralization and local autonomy, before any long-run stability can be achieved.* But the objectives are clear, and slow development toward these aims may be expected.

Unlike the French, British colonial aims are not expressed in detail on paper, but the "final status" toward which most of the colonies are moving is clear. Where human and physical resources allow, the British are striving toward new Dominions by federating contiguous colonies— in Central Africa (the Rhodesias and Nyasaland), East Africa, West Africa, Malaya, and the British West Indies. Some small territories, mostly islands and strategic outposts, will be locally self-governing units, with foreign affairs and defense in the hands of Great Britain. The status of a few small protectorates, a number of which "fit" geographically into other nation-states, may be decided by self-determination or some other acceptable means.[10]

The newly federated states will presumably have eventual full independent sovereignty much the same as do existing members of the Commonwealth. Some may choose to be completely independent, like Ireland and Burma, others to be Dominions, still others to be independent members of the Commonwealth, like India recognizing the Crown as head of the Commonwealth but not sovereign over their own

---

Luchaire, *Manuel de droit d'outre-mer*, Paris, 1949, p. 134). French citizenship was extended to all peoples in the Republic by the constitution, but the means by which nationals of overseas territories exercise their rights as citizens is laid down by law (Article 80), thus allowing one million European French in the three Algerian departments to elect the same number of delegates to the French Parliament as eight million Moslems, and similar discrimination exists in Madagascar and French Equatorial Africa. Also, while local autonomy has in principle been granted the Indochinese, in practice economic and financial affairs are by treaty under a quadripartite board with members from each of the three states and France. The provisions of the treaties which concern the board are vaguely worded and allow considerable latitude for French control. For a brief criticism of French centralization in the metropole, cf. A. Cobban, *National Self-Determination*, Chicago, 1947, p. 143.

* [Editor's Note. The 1958 Constitution of the Fifth French Republic provided considerable modification in this direction. The French Community, as it is now called, is much more decentralized than the French Union. Secession is even allowed.]

[10] About fifteen colonies would be left without full sovereignty (i.e., with only local autonomy) if the tentative hopes for federated Dominions were realized: the Bahamas, Bermuda, Cyprus, the Falklands, Fiji, Gibraltar, Gilbert and Ellice, Hong Kong, Malta, Mauritius, Pitcairn, Seychelles, Singapore, the Solomons, and St. Helena. Some of these, of course, like Cyprus and Hong Kong, might be ceded to other nations, as may be eventually expected of Aden, Basutoland, Bechuanaland, British Somaliland, Brunei, Sarawak, and Swaziland.

country. Attainment of full sovereignty in any form, however, will be a gradual and pragmatic process.

The "final status" for the emasculated Netherlands Kingdom is nearer fruition than that of any other colonial empire. Surinam and the islands of the Netherlands West Indies, which now have complete control over their own domestic affairs, are to be full partners in a federation joined together under the Dutch Crown. Foreign affairs and defense are to be in the hands of a superstructure still to be established, which the Netherlands will control as a result of its preponderant wealth and population but in which the two territories will have a voice. On paper, Netherlands territories have a status similar to that of the French Associated States, but, partly because of the metropolitan country's majority in the Kingdom, a real voice, without loss of control, may be given the overseas territories in foreign affairs and defense, and local autonomy is accepted more literally by the Dutch than by the French.

Assuming some modifications and loosening of the French Union concept, French, British, and Dutch colonial relationships are moving toward a framework not very different from that of the American "Empire." Statehood for the two incorporated [11] territories of Alaska and Hawaii will leave this country with the unincorporated territories of Puerto Rico, the Virgin Islands, Guam, and American Samoa and the strategic trust islands in the Pacific. The new constitution for Puerto Rico presumably establishes some pattern by which the unincorporated territories may become locally autonomous units, with foreign affairs and defense in the hands of the United States, protected only by a resident commissioner (now provided only for Puerto Rico) in Washington.

The inferences which may be drawn from an analysis of existing colonial relationships—that what is involved is a variety of problems, primarily related to Europe and Africa, which are constantly evolving toward a series of pragmatically determined "ends"—have an important bearing on United States policy. This, then, is the colonialism that concerns this country. The question now must be raised as to why we

---

[11] In 1901 the Supreme Court in De Lima vs. Bidwell and Downes vs. Bidwell drew the distinction between incorporated and unincorporated territories; the former, established by the express or implied will of Congress, are subject to all provisions of the Constitution not obviously meant for states, while for the latter only certain "fundamental" provisions of the Constitution apply.

are interested in it, i.e., what aspects of the national interest bear upon this group of problems categorized as "colonial."

[III]

In the concept of the national interest of the United States is embodied a large number of components which are impossible to ferret out, classify, and order; the concept defies a complete and accurate definition acceptable to all Americans, or even to the bulk of them.[12] But if political interests are considered intermediate ends rather than final ends—they are final ends only insofar as the existence of certain political conditions abroad is of interest to us for their own sake, e.g., if democracies everywhere add to the happiness of people in the United States or contribute confidence in our own institutions—then security and economic considerations form at least a very large part of the national interest involved in colonial problems. Certain less tangible, perhaps moral considerations, such as the effect of colonies on the institutions of the mother country, or of our support of colonial relationships on our own way of life, are not here excluded. But they enter by a back door, at the point where policy becomes reprehensible to the mother country or to ourselves, and may be postponed until reappraisal of our policy in the next section.

In considering security and economic factors against a "cold war" background, distinction between the two is probably not a useful dichotomy, especially in relation to colonialism because of its bearing on the raw materials problem, which is both a matter of security and economic welfare, and its bearing on the economic interests of European countries which are, in turn, a strategic interest of the United States. Artificial division may be avoided by merely moving along a spectrum of our interests from pure security factors, such as military bases and manpower, through the raw materials problem, which is of some direct economic and strategic interest to us, to other economic considerations which largely affect Europe but are of indirect interest to this country.[13]

---

[12] George F. Kennan has made a start at defining "national interest" by indicating what it is not. Cf. "The National Interest of the United States," *Illinois Law Review*, XLV (January-February 1951), pp. 730-42. I will not enter here into whether or not the national interest should be the objective of American policy but will accept this as a dictum, following Kennan and others in believing that it is all we can "know" and that our first responsibility is to ourselves.

[13] The extent of United States national interest involved in colonialism has received little attention, Professor Jacob Viner's wartime study being the only comprehensive investigation. Cf. J. Viner, *et al.*, *The United States in a Multi-National Economy*, New York, 1945, Chapter 1.

Perhaps the most obvious of our interests involved in colonial matters are the air and naval bases in dependent territories which help us maintain control of the Atlantic and Pacific oceans, defend the Panama Canal and inter-American supply route, afford us important strategic bombing bases which can be supplied by seapower, and provide keys to naval operations in the Mediterranean.[14] The vital importance of most of these bases was proven in the last war, the only new element being Moroccan and Greenland airfields for strategic bombing purposes. Their value, especially in the case of Morocco, lies in their location within range of Russian industrial targets, outside possible land penetration on the Continent, and yet at points which are easily supplied by seapower.

The value of potential military manpower in colonial territories is of more doubtful importance. Only for France has this factor been a major consideration in the past. In World War I there were 275,000 colonial troops in metropolitan France fighting the Germans,[15] and Clemenceau insisted in 1918 that his major concern with respect to overseas territories was "an unlimited right of levying black troops to assist in the defense of French territory if France were attacked in the future by Germany."[16] A still larger number of colonial troops were in France in World War II, and it was reliably reported in February of 1940 that 700,000 colonials were mobilized.[17] There was also some utilization of imported civilian workers from the colonies. But the changed spirit in French overseas territories, characterized by strong objections to "exploitation" of the colonial soldier and inequalities between him and his French counterpart, will undoubtedly diminish the value of this manpower source in any future period of hostilities. In overseas territories of other European countries, manpower has been used only sparsely outside of the colonies themselves.

As in the case of these purely strategic considerations, the important bearing of colonialism on world raw material supplies is of direct interest

---

[14] These bases include United States trusteeship islands, Guam, Samoa, Singapore, Hawaii, Alaska, and a network of small islands scattered over the Pacific; Bermuda and the Azores (technically an integral part of Portugal) in the Atlantic; Trinidad, Puerto Rico, and inactive leased bases in the British West Indies for defense in that region; Morocco and Greenland as strategic bombing bases with naval protection; and Gibraltar, Malta, and Cyprus in the Mediterranean. The United States maintains or has specific plans to operate bases in all of these territories except Singapore, Gibraltar, and Malta, where the British have important facilities.

[15] *The Round Table*, No. 119 (June 1940), p. 551.

[16] Quoted from David Lloyd George's *Memoirs of the Peace Conference*, in H. Arendt, *The Origins of Totalitarianism*, New York, 1951, p. 129.

[17] *New York Times*, November 30, 1939, p. 8, and February 9, 1940, p. 3.

to both Europe and the United States. The recent boom in primary product prices following the outbreak of the Korean conflict focused attention on a basic, long-term problem which the industrial countries of the West have been slow to recognize, that is, the progressive failure of raw material supply to keep pace with demand since 1913. W. Arthur Lewis has calculated that on the basis 1913 = 100, manufacturing production had reached 247 in 1950, while primary production stood at 155.[18] The annual increase in agricultural production especially, both of food and raw materials, has declined from 1.1 per cent between 1913 and 1929 to 0.3 per cent between 1937 and 1950. Growth in manufacturing production over the same period has forced industrial countries into greater and greater dependence on overseas sources for supplies of raw materials.

These developments pose a twofold problem for the West: (1) the need for ever-increasing assurance on delivery of primary products absolutely essential in wartime; and (2) the need for generally expanding raw material supply to offset the tendency for the terms of trade to move against the industrial countries, i.e., to offset industrial centers having to pay more and more in terms of goods for a given volume of necessary food and raw materials. It should be noted that expansion of production would probably also be in the interests of primary-producing countries, since gain from trade may increase although the terms of trade move adversely or are prevented from moving favorably by increased output. For the United States, this latter problem is not so important; for Europe, and especially Great Britain, it is crucial.

Existing and potential production in colonial territories are vital to meeting these needs of Western industrial countries. Colonies today produce 53 per cent of the non-Soviet world supply of bauxite, 26 per cent of chrome ore, 21 per cent of copper, 50 per cent of manganese ore, 40 per cent of phosphate rock for fertilizer, 48 per cent of tin, 50 per cent of rubber, and a very large percentage of certain specialized agricultural products such as cocoa beans, copra, groundnuts, palm oil and kernels, and sisal.[19] Dependence on colonial supply is also very high for industrial diamonds, graphite, cobalt, mica, and a number of other products which do not bulk large in world trade. For the United States,

---

[18] W. A. Lewis, "Food and Raw Materials," *District Bank Review* (Manchester), September 1951, pp. 1-11.

[19] Percentages are computed from 1949 production figures in the United Nations *Statistical Yearbook*, 1949-50.

the proportion of imports of certain strategic materials from European dependencies is significant. For example, 97 per cent of our columbian ore came from Nigeria and the Belgian Congo in 1950, 82 per cent of our bauxite from Surinam and British Guiana, 81 per cent of our palm oil, 68 per cent of our cobalt, and 52 per cent of our industrial diamonds from the Belgian Congo, 51 per cent of our tin and 48 per cent of our rubber from Malaya, and 23 per cent of our manganese ore from the Gold Coast and French Morocco.[20]

Even with large-scale stockpiling, both Europe and the United States will continue to be interested in the steady flow of strategic raw materials from colonial territories, the most important producers being in the southern and western portions of Africa, in the Caribbean, and in Malaya. In addition, regular operation of the oil refineries in the Netherlands West Indies and Trinidad, which together refine much of the Venezuelan crude, is of primary concern. In the long run, however, expansion in colonial raw material production may prove to be of even greater importance than the uninterrupted export of existing output. This has been recognized in the allocation of ECA-MSA funds and by the European metropolitan countries which have fostered large-scale development schemes for their overseas territories.[21] Colonies are especially important in this respect because of the reluctance of independent underdeveloped countries to undertake raw material, as opposed to industrial, expansion, and the uncertainties and restrictions which limit the flow of private capital into these regions. Realizing the potential of

---

[20] The areas of supply listed are the principal sources. Cf. Mutual Security Agency, *The Overseas Territories in the Mutual Security Program*, March 31, 1952, p. 2. This country's dependence on colonial territories is steadily increasing, as is shown by comparing 1950 figures with those of 1943 compiled in United States Military Academy, *Raw Materials in War and Peace* (New York, 1947), although the imports above were partially for stockpiles.

Professor Edward S. Mason has argued that for the United States, alone and at war, loss of any or all of the raw material supplies outside of the Western Hemisphere would, after full allowance is made for substitution, involve a relatively small decline in the output of war materials. Cf. "American Security and Access to Raw Materials," *World Politics*, I (January 1949), p. 150. While this may be correct, and it might not be in our own interests (excluding supply considerations of our allies) to divert military forces in order to protect strategic material supplies in Africa or in the Far East, it is surely beneficial to avoid the substitution costs and the production of some inferior goods if possible. And against a "cold war" background, preservation of Western Hemisphere supplies by use of the products of other areas is clearly to our advantage.

[21] For an account of the development plans in Africa, cf. Organization for European Economic Cooperation, *Investments in Overseas Territories in Africa, South of the Sahara*, Paris, 1951.

colonies in primary product supply is a slow and difficult process because of the many social, rather than technical, obstacles. But if the tendency for the terms of trade to shift against manufactured products is to be stemmed, it is for the most part colonial raw material production which must be increased.

This actual and potential supply is one of the major "plus" items in the colonial contribution to the economic health of Europe, which has in recent years become a major concern of the United States. Colonies also contribute to the other side of the trade coin; they serve as export markets, and they provide European countries with income from the sale of services and the return on investment, and, most important of all in the last few years, they either earn or lose dollars. The question is whether or not these benefits to metropolitan countries are sufficient to outweigh the cost of colonies—the old question of whether or not colonies "pay," which Grover Clark answered in the negative in considering the long history of imperialism before the last war.[22] But if colonialism has not "paid" in the past, it may still in present circumstances contribute to the economic welfare of European mother countries because current benefits exceed current costs, which is probably the case for all of the metropolitan countries except France, or because of the need for protecting vested interests already existing in colonial territories.

The gain from the considerable volume of colonial trade, which in 1948-1950 averaged annually between five and six billion dollars for all Europe with overseas dependencies, and the income derived from provision of banking, insurance, and shipping facilities are important economic benefits of colonialism. Close political association normally tends to beget business confidence, promote complementary production, foster economic contacts and the provision of information, and generally create a framework of similar business customs and practices which is favorable to international exchange. Without political ties, such a large volume of trade, which for France and Great Britain amounts to two billion dollars each, or one-third of the former's and one-seventh of the latter's total trade, would be unlikely.[23]

For Great Britain in the postwar period there have been, in addition,

[22] G. Clark, *The Balance Sheets of Imperialism*, New York, 1936.

[23] Trade data are derived from United Nations, International Monetary Fund, and International Bank for Reconstruction and Development (Joint Publication), *Direction of International Trade*, Series T, Volumes I and II.

the dollar earnings of the colonies, which amounted to $798 million over the period 1946-1950 and made up about 15 per cent of the United Kingdom dollar deficit.[24] Dutch, Belgian, and, to a minor extent, Portuguese colonies are small dollar earners, while French territories used dollar resources of the metropolitan country to the extent of $718 million between 1946 and 1950, or in other words contributed 15 per cent of the total Franc Area deficit with the Dollar Area.[25] In the immediate future, colonies are expected to continue to drain France of dollars, although development of known raw material supplies and new geological discoveries may change this over a longer period.

In addition to the benefits derived from commodity trade and the dollar earnings of all except French territories, colonial powers have "at stake" a considerable amount of existing investment and the earnings from this capital. For example, probably between one-eighth and one-quarter of total British overseas investment, or between one and two billion dollars, are in British colonies. The amounts for other metropolitan powers are undoubtedly considerably less, although no data are available for even rough estimates.[26] Protection of investments and investment income and the potential future investment opportunities in raw materials and small manufacturing is a primary concern of all colonial powers. What do they pay for this protection and for the benefits which accrue from colonialism? For Great Britain the cost is amazingly low—between 1946 and 1950 expenses to the British taxpayer were probably less than £100 million ($280 million), or less than one-quarter of the amount of the United States contributed to the tiny island of Puerto Rico over the same period and only about one-tenth of the French colonial expenditures which can be estimated from the metro-

[24] Cmd. 8065, pp. 24-5, and Cmd. 8195, p. 36. This does not include an unallocated dollar deficit on the whole Sterling Area account of $876 million as a result of payment agreements with non-sterling countries, but this should be more properly attributed to the United Kingdom than to the colonies. It also does not include gold sales to Britain by the colonies, which increase dollar earnings by $50-$100 million over the period.

[25] International Monetary Fund, *Balance of Payments Yearbook*, iii (1949-50), pp. 197-201.

[26] Total known British capital in the colonies from data on securities traded amounted to £245 million in 1948 ($700 million at the current rate of exchange). Cf. Bank of England, *United Kingdom Overseas Investments, 1938 to 1948*, London, 1950. Material presented at the Washington loan negotiations and subsequent balance of payments data indicate that private investments not registered on the stock exchanges would bring total investment up to around twice this known amount.

politan budget.[27] These figures for France and Great Britain total "housekeeping" costs, development grants, and military expenses which can be allocated to the colonies. None of the cost of the British Navy, however, is included. A large part of French expenses have, of course, been for the war in Indochina, which has cost the French more than the total of Marshall Plan aid and amounted in 1951 alone to francs equivalent to one billion dollars. But even if Indochinese costs are excluded, French colonial expenses in the postwar period have been roughly three or four times those of Great Britain. For smaller European metropolitan countries, the costs of colonialism now are very small, although the drain of Indonesia on the Dutch was considerable until settlement was effected.

When the current benefits and vested interests of colonialism to Europe are measured against the costs, it is clear that preservation of some colonial relationship is to the economic interest of all metropolitan countries, with the possible exception of France (and, it may be added, the bond is probably in the economic interest of most of the overseas territories also). Even if the Indochinese question is excluded and assumed to be swallowed up in larger world problems, it is questionable whether or not current French benefits from colonialism outweigh the total expenditures, which are now at an annual rate of $300-$400 million, and the annual dollar deficit of $150 million. The economic advantages to the French depend largely on the potential future value of the colonies.

It is clear that the most important direct United States interests in colonial territories, military bases, and the expansion and steady flow of strategic raw materials coincide with the interests of European metropolitan countries. Similarly, our national interest is fostered indirectly by the colonial contribution to the economic health of Europe. These interests of the United States are largely new phenomena which have superseded the relatively minor considerations of commercial policy in the colonies, a frequent source of conflict between European countries

---

[27] The British taxpayer cost for the period January 1, 1944, to July 20, 1949, was given in Parliament as £180.4 million, but this includes the total of £120 million allotted under the Colonial Development and Welfare Act in 1945 for a ten-year period. Cf. *The Economist Records and Statistics Supplement*, August 20, 1949, p. 163. The £100 million estimate above was arrived at by adding the amounts actually used from the Development and Welfare Fund through 1950 to other costs given in the above source. Expenditures of the United States in Puerto Rico are given in the latter's balance of payments data. The breakdown of the French budget is presented in supplements to Ministère des Finances, *Statistiques et études financières*.

and the United States in the past. There is still considerable discrimination against United States exports to European dependencies and even against investment by this country. No discrimination exists, however, in the matter of major concern to us—equal access to raw materials and investment in such products as are necessary for this country's economy. Discrimination by preference arrangements (in which, of course, this country is also guilty), legislation restricting foreign investment, which exists only in the French territories and is now being by-passed by the grant of special permission, and import and exchange controls are perhaps annoying. But insofar as the economic interests of this country are concerned, such restrictions are of minor importance.

[IV]

We come now to tying together the three strands of our argument: United States policy toward traditional colonialism, the nature of and recent developments in dependent relationships, and the extent and nature of national interest which is involved in colonial problems. A reformulated American policy should be based on protection and furthering of our economic and strategic interests in colonial territories with the proviso that our actions or support of the actions of others should not (1) react adversely on our interests elsewhere, or (2) be morally corrupting to our own culture or institutions.

It is first clear that a narrow concept of the national interest dictates general support of the European colonial powers. Insofar as our security and economic interests are concerned, the best possible situation is a series of "happy" colonial relationships, which would serve as protection for military bases, allow for the maximum amount of development of raw material supplies, and contribute to the economic welfare of Europe. The main burden of colonialism for the mother country—extensive military expenditures—would be avoided. There would also be no problem of possible secondary effects on colonies in one area produced by a grant of independence in another.

If such is the case, the first political objective of the United States should be the discouragement of sentiment for independence rather than the promotion of it, while at the same time working quietly, but with force, to push the mother country into making reforms which may be necessary for any "happy" relationship. Certainly modification of the French Union concept is needed for long-run stability. Many territories cannot ever realistically aspire to full sovereignty, because of meager human and natural resources, and in others no real sentiment for full independence now exists. The "small print" of United States policy has sometimes recognized both these exigencies, but it has usually been swallowed up in the broader sweep of our words and deeds fostering the general concept of independence and condemning colonialism. The Caribbean area is a case in point.[28] Colonial territories in this region are of significant strategic importance to the United States because of naval and air bases for the protection of the Panama Canal and the inter-American supply route, and bauxite (British Guiana, Surinam, and Jamaica), crude oil (Trinidad), and oil refineries (the Netherlands Antilles and Trinidad). Because of the patchwork of races and cultures, there is no fervent "nationalism," nor is there, at present, any real demand for independence produced by xenophobia, although the desire for local autonomy is quite real in most of the territories. It is extremely doubtful that any of the dependencies could at present stand alone as fully sovereign states. To grant the fiction of legal sovereignty to territories which are heavily dependent economically or militarily or both is always to run the risk of abusing the theory of sovereign independence and to invite confusion and bitterness and create tensions and misunderstandings worse than anything involved in the more honest and applicable institution of colonial status. All of the colonies have arrived at, or are clearly in sight of, a final status of local autonomy, or assimilation as overseas departments in the case of the French territories, which is satisfactory to most of the indigenous inhabitants. In spite of all this, the United States did not object strongly or vote against (it abstained) an inter-American resolution at Bogota in 1948 which favored "putting an end to colonialism and the occupation of American territories by extra-continental countries" and set up an American Commission of Dependent Territories "to find an adequate solution" to the colonial question in the Western Hemisphere.[29]

If support of some form of "happy" dependent relationship is indicated when it is feasible or is the only realistic arrangement, what of situations where it is impossible, where rabid nationalism or xenophobia is likely to create instability for as long as any type of political ties endure? When, if at all, is such a territory to achieve independence? The

---

[28] The Ford Foundation made it possible for the author to spend the month of January 1952 in the British, United States, French, and Netherlands territories in the Caribbean.

[29] *New York Times*, May 1, 1948, p. 7.

only real test available for such a situation is the final recognition by the mother country that its own national interest is no longer served, on balance, by the continuation of the effort to hold the colony in subjection. This point was reached in England with respect to the thirteen colonies at the time of Cornwallis' surrender; it was reached with respect to Cuba in the final weeks before the outbreak of hostilities between the United States and Spain; it was reached by the British with respect to India in the immediate aftermath of World War II, or perhaps somewhat earlier; it was reached by the Dutch with respect to Indonesia in 1947, but only in the light of the fact that the opposition of a large part of the international community had added to the opposition of the colonial peoples involved. It is probably being reached by the French at the present time, in the sense that there appears to be a decisive swing of authoritative French opinion to the view that the maintenance of the colonial status for Indochina is no longer justified by French interests alone; in other words, the colonial problem of Indochina is being swallowed up by larger world problems.

In any case, when this stage is reached there has been an important turning point—and perhaps the only fully decisive one—in the colonial relationship. Experience has shown that except where a mother country has reasons of its own—ideological or economic—for wishing to relinquish its control over a colonial territory, the only really pertinent test of fitness for independence has generally been the ability of the colonial people to make itself so much of a trouble and nuisance to the mother country as to render the continuation of the relationship unprofitable to the latter. Situations of this sort can be created by a variety of components, of which the degree of resentment of the colonial people and of the resultant civil disorder and resistance is only one. Other things, such as geography, economic value to the mother country, the importance of the creation of precedent, effect on the interest of third powers, and domestic preoccupation of the mother country—all these play an important part in determining when the crucial point has been reached at which a colonial relationship may be regarded as exhausted and conducive to no further constructive purpose.

Such a conclusion assumes that the national interest of the United States coincides with that of the European mother country, which is a plausible general proposition, although certainly not true in every case. For example, a dispute *between* two European countries with respect to a colonial issue obviously cannot find the United States on both sides simultaneously. We must be careful of situations in which the national interest of the metropolitan country is distorted by pressure from private interest groups, by considerations of pride or prestige, or by our own contributions to the economic burden involved. It is in the case of the French colonial empire that misjudgments of this kind are most likely. Here again, however, the interdependence of colonial developments must be recognized—of Libyan independence on all of French North Africa, and resolution of the Tunisian case on Algeria and Morocco, and even, in the longer run, on French territories further south. There is a lesson to be learned from the case of Libya, which achieved its independence, against the better judgment of all who studied carefully its capacity to assume the responsibilities involved, by virtue of a single vote in the General Assembly—a vote which can be attributed more to the tiny republic of Liberia, which had no essential interests involved, than to any other country.[30] That Libyan independence has had much to do with the disturbances in Tunisia, Algeria, and Morocco can hardly be doubted.

Support of the national interest of the mother country raises the issue of the menace to peace of colonial discontent, either directly through a spreading of the conflict, or indirectly through the encouragement of Communism in unstable political situations. Chronic disturbances do cause frictions and tensions, but the objective of political stability can be dangerous if it is made a fetish and pursued to the exclusion of other pertinent considerations. Walter Hines Page once said of the British, "They have a mania for order, sheer order, order for the sake of order and—of trade." [31] At some stage in some territories independence may clearly be the best step, but the United States has, in effect, frustrated the objective of political stability in recent times by fomenting revolutions through its condemnation of colonialism and general advocacy of indiscriminate independence.[32] Prevention of inroads by Communism in

---

[30] The crucial vote on tripartite trusteeship for the area among France, Great Britain, and Italy came in 1949 following the failure of four-power agreement and submission of the issue to the General Assembly. British administration of Cyrenaica and French administration of the Fezzan were barely approved by the necessary two-thirds majority, but Italian trusteeship lacked one affirmative vote. Liberia, which had voted in favor of Great Britain and France, abstained in the case of Italy. Defeat of this section caused the entire South American bloc to smother the whole resolution, and Libyan independence was decided upon at the next session of the Assembly.

[31] Quoted in A. K. Weinberg, *Manifest Destiny*, Baltimore, 1935, p. 423.

[32] Cf., e.g., the 1950 statement of George C. McGhee, then head of the African Affairs Division of the State Department, advocating the "advancement toward independence" of colonial territories in Africa (United States Department of State

colonial regions may very well be easier when control is in the hands of a European country than when there is considerable political instability following newly won independence, although probably the spread of Communism has actually been fostered in some areas under French control, such as the Caribbean islands, because of the strength and Messianic aims of the party in the metropole.

The pursuit of what may be termed by some a "hard," by others a "realistic," policy on colonial questions must meet the test of two criticisms, which together form the basis for the traditional and existing American attitude. It must not be only a short-run policy which would damage our long-run interests outside of Europe. And it must not react adversely on our own culture and institutions.

So far as our long-run interests outside of Europe are concerned, the problem is a real one and should be recognized as such, but at the same time the potential damage is easily exaggerated because of failure to distinguish between the sentimental and the real factors involved. Rupert Emerson makes the strongest case for the importance of this issue by arguing that this country should align itself with the forces of the future rather than of the past.[33] The thesis is partially based on the assumption that nations, like elephants, have long memories. The Irish have proved that this can be the case, but India and other former dependencies which have chosen to join the Commonwealth of Nations, as well as such countries as Haiti, which frequently breaks away from the Central and South American bloc in the United Nations to vote for France but for no other European power, are proving the adverse also. The argument, secondly, places great weight on the importance of United States popularity among peoples and governments in other parts of the world. That this factor should not be entirely discounted is clear; but at the same time it should not be overrated and become an aim of foreign policy, rather than merely a consideration to be taken into account.[34]

Bulletin, XXII [June 19, 1950], pp. 999-1003), or John Foster Dulles' statement before the General Assembly in 1947: "The colonial system is obsolete and should be done away with as soon as possible," quoted in W. R. Crocker, *Self-Government for the Colonies*, London, 1949, p. 10.

[33] R. Emerson, "American Policy Toward Pacific Dependencies," *Pacific Affairs*, XX (September 1947), pp. 259-75.

[34] An example of what seems to be disproportionate weighting of this factor is the following statement: "To win praise instead of disapproval, the United States must find an answer to a most difficult question: What policy compatible with our democratic values can we adopt toward our own colonies and those of other powers

Our main difficulty in this respect is that we often fail to distinguish between "anti-colonialism" which is an expression of national interest and "anti-colonialism" which is an expression of grass-roots moral fervor. When Argentina and Guatemala object strenuously to European colonies in the Western Hemisphere, it must be remembered that the maps of each country are already drawn to include the Falkland Islands in the case of the former, and British Honduras (Belize) in the case of the latter. Similarly, the demands of Egypt and other Arab countries with respect to parts of Northern Africa are hardly an expression of disinterested morality. When the issue is one of opposing national interests, we should recognize it as such and act accordingly. Because of the substantial concern of Europe and ourselves in colonies and the interdependence of actions in the different territories, the national interest of the United States will generally lie with the colonial powers.

The effect of a more realistic policy toward the existence of colonial dependence on our ideological position in the world turns mainly on the nature of colonial relationships and how we present our case. If colonialism is unjust tyranny, not only are we morally wrong in the eyes of world public opinion, but we should be in our own eyes also, i.e., our policy is likely to corrupt the national objectives we are endeavoring to preserve. In a forceful exposition on the historical development of imperialism, Hannah Arendt argues that no democracy can keep another people in subjection and survive, that a successful empire comprising different cultures necessitates a totalitarian regime at home.[35] Similarly, Reinhold Niebuhr states:

> The economic consequences of imperialism were certainly not as unambiguously evil as the Marxist propaganda claims; for it introduced technical skills and education to the agrarian world. Perhaps the most deleterious consequences of imperialism are in the spiritual rather than the economic realm. For arrogance is the inevitable consequence of the relation of power to weakness. In this case the arrogance of power reinforced ethnic prejudices; for the industrial world was "white" and the non-technical world was "colored." [36]

Such considerations must surely be kept constantly in mind, but two observations are in order concerning their relevance to present circum-

---

which will reconcile these two demands [freedom and welfare] and thus diminish conflicts within dependent areas and concerning them?" (A. B. Fox, *Freedom and Welfare in the Caribbean*, New York, 1949, p. 3).

[35] Arendt, *op. cit.*, Part Two.

[36] R. Niebuhr, *The Irony of American History*, New York, 1952, pp. 112-13.

stances. First, colonialism today, while it obviously has some defects from any "objective" viewpoint (if such were possible), is not the old-fashioned tyranny that it once was in many parts of the world. It was pointed out in Section II that most colonial relationships are steadily evolving toward a series of varied, pragmatically determined "ends" that are at neither the extreme of complete subjection nor of full independent sovereignty. Secondly, there are so-called "rights" involved on both sides of colonial issues, none of them being in themselves absolute. People in the United States tend to visualize a colonial relationship as involving only one "right"—the "right" of self-determination—and this "right" is seen as being infringed upon. In his careful study, Alfred Cobban answers this argument succinctly:

> In short, are there not geographical, historical, economic, and political considerations which rule out national self-determination in the form of the sovereign state for many of the smaller nationalities of the world? . . . The true rights of man are his liberties—political, economic, national, religious—and these may necessitate some degree of separate state-hood, or they may not, and such political independence may be objectively possible, or it may not. Circumstances, in the end, are the determining factor.[37]

Support, rather than general condemnation, of colonialism is clearly the path for the United States where such a relationship is the only feasible alternative because of meager resources, or where the relationship is not subject to dispute. In other cases, a reasoned policy of general non-interference, in words as well as actions, recognizing the extent of national interest involved and the fact that in colonial issues, as in most problems, there are no absolutes, no clear "rights" and "wrongs"— a policy devoid of sentiment but not of moral content—should not be damaging to ourselves nor, if honestly expressed, to our ideological position in the world. If we recognize that political status may be, and in some cases must be, relative, bordering on neither the extreme of subjugation nor of full independent sovereignty, we should not feel guilty about presenting this possibility to the rest of the world. Such a policy will be harshly criticized in some sectors, of course. But we should not let our "rabbit ears," often so sensitive to foreign criticism, dominate decisions in which a substantial degree of the national interest is at stake and in which there are no clear moral "rights" and "wrongs."

---

[37] Cobban, *op. cit.*, p. 74.

United States Policy and Colonialism*

by William Henderson

The issue of colonialism has been one of the most perplexing problems which the United States has had to face in the post-war period. On the whole we seem not to have handled it very well. Our relations with the newly emerging nations of the non-Western world are for the most part far from satisfactory, and the attitudes of their peoples toward the United States are characterized, not by friendliness or a sense of partnership, but rather by deep-seated feelings of resentment and suspicion. Few indeed would any longer acknowledge us the champions of anti-colonialism. However fantastic the charge may seem, we are today more often counted among the imperialists, and looked upon as a threat to liberties but lately won after long and costly struggle.

There is a wry and tragic irony to this. Americans are, after all, the children of revolution. Opposition to colonial rule, and sympathy for the oppressed and downtrodden of all nations, have been among our proudest traditions. In the past they earned us the respect and admiration of the non-Western world. It is true that our actions usually spoke much more quietly than our words, if indeed they spoke at all, but few questioned our essential sincerity. The palpable difficulties standing in the way of effective action in particular cases were sufficient to rationalize, abroad as well as at home, the yawning gap between emotional response and practical performance.

Since the end of World War II, however, we have been called upon to live up to our ancient promises. The rise of the United States as the richest and most powerful nation on earth, at a time when nationalism had struck deep roots throughout most of the non-Western world and classical colonialism had entered upon an epoch of headlong retreat, aroused great expectations in the farthest reaches of Asia and Africa. For the most part these expectations have been disappointed. To the non-Western world the United States has often seemed unwilling or unable to project its traditional posture with respect to colonialism, and its concern for the political, social and economic development of dependent peoples, into the realm of practical policy. Our failures, for so

* From the *Proceedings of the Academy of Political Science*, Vol. XXVI, No. 3 (1957), pp. 53-63. Reprinted by permission of the Academy of Political Science.

they are judged whether rightly or wrongly, have been widely interpreted as pusillanimity or worse. They have given rise to bitterness and contempt, as well as the suspicion that we have lost interest in the advancement of the world's backward and underdeveloped areas.

Many thoughtful observers have urged that the United States should forthwith adopt a position of outspoken and uncompromising opposition to colonialism everywhere on the face of the globe, in an effort to regain lost ground among the emerging nations of Asia and Africa. Even if this were a realistic alternative for United States policy, which it is not, it would go only a small part of the way toward meeting the anticolonial strictures of the peoples of the non-Western world.

When these peoples speak of "colonialism," they have in mind many different things. The continued domination of the world's remaining dependent territories by a handful of Western countries is perhaps the most obvious. But they refer also to the bitter memories of their colonial past and to the long struggle for independence; to the overwhelming problems inherited from the colonial period of their history, for which they not unnaturally blame the former imperial Powers; to their morbid and for the most part unreasoned fears that these nations, including the United States, may attempt to reassert control over them, by economic if not by political means; to their resentment against what they consider to be the arrogance, highhandedness and race prejudice of the leading Western nations; to their sense of inferiority and frustration in face of the material accomplishments and political maturity of the West. There is no single "policy on colonialism" by which the United States can effectively respond to this generalized sentiment of hostility. It will be assuaged only as time heals the wounds of history, and solid progress ameliorates the poverty and backwardness of the non-Western world.

This is not to suggest, however, that the United States is powerless in this situation. We can do a great deal to speed up the process of adjustment and reconciliation. On the most superficial level, we should in every possible manner show deference to the sensitive pride of the newly independent nations of Asia and Africa, and give constant public evidence of our respect and esteem for them and for their brothers who are not yet free. One obvious expedient is to support whenever feasible the candidates of non-Western nations, whether neutralist or openly aligned with the United States, for leading positions in the organs of the United Nations and other international bodies. We should strive to persuade these countries, publicly as well as privately and by every available means, of the essential parallelism between their most basic interests and our own, and that we seek neither to subvert their freedom nor selfishly to exploit them in a material sense. We must be interested in their future progress as people, and not merely as pawns in some larger international strategy.

Washington could greatly develop the habit of consultation with the governments of the non-Western world on the whole range of American policies and programs applicable to their respective areas. The exercise might not gain us much in the way of added support, at least at first, but we would be demonstrating our consideration for the opinions of the peoples who are, after all, most directly concerned. The United States should make every effort to comprehend the non-Western point of view, and to concede to it wherever possible. We cannot be expected to applaud neutralism, but we can try to understand it and to develop a more satisfactory response to it than has hitherto characterized our relations with the neutralist nations of the world. Finally, the image of ourselves which we project to these peoples is immensely important. Above all, we must rid ourselves of those qualities of arrogance and prejudice which they resent so deeply.

Perhaps the most effective contribution which the United States can make to the peaceful development of viable modern states in the non-Western world is through wisely conceived and soundly administered programs of economic and technical assistance. They are in the first place the most important means by which we can influence the political evolution of underdeveloped countries. In a recent book Professors Millikan and Rostow have summarized the ways in which foreign economic aid, by making possible real economic growth, can hasten the development of political maturity.[1] The prospect of significant economic progress provides a constructive outlet for popular energies which are now too often dissipated in keeping alive the torch of an outmoded anti-colonialism. Since it is a goal shared by the whole population, it can become an important force making for unity and cohesion in societies often threatened with complete disintegration. Aid programs, by insisting on balanced economic development, can help to bridge the broad gulf between the city and the countryside by compelling the urban leadership to think about and work with their country cousins more than they have ever done before. Such across-the-board economic

---

[1] Max F. Millikan and W. W. Rostow, A Proposal, Key to an Effective Foreign Policy (New York, 1957), chs. 3-4.

development also serves to uncover new sources of leadership, hitherto drawn almost entirely from the urban intellectual élite and cut off from the great masses of the population.

American aid has the distinctly economic objective of laying the economic bases for healthier, happier and more prosperous societies in the non-Western world. While economic conditions are not the only source of instability in these areas, they are certainly one of the most important. The need to raise living standards is all the more pressing since expectations of a better life have been growing rapidly in recent years. In order to improve prevailing economic conditions in the foreseeable future, sustained economic growth at a fairly rapid rate is essential. But the newly emerging nations do not possess the resources in capital, skills and experience necessary to accomplish this purpose on their own. It is here that the United States, through its programs of economic and technical assistance, can make a major contribution to the economic development of these countries.

Finally and perhaps most important of all, the elaboration and implementation of programs for significant economic development, which could be made possible by American aid, would have a profound effect in generating a sense of purpose and direction within these countries. Economic development does not necessarily insure an orderly political evolution, at least in the short run. On the contrary, its most immediate consequence may often be a striking increase in unrest and instability because of the variety of sudden shocks and changes which it engenders throughout the whole structure of society. But this is a risk worth taking if at the same time there emerges a feeling of confidence in coping with pressing problems, faith in the future, and a sense of meaningful progress in a democratically oriented society. It is this sentiment, even more than the fact of quantitative economic growth, that the United States should seek to stimulate.

The proper conditions of eligibility for American economic and technical assistance may be derived from the long-range policy objectives we are aiming at. Our basic interest is to encourage the development of these countries as independent, progressive and democratically oriented states. It is not, or should not be, to purchase or compel their alignment in the cold war on the side of the United States. Insistence on onerous political conditions will often cause our aid to be rejected by nations which have opted for a neutralist posture in world affairs. The only conditions which should be imposed are criteria relating to productive use of the aid. Even the acceptance of aid from the Communist-bloc countries should not be considered a disqualification for further American help unless the volume or circumstances of such aid seriously threaten the independence of the recipient.

Undoubtedly the aspect of colonialism which most deeply engages the emotions of the non-Western world today is the continuance of Western colonial rule over a large portion of the earth's surface, especially in Africa. Whether or not they themselves have won freedom, these peoples profess to see little if any justification for the perpetuation of Western domination, at least in its present forms, even in the most backward areas. Being less familiar with Communist imperialism and the Soviet empire in Eastern Europe, they are less concerned by them. But Western rule, which is to say the domination of the white man, over dependent territories of the non-Western world is intolerable.

For a variety of reasons the United States has been unwilling during the past decade to adopt an intransigent position in opposition to Western colonial rule. In the first place, many of the world's remaining dependent territories are clearly not prepared for independence. A more or less protracted period of tutelage in such areas as West New Guinea and Portuguese Angola is an unavoidable necessity until the political, social and economic bases of freedom have been firmly and securely established. In some colonial territories premature independence would almost certainly create more problems than it solved, and might lead to a resort to radical solutions as a way out of the morass, and ultimately to a Communist seizure of power. British Guiana has recently afforded an instructive lesson in this respect. In Southeast Asia the great commercial entrepôt and military bastion of Singapore is another.

In many instances, moreover, the administering Powers deserve real credit for the manner in which they have discharged their responsibilities toward their dependent territories. Great Britain's post-war record is particularly noteworthy, and should not be forgotten despite such episodes as Cyprus and Suez. The United States has an important stake in the raw materials of various dependent territories, such as the uranium of the Belgian Congo, and in the strategic location of others. These interests might be jeopardized by the sudden end of colonial rule. We are a colonial Power ourselves, and thus far Washington has shown little disposition to surrender our hold on such territories as the Ryukyus and the former Japanese-mandated islands of the Western Pacific.

But most of all, an outspoken anti-colonial posture would place an intolerable strain on our relations with our oldest and most valued allies, especially Great Britain and France. There are limits beyond which these nations will not go in order to preserve unity with the United States when they consider their vital interests to be at stake. Suez, which was not a clear-cut colonial issue, demonstrated this with tragic clarity. We cannot irrevocably antagonize the colonial Powers with respect to their dependent territories, and then expect them to coöperate with us on the exposed fronts of the cold war. This is not the place to argue the importance of these European nations to the United States as against the benefits to be harvested among the peoples of the non-Western world by adoption of an outspoken anti-colonial position. Suffice to say that an irreparable break with our traditional allies is unthinkable, as much for spiritual as for practical reasons; and further that the sympathy we should gain among the newly emerging nations, while it would certainly improve our immediate relations with them, would probably not fundamentally affect their present international orientation or their deep-seated hostility to the West. On the whole we should have made a bad bargain.

The basic dilemma for the United States has been to find a position with respect to dependent territories which satisfies both the European colonial Powers and the emerging nations of the non-Western world, which at the same time takes into account in a responsible manner the needs and aspirations of the dependent peoples themselves, and finally which safeguards our own important stake in many of the dependent territories. The search has proved a frustrating business.

On paper the United States still adheres to its traditional anti-colonialism, and the political air is often set to ringing with proud assertions of our bias in this respect. Thus President Eisenhower on November 14, 1956, declared that "we simply insist upon the right of all people to be free to live under governments of their own choosing."[2] At the same time we recognize that the attainment of self-government or independence should be preceded by the establishment of institutional bases capable of sustaining freedom. As Thruston B. Morton, then Assistant Secretary of State for Congressional Affairs, wrote on June 20, 1955:

> . . . the question of timing in the transition from colonialism to self-government or independence is of the utmost importance and delicacy. At

---

[2] *New York Times*, November 15, 1956.

a time when international communism is trying to take over all weak governments, we have to be sure that the transition . . . takes place under such circumstances that truly free institutions will be maintained.[3]

In the daily conduct of affairs, however, the United States has been much less forthright than this general policy position would suggest, and, one might say, a good deal more equivocal. From time to time the United States has exerted considerable pressure, usually in private, on the colonial Powers to hasten the advancement of their dependent peoples. But as particular colonial issues come to the fore, especially in the United Nations, Washington generally does not have a concrete and long-range policy worked out in advance, derived from a coherent set of principles as they relate to the merits of the case at hand, and on which we are prepared to take a public stand. We prefer to climb up on the fence and essay the rôle of middleman between the administering Powers and their anti-colonial critics. In most instances we systematically try to avoid taking positive positions on either side of the question at issue.

This is an understandable posture, and in some respects even a commendable one. We have often stimulated the administering Powers to more rapid accomplishment, and mediated their differences on colonial issues with the emerging nations of the non-Western world. On the other hand, our behavior has failed to satisfy the colonial Powers, which believe that they should have a far greater measure of support in their efforts to come to grips with the undeniably difficult problems of their dependent territories. They resent even the vaguest and most general criticism, and they look upon us as undependable and too soft. Still more important, perhaps, is the fact that we have failed to respond adequately to the prevailing anti-colonial temper of our time. Equivocation with respect to colonial issues has greatly damaged the prestige of the United States at a time when Communist influence is making striking inroads throughout the non-Western world.

There is no easy way out of our dilemma. It may be argued, however, that the United States should in the near future consider the wisdom

---

[3] Letter dated June 20, 1955, from Thruston B. Morton, Assistant Secretary of State for Congressional Affairs, to James P. Richards, Chairman, Committee on Foreign Affairs, House of Representatives, commenting on House Concurrent Resolution 149.

of taking several calculated steps away from a colonial policy largely based on the shifting sands of expediency toward a position more nearly in harmony with the essentially sound anti-colonial traditions of our history. From all indications current Communist world strategy aims at bringing about and maintaining a relative relaxation of international tensions for the indefinite future. So far in the post-war period American foreign policy has given the highest priority to safeguarding the security of the United States from Communist ambition, primarily through the strengthening of Western Europe and the construction of a world-wide network of defense alliances. Much has been sacrificed to these ends. Perhaps the time has now come when we can with safety turn greater attention to the non-Western world, and initiate courses of action aimed at replenishing, at least to some extent, our sadly depleted reservoirs of good will among the uncommitted peoples of Asia and Africa.

This is not to suggest that the United States should embark upon a crusade against colonial rule wherever it still persists, or that we should get into the business of stirring up demands for independence. If we can avoid involvement in a given colonial issue without loss of prestige, we would usually be wise to do so, although there may be rare opportunities when deliberate intervention on the side of anti-colonialism would yield rich dividends in the non-Western world at little cost to our relations with the European colonial Powers. In most instances, of course, the United States will necessarily be involved simply because of its own leading position in international affairs.

On such occasions, the United States should, where it is persuaded of the merits of the case and unless compelling circumstances dictate otherwise, openly assert its support for a peaceful solution based ultimately on the freely expressed wishes of the people in the territory concerned. In the final analysis, whether the issue involves Goa, or Togoland, or even Algeria, the peoples of all dependent territories must eventually be given the right to determine their own political future. We should then strive, tactfully but firmly, to promote this objective by every pacific means at our disposal. We should make clear that we are doing so, and that we shall continue to do so until it has been reached. At the same time the United States should publicly take account of circumstances complicating the orderly evolution of particular dependent territories. Every colony has its own peculiar problems. There is no single formula or timetable. The minority Turkish community cannot be ignored in planning the future of Cyprus, for example, and still less the position of the French in Algeria. In such racially tangled situations, where tensions have reached or passed the breaking point, some kind of accommodation must first be sought among the various resident peoples.

The United States can have an important rôle in the development of adequate political, social and economic foundations in dependent territories by making available large-scale economic and technical assistance, provided that we are satisfied as to the sincerity of purpose of the administering Powers. Where this condition is fulfilled, we should play our part in association with the administering Powers, rather than apart from them, since they are the best guarantee that the evolution of the dependent territories for which they are responsible will proceed in a peaceful and democratic fashion. We should also endeavor to increase the rôle of the United Nations in the solution of outstanding colonial problems, although in concrete instances this will usually be difficult to accomplish, and we should always be careful not to break the back of that organization through the imposition of tasks it will not be able to discharge.

In other words, the touchstone of United States policy on concrete colonial issues should not be immediate freedom regardless of the consequences, but rather meaningful progress toward self-government in accordance with an intelligible time schedule, and ultimate independence where this is the clear choice of the majority. Such a posture would undoubtedly place a strain on our ties with the European colonial Powers. But almost any policy involves certain hazards. The essential reasonableness of this position, together with the fact that for the most part these Powers have themselves subscribed, whether tacitly or explicitly, to the principle of increased autonomy for their dependent territories, would probably preclude an uncontrollably violent reaction. We must also recognize that the same rules would have to be applied to our own dependencies, regardless of our stake in them; and their implementation in the dependent territories of other colonial Powers involves inevitable risks with respect to important American strategic and other interests.

On the other hand, this approach would by no means satisfy the intemperate demands of the newly emerging nations of the non-Western world. We might even be accused at first of throwing up a smoke screen to facilitate the preservation of European colonialism. But we should at last have gained a firm position on which to stand. We shall not have been apathetic, and we shall have tried hard not to be irresponsible. In the long run the dignity of a consistent, enlightened and reasonable colonial policy would gain us respect, even if it did not win us affection.

FOR FURTHER READING:

Thomas R. Adam, *Modern Colonialism: Institutions and Policies* (New York: Random House, 1955).

Chester Bowles, *Africa's Challenge to America* (Berkeley: University of California Press, 1956).

John C. Campbell, *Defence in the Middle East: Problems of American Policy* (New York: Harper and Brothers, 1958).

Clyde Eagleton, "Excesses of Self Determination," *Foreign Affairs*, Vol. XXXI, No. 4 (July, 1953), pp. 592-604.

Russell H. Fifield, *The Diplomacy of South East Asia: 1945-1958* (New York: Harper and Brothers, 1958).

Robert C. Good, "The United States and the Colonial Debate," in Arnold Wolfers (ed.), *Alliance Policy in the Cold War* (Baltimore: The Johns Hopkins Press, 1959), pp. 224-270.

George McTurnan Kahin (ed.), *The Asian-African Conference* (Ithaca: Cornell University Press, 1956).

The Political Quarterly, Special Number, "The Passing of Colonialism," Vol. XXIX, No. 3 (July-September, 1958), pp. 209-316.

Benjamin Rivlin, "Self-Determination and Dependent Areas," *International Conciliation*, No. 501 (January, 1955), pp. 195-271.

Emil J. Sady, "The United Nations and Dependent Peoples," in Robert E. Asher and others, *The United Nations and the Promotion of the General Welfare* (Washington, D.C.: The Brookings Institution, 1957), pp. 815-1017.

Robert Strausz-Hupé and Harry W. Hazard (eds.), *The Idea of Colonialism* (New York: Frederick A. Praeger, 1958).

Philips Talbot and S. L. Poplai, *India and America: A Study of Their Relations* (New York: Harper and Brothers, 1958).

Chapter XII

ECONOMIC DEVELOPMENT

Economic development is one of the most important topics in the contemporary public debate on United States foreign policy. It is related to colonialism as many of the same states are involved and as independence needs to be buttressed with economic growth. Further, many anti-colonial spokesmen, rightly or wrongly, blame present economic backwardness on past colonial policies. At the same time, economic development is probably a more important issue. The "revolution of rising expectations" is one of the fundamental forces in present world politics. Underdeveloped areas comprise the largest portion of the world—most of Africa, Asia, and Latin America can rightly be included in this classification (see Map III,* next page). The people in these areas, almost half the world's total, are determined rapidly to develop their economies. Whether they will be able to achieve this goal and in what manner are questions of basic importance for the future of world politics. As a great power the United States is naturally interested in the outcome of these questions, and Soviet-American tensions heighten this interest.

The United States began major programs to assist underdeveloped areas over a decade ago with President Truman's announcement of the Point Four Program in his 1949 inaugural address. This program of technical assistance has been continued under various names bilaterally

---

* Map III, "The Underdeveloped World," is reprinted by permission from *Economic Development Assistance* (New York: Committee for Economic Development, 1957), pp. 8-9.

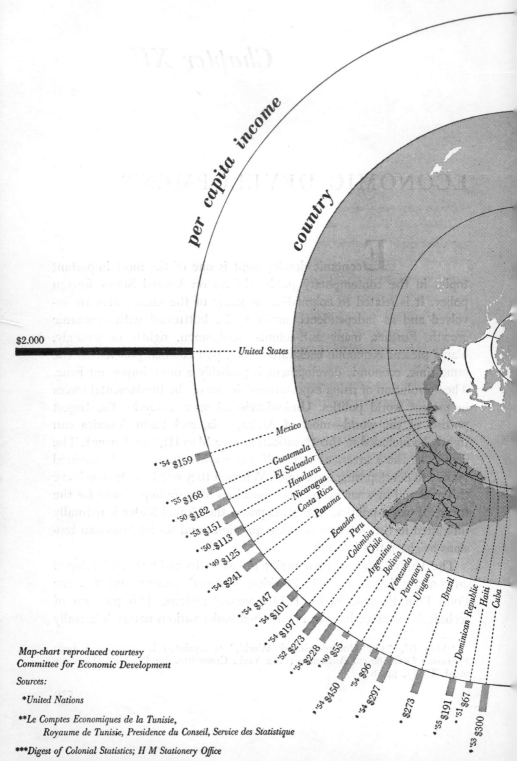

per capita income

country

$2.000 ——————————————————— United States

Mexico

'54 $159 —— Guatemala
— El Salvador
— Honduras
'55 $168 —— Nicaragua
'50 $182 —— Costa Rica
'53 $151 —— Panama
'50 $113 —— Ecuador
'49 $125 —— Peru
'54 $241 —— Colombia
Chile
'54 $147 —— Argentina
'54 $101 —— Bolivia
'52 $273 —— Venezuela
'54 $228 —— Paraguay
'49 $55 —— Uruguay
'54 $450 —— Brazil
'54 $297 —— Dominican Republic
$273 —— Haiti
'55 $191 —— Cuba
'51 $67
'53 $300
$96

Map-chart reproduced courtesy
Committee for Economic Development

Sources:

  *United Nations

**Le Comptes Economiques de la Tunisie,*
   Royaume de Tunisie, Presidence du Conseil, Service des Statistique

***Digest of Colonial Statistics; H M Stationery Office*

75 countries, 1,150,000,000 people

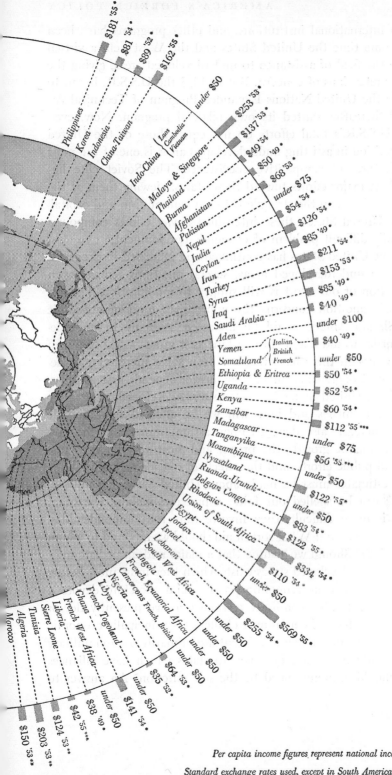

Philippines — $181 '55 •
Korea — $81 '54 •
Indonesia — $89 '52 •
China-Taiwan — $162 '55 •
Indo-China { Laos, Cambodia, Vietnam } — under $50
Malaya & Singapore — $253 '53 •
Thailand — $137 '53 •
Burma — $49 '54 •
Afghanistan — $50 '49 •
Pakistan — $68 '53 •
Nepal — under $75
India — $54 '54 •
Ceylon — $126 '54 •
Iran — $85 '49 •
Turkey — $211 '54 •
Syria — $153 '53 •
Iraq — $85 '49 •
Saudi Arabia — $40 '49 •
Aden — under $100
Yemen — $40 '49 •
Somaliland { Italian, British, French } — under $50
Ethiopia & Eritrea — $50 '54 •
Uganda — $52 '54 •
Kenya — $60 '54 •
Zanzibar — $112 '55 •••
Madagascar — under $75
Tanganyika — $56 '55 •••
Mozambique — under $50
Nyasaland — $122 '55 •
Ruanda-Urundi — under $50
Belgian Congo — $83 '54 •
Rhodesia — $122 '55 •
Union of South Africa — $334 '54 •
Egypt — $110 '54 •
Jordan — under $50
Israel — $569 '55 •
Lebanon — $255 '54 •
South West Africa — under $50
Angola — under $50
French Equatorial Africa — $64 '53 •
Cameroons French British — under $50
Nigeria — $35 '52 •
Libya — $141 '54 •
French Togoland — under $50
Ghana — $38 '49 •
French West Africa — $42 '55 •••
Liberia — $124 '53 •••
Sierra Leone — $203 '53 ••
Tunisia — $150 '53 ••
Algeria
Morocco

Per capita income figures represent national income divided by population.

Standard exchange rates used, except in South America where multiple rates exist.

and through international institutions, and other programs have been added. For some time the United States and the West held a virtual monopoly in the field of assistance to underdeveloped areas, giving the lie to Soviet pretensions of concern. But in 1953 the U.S.S.R. began to participate in the United Nations Expanded Program of Technical Assistance and thereafter started its own bilateral program. Now, even though the U.S.S.R.'s total efforts do not equal those of the United States, competition in assisting underdeveloped areas is one of the most prominent features of competitive coexistence. The Soviet elite has chosen to direct major efforts toward these states, viewing them as the possible key to victory in the struggle between communism and capitalism. For the United States, these intensified Soviet efforts compound the intrinsically difficult problem of economic development.

Although the United States has continued and increased its programs of assistance to underdeveloped areas, several questions remain open and the direction of our effort is still subject to modification. Perhaps the most basic question concerns the appropriate level of economic assistance: Should American aid be increased as many in underdeveloped countries would like, held constant as it more or less has been since 1953 (although there have recently been some increases), or decreased as some Congressmen urge? The answer depends first upon assumptions about United States interests in underdeveloped areas: How vital are these countries and how will we be affected by economic development there? It also depends upon assumptions about the possibilities for economic growth, the proper and most advantageous role for private and public efforts, and the effects of outside economic help. In addition, estimates must be made about United States capabilities. Our interests can be spelled out fairly concretely; making the other assumptions is more difficult, they involve numerous imponderables. Other basic questions are: What sort of aid should we give and to whom should it be given? Should we assume that a major and immediate military threat to underdeveloped states exists which they must meet before they can make significant economic progress and therefore devote a large share of our funds to military assistance as we presently do, or should we assume that the communist challenge is principally economic and social in nature and therefore concentrate primarily on non-military assistance? Should preference be given to states which have alliances with us, or should economic need be the sole criterion? An answer to the last question depends upon an evaluation of our alliances in under-developed areas and the psychological reactions of very different peoples. Finally, there is the question of how American aid should be given: Should we continue our present emphasis on bilateral rather than multi-lateral programs, or should this division be altered? To decide one must estimate the relative effectiveness of American and international agencies and the receptivity of underdeveloped areas to various programs.

The selections reproduced in this chapter deal with these and other basic questions. In the first selection, C. Douglas Dillon, Under Secretary of State, presents the official evaluation of the need for economic assistance to underdeveloped areas and describes the various bilateral and multilateral programs in which this country participates. Mr. Dillon's article indicates the multi-faceted nature of our present program. He emphasizes the importance of the strength of the United States economy, the necessity for military assistance, the need for increased trade, and the role of private enterprise. These factors have been emphasized by the Eisenhower administration in its approach to foreign economic assistance.

The second selection is taken from a book by Edward S. Mason, Dean of Harvard University's Graduate School of Public Administration and frequent consultant to the United States Government on economic problems. He analyzes in detail the Soviet challenge in underdeveloped areas and American interests in economic development. He concludes that our political and security interests are the most basic, that they justify our program and should determine its nature. It is interesting to note how this hardheaded realism conflicts with Secretary Dillon's plea for presenting American foreign assistance programs in a more altruistic light. On the basis of his analysis, Mr. Mason thinks that the United States should give more assistance to underdeveloped areas and that less emphasis should be placed on military aid.

Max F. Millikan and W. W. Rostow take an even stronger stand in this direction in the third selection. Both men are members of the economics faculty at the Massachusetts Institute of Technology and both are affiliated with M.I.T.'s Center for International Studies; Mr. Millikan is the Director and Mr. Rostow a senior staff member. The Center began a major research project on problems of economic development in 1952, and in 1957 as a result of this work Messrs. Millikan and Rostow published a widely read book advocating increased assistance to underdeveloped areas.* The article reprinted here is a follow-up to this book, reëmphasizing its policy conclusions. Messrs. Millikan and Rostow argue for an increased United States foreign assistance program generally, and particularly for increased aid to India, a state which they feel is crucially important in world politics and now ready for economic development.

Some of the questions and doubts about the utility of the present United States foreign assistance program are presented in the final selection by Zbigniew Brzezinski, a member of the Government Department at Harvard University. Barring a vastly increased foreign assistance program, which he does not foresee, Mr. Brzezinski is doubtful that underdeveloped areas will achieve economic development under democratic regimes. He thinks that circumstances are likely to force underdeveloped countries to adopt totalitarian methods, and that patterns of communist rule will be used as models. He carefully analyzes the appeal of communism for the ruling elites in underdeveloped countries. The policy Mr. Brzezinski advocates for the United States is that of being a "sympathetic observer" to the process of economic development. This article and the others reproduced here introduce the complexities of the problem of economic development.

---

* A *Proposal: Key to an Effective Foreign Policy* (New York: Harper and Brothers, 1957).

Imperatives of International Economic Growth*

by C. Douglas Dillon

I want . . . to examine . . . the demand being made upon our resources and upon our consciences to help raise the living standards of the peoples of Asia, Africa, and Latin America. These are the areas where most of mankind lives and where the struggle between freedom and totalitarianism may ultimately be decided. The need to help these peoples forward on the road to economic progress would confront us even if communism and the Sino-Soviet bloc simply didn't exist.

To me, the yearning of the peoples of Asia, Africa, and Latin America for a better way of life presents us with the ultimate challenge of our times—and our greatest hope for the future. It is clearly a moral challenge. If we fail to respond adequately, we shall stand accused as a people who proclaim our own satisfaction with the benefits of freedom but who are slothful in carrying the spirit of freedom to others around the world. The plain fact is that our posture before the world can be no better than the manner in which we fulfill the obligations that flow from our status as the most materially favored nation in all history.

ECONOMIC IMPERATIVES FOR DEVELOPED COUNTRIES

Our objective must be to help raise other peoples' standards of living. In so doing we shall also help to raise standards of personal and political freedom—a goal which is impossible of achievement in the absence of economic growth. With these objectives in mind let us consider the imperatives of international economic development.

The first imperative—and a major one—is to maintain a sturdy, growing economy in the United States. Our ability to extend aid, to offer the capital which is so badly needed in the newly emerging countries, is conditioned upon our domestic strength. Our prosperity also helps to assure them a market for their output. The movement of goods is, of course, closely related to the movement of capital. Not only must we import in order to export. We must import to keep investment flowing overseas. For, without the prospect of returns, the expanding flow of private investment is impossible.

---

* From the *Department of State Bulletin*, Vol. XL, No. 1023 (2 February 1959), pp. 165-168.

The second imperative—and one with which we must reckon increasingly as we continue to prosper—is the need to narrow the widening gap between living standards in the industrialized West and the underdeveloped nations. Ironically, while our own living standards and those of our allies in Europe are rapidly improving, living standards in the newly emerging nations are advancing much more slowly—due largely to the tremendous growth in population. Heroic efforts to narrow this gap must be made this year, not a decade hence, when it will be too late. We can be thankful that we are not alone in our recognition of this imperative. As they have emerged from the devastation of war, Britain, France, and Italy have been turning their attention increasingly to assisting the world's underdeveloped areas. Germany has recently entered this field with characteristic vigor, as have our neighbor, Canada, and other members of the British Commonwealth. So has Japan. The Japanese are now beginning to share their skills and resources with their neighbors.

But this gap cannot be closed by our efforts alone, nor even by the combined efforts of ourselves and our allies. The peoples of the newly emerging nations must make the major contribution to their own progress. I have visited many of these countries and talked to their leaders. A fresh wind is sweeping through them. Their peoples are no longer content to sit back and envy the more developed countries. They have been caught up in what has been aptly described as the revolution of rising expectations. Their leaders are desperately trying to meet these expectations. They need our help in their great effort.

Military security and internal stability must be present to provide the framework in which economic progress can take place at a steady and acceptable rate. Many of the newly emerging nations, especially in Asia and Africa, are plagued by the tensions inherent in the transition to new-found political independence. Our mutual security program has been of assistance in this respect by making available equipment, training, and defense support for indigenous military and civil forces.

A third imperative is the maintenance of adequate markets on which the developing countries can place their goods. These countries must sell their products in order to obtain the industrial equipment needed for development. We have made significant strides toward keeping our market open to the surplus production of all countries of the free world through the extension of our Reciprocal Trade Agreements Act on a realistic, long-term basis. We are also working with other countries to expand trade through the operations of the General Agreement on Tariffs and Trade. We must continue to pursue ways to remove artificial restraints upon world trade—our own and those imposed by others. Since many of the less developed countries now find their exports concentrated in a few primary commodities, we must stand ready to study ways to help avoid disastrous price fluctuations and to assist them in diversifying their economies.

NEED FOR TECHNICAL AND MANAGERIAL SKILLS

A fourth requirement for the newly emerging nations is the crying need for the technical and managerial skills which are the bedrock of development. Without them no amount of capital will bring about growth. The United States has, over a period of years, made important contributions in this area: bilaterally, through our International Cooperation Administration and, multilaterally, through the United Nations and the Organization of American States. The need for technical skills is fully recognized by the developing nations themselves. For example, the recent annual report of the Colombo Plan's Consultative Committee, said:[1]

> In a year which has seen intensive consideration given to increasing the capital resources of leading lending institutions, it is now urgent that the less developed countries give greater attention to the development of the human skills which can assure the appropriate and effective utilization of these capital resources.

A fifth necessity is private investment. If we are to be of maximum help to less developed countries, our private resources—which are far larger than those Government can possibly provide—must be welcomed and drawn upon to the greatest extent possible. We are constantly seeking ways to stimulate the flow of private American investment abroad. The investment guaranty program of the ICA has been steadily expanding. Through tax treaties, through our system of credit for foreign income taxes paid, and through other provisions of the Internal Revenue Code, the United States is endeavoring to avoid double taxation and thus facilitate American investment abroad. In our current tax-treaty negotiations we have introduced an important innovation. We are preparing to give tax credit for certain income taxes waived by less de-

---

[1] For an extract from the annual report, see the *Department of State Bulletin* of Dec. 1, 1958, p. 853.

veloped countries as an inducement to investment, as if they had, in fact, been collected abroad. Currently we are studying ways to ascertain how the Government can more effectively enlist the aid of private enterprise in achieving the objectives of our foreign policy. A group of distinguished citizens drawn from the Business Advisory Council of the Department of Commerce is now working actively on the preparation of concrete suggestions, and the President has stated his intention of submitting legislation on this subject to the Congress.

A sixth requirement is for public loans on normal bankable terms. Such loans are now being extended by the International Bank for Reconstruction and Development and the International Monetary Fund. These organizations have a special virtue, for they draw on both the public and private resources of the entire free world. The United States has believed in, contributed to, and supported these agencies from the very beginning. The directors of these institutions, acting upon an American suggestion, have proposed to expand their resources.[2] The United States also extends bankable loans for development through the Export-Import Bank, which has made an outstanding contribution to economic progress.

A seventh requirement is for development financing which will provide flexible terms of repayment. Many sound projects which are essential to development cannot qualify for bankable loans. It was to help finance such projects on a businesslike basis that the United States Congress established the Development Loan Fund. It works closely with our Export-Import Bank and with the World Bank to stimulate an increased flow of bankable loans for development programs. One of its objectives is to help stimulate private enterprise, which is so essential to the stability of the less developed areas. In its first year of operation it has proved itself as a highly effective tool for economic development. It deserves your full and active support.

The United States is also working with its sister republics of the other Americas toward the establishment of an inter-American financial institution. And we are suggesting the establishment of an International Development Association closely affiliated with the International Bank. Such an association would be a multilateral version of our own Development Loan Fund. It would provide a means whereby other countries able to do so could join in financing development projects. We are now

---

[2] *Ibid.*, Nov. 17, 1958, p. 793.

actively examining the feasibility of such an institution with our friends and allies. This proposal, as many of you know, sprang originally from an imaginative concept of Senator Monroney, who has long been a leader in our nation's efforts to aid the newly emerging peoples.

ECONOMIC IMPERATIVES FOR UNDERDEVELOPED COUNTRIES

Now I have been discussing the imperatives which depend heavily upon the initiative and the resources of the more developed nations. There are other imperatives of economic development which rest largely with the peoples of the underdeveloped nations themselves. I shall mention them briefly:

1. The need to create a climate in which foreign private investment can flourish;

2. The need to stimulate national savings so as to accumulate the domestic capital which is needed to insure stability and economic progress;

3. A willingness on the part of indigenous capital and business to welcome competition and assume risks normal to healthy free enterprise;

4. The reduction of traditional social and cultural barriers to economic progress, whether based upon class, race, or tradition;

5. The need to emphasize scientific, technical, financial, and commercial studies in their educational systems—plus a willingness on the part of the more talented individuals to seek training in skills directly related to economic progress rather than to pursue education primarily as a means of enhancing social prestige.

These needs are rooted in problems based on attitudes, tradition, and established social patterns. They are resistant to change. They will not all be met tomorrow. But they must eventually be met if the newly emerging peoples are to make a successful transition to a state of steady economic growth.

REDEFINING OUR NATIONAL PURPOSE

Finally I come to an imperative which is of crucial importance to this nation. I refer to the need for redefining our national purpose in extending aid to other countries of the free world.

I sometimes wonder if we haven't fallen into a trap of our own making when, in seeking support for our mutual security program, we present it to the American people mainly as an answer to the menace of Communist aggression. We find that our motives are sometimes misunderstood abroad. I wonder if we haven't allowed ourselves to be identified in the eyes of large parts of the world as defenders of our own *status quo*, rather than as a people whose motivations are founded upon principle and whose response to the needs of others arises out of a deep sense of moral responsibility.

We must clearly establish the fact that all of our endeavors in the foreign aid field are designed as part of one common free-world enterprise. We must consolidate a communion of interest with the aspiring peoples. I know of only one way to shape an image of integrity and responsibility. That is to exhibit integrity and responsibility. This we have most assuredly done. But perhaps we have allowed our good deeds to be obscured in the fog generated by our problems with the Soviet Union.

I neither overlook nor minimize the dangers to this country inherent in masses of men and weapons, as well as technical and industrial resources, in the hands of an implacable Communist enemy. Without question, economic and technical assistance to the newly developing nations is in our national self-interest. However, we do ourselves a grave injustice and distort our true image before the world if we give our foreign aid program a wholly selfish cast. For this program rests squarely in the great tradition of idealism that has motivated the American people since our earliest beginnings.

The Marshall plan, the point 4 program, and the present mutual security program have no parallel in all history. The willing acceptance by the American people of the challenge to help free other peoples from the bitter slavery of poverty is one of the greatest moral achievements of this century. We should not permit it to be derided by the cynical or deprecated by the uninformed.

. . . our foreign aid programs grew naturally out of our social, cultural, and religious heritage. We have accepted a great challenge from which we cannot draw back. If we answer it successfully we shall be assured a place in history as one of the great humanitarian peoples of all times. In the words of Arnold Toynbee:

> Our age will be well remembered, not for its horrifying crimes or its astonishing inventions, but because it is the first generation since the dawn of history in which mankind dared to believe it practical to make the benefits of civilization available to the whole human race.

We are the natural leaders of that generation. Our duty and our path are clear.

American Interests in Underdeveloped Areas*

by Edward S. Mason

Since the War—1946 to 1954 inclusive—the United States has committed nearly 50 billion dollars in loans and grants to foreign aid programs, military and economic. Approximately 2 to 3 billions of this have taken the form of technical and economic assistance to the development of so-called underdeveloped areas. Speaking in the vernacular, 2 billion dollars "ain't hay"; neither, however, considering the sumptuousness of the table set for other types of economic and military assistance, can it be called caviar. The program of technical and economic assistance to underdeveloped areas has been to date a relatively small program. Should this program be continued? If so, should it be enlarged or should it be diminished? These are the questions before us.

The answer depends in part on whether the areas in question are susceptible to economic development and, in particular, whether substantial development can be brought about by foreign assistance. In order to get ahead with the argument let me indicate in advance my tentative conclusions on this subject; substantial economic growth is possible in the areas in question and can be facilitated by foreign assistance. Assuming this to be a fact, the question becomes, what interest has the United States in using taxpayers' money to promote the economic growth of underdeveloped areas?

Before getting down to business it is necessary, however, to define and limit our problem somewhat further. The term undeveloped—or underdeveloped—area, which is currently so much used, and abused, carries with it the implication of capability for development or growth. But, if capability for growth is the criterion, it is by no means obvious that Africa, southern Asia and the Middle East are the true underdeveloped areas. In terms of unexploited natural resources it would appear to be Canada or Australia rather than India or Indonesia that are under-

---

* From *Promoting Economic Development*, pp. 8-32, by Edward S. Mason. Copyright 1955 by Claremont College, Claremont, California, for the Associated Colleges at Claremont. Reprinted by permission of the publishers.

developed. In terms of what enterprise and technological improvement may be expected to accomplish over the next few decades, perhaps the United States is the underdeveloped area rather than the Middle East. As used here, the term merely means poor—an underdeveloped area is one with a low per-capita income.

The term poor is used advisedly. The first impression of a new arrival from the United States in the Middle East or in southern Asia is that the economic situation is somehow anachronistic. How can these conditions exist in the twentieth century? The fact, of course, is that poverty is the rule among nations. Three-quarters of the world's population live this way. The western fringe of Europe, most of North America, and a few other scattered areas form the exception not the rule.

But, although all underdeveloped areas are characterized—or rather defined—by low per-capita incomes, there are, of course, enormous differences among them with respect both to potentialities of economic growth and to the character of United States interests in the area. Limitations of time and knowledge constrain me to a concentration on that underdeveloped area known as southern Asia and I shall be particularly concerned with the problems of Pakistan.

The area as a whole, as I define it, includes, in addition to Pakistan, India, Ceylon, Burma, Thailand and Indonesia. There are sufficient differences among these countries to indicate a variety of problems faced by the United States in the determination of policy. Nevertheless, the similarities are such as to permit certain generalizations relevant to the whole area. All the countries of southern Asia are heavily populated in relation to available natural resources; there are no broad, fertile, untouched expanses of territory like those opened to settlement and development in the Western Hemisphere during the nineteenth century. All the countries in question have been the seats of civilizations that were old before the Western Hemisphere was suspected. Forms of social organization and ways of doing things have been sanctioned by centuries of usage; there exists here no virgin social wax on which may be easily impressed the pattern of western ways and habits of thought. All the countries in the area, with the exception of Thailand, have had a long colonial experience which, from the point of view of potential economic development, has its advantages as well as disadvantages. All these countries, again with the exception of Thailand, are newly come to independence, and have, as a result, governments of varied but limited experience. All have the predominantly agricultural economies characteristic of underdeveloped areas. At the same time all are governed by regimes that not only profess but actually have an intense interest in economic development.

The whole area may be said to be shaken by the impact of the Communist revolution in China. But the susceptibilities of the various countries to internal subversion and the reactions of their governments to the external threat of Communism is decidedly various. Indonesia and India have strong indigenous Communist movements. Thailand, Burma and Indonesia have strong Chinese minorities, imperfectly assimilated and a source of danger in the event of further Chinese expansion. Both India and Pakistan have strong religious minorities remaining after partition. There are 10 million Hindus in Pakistan, mainly in East Bengal, and 40 million Moslems in India. Both minority groups complain—and with justice—of persecution.

Pakistan and Thailand have taken their stand firmly with the United States and are receiving military aid. All the countries in the area, however, have qualified for technical assistance and India, in addition, has been receiving special economic assistance. India aspires to the leadership of a neutralist bloc in southern Asia and Indonesia, Burma and Ceylon have been willing to date, though in varying degree, to follow the Indian example. No country in the area can be said to have a thoroughly stable government though the sources and degrees of stability differ greatly. . . .

To repeat, the question now before us is whether United States programs in support of economic development in southern Asia should be increased, diminished or discontinued. Again let me say that one of the assumptions underlying this discussion is that it is possible to promote economic development in this area by means of aid from abroad.

International as well as domestic politics has been described as the art of winning friends and influencing people. Whatever relevance this statement may have to the domestic scene it fails to describe the basis of sensible action in the international arena. Influencing people may be a proper matter of concern but winning friends seems to me of negligible importance. Lord Palmerston is supposed to have said with respect to British foreign policy, "Britain has no permanent friends: she has only permanent interests." We Americans are, perhaps, too prone to rejoice in superficial evidences of friendships among nations and to lament when the evidence shows that the United States is not universally loved. As long as the tie between us and other countries is a persistent similarity of interest there is little need to worry about whether Americans are or are not beloved. The time to worry is when interests diverge or are thought to diverge.

What, then, are the substantial American interests in the development of underdeveloped areas? They are usually described as humanitarian, economic and security interests.

Humanitarianism as a fundamental motivation has certainly played an enormously important role in American action, whether public or private, in the undeveloped areas of the world. It requires a certain amount of missionary spirit for a man to be willing to leave his family for two years and to settle down in a primitive Iranian or Indian village to teach the local farmers how to improve their agricultural practices—even though that man is on the United States government payroll. And American history is studded with private humanitarian ventures, both religious and secular in the countries with which we are concerned. Furthermore, as Professor Viner has pointed out, "It is an unexpected tribute to our national modesty that there seems to be no American history of our record in this connection. . . ." [1]

Nevertheless, humanitarianism can hardly be described as a national interest or as an important objective of public policy. Even in those cases where the United States has acted to combat the effects of natural disaster there has usually been an ulterior motive. The so-called $100 million wheat loan—read gift—to Pakistan, for example, made in 1952 to alleviate the effect of crop failure in West Pakistan was not unrelated to the highly important domestic problem of the disposal of agricultural surpluses. And even the magnificent United States Government health program undertaken during the summer of 1954 in East Bengal in an attempt to curb a cholera epidemic expected with the recession of disastrous floods, was undertaken to serve other than humanitarian purposes. The dedicated American civilian and military personnel wading through the flooded cobra-infested Ganges delta to inoculate 2 million Bengali were certainly and strongly imbued with humanitarian impulses, but in government circles the talk was of the magnificent propaganda effect of this effort in southeast Asia. It is no criticism of the United States or of any other country to say that humanitarianism is not an important national interest; governments simply do not act on the basis of such unadulterated considerations.

---

[1] "The Role of the United States in the World Economy"—paper prepared for a session of the Bicentennial Celebration at Columbia University, May 27-29, 1954.

Nevertheless the humanitarian motivations that have led countless Americans, both in and out of government, to give their lives to the improvement of conditions in underdeveloped countries have an important bearing on United States action with respect to these countries. Devoted efforts to educate and to alleviate suffering and disease have created a reservoir of good will in these countries which—*if it is joined to a persistent similarity of interest*—makes effective cooperation infinitely easier. The American University in Beirut and Roberts College in Istanbul have educated generations of Arab and Turkish leaders and have created attitudes toward the United States that tend to survive anything except a disastrous conflict of interest. The persistent and increasingly successful effort of Sister Benedict to create in Dacca, the capital of East Bengal, the only modern hospital available to a population of 42 million, is a magnificent achievement which influences the attitudes of thousands of Bengali toward the United States and toward Americans. The Seventh Day Adventist Hospital in Karachi is by far the best hospital in this capital city of over a million. It has been administered and staffed by a number of devoted Americans whose influence has been large and pervasive. Furthermore, these are but a few examples of hundreds of effective American humanitarian enterprises in the areas with which we are now concerned.

When, however, the reservoir of good will created by humanitarian activities is not joined to a similarity of national interest or when there occurs a shift in national interests this reservoir quickly evaporates. The leading example, of course, is China. Americans labored devotedly in this vineyard for decades and this, no doubt, accounts in part for the acute sensitiveness of our reaction to events in China now that that country has turned against us.

It is nevertheless in the national interest of the United States, evenly narrowly concerned, to encourage these humanitarian efforts. Any intelligent administrator of foreign policy would consider this "good business." But it is good precisely because it is not business, and it is in the national interest precisely because these ventures are undertaken with little or no thought of serving the national interest. Humanitarianism has been an important motivation for thousands of Americans working in undeveloped areas throughout the world. Their efforts have created a stock of good will toward the United States that can and does influence the conduct of foreign affairs. But undertaking good works abroad without regard to national benefit is not now, and never has been, an objective of public policy. The morality of governments does not stretch this far.

I stress this point because there is much misunderstanding in certain underdeveloped areas concerning the amount of assistance that can be expected from the United States and the terms on which it is likely to be available. In certain circles abroad the dispensing of aid by the United States is regarded as not only a duty, but a privilege. To a generation of Indian students brought up on Lord Keynes it is obvious that the United States lacks investment opportunities sufficient to absorb her annual volume of savings and that the underdeveloped areas in general, and India in particular, are doing us a favor by maintaining employment in the United States when they receive economic assistance. To others it is equally apparent that the wealthy nations of the world have a moral obligation to give to the less wealthy.[2] They point out that in the advanced capitalist countries of the West there has been, during the last half century, a strong tendency toward equalization of incomes through progressive taxation and the provision by the state of various welfare services.

What this argument neglects is the fact that such income redistribution as has taken place has not been the result of voluntary offerings by the well-to-do; it has been compelled by government. And in the international arena there is to date no power that is likely to be able to compel well-to-do nations to share their substance with the less well-to-do. If the United States does, in fact, embark on a program of economic assistance to the underdeveloped areas it will be because we believe that substantial United States interests will be furthered thereby.

The real objectives of public policy, as Adam Smith recognized long ago, are defense and opulence. It is the economic and the security in-

---

[2] Our admirable former Ambassador to India, Chester Bowles, apparently believes we have such an obligation. Cf. "The U.S. and Asia" in A Guide to Politics, 1954, editors Quincy Howe and Arthur M. Schlesinger, Jr., p. 75. "We should recognize frankly that the wealth drawn by the European powers from Asia and invested in the United States played a large part in our own economic development. Not as a charity but as an act of simple justice we should provide non-military grants and loans now to help free Asians build a better future."

In the first place it is dubious whether European investments in the United States depended to a considerable extent on "wealth drawn from Asia." In the second place what we secured from Europe in the way of capital assistance were private investments on which the investors expected to—and usually did—secure a sizeable return. These were not grants-in-aid or Government "loans" made with no expectation of repayment.

terests of the United States in the development of the underdeveloped areas of the world that need to be examined.

The case for our economic interests can be put very simply. It is said that the American economy cannot hope to grow and flourish in the midst of a poverty-stricken world. It is also said that the United States must necessarily become increasingly dependent on the underdeveloped areas of the world as sources of raw material supply and that *ipso facto* we must increasingly look toward these areas as markets for our finished products. There is a little merit in this case but so little that it does not, in my opinion, justify a substantial program of foreign aid and technical assistance on these grounds alone.

The American economy has, in fact, grown mightily for the last century and a half in the midst of a world that for the mass of the population was poverty stricken, and there is no overriding reason why we cannot expect to continue to do so. Since 1800 the national income of the United States has, roughly, doubled every twenty-five years and per-capita income has, at least, doubled every half-century. During this period per-capita incomes in most of what are now the underdeveloped areas of the world have changed very little. The fact is that, over this long period, the distribution of per-capita income among the countries of the world has grown less, rather than more, equal. Western Europe, North America and a few other areas have shown a continuous increase but the vast population of Asia has remained relatively stagnant.

The Communists tell us, of course, that the capitalist West has flourished at the expense of the undeveloped colonial areas of the world. The West has grown rich because the others have remained poor. Nothing could be farther from the truth. Throughout most of its history the United States has been without colonial possessions and into such colonies as we have had we have put far more than we have ever taken out. In western Europe the Scandinavian countries have managed to fare better without colonies than have most of those with colonial possessions. And for the colonial powers themselves, the economic advantages derived from overseas territories have varied directly with the rate of economic development in those territories.

There can be no doubt that acceleration in the rate of development of the underdeveloped areas of the world would benefit not only these areas but all countries trading with them. Among these countries is the United States which would certainly fare better in a world that is less, rather than more, poverty stricken. But economic advancement elsewhere is not a necessary condition to our own continued economic development. Neither our total exports nor our total imports amount to as much as 5 per cent of national income. And though expanding international trade would facilitate economic growth in the United States it is not a prior condition to growth. Looking at the situation from a narrowly economic point of view I find no justification for the plea that a sizeable foreign aid program to promote economic development elsewhere is necessary to our own continued economic prosperity.

This judgment is reinforced when attention is directed specifically to the importance to us of the underdeveloped areas as sources of raw materials and as markets for our finished products. It is, of course, true that during the last quarter century we have become a net importer of raw materials and foodstuffs. It is also true that with trade barriers no higher than they are now our dependence on foreign sources of raw material supply will inevitably increase. Furthermore, the outflow of dollars required to finance raw material imports will provide increasingly important markets for the export of American manufacturers. We may, in the expected course of events, therefore, look forward to an increasing and mutually beneficial trade with the raw material exporting, underdeveloped areas of the world.

It does not follow from this, however, that a check to the growth of this trade would have profoundly adverse effects on the United States economy. Nor does it follow that we should do everything possible, and embark on a large foreign aid program in order to promote this trade. The United States is relatively invulnerable to a disappearance of foreign sources of raw material supply given time to make the necessary adjustments. To have to rely on higher-cost domestic sources— either natural or synthetic—would be, of course, unfortunate, but it would not be disastrous.[3]

Directing attention specifically to southern Asia, we find this area to be a primary source of some important United States raw materials imports including tin, rubber, manganese, jute and mica. A sudden cessation of imports from the area would, of course, present difficulties. But given time to make the adjustments, synthetic can replace natural rubber, other fabrics plus paper can substitute for jute, manganese can be obtained from other sources or even from domestic output though this is high-cost. Even tin, in its most important uses, can be replaced

---

[3] This position is argued at greater length in a paper of mine, "An American View of Raw Material Problems" in the *Journal of Industrial Economics*, November, 1952.

by plastics, glass or other materials. The strength of our own raw material position plus the possibilities of substitution are such as to make this country relatively invulnerable to the loss of any limited foreign source of supply.

Let us be clear, however, where this argument leads us. I am not presenting a case for economic isolationism. The economic growth of the United States is made somewhat easier if growth likewise takes place in the underdeveloped areas of the world. It is better for us economically if we can depend on low-cost foreign sources of raw material supply than to be forced to exploit high-cost domestic sources or to develop synthetic substitutes. Furthermore, it must be recognized, in framing our commercial policies, that changes of small consequence to the American economy may have large effects abroad. But the favorable repercussion on the United States economy of an accelerated rate of growth in underdeveloped areas is not—in itself—likely to be such as to justify a large United States foreign aid program designed to promote this development. We can obtain a larger return for our money elsewhere.

If humanitarianism and economic interest are rejected as insufficient justification for United States foreign technical assistance and economic aid to underdeveloped areas, where then is justification to be found if indeed it can be found at all? Or, to put the question in less prejudicial fashion, is there a persuasive case either for or against the use of United States taxpayers' money to promote economic development abroad? If there is such a case it is presumably to be found in the realm of American security interests. But it must be recognized that United States security policy, with respect to underdeveloped areas in general, and to Asia in particular, is in a singularly unformed and ambiguous state. Furthermore, the formulation of such a policy confronts a series of issues that, though highly debatable, have been to date inadequately debated in this country. If aid is to be given should it be exclusively military or partly economic and, if the latter, in what proportions? Should aid of whatever sort be limited to those countries able and willing to defend themselves against Communist aggression? How far should able and willing to defend against Communist aggression be interpreted to mean able to put a military force in the field and willing to accept United States leadership in foreign affairs? Is United States leadership to be exercised through bilateral dealings or mainly by way of regional alliances? Is a neutralist foreign policy on the part of an undeveloped country reason enough to deny aid regardless of the danger of internal subversion? If economic development is judged to be a bulwark against subversion, to what extent can and should the United States intervene in the domestic affairs of those countries to which we are willing to extend aid, in order to make this aid effective? These questions are all relevant to United States security policy and all difficult to answer. Before attempting a discussion of them let me review briefly what seem to me the main lines of development of United States security policy since the War.

While a Utopian "One Worldism" obviously seized the imagination of some Americans in high positions during the War, this notion barely survived the cessation of hostilities. Washington knew for certain by the time of the Potsdam Conference in 1945 that our war-time ally, the Soviet Union, was going to prove an exceedingly intractable opponent in any post-war settlement. We were at that time, however, still a long way from a recognition of the fact that the world was already divided. From 1945 until 1947, when our attention was centered almost exclusively on Europe, the objective was to bring into being a disarmed and neutralized Germany and Austria and a Europe exclusively aligned to neither side. The rapid acquisition by Russia of its satellite powers in the Balkans, culminating with the subversion of Czechoslovakia, and the failure in four successive Four-Power Conferences to put into effect agreed policy toward Germany and Austria, put an end to all that.

The change in American orientation was heralded by the Greek-Turkish Aid Program designed to prevent these countries too from becoming Russian satellites, initiated in March, 1947, and by the enunciation of the Marshall Plan in June. By the end of the year the last Four-Power Conference had been held, and in the spring of 1948 Congress had set the Marshall program in motion. But, though the principal motivation of the Marshall Plan was to promote the security of the United States the means were exclusively economic assistance. The danger was conceived to be the internal subversion of western Europe rather than military invasion and the appropriate remedy was considered to be relief and reconstruction. Although the United States began pressing for the rearmament of Western Germany in 1950 and the preliminary discussion of the North Atlantic Treaty Organization dates from 1948 the shift from predominantly economic to predominantly military assistance to western Europe, symbolized by the change in name of the Economic Cooperation Administration to Mutual Security Agency, did not take place until 1951.

In the Far East, an area relatively neglected in the early post-war period, the United States watched the Communist absorption of China with something like the paralyzed fascination of a bird entrapped by a snake. Although the debacle in China led us to revolutionize our thinking on the prospective role of Japan in our defense strategy, our military expenditures continued to decline—with the approval of both parties let it be said—and amidst the general acclaim of the United States populace—until the beginning of the Korean War.

Korea marks the end of an epoch. During the three years of that frustrating and indecisive war, United States military expenditures continually increased. And elsewhere in the world a program of economic assistance became almost exclusively a military assistance program. In Europe the accent was on the rearmament of the NATO countries and the promotion of a European Defense Community that was ultimately to fail. In the Far East Formosa was fortified, Japan became our principal military staging area and was freed by the Japanese Treaty, within limits, to undertake rearmament; assistance was given to France in her unsuccessful war in Indo-China. In the Middle East, Greece and Turkey continued to be the recipients of large military aid programs and a beginning was made to the military support of the Middle Eastern countries. Spain began to receive military assistance and a military aid program was designed for Pakistan. Economic assistance was very largely converted into a supplement to rearmament and programs of economic aid and technical assistance unrelated to military program dwindled to very small proportions.

At the risk of extreme simplification the security policy of the United States during the post-war period may be said to have passed through three stages. The first, which lasted roughly from the end of the war to the initiation of the Marshall Plan, witnessed an attempt to accomplish, with the cooperation of our late allies, a disarmament and neutralization of our late enemies and at the same time to limit so far as possible spheres of exclusive influence. The second stage, running approximately from the initiation of the Marshall Plan to the Korean War, saw a recognition of a division of the world into contesting groups and an assessment of the danger to the United States chiefly in terms of subversion, with economic assistance to endangered areas as the principal remedy. In the third and current stage, United States security policy appears to envisage the threat as primarily military and the appropriate response a build-up of our own military strength and the assistance of those allies able and willing to cooperate with us in the sphere of military operations.

This development of United States policy has been accompanied by internal divisions and recriminations that have threatened at times to become as serious a menace to our own security as the actions of an external enemy. The so-called "great debate" on United States foreign policy has frequently descended to the level of a bar-room brawl. Honest mistakes of judgment on the part of responsible officials have been called treason and differences of opinion have been treated as unmistakable evidences of subversion. All this has not contributed much to the formulation of sensible answers to a very difficult set of problems. And a continuation of this state of mind may well make the formulation of an intelligent American security policy in southern and eastern Asia impossible.

In the current debate on United States policy in Asia it is easy to see the logic of the extreme positions. It is much less easy to discern a position that makes sense in the light of *all* the facts. The arguments for the extreme positions have their beginning in diametrically opposed conceptions of the nature of the Communist threat. On one side is the view that this threat is exclusively or primarily military. The regimes in Russia and China are aggressive nationalisms out to conquer the world or such parts of it as are vulnerable to military penetration. Consequently the only appropriate response is a military response. Economic assistance is justifiable only to the extent that it results in military strength.

This analysis supports a policy of building military strength in those countries that share this view of the nature of the threat and are able and willing to oppose it. In Asia this appears to mean Japan, Korea, Formosa, the Philippines, Thailand, Pakistan, and Turkey with the possibility that a few others might, in the course of time, be added. Assistance to those countries that do not share our aims is, according to this argument, worse than useless. It could lead to the strengthening of countries that may eventually become our enemies. At best it discourages our friends by making it clear that the reward of economic assistance has nothing to do with right thinking and good behavior. To those who think of the threat as exclusively military the idea of drawing a line beyond which aggression will automatically provoke massive retaliation appears to have great appeal. Furthermore, since to them the threat is exclusively military, the desire and ability to make war becomes the only test of what governments we should be willing to support.

To the extremists on the other side the threat lies exclusively or primarily in the appeal of Communism to the underprivileged masses and the struggling, newly independent governments of Asia. The nature of the appeal of Communism is variously interpreted. The Soviet Union has accomplished a rapid economic development through industrialization. Economic development and industrialization are passionately desired in Asia. Communism is a revolutionary movement that has swept away privileged position and feudal relationships in other parts of the world and might do the same thing in Asia. Communism, in the eyes of most Asians, does not share the taint of colonialism and in the eyes of some it is the new broom that could clear the vestiges of colonialism out of Asia.

The appropriate course of United States Asian policy, for those who interpret the Communist threat in this manner, runs in quite a different direction from building up positions of military strength. We should, in their view, seek to align ourselves with the "progressive," democratic forces in Asia; we should make economic assistance available to democratic governments without regard to their ability or desire to arm themselves against Soviet aggression; we should refuse assistance to governments dominated by feudal elements and align ourselves squarely against colonialism. People of this persuasion envisage the struggle as an ideological, politico-economic conflict between totalitarianism and democracy with victory going to the side that demonstrates the greatest capacity for helping the mass of the population to a better standard of living. In this struggle our greatest weapon is conceived to be economic assistance and, if Communism is turned back in Asia, it will be because, with United States help, popular governments have been able to show their citizens that economic growth is possible under democratic institutions.

If the Communist threat in Asia were exclusively either military or ideological the designing of an appropriate American response would be easy. In fact, however, it is both. It is at the same time an aggressive nationalism that can be countered only by positions of military strength and a revolutionary movement of great appeal in southern and eastern

Asia that can be effectively countered only by giving the Asian masses some hope that their aspirations can be satisfied by non-Communist means. Since this is so, a successful United States policy in Asia must meet both threats. We could, by partial action, succeed in building up positions of military strength only to watch them become surrounded by a sea of revolutionary Communism. We could also, by partial action in the other direction, contribute to economic development in a group of sitting-duck democracies only to see them overwhelmed by military aggression.

It must be obvious, however, that devising an American policy that meets the Communist threat in Asia in whatever form this threat assumes is a complicated and difficult task. It is not a problem that can be solved by a doctrinaire approach. If military strength is a necessary ingredient in an effective program it may have to be purchased by support of governments that do not meet all the requirements of a forward-looking democracy. If countering the social and ideological appeal of Communism is an essential part of the program we may have to give economic support to governments with whose foreign policies we are far from sympathetic. Nor can the United States deal with the countries comprised within its Asian policy in isolation from each other. What we do in our relations with Korea and Formosa will have repercussions in India. What we do in India will affect our relations with Thailand, Burma and Indonesia and, it goes without saying, Pakistan.

Since I am convinced that the threat in Asia is both military and socio-ideological, both a military and a non-military response seem to me necessary. War in Korea and later in Indo-China inevitably channeled United States action in a military direction. But even after Korea and Indo-China and elsewhere in Asia our policy has become predominantly—and to my mind too predominantly—military. This policy has brought us certain obvious assets; it has also produced some liabilities and has saddled us with certain responsibilities that are not always fully realized.

Our military action has brought us staunch allies, well drilled and well equipped armies and strategic space in Korea and Formosa. It has also joined us to regimes heavily motivated toward reconquest of lost territories and ready to involve themselves and us in world war at the drop of a hat if and when this becomes feasible. The acquisition of these allies can be considered an asset if, and only if, adventurism is strictly controlled. A failure of the United States to insist on responsible action would have adverse repercussions far beyond the limits of Asia.

American post-war leadership has converted Japan from a war-time enemy to the potential bulwark of the Free World's Pacific defenses. United States military expenditures in Japan since 1950 have greatly assisted economic recovery and Japan can be expected within the near future to shoulder a substantial share of our joint military burden. She can be expected to do so—that is—if ways and means can be found to develop export markets sufficiently large to permit payment for Japan's necessary imports. Japan has an acute balance of payment problem which can only be permanently solved by bringing southeast and southern Asia into more active trading relations. The East Asia Co-prosperity Sphere, or at least a large part of it, will have to be revived as a trading entity if Japan is going to be able to make its desired contribution to the defense of the Pacific. Our security objectives with respect to Japan can obviously not be attained by exclusively military means.

On the other side of Asia, Turkey, and now Pakistan, are recipients of United States military aid. Both countries have sound military traditions and share with the United States a desire to oppose aggression. Both countries occupy strategic locations and the support of Turkey and Pakistan to the defense of the Free World is of great importance. It has already been realized in Turkey, however—and it is an obvious fact in Pakistan—that to build up military strength in an underdeveloped area at the expense of economic development is a dubious contribution to security. In the first place, unless the receiving country is to be permanently dependent on military assistance from the United States, it must develop the capacity to maintain its armed forces largely from its own output or from foreign exchange earned by its own exports. Even from the narrowly military point of view, then, economic development is a necessary requirement to adequate defense. In the second place, peoples have to be willing as well as able to fight and their willingness seems to be a good deal affected by whether they see some prospect under the existing political regime of living a fuller life. To undertake armament at the expense of economic development runs great risk of inducing such political instability as to make the contribution to security negligible. With this in mind the United States has already accompanied military assistance to Turkey with an economic aid program and we now find ourselves under the same necessity in Pakistan.

In sum, the military aspects of our security policy in Asia have brought us some vitally important acquisitions of strength. At the same time it has become obvious that if military strength is going to be sustained in underdeveloped areas of the world with the support of the populations of the countries in question, prospects for economic growth and betterment must also be sustained and this is going to require economic assistance from the United States. It is likewise clear that if these positions of strength are going to serve the interests of defense, irresponsible action must be held in check. As long as these implications and responsibilities are recognized there is little to criticize on the military side of our security program. But, as I have attempted to emphasize, the Communist threat in Asia is by no means exclusively military.

The view, however, that the United States considers the Communist menace to be exclusively military and that we are prepared to meet it only on military grounds is widespread and pervasive in Asia. Furthermore, it is not so obvious to the people of Asia as it is to us that our intentions are strictly defensive. In fact, a picture of the United States has been developing in southern and southeast Asia that, if they were confronted by it, would shock most Americans. The Communists, it is true, have had their share in painting this picture. But it has been made all too easy for them in recent years by the heavy military bias in our own foreign policy.

The governments of the countries with which we are here principally concerned are neither definitely pro-Russian nor anti-Russian. They are neither definitely pro-American nor are they anti-American. The neutralism implied in this position covers a wide range of differences of opinion among governments regarding the nature of the Communist threat, but in general most of them are strongly of an opinion that their security will not be advanced by adhering to a military alliance in conjunction with the United States. They have made their position quite clear in negotiations concerning the Southeast Asia Treaty Organization. India, Ceylon, Burma, and Indonesia have refused to participate.

The attitude of the people of these countries toward Communism as a political movement and a form of social organization is certainly ambivalent. To most of the religious people of the area whether Moslem, Hindu, Buddhist or other, the Communist doctrine of the totalitarian state with its relation of government to the individual is abhorrent. In southern Asia as elsewhere religion is a strong bulwark against Communism. The revolutionary force and bloodshed that has everywhere attended the advance of Communism certainly runs counter to a strong Asia tradition of non-violence, particularly in India. The western heritage of democracy and the rule of law has penetrated deeply into important circles in all the countries of southern Asia and particularly into the ranks of the western trained civil service.

At the same time the success of the Soviet Union in achieving economic development and industrialization has made a deep impression in Asia. For one hundred and fifty years the economies of southern and southeast Asia have been relatively stagnant while western Europe and North America have grown rich. In a few short years the Soviet Union has doubled its national income and has become a first-rate industrial power. The Soviet Union has done this, in part, by borrowing the West's most modern technical methods and she has done it while sweeping away feudal positions of privilege of a sort that are conspicuous in many parts of southern Asia. Could not Communism also accomplish this for Asia? Although the excesses in revolutionary China have awakened revulsion elsewhere in Asia and although the military aggression of the Chinese government has brought dismay in many quarters, the optimism of Chinese economic forecasts and the evidence of growing military strength have made a great impression.

What needs to be said about these 5 to 6 hundred million people of southern Asia and about their governments is that to date they are uncommitted between East and West. Nor are most of these people motivated by strong ideological views about either Communism or Capitalism. They *are* passionately interested in better standards of living and they look to their newly formed governments, mostly independent for the first time from European control, to give it to them. Economic development has, therefore, become almost the single-minded preoccupation of governments throughout this area. These relatively untried and somewhat shaky democratic regimes are likely to stand or fall depending on how well they satisfy the rising expectation of their populations.

At best it will not be easy to raise per-capita incomes in this over-populated area of the world. Nor is the task made easier by the touchy nationalism and the raw inexperience of the governments in question. I am convinced that it is impossible without a substantial increase in foreign assistance and this means largely United States assistance. The only argument for continued and increased American assistance that appeals to me is the security argument; that the safety of the United

States will be increased if some substantial measure of economic development can be brought about in southern Asia.

It would, however, be a mistake to embark on a foreign aid program for southern Asia on the assumption that to do so will assure the desired results. The argument for such a program may be persuasive but it cannot, inevitably, be conclusive. In summary the argument is as follows: (1) that an increase in per-capita incomes can be achieved but is unlikely to be achieved without substantial foreign economic assistance; (2) that an increase in per-capita incomes is a necessary condition to the maintenance of power by non-Communist regimes in southern Asia; (3) that the provision of economic assistance to those countries that are not with us will leave unimpaired our relations with these countries that are with us.

The questions whether economic development is possible in southern Asia and, if so, whether it is dependent on foreign economic assistance . . . by no means have obvious answers. The present poverty of the area severely limits the volume of domestic saving. The shortage of entrepreneurial ability and executive capacity both inside and outside of government is a serious handicap to the effective use of increased quantities of capital. And even if these limitations do not prevent a substantial increase in national income the rate of population growth may be such as to prevent the increase in national income from becoming an increase in per-capita income.

Assuming, however, that the economic well-being of the populations of southern Asia does improve can we say with assurance that the threat of Communist revolutionary overturn is at an end? At best we can say only that such an improvement is a necessary condition of political stability; it is almost certainly not a sufficient condition. The problem is obviously much more complex than any such simple relationship would suggest. About all we can say is that great expectations of economic improvement have been generated in southern Asia and that a failure of present democratic regimes to satisfy these expectations, at least in part, is likely to endanger the continued existence of these regimes.

Finally, what can be said about the impact of an American aid program that does not discriminate between friends and neutrals? In order to see this problem clearly consider the differences in our current relationships with Pakistan and with India. Pakistan is cooperating fully with us in a program designed to build positions of military strength around the periphery of Asia. India seeks the leadership in Asia of a group of countries who not only refuse to participate in a mutual defense policy but denounce attempts by this country to organize an effective defense in Asia as military provocation. In dispensing such economic and technical assistance as we are prepared to undertake in southern Asia, are we to take no account of willingness to cooperate in terms of our broad security policy?

The answer, in part, is that of course we do take account of willingness to cooperate. The very large increase in economic assistance to Pakistan in 1954-55 was not unconnected with that country's security policy. In part the answer is that we have an interest in contributing to the ability of a free country to defend itself against Communist aggression whether or not that country shares our views as to how our mutual security can best be promoted. Finally, if continued economic stagnation with associated political instability in southern Asia seems likely to broaden the area of Communist expansion, there is an argument on security grounds for promoting the development of underdeveloped countries entirely apart from narrow military considerations.

I accept this argument myself since I believe the Communist danger in Asia is both a military danger and a danger of politico-economic subversion. At the same time, while supporting an economic assistance program for India, and associated countries, I see no particular need for treating Mr. Nehru's neutralist susceptibilities with any special tenderness or consideration. If Pakistan is willing to associate herself with us in mutual defense arrangements in Asia there are strong reasons for initiating a military aid program in that country whether India likes it or not. Mr. Nehru is entitled to his assessment of the nature of the Communist menace, but so are we.

Foreign Aid: Next Phase*

by Max F. Millikan and W. W. Rostow

[1]

In the past year American economic foreign policy has moved perceptibly, if indecisively, back towards the path marked out by the Point

* From *Foreign Affairs*, Vol. XXXVI, No. 3 (April 1958), pp. 418-436. Copyright 1958 by the Council on Foreign Relations, Inc., New York. Reprinted by special permission from *Foreign Affairs*.

Four Program launched in 1949, the Gordon Gray Report of 1950 and the Nelson Rockefeller Report of 1951—a path from which the United States was diverted by the Korean War and the subsequent concentration on the build-up of military pacts (backed by military aid) around the periphery of the Communist bloc.

The acceleration of economic growth in non-Communist Asia, the Middle East, Africa and Latin America is beginning to be recognized, in fact as well as in word, as a major national objective, quite apart from military aid and the use of money to help salvage crisis situations. The Development Loan Fund exists; some $290 million has been scraped up to postpone too drastic a cutback in the Indian Second Five-Year Plan; surplus food and fibers available under Public Law 480 are beginning to be understood, both abroad and in Washington, as potentially a major constructive instrument for economic development; and before or during the NATO meeting of last December significant gestures, at least, were made by the German, Italian and American Governments looking toward coördination of the free world's development effort.

Whether there will now emerge into maturity an American and free-world economic development policy capable of protecting the common interest in a world dominated by expensive military stalemate on the one hand, and by the accelerating nationalist revolutions of Asia, the Middle East and Africa on the other, hinges in part at least on a clarification of three major issues. These are: the nature of the American interest in the revolutionary areas; the relations between private and public capital in the early stages of economic growth; the special position and problems of India.

[II]

The American interest in economic development flows from the historical status of most of the nations and regions of Asia, the Middle East, Africa and Latin America.

Economically, these stand somewhere along the path between a relatively static agricultural society and a society capable of applying promptly and productively the fruits of modern science to its natural and human resources. These transitional societies have absorbed varying degrees of modern economic activity; but they have not yet woven them together in such a way as to make economic growth a regular, automatic condition: productive investment is not yet high enough regularly to yield increases in output substantially greater than increases in population. Politically, they are somewhere in the transition from regionally based hierarchical societies, rooted in traditional land relations, to centralized states capable of providing a unified national framework for modern economic, social and political activity.

Both historically and at present the building of modern economies and centralized modern governments has been driven along less by the profit motive than by the aspirations for increased national and human dignity. Merchants and the profit motive played their part in the modernization efforts of Bismarck's Germany, Meiji Japan, Witte's Russia and Ataturk's Turkey; but soldiers, civil servants and nationalism were the more powerful agents. And so it is today in Asia, the Middle East and Africa.

In these transitional stages, nationalism may be turned in varying proportions to these three objectives: towards the consolidation of the central power of the new state over the old regional interests (as with Diem and his sects in post-1954 South Viet Nam); towards external adventure, to redress real or believed old humiliations (as with Nasser in the Middle East since 1955); or towards the economic and social modernization of the domestic society (as with the Indian Five-Year Plans). No successful politician in a transitional society can afford wholly to neglect any one of these tasks; that is, he must build up the power of the central government, assert a position of increased authority and sovereignty on the world scene, and launch some kind of program for economic and social modernization. And these three elements of policy cannot be cleanly separated.

How do these objectives relate to each other? If the local political leader concentrates merely on consolidating his central power or on rallying his people around an external objective, he may well achieve short-run success; but he will not meet the demand for economic and social progress pressing up steadily from the grass roots. He runs the longer-run risks of creating a centralized state without a viable political basis; or of exhausting his popular mandate in efforts to assert the sovereignty and power of the new nation against the external world, efforts which fail to satisfy his people's rising expectations for material advance. To be successful, a politician in a transitional society must, in the end, link nationalist fervor and the new centralized state to programs of economic and social substance.

The length of time and the vicissitudes of transition to modern economic and political status thus depend substantially on the degree to which local talent, energy and resources are channelled into the constructive tasks of modernization. The powers of the central government must, of course, be reasonably well established as a prior condition, and the government must present to its people a record of enhanced international standing; but the long-run influence of the central government depends, in the end, on its becoming a major source of energy, initiative and resource for modernizing the economy—a lesson Soekarno is being taught, painfully and late.

Communist policy is based squarely on an understanding of this precarious transitional process. Increasingly since the summer of 1951, Moscow and Peking have sought to associate Communism (as well as the Soviet Union and Communist China as governments) with the aspirations of the political leaders and peoples of the transitional areas for national independence, economic development and peace. On the other hand, Soviet diplomacy and propaganda have systematically sought to divert their attention from the tasks of modernization towards "bloody shirt" policies; that is, an obsessive concern to redress real or believed past humiliations—colonialism, Israel, Kashmir, West Irian, etc. In this connection, the resolutions generated out of the recent Cairo conference of the Afro-Asian bloc are worth careful study.

This strategy does double work for Moscow. In the short run, it creates costly disruption within the free world; it threatens the supply of essential raw materials to Western Europe; it threatens to disrupt the American air base structure; and, on the colonialism issue, it further splits the United States from Western Europe. In the long run, it creates the conditions which will help the Communists take over power. It creates these future conditions by diverting the energies of the new nations away from the tasks of economic and social modernization; and thus the people's hopes for improved welfare are frustrated. It is the Communist intent that, when these hopes for progress are sufficiently frustrated, men and women in these areas will turn to Communism. The local Communist parties are already steadily at work seeking to heighten and to exploit these frustrations.

The Communist policy being pursued in Asia, the Middle East and Africa is modelled closely—and, we believe, quite consciously—after the Communist success in China. Sun Yat-sen turned to Moscow for guidance and support after he failed to get economic and political support from the United States. In the 1920s and 1930s Moscow did, to a degree, support the Kuomintang while seeking to give it an anti-

Western cast; but the Chinese Communists at the same time, with Moscow's help and encouragement, pursued a policy first of infiltration of the Kuomintang and then of military and political obstruction designed to make it impossible for Chiang Kai-shek to achieve the social and economic progress which Chinese men and women ardently sought. And this double pattern persisted virtually down to the end: while the Soviet Union remained solemnly committed to support Nationalist China diplomatically, it turned captured Japanese arms over to the Chinese Communists in 1946. Chiang Kai-shek's view of reform as a second priority played, of course, into the hands of Communist policy throughout this sequence.

There is little doubt that Moscow and Peking regard Nasser, Nehru, Soekarno and the other non-Communist leaders of the new nations as the Chiang Kai-sheks of the future.

It is in this perspective—of short-run and long-run Communist strategic objectives—that the Soviet economic offensive should be viewed. In Jugoslavia, Egypt, Syria and Afghanistan, Moscow has urgent short-term strategic objectives; and those four countries get about three-fourths of Soviet aid outside the Communist bloc. In India, Indonesia, Burma, Ceylon and elsewhere, the amounts of aid doled out are sufficient to build up a measure of good will and a favorable image of Communist intentions; but they are grossly insufficient to supply the foreign exchange requirements for a serious economic development effort.

Nevertheless Moscow is laying out considerable capital in this effort at a time when there are ample alternative claims on Soviet resources for civil and military purposes within the Communist bloc. The problem of getting agreement within the Soviet Presidium for this rather expensive program is undoubtedly eased, however, by the increasing dependence of the Communist bloc on imported foodstuffs and raw materials. Mikoyan is probably able to claim that he can make the effort virtually pay for itself: the old Soviet principle of balancing the foreign policy books every night can be roughly maintained.

In facing Communist policy, then, we are not engaged in a popularity contest or in a numbers racket centered on total figures for aid and trade. We are confronted with a systematic effort—diplomatic, psychological, economic and political—to exploit the weaknesses, confusions and temptations of new nations in the transitional period so as to clamp Communism down firmly on them before steady economic growth and the political resilience of a modern state emerge.

Indeed, in the sweep of history, Communism as we have known it thus far in the twentieth century is likely to be viewed as a diseased form of modern state organization, capable of being imposed by a determined minority on a confused, frustrated transitional society. Conversely, a society which has passed through its economic take-off and restructured its political and social institutions around the requirements of modern statehood is likely to have a high immunity to the Communist appeal. Russia almost made it, but the First World War came at a bad time in the Russian evolution.

If this view is correct, the central objective of American policy in the transitional areas is to use whatever influence we can bring to bear to focus the local energies, talents and resources on the constructive tasks of modernization. American military strength must be used to give these nations relative security, with a minimum diversion of their own efforts; and when it is mutually judged necessary to generate local military forces, these in turn should be made to contribute wherever possible to the constructive tasks of modernization. The nineteenth century rôle of the American Corps of Engineers is a suggestive guide. Diplomatically, our stance should put a greater premium on the posture of governments towards the modernization of their own societies than on their day-to-day position in the politics of the cold war. Finally, our economic foreign policy must make it both possible and attractive for local politicians to set the aspirations of their peoples on long-term programs of modernization rather than on tempting but diversionary "bloody shirt" nationalism.

This incentive cannot be created unless American resources available for economic development are sufficiently big and offered with a continuity and on terms such that a serious operating politician can plot a long-period course with reasonable confidence.[1]

Thus the American interest in Asia, the Middle East and Africa is fundamentally political. The American interest lies in assisting the new nations to advance toward modern economic and political status while maintaining their independence and assuring the possibility of a domestic evolution which employs the political techniques of consent and safeguards the liberty of the individual. If we are prepared to recognize —as we should—that democracy is a matter of degree and of the direction of change, then our objective can be described as the creation of a

---

[1] Such was the purpose of the policy outlined last year by the present authors in "A Proposal: Key to an Effective Foreign Policy" (New York: Harper, 1957).

world of independent, democratically oriented states which have built economic growth into their societies as a regular condition. This is an objective we should be prepared to state frankly, without embarrassment. It requires an American economic development effort larger and with more continuity, one with criteria for lending vastly less ambiguous (and economically more hard-headed) than our present programs. We are unlikely to get such an effort under way until its purposes in relation to Communist strategy are widely understood.

[III]

There is a second prerequisite for a mature and effective American economic development effort. This is increased clarity and consensus on the relation between private and public enterprise both within the areas receiving American government loans and as between the public and private sources of capital and technical assistance in the United States.

In the course of the last year's reëxamination of American economic foreign policy, there were interesting and forceful assertions of three propositions: first, that private enterprise is superior in efficiency to public enterprise, even in the underdeveloped areas; second, that substantial untapped potentialities exist in public policy both for expanding American private capital exports and for increased collaboration between public and private sources of American capital; and third, that the American Government could do more than it is now doing to create a more favorable climate for private investment in the underdeveloped areas. These views were presented against the background of what appeared to be a relatively substantial increase in American private investment abroad, opening up a somewhat more optimistic vista of the future rôle of private capital exports than that generally accepted in the recent past.

So far as the ideological debate on public versus private enterprise is concerned, several things have been happening. In Western Europe and in other industrial societies, the old banner of nationalization has faded markedly within the Social Democratic parties. Men have come to learn that Marx was wrong when he regarded the public ownership of property as the only effective form of ensuring that the public interest in the economy is respected. Ways have been found for protecting the legitimate public interest in economic activities without burdening the state with heavy operating bureaucracies which, on the whole, tend to impede rather than to encourage good public as well as good economic policy. The slogans of youth are not easily surrendered, and political banners fade slowly. There is little doubt, however, that in the postwar decade the Social Democratic movements have shifted as rapidly as they safely could away from the commitment to nationalization which had grown up in the first four decades of the century.

This transition may, in time, be expected to have its impact on the politics of the underdeveloped areas, since so many of the leading figures there were strongly marked by Western Social Democratic views, and many important connections remain. More relevant, however, than the vicarious experience of Europe is the evidence accumulating in those underdeveloped areas which have gathered economic momentum: that the expansion of the local private sector, including the development of vigorous efficient modern businessmen, can constitute a valuable support to the government's larger economic and social objectives; and that, within reasonable limits, it can be made politically quite safe and economically quite wholesome to permit private foreign enterprise to operate within their countries. These trends are mainly to be observed in Latin America, but they color hopefully some American visions of the future in Asia, the Middle East and Africa; for it now appears possible that vigorous private sectors can emerge more rapidly than our somewhat static sociological analyses of entrepreneurship would suggest. Once the expectation becomes general that next year's output is likely to be larger than this year's, businessmen begin to think about plowing back profits, expanding capacity and introducing new machinery, rather than merely clinging to the older pattern of fixed output with big profit margins syphoned off to keep the family comfortable. These transitions in the outlook and operations of businessmen obviously take time; but they seem to come more quickly than many had thought, once the economy as a whole begins to gather momentum.

In this mood, a good many measures have been put forward designed to expand the rôle of American private direct investment in the underdeveloped areas. These include: improved administration of the government guarantee programs; more substantial tax incentives for private investment overseas; the merging of government and private funds in particular projects; the expanded use of management contracts; the more firm negotiation of treaty and other conditions designed to protect American private investment; and the spreading of information on the virtues and efficiency of private over public enterprise.

Even the most ardent of the recent advocates of private over public investment have been clear, however, about two things. One is that certain kinds of government investment are not only required in the underdeveloped areas but are essential to create a setting within which efficient and profitable private operations can grow: notably, investment in education, health, agricultural extension work, irrigation, transport, fuel and power. The second is that American influence to encourage the strengthening of private sectors in underdeveloped areas and to enlarge the flow abroad of American private capital is a matter in which great tact must be observed. What is basically involved is that other peoples come to accept, sometimes in the face of long-held views rooted in difficult past experience, that a vigorous private sector and foreign private investment can be made to reinforce rather than to disrupt public purposes to which they are committed.

In short, it should now be possible to crystallize a clear and well-balanced American attitude toward the issues of public and private enterprise in economic development and to mount an American policy that harnesses them in more vigorous collaboration than we have had in the past.

What such a generally hopeful perspective and policy must take into account, however, is that what we call underdeveloped areas are at very different stages on the path from traditional to modern status. The currently successful cases of private international investment tend to cluster about two extreme points along this path—that is to say, in areas which have barely moved beyond the traditional stage and where oil and other extractive foreign enterprises operate in relative (but rapidly decreasing) comfort, as in the Middle East and parts of Central Africa; and again in such new nations as Mexico which have, in fact, passed through the take-off into sustained growth and are rapidly becoming thoroughly modernized societies. Vigorous, competent businessmen have emerged in large numbers only in these latter advanced societies, and only there has the attitude towards foreign private enterprise been generally hospitable.

In between lies the difficult transitional period in which a good deal of Asia, the Middle East and Africa finds itself. In economic terms, an extremely high percentage of investment in this transitional period must go into social overhead capital. At the local end this means a high proportion of government investment. At the American end, this means a high proportion of inter-governmental loans, unless the pre-1914 private

market for foreign government bonds suddenly recreates itself. Moreover, in these transitional periods, while the new crops of modern
industrial businessmen are emerging it is likely to be a simple fact of
life that civil servants and politicians (and, sometimes, soldiers) will
perform more of the functions of entrepreneurship than American experience would find normal. Economically, this stage can give way to a
more familiar and congenial balance between public and private sectors
only when the whole modernization process has gathered momentum.
American advice and negotiation can help in this evolution; but economic progress itself is the decisive variable.

The nature of this intermediate stage explains why governments—
and inter-governmental loans—may have to play temporarily a disproportionately large rôle even outside the area of social overhead capital.
The risk of investment—and the time before payoff becomes possible—
does not lie in the nature of the individual project or its intrinsic soundness by conventional banking standards. The question is: When will
the economy as a whole enter the stage of self-sustained growth? Private
investors understandably draw back from gambling on the timing of
such profound historical changes. Governments—theirs and ours—must
live with and operate on precisely such risks; because, without adequate
governmental investment, the take-off may not occur rapidly enough to
meet the political pressures for it.

The nature of this intermediate stage explains also why such devices
as dollar loans repayable in local currencies make sense. Many nations
moving forward—whose take-offs are in the American interest, but
which have not yet occurred—can use capital productively but they
cannot generate sufficient foreign exchange and international credit-
worthiness until they achieve the stage of self-sustained growth. Soft
loans are one way of covering this interval whose length cannot be predicted with confidence. The temporary accumulation of local currencies
is, thus, a minor embarrassment in an essentially rational course of
action.

Politically, in between the two relatively comfortable stages for foreign private enterprise occurs the passage of local history in which a
modern centralized government is created and effectively takes hold. It
is to be expected on the basis of history that at some stage in the political transition the nationalist emotions which drive local politics create
a somewhat critical, if not hostile, atmosphere towards foreign investment, notably if the foreign positions in the economy became en-

trenched during a colonial or semi-colonial past. Knock-down, drag-out crises in the status of foreign enterprise are, of course, not inevitable; but changes in relationship and attitude are inevitable as the new nations take shape and become increasingly conscious of their sovereignty. A wiser and more forehanded free-world policy towards, for example, Indonesia and Egypt in recent years might well have prevented or softened the current crises in the status of foreign enterprise there; and Western oil companies (and their governments) would do well to avoid clinging rigidly to old formulas in the Middle East. But it is in the nature of the historical process taking place that a certain amount of awkwardness and readjustment will be required.

Thus it will take an understanding of what it is like to move from a traditional to a modern society—a sense of history and patience as well as a vigorous collaboration between American public and private authorities—to see us through into the stage when most men and governments in the world come to perceive that private capitalism, domestic and foreign, has an expanding rôle to play in the new nations capable of reinforcing their larger political and social objectives.

[IV]

India provides a critical focus for our economic development policies for the next decade, and a test of their meaning. There are a number of reasons for this. In the first place, the population of India includes about 40 per cent of all the people in the underdeveloped countries of the free world. Politically and strategically India is even more important than the numbers of her people would suggest. The success or failure of Indian development efforts will affect the course of events from the Celebes to Morocco. We have not yet devoted the attention and resources to Indian development problems that the American interest requires.

There are compelling technical economic reasons why, at the moment, we should be concentrating a much larger share of our capital assistance on India than even her size would dictate. To allocate development assistance to countries in proportion to their population or their relative claim on our sympathies is to misconstrue the relation between capital and the development process. The requirements for outside capital of countries seeking development vary widely depending on the stage of development they have reached. In the early precondition stages in which many of the underdeveloped countries find themselves, the amounts of capital they can productively absorb are sharply limited by shortages of skills, education, administrative capability, essential social overhead such as roads, ports, communications and the like, and by the absence of the attitudes, motivations and political leadership that make growth possible. Technical assistance and limited amounts of capital may have to be supplied for some years before the country is technically and politically ready for the take-off—the concentrated effort to launch a growth process that will be self-sustaining.

But there does come a time when the stage is set for the big push. The country finds itself in a position to launch simultaneously a wide variety of interdependent activities which reinforce each other, and whose combined effect is to produce for the first time a substantial forward movement in all major sectors of the economy at once. India is, in our judgment, at this critical turning point. For a decade or so, during this take-off, requirements for foreign capital are at a maximum. Then, if the process is successful, the country's own rising income increasingly provides the new resources which can be plowed back into investment to stabilize growth as a regular feature of the economy; and the fact of regular growth itself permits the country, once the take-off has occurred, to acquire external capital from private or other orthodox sources.

The evidences that India is ready for the take-off—indeed has already started it—are many. Over the past eight years her output of goods and services has grown by about 25 per cent. This growth has occurred in agriculture, in large-scale industry, in small-scale industry, in transport and services. In all these fields there are investment projects on the drawing boards, Indian designed and engineered, to continue the expansion. There is a growing class of competent administrators, both public and private, to undertake the work. There are clear signs of growing domestic markets to buy the new output when it is ready. There are many more things which Indian leaders must do vigorously if they are to accomplish the take-off, but they now have it in their power to take most of the necessary steps themselves.

There is, however, one major economic threat to the maintenance of momentum which can be met only by action outside India: there is a shortage of foreign exchange with which to acquire the resources needed from abroad for the investment program. The drain which India has recently suffered on her foreign exchange reserves has been caused not, as in the case of some countries, by a decline in her export earnings nor, as in others, by an expansion of domestic consumption. Rather it has come about mainly by an import of capital goods, primarily for the private sector, much larger than anticipated by Indian government planners. This drain has been accentuated by two relatively poor harvests; but the essential reason that India's foreign balance is in trouble is not that her development efforts have not been succeeding but that investment has gathered more momentum than anyone anticipated. The problem facing India today is how this momentum can be preserved.

The availability of help and resources from outside is important at all stages of the growth process. But there is a peculiarly critical moment in that process, which India has now reached, when external capital in adequate amounts and over a long enough period becomes the key determinant of what happens. After the take-off, as in Mexico, the external environment is important, but non-governmental sources of capital can carry most of the load. Before the take off technical assistance and some outside capital for social overhead are necessary; but the critical bottlenecks are the needed transformations in the social, political and economic structure of the nation for which its own leadership must take prime responsibility. A time comes, however, when the domestic prerequisites for success have been largely met and when the availability of substantial external resources on an investment basis is the single most important condition of success. India is the prime case in the year 1958 of a country in this position. No one can, of course, guarantee that if the foreign exchange bottleneck is removed, success is assured. Development is always a gamble. But the risk in the Indian case appears eminently worth taking from the American point of view.

We have taken a first step toward meeting India's immediate needs by arranging for a series of credits with the Export-Import Bank, the Development Loan Fund and our agricultural surplus disposal program. They aggregate $290 million for the current year. In our judgment this requires extension of three sorts. First, the annual volume of American loans needs to be increased to at least $500 million; second, a serious effort needs to be made to find substantially more capital from sources other than the United States, such as Western Europe; finally, India requires some assurance that she can count on this general level of new credit for a period of some years.

In terms of the preceding analysis of the American interest in economic development, the Indian scene has two characteristics that lend special urgency to an adequate program of American loans to that country. The first is that the present Indian leadership has quite clearly centered its bid for national unity on a common effort to achieve constructive economic goals, in a framework of democratic consent. Economic development goals are a live political issue in India, as they are not (to anything like the same extent) in any other underdeveloped country. Indian foreign policy, anti-colonialism and the Kashmir issue frequently reach the headlines of the Western press; and, of course, they play a significant rôle in domestic Indian politics. But the Congress Party will not stand or fall at home, as Nasser and Soekarno may, on its external successes. Indians will judge the Congress Party on how far and how fast it achieves the modernization of India by the voluntary and essentially democratic methods it has chosen to employ.

In India we have the opportunity of confronting the Communists with a serious dilemma. They would, of course, like to exploit Indian-Western tensions. But these are not as much at the center of the thinking of Indian intellectuals as is the case, for example, in the Middle East. The Russians would like to appear as the friends of Indian economic development, which has come to have genuine importance to a great many Indians. But ultimate Communist success in India depends on the failure of the economic development efforts sponsored by what Communists would describe as the present bourgeois régime. As long as the West fails to insure adequate resources for a successful Indian take-off the Communists can successfully pursue the tactic of providing enough help to be symbolically persuasive of their good intentions, but not enough to make a significant difference to the outcome of the Indian Second Five-Year Plan. Thus the success of current Communist tactics in India depends on an American and Western European failure to cover the foreign exchange gap.

The present leaders of the Indian state of Kerala, which went Communist at the last elections, are likewise giving evidence that they are faced with a dilemma. If within the state for which they have responsibility they pursue aggressive and coercive Communist policies, which the Indian electorate finds uncongenial, they may lose their slim parliamentary majority. On the other hand, if they are constructive and reasonable, suppressing their distinctively Communist policies and coöperating with private interests and with the national government, they weaken their case that only Communism can satisfy Indian aspirations for economic advance. Their great hope, of course, is that the national effort will fail and that they can contrast national failure under Congress leadership with at least partial success in Kerala. We have it in our power to help frustrate this Communist hope; but it will take substantially more than we are now doing.*

Let us be clear about the nature of the danger confronting us. There is no immediate threat of an extension of Communist control from Kerala to the national government in India. The commitment of most elements of Indian leadership to the methods of consent and non-violence is so deep that even if economic development lags, an early Communist take-over is exceedingly unlikely. What is likely over the years, if development loses its momentum, is increasing conflict and confusion within the Congress Party, a resurgence of sectional and linguistic interests perhaps breaking into violence, a heightening of the political and social tensions created by mass unemployment—in short, a reversion to the kind of political instability which tempts otherwise moderate persons to support anyone who can maintain order. While there is no Communist-inspired crisis at present, the prospects are poor for stable and effective democratic government if the present development program fails.

It is precisely in the fact that no serious political crisis is on the immediate horizon in India that our great opportunity lies, for we have learned in many other places around the globe that the salvage of situations which have been permitted to degenerate into crises is an exceedingly expensive, precarious and time-consuming business. In India there is still time in hand for us to use. We can demonstrate that we have a national interest in the development of the underdeveloped countries that lies deeper than our concern to chalk up day-to-day points in the game of cold-war diplomacy. Indian-American relations are important for their own sake. But they are even more important as an earnest of America's determination to play a constructive as well as a fire-fighting rôle in world affairs. In India, where a serious and promising attempt is

---

* [Editor's Note. After much controversy and a successful non-Communist passive resistance campaign, Indian President Rajendra Prasad dismissed the Communist-ruled Kerala State Government on July 31, 1959, on the ground that it was unable to govern peaceably and in accordance with the Indian Constitution. In special elections on February 1, 1960, a coalition United Democratic Front formed by the Congress Party, the People's Socialist Party and the Moslem League defeated the Communist Party. However, the Communist Party increased its share of the popular vote from 35 per cent to 42½ per cent although its representation in the 126-member Kerala Assembly fell from 60 to 27.]

being made to forge a new nation around the ideals of domestic progress by democratic procedures, it would be most shortsighted of us not
to do what we can to make the effort a success.

The second characteristic of the Indian scene that gives it special
urgency is the interesting relation between private and public economic
activity that has begun to reveal itself in the last two years. The fact that
public and private investment are not alternatives but can support each
other in the early take-off stage of development has been nicely demonstrated by the Indian experience. In spite of an explicitly socialist governmental ideology, private investment in India has recently been boom-
ing. The private sector has, in the first 18 months of the Second Five-
Year Plan, undertaken as much investment as the planners initially
expected it to undertake over the entire five years. An analysis carried
out at the Center for International Studies, M.I.T., of the composition
of the unusually heavy volume of imports into India over the past two
years reveals that the big increase has been in capital goods imported on
private account. The purchasing power created by public investment
and the improved transport, communications, power and other services
resulting from the activities of the public sector have created an environment in which private investment opportunities have multiplied. As
mentioned earlier, it is this buoyancy of private economic activity which
has been principally responsible for the foreign exchange difficulties
with which India now finds herself confronted.

These difficulties—essentially growing pains—pose a serious dilemma
for Indian policy. If additional foreign resources are not forthcoming,
India must cut down her imports by strict controls to much lower levels.
Her leaders are now politically committed to a variety of public projects.
But even if they were not so committed, technical economic considerations would suggest that a sharp cut in investment in social overhead
might ultimately throttle private as well as public activity. Further expansion of the private sector is conditioned upon a steady rise in purchasing power and a continuing expansion of transport, power and other
services. Even steel might become a bottleneck if present plans were
sharply cut back. On the other hand, if the core of the public program
is to be maintained, imports can be sharply reduced only by restricting
severely the licensing of capital imports for private Indian business.

In short, the volume of public and private investment required over
the next decade to make full use of visible Indian resources for growth
calls for a supply of foreign capital substantially above current levels.

If this supply is forthcoming, there is an excellent prospect that Indian productivity and output will expand sufficiently over the next decade or so to permit India to carry without difficulty the higher level of foreign indebtedness which would result. If the supply is not forthcoming, not only will Indian development be threatened, but also a chance will have been missed for a practical demonstration of the complementarity of public and private activities which would be enormously persuasive in other underdeveloped countries with socialist preconceptions.

The conclusion might be drawn from this line of argument that what we need is not a more vigorous program of economic assistance in general but rather a special program specifically focussed on and tailored to Indian requirements. This, in our view, misses the essence of our case. A successful Indian program is important at least as much for the model it can set for political leadership in other underdeveloped countries as for its own sake. If our economic assistance program sets up the kinds of criteria for foreign loans that we believe desirable, emphasizing the productivity of such loans for domestic development, India will, over the next two or three years, qualify for a larger share than her population would suggest. But the program as a whole should be so designed as to provide maximum incentives for the leaders of countries less far along to concentrate their energies on preparing their countries to make similar take-off efforts at a later stage. Our attitude should be that we are ready to help any country that has demonstrated its determination to focus its energies seriously on the problem of meeting the economic and social aspirations of its people. This requires a Development Loan Fund with larger resources and a longer Congressional lease than exists under present legislation.

We should not be drawn by the exigencies of cold-war diplomacy into making investments which are unproductive and economically foolish from the standpoint of the development of the recipient. We will gain little long-run advantage from competitive blackmail. But we stand to gain a great deal as time goes on from a clear demonstration that we believe our interests and those of countries prepared to make a real development effort based on political consent are sufficiently common to justify sustained American investment.

India, under its present political leadership, has made the commitment to harness its nationalist aspirations to the tasks of modernization. The American stake in India is that this commitment shall not fail of its purpose. The more difficult task for American policy is to use our limited but real margin of influence to make it as easy and attractive for other transitional nations to do likewise. Among the many aspects of American policy which can contribute to this outcome, not the least important are the actions we take at this promising but difficult period in Indian history.

[v]

If we can, during the current examination of the foreign aid issue, clarify our national purposes in the program as a whole, establish the possibilities and limits of the rôle of private capital within it, and grasp the significance of the special case of India, it should be possible over the next year to build a stable and effective economic development policy for the longer pull. Essentially, three elements are involved: continuity, scale and coördination.

It is evident that the Development Loan Fund will not be able to fulfill its mission until its Congressional lease on life, is, by one device or another, extended. The Congress may wish to postpone such action until 1959, since the Fund is only now beginning to disburse loans; and it is reasonable for definitive action to await evidence of vigorous and effective administration in terms of criteria of productivity. Similarly, it is evident that the present *ad hoc* emergency aid to India will not do the job and that the flow of American lending must be put on a longer-term basis if Indian leaders are to proceed with confidence and the Second Five-Year Plan is not to falter dangerously.

With respect to scale, it seems likely that the Loan Fund and the level of assistance to India will both have to be somewhat expanded. It is difficult to be dogmatic until further examination is undertaken; but it seems altogether possible that the Development Loan Fund will be able to justify an annual disbursement rate of about $1 billion in loans when it has worked itself properly into business. So far as India is concerned, it seems likely that American loans on something like the order of $500 million per year will be necessary for the duration of the next Five-Year Plan and, perhaps, for some time thereafter.

The maturing of the development program requires, finally, that methods of coördination improve both in Washington and on the international scene. As the Loan Fund has emerged it is simply one of a number of American instruments for accelerating economic growth in the underdeveloped areas. Grants and technical assistance flow from the I.C.A.; the Export-Import Bank dispenses dollar loans, and is likely to do so on a rising scale; food and fiber surpluses are being increasingly used for development purposes—as working capital—rather than merely to salvage famine situations; and the Government, in its guarantee program and other arrangements can influence to a degree the flow of private capital abroad. Finally, the United States has some influence in the allocation of the hard currency loans available from the International Bank for Reconstruction and Development. There is evidently a need in Washington for strong central leadership in orchestrating these instruments around a coherent policy towards each of the nations applying for development assistance. The individual institutions and programs involved have grown up, each with its own history, criteria and *mystique*. Purposeful direction, backed by strong staff work, will be required in the Department of State to make them serve the nation's interests. In this connection, the *ad hoc* organization of $290 million for India was, on the whole, a hopeful exercise.

In addition, there remains the challenging and extremely important task of finding a method and an instrument for coördinating the economic development programs, now mainly bilateral, within the free world. There are powerful political undercurrents in Western Europe, Japan, Canada and elsewhere, which look to such a coördinated effort as a means of giving increased unity, meaning and vitality to the free world alliance. On the other hand, as the NATO conference of December 1957 revealed the countries of Western Europe are reluctant to commit themselves to an expanded and coördinated development effort until the American Government—in both its branches—exhibits the determination to build a serious and sustained program around economic (as opposed to military) aid. The passage of the current proposals before the Congress should open the way, over the next year, to the exploration of the enormous constructive potentialities of a common free-world economic development program in Asia, the Middle East, Africa and Latin America.

The Politics of Underdevelopment*

by Zbigniew Brzezinski**

"We are living in an age in which all roads lead to communism," Molotov proclaimed confidently in 1947. Kaganovich re-echoed him in 1955 by maintaining that "if the nineteenth century was a century of capitalism, the twentieth century is a century of the triumph of social-ism and communism." This serenely optimistic viewpoint sees the vic-tory of communism as all-inclusive, leaving no room for any mutual adjustment between the Communist and non-Communist worlds. In-deed, the First Secretary of the CPSU, Nikita S. Khrushchev, has re-peatedly made it clear that the concept of coexistence relates simply to a transitory phase prior to the final assertion of the Communist mode of life over the entire globe. It would be idle to dismiss these claims as mere expressions of blind fanaticism, for whatever the element of fanaticism in the thinking of Soviet leaders may be, such proclamations of faith in final victory are also supported by observation of recent trends in world affairs. These trends have shown a marked expansion in the territorial base and ideological appeal of the Soviet system. This ex-tension, as has often been noted, has been most marked in areas that are economically underdeveloped and essentially pre-industrial in na-ture. On the whole, the recent Communist expansion has been most successful in environments approximating that of Russia prior to the Bolshevik Revolution.

The purpose of this paper is to discuss some political implications of the aspirations of the newly independent Asian peoples (and soon, it is to be expected, of the African peoples as well), in the context of the existing global competition between the Communist world, specifically the USSR and China, and the non-Communist world, particularly the United States. Almost inevitably, the projections developed and the conclusions reached will be largely speculative and merely represent an attempt to assess the shape of future developments if present trends continue. Of course, it is quite possible that some completely unfore-seeable factor or combination of factors, such as the impact of an out-

* From World Politics, Vol. IX, No. 1 (October 1956), pp. 55-75. Reprinted by permission of World Politics.
** The author expresses his sincere appreciation for the support given him by the Russian Research Center, Harvard University.

standing personality, war, or domestic developments in the USSR or the
United States, might intervene to change the course of history entirely.
This paper does not attempt predictions; it is simply an essay on the
meaning and potential significance of existing trends. Its broad thesis is
that in the present epoch non-democratic forces enjoy a definite advantage over the democratic countries in being able to export their political structure to the newly liberated peoples not only through conspiratorial action, but also through the dynamics of the situation, given
the economic and political aspirations of these peoples. As a result, the
totalitarian pattern of political and social organization is more likely
than not to engulf an even larger portion of mankind. If this happens,
it will be exceedingly difficult for these new totalitarian systems to avoid
following the Communist model and they will tend to gravitate toward
the Soviet orbit. That this may have dire consequences for the democratic world need hardly be said.

Just prior to World War II, the population of the globe was estimated at roughly 2.1 billion. Of these, 170 million were living under a
Communist regime, about 1.1 billion were living in countries enjoying
national sovereignty in political systems other than Communist, and 815
million were living under colonial tutelage. The revolutionary changes
produced by the war and the subsequent period of dislocation, internal
strife, Soviet expansion, and the spread of violent nationalism brought
about a drastic rearrangement in the political distribution of the peoples
of the world. The Communist orbit expanded rapidly, chiefly by absorbing many of the peoples living in sovereign nation-states, while the
majority of the colonial peoples were granted, or won, their independence. In 1955 the estimated population of the world stood somewhere
in the vicinity of 2.5 billion. Of these, 955 million were now in the
Soviet bloc, 650 million were still in the sovereign nation-states that existed in 1939, 170 million were under colonial administration, and 750
million people were living in recently created states which formerly were
part of various colonial possessions. It is to be expected that this final
category will grow even larger in the near future, in view of events in
Morocco, Algeria, British Central and West Africa, etc. Unlike the experience of nineteenth- and twentieth-century Europe in the age of
nationalism, the emergence of former colonies into independent statehood comes at a time when the world is divided into two political blocs
—one highly integrated and, by its own definition, fundamentally an-

tagonistic to the other, which is rather loosely held together by a series
of treaties, certain common traditions, and a Christian heritage. These
two blocs offer radically different approaches and solutions to existing
economic, social, and political ills in the newly liberated and largely
underdeveloped countries. It is not unlikely that the fate of either bloc
will depend to a large degree on the course that these newly liberated
areas follow, given the existing polarization.[1]

In the initial stages of their statehood, these new sovereign states have
adopted, by and large, the political forms of the Western democratic
world. It must be remembered, however, that these forms are the product of a long evolution, by trial and error, and arose in response to certain political and economic difficulties. They are thus inextricably linked
to the history of the Western nations, and for this reason more capable
of withstanding many a contemporary storm. French republicanism, for
instance, is so much a product of French historical development (both
political and economic) of the last 150 years—and the intellectual tradition behind it is older still—that despite an almost permanent crisis
situation it has been able to maintain its institutional forms successfully.
Such is generally not the case in these new states. On the contrary, their
intellectual climate, fraught with memories of inequality, of shame, of
submission to racially and culturally alien masters, and frequently of
economic misery, is characterized by a violent rejection of the past. To
these new states, it is the future that justifies the present, and the present is accordingly to be subjected to major reconstruction, eradicating
the vestiges of all that was unwanted in the past. Thus, the test of the
political institutions to be adopted from alien patterns by these new
states will be largely a matter of their ability to operate in response to
requirements yet to be put before them. Democracy will survive only if
it can both satisfy the aspirations of the people and deal effectively with
the consequences of satisfying them.

The dominant aspirations of the new states are largely a product of
the thinking and activity of a small minority of leaders, drawn from
and supported by a relatively restricted intelligentsia. These intellectuals

---

[1] It does appear, however, that the Soviet bloc, larger and geographically more
coherent, is more likely to endure in the form it has had in the past, if the post-
colonial areas veer to the other bloc, than the loosely organized and in some respects
directionless and self-doubting non-Communist bloc is, if these new sovereign states
veer toward communism. It is to be observed, furthermore, that in periods of crisis
a democracy tends to develop many non-democratic characteristics. The debatable
question of the inner resiliency of the respective blocs is, however, beyond the scope
of our present inquiry.

(the word is used loosely), chiefly Western-trained but also containing a sprinkling of Communists, are on the whole elitists, despite their protestations. This is true of men like Nehru or Soekarno, and even more so of the younger generation of leaders around them. Lacking the Western religious tradition which influenced to such a great extent the concept of the dignity of man, and surrounded by millions and millions of retarded, illiterate, often filthy, and certainly pliant masses, they tend to approach their fellow countrymen with a thinly concealed contempt, or at least an implicit sense of superiority. They feel that, to be operative, such concepts as individual freedom or the dignity of man must be preceded by a drastic educational and economic readjustment of the existing societies, a readjustment which they themselves are prepared to effect. This sense of elitism and their consciousness of intellectual achievement and leadership incline them particularly toward a faith in the accomplishments of social engineering as an answer to existing ills. Man's reason can provide the answer, and man's reason put into action can produce the desired results without a lengthy evolutionary process, such as that undergone by the West. The leadership and the intellectuals of these countries thus tend to believe in man's capacity to steer political and economic development at an accelerated pace toward the achievement of desired ends.

Viewing the past with distaste, deeply conscious of their economic and social backwardness, fully aware that both the USSR and the West are far ahead of them in power, prestige and, in the case of the latter, standard of living, the intellectuals tend to see one factor as paramount in causing this state of inequality: the technological revolution of industrialization. They realize that in the age of technology both power and wealth depend on a solid industrial base, and they note with bitterness that the colonial powers, and their local, conservative, and largely landed allies (sheiks, maharajahs, sultans, etc.), prevented—or at least did not further—industrial development in the colonial areas. But it is not only the industrialization of Western Europe and the United States that has created such a strong impression; they note with particular envy the rapid industrialization of the USSR and its consequent (as it seems to them) rise to world prominence as further proof that industrialization must be achieved if their aspirations, both national and social, are to be fulfilled. Industrialization has thus become a sort of panacea—a key to the future.

If these leaders, already operating largely within the framework of institutions of the Western type, had had only the Western experience as a guide, they might well have leaned toward industrial development on the basis of foreign credit, balanced between a consumers' goods policy and a capital investment policy, gradualist in character. Such a program might even have enlisted the support of some of the local wealthy elements anxious for a large supply of consumers' goods. But the Soviet experience points to an alternative route, in many ways more attractive because it is a shortcut.[2] Not that it contains no disagreeable elements—this the intellectuals would be the first to concede. But it is important to remember that these disagreeable elements are less important to them than to their Western counterparts. To the Western intellectual, Communist totalitarianism means, after all, the destruction of values and standards built up through many years. To an Asian, Communism is merely an alternative to liberal democracy, and an alternative which produces the desired effects faster. Furthermore, accepting the Leninist concept of imperialism, they feel themselves free of any responsibility for the unhappy situation prevailing in their countries, blaming it all on their "capitalist oppressors." This, of course, makes the Western model even less acceptable. In addition, some of them are confident that they can avoid these undesirable consequences—a matter to which we will return. The point here is that rapid industrialization appears not only possible but also desirable. Few human beings are truly patient—and the Asian leaders have just been liberated after years of frustration. Their will to action is therefore that much more intense. It is hence quite natural that almost all of the newly liberated countries have adopted programs of industrial development.[3]

These programs—and it must be emphasized that they are still largely modest and preliminary in character—have been initiated in a setting where there is little confidence in slow and chiefly self-directed economic development. The Indian Congress Party has thus made it crystal clear that its goal is a "socialist pattern of society." Private investment can hardly be expected to find comfort in such intentions. Furthermore, the basis for a capitalistic type of economy seems to be

---

[2] Japan might have been an alternative model, but the collapse of the Japanese Co-Prosperity Sphere has eliminated the possibility.

[3] To cite one example, the Indonesian National Planning Board in its 1954 estimates for the first Five-Year Plan envisages the following pattern of development: agriculture and social improvements—12 per cent; transport and roads—25 per cent; industry—25 per cent; irrigation—25 per cent; education and health—13 per cent (*Indonesia*, VII, No. 1 [August-September 1955], p. 11).

lacking. These areas, in general, do not have a large bourgeoisie which could provide the basis for entrepreneurial action, nor do they have local capitalists with the necessary financial resources. They do have large, dormant masses and a few privileged rich with a vested interest in the status quo. In short, there are no cadres other than the intellectuals to launch the desired changes. And, according to all accounts, these people are predisposed toward not only a state-planned and directed economic development, but one intended to produce tangible returns at an early date.[4]

Of course, one cannot dismiss altogether the possibility that Asian industrial development will continue at a moderate pace. At the present time, however, the influential intelligentsia and the youth (university students in particular) appear to be hypnotized by the image of large-scale industry. Evidence of this was furnished by the enthusiastic responses that Khrushchev and Bulganin evoked by their frequent adjurations that these areas industrialize.[5] It would be imprudent, therefore,

[4] According to the *New York Times*, February 10, 1956, the new Indian Five-Year Plan calls for ". . . total capital outlay by the Government of $10,080,000,000, and $4,830,000 by private enterprise. Of the Government outlay, $4,777,500,000 will be spent on industry, minerals, transport, communications and power.

"By the end of the second plan in 1960-61, food production is expected to go up by 10,000,000 tons, or 15 per cent, cotton by 34 per cent and sugar by 29 per cent. Nearly 21,000,000 acres of new land would have been brought under cultivation.

"Output of steel is to rise from the present 1,300,000 tons to 4,300,000 tons, coal from the present 37,000,000 to 60,000,000 tons, and cement from 4,800,000 to 10,000,000 tons."

The emphasis on industrial development becomes even more evident when one compares the financial outlay for industrial development in the first and second Five-Year Plans: first plan, $1,543·5 billions; the second, $4,783·5 billions, or a 300 per cent increase.

[5] They pursued this line with dogged determination. For example, Khrushchev said at the Taj Mahal: "You are going through the wonderful spring of your country's national liberation and independent government. But I would like to warn you that freedom and independence can only be made lasting if you develop your industry, particularly machine building [Applause]" (*Pravda*, November 21, 1955). Khrushchev told the Indian Parliament: "The course of social development shows that in order to become truly independent and to ensure the welfare of its people each country must have its own developed economy, independent of foreign capital. History teaches that the colonizers' efforts to bring about the foreign enslavement of a less developed country can take the most varied forms. They try in every way to hamper the development of native industry in these countries, fearing that the establishment of its own industry, the creation of its own intelligentsia and the raising of the living standards of its people will strengthen a formerly dependent country, and help it along the path of independent development [Applause]" (*Izvestia*, November 22, 1955). And, again, in the same speech: "In order to create conditions for the country's full independence, it is necessary to create a firm foundation in the form of good industry, and to rely on it. In so doing, it is important to rely first of all on your own resources, especially since certain rich countries, in giving aid to others, want to place those whom they aid under their authority." Speaking at

to assume that the Asian elites, wielding power to the extent that they do, will be either willing or able to have patience and act in terms not of their own lifetime but of that of their grandchildren. A very real likelihood exists that the present modest beginnings in industrialization will be followed by an acceleration in pace, particularly when Chinese economic development begins to gather momentum. What will be some of the political consequences of a more rapid industrialization?

Industrialization involves a number of things. It means building factories; it means the displacement of the small handicraft entrepreneur; it means increasing overpopulation of the urban centers; it means the flow of labor away from rural areas; it means the breakdown of the kinship system, rooted in the villages; it means, in brief, a tremendous change in the existing way of life. But the status quo always has some adherents, who vary in number depending on the attraction of the status quo. In the areas that were formerly colonies, the status quo is buttressed by centuries of tradition, ancient authority and privilege, and the caste system. Industrialization, especially as it begins to spread, will inevitably come into conflict with a variety of established interests. Landlords will resent the loss of cheap labor, local patriarchs will object to the shedding of tradition by the youth flocking to the factories, pre-industrial entrepreneurs will fear the economic consequences of industrial competition, the middle class will be apprehensive of the economic squeeze resulting from capital investment in largely impoverished areas. Resistance, both passive and active, is likely to develop.

It will be accompanied, one might expect, by considerable dislocation. Agricultural production may suffer temporarily; consumers' goods may become scarce; all sorts of temporary adjustments to the requirements of the situation may follow: barracks for the new factory labor, a variety of government measures to prevent serious economic crises, obligatory state loans to raise capital, low wages and high taxation.[6] An atmosphere of

---

Madras, Khrushchev said: "From personal experience we know that it is not enough to gain national independence; one must strengthen the independence gained in order to be able to defend it. [Stormy applause] The path toward strengthening the independence gained is the path of setting up one's own powerful industry and the path of steadily raising the people's welfare. [Applause] We sincerely wish the Republic of India to have its own powerful, highly developed industry and its own national economy, independent of foreign states" (*Pravda*, November 30, 1955).

[6] The middle-class elements in India cannot take much comfort in the suggestion made by a taxation inquiry commission, and re-echoed by the Indian Planning Committee, that a "reasonable" ceiling on personal income would be 30 times the national average, which is 280 rupees. The ceiling would then be 8,400 rupees, or $1,764.

conflict may be artificially stimulated to raise morale and induce mass enthusiasm. Discontent, however, will probably not be alleviated by these measures as wants and sacrifices increase and the standard of living is leveled. A crisis situation may develop rapidly.

In such circumstances, those in leadership will be faced with a dilemma: the more moderate, democratic elements, abhorring violence, may suggest slowing down; others, more fanatical or extremist, may demand that industrialization be pushed forward. History shows, unfortunately, that in moments such as these power is usually retained by those willing to keep abreast of the social dynamics, once they have been set in motion. The moderates, to keep power and maintain a moderate program, would have to turn to the conservative elements, finding in them their last refuge and hope. In time, the moderate program might even become one of reaction. This, some of the moderates would not be willing to face. Some might hesitate, others might drift to the extremists. Measures to overcome social resistance would follow accordingly, even though modestly at the beginning.[7]

The modern society is so complex, however, that to effect real change, such as large-scale industrialization, especially in the face of resistance, a high degree of governmental control is necessary lest society disintegrate into anarchy. Western democrats, despite their willingness to engage in governmental planning and direction, have always been careful to avoid a complete commitment of the governmental powers to an artificially induced process of social and economic change. Similarly, in Russia in 1917, it was the fact that the more democratic elements shied away from a total application of coercive power to a society in a stage of transition that gave such a tactical advantage to the Bolsheviks. It is doubtful that all of the present and particularly the future leaders of these new Asian states, given their elitist and dedicated character, will be able to resist the temptation of employing the power at their disposal, both to organize society and to eliminate resistance. Opposition may even encourage the use of force because, once the process of internal revolution has been launched, resistance inevitably takes on the form of interference with the progress of new measures; this, in turn, seems to those in control an attempt to destroy the future so firmly outlined in their minds, and the charge of sabotage follows. Furthermore,

---

[7] For a reasoned discussion of the general problem of power, see Barrington Moore, Jr., "Notes on the Process of Acquiring Power," *World Politics*, viii, No. 1 (October 1955), pp. 1-20.

once the programmatic plans of the leaders have been launched, not to
employ force is to risk anarchy and civil war. Force thus acquires justification in the eyes of those willing to wield it, and far-reaching political control becomes necessary.

But more than this is needed to account to the people for the sacrifices, confusion, and dislocation that an action-program involves. They
require a simple but convincing explanation of past evils and a guarantee of future happiness. There is no doubt that ever-growing numbers
of people throughout the world are asking questions and searching for
the meaning of the baffling conflicts and struggles they are undergoing
and the sacrifices that are demanded of them. They must be made to
believe that their efforts have some meaning and that these efforts are
bound to succeed. True, some of the disruption may be explained by
pointing to enemies who are preventing the attainment of utopia (e.g.,
Nasser and Great Britain, Soekarno and the Netherlands). But these
regimes need further justification—they must raise capital for investment, they must push forward since their image of the future is to be
realized within a generation or two. Effort and sacrifice must be mobilized and channeled. In Asia, within the context of a movement of reform and change, of rejection of the past and efforts to rebuild society
through the instrumentalities of the state, the people's need for an explanation may lead to the emergence of an official state ideology which
explains the past and provides the key to the future. Social control,
reaching deep into society, may thus become more and more necessary.
Pluralism, the basis of democracy, may become an awkward impediment
to the monolithic unity essential to success.

The question arises, however, of how this control is to be organized
so as to be effective and how this ideology is to be developed and carried
forward. It is one thing to rule a status quo society through a traditional form of dictatorship which avoids all major change. Such a dictatorship can rely on the support of a number of vested interests and traditions, and hence can rule from above without penetrating society very
deeply, depending merely on this balance of interests to maintain itself in
power. At the same time, authority is accepted by the population as part
of the traditional order, especially since that authority, subscribing to
the traditional norms, does not seem to invade all aspects of their daily
existence. The situation becomes radically different when a regime,
ruling largely from above (as is now the case in Asia, with the educated
minority at the helm), proceeds to tear up the social fabric. It then has

to devise an institutional apparatus that can be used to penetrate society, rally it around the official action-program, and channel its energies. In modern times, the single-party system has emerged as such an instrument of institutionalized revolution, and the Asians have not been blind to this development. The need for a single party is all the greater in a society where age-old social forms are crumbling and the people, torn from their villages and accepted norms, seek a new sense of belonging and new institutional forms to provide the security they desire.[8] This party then becomes the chief instrument of rule (*vide* the Congress Party) and inevitably—although not necessarily at once—the standard-bearer of the ideology.

Indeed, if one looks at the existing situation, it readily becomes apparent that those countries which are already turning away from the past (e.g., India and Egypt[9]) are moving in this direction. Others, still wobbling between the legacy of the past and the promise of the future, and with very uncertain control of the present (e.g., Indonesia and Burma, in both of which the Communists have recently scored electoral successes), do not give much indication that their multi-party systems are likely to endure for long. The one-party system with an official ideology appears more likely to succeed in launching, and certainly in executing forcefully, the type of program that the more ambitious elements among the newly liberated peoples desire. Even when such programs are launched in a setting which largely resembles the Western democratic model, it is probable that the revolutionary consequences of such a program will eventually place power in the hands of a single party with the will to push the measures through and with an ideology that justifies them. The totalitarian pattern is incipient in such a development, to say the least.

It could be argued that this in itself need not be alarming. After all, the great majority of mankind has lived for centuries under non-democratic forms of government. Constitutional democracy is a relatively recent phenomenon which, at best, is the realization of a certain potential inherent in some men and societies. That such are in the minority

---

[8] Cf. F. G. Friedman, "The Impact of Technically Advanced Civilization on Underdeveloped Areas," *Confluence*, IV, No. 4 (January 1956), pp. 391-406.

[9] In Egypt, President Nasser's book on the goals of the revolution, together with the constitutional draft, already comprise the embryo of such an ideology. At the same time, press restrictions assure the government a complete monopoly in the field of mass communications.

is not surprising. Furthermore, democracy has succeeded in emerging from and surviving in seas of non-democratic systems.

The point is, however, that a vast difference exists between traditional dictatorial systems and the new totalitarian variety. The latter are revolutionary, universalistic in their goals, and dedicated to the destruction of all systems that differ from themselves.[10] The development of these new totalitarian systems, furthermore, would take place in the context of a world-wide struggle between the Soviet and the Anglo-American blocs. The failure of the Fascist and Nazi types of totalitarianism has left few models for new totalitarian regimes to emulate, and it must be remembered that these new countries, insofar as their social and economic conditions are concerned, are very similar to China and the USSR prior to their industrial drives. It is also to be anticipated that the Soviet orbit will tend to encourage the undertaking of large-scale internal changes in the expectation that these will produce irreversible trends favorable to an ultimately Communist pattern, especially since they will be occurring in the context of anti-colonialism. That seems to be the implication of Shepilov's remarks at the Twentieth Party Congress:

"One of the characteristic features of our epoch is the combination of the socialist revolution in individual countries with the struggle on a mass scale of any and all oppressed and dissatisfied people. Great Lenin rejected as pedantic and ridiculous the point of view that somewhere an army will take positions and say: 'We are for socialism,' and in another place another army will say: 'We are for imperialism,' and that would be the social revolution.

"What happens in actual fact, under the conditions of the general crisis of capitalism, is the confluence into one mighty stream of the popular liberation struggle of many socialist and non-socialist currents and streams, which wash loose and undermine from various sides the worn-out capitalist building." [11]

---

[10] This distinction is developed in the writer's *Permanent Purge: Politics in Soviet Totalitarianism* (Cambridge, Mass., 1956) and in an article, "Totalitarianism and Rationality" (*American Political Science Review*, L, No. 3, September 1956), where the following definition of totalitarianism is offered: "Totalitarianism is a system where technologically advanced instruments of political power are wielded without restraint by centralized leadership of an elite movement, for the purpose of effecting a total social revolution, including the conditioning of man, on the basis of certain arbitrary ideological assumptions, in an atmosphere of coerced unanimity of the entire population."

[11] *Pravda*, February 17, 1956.

In Shepilov's analysis, the destruction of capitalism will leave the uncommitted lands only one alternative—socialism; and socialism has been clearly defined as a society like that of the USSR. Implicit, therefore, in the statements made before the Twentieth Congress is the belief that although there may be varied ways of reaching socialism, there is only one kind of socialism, that which has already been erected in the USSR. The destruction of the capitalist structure will leave the world only one choice. In the Communist view, rapid industrialization is to be encouraged, for it makes it less likely that the new nations will be able to maintain their democratic forms.

The confidence of Communist leaders is buttressed by the fact that the USSR and China are excellently equipped to influence these new states. Unlike the West, they share with them a history of underdevelopment and a sense of national inferiority. These the USSR has overcome, to a great extent, by constructing its own industrial base. Furthermore, both the USSR and China are in a uniquely strategic position to aid and abet the new Asian nations and lead them by example.[12] Their geographical proximity makes them logical partners in trade and economic development. Unlike the West, with its relatively longer history of gradual development, both the USSR and China can point to themselves as models for a rapid achievement of the desired objective—intensive industrialization. They also share with these nations a large peasant class that accepts authority which is distant from it and is traditional, that fears the machine and yet wants to harness it, that senses the breakdown of the existing social framework and is at a loss as to what to do about it. Into this situation step the Marxist program and the Communist Party.[13] At the same time, the USSR and China claim that the future is theirs, and there is no doubt that many Asians (and Africans) have become convinced that what they say is true. The electoral successes of the Communists in Burma in the spring of 1956 certainly seem at least a partial indication of this. With excellent insight

---

[12] The Soviet leaders, while on their Asian tour, frequently emphasized their willingness to share with Asiatic students the latest Soviet industrial know-how. The USSR indicated in February 1956 that it was prepared to grant 200 scholarships to Asian students to study Soviet techniques. Also, the USSR is now constructing a large technological institute in Rangoon, a hospital, an exhibition hall, and a sports center. In India, the Soviets have undertaken to build a steel mill with a capacity of one million tons.

[13] See the stimulating discussion of this problem by Adam B. Ulam, "The Historical Role of Marxism and the Soviet System," *World Politics*, viii, No. 1 (October 1955), pp. 20-46.

into this state of mind, Khrushchev and Bulganin repeatedly stressed the theme of the inevitable victory of communism on their Asian tour.

It would therefore be idle to assume that the Communist countries will limit themselves to gracious encouragement. In the Communist conception, political developments the world over are part of an unfolding process of struggle between diametrically opposed economic and political systems. This being so, the fate of these new states will be determined in terms of their future coalescence with one or the other bloc. Recent Soviet statements indicate that the Soviet leaders have already become confident that present trends in these states are bringing them into the Soviet orbit, which they identify by the Aesopian term, "the peace-loving bloc."

This theme, so heavily stressed at the Twentieth Party Congress, was to some extent anticipated in an article which appeared in *Nowe Drogi*, the organ of the Central Committee of the Polish Communist Party (United Workers' Party), in January 1956. The author of the article, a specialist in Asian affairs, first points out that Asia has witnessed two types of national liberation, one led by the Communist parties and one which has left "the frame of the social structure untouched." He then frankly admits that until recently the Communists "were not able to appreciate fully the significance of the fact that four hundred million Hindus and eighty million Indonesians obtained state independence and national sovereignty. We tended to simplify the matter, seeing in the act of proclamation of the independence of India and Indonesia something in the way of a maneuver making possible further continuation of colonialism under a new label." [14] It is now clear, he says, that these events were the beginning of an even greater struggle.

After quoting the premier of Indonesia to the effect that the major task of the day is the removal of colonial vestiges from the Indonesian economy, the article continues: "The struggle for economic independence, for complete self-sufficiency of the liberated countries, is not an easy matter. . . . The most consequential fighter for full and real independence of the liberated countries is their Communist parties." [15] These new countries thus have a choice: either to remain exploited and hence not really independent, or to become economically independent. And here the organ of the Central Committee comes to the heart of the

---

[14] Stefan Arski, "Wielka podroz" ("The Great Journey"), *Nowe Drogi*, i, No. 79 (1956), p. 14.
[15] *Ibid.*, p. 15.

matter: to become economically independent, the new countries must take "the way of independent industrialization." [16]

Such industrialization, says the article, must avoid any Western entanglements, "for industrialization may become a trap of even greater dependence when it is carried on through 'aid' from great capitalist countries, and particularly the United States. First of all, such industrialization does not develop according to criteria of the economic interests of a given country, but is dictated by the interest of foreign capitalists. . . . Secondly, such industrialization involves burdensome political conditions which sooner or later will vitiate their independence. . . ." [17] China avoided such a situation because the leadership of its revolution was in the hands of a Communist Party. Its industrialization is entirely independent of foreign capital. The other Asian nations might easily lose their independence, *Nowe Drogi* points out, if it were not for the changed international situation: "Fortunately, a new political and economic factor has appeared in the arena: the strength of the countries of the socialist camp and their economic potential. This factor has become a great stimulant to the political and economic emancipation of the young Asian and African republics. On the one hand, it neutralized and paralyzed the direct military and political pressure of the imperialist camp; on the other, it opened up previously unknown perspectives of economic independence and independent industrialization." [18] The article concludes by suggesting that, with the Western monopoly broken, these new countries can count on Soviet aid and proceed to industrialize at will. "These nations find support in the political and economic might of the socialist camp. . . . The result of the struggle in the final analysis depends on the fact that Russia, India, China, etc., constitute the great majority of mankind' (Lenin)." [19]

This matter being crucial to the victory of world revolution, we can expect Communist propaganda to continue to emphasize the importance of Soviet industrial achievements, and to suggest that only the "imperialistic capitalists" of the West would urge the Asians not to

---

[16] *Ibid.*, p. 18.

[17] *Ibid.*

[18] *Ibid.*, p. 19. The ideological aspects of this were discussed recently by D. Tumur-Ochir, "O nekapitalisticheskom puti razvitiia otstalykh stran k sotsializmu" ("On the non-capitalist way of development of the backward countries toward socialism"), *Voprosy filosofii*, No. 1 (1956), pp. 47-63. Tumur-Ochir, using Soviet Mongolia as a case study, develops the thesis that the Soviet experience demonstrates a desirable non-capitalist way of development of backward countries.

[19] *Nowe Drogi, op. cit.*, p. 23.

engage in it. The local Communist parties can be expected to be particularly vociferous in urging rapid industrial expansion on the Soviet and Chinese model, and to attempt to take advantage of any split within the leadership that might arise when the difficulties of such a program become more apparent. And in areas still under colonial control, the Communists have the added advantage of being able to pose not only as the architects of an industrial society but as fighters for the liberation which must precede such industrialization. In a sense, the local Communist leadership may even calculate that the economic situation in most of these states, especially in terms of raw materials, makes industrial development difficult, and may therefore urge its adoption so as to accentuate the crisis and make the choice between moderation and extremism that much sharper. Their opportunity may be even greater when modest industrial development begins to bear fruit—appetite grows with the eating—and pressures for further expansion mount accordingly.

This strategy of the local Communist parties is made all the more effective in that they can claim to possess a monopoly of understanding the nature of Soviet development. In this, they enjoy a considerable advantage over other competing political groups: the adherents of free enterprise are few and are handicapped by the fact that most Asians identify capitalism with colonialism, while Asian social democrats have no real experience on which to base their actions, except perhaps that of Israel. Western European socialism is, after all, a product of capitalism and nowhere has a truly socialist state been set up without a prior capitalist phase. Dismissing the Western experience as inapplicable, the Communists can point to themselves as the only group equipped to push through a program like the Soviet Union's. And if internal difficulties mount, and some moderates become disillusioned and even veer away from industrialization, it may be the local Communist Party which will emerge in the guise of a leader, willing and determined to push through the original policy. Their task may appear all the more attractive to some of the semi-democratic leaders since Khrushchev's declaration that dictatorship of the proletariat in its violent form is no longer the logical consequence of Communist activity, and his acceptance of alternative ways of achieving socialism. Thus dedication to the goal, existing conditions of crisis, a splitting-away of adherents, and a general tendency toward political totalitarianism may force the leadership to cooperate more and more with the local Communist parties. Whether this in itself will mean that they will become Communist totalitarianisms remains to be seen. At the moment, however, there appear to be no viable institutions or alternative programs of sufficient appeal and scope to match the Communist Party organization, with its Soviet support, and its ideological explanation of the past and "scientific" assessment of the future, once the disintegrative consequences of rapid industrialization begin to make themselves felt in largely backward and traditional societies.

The West must therefore consider the real possibility that the areas now in flux will ultimately fall within the Communist orbit. Can this outcome be prevented? And if so, how? Basically, there seem to be two available courses of action. One is to encourage those social and political elements which are opposed to rapid and large-scale industrialization. To some extent, this alternative finds cogency in the fact that such elements are usually sympathetic to the West. Why then, the argument runs, should we undermine them either by helping their nations to industrialize too fast, or by failing to obstruct such developments, which can only destroy them and produce consequences inimical to us? Instead, we should grant them military aid to buttress their spirit of resistance to external aggression, and indulge in limited ventures like the Point Four Program to alleviate the more obvious sources of social unrest. Stable and sympathetic governments will be the result. Certainly, the apparent success of our policy toward Thailand and, to a lesser extent, Pakistan and Iran may be considered a justification of this line of reasoning.

It is not easy to dismiss such an argument. It has considerable support in this country, and it is doubly attractive because its positive consequences become manifest immediately. Its weakness, however, lies precisely in its strength—the positive consequences it produces are essentially static in character and do not take into account the changes that are occurring in those areas. Such a policy, in the short run, might be successful; it would probably result in pro-Western but rather conservative regimes which would rely for their internal support on a balance of various established interest groups. In the long run, it would probably produce a complete collapse. It would result in the alienation of the younger generation—the students, young journalists, former fighters for independence—it would be exploited by the Communist parties as indicating our determination to maintain economic supremacy in these areas, a charge believed even by Asian observers friendly to us,[20] and it could produce only temporarily stable and conservative dictatorships, the fall of which would precipitate an even more rapid rise of hostile totalitarianisms. Such a policy would be meaningful only in the context of a determination on our part to resolve our differences with the USSR in a radical and final fashion in the near future.

But if we are to continue to be faced by a fundamentally hostile and energetic Soviet bloc, then our efforts vis-à-vis these areas must aim at a more positive relationship with them which takes into account the future consequences of our present actions. Given the desire of these nations to industrialize, and recognizing the political danger of the shocks that rapid industrialization produces, the other alternative is to attempt to ease the pains of that industrialization. Our hope would be that, with these pains eased, more moderate elements would succeed in maintaining themselves in power and a growth of democratic tradition would ensue. In the context of such an analysis, the current political views of Nehru or Soekarno become less important; the chief aim is that they succeed in satisfying the dominant aspirations of their articulate elites without opening the floodgates to totalitarianism, ultimately of a Communist variety. If they succeed, they may be able to raise cadres imbued with their own spirit (which is fundamentally unlike that of the Soviet Marxists), which, when time washes away the more bitter (and exaggerated) memories of colonialism, will tend to coalesce with the West.

Some argue that, to do this, the West will have to be willing to help these areas with a vast program of sharing its industrial know-how and financial resources.[21] The burden of that aid would fall on the United States, although the United Kingdom and the German Federal Republic ought to carry their share. The object of this aid would not only be to change somewhat the intellectual atmosphere in which the development programs are now being undertaken, but also to minimize the degree of social coercion which dependence on their own efforts will inevitably produce in these backward countries. Foreign capital might make it possible for these regimes to increase the production level of consumers' commodities and also to limit the commitment of national

---

[20] Cf. A. K. Brohi, "Asia and the Western Man," *Confluence*, IV, No. 3 (October 1955), pp. 302-12.

[21] The scale of this program is suggested by the fact that India alone needs $2,520,000,000 to close the gap between the estimated cost of the development program through 1961 and the resources it will be able to raise internally (*New York Times*, February 10, 1956).

energy to heavy capital development, part of which would then be shouldered by foreign capital. In this manner, the social pressures in the direction of totalitarianism would be lessened.

The difficulty with this argument, and the writer's consequent pessimism about it, are based on a twofold consideration. It seems highly unlikely that Western capital will be available in sufficient quantities to produce the desired effect. Such capital could be forthcoming through private investment or through state loans. Foreign private investment in the new Asian countries, except for a few modest ventures, is not likely to develop, because the necessary confidence is absent. Private investment, by its very nature, depends on profit, and these states offer little encouragement to private business not only because of their political instability and hostility to the West, but also because their announced goal is a socialist society. In fact, foreign investment is viewed by many Asians as another form of colonialism, and stringent measures to ensure native control of foreign companies have been adopted. Under these conditions, any long-range investment program is faced with the prospect of expropriation and socialization. The Abadan incident serves as a warning. Short-range ventures, based on high interest, are unlikely to have the desired social effect and their open profit motive is not apt to engender much sympathy among the Asian elites.

The second alternative, therefore, is for the United States, as well as the United Kingdom and the German Federal Republic, to engage in large-scale programs of economic aid. A few influential voices on behalf of this policy are being heard in the United States on both the Democratic and the Republican side of the political fence. Such a policy would mean large-scale investment and, probably, major purchases of Asian surpluses and staples. Multi-billion dollar programs of this kind, when coupled with existing military expenditures, would demand at least the maintenance of, if not an increase in, the present level of taxation. This degree of taxation, in the eyes of the political opponents of such a program and of the American public in general, would seem designed to give aid to regimes whose foreign policies could be construed as hostile neutralism. The fact that this may be irrelevant to the future of world politics would certainly not be readily apparent or even explicable. Under these circumstances, it is highly unlikely that it would be politically feasible for any United States administration to engage in a long-range program of this sort. Only if the need for it became overwhelmingly obvious in the face of imminent danger would the program be possible. Then the

American people would probably respond, as they did in the past with the Lend-Lease Program and the Marshall Plan. Unfortunately, in this case we are dealing with imperceptible developments which, by the time they become perceptible to public opinion in the West, will be irreversible.

The second major consideration that makes for pessimism about the prospect for success of even a reasonably forward-looking American policy with respect to these areas is the very assumption on which the foregoing discussion was implicitly based. Western capital, if generously applied, might help the underdeveloped countries to start fulfilling some of their most urgent aspirations while alleviating some of the more dangerous consequences of such reforms and undertakings, and at the same time winning friends. But this assumes that there is a fixed time limit in the aspirations of the elites of these countries. Unfortunately, there is some likelihood that these elites would merely utilize our aid to speed up the achievement of the goals (or maximize them), matching our aid with the maximum of effort. Any attempt by us to encourage them to slow down would be exploited by the Communist parties as foreign intervention (and be so viewed by most Asians) and would negate our purpose. Many Asians sympathetic to us still feel that ". . . most, if not all, of the countries in Asia are not yet free from economic bondage. Although the European powers have disappeared from the stage, they continue to pull wires in the wings." [22] Our efforts to slow down their pace would certainly be interpreted as further proof of this. In such an event, the USSR would probably express its willingness to aid them while encouraging maximum internal effort—advice more to the taste of many Asian intellectuals.

The political consequences in either case would thus be the same. The great tragedy of the present situation is that any effort to slow down the development of these areas will immediately play into the hands of the extremists, particularly the Communists, who are waiting on the sidelines. The only hope of the moderates is therefore to go along, but once the program is launched, the danger that they will eventually be obliterated mounts. Immoderate methods of wielding power are necessary in such situations, and modern totalitarianism seems to be well equipped to meet this requirement.

Insofar as the immediate future is concerned, it thus appears that the democratic world is severely handicapped, both ideologically and in-

---

[22] Brohi, op. cit., p. 306.

strumentally, in intervening in the political struggle which is implicit in the economic development of these new nations. Its basic assumptions make it difficult to respond on either ground with the desired effect and still remain true to itself. From the ideological point of view, a true democracy is always handicapped when faced by a militant, universalistic totalitarianism, for it is contrary to the spirit of democracy to formulate a closed, foolproof system of thought which can compete with the totalitarian ideology. Instrumentally, the democratic system, being the complex product of long philosophical tradition and institutional growth, is not able to organize those who subscribe to its ideals into effective action-oriented movements as the totalitarian conspiracies do. As a result, the major focus of democratic efforts to influence the new nations is on external action, i.e., governmental action, usually in the form of grants and loans. Unfortunately, efforts to channel aid in such a way as to make it maximally effective are viewed with suspicion or are rejected outright.[23] It appears that existing hostility to the West is not diminished even by liberal grants, while Communist trade or loans are viewed with favor by many.

It thus may well be that the time has come for the United States to reconsider its aid policy. The moment may have arrived for a radical shift from the position of an active external "doer" (so characteristic of United States policy since the great success of the Marshall Plan) to that of a sympathetic observer, willing to engage in such activities as will benefit both us and the Asians without exacerbating the presently unfavorable trends. It is not within the scope of this article to outline in detail the nature of such activities but primary among them could be economic trade on the largest scale possible (this might even leave some room for behind-the-scenes government sponsorship), to make available to the Asians (if they want it) our machinery in exchange for whatever they have to offer. Such a policy would also make it clear that, while we are willing to help the Asians, we do not want them to become dependent on us, since trade is a matter of partnership, while aid is not. Simultaneously, we could offer, on bilateral grounds, military aid to those nations that want it, without necessarily engaging in cumbersome and largely illusory structures, such as SEATO, which merely serve as

---

[23] E.g., Asian countries have been unwilling to take advantage of the American offer of $100,000,000 for regional development under the Colombo Pact because they do not want to engage in regional cooperation; Indonesia is not using its $100,000,000 credit with the World Bank because it is unwilling to accept help in surveying and other technical prerequisites.

irritants to the uncommitted Asians. A simple declaration to the effect that we will defend any free nation against Communist aggression would probably be as effective militarily and more acceptable politically.

In other words, we would cease struggling actively for Asia under conditions manifestly unfavorable to us while in fact creating the basis for cooperation should the time come when the Asians desire it. In the final analysis, the fate of Asia is up to the Asians and neither the West nor the USSR is in a position to steer the economic and political development of these areas. There are certain trends now in motion that are highly inimical to us and these we ought to avoid augmenting. We can neutralize direct Soviet efforts at conquest by a firm military stance, but there is little we can do to prevent internal subversion. Our present involvement, albeit with the best of intentions, can only produce adverse results in certain key areas, such as India or Indonesia. A policy of competing with the USSR in extending aid can only serve to strengthen the already prevalent belief that it is politically activated, without substantially eliminating the political dangers of a rapid economic revolution. But a policy of sympathetic observation and disengagement can do much to eradicate the hatred of colonialism and the suspicion of imperialism which even our present actions breed. The result might be a clearing of the atmosphere which would create a more favorable climate for eventual democratic victory.[24] The time may eventually come when some Asians will perceive more accurately the nature of our motives, especially when the mist of alleged American imperialism lifts to reveal the real motives of Soviet aid. The latter may become even clearer when the Communists proceed to exploit the internal difficulties caused by rapid industrialization.[25] That such awakening may come too late is possible, but that happens to be precisely the nature of our disadvantage in the present epoch in Asia. In such delicate circumstances, it is sometimes more difficult and more fruitful to do little than to do too much.

----

[24] This victory, however, is unlikely to mean that an industrial India or Burma would resemble the United States or even the United Kingdom. The most we can hope for (although present trends are to the contrary) is that, despite the probable socialization of their economies, they will succeed in retaining political freedom and the values connected with it.

[25] Alexander Gerschenkron makes the point that the tendency toward political radicalism in Russia consequent upon industrialization waned after the critical period passed. Cf. his thought-provoking study, "The Problem of Economic Development in Russian Intellectual History of the Nineteenth Century," in Continuity and Change in Russian and Soviet Thought, ed. by Ernest J. Simmons, Cambridge, Mass., 1955.

FOR FURTHER READING:

Jonathan B. Bingham, *Shirt-Sleeve Diplomacy: Point Four in Action* (New York: John Day, 1953).

William A. Brown and Redvers Opie, *American Foreign Assistance* (Washington, D.C.: The Brookings Institution, 1953).

Norman S. Buchanan and Howard S. Ellis, *Approaches to Economic Development* (New York: Twentieth Century Fund, 1955).

Philip M. Glick, *The Administration of Technical Assistance: Growth in the Americas* (Chicago: University of Chicago Press, 1957).

William A. Hance, *African Economic Development* (New York: Harper and Brothers, 1958).

Albert O. Hirschman, *The Strategy of Economic Development* (New Haven: Yale University Press, 1958).

Paul G. Hoffman, "Operation Breakthrough," *Foreign Affairs*, Vol. XXXVIII, No. 1 (October, 1959), pp. 31-45.

Charles P. Kindleberger, *Economic Development* (New York: McGraw-Hill, 1958).

Albert Lepawsky, "The Bolivian Operation: New Trends in Technical Assistance," *International Conciliation*, No. 479 (March, 1952), pp. 101-140.

Max F. Millikan and W. W. Rostow, *A Proposal: Key to an Effective Foreign Policy* (New York: Harper and Brothers, 1957).

Walter R. Sharp, *International Technical Assistance* (Chicago: Public Administration Clearing House, 1952).

Eugene Staley, *The Future of Underdeveloped Areas* (New York: Harper and Brothers, 1954).

James W. Wiggins and Helmut Schoek (eds.), *Foreign Aid Re-examined: A Critical Appraisal* (Washington, D.C.: Public Affairs Press, 1958).

Chapter XIII

FOREIGN TRADE

Foreign trade issues in the public debate on American foreign policy are perhaps less dramatic and may appear less urgent than many others, but they are nonetheless of basic importance, particularly in view of the recent Soviet emphasis on the economic aspects of competitive coexistence. Foreign trade has great significance for both underdeveloped areas and highly developed states; for the former it can either facilitate or hinder their economic growth and for the latter it is a fundamental determinant of their economic health and stability. Our times clearly demand sound international trade policies. Achieving sound policies in this sphere, however, is a peculiarly complex and demanding task. Many of the issues involved appear highly technical and frequently they depend on long-range and therefore somewhat unreliable estimates. In a relatively free, market-guided economy the level of foreign trade is determined by a myriad of individual decisions, which government can at best only influence. And many governmental decisions which vitally affect foreign trade are taken, and to a certain extent must be, largely on the basis of their domestic impact. Foreign trade issues in the public debate, more than many others, emphasize the close connection between politics and economics.

Since 1934 the United States has pursued basically liberal foreign trade policies which have been aimed at reducing barriers to international commerce. In that year the Reciprocal Trade Agreements Act was passed, and we began to reduce our tariffs from the high levels they had reached in the Smoot-Hawley Tariff of 1930. This Act has been periodically renewed and additional measures have been taken to reduce tariffs and other obstacles to trade. On an international level the United States played a decisive part in the establishment of several institutions with this purpose: the International Bank for Reconstruction and Development (IBRD); the International Monetary Fund (IMF); the General Agreement on Tariffs and Trade (GATT); and the Organization for European Economic Cooperation (OEEC). Cordell Hull, Secretary of State from 1933 through 1944, did much to give American policy this orientation. He believed that freer trade would benefit the world and the United States economically and that the resulting increased contacts and opportunities would promote world peace.

It does not appear likely that the United States will retreat in any major way from its liberal position, and this does not seem to be an issue in the public debate. Much current discussion centers on the need for and pace of further liberalization. Whether more international institutions are needed is also a point frequently considered. Since the last stages of the Second World War many have felt that a broad organization dealing with trade policy should be established. The United States' latest effort in this direction was the 1955 proposal for an Organization for Trade Cooperation (OTC); a proposal accepted by the world's major trading states, but which has not yet received Congressional ratification. Other current issues have a broader focus, dealing with general aspects of economic policy. Their ultimate concern is the long-range strength and health of Western economies. How much of a threat is inflation here and abroad? What is the foreign trade impact of anti-inflationary measures? How should agricultural surpluses be handled and how can primary commodity markets be made more stable? On the assumption that large market areas are needed for economic growth and stability, the United States has generally favored the development of regional groupings. The most significant regional grouping yet formed is the European Economic Community (EEC): the attempt by Belgium, France, Germany, Italy, Luxemburg, and the Netherlands to establish a common market. Recently some have begun to wonder whether these regional groupings may not conflict with our global efforts to reduce obstacles to trade and to ponder their impact on American exports. All foreign trade questions have been put into a new perspective by the recent outflow of gold from the United States; with our military and foreign assistance expenditures we are currently spending more abroad than we earn. In the long run either United States exports must be increased or our foreign expenditures curtailed.

The first selection in this chapter, an excerpt from the report of a panel of the Rockefeller Brothers Fund Special Studies Project, headed by Milton Katz, Director of International Legal Studies at Harvard Law School, provides basic facts for an analysis of foreign trade problems and also sets forth broad policy recommendations. It indicates the importance of foreign trade to various areas and states, and illustrates the central role of the United States in the Western economy. Although foreign trade comprises only a small portion of our gross national product, our trade looms large in the economic life of other Western states. Despite the significant economic impact of foreign trade on several segments of American society, therefore, its political implications in terms of over-all Western economic health are probably more important to the United States. To insure this economic health, the report recommends further trade liberalization.

The broader focus of the current public debate is indicated by the second and third selections. Miroslav A. Kriz, formerly head of the Foreign Research Division of the Federal Reserve Bank of New York and now an Associate Economist with the First National City Bank, analyzes the strength of Western economies in the second selection. His concern with inflation and adequate monetary reserves parallels much of the thinking within the Eisenhower administration. While Mr. Kriz advocates further trade liberalization, he is satisfied with past progress in this sphere, and his primary interest is in a strong and growing economy. This is also the principal interest of the author of the third selection, Bertrand de Jouvenel, Director of the Société d'Études et de Documentation Industrielles et Sociales (Paris) and author of various works in political philosophy. M. de Jouvenel, however, would not accept Mr. Kriz's estimate of the danger of inflation, or his approval of anti-inflationary measures. In M. de Jouvenel's view, the anti-inflationary policies recently pursued by the United States and others have held down Western economic expansion.

The last two selections deal with the 1958 renewal of the Reciprocal Trade Agreements Act. Of these, the first is taken from John Foster Dulles' testimony before the Senate Committee on Finance in support of the Act's renewal. He places the Trade Agreements Act in the context of Soviet-American tensions. His arguments concerning the need to have authority to negotiate with the European Economic Community are especially relevant in view of the present United States balance of payments. Congress accepted most of Mr. Dulles' arguments, and he in turn was basically satisfied with the resulting legislation. Some, however, were not. The last selection presents a sample of this contrary opinion. In it, John M. Letiche, of the Economics Department at the University of California (Berkeley), analyzes the 1958 Act and on the basis of this argues that the United States has lost leadership in the foreign trade field.

Foreign trade issues in the public debate are frequently prosaic and difficult and many times the real problems are obscured. Yet the importance of such issues cannot be denied. The decisions taken will vitally affect the fate of the West.

Trade Policy*

by the Rockefeller Brothers Fund Special Studies Project

Ultimately the vitality of the economy of the free world will reveal itself in a high level of international trade. Here much depends on United States policy.

Before policy with respect to our foreign trade can be formulated, it is requisite that the broad outlines of world trade structure be understood.

In 1956, the total value of goods moving in international trade, exports and imports combined, totaled approximately $206 billion, or about 18 per cent of the world's total production of both goods and services. If the international trade in services, shipping, tourism, banking, and insurance were added, the degree of interdependence in the world economy would be seen to be considerably higher still.

The degree to which the countries in any given area are dependent upon the maintenance of trade with the outside world is better indicated by comparing the combined imports and exports of each with the total value of goods and services it produces. We then find that the trade of Western Europe and of the other industrialized free world nations, excluding the United States, averages about one-third of their total national product. For the less industrialized group of free world nations, the percentage is even higher, at about 37 per cent. For the Communist bloc as a whole it is 7 per cent, and for the U.S.S.R. only 5 per cent.

An understanding of these basic elements of the over-all world trade pattern is essential to the formulation of a constructive United States commercial policy. We must take account of the fact that, comparatively, the impact of fluctuations in the level of United States imports and exports upon the economies of other countries is greater even than the considerable effect of such fluctuations upon our own economy. Within the free world trading system, United States exports account for 20 per cent of all exports, and its imports for 14 per cent of total imports. But in terms of our domestic economy, combined imports and exports represent only about 8 per cent of annual output. This relatively small—although, as we shall see, highly significant—proportion which foreign trade bears to our own total output often leads us to underesti-

---

* From *Foreign Economic Policy for the Twentieth Century,* a report by the Rockefeller Brothers Fund Special Studies Project, pp. 37-42. © 1958 Rockefeller Brothers Fund, Inc. Reprinted by permission of Doubleday and Company.

mate, and indeed to misunderstand, the importance of that trade to *other* nations. What is a small item on our import list may be a major source of revenue for an exporting nation, as for example our imports of Swiss watches, Scotch whisky, or Latin American coffee and copper. Thus, a small fluctuation in the level of United States imports or exports may have a major impact on the economies of other nations—including many in whose political and economic stability we have a deep concern.

Despite its relatively small percentage weight in our over-all economy, a vigorous and expanding foreign trade is essential for the vitality of our economy. We import half or more of a wide variety of metals and minerals essential to United States industry. Three-fourths of our newsprint is imported, all of our natural rubber, 18 per cent of our iron ore, and over 15 per cent of our petroleum.

Between 9 and 10 per cent of all the durable goods produced in the United States is sold abroad. Significantly enough, these sales provide the margin between profit and loss for a large segment of American industries. Exports represent from one-fifth to one-third of the total sales of American production of civilian aircraft, textile, steel and rolling mill machinery, and sewing machines. They represent 19 per cent of all motor truck and bus sales, 16 per cent for diesel engines, 14 per cent for agricultural machinery, and 11 per cent for machine tool production. American farmers depend upon foreign markets for the sale of 20 to 40 per cent of their wheat, rice, cotton, rye, barley, hops, grain sorghums, soybeans, leaf tobacco; and the same is true for domestically produced calf skins, fats and oils, dried fruits and processed milk.

Even this does not exhaust the United States dependence on foreign trade. For 1957, the total value of United States goods and service exports totaled $26 billion. But the total sales of 2,500 branches and subsidiaries of United States companies located abroad were estimated at $32 billion and at least 40 per cent of these were sales in international rather than local markets. About 4.5 million workers, or 7 per cent of the entire United States labor force are directly dependent upon foreign trade for their livelihoods. Foreign trade provides more direct employment in the United States than the automobile, steel, chemical and textile industries combined.

Against the background of this degree of interdependence between the United States and other areas, it might be expected that the foreign commercial policy of the United States would be encouragement of exports and imports to the utmost, if only from the point of view of our

most immediate economic self-interest. When we add the vital importance of expanding production and trade for all of the other nations
of the free world, it would appear that the case for a liberal trade policy
should command virtually unanimous national agreement.

Yet it is clear, from the debates over the renewal of the Trade Agreements Act and the President's authority to reduce tariffs, that this is not
so. The case for a freer trade policy must be repeated year after year and
the same arguments must be refuted each time. Nearly everyone recognizes the advantage of a liberal trade policy. But it seems that we hesitate to pay the price it demands. Understandably, those who suffer by
lower tariffs are reluctant about a freer trade policy. Yet economic wisdom demands acceptance of the fact that if other jobs, sales and profits
are to accrue from United States exports, we inevitably must be willing
to accept the imports upon which payment for our exports depend. It
is unavoidable that some of our imports will compete with segments of
domestic production as do our exports in many of the markets in which
they are sold.

Every serious study that has been made in this field to date indicates
that the preponderant bulk of American industry is well able to meet
such competition. Indeed, one of the most important arguments in favor
of trade liberalization is that it will broaden competition and thus increase the competitive discipline that is a major safeguard against inflation. Especially when consumer demand in the United States is pressing against our capacity output, freer access of foreign producers to our
market will help to keep prices from rising. Under any gradual progression toward tariff liberalization, the displacements are not likely to be
on a broader scale or of deeper dimension than those that are continuously occurring through domestic competition within and between
industries.

The major fault of United States commercial policy, in recent years at
least, has been its failure to provide assurance of direction and continuity. Judged by current world standards, our prevailing tariff levels
and commercial policy procedures are not unduly restrictive. But our
market is so large and so generally competitive that it requires a sustained
and expensive effort for foreign business interests to establish a foothold
in it. Relatively few have the resources or the fortitude to make the
effort when they are faced with the possibility or even probability that
our rules will be changed if they are successful.

We therefore believe it essential that the Reciprocal Trade Agreements Program be made a permanent part of our national policy. There should also be a broadening of Presidential discretion to allow for consideration of broad domestic and foreign policy interests. Escape clauses, peril point provisions, and even defense essentiality procedures should be reconsidered so that the criteria for decision are based upon the whole balance sheet of national policy instead of items of short-run advantage and disadvantage. Beyond the Reciprocal Trade Act the United States should use its influence in bringing about an increasingly free world trade. The regional groupings if properly conceived can be an important step in this direction. We need above all to be clear about this aim and we require sufficient resolution to adhere to it.

Thus our trade policy necessarily becomes a central part of our foreign economic policy, and must be considered on this plane. Without a policy of vigorous promotion of multilateral trade, our larger foreign economic policy cannot promote a just and workable international order, or forward our own aspirations for growth.

The Tasks of Economic Statesmanship in the World Today*

By Miroslav A. Kriz

Among the problems that the free world is facing, the increasing of its economic and financial strength is second only to the maintenance of its political and military supremacy. Indeed, as the free world enters the era of "competitive coexistence" with Russia and the countries in Russia's orbit, the issue of its economic and financial strength under armed peace comes into the foreground.

The free world, it is true, is enjoying unprecedented prosperity, and the economies of most of the free nations are inherently much stronger than in the earlier post-war years, domestically as well as internationally. Yet the rebuilding of efficient and resilient economies, not to mention the further advance toward freer and more multilateral world trade and payments, is once more being impaired by renewed inflationary pressures. Sterling, in which nearly half of the world's trade is conducted, is again experiencing difficulties. To be sure, remedial action, largely

* From the *Political Science Quarterly*, Vol. LXXI, No. 3 (September 1956), pp. 321-340; copyright 1956 by the Editors of the *Quarterly*, and reprinted with their permission and Miroslav Kriz's.

monetary, has been taken in many countries to reëstablish a more nearly sustainable balance, but much remains to be done to restore and permanently secure such a balance. This, therefore, is a good time to weigh the elements of strength and weakness in the free world's economy and the difficult and delicate tasks challenging the economic statesmanship of the free nations.[1]

[I]

The free world has moved a long way since the earlier post-war years when the so-called "dollar shortage" was measured in billions and the need for America's financial aid in many countries was desperate. The chief reason why international payments difficulties appeared then as essentially a dollar problem was that Western Europe, with its associated overseas currency areas, was unable to secure from its own output sufficient foodstuffs, raw materials, and industrial goods to match its greatly increased needs. Besides, Western Europe was receiving far less than before the war from Eastern Europe, the Far East, and Latin America; and, so far as it was possible for this reduction in supplies to be made good elsewhere, it was done through imports from the United States and Canada. These and other shifts in trade accounted for much of the "dollar shortage."

Far from demonstrating the prevalence of an intractable "disequilibrium," the post-war "dollar shortage" thus was, for the most part, a sign of the large rehabilitation and reconstruction outlays by Western Europe and its associated overseas currency areas, and of the free gifts and loans made by the United States and Canada to speed up the post-war recovery. From 1946 through 1953, the United States, through gifts and loans, transferred to the rest of the world 33 billion dollars' worth of goods and services, excluding military supplies; this was equal to more than one fourth of all United States exports during these years. By 1953, however, the recipients of American aid had succeeded in greatly increasing their own output and in restoring a large measure of fiscal and monetary order, and as a result the "dollar shortage" has disappeared. Even though inflationary strains and balance-of-payments difficulties have reëmerged in certain countries and areas—these are among the elements of recent weakness that I shall discuss later—the improvement achieved in international payments has been truly remarkable. . . .

---

[1] The views stated here are those of the writer and do not purport to reflect those of the Federal Reserve Bank of New York.

This improvement was basically the outcome of the growth in output and productivity in the nondollar world and of the redirection of world trade. In Western Europe, industrial production stands about 70 per cent higher than before the war; and agricultural and mineral output has likewise reached record levels. Although the rise in the gross national product has not been as striking as in industrial output, and although allowance must be made for the increase in population, Western Europe's recovery has been much faster and greater than after the First World War.

In other regions, record levels of agricultural and mineral output have likewise been reached, and industrialization has proceeded fast. This has been in part the outcome of official development expenditures so far undertaken, but the influence of a high level of world demand, which in turn induced a growing volume of private investment, must also be recognized. Export prices have necessarily continued to fluctuate, and price variations have been wide for certain agricultural products like coffee; but prices have remained favorable by any earlier standards except those of the world-wide commodity boom that followed the Korean outbreak in mid-1950. The demand for primary commodities has remained high because of the sustained level of business activity in the United States and other principal markets. The volume of investment in both the public and the private sectors has never been larger, and machinery and other equipment have become more readily obtainable in the industrial countries. However, economic development has not always been as great as might be hoped, and has often been distorted by inflation; furthermore, in view of the rapidly increasing population and with levels of per capita consumption remaining in many areas below pre-war levels in spite of all that has been done, the free world must not be complacent about its achievements. The reëmergence of agricultural surpluses, noted later, is another weak spot in the world economy today.

Nevertheless, as agricultural, mineral and industrial output has expanded to all-time record levels, most nondollar countries have been able gradually to replace the abnormal post-war imports from the United States by their own output or by imports from nondollar sources. Their own exports, on the other hand, have also risen substantially. . . .

These and other factors are best summed up in the trends of gold and dollar holdings of foreign countries. Such holdings had been depleted by 6.0 billion dollars between December 1945 and September 1949, the date of the world-wide currency readjustments; but they rose by 11.8

billion dollars between September 1949 and December 1955, when they stood 92 per cent above the pre-war level. Of these 11.8 billion dollars, 2.6 billion accrued from new foreign gold production (probably including some gold acquired from Russia), while 9.2 billion can be accounted for by transactions with the United States as well as with international financial institutions, whose dollars were of course derived principally from the subscriptions by the United States government or borrowing in the United States. The gold and dollar acquisitions resulting from transactions of foreign countries with the United States have been the outcome of a number of factors, some fundamental, like those already mentioned, and some temporary or merely accidental, like those on which I shall comment below among the elements of weakness; but these temporary or accidental factors cannot hide the fundamental improvement in international payments.

. . . International payments are much freer today, and this, too, is a fundamental element of strength. . . . Countries that have relaxed their dollar-import restrictions, like West Germany, the Netherlands, the Union of South Africa, and to a smaller degree the United Kingdom, are importing considerably more dollar goods . . . ; to a lesser extent, this is also true of other countries in Europe and elsewhere.

Sterling in particular is much freer than in 1953. In the United Kingdom, most raw materials and foodstuffs can now be imported without discrimination, while in South Africa there is no trade discrimination whatever and in other sterling countries a substantial part of imports may be purchased from the cheapest sources, without preference having to be given to nondollar currencies. The remaining dollar discrimination in the sterling area, even though not negligible, is relatively small in comparison with the area's total imports. Furthermore, because of the widening in early 1954 of the transferable-account area to include almost all nonsterling nondollar countries, transferable sterling can be used for payments to and from practically all nondollar countries, and can be converted at the official rate into all currencies except those of the dollar area; large segments of international trade and payments have thereby been made multilateral. Since early 1955, transferable sterling, which previously could be converted into dollars only at a considerable discount, has in effect been convertible at a rate within 1 per cent of the official sterling-dollar rate. All this must be kept uppermost in our minds in judging the area's present conditions and prospects. It is particularly notable that, despite the area's renewed payments difficulties, there has been, with the principal exception of Australia, no relapse into the more stringent trade and payments controls that had characterized the earlier post-war years.

The economies of much of the free world are thus inherently much stronger than only a few years ago. Many countries are, however, still facing great economic and financial difficulties, domestic as well as international, which may well give rise to many doubts about the advance thus far made toward freer trade and payments.

[II]

Among these doubts, I may allude, to start with, to the fact that the closing of the dollar gap has taken place in an environment in which the productive efficiency of most European industries, and Europe's ability to live in a more competitive world, have not yet been tested fully. Most of the dollar liberalization has so far been concentrated on raw materials and certain foodstuffs; indeed, its main purpose has been to cheapen such imports and thereby exert a downward pressure on domestic prices. The cheaper dollar imports have actually helped to improve the terms of trade and lower the manufacturing costs of certain European industrial countries; but these countries have not yet encountered the competition of American manufactured goods in their own economies or in various sheltered markets. Altogether apart from the discriminatory import quotas, the tariffs in a number of countries isolate various domestic industries more effectively than before the war. The ultimate reasons for trade restriction lie today as much in the desire to protect individual industries (and also agriculture, where social and strategic considerations are important) as in the state of the balance of payments.

The second reason for skepticism is the very uneven distribution among foreign countries of the post-war rise in the gold and dollar holdings. The largest gain has been made by Continental Western Europe—7.2 billion dollars from September 1949 to the end of 1955, with France and West Germany the principal beneficiaries but Italy and the Netherlands also showing sizable increases. Canada's holdings of gold and United States dollars have likewise risen (by 1.2 billion dollars); the strength of Canada's international economic position was also reflected during most of the recent years in the premium at which the Canadian dollar stood over the United States dollar. Outside of Continental Western Europe and Canada, however, the rise in gold and dollar holdings has, at best, been moderate.

The gold and dollar holdings of nonsterling Asian countries and of Latin America have risen, but within each group the distribution of the rise has been very uneven; the holdings of some countries have actually declined.

Altogether, therefore, only certain countries in Continental Western Europe, and Canada, have gold and dollar holdings that can be regarded as adequate. Even more important, the currencies of Continental Western Europe, essentially regional as they are, are collectively backed by gold and dollar reserves nearly four times as large as those supporting sterling, which, along with the United States dollar, is the world's key currency. Yet, conditions have, on the whole, been favorable to sterling, since world trade has been expanding and the terms of trade have not been too unfavorable to the sterling area.

Another disturbing development is the persistence of Western Europe's dollar deficit on trade and other nonmilitary accounts. Some of Western Europe's rise in reserves has thus merely reflected—even though not in a simple and direct fashion—receipts of dollars under military and other aid programs of the United States. France in particular received sizable reimbursements for expenditures incurred in Indo-China; countries that do not receive direct aid have benefited indirectly from the flow of such dollars (for instance through the European Payments Union, of which France was at various times the largest deficit country). In addition, United States military expenditures abroad, which of course do not count as a form of aid, have likewise been important. These dollar receipts differ from normal commercial transactions, since they are based on strategic and military considerations rather than on private economic motives; but there is not much likelihood of their being terminated in any discernible future, even though they are likely to decline gradually.

The failure of the United Kingdom, and of the sterling area as a whole, to rebuild monetary reserves has been due in large measure to the persistent rise in demand for goods—for consumption as well as for investment in industrial plant and elsewhere—which has tended to outstrip available resources. It has thus led both to increased imports and to smaller exports than might otherwise have been achieved; as a result, balance-of-payments difficulties have reappeared, most recently in 1955.

Sterling is, however, also one of the three main forms—with gold and the United States dollar—in which other countries hold their external liquid resources, whether as working balances for current trade or as currency reserves; Britain thus has large currency liabilities. Furthermore, sterling is vulnerable in the exchange markets whenever bankers, merchants and others go short of sterling, for instance by delaying to the last moment a necessary sterling purchase; pressures on sterling have occurred at times during recent years, and this tendency, too, has been an element of weakness.

Still other elements of uncertainty are of a political character. Among these are the future political status of Malaya—which, thanks to its rubber and tin earnings, is the largest single net contributor to the sterling area's dollar pool—and the future of the Middle Eastern oil, to mention but two examples. Furthermore, as the inevitable counterpart of its rôle in world affairs, Britain carries a burden of defense outlays far larger than could have been foreseen at the end of World War II; she has to be in a position to sustain this burden for a long time, and may even have to live with it indefinitely. A large portion of these outlays is in dollars; these political and strategic commitments—commitments that Germany and other Continental European nations except France do not have—may well make the difference between a precarious dollar balance and a surplus.

The United Kingdom, and also France and the Netherlands, have also been affected by the loss of much of their overseas investments; on the other hand, they have incurred large dollar indebtedness. The change in Britain's status from the world's greatest creditor to the world's greatest debtor has further increased the magnitude of the necessary adjustment in her balance of payments.

I have dwelt at some length on the elements of weakness that surround sterling, since the pound is a world currency, and in the long run will retain its international status only if it can hold its value and be freely used by people outside the United Kingdom. There are, however, still other elements of weakness, in the world at large, political as well as economic and financial. Conspicuous among them is the problem of agricultural surpluses—not only in the United States, but in many other countries as well. The possible impact upon their trade of the United States government measures for the disposal of agricultural surpluses is a matter of concern to many primary-producing countries.

Russia's offers to purchase surpluses of countries like Egypt (cotton),

Burma (rice), Cuba (sugar), and Argentina (livestock) are other examples of the type of problems now coming up. These seemingly genuine business transactions may appear attractive to countries that are obviously glad to sell otherwise unsalable surpluses, but payment will be made in rubles (or other Soviet-bloc currencies) that the trading partners will be forced to use for Soviet-bloc goods that may be unsuitable, poor in quality, or overpriced by Western standards. The Western nations must not, however, be complacent about Russia's moves on the ground that they will necessarily defeat themselves.

[III]

These elements of weakness are deep-seated and disturbing. Nevertheless, there are reasons to believe that the free world may be reasonably successful in building up efficient and resilient domestic economies, linked together by a smoothly working network of trade and payments. Looking backward to the state of chaos and the seemingly intractable problems of the early post-war years, and then comparing these with the halfway house that has been reached today, the free nations can, I think, feel encouraged; and, although the magnitude of the task ahead is appalling, there are reasons to hope that the undertaking begun years ago may not remain unfinished.

Perhaps the most encouraging aspect of the problem is the growing awareness that there is no escape from economic necessity, since in the long run a country cannot consume or invest or spend for government purposes more than it produces; it can live beyond its means only so long as it spends its gold and foreign exchange reserves or receives loans and grants from abroad. Therefore, the only choice that exists is whether to equalize claims of consumption and investment with resources in a rational way, which will prevent inflation, or in a haphazard and economically and socially injurious way, which tolerates inflation; the equalization will have to be effected in the one way or in the other.

There is also a much greater awareness today than a few years ago of the economic and social costs of inflation, and of the relation of the surplus or deficit in a country's international payments to its management of its affairs at home. Only a few years ago it took as much courage to suggest, in certain countries, that a reduction in government spending, or in the rate of private or public investment, or in personal consumption, was desirable, as it took twenty-five years ago to state the case for a policy of economic expansion as a way out of the depression.

Today, in contrast, many governments are endeavoring to impress upon public opinion the necessity for preventing consumption and investment from outstripping available resources, and thus stopping inflation and rehabilitating the currency. It is particularly noteworthy that not only the developed countries of Western Europe but also the developing countries in other parts of the world are now endeavoring to restore and maintain reasonable monetary stability. There are, of course, cases where monetary policy can do little, though the wrong policy can do a great deal to make matters worse. In countries that depend for a substantial part of their national income on the export of a few primary commodities whose prices are liable to sharp fluctuations, there are limits to what monetary policy by itself can do; this has been a serious problem for primary-producing countries. Another limitation upon monetary controls is the lack of developed money and capital markets.

The problem of reëstablishing a workable economic balance is still great in certain primary-producing countries where inflationary pressures have prevailed during most of the recent post-war years. On the other hand, Western Europe and Canada are undergoing inflationary strains and balance-of-payments difficulties that are marginal by any comparison with the earlier post-war years. The required reduction in the flow of spending appears therefore to be small, at least in aggregative terms. In Great Britain, for instance, what is required is an addition to exports, or a reduction in imports, or a combination of these, equivalent to about 1½ per cent of the gross national product.

Another encouraging sign is that the economies of Western European nations, though by no means as flexible as that of the United States, are more adaptable to changing circumstances than in the earlier post-war years. One of the most notable examples of adjustments in the pattern of production to meet changes in overseas demand is the very remarkable, though still insufficient, rise in Britain's exports amounting to two thirds in volume over pre-war exports. The increase in exports of metal and engineering products is particularly encouraging. Fully half of British exports now consist of such products; and, compared with those before the war, such exports have increased two and one-half times. It is, of course, for these products that there is the most sustained demand in world markets. The changes that Britain has made, and is still making, in her economy to meet this demand, even at the cost of cutting her own investment (as will be noted below), are just the type of adjustment that is required of a country dependent on foreign trade, if it is to reassert its position in a competitive world. Nevertheless, even so marked an expansion in exports has been inadequate to meet the demand for imports and the other claims on the United Kingdom's exchange resources.

There has also been a profound difference in the type of policies followed. During the earlier post-war years, in part because of the overhang of wartime inflation, most of the free nations relied principally on direct or physical controls over prices, allocation of materials and investment; but they have probably indulged, as the result of government deficit financing and bank lending to business, in more laissez faire with regard to redundant money than, at least in retrospect, appears to have been necessary. Today, the dynamic forces that alone can ensure a viable economy have been released while the necessary general controls over the economy are being exercised mainly through monetary policies. Furthermore, in countries with more developed money markets and banking systems, monetary policies are now working more strongly, and with a more powerful momentum, than at any time during the post-war years. Not only have the official discount rates been raised since early 1955 in sixteen foreign countries—sometimes to the highest levels since the war or even, as in England, to the highest level since the early thirties—but they have also greatly gained in power as a monetary policy instrument since 1950-52, the last previous phase of monetary restraint. Rigid central bank support of government bonds also has been abandoned, and much less reliance is being placed on selective credit controls (except for the revived consumer credit controls). . . . Money has thus been made not only dearer but also scarcer, and this has been accomplished primarily through the traditional method of acting directly on the credit base. These and other features of general monetary restraint are a measure of the firmness of the new monetary policy.

The test to which monetary policy is currently being subjected is, however, very severe. In the past, many countries have been, at times, too ready to tolerate a higher volume of demand for goods than their overloaded economies could meet. As the British Chancellor of the Exchequer pointed out recently, the most "interesting clue" to Britain's economy is that "in the eight years from 1946 to 1954 we turned out 26 per cent more goods and services, but we paid ourselves 80 per cent more money for doing it." Of this 80 per cent of "more money," the largest portion was in wages and salaries; wage restraint is therefore an indispensable accompaniment of monetary restraint, more particularly since monetary conditions are closely linked to wages.

Furthermore, monetary policy, directed at restricting spending in the private sector of the economy, has not always been accompanied by a reduction in government outlays, including those of the nationalized enterprises, or by tax raises to help counter the excess demand for goods. In present-day economies, characterized by much larger government sectors than before the war, such lack of appropriate fiscal action has often impaired the efficacy of monetary policy. It is notable, therefore, that some measures taken in England were specifically aimed at reducing the spending in the government sector. Another difficulty has been the tendency in a number of countries, particularly in Scandinavia and until quite recently also in England, to soften the impact of the rise in interest rates in so far as it affects residential housing.

A still further difficulty of monetary policy, even where aided by fiscal policy, is in making it induce a shift in the use of the productive resources, of the type required in a country like Britain. The main reliance is being placed on drawing down stocks and cutting new investment in plant and equipment. But stocks cannot be reduced below certain levels if efficient production is not to be impaired; hence most of the retrenchment will have to fall on new fixed investment. The difficulty, to be sure, is not that British investment is too high by any absolute standards (it had been, on the contrary, too low for decades) or that British production is too low (it is one of the highest per capita in the world), but that room has not been made for investment by reducing consumption and government expenditures. Consumption is now to be cut somewhat, but the brunt of the retrenchment will fall on fixed investment, as in 1947, 1949 and 1951. The diverting of resources from new investment thus involves a painful sacrifice in terms of viability prospects, but is, in the short run, a political and economic necessity. It has also the immediate advantage of enabling Britain to increase, in not too distant a future, her exports of machinery and equipment. Delays in deliveries and a lack of incentive to seek export markets, which are by-products of inflation, seem to have accounted, more than excessive costs, for Britain's failure to increase her exports further in an expanding world market.

[IV]

Another ground for reasonable hope in the ability of the free nations to build up efficient national economies is what may be regarded as the fairly satisfactory state of the economic relationships of the United States with the other parts of the free world. Among these relationships, I would emphasize the steady growth in United States output and hence in imports, as well as the record of United States trade policy which, despite many difficulties, has not been one of retreat.

The rôle of the United States in the world economy is, of course, more important than that of any other single country; but, contrary to assertions made in many quarters in the earlier post-war years, the world economy is not entirely dominated by the United States. Whenever America sneezed, the rest of the world was expected to catch pneumonia. So it seemed, indeed, in 1949 when a drop in industrial output in the United States preceded world-wide balance-of-payments disturbances; even then, however, this inference was not quite justified since the principal nondollar currencies were undoubtedly out of line with the United States dollar. When in 1951 similar disturbances occurred, at a time when American output and income were rising, it became clear that it was not the behavior of the United States, but rather factors indigenous to other parts of the world—which by then had "outinflated" the United States—that were primarily responsible for renewed balance-of-payments difficulties. Then came 1953, but, despite the mild recession in the United States, expansion continued in Western Europe and much of the rest of the world. Actually, industrial production in countries outside North America—equivalent to about two thirds of North American output—continued to rise at a rate that offset the drop in North American output, with the result that the level of world industrial production as a whole was maintained despite the American recession. This experience has shown that many foreign economies have become resilient enough to adjust themselves to moderate fluctuations in the level of business activity in the United States.

The United States has absorbed during recent years a growing volume of imports. The recession in the United States from October 1953 to September 1954, which was marked by a contraction of about 2.5 per cent in gross national product and 7 per cent in industrial output, was accompanied, it is true, by a decline in imports of 9 per cent in volume, but even during the year ended September 1954, prior to the sharp recovery that began at that time, United States imports were 20 per cent larger in volume than as recently as 1949. Moreover, from the third quarter of 1954 to the last quarter of 1955, imports rose about 30 per cent in volume.

An even more significant development of recent years has been a steady advance in United States imports of finished manufactures. The value of these imports increased from 960 million dollars in 1950 to some 1,800 million in 1955. Of this increase, over half represented purchases from Western Europe. The rise in imports of manufactured products has greatly contributed to the better international balance that has emerged. Nevertheless, our imports cannot be regarded as especially high in terms of the gross national product: today they are less than 3 per cent of the goods and services that the country is producing—a considerably smaller proportion than in the twenties.

The trade policy of the United States has likewise been important. Trade policy is necessarily a compromise between many economic and other forces; if we look, however, not at the "victories" and "defeats" in the contests over foreign trade policy, but at long-term trends, there has been a real continuity in our trade program since the mid-thirties. Once again in 1955 the Trade Agreement Act was extended and amended so as to provide increased authority for tariff negotiations; under this authority, the United States has negotiated, in the fourth round of tariff negotiations under the auspices of GATT, for further reciprocal tariff concessions over the next three years. Perhaps even more significant, the so-called "escape clause," under which the Tariff Commission can make recommendations to the President for higher tariff rates on the ground of injury to domestic industry, has been invoked in 62 cases since it became law in 1948; but only 16 of these cases were approved by the Commission, and of the latter's recommendations the President rejected 10 and put only 6 into effect. Statistically, this is not a bad record; and, even though the individual tariff increases that were finally effected threatened to cut deeply into the exports of the foreign countries concerned, in at least the two most publicized cases—watch movements and bicycles—the actual effect has been negligible. It may be added that consideration of national defense had apparently a bearing on the increased duty on imported watch movements; in the bicycle case, the actual tariff rise was held to less than initially recommended on the grounds, worth stressing here, that foreign producers and American importers had, by their "ingenuity and resourceful efforts," created an American market for lightweight bicycles. This stand, which should help allay the reluctance of other foreign manufacturers to undertake similar export efforts in this country, was unfortunately lost sight of in the criticism that once more the "escape clause" had been invoked against successful imports; and some damage was done to the much-needed understanding between the United States and its trading partners.

Much else could be said about the record of United States trade policy—among other things, that although many tariffs are high and many of our customs procedures are slow and cumbersome, many other United States tariffs are low and more than half of our imports enter free of duty. Even more important, however, is the increased awareness, both here and abroad, that there are very definite limits to what can be accomplished by further tariff reduction alone; and that what matters more than tariffs is the rising level of employment and incomes in the United States, which in turn calls for larger imports. The full answer to the question of what the United States can best contribute to international balance is therefore a continuing expansion of imports—which are now at the highest level ever recorded—in response to the growth of the American economy.

For several decades, there has been little experience for any considerable period of time with United States tariffs under conditions that might be regarded as more or less normal. The Trade Agreement Act was enacted during the depression, and the outbreak of war disrupted the new trade pattern that was then arising as a result of the many tariff reductions. Tariffs were further reduced after the war, but the earlier post-war years, and again the years immediately following the Korean war, were likewise abnormal. It is only today that the free world—including the United States—can begin forming a judgment on how American trade policy is actually working.

[v]

The strains and stresses in world trade and payments today thus differ fundamentally from the "dollar shortage" that plagued the free world during the earlier post-war years. The earlier inflations and the balance-of-payments predicaments had arisen because of the transition from war-time destruction and post-war distortion in trade and payments; in contrast, today's problems are for the most part the inevitable accompaniment of rapid economic growth of dynamic economies that have not yet learned how to maintain a high level of employment without at the same time giving rise to inflationary pressures and balance-of-payments deficiencies.

For this very reason, payments difficulties are no longer world-wide in scope and character. For this reason, too, they can be dealt with primarily by the countries concerned, on their own initiative and responsibility. We want, to be sure, a balance in international accounts at a level of living standards that will be socially and politically endurable; but it should be possible, I think, to achieve this with output and productivity at record levels in much of the world and—at least in the developed countries—much higher per capita than before World War II. The speeding-up of economic development in the less-developed countries of the free world, on the other hand, will require aid by all other free nations capable of maintaining a large export surplus and of providing resources for foreign investment. The principal contribution that the United States can make is for it to pursue economic policies that will facilitate the attainment and maintenance by the other free-world countries of a sustainable balance in their international payments at a high level of employment, income, and standard of living. Along these lines, the steadily rising volume of imports in response to growing output and the basic continuity in the United States trade policy, together with a long-range programming of economic aid now considered by the Administration, hold much promise.

Much more is, however, at stake than a further step-by-step advance toward freer and more multilateral trade and payments along the lines of the policies of recent years. It is important that the earlier momentum be not lost; but at a time when Russia and the countries in her orbit have entered into "competitive coexistence" with the free world, it is even more essential that the free nations reassert their willingness to reduce trade barriers further among themselves and speed up the economic growth of the less-developed regions. The free world consists, of course, of many sovereign nations, each with its own aspirations and its own way of life. Because of the political and atomic stalemate among the Great Powers, many of these nations, in Western Europe, as well as in Asia and Africa, are unwilling to commit themselves politically; they are, however, fully aware that the threat to their independence comes from Russia, and are therefore anxious to strengthen their economic and cultural ties with the United States. This calls, I think, for a much greater stress on trade among the free nations and on other economic aspects of their relationships. At this particular juncture, therefore, it seems of utmost importance to unite the economies of the free world into a smoothly working and, as far as is feasible today, self-sustaining network. Not only the well-being of each nation but also the political and military strength of the entire free world depend importantly upon countering Russia's attempts at economic penetration by recreating as close an economic and financial unity as possible.

American Policy and the Free World Economy*

by Bertrand de Jouvenel

The United States government, beginning in 1955, has tried to curb domestic inflation by a series of measures designed to stabilize the purchasing power of the dollar. The question must be asked not only as to whether these measures proved effective but, also, how they influenced the economic fortunes of the Free World as a whole. The following discussion is addressed to an examination of trends for the period 1957-1958 in the balance of payments of the United States' major allies, especially Great Britain and France.

THE LOGICAL ASSUMPTIONS

A few years ago it seemed safe to assume that the world political situation, as seen from Washington, would be a major determinant of American economic policy and that, in turn, U.S. policies would exert a major influence upon world economics. Americans regarded Soviet Russia as a potential military danger and the communist bloc as an "alienated" portion of the planet. They were intensely concerned with blocking communist gains in those heterogeneous countries which are lumped together under the term "Free World." Such gains, whatever form they took, seemed to Americans politically dangerous: geographic increments to the communist bloc as, for example, North Vietnam, or the growing prestige of the communist states in the public opinion of

---

* From *Orbis*, Vol. III, No. 1 (Spring 1959), pp. 63-74. Copyright 1959 by the Trustees of the University of Pennsylvania. Reprinted by permission.

non-communist countries, or, although this appeared then unlikely, increasing commercial, financial and diplomatic ties between communist and non-communist countries as, for example, Egypt. Given this general outlook, it could reasonably be surmised that American economic policy would be oriented by three imperatives: 1) the defense establishment of the U.S. must be maintained well ahead of the Russian; 2) production must be expanded in the U.S. and allied industrial countries (Western Europe, Japan), thus refuting the myth of "capitalist stagnation" and giving the lie to the accusation that capitalism breeds depressions; and 3) countries relying upon primary exports, most of whom were uncommitted in the East-West conflict, must be tied to the U.S. and Western Europe by strong bonds of economic interest.

A rapid and steady increase of activity in the industrial countries affords an increasing market to primary exporters. The swelling inflow of foreign currencies enables the latter to acquire foreign manufactured equipment for purposes of internal development. Indeed, favorable prospects for the sale abroad of their primary goods bring to the producing countries additional benefits, such as private foreign capital for investment in natural resources and transportation facilities. Such an inflow of foreign capital generally induces the government of the receiving country to accord fair treatment to foreign investments: more often than not discriminatory measures against foreign investors are taken only when the inflow of foreign capital has ceased. In turn, the feeling of confidence engendered abroad by a country's promising export outlook and its respect for contracts induces foreign suppliers to grant longterm credits. All these advantages are bound up with a ready market for the country's staple commodities. Foreign aid can be a welcome addition to earnings from staple commodities, but it cannot compensate for declining exports.

THE SLOW-DOWN SIGNAL

To the foreigner, American public opinion is disconcerting for it appears to move in what seems to be a massive and sudden manner from one object of attention to another. Containment of the communist world had been up to 1952 the main object of attention; in 1953 it was entirely superseded by the purpose of cutting down government expenditure, a purpose which was achieved exclusively through the cutting back of defense expenditure.[1] As is well known, the more drastic cutback of orders for defense[2] caused a slack in the economy in 1953 and 1954—a slack which was taken up by a boom in consumer durables and housing, followed at a year's interval by a boom in investment expenditures.[3] From the summer of 1955 onwards, the fear of "inflation" became the dominant American concern, and the "line" to be held henceforth was not the "Popilius line" against communism[4] but the "price level."

Notice of intention was given by three increases of the Federal Reserve rate which occurred in rapid succession in the summer of 1955. These actions were understood throughout the Western world as signals that the United States proposed to "slow down" and that other countries had to apply the brakes in order to stay in step. This, far more than the American recession itself, has influenced the general pace. It should be remembered that, if the three "warning shots" by no means arrested the rate of investment in the U.S., they did, in fact, halt the expansion of overall industrial production. Taking January 1953 as 100, the index of industrial production reached 107 in October 1955, remained at about that level for two years, rose briefly to 110 in the last quarter of 1956, and declined to well beneath 100 in the first months of 1958.[5]

It is not possible here to examine the doctrine which guided American policy—a doctrine which placed a supreme value upon the preserva-

---

[1] This appears very clearly if one consults the quarterly figures of "Government purchases of goods and services": these fall from 85 billion in the second quarter of 1953 to 74.5 in the fourth quarter of 1954—a decline of 10.5 billion. In the meantime, National Security expenditures fell from 53.5 to 40.5, a decline of 13 billion. All other expenditures rose from 31.5 to 34.0, i.e., by 2.5 billion: they were, however, differently distributed between "Federal" and "State and Local."

[2] The amount of defense order placement fell from 9.3 billion in the first quarter of fiscal 1953 to less than one half billion in the last quarter of fiscal 1954, according to a statement by M. W. J. McNeill to the Conference of Business Economists in February 1958.

[3] The consumer durables boom began in the second quarter of 1954, the investment boom in the second quarter of 1955. The apex of the former was reached in the third quarter of 1955, when maximum coincidence between the two booms caused temporarily an excessive pressure, soon relieved by greater productive capacity.

[4] The Roman ambassador who told Antiochus, "Do not cross this line!" may well stand for a symbol of "containment."

[5] It should be noted that, while industrial production in this five-year period never moved above 10 per cent of its initial level, and at the end of the period had fallen beneath the initial level, manufacturing capacity, according to the McGraw-Hill Index, moved up 30 per cent. The fact that the previous figure relates to industry, the latter to manufactures makes no significant difference.

tion *ne varietur* of the buying power of the dollar,[6] and sought to achieve this end by creating a "slack" in the economy. The effectiveness of the method, under present institutional conditions, is doubtful; its political dangers are certain. Even though the policy of "slack" is addressed to a reduction of profits[7] rather than of labor income,[8] it is regarded by wage-earners as directed towards weakening their bargaining power. The ensuing social tensions are grist for the mills of Soviet propaganda, which seizes with avidity upon the increase of unemployment and the stagnation or decline of production.

CONSEQUENCES OF DISINFLATIONARY POLICIES

Rising prices, it is said, reflect excessive overall pressure of demand upon physical resources and thus call for a curb upon demand in order to preserve the buying power of the currency. This was the gist of the argument which swayed American opinion in 1955-56 and which was immediately echoed in West Germany—if, indeed, it did not originate there. The U.S. and West Germany boasted of vast export surpluses. According to the classical theory of international equilibrium, the balance between countries incurring an external payments deficit and countries registering an external payments surplus is restored through complementary adjustments made by both the deficit and surplus countries. In the deficit countries, the process is deflationary (prices go down absolutely or relatively to the international price level, and interest rates fall relatively to the international average). According to the classical doctrine, the inflationary developments affecting surplus countries are just as necessary to the restoration of equilibrium as the deflationary developments affecting deficit countries.

In 1955-56, however, the surplus countries, seeking to maintain the internal buying power of their currencies, pursued policies which ccould not fail to increase the international disequilibrium, for these policies, suitable as they are to deficit countries, are the least likely to remedy the

---

[6] A currency with an invariant buying power was regarded as an impossibility by all the classical economists from Ricardo to Rist.

[7] According to the "leftist" doctrine of full employment the working man's security in his job can be matched by the entrepreneur's enjoyment of higher profits.

[8] Labor income is, in any recession or depression, less affected than profits. Now there can be, on the part of government, no hesitation to grant financial relief to the unemployed. On the other hand, those suffering only from the elimination of overtime feel entitled to higher wage rates in order to restore their weekly earnings.

plight of surplus countries. A squeeze in deficit countries and a swelling in surplus countries—this is the sensible and well-proven treatment; but the economic doctors of the surplus countries recommended a domestic contraction. The natural consequence was to force upon the deficit countries a far greater squeeze than would have been called for if the surplus countries had let inflation run its course.

Disinflation in the surplus countries, the U.S. and West Germany, could not but impair the external balances of the other countries and therefore gave them no other choice except deflation or devaluation. All the industrial countries of Western Europe (except France) tried to "keep up with the Joneses" by energetic measures of squeeze. As a result, most of them practically held their industrial output to the January 1956 level. Such was the case of Britain, the Netherlands, Belgium, Denmark and Norway, while Italy braked production only in the spring of 1957 and Sweden and France did not slacken perceptibly their economic pace. Notwithstanding the measures taken, most European countries in the first semester of 1957 suffered a serious drain of exchange reserves. It was then believed that most European currencies would be devalued in relation to the dollar and the German mark. This belief itself started a stampede towards the mark. The rush was accelerated when, on August 10, 1957, France devalued her currency. In the first days of September the British authorities admitted a loss of 223 million pound sterling, incurred in the month of August, and *The Manchester Guardian* deemed it necessary to caption its front page with "Devaluation Excluded!" The pressure upon sterling was such that the Bank of England raised its discount rate to 7 per cent—a measure without precedent in peacetime.

Obviously a much lower rate would have been adequate if money had not then been so dear in the surplus countries. Prime commercial paper in New York had gone up to 4.5 per cent, implying a real cost of 5⅝ per cent to the borrower. Bonds bringing 8 per cent interest were issued in West Germany, a rate completely at odds with the abundant inflow of gold and dollars which should have produced monetary ease within the country.

The high price of money in London adversely affected the whole sterling bloc. Balances from the overseas sterling area were attracted to London, thus whittling down the credit facilities available in the overseas countries. This, however, was only a minor trouble, for the overseas countries were severely affected, like other primary exporters, by the stagnation of the American economy.

Between the first quarter of 1957 and the first quarter of 1958, the global value of the exports of the overseas sterling area fell by 12.5 per cent—a decline which may be presumed representative of the conditions experienced by all other countries exporting primary commodities. For sterling area countries alone, the drop was $127 million per month. Practically half of this loss was accounted for by the decrease in the value of rubber and wool exports.[9]

While the overall consumption of raw materials by Western Europe (O.E.E.C. countries) is little more than one half the American consumption, imports by Western Europe are about double the American imports, because the U.S. obtains rather more than three fourths of its raw materials from domestic sources while Western Europe satisfies less than one fourth of its demand from its own territory.[10] It follows that a 2 per cent fall in U.S. demand is compensated by a 1 per cent rise in European demand. Therefore, raw materials exporters were not hurt gravely by the first post-war American recession, since the decline of American demand was offset by coincident Western European expansion. In 1957, however, the "slack" forced upon Western Europe by the combined disinflationary policies of the U.S. and Western Germany resulted in a far greater deterioration of the situation of primary exporters.

BRITAIN AND THE POUND

The British authorities, responding to American and German disinflationary policies, deliberately sacrificed economic expansion to the purpose of strengthening the position of the pound. They succeeded in their purpose. The gold and dollar reserves backing the pound rose from a low of $1,850 million in September 1957 to as much as $3,080 million at the end of July 1958, the highest figure since 1950.

---

[9] See the British *Board of Trade Journal*, Aug. 1, 1958.

[10] See the important article by Gertrud Lovasy on "Prices of Raw Materials in the 1953-54 U.S. Recession," *International Monetary Fund Staff Papers*, February 1956. We stand in dire need of a survey of the balance of "third countries as a whole." The E.C.E. in Geneva put F.O.B. exports of primary countries to the U.S. in 1956 at $6.1 billion, while to Western Europe they were $12.2 billion. See Table IX, A 14, of the 1957 report.

Another feature of sterling strength was much in evidence during the summer of 1958. Let me briefly recall the distinction between "convertible" and "transferable" sterling: sterling accruing to residents of the dollar area are "convertible," i.e., the British authorities assume the obligation of turning at call sterling into dollars within the exchange margins covenanted with the International Monetary Fund (floor price of the pound: $2.78, ceiling price: $2.82). On the other hand, sterling accruing to others than residents of sterling area countries are merely "transferable," i.e., they can be used for international payments but, if sold against dollars, no selling price is formally guaranteed by the British authorities. In the summer of 1958, for the first time since the war, such "transferable sterling" sold above the "floor" price for convertible sterling. Thus, in practice all sterling accruing to foreigners have become convertible within the I.M.F. range of "parity." [11]

Gratifying as was the strength of sterling, it has been paid for dearly. In April 1958, 3,600 firms replied to a questionnaire sent out by the Association of British Chambers of Commerce to ascertain the effects of the credit squeeze. Among the firms replying, 53 per cent stated that their turn-over had been reduced, 43 per cent of the firms replying foresaw further contraction in the course of 1958. The Federation of British Industries estimated that 36 per cent of its members were not working at capacity. Indeed, special surveys can but enhance the vividness of the picture of stagnation offered by the industrial production index. The over-all seasonally corrected index for the last quarter of 1955 was 140 (1948 = 100); it was 138 for the first quarter of 1958 and 136 in May.

What is more, this stagnation by no means slowed down the rise in retail prices. During the four years terminating at mid-January 1956, the all-items index of retail prices rose by a total amount of 15.8 per cent, i.e. at the average yearly rate of 3 per cent. During the two years of stagnation terminating at mid-January 1958, the index rose by 8.1 per cent, i.e. at a 4 per cent yearly rate. It seems that some "slack" does not arrest price increases. Notice also that there has been no slow-down in the rise of wage-rates, which moved up from January 1952 to January 1956 at an average yearly pace of 5¼ per cent; from January 1956 to January 1958 they rose by as much as 12 per cent. The progress of earnings (as against rates), however, decelerated.

There seems little reason to doubt that the rise in the labor cost per

---

[11] Since this article was written, the British Government, in December 1958, made sterling fully convertible.

unit of output proceeded just as fast under conditions of declining productivity as it did in years of expansion. Indeed, the precedent of stagnation in 1952, when labor costs per unit of output increased substantially, strengthens the argument that labor costs per unit advance faster in years of stagnation than they do in years of expansion. Apparently the rate of advance in the cost of labor per hour does not slacken while the advance in output per hour does.

Surprisingly, the rise in wage cost per unit of output did not seem to have affected the export of British manufactures, which stood at the same nominal level in the first quarter of 1958 ($1,934 million) than in the first quarter of 1957 and formed a slightly higher percentage of the Free World exports of manufactures (19 per cent instead of 18.5 per cent). It is probable that the cost comparison approach to problems of international trade is, within limits, less relevant than the "absorption" approach.

THE UPSURGE OF THE FRENCH ECONOMY

The French economy offered the most striking contrast with the British. Firstly, French economic expansion proceeded at an altogether faster pace than the British. Secondly, since the beginning of 1956, this expansion did not slacken as did the British. Thirdly, since the international standing of the currency had not been given in French policy anything approaching the high priority accorded by British policy, the balance of payments and French exchange reserves compared unfavorably with those of Britain.

French economic expansion did not reach its greatest vigor in the immediate post reconstruction period (1949 to 1953). French expansion was slightly more rapid than the British. From 1949 to 1953, the French Gross National Product at constant prices grew at a yearly rate of 4 per cent (Britain 2.5 per cent) and French industrial production grew at a yearly rate of 5 per cent (Britain 3.5 per cent). In the period from 1953 to 1957, the pace was greatly quickened and the French GNP grew by 5.6 per cent yearly (U.K. 2.9 per cent), while industrial production in France increased 9.4 per cent (U.K. 3.5 per cent).[12]

The O.E.E.C. indexes for the first quarter of 1958 showed French industrial production as 157, compared with Western Germany's 152.

---

[12] *Etude sur la Situation Economique de l'Europe*, 1957, Chapter II, p. 3.

These two countries were well ahead of all others, the index for the U.K. standing at only 114 and the index for the U.S. at 97. It may come as a surprise to many readers that, since 1953, French industrial production has progressed even faster than the German. Even more remarkable perhaps are the figures relating to the progress of output per head in manufacturing. According to the U.N. Bureau of Economic Affairs, the annual percentage change from 1950 to 1956 in output per man-hour in manufacturing was 7 per cent in France as against 6.7 per cent in Western Germany and 1.2 per cent in the United Kingdom. Taking only the industrial indices from 1954 to 1956, the yearly gain in output per man-hour was as high as 9.3 per cent in France, as against 5.4 per cent in West Germany and 1.9 per cent in the U.K.[13] . . .

There are ample grounds for finding fault with French economic policies. Yet, many serious failings in terms of financial soundness notwithstanding, the vigor of France's economic development is truly astounding. Practically all the weak spots of the French economy seem to be the consequences of mistakes made before World War II and the destructions which the war left in its wake, and of the delusions fostered by the Provisional Government of 1944. Living standards, except for housing, seem in every respect higher than anywhere else on the Continent. These high average standards of living are combined with a remarkably high degree of release from anxiety through guaranteed social benefits. A high rate of investment holds the promise of further progress. Harmony now obtains between employers and employees; the communist vote is not a measure of social antagonism but rather a barometer of consumer discontent.

France flourishes, even though she bears (quite apart from military expenditures) an inordinate burden of overseas expenditure. Incidentally, there exists no estimate of the net contribution of the French economy to the overseas territories. Pending correction, this may be assessed at 15 to 20 per cent of net Metropolitan savings.

France's great economic weakness lies in the practically chronic payments deficit of the franc area in relation to the rest of the world. The enormous deficit in 1946 ($2,048 million) was rapidly whittled down to 706 million in 1949 and to 238 million in 1950. It jumped back to 1,063 million in 1951; it was reduced to 220 million in 1953. In 1954 and 1955, the balance of payments was favorable. But the franc area went

---

[13] *World Economic Survey 1957*, Chapter I, Table 8.

back into the red in 1956 (835 million) and 1957 (1,427 million). These deficits would have been even larger but for the expenditures of the U.S. Government within the franc area. Inability to keep consumption of foreign currencies within the limits of earnings in foreign currencies: this is the basis for the harsh judgments passed upon the French economy as a whole. It is commonly said: "The French do not keep their house in order; just compare their record with that of the Germans!"

France can accept the challenge. The financial rubble left behind by the war was cleared away in Germany by a brutal monetary reform which the Allied Powers found it easier to impose than would have been the case of a national government dependent upon public opinion. The government of experts which had served Germany so well had ample time, thanks to a Basic Law passed in the climate of foreign occupation, to demonstrate the validity of its economic theories. The German government was much less vulnerable to demands and pressures arising in the social field than successive French governments. German economic policy was free of the twin burdens which have weighed heavily upon the French post-war economy: military expenditures and aid to overseas territories. During a decade marked by an avid international demand for industrial equipment, French exports of that nature were balked by the demands of national defense and of the overseas dependencies. The overseas territories of the franc area are about as large as Canada, with about three times the Canadian population. Suppose they all formed one independent country: It would not seem strange that its development process should absorb about a billion dollars of foreign aid or investment per year. Whatever the nature of the political links between France and these overseas countries—whether they are tightened (integration), loosened (federation) or severed (independence)—it will be imperative for the Atlantic countries to give increasing financial aid to France's dependencies overseas.

France might do well to present its foreign critics with a balance of payments of Metropolitan France with the rest of the world (including the overseas franc area), and a balance of payments of the overseas franc area with the rest of the world (including France). This comparative study would reveal that Metropolitan France has not done so badly. More important still, it would show that bringing the franc area into balance with the rest of the world is fundamentally an absurd goal. To aver that this can be done is tantamount to saying that the overseas

franc area should be developed solely and entirely out of French savings
—an implausible proposition. While the progress of France has not
been as fast as that of Germany, it has been more vigorous than that of
Britain. Britain, it seems, has paid too high a price in a lagging productivity for the strengthening of the pound.

It is in the general interests of the Free World that a great and inven-
tive country like Britain should not be condemned to stagnation by disinflationary policies "made in the U.S." and "made in Germany." It is
equally in the Free World's interest that France should not be forced
to stint her lusty economy for want of dollars that could foster economic
development overseas. It seems extremely dangerous to let the uncommitted nations of the world, because they cannot find adequate outlets
for their primary materials, drift into bilateral trading relationships with
the Soviet bloc. Everything must be done to spur the dynamic expansion of the U.S. economy rather than rest content with a mere "recovery." Barring such affirmation of America's vitality and creativity,
the fragile edifice of the Free World will fall to pieces.

Vital Importance of the Extension of the Trade Agreements Act*

by John Foster Dulles[1]

We live in a world which is new in terms of its political structure and
its economic demands. Twenty countries have won their political independence within the last 15 years, and this trend is likely to continue.
Seven hundred million people are directly involved in this rapid transformation from the long-established system of colonialism. The very
rapidity with which this transformation is occurring presents a major
problem—how to achieve and maintain political stability.

Mass aspirations follow these new grants of independence. They are
contagious and spread to other lands. The demands for improved living
conditions are insistent. No possible sources of assistance are dismissed
out-of-hand. Present free-world nations may prefer to buy and sell within

---

* From the *Department of State Bulletin*, Vol. XXXVIII, No. 993 (July 7,
1958), pp. 34-37.

[1] Statement made before the Senate Committee on Finance on June 20, 1958.

the free world. But, if they are frustrated in their efforts to do so, they can be expected to direct their search elsewhere.

Although no international wars are being fought today, our security is menaced not only by the vast Soviet military buildup but by the efforts of international communism to turn the worldwide changes to selfish use as stepping stones to world domination.

If we are to combat this evil successfully, a better international order must be built and the United States must be in the forefront of that effort.

Fortunately for us, the free world is not disunited. It works together and provides dispersed power to retaliate against armed aggression. Military unity is imperative and must be continually strengthened. But this requires high morale throughout the free world and a willing spirit of close cooperation. Such an atmosphere is not created and maintained through military cooperation alone. Economic security is indispensable to all our allies and friends. It is essential that their relationship to the United States contribute not only to their military security but also to their economic well-being.

The strategy of Communist imperialism involves the subversion of country after country until the United States is isolated and subject to economic strangulation. You have heard repeatedly Mr. Khrushchev's threat of "war" in the peaceful field of trade and his boast that the Soviets will win this war because of the superiority of their system. I have said before—and I say again—it would be reckless to treat this threat as negligible.

The Soviet Union is rapidly developing its weapons for waging economic warfare against the United States and has achieved an industrial level which enables it to export manufactured goods in increasing quantity and variety and to take in exchange large amounts of natural products, whether agricultural or mineral, for their own use or to dump on free-world markets. Through pursuing this course they hope to gain dominance, first economically, then politically, in many countries which need an assured foreign market.

Our Government has by treaty or resolution declared, in effect, that the peace and security of the United States would be endangered if any of nearly 50 countries were to be conquered by Communist imperialism. But *declaring* this is not enough. We have to convince both friend and foe that we will do what is needed to prevent the Communist conquest.

So we have the policies and actions represented by our mutual security program and by the Trade Agreements Act.

Some seem to believe that national policies which aim to assure a congenial and friendly world environment are un-American or unpatriotic. The fact is that from our beginning United States doctrine has proclaimed that our own peace and security are bound up inextricably with conditions of freedom elsewhere. Today that doctrine, the doctrine of interdependence, is the cornerstone of free-world policy.

How has trade figured in these developments? During the depression of the early thirties, many countries tried to restore their economies by tariffs, quotas, and currency manipulations. We did those things and did them without regard to the effect upon others who were largely dependent on international trade. But the domestic relief we expected did not come. And by 1934 the decline in world trade brought to power, in several countries, leaders so nationalistic and aggressive as to constitute a major cause of World War II. They sought to expand their national domains at the expense of weaker neighbors on the ground that they could not assure their people a living standard by normal methods of peaceful trade. The price we all paid in World War II will, I hope, help us to avoid such shortsighted action in the future.

So far as the free world is concerned, the trend since that war has fortunately been in the other direction. In this movement to liberalize trade the United States has been an indispensable leader. Our Trade Agreements Act, first enacted in 1934 and since extended 10 times, has reflected our desire and purpose to promote the mutually advantageous expansion of world trade.

Some elements of United States industry try to improve their competitive position by implying that any competition from abroad, merely because it is "foreign," should for that reason be barred. This viewpoint, I repeat, cannot be accepted as United States policy without endangering our whole nation. This is not to say there are no cases where foreign competition should be restrained. There is a wide range of such cases, and protection is in fact accorded. It is true, however, that any general disposition to exclude foreign goods simply because they are competitive would gravely disrupt economic, political, and spiritual relationships which are required for our own welfare and for the defense of our peace and freedom.

You may ask what is the proper relationship between the progress of the trade program and the interests of domestic procedures. Let me say this. Almost every national policy hurts some and benefits others. The form of our taxation; the nature of our defense purchases; the location of government operations—all of these and many other national policies inevitably tip the scales of competition. Often, and certainly in the field of trade, the few who may be hurt, or fear that they may be, are more vocal than the many who may gain. That is their right. But the Congress has a duty; that is to serve the overriding national interest.

Important as the trade agreements program has been since its inception in 1934 and since World War II, I anticipate a progressively more vital role for the program in the future.

The program is one of our most effective tools for combating the emerging Soviet strategy of political economic penetration into uncommitted countries through the offer of trade and economic aid. Since 1954 economic assistance extended by the Communist bloc to countries outside the bloc has amounted to $1.5 billion. Since 1954 the exports of the Communist bloc to the free nations have grown 70 per cent. In 1957 they amounted to some $3.1 billion. Furthermore, the number of bloc trade agreements with the free nations has more than tripled in the last 3 years, rising from 49 at the end of 1953 to 149 at the end of 1957. From what we know of the economic potential of the Communist bloc there is reason to believe that this performance can be greatly augmented within the next few years. The state-controlled economy of the Soviets is well suited to swift changes in quantities and destination of exports. The shortage of virtually all consumer goods within the Soviet area means that additional quantities of a wide variety of imported materials can be absorbed with ease.

The danger of the Soviet economic offensive arises from the fact that to the leaders of Communist imperialism economic ties are merely another means of gaining ultimate political control. If through trade and economic assistance they can bring free nations within their economic orbit, they will have paved the way for political victory. Even though responsible leaders in the recipient countries also know this, desperation for markets in order to meet the aspirations of their people can tempt those governments to gamble their political independence rather than refuse Communist aid and trade.

To this challenge our basic answer is our trade agreements program, coupled with our own aid program. The free world as a whole certainly offers by far the largest market for the raw materials that provide most of the money income of the less developed countries. This offer can only be realized, however, so long as the dominant free-world trade trend is in the direction of opening markets and expanding trade to the maximum.

In Western Europe we see unfolding a great new movement toward economic unity. This is the European Economic Community established by the Treaty of Rome, which entered into force on January 1, 1958. Through this treaty six nations on the European continent—Belgium, France, the German Federal Republic, Italy, Luxembourg, and the Netherlands—have agreed to eliminate all barriers to trade among themselves and to act toward others as a single economy. They will form a single Common Market of 170,000,000 customers with a total import trade which, last year, was larger than that of the United States. This new market will in time have a single uniform tariff and a common trade policy, which it will apply to imports from the United States and other countries of the free world.

This development has been encouraged by the United States, both the Congress and the executive branch, since the early days of the Marshall plan. It should now be our policy to cooperate with the new Economic Community of Europe to the end that both the United States and the European Economic Community will contribute to the economic strength and well-being of the free world as a whole.

The next 5 years will be the critical, formative years of the European Economic Community. This is a major reason why it is essential that the trade agreements program be renewed this year for 5 years. During this period long-lasting decisions will be made as to the level of the European common external tariff and as to the other commercial policies which the Community will adopt. The best opportunity we will have to negotiate with the Community the tariff reductions most advantageous to our export trade will be before the new tariff becomes firmly established. We would seek to negotiate tariffs lower than those to which the countries comprising the European Economic Community are presently committed.

The procedure and timetable which its members contemplate for the establishment of the Common Market illustrate the need for extending our program for not less than 5 years.

The first step in reducing internal tariffs, within the Common Market, will be taken next January 1, when internal duties are to be reduced by 10 per cent from their present levels. Thereafter there will be progressive reductions until internal tariffs are completely eliminated by the end of 1972. These reductions are important to us because after the first of next year goods produced within the Common Market will have a steadily increasing advantage within the Common Market area over American and other free-world goods.

With respect to external tariffs the plan is this: The European Economic Community has informed us that they expect to have their proposed, or "target," tariff (which they are now negotiating among themselves) available for examination by us and others about the end of 1959.

The objective of this examination will be to ascertain whether the target tariff accords with the obligations which the Common Market countries have previously assumed under the General Agreement on Tariffs and Trade. In this context we shall want to be satisfied that the target external tariff is not on the whole higher nor more restrictive than the separate tariff schedules of the six countries now in effect.

We shall also look at the individual items to be certain that the commitments which others have made to us are maintained.

After we have completed this examination, we will have to prepare the United States position for negotiations and choose the items on which we might be willing to consider tariff concessions. This will include peril-point investigations by the Tariff Commission. This whole process will take at least 18 months from the date on which we receive the target tariff. This timetable makes clear that under the best of circumstances negotiations with the European Economic Community cannot begin until 3 years from now. The negotiations themselves would take at least a year, bringing us at least to mid-1962. It is only prudent to allow another year for slippages. Finally, other countries will not be willing to make the complex preparations for these negotiations unless they are sure that the United States Government has authority to see them through to completion. For all these reasons the full 5-year extension is a necessity.

United States Foreign Trade Policy*

by John M. Letiche

The stark fact of international trade policy is that its leadership has in
the last few years been transferred from the United States to Western
Europe. The reasons for this transfer have been neither simple nor
singular, but a review of the voluminous literature on the recent renewal of The Trade Agreements Act reveals the major causes of this
development as well as its relevance to contemporary conditions.[1]

I. TRADE AGREEMENTS EXTENSION ACT OF 1958

Public Law 85-686 marks the eleventh time that the Congress has
extended the President's authority to negotiate reciprocal tariff reductions with foreign countries since its original enactment in 1934. Previous extensions had been for 3 years or less; the current one is for 4 years
—through June 30, 1962. The President is empowered to reduce tariffs
to the lowest rates obtainable by any one of three alternative methods:
(1) The July 1, 1958 rates may be lowered by 20 per cent. The reductions would have to be made gradually: 10 per cent of the total reduction would generally be the maximum in any one year. (2) The July 1,
1958 rates may be lowered by 2 percentage points. Such reductions
would also have to be made gradually: no reduction of more than 1 percentage point would generally be made effective in any one year. This
alternative authority, which has not been provided for in previous legislation, would be significant in cases where 2 percentage points would
permit a larger reduction than the maximum reduction obtainable
under the first method. Thus, if the July 1, 1958 tariff rate on a commodity were 5 per cent, the second method would permit a reduction
to 3 per cent, whereas the first method would permit a reduction to only
4 per cent. (3) The July 1, 1958 rates which were higher than 50 per
cent ad valorem may be lowered to that rate. Similar authority was

---

* From *The American Economic Review*, Vol. 48, No. 5 (December 1958), pp.
954-966. Reprinted by the courtesy of the American Economic Association and the
author.
    [1] The volumes under review [5] [7] [10] [11] [12] [13] [14] are staggering in
length. If the usefulness of Congressional hearings is not to be further impaired,
more effective procedures which economize on testimony will have to be devised.

granted in previous trade agreements legislation. Reductions under this method would also have to be made gradually and seriatim. One-third of the total reduction is the maximum that may be made effective in any one year. This alternative method would be significant in cases where rates exceed 62 per cent, for it would permit a greater reduction than that obtainable under the first method.

Regardless of the form of tariff reductions, in no case may there be more than 4 stages; nor may separate stages be less than a year apart; and the last stage may not be later than 3 years after the first. If the authority to reduce tariffs is not put into effect before July 1, 1962, the power to do so does not automatically lapse. The President's authority to enter into new trade agreements expires on July 1, 1962, but he may enter into agreements before this date with the proviso that the full authorized reduction authority shall be put into effect thereafter. However, no part of a reduction may be put into effect for the first time after June 30, 1966.

P.L. 85-686 provides for the continuation and strengthening of the safeguards for American industry and labor against serious injury from imports. As in previous trade agreements legislation, the proposed changes in U.S. tariff rates would be subject to the peril-point provisions. These provisions direct the President, before entering into negotiations, to furnish the Tariff Commission with a list of articles, together with their tariff rates and other customs treatment, which may be considered for modification. The Tariff Commission, in turn, is directed to make an investigation and report to the President its findings as to (1) the peril-point or rate below which U.S. duties may not be reduced without resulting in serious injury to domestic industry; and (2) the minimum increases in U.S. duties or additional import restrictions required to avoid serious injury. The new law extends the period within which the Tariff Commission has to make its investigations and to report to the President from 120 days to 6 months so that the Commission may make more extensive investigations. In addition, the law amends the peril-point provisions by directing the Tariff Commission, as previous legislation did not, to institute an escape-clause investigation promptly whenever it finds any article on the list upon which a tariff concession had been granted in the case of which an "increase in duty or additional import restriction is required to avoid serious injury to the domestic industry producing like or directly competitive articles" [7, p. 3, Sec. 4 (b)]. A new provision states that in each such investigation the Tariff Commission shall, to the extent practicable and without excluding other factors, ascertain for the last calendar year preceding the investigation the average invoice price on a country-of-origin basis at which the foreign article was sold for export to the United States and the average prices at which like or directly competitive domestic articles were sold at wholesale in the principal markets of the United States.

The escape-clause provisions put into effect by previous legislation are also continued, but with several new amendments. Under previous legislation, the Tariff Commission was required, upon application of an interested party, to make an investigation to determine whether imports of a particular commodity subject to a trade agreements concession were causing or threatening serious injury to a domestic industry. If the Commission found evidence of injury, it was required to submit a report to the President within 9 months with a recommendation for remedial action. The President made the final determination regarding the acceptance of a Tariff Commission recommendation that a duty be raised or a quota be imposed on imports. These procedures are maintained under the new law except that it provides for Congressional review when the President rejects recommendations of the Tariff Commission for import restrictions to shield domestic industries claiming injury from competition. It empowers Congress to reverse the President in such cases by two-thirds majorities in both houses. Another amendment reduces the time that the Tariff Commission has to make escape-clause investigations and reports thereon from 9 to 6 months. The powers of the Tariff Commission to obtain information by subpoena, and related powers, are extended and expanded. Furthermore, the law now provides the President with authority in escape-clause cases to impose a duty as high as 50 per cent ad valorem on a duty-free item which has been bound in a trade agreement. Previous legislation forbade transfer by the President of articles from the free list to the dutiable list. Finally, as regards eligibility to file an application for an escape-clause investigation, the Trade Agreements Extension Act of 1951 is amended by striking out the phrase "any interested party" and substituting "any interested party (including any organization or group of employees)" [7, p. 4, Sec. 5 (a)]. This provision was added in order to make it clear that such bodies could make application even though management was not a party to the application.

The national security amendment of the previous legislation has been stiffened rather than liberalized. Under the terms of the amendment, the President may not decrease duties on imports, but may restrict imports that are found to threaten the national security. More detailed standards and criteria are provided for the guidance of the President and the Director of the Office of Defense and Civilian Mobilization (ODCM):

> For the purposes of this section, the Director and the President shall, in the light of the requirements of national security and without excluding other relevant factors, give consideration to domestic production needed for projected national defense requirements, the capacity of domestic industries to meet such requirements, existing and anticipated availabilities of the human resources, products, raw materials, and other supplies and services essential to the national defense, the requirements of growth of such industries and such supplies and services including the investment, exploration, and development necessary to assure such growth, and the importation of goods in terms of their quantities, availabilities, character, and use as those affect such industries and the capacity of the United States to meet national security requirements. In the administration of this section, the Director and the President shall further recognize the close relation of the economic welfare of the nation to our national security, and shall take into consideration the impact of foreign competition on the economic welfare of individual domestic industries; and any substantial unemployment, decrease in revenues of government, loss of skills or investment, or other serious effects resulting from the displacement of any domestic products by excessive imports shall be considered, without excluding other factors, in determining whether such weakening of our internal economy may impair the national security [7, pp. 6, 7, Sec. 8 (c)].

A provision has been inserted requiring that the Director of the ODCM issue regulations for the conduct of investigations under this section. In addition, procedural changes have been made toward eliminating multiple investigations possible under previous legislation and requiring that the ODCM publish a report on the disposition of each national security case. The Director, with the approval of the President, shall also submit to the Congress a report on the administration of investigations and action to prevent a threat of impairment to national security.

The new law authorized the President to raise duties as much as 50 per cent over the rates which existed July 1, 1934. In the case of specific duties the President is empowered to convert such duties to their July 1, 1934 ad valorem equivalent, using 1934 values, and to increase such equivalents 50 per cent. Previous legislation provided the President with authority to increase rates as much as 50 per cent over the rates existing on January 1, 1945. Since the 1934 rates were substantially higher than the 1945 rates, this change in the base date increases the extent to which duties on such items can be raised.

The law continues the requirement that the President submit to the Congress an annual report on the operations of the trade agreements program, but in addition, directs him to include in such reports a statement on results of action taken to obtain the removal of foreign restrictions, including discriminatory practices against U.S. exports and the measures available for seeking the removal of such remaining trade barriers. It declares it to be the sense of the Congress that during the course of negotiating a trade agreement, the President should seek information and advice from representatives of American industry, agriculture, and labor.

II. THE HEARINGS

Prior to this extension of the Trade Agreements Act, U.S. foreign economic policy underwent thorough Congressional evaluation. As compared with previous *Hearings*, those under review reveal a critical sense of relevance and urgency. Numerous executives, representatives of the press, government, and private associations furnished responsible testimony concerning the national interest. More than 30 university economists were invited to prepare papers on the objectives, administration and operation of domestic and foreign economic policy. With one exception, these papers were carefully prepared, representing the highest quality of professional work. But the resulting legislation is disappointing; it is not to be matched with the need, even though it represents victory in a hard-fought battle by Congressional advocates for a more liberal foreign-trade policy.[2] Powerful pressure groups have been successful in obtaining so many exceptions to our trade program that its effectiveness has been seriously undermined. If left unchecked, this trend may make it very difficult to maintain the political and economic solidarity of the noncommunist world.

The agenda of the Subcommittee on Customs, Tariffs, and Reciprocal Trade Agreements included testimony on U.S. trade policy and the national interest; on the emerging pattern of foreign trade and payments;

---

[2] The bill was approved by the House Ways and Means Committee in an 18-to-7 vote. Committee Democrats voted 14-to-1 for the measure, Republicans 6-to-4 against. In a standing vote, the bill was passed in the House 161-to-56. In the Senate, it was passed 72-to-18; Democrats voted in favor 40-to-6, Republicans 32-to-12.

on foreign commercial policies and their relation to U.S. economic activity, with particular emphasis on the escape clause and peril-point procedures, the national security amendment, antidumping, counter-vailing duties, unfair competition, quotas, the Buy-American Act, section 22 of the Agricultural Adjustment Act, and restrictive trade practices engaged in by foreign countries. . . .

The general impression one obtains from comparing the testimony reported and the resulting legislation is that the U.S. Congress can be relied upon to pass responsible legislation in this field whenever the American national interest and her international responsibilities are made reasonably clear. But the testimony also reveals that the pressures upon individual Congressmen with respect to the multifarious "special cases" are overwhelmingly strong. For this reason the U.S. Congress is not well suited to deal with the particular problems of specific commodities or local dislocations. The restrictive provisions of P.L. 85-686 bear witness to this fact; and for the same reason its implementation may not correspond with the need.

For the effective implementation of U.S. foreign-trade policy, strong and consistent leadership from the administration is a primary requisite. In effect, leadership in this field has recently been transferred from the United States to Western Europe because a vacuum has been created. We have espoused a more liberal trade policy on the one hand, and imposed new quantitative restrictions on the other. The U.S. Tariff Commission was at one time the most outstanding government agency of its kind. Now it consists of a majority of protectionist appointees and is championed by the American Tariff League. At least since 1952, the U.S. tariff has in fact not been more restrictive than those of the larger European countries.[3] The escape-clause and peril-point provisions have been judiciously administered. But the instability of the American market—and especially the uncertainty concerning American foreign trade policy during recessions—has been at the root of the difficulty.

The evidence on the long-term trend of U.S. foreign trade and payments suggests that strong underlying forces are operating toward equilibrium in our international accounts. But the testimony furnished

[3] For 10 countries, the unweighted average of the 1952 percentage tariff rates on the same 78 representative commodities (including foodstuffs, raw materials, semi-finished goods and manufactures) were as follows: Italy 24, France 19, Austria 17, United Kingdom 17, Germany 16, United States 16, Canada 11, Benelux 9, Sweden 6, Denmark 5. Calculated by the Secretariat to the General Agreement on Tariffs and Trade [6, p. 62]; also cited in [1, p. 421].

in the *Hearings* under review indicates that protection will be accorded to the weak segments of the American economy. The only question is whether it will be administered in a manner which is conducive or inconducive to the long-term economic growth and international equilibrium of the United States as well as its friends and allies.[4] Congress has provided the President with legislation which, if liberally interpreted, can be used as a catalyst to integrate the trading policies of the non-communist world. Just as we have given our support to the establishment of the European Economic Community, so it is now urgent that we provide the leadership in the General Agreement on Tariffs and Trade Organization by ratifying the Organization for Trade Cooperation and supporting Britain and those other members of the OEEC who are genuinely striving to create a reasonably free outward-looking common market. Not only would this serve the best interest of Europe and the United States, but it could help to solidify our respective trade relations with Canada, Latin America, and the newly developing countries of Africa and Asia.

REFERENCES

1. DONALD MACDOUGALL, *The World Dollar Problem*. London 1957.

2. MARC OUIN, *The O.E.E.C. and the Common Market*. Paris 1958.

3. ROBERT TRIFFIN, *Europe and the Money Muddle*. New Haven 1957.

4. JACOB VINER, "The Gordon Commission Report," *Queens Quart.*, Autumn 1958, 64, pp. 305-25.

5. *First Annual Report on the Operation of the Trade Agreements Program*. Message from the President of the United States, 85th Cong., 1st sess. Washington 1957. Pp. iv, 248.

6. General Agreement on Tariffs and Trade, Secretariat, *International Trade*. Paris 1952.

7. Trade Agreements Extension Act of 1958, August 20, 1958. Public Law 85-686, 85th Cong., H.R. 12491.

8. U.S. Congress, Joint Economic Committee, *Defense Essentiality and*

---

[4] Structural shifts and recent trends in the United States balance of payments are discussed in an article by Fred H. Klopstock and Paul Meek, and in a paper by the United States Department of Commerce [11, pp. 303-17]. The problems of internal and external adjustment are dealt with in the same publication by Samuel Lubell, C. P. Kindleberger, Stephen Enke, Howard Piquet, W. S. Salant, D. D. Humphrey, Klaus Knorr, D. G. Johnson, S. H. Ruttenberg, and I. B. Kravis.

Foreign Economic Policy (Case Study: The Watch Industry and Precision Skills). Washington 1956. Pp. 476.

9. ———, *Defense Essentiality and Foreign Economic Policy*. Report. Washington 1956. Pp. 35.

10. U.S. Congress, House Committee on Ways and Means, *Administration and Operation of Customs and Tariff Laws and the Trade Agreements Program*. Hearings before a subcommittee, 84th Cong., 2nd sess. Washington 1956. Pt. 1, pp. v, 549; Pt. 2, pp. vi, 697; Pt. 3, pp. v, 518.

11. ———, *Foreign Trade Policy*. Compendium of papers collected by the staff for the Subcommittee on Foreign Trade Policy. Washington 1957. Pp. v, 1157.

12. *Renewal of Trade Agreements Act*. Hearings, 85th Cong., 2nd sess., Feb. and Mar. 1958. Washington 1958. Pt. 1, pp. xi, 1499; Pt. 2, pp. xv, 1435.

13. ———, Subcommittee on Customs, Tariffs, and Reciprocal Trade Agreements, *Report to the Committee on Ways and Means on United States Customs, Tariff, and Trade Agreement Laws and Their Administration*. Washington 1957. Pp. vi, 223.

14. ———, Trade Agreements Extension Act of 1958. Report, 85th Cong., 2nd sess. Washington 1958. Pp. iv, 135.

FOR FURTHER READING:

Percy Bidwell, *Raw Materials: A Study of American Policy* (New York: Harper and Brothers, 1958).

William A. Brown, *The United States and the Restoration of World Trade* (Washington, D.C.: The Brookings Institution, 1950).

Geoffrey Crowther, *Balances and Imbalances of Payments* (Boston: Harvard University Graduate School Administration, 1957).

William Yandell Elliott (ed.), *The Political Economy of American Foreign Policy* (New York: Henry Holt and Company, 1955).

Richard N. Gardner, *Sterling-Dollar Diplomacy: Anglo-American Collaboration in the Restoration of Multilateral Trade* (London: Oxford University Press, 1956).

Michael L. Hoffman, "Problems of East-West Trade," *International Conciliation*, No. 511 (January, 1957), pp. 259-308.

Samuel Lubell, *The Revolution in World Trade* (New York: Harper and Brothers, 1955).

Raymond F. Mikesell, *United States Economic Policy and International Relations* (New York: McGraw-Hill, 1952).

Clarence B. Randall, *A Foreign Economic Policy for the United States* (Chicago: University of Chicago Press, 1954).

Robert Triffin, *Europe and the Money Muddle* (New Haven: Yale University Press, 1957).

Raymond Vernon, "Organizing for World Trade," *International Conciliation*, No. 505 (November, 1955), pp. 163-222.

Chapter XIV

THE UNITED NATIONS

At the conclusion of the Second World War many in the United States hoped that it would be possible to rely on the United Nations to supervise the liquidation of colonialism, to serve as the center for international economic and social cooperation, and, above all, to preserve peace and security. In short, the United Nations was envisaged as the focal point for all major foreign policy efforts. Postwar reality has been far different. The United States' major security problem, the threat of Soviet aggression, was one which the United Nations was constitutionally and at times perhaps temperamentally incapable of solving. Thus we were forced to rely on alliances rather than collective security for our defense. Cold-war tensions pervaded the U.N.'s economic and social work and we also discovered other real or imagined deficiencies and so chose to channel our major economic efforts, the European Recovery Program and most economic development assistance, outside the world organization. The pace demanded by the U.N.'s anti-colonial majority for the liquidation of colonialism proved too rapid for our colonial allies and occasionally even for us, and we therefore frequently sought to deemphasize the United Nations in dealing with colonial problems.

But although the United Nations has not had the central role many had hoped, it has still been important. Most states are members and most foreign policy issues continue to be raised in the world organization. United States policies, as well as those of other states, are brought before it, and scrutinized with both emotion and care. The United

657

Nations is one of the few places where Soviet and American diplomatists confront each other directly in the immediate presence of a world
audience. In Korea, through constitutional manipulation we found that
the U.N. could aid in the protection of our security interests. In addition to its political aspects, the United Nations has developed important
economic and social programs and has played a significant role in bringing several states to independence. For new states, it provides a source
of assistance and guidance. And decisions in the United Nations inevitably have an important effect on the future as well as the present. At
the same time that the United Nations offers all these opportunities, it
also creates serious difficulties for the United States: its voting procedures force us to take sides when it might be more convenient not to
be counted; its meetings provide a forum from which the Soviet bloc
can fan the flames of smoldering conflicts in the Western world and
ignite others; its freedom of discussion allows irresponsible diplomatists
to introduce proposals which, despite their unworkability, are nevertheless difficult to reject because of their demagogic appeal.

The problem for the United States, and the one on which the public
debate should concentrate, is how best to use the opportunities provided
by the United Nations and how to minimize the difficulties. The United
Nations has a dual nature. On the one hand it is an ideal and on the
other, a political institution. The U.N. Charter is a statement of man's
hope for a better world: it lists goals and provides a standard by which
conduct can be measured. The U.N. we see on the East River at Turtle
Bay, however, is a political body. For this, the Charter provides a legal
base, but one which like all constitutions is constantly subject to revision and modification. The political U.N. can only equal the total of its
parts, the various national policies pursued there (which may or may not
be motivated by the Charter's ideals) and the work of the Secretariat.
It is this United Nations which creates the opportunities and difficulties
for United States foreign policy, and it is the one which should be the
subject of the public debate. The U.N. as a political institution is complex; the term "United Nations" as used frequently in common discourse and here, refers not only to the principal organs of the U.N.
itself—the General Assembly, the Security Council, the Economic and
Social Council, the Trusteeship Council, the International Court of
Justice, and the Secretariat—but also to the various specialized agencies
brought into relationship with the U.N. Each body presents distinct
opportunities and difficulties, but it is nevertheless convenient to treat

them together, for policy in one depends heavily on policy in the others, the various bodies are closely interrelated, and the need for balance and careful orchestration is great.

In the first selection in this chapter, Stanley Hoffmann, formerly an officer of the *Association Française de Science Politique* and now a member of Harvard University's Government Department, seeks to define the opportunities the United Nations offers, using an analysis of contemporary world politics as his base, and then suggests fruitful lines for future policy. He believes that the U.N.'s collective security functions should be deëmphasized and its economic and social tasks stressed instead. He advocates the development of a regional functionalism as the best means of working toward gradual modification of the present multi-state system.

Vernon V. Aspaturian, of the Political Science Department at Pennsylvania State University, examines the pattern of political power within the United Nations in the second selection. He believes that our successful efforts to strengthen the General Assembly's power and the increased voting strength of the Asian-African bloc in this body have combined to make the United Nations less useful for United States foreign policy. He thinks the U.N. is now dominated by an anti-colonial majority, that this majority will pursue policies inimical to United States interests, and that it is impossible for the United States effectively to lead this majority.

The third selection, by Lincoln P. Bloomfield, who formerly was special assistant to the Assistant Secretary of State for International Organization Affairs and is now Professor of Political Science at the Massachusetts Institute of Technology, offers a more optimistic view. He analyzes past United States policy and argues that a reformulation is needed. On the basis of an examination of our security interests, he envisages several functions for the U.N. short of the impossible collective security.

The next-to-last selection, by Robert E. Asher, now a member of the senior staff of the Brookings Institution in Washington, D.C., and formerly a Special Assistant to the Assistant Secretary of State for Economic Affairs, gives a survey of the economic work of the United Nations and suggests a number of areas in which he feels new initiatives by the United States might prove fruitful. Although some of the measures he suggests have been put into effect—the technical assistance program has been supplemented by the creation of the United Nations Special

Fund and steps have been taken to establish the International Development Association—they have not had the magnitude he advocates. The main force of his argument still holds.

More than the others, the final selection by Inis L. Claude, Jr., a member of the Political Science Department at the University of Michigan, emphasizes the implications for the future of policy in the United Nations. He criticizes those who bemoan the U.N.'s lack of coercive power, and argues that coercion is not necessarily the best means of developing a more peaceful world. He thinks that a more fruitful method is to be found in attempts to increase world consensus, and analyzes the opportunities for this afforded by the United Nations. These opportunities are the ones which should be seized by those who hope ultimately to lessen the moral dilemmas caused by the present lack of consensus in world politics.

The Role of International Organization: Limits and Possibilities*

by Stanley Hoffmann

No field of study is more slippery than international relations. The student of government has a clear frame of reference: the state within which occur the developments which he examines. The student of international relations, unhappily, oscillates between the assumption of a world community which does not exist, except as an ideal, and the various units whose decisions and connections form the pattern of world politics—mainly, the nation-states. International organizations therefore tend to be considered either as the first institutions of a world in search of its constitution or as instruments of foreign policies. The scholar who follows the first approach usually blames, correctly enough, the nation-states for the failures of the organization; but he rarely indicates the means which could be used to bring the realities of world society into line with his ideal. The scholar who takes the second approach stresses, accurately enough, how limited the autonomy of international organizations has been and how little they have contributed to the achievement of their objectives; but because he does not discuss his fundamental assumption—the permanence of the nation-state's driving role in world politics—he reaches somewhat too easily the conclusion that the only prospect in international affairs is more of the same.

It may well be that this conclusion, too, is justified, but it should not be arrived at through a shortcut. The approach which seems the most satisfactory, though not the simplest, should be the following one. First, the objectives defined by the Charter of the United Nations are to be considered as the best moral goals statesmen can pursue; that is, the maintenance of peace and security, the promotion of economic, social and cultural cooperation, respect for human rights, and the establishment of procedures for peaceful change. (Implicit in this assumption is, of course, another one: it is legitimate that statesmen should assign moral ends to their policies, and that states' activities should be submitted to moral judgments, the absence of a single, supranational system

* From *International Organization*, Vol. X, No. 3 (August 1956), pp. 357-372. Reprinted by permission.

of values notwithstanding.)[1] Secondly, the means through which these objectives are to be sought are necessarily international agreements; no conquest of the world by one nation, or even by an alliance of nations, could bring them about; consent is indispensable, even if it means that they can only be reached gradually and partially. Thirdly, it cannot be assumed at the outset that the present structure of international society *must* be the permanent framework of action, for it may well be that the objectives cannot be reached within such a framework, as, for instance, the World Federalists have argued. Changes in the structure may thus appear necessary. But one has to avoid utopias; if it is unwise to postulate the perpetuation of the present system, it is equally unwise to advocate ways which an analysis of world politics reveals to be blocked.

The problem which we want to discuss briefly can thus be phrased in the following terms: given the present structure of world society, what *should* and what *can* international organizations do to promote the objectives which we have mentioned?

[1]

A short analysis of present world society reveals a number of paradoxes and contradictions.

In the first place, the scene is dominated by two opposite developments. On the one hand, there is the phenomenon usually described as bipolarity of power. On the other hand, at the same time that military and economic strength has become centered, temporarily perhaps, in only two superpowers, there has been a trend toward further political disintegration of the world. As the process of "social mobilisation" of hitherto "passive" peoples progresses,[2] the number of sovereign states has increased,[3] and the continuing break-up of former empires will undoubtedly add new ones. Both developments, contradictory as they appear, make the return to a concert of the great powers impossible; the

---

[1] We have argued this elsewhere at greater length. See "Quelques Aspects du Rôle du Droit International dans la Politique Étrangère des Etats" in: Association Française de Science Politique, *La politique étrangère et ses fondements*, Paris, Armand Colin, 1954, p. 264-270. See also A. H. Feller, "In Defense of International Law and Morality," *Annals of the American Academy of Political and Social Science*, July 1952 (Vol. 282), p. 77-78.

[2] See Karl Deutsch, *Nationalism and Social Communication*, John Wiley and Technology Press, 1953.

[3] See E. H. Carr, *Nationalism and After*, New York, Macmillan, 1945, p. 53, for predictions to the contrary.

necessary solidarity and fluidity of power are both gone.[4] And yet, the technological gap between the advanced and the backward nations is greater than ever before.

In the second place, the process of interlocking interests and activities, which internationalists once hopefully described as leading inevitably to a world community, has indeed continued. The distinction between internal and international affairs is now ruled out; it has therefore become impossible to prevent one nation from influencing and intervening in the policies of another. The superb autonomy and specialization of diplomacy is over, and nearly the whole world has become a "Turkish question." At the same time, however, the psychological effect of this development has been rebellion and seeking refuge in a conception made for, and reminiscent of, a more idyllic age: the concept of national sovereignty and independence. The contradiction is nowhere more apparent than in the U.N. itself. The organization has contributed immeasurably to an internationalization of all problems, and to a kind of equalization of diplomatic standards and practices for all members; but at the same time its operations are based on the principle of equality and the myth of sovereignty. The smaller states use sovereignty as a fortress, and the superpowers as a safeguard of their own freedom of action against friendly or hostile restraints.[5]

In the third place, the two sets of factors previously mentioned have produced a fundamental change in the politics of the two leading powers. The great powers of the nineteenth century used limited means for limited objectives. The relations between these powers could easily be described in equations, or at least in mechanistic terms—balancing process, equilibrium, etc. The superpowers of today have trans-national objectives; each one stands both for a certain organization of the world, and for a certain distribution of social forces and political power in each nation.[6] The means they use, with one important exception (the resort to general war), are also much broader. Their emphasis, in the choice of means, is far less on *national* power, far more on gaining allies. As some

<hr>

[4] See Kenneth Dawson, "The U.N. in a Disunited World," *World Politics*, January 1954 (Vol. 6, No. 2), p. 209, and this writer's *Organisations internationales et Pouvoirs Politiques des États*, Paris, Armand Colin, 1954 part I.

[5] See Max Beloff, *Foreign Policy and the Democratic Process*, Baltimore, John Hopkins Press, 1955, lecture IV.

[6] Raymond Aron, "En quête d'une Philosophie de la Politique Étrangère," *Revue Française de Science Politique*, January-March 1953, p. 87-91.

theorists have shown,[7] this "multiple equilibrium" opens new channels of influence for the two superpowers and creates, at the expense of both, new procedures of restraint quite different from the restraints imposed on the big powers by the European concert. No big power can "go it alone" and define its interests to the exclusion of other nations' interests; the only, though very real and important, choice it has is between more and less broad international definitions of ends and means, depending on the kind and amount of international power it wants to mobilize.

In the fourth place, the smaller nations are torn between two modes of behavior in which they usually try to indulge simultaneously, as well as between two attitudes toward both the nation-state and the U.N. The two modes of behavior represent two levels of world politics. On the one hand, the smaller states try to protect themselves, *collectively*, against the rivalries of the two superpowers. Individually, they would be the victims of the great conflict; together, they have the best chance of restraining the big powers and of gaining a number of advantages in return. Some seek such a common escape in a broad alliance with the United States (Rio Treaty, NATO, SEATO), others in a neutral belt. But in either case, thus protected against the "nationalistic universalism" of the superpowers,[8] they practice traditional nationalism quietly. The smaller nations live in two ages at the same time. As for the two attitudes toward the nation-state and the U.N., each one is taken by a different group of states. The new nations focus on the nation-state their highest ambitions of international power, economic development, and social unity. Furthermore, their attachment to the nation-state is proportional to the intensity of their will not to get involved in the big-power conflict: a feeling that neutralists in Europe have echoed and expressed sometimes in impressive theoretical arguments.[9] These nations, at the same time, look on the U.N. with great enthusiasm; they see in it an instrument for the advancement of the smaller nations (in number and in power), and a mechanism for restraining the superpowers. On the contrary, the older nation-states of continental western Europe are more

---

[7] Jiri Liska, "The Multiple Equilibrium and the American National Interest in International Organization," *Harvard Studies in International Affairs*, February 1954; Ernst B. Haas, "Regionalism, Functionalism and International Organization," *World Politics*, January 1956 (Vol. 8, No. 2), p. 238.

[8] Hans J. Morgenthau, *Politics Among Nations*, New York, Alfred A. Knopf, 1954, p. 230-234.

[9] See for instance J. M. Domenach, "Les Nationalismes," and G. E. Lavau, "La Souveraineté des Etats," in *Esprit*, March 1955.

disabused of the nation-state, even though it retains the citizens' basic loyalty; and they look at the U.N. with greater misgivings, both because they have been outvoted so often in the U.N. on colonial issues, and because they contest the wisdom of spreading all over the world the disease of nationalism which they, too, contracted once, and from which they have suffered grievously.

This brief description leads to a few remarks concerning the scholar's or the politician's usual approaches to the understanding of world politics. First, it shows the fallacy of simple models or categories of analysis. The assumption of a Hobbesian state of nature among states is misleading. It exaggerates the degree of opposition between loyalty to the nation and cooperation among nations,[10] as well as the degree to which the more unmitigated forms of "power politics" are being used by nations; it leads to the presently hopeless solution of world government as the only alternative to a world of militarized, anti-liberal, indeed carnivorous nations.[11] Now, this is not at all the way in which many people think of the nation-state. It oversimplifies the reasons for the rise of anti-liberal forces which are not engendered only by the clash of sovereignties and nationalism; it leaves out all the restraints which, in the 19th century, made the state of nature a rather Lockian one, and, in recent years, shaped a system so new and complex that no theorist has anticipated it. The model of Hobbes is not more accurate than the model of the world community—which may explain why it is so easy to jump from the first to the second.[12]

In the second place, the analysis of foreign policies in terms of power, or of power and purpose,[13] is also insufficient. The concept of national power is no guide in a century where ideas are the most powerful weapons, if it does not include the strength of ideological appeals. Even if it does, it fails to explain the differences between the ends and means of

---

[10] This exaggeration has been criticized by Arnold Wolfers, "The Pole of Power and the Pole of Indifference," *World Politics*, October 1951 (Vol. 4, No. 1), p. 39, and by Karl Loewenstein, "Sovereignty and International Cooperation," *American Journal of International Law*, April 1954 (Vol. 48, No. 2), p. 222.

[11] See Thomas I. Cook, "Theoretical Foundations of World Government," *Review of Politics*, January 1950 (Vol. 12, No. 1), p. 20.

[12] See Ernest S. Lent, "The Development of United World Federalist Thought and Policy," *International Organization*, IX, p. 486-501.

[13] See, respectively, Morgenthau, cited above, and Thomas I. Cook and Malcolm Moos, *Power Through Purpose: The Realism of Idealism as a Basis for Foreign Policy*, Baltimore, Johns Hopkins Press, 1954.

foreign policy in periods of limited conflicts and relative stability, and in revolutionary periods.[14]

Thirdly, the usefulness of reasoning on the basis of internal or even international precedents appears very limited. Those who show, not without truth, the distorting effects of the nation-state on the thinking of the citizens, are sometimes the first to use examples drawn from the development of constitutionalism.[15] Those who deplore the forces which have destroyed the simple and autonomous mechanisms of nineteenth century diplomacy are too easily inclined to use it as a standard and as a still attainable ideal.

Finally, the statesmen's view of world politics is sometimes equally over-simplified. Western statesmen have tended to assume too readily that there are two completely separate spheres of world politics today: the conflicts with the communist bloc, all around the iron curtain, and the relations with the rest of the world, where all the objectives of the U.N. may be gradually reached, where anti-Soviet collective security and solid, supranational communities can be organized without any Soviet leap over the barriers of containment.[16] The Soviets have tended, and still tend, to assume too easily that, in the non-Soviet world, all is tension and conflict, as if the alignments established as buffers against the cold war did not dampen minor antagonisms.[17]

[II]

Before examining what international organization should and could do in such a world, let us see what its recent role in international politics *has been*.

The U.N. was built on two assumptions; both have proved to be unjustified. The first was, of course, the survival of a concert of great powers. The second was what one might call the Kant-Wilson hypoth-

---

[14] See Aron, cited above, and Association Française de Science Politique, cited above, p. 370-373.

[15] This tendency is criticized by H. J. Morgenthau, cited above, Ch. XXIX, and by Gerhart Niemeyer, "A Query about Assumptions of International Organization," *World Politics*, January 1955 (Vol. 7, No. 2), p. 337.

[16] That this view was held by Secretary of State Acheson appears in many of the documents reproduced by McGeorge Bundy, *The Pattern of Responsibility*, Boston, Houghton Mifflin, 1952. It remains true that this picture was a fairly accurate basis for policy in Stalin's time.

[17] See Khrushchev's speech at the 20th Congress of the Communist Party of the USSR, *New York Times*, February 15, 1956.

esis. The organization was supposed to harmonize the interests of sovereign states, conceived as nineteenth century nations. Their international policies would therefore be distinguishable from their internal problems. Their usual antagonisms would be limited in scope, or at least seldom involve their national existence. This was the assumption of a world squarely based on the nation-state—the hypothesis of inter-space cooperation for and with peace and security.[18] There was nothing revolutionary about it; historically, it was rather reactionary, in so far as it tried to revive conditions whose disappearance had brought about two world wars. Both assumptions implicitly envisaged the establishment of a widely acceptable *status quo*, on the basis of which the organization would operate. The tragedy has been the conflict between these underlying hypotheses and the two major realities of world politics: the bipolarity of power and the further disintegration of the world.

The consequence of the conflict between the first postulate and bipolarity has been the failure of the collective security mechanisms of the Charter. The conflict between the second postulate and the multiplication of nation-states, due to the anti-colonial revolution has led the U.N. to use as channels of peaceful change the procedures created for the settlement of ordinary disputes. It was hoped that the U.N. might thus harness that revolution. However, change has taken place, not as the consequence of, but either outside of or before the decisions of the U.N., and it has been violent and often savage. The U.N. has given the impression of merely smoothing some of the edges and of running after the revolution so as not to be left too far behind.[19]

In order to avoid complete paralysis on cold war issues because of the first conflict, and to transcend the procedural limitations which have made it difficult to cope with the second, the organization has escaped from its original Charter and changed into a "new United Nations." [20] However, the new, unofficial charter is based upon an assumption which conflicts not only with the old ones, but also again with the reality. Both the "Uniting-for-Peace" resolution, charter of the "cold war" role of the U.N., and the more fragmentary code of practices adopted by the U.N.

---

[18] See Max Beloff, "Problems of International Government," in *Yearbook of World Affairs*, 1954, London, Stevens & Sons, p. 4-8.

[19] See Raymond Aron, "Limits to the Powers of the U.N.," *Annals of the American Academy of Political and Social Science*, November 1954 (Vol. 302), p. 205.

[20] See H. J. Morgenthau, "The New U.N. and the Revision of the Charter," *Review of Politics*, January 1954 (Vol. 16, No. 1), p. 3.

in dealing with the anti-colonial revolution[21] were obviously necessary in order to keep the U.N. in line with the main currents of international politics. But the policy of collective assertion, parliamentary debates and majority votes assumes the existence of a sort of world community, where decisions similar to those reached in the framework of a constitutional system would make sense—[22] a far cry from both the hierarchical big-power rule and from the inter-state league of the Wilsonians. All these contradictions have engaged the U.N. in a series of vicious circles.

On the cold war front, bipolarity has made the resurrection of a concert of power against the one threatening big state fairly ineffective. The fear many small nations have of becoming engulfed in the cold war has, of course, undermined the whole argument behind the Uniting-for-Peace Resolution. Furthermore, the impossibility of tracing a clear line between internal and international affairs has obscured the idea of aggression; when aggression is easily disguised as social liberation, it is not astonishing to see the very nation which advocates a clear-cut definition of aggression suggest that civil or national-liberation wars be left out of the organization's reach.[23] Finally, the fact that recommendations have to be made by a ⅔ majority increases the small nations' power to destroy the new system either by refusing to make it work or by irresponsible recommendations which not they, but the big states, will have to carry out; the balance between proclamation and performance is a difficult one.[24] Both the difficulties and the dangers of putting into effect the "Uniting-for-Peace" machinery show that the primary emphasis in the U.N. cannot be put on collective security.[25]

The attempts to cope with the nationalist revolutions and the prob-

[21] Elimination, through a variety of devices, of the domestic jurisdiction clause; assertion of a right of the U.N. to define a collective and substantive policy, rather than limiting the organs to the more purely conciliatory procedures of the Charter: See Leland M. Goodrich and Anne P. Simons, *The U.N. and the Maintenance of International Peace and Security*, Washington, Brookings Institution, 1955, p. 155, 160, 609; and H. J. Morgenthau, cited above, p. 315-338.

[22] See Aleksander W. Rudzinski, "Majority Rule Versus Great Power Agreement in the U.N.," *International Organization*, IX, p. 366-385, 368.

[23] See Ales Bebler, "The Yardstick of Collective Interest," *Annals of the American Academy of Political and Social Science*, November 1954 (Vol. 302), p. 85.

[24] See the comments of George Kennan, *Realities of American Foreign Policy*, Princeton University Press, 1954, p. 40, and the suggestions of H. Field Haviland, Jr., in *Annals of the American Academy of Political and Social Science*, November 1954 (Vol. 302), p. 106.

[25] See the remarks of Sir Gladwyn Jebb, "The Role of the United Nations," *International Organization*, VI, p. 509-520, and René de la Charriere, "L'Action des Nations Unies pour la Paix et la Sécurité," *Politique Étrangère*, September-October 1953.

lem of change are not much more satisfactory. Conditions are so revolutionary that the U.N. has been unable to use effectively conciliatory procedures tailored only for conflicts between stabilized sovereign states. But world politics remain so strongly based on the sovereign state that the U.N. cannot get its assertions of competence and declarations of policy accepted by those of its members whose sovereignty is thereby infringed. If the members of the majorities point out that sovereignty means little in an era when internal tensions become matters of international concern, the outvoted members can always argue that the majorities' policies lead not to greater integration of the world, but to an increase in the number of sovereign units eager to shield their own activities behind Article 2, paragraph 7.[26] The issues between states, in an era where conflicts do indeed involve the very existence of nations, the birth of some, the dismantling of others, cannot be settled by resort to a world court: hence the constant refusal of the Assembly to submit such questions to it. But precisely because the issue is the life and death of the basic units in world politics, it is useless to expect the more threatened ones to submit to majority votes.[27]

The result, not unexpectedly, is frequently deadlock followed by a retreat of the U.N. The policies advocated by it are not carried out, and after a decent resistance the U.N. ceases to recommend them.[28] The committees established for the implementation of these policies fail to obtain the cooperation of the other party, and when the walls of Jericho refuse to collapse, it is the committee which is broken up.[29] At the same time the more modest task which the original Charter did allow the U.N. to perform—what we called the smoothing of edges, the curbing of the worst forms of unavoidable violence—becomes more difficult for two reasons. The decision of the U.N. to take a substantive stand re-

[26] See the debate between Clyde Eagleton and Quincy Wright in *Proceedings of the American Society of International Law*, 1954, p. 32-34, 67, 116, 119. The long discussions in U.N. organs on human rights show similar arguments.

[27] See Clyde Eagleton, "Excesses of Self-Determination," *Foreign Affairs*, July 1953 (Vol. 31, No. 4), p. 592, and "The Yardstick of International Law," *Annals of the Academy of Political and Social Science*, November 1954 (Vol. 302), p. 68.

[28] An examination of U.N. substantive recommendations on Palestine, Kashmir, Spain, and South Africa's apartheid policies, and of their gradual watering down or abandonment is the basis of this assertion (see Goodrich and Simons, cited above, chapters IX to XII). The success of U.N. intervention in Indonesia remains an isolated instance in this respect (i.e., substantive recommendations on issues not directly connected with the cold war).

[29] See the fate of the committees created for dealing with German elections, with apartheid policies and with the problem of Indians in South Africa (see Goodrich and Simons, cited above, chapters VIII and XIII).

duces the chances of conciliation by increasing the opposing party's resistance and distrust. Furthermore the two main trends of present world politics have interacted. The cold war has first thrown a shadow over, then a monkey wrench into, U.N. attempts at securing peaceful change. The break-up of the original concert of powers in these matters[30] has increased the chances of change through violence; it has emancipated the anticolonial nations from a possible big-power tutelage; in so far as the Soviets support them, while the U.S. is allied to the colonial powers in such institutions as NATO and SEATO, it has become far more difficult for the U.N. to oblige the antagonists or the reluctant side in a colonial conflict to renounce violence.[31]

It may have been vain to expect, in a world where the two main trends create for existing states a good deal of trouble, that an international organization established for coping with the irrepressible, minimum degree of insecurity that persists during stabilized periods could do much to eliminate the glaring insecurities of today. Maybe the organization could, indeed, be nothing but a "gentle civilizer." But the civilizer has not always been gentle. It has rather tended to increase the degree of insecurity, while both the cold war and the peculiar voting system which gives the loudest notes to sing to the weakest voices have prevented it from harnessing the forces it helped to set in motion. The reliance on, and exploitation of, the vague, broad and yet-to-be achieved principles and purposes of the Charter have combined the maximum of ambiguity with the maximum of resistance from the members. The result has been a somewhat disturbing division of labor between the world body and the regional organizations; the problems that could be solved were quite legitimately dealt with by the latter,[32] but the U.N. has become the recipient of those problems which just cannot be solved diplomatically, *a fortiori* by parliamentary votes in the Assembly.[33] This was particularly apparent in the case of all the cold war conflicts which were submitted to the U.N. by both parties for propaganda purposes; on these issues, and on most of the colonial problems as well, Mr. Kennan's

---

[30] See a study of these "ad hoc concerts" in Ernst B. Haas, "Types of Collective Security: An Examination of Operational Concepts," *American Political Science Review*, March 1955 (Vol. 49, No. 1), p. 40.

[31] See Coral Bell, "The U.N. and the West," *International Affairs*, October 1953 (Vol. 29, No. 4), p. 464.

[32] In particular in the case of the Organization of American States.

[33] I. L. Claude, *Swords into Plowshares*, New York, Random House, 1956, p. 122, comments that the Commonwealth has been the greatest exporter of insoluble disputes to the U.N. (Kashmir, Indians in South Africa).

rather cruel description of the Assembly's votes as a series of "tableaux morts" [34] is an apt one.

Self-restraint or resignation to very limited and superficial soothing tasks might have killed the organization. But taking worthy stands and cheering itself up until it gets hoarse has not really saved it as a force in world affairs—though such attitudes might have made it useful as an instrument serving a number of widely different foreign policies. The rules of the "new U.N.," like the rules of the original Charter, create both too rigid and too big-meshed a net of obligations for member nations. It is too rigid, in so far as compliance with these rules has proved to be impossible. It is too big-meshed, because in order to be applicable to so many different states, these obligations inevitably had to be few and vague. Thus, the rather obvious and recognized solidarity of interests among smaller groups of states is not sanctioned by any set of norms and institutions common to them. These great gaps increase insecurity, the chances of conflicts, and uncushioned power politics.

[III]

The following considerations on what the role of international organization *should be* in the present world are based on the following postulates. *a*) The nation-state, conceived as a legally sovereign unit in a tenuous net of breakable obligations, is not the framework in which the ideals we have defined at the outset can *all* be realized or approximated. It can hardly be maintained that it affords the greatest possibilities of economic advance, and even, in many areas, of orderly political and social change. *b*) Experience to date has shown that political organization on a world scale cannot, by itself, advance beyond the stage of the nation-state: its fate is linked to the nation-state. Three consequences flow from these postulates.

The first consequence concerns the role of the political organs of the U.N. If they cannot shape new forces, they should at least prevent the nation-states from getting even further away from the distant objectives which the U.N. proclaims. The two tests—rather negative ones, one may fear—which each decision or recommendation should meet are, first, a test of responsibility: will it decrease, increase, or leave unchanged the state of tension with which it is supposed to deal? If it will not contribute to decreasing tensions, it should not be made, except if

---

[34] George Kennan, *Realities of American Foreign Policy*, cited above, p. 42.

inaction is clearly bound to produce even worse consequences than intervention. This test is particularly necessary in colonial affairs. . . . Secondly, a test of efficiency: is the measure advocated, sound as it may be, backed by a sufficient combination of interests and forces? Otherwise, it will be an empty gesture.

The second consequence suggests the need for building new institutions which will help the nation to go beyond the stage of the nation-state. A case can be made—and has often been made[35]—against excessive and premature attempts at establishing "rigid legal norms" and institutions; it has been said that the process of integrating nations must be left to the free interplay of political, economic and social forces within them. Undoubtedly, no organization can be effective if there are no such favorable forces; it cannot create them. But where they do exist, a network of legal obligations and institutions can consolidate the common interests at the expense of the divergent ones, and act as the indispensable catalyst of an emergent community; otherwise there would be no opportunity to select, seize, save and stress the unifying forces. The reason why the nations tend to organize themselves as states and why the highest allegiance of the citizens usually belongs to the state is that this form of political organization affords them protection, security, justice, gratifications and services. Therefore, the only way to transfer loyalty to another set of institutions is to create new agencies which will provide the citizens with some of these advantages and help in gradually building communities larger than nations.

But these new agencies will be solid and effective only if they are accepted freely by the peoples they are supposed to link. This means, in the first place, that the peoples will have to reach the "national stage" first. Recognition of the insufficiency of the nation as framework of social organization can only come *after* the nation has achieved a large measure of self-government. Consequently, in areas where no nation-state has yet been established, the national stage cannot, in all probability, be skipped. However, independence might be accompanied by an agreement on "interdependence" with other countries for clearly defined and accepted functions.

In the second place, wherever the nations, new or old, have all the

---

[35] See George Kennan, *Realities of American Foreign Policy*, cited above, p. 105-106.

attributes, blessings and curses of the sovereign state, a difficult task of incitement and negotiations will have to be performed. Political federation is probably ruled out in the early stages. Except perhaps in the limited European area where disillusionment with the nation-state is strongest (but how far does it go?) one cannot expect, even under the stress created by necessities of defense or economic development, that nation-states will agree to the kind of wholesale transfer of powers which political federation requires. Suicide, so to speak, if it takes place at all, will have to be piecemeal. Political power cannot be expected to be abandoned first. Nor is it sure that political federation is always a desirable goal. The main enemy of international stability and individual liberty, in those countries where the nation-state has ceased to be a refuge and become a prison, is not the nation, but the state; it is the concentration of political, economic, military power, etc. . . . in one set of institutions. The creation, by amalgamation of existing nation-states, of a new state similar in its essence to the previous ones and even larger in area can hardly be called an improvement. A federation strong enough to survive the strains of birth and youth might soon develop into a super-nation; the trend toward centralization, observed in all federations, could lead to such a result.[36] A decrease in the number of leviathans is no gain if it is compensated by an increase in their respective power. Thus, the only practical way to reach the aim—a decentralization of allegiance—seems to be the establishment of functional institutions based on trans-national interests. In order to be effective, these agencies would have to be geographically limited. Or, if in certain cases a regional limitation makes little sense economically,[37] they should possess some ideological, historical or technical justification. They would therefore, as a rule, not be universal institutions like the U.N. and its specialized agencies, but, for instance, organizations in which certain underdeveloped countries sharing one common economic problem would cooperate with more advanced nations which have solved or faced the same prob-

---

[36] See François Perroux, *L'Europe Sans Rivages,* Paris, Presses Universitaires, 1954, especially part II; Percy Corbett, "Congress and Proposals for International Government," *International Organization,* IV, p. 383-399, 390, and Jean Rivero, "Introduction to a Study of the Development of Federal Societies," *International Social Science Bulletin,* Spring 1952 (Vol. 4, No. 1), p. 375.

[37] See the case against regionalism in economic organizations in Raymond F. Mikesell, "Barriers to the Expansion of U.N. Economic Functions," *Annals of the American Academy of Political and Social Science,* November 1954 (Vol. 302), p. 39-40, and Perroux, cited above, especially p. 399-415.

lem at home or in their colonies. The nation-state would thus be caught in a variety of nets. Gradually, unobtrusively perhaps, a large measure of economic power would be transferred to the new agencies. They would for a long time to come leave to the state a kind of negative power to destroy the net; nevertheless, they could reach and provide the individuals with tangible services.[38] They would not constitute an immediate rival for the states and would therefore expect more consent or at least less violent resistance. The most effective attack on sovereignty is not a frontal one—it is one which slowly but clearly deprives sovereignty of its substance, and consequently of its prestige. The build-up of interlocking functional communities is required both by the presently strong attachment to formal sovereignty and by the actual interlocking interests which can become a positive force in world politics only if they are institutionalized.

As a third consequence of our two postulates, the U.N. should concentrate on, and develop, its role as a "center for harmonizing the actions of nations in the attainment of (the) common ends," which these joint interests suggest. Indeed the U.N. should either take the initiative or at least assume responsibility for the establishment and coordination of the regional or functional communities we have advocated. Two reasons militate for such a policy. In the first place, it is necessary to provide the U.N., checkmated on political issues, with a new area of activities in its own interest. Secondly, the west, increasingly unable in political matters to get its views accepted by others through a process of "collectivization of interests,"[39] but unable also to discard the world body, must find constructive ways of seizing the initiative. In the inevitable clash of ideas between east and west, the west cannot merely offer to the nations the ideal of internal democracy; it must also present the image of a more satisfactory world order. The Soviet Union, which wants to prevent a consolidation of the non-communist world, plays upon the strong attachment which is still felt to the nation-state and to nationalism, sovereignty and independence. The west cannot fight back on this ground; it would mean giving up the objectives we have men-

---

[38] See I. L. Claude, "Individuals and World Law," *Harvard Studies in International Relations*, 1952.

[39] Hans Morgenthau, cited above, in *Annals of the American Academy of Political and Social Science* and *Review of Politics*; Edward H. Buehrig, "The United States, the United Nations and Bipolar Politics," *International Organization*, IV, p. 573-584, 583.

tioned. Nor can the west propose such revolutionary changes that the Soviets might successfully exploit this continuing attachment to the shelter of sovereignty, as well as charge the west with hypocrisy, since none of the leading western states is ready to sacrifice large areas of its own sovereignty.

Again, a progressive middle road seems to be the right one. This is precisely where the U.N. can operate. Militarily, the role of the U.N., as we indicated, can only be a very limited one; it is therefore normal that initiatives for collective defense be taken outside of it. But initiatives for economic action should be made within the U.N. This would be politically advantageous. The suggested regional or functional institutions can hardly function without western economic assistance. Now, the new nations have shown a distrust of purely western initiatives, interpreted as cold war moves, and a respect for the U.N., which suggest that the U.N. should be selected as the channel for such assistance. It is also wise technically; there is a need for coordination of the present and future technical institutions, which can best be exercised by the U.N.[40] As the French Foreign Minister, M. Christian Pineau, has recently suggested,[41] an agency for world economic development should be created within the framework of the U.N. This agency would coordinate and control specialized agencies such as the International Monetary Fund and the International Bank for Reconstruction and Development, as well as the U.N. technical assistance activities and more recently created or proposed U.N. institutions such as the International Finance Corporation and the Special United Nations Fund for Economic Development.[42] It should give its aid, gifts, loans, technical assistance, raw materials or energy, etc., to the regional or functional organizations we have recommended, rather than to states directly. These organizations would be sponsored by the U.N. agency and established among the under-developed nations (with or without direct participation of the industrialized ones). They would be the pioneers of supra-national development. The U.N. agency, being international by virtue of the Charter, would play the more modest but essential role of an instigator.

---

[40] See Edgar S. Furniss, Jr., "A Re-examination of Regional Arrangements," *Journal of International Affairs*, May 1955 (Vol. 9, No. 2), p. 79-89.

[41] See a summary of M. Pineau's project in *Le Monde*, May 5, 1956, p. 2.

[42] M. Pineau's plan envisages also the establishment, within the world agency, of a board which would buy and sell surplus commodities produced by underdeveloped areas, and stabilize the market prices of raw materials.

[IV]

The last question we have to discuss is obviously the most difficult one: *can* international organizations play the role we have tried to assign to them?

First, as for limiting the political organs of the U.N. to the rather limited tasks we have suggested, there is little doubt about the answer. On colonial and self-determination issues, the small powers, which are indispensable in the decision-making process, cannot be led to abandon the policy they have promoted in recent years; the Soviet bloc may be expected to fan the flames, and the United States cannot easily try to stop the movement—the more so, since it needs the small powers in case of a return to acute cold war tension. The answer here is: no. However, on the issue of collective security and also in the settlement of ordinary disputes, the organization might be condemned not just to violate the two tests we have indicated, but not even to reach the stage where proposals would be submitted to the tests. Both the reluctance of a majority of members to face the cold war and the neutralization of U.N. procedures by the conflicting maneuvers of the big powers could lead to such a paralysis. Writers who have shown how useful an instrument of American foreign policy the U.N. is[43] have attached too much importance to the Korean miracle and the mechanical "50 to 5" votes and underestimated the eventuality of Russian exploitation of U.N. procedures. However, any American attempt at penalizing the small powers either by direct pressure or by de-emphasizing the importance of the U.N.[44] would leave the field wide open to the Soviet Union. The Soviets, who adopted in the worst years of the cold war an attitude of disdain for the U.N., have now realized what possibilities of counterattack they have neglected; nor can the United States afford to abandon the U.N. in favor of pure bilateralism or regionalism. Each of the superpowers is, in a way, caught in the U.N. In spite of the partial excesses and the partial paralysis, the political organs must be preserved. By promoting diplomatic intercourse among all nations, they allow the more under-developed ones to use their participation as both a compensation for and as a weapon against the gap that separates them from the more advanced

---

[43] Advocated, for instance, by George Kennan, cited above, p. 59-60.
[44] Hans Morgenthau, cited above and "The Yardstick of National Interest," *Annals of the American Academy of Political and Social Science,* November 1954 (Vol. 302), p. 77; Jiri Liska, cited above.

states. Also, if the world should return to multi-polarity and stabilization, the U.N. must be there to perform at last the services that had been prematurely expected in the days of euphoria.[45]

Secondly, could the U.N. play the new economic and social role which we have suggested? The obstacle here seems to be the reluctance of the United States and Great Britain to allow the U.N. to play such a role, and to transfer a major part of their foreign aid funds to the U.N. It has been suggested that the west might lose its freedom of movement on the economic front of the "cold war" if it accepted a system in which the smaller powers, and the USSR itself, could control the use of western resources. This argument is debatable on two counts. It is better to risk providing the nations concerned with a sort of right of veto or a brake on the activities of a U.N. economic agency than to sow the seeds of grave economic rivalries, misallocation of resources, and social and international tensions by taking no initiative at all. Such would undoubtedly be the effects of the uncoordinated policies of nations which may all want to industrialize themselves without regard for the regional distribution of opportunities and the scarcity of investment funds. To resort to purely western initiatives made outside of the U.N. is to court failure, as the new nations fear colonialism in disguise and western "cold war" intentions. To wait for local initiatives is not very wise either. A study of existing economic agencies shows that, with the significant exception of the European Coal and Steel Community and new continental European projects, American or British initiatives have been decisive.[46] The institution we suggest, which could be an irritating check on western policies, would also provide the west with a big and subtle channel for getting the main points of its policies across far better than through direct aid to a few selected allies; the dose of economic medicine administered to the peoples of under-developed areas through such an institution may be excessively sweetened in consequence of their objections, but it will still be administered to more.[47]

Furthermore, the opportunities that a U.N. agency might give to

---

[45] See the concluding remarks of E. B. Haas, cited above, *World Politics*, January 1956.

[46] The contrast between the Colombo Plan and the failure of the Simla Conference, where the initiative was left to the local leaders, is a case in point. See William Henderson, "The Development of Regionalism in Southeast Asia," *International Organization*, IX, p. 463-476.

[47] See Benjamin V. Cohen, "The Impact of the United Nations on United States Foreign Policy," *International Organization*, V, p. 274-281.

Soviet maneuvering are not greater than the opportunities the Soviets already have for exploiting nationalism and driving wedges between those nations closer to the west and the uncommitted ones. If the main western powers carry their hostility against the restraint exercised at their expense by the small nations so far that the more traditional emphasis on bilateral diplomacy and "self-interest," narrowly defined, is preferred, then indeed Soviet strategy will have won. Bilateralism breeds separation, and further opportunities for political and economic conflicts. It allows the Soviets to outbid the west, or at least to drag the west into an endless bidding game. On the contrary, if the west did take the initiative in proposing a world agency on the lines we suggest, and if the Soviets refused to join in order to "go it alone," their own unilateral offers of aid would then become as politically suspect as western offers have sometimes become. The example of SUNFED should be kept in mind. The Soviets, in the beginning, were as cool to the Fund as were the western industrial nations. Strengthening an important area of the non-communist world could hardly have been welcome to the Soviets; but in 1954 and 1955 they saw that they could exploit western reluctance at no cost to themselves, and they rallied to the underdeveloped nations' claim for a rapid establishment of a Fund. Western reticence and insistence on priority for bilateral aid may prove to be a serious mistake. American opposition, at first, to close bonds between the proposed Atoms-for-Peace organization and the U.N., and the shift, between 1953 and 1954, from a revolutionary and truly supranational institution to a mere clearing house, can also be criticized on these grounds. The more rapidly the world moves out of the situation of bipolarity, the more useful it will be for the west to deal with the under-developed, uncommitted members of the "third force" through a world organization, where their moves and maneuvers can be more easily controlled than if they too enjoyed total freedom from international restraints.

Finally, it remains necessary to discuss the chances of success of regional or functional institutions sponsored by a U.N. agency of the kind we have suggested. The record of existing regional and functional organizations such as NATO, the Colombo plan, the OEEC, the European Coal and Steel Community, and the OAS, does not really answer the question, because most of them have not been launched for the purposes and in the conditions we have advocated. However, the main conclusions have to be taken into consideration. In the first place, outside of the Soviet bloc in which regionalism is an instrument of Soviet hegemony, there has been no political integration. In political matters, interstate cooperation remains the most one can expect. Secondly, the greatest measure of effective supranational integration has been achieved, ironically enough, in military alliances.[48] This is an ominous sign indeed, whose meaning can best be seen in connection with a third conclusion. The most successful non-military organizations are those which are squarely based on their members' calculations that the common agencies will bring benefits to them as nations; the framework of expectations remains the nation-state, not the larger area served by the agencies. States are more willing to confess their military insufficiency than their economic and social weaknesses. When it is a question of welfare, not of survival, the urgency seems smaller. This explains why NATO has never been able to play the same role in economic and political matters as in military affairs.[49] The only relative exception to the last conclusion is western Europe, for the reasons which were indicated above. It is no accident that the only area in which individuals may appeal, in case of a violation of their rights, to a supranational body is part of the territory covered by the Council of Europe; and even there the process is a slow and limited one.[50]

Thus, the precedents show a need for caution and realism. Many serious objections must be contemplated. First, there are obstacles to the very establishment of the institutions we have advocated. The most obvious one is, again, the cold war. How will it be possible even for a U.N. agency to convince the new uncommitted nations to harmonize their development plans and, as it may appear necessary, to "de-nationalize" a part of their economic resources and policies, when they are encouraged to stick to the nation-state by Soviet strategy and may even receive Soviet help if they refuse to join western-inspired arrangements? There is no doubt about the crippling effect Soviet policy could have; but this is not a reason to give up trying, since this is precisely what the Soviet Union would like to force the west into. Furthermore the Atoms-

---

[48] The record of the European Coal and Steel Community, impressive as it is, does not rival NATO's and justifies Lincoln Gordon's question whether similar results could not have been reached without the apparatus of supranationality ("Myth and Reality in European Integration," *Yale Review*, September 1955 (Vol. 45, No. 1), p. 80-103, 92).

[49] See on this subject Norman J. Padelford, "Political Cooperation in the North Atlantic Community," *International Organization*, IX, p. 353-365.

[50] In addition to trusteeship territories, of course. See P. Modinos, "La Convention Européenne de Droits de l'Homme," *Annuaire Européen*, Vol. 1, The Hague, Martinus Nijhoff, 1955.

for-Peace case shows that the west disposes here of such a powerful lever that even the Soviet Union cannot afford to remain aloof and hostile—or else, as in the Marshall Plan precedent, in spite of all her threats and baits, the nations which see the advantages of such common enterprises will join at great cost to Soviet prestige.

A second obstacle can be called the vicious circle. The new institutions cannot be created without the consent of, and, especially in case of U.N. sponsorship, without a controlling role for the recipient nations. Will they not therefore be able to veto, for nationalistic reasons, more ambitious plans of supranational development, and end up with nothing more than the more timid and traditional inter-governmental cooperation schemes, loaded with safeguards and rights of veto? This may well be. But even modest schemes are better than unbridled competitions, and additionally, in so far as most of the functional plans would depend on support from the industrialized nations of the west, the bargaining power of the latter should not be underrated. The needs of the under-developed nations are such that if they had to choose between the discomforts of isolation and the sacrifice of sovereignty involved in joint development projects, it should not be lightly assumed that they would prefer the first—unless the west couched its appeal too much in cold war terms, or asked at the outset for too many sacrifices of sovereignty. The possible advent of a "third industrial revolution" should give to the western nations, who have such an advance in atomic energy experience, a very powerful counter. The debates in the 1955 General Assembly on Atoms-for-Peace have shown that the under-developed nations are willing to accept and even to promote joint undertakings as an alternative to the western tactics of bilateral agreements, which they resent.

A third obstacle could prevent either the establishment or the efficient functioning of the suggested institutions. Will not the basic political antagonisms between states paralyze these agencies? Will not, for instance, the fear that the members might have of each other's ambitions or power prevent any joint undertaking? Or will not the nation which has the greatest resources and skills, or whose economic development will appear to be the most necessary for the whole area's advance, seize these advantages and impose gradually its domination over the other members under the cloak of supranational arrangements? Here again, one must recognize that the risk does exist and that such fears may either play a deterrent role or saddle the institutions with crippling provisions for balancing purposes. It would indeed be naïve to expect these institutions to put an end to "power politics." They would provide new channels, new restraints and new fields of action for it. But it would be equally naïve to expect, in the absence of any joint undertaking, that the effects of uneven distribution of power would not be felt. They cannot be eliminated; but they can be softened and used for the common good if adequate common mechanisms are established. Thus, this objection is, and should be, a cause for great caution in the establishment of new institutions,[51] but definitely not for inaction.

The last objections bear upon the effects such mechanisms, if they are successfully established, might be expected to produce. On the one hand, it is suggested that the decentralization of allegiance to which we have referred will not take place because the various states will still act as a screen between the individuals and the supranational bodies. State borders might lose their political significance, but their psychological effects will be preserved, and the states will have a vested interest in not allowing too big a transfer of loyalty to the new units.[52] On the other hand, one might say that even if the states did not insist on keeping their subjects' full allegiance, the transfer of loyalty to utilitarian, technocratic bureaucracies deprived of any contact with the peoples they work for is very unlikely indeed. There really is no easy refutation of this argument; the dreams of rational internationalists have been shattered more than once; there is little doubt that the splitting of loyalties can only be the result of a very long process, and that it will require a period of peace in which the state's prestige and resistance to encroachment on its powers can be eroded. Common economic interests have not prevented nationalist explosions; nor can the institutionalization of these interests be expected to suppress them. In most parts of the world, on the most elemental and vital problems, the nation-state will keep the final say. But this is not an argument against trying both to remove the greatest possible number of questions from the sacred zone of nationalism and sovereignty to the unglamorous sphere of international cooperation and to create such patterns that even when the last word remains

---

[51] Safeguards that make cooperation possible, even though it will be slow, are better than schemes which disintegrate because they were too bold. The failure of EDC shows how necessary it is to provide for common mechanisms which do not create, among the weaker members, fear lest the potential superiority of one of the partners will be accentuated by the process of integration.

[52] See Hans Morgenthau, *Politics Among Nations*, cited above, p. 500; contra Quincy Wright, "International Organization and Peace," *Western Political Quarterly*, June 1955 (Vol. 8, No. 2), p. 149. See also I. L. Claude's discussion in *Swords into Plowshares*, cited above, p. 382-387 and 400-402.

with the state, this word will be in no small way conditioned by the state's commitments and by the growing habit of common action.

[v]

If we state, then, what can be done, and compare it with what should be done, the prospects appear both modest and not at all hopeless. Far less can be done than the most ardent internationalists desire or sometimes expect. But somewhat more can be done than the spokesmen for reliance on "wise statesmanship" or on the manifestation of "perennial forces" seem to believe, and certainly quite a lot more should be tried.

The defenders and promoters of international organizations would have a much stronger case if they recognized frankly the two following limitations. First, there is no sudden mutation in world politics, and the forces that may some day break the crust of the nation-state can only be helped, not created, by international organization. This is why the basis of action remains the state, why the chances of truly supranational institutions, even limited to certain functions, are far smaller, in most parts of the world, than those of organs of international cooperation, why even ambitious supranational schemes might not operate very differently from these, and finally why in the new bodies "power politics" will continue. But this is not what matters. Power politics also survive in the internal affairs of any nation. What counts is the framework and the general direction of the process.

Secondly, the mushrooming of international institutions will not solve the fundamental issue of security.[53] They can be created on all sides of the big abysses that separate the nations and threaten world peace—the cold war, the colonial revolution; they cannot bridge the gaps. Here the balance of power between the superpowers, and between the crumbling empires and the rising new nations, are the decisive factors. The most international organization can do is to provide restraints on the superpowers and centers of cooperation between old and new nations after the colonial issue has been decided by force or by local agreements.

Once these limitations are accepted, the role of international organization should appear in its true light. Even if it were not much more than that of an "amiable civilizer," it would still be a far bigger one than many challengers seem to suggest. They usually leave this role to traditional diplomacy. International organization as a fragile but still badly

---

[53] See Arnold Wolfers, cited above, and E. H. Carr, cited above, p. 52-53.

explored diplomatic method can, within its own limits, help the nations to transcend the limits of the nation-state.

The Metamorphosis of the United Nations*

by Vernon V. Aspaturian

"If the United Nations was made substantially universal," John Foster Dulles once mused as a private citizen, "that might end the preponderant voting superiority of the United States and its friends which, while pleasant, is somewhat fictitious." With the admission of sixteen new members last year and five more during the current session of the General Assembly, the organization has increased its membership by one-third, is on the brink of universality, and the United States has lost its "preponderant voting superiority." Though this change was to be expected, its consequences are unpredictable; it creates some new opportunities for the U.N., but it also imposes some harsh limitations on its moral and political benefactions.

The preëminent role of the United States in mobilizing the Assembly majorities in the Egyptian and Hungarian crises has generally obscured the fact that the United States has forfeited its long-held mastery over the General Assembly to the amorphous and insurgent anti-colonial forces there. The current Assembly of eighty-one nations not only represents an expanded organization, but symbolizes a changed United Nations, as distinct from last year's organization of sixty states as it, in turn, was different from the one founded by fifty states in San Francisco more than a decade ago. The United Nations is no longer, as it was in the years right after the Second World War, an exclusive club reserved for "peace-loving" states and dedicated to preserving the existing political order against the revival of fascism, nor is it any longer the anti-Soviet coalition of the Korean War; instead, it now threatens to become an organization whose main obsession is to purge the world of the real and imagined inequities of Western colonialism.

Although the United Nations in ten years has acquired a certain psychological transcendence of its own, the notion that it is a separate

---

* From *The Yale Review*, Vol. XLVI, No. 4 (June 1957), pp. 551-565. Copyright 1957 by the Yale University Press. Reprinted by permission.

organism endowed with an autonomous vitality, standing morally and physically above and apart from its membership, is an illusion that enmeshes its purposes and works in a web of confusion and partisan strife. The United Nations is an organization contrived by man, not an organism begotten by him; it does not function as an impartial arbiter, because its members, who are judges as well as participants in disputes, represent special causes and interests; it is not an institution to be venerated as an end in itself, but remains a pragmatic instrument whose worth is measured only by its ability to fulfill its purposes.

The moral judgment of the U.N. does not materialize out of an impartial vacuum, but is always dependent upon the motivations of those members who make up the "preponderant voting superiority," just as its effectiveness is not automatic, but rests upon the responsibility and power of its members, especially the United States and the Soviet Union. The United Nations can never be a surrogate for the foreign policy of its members, but it can often be an instrument of that policy.

The present anti-colonial majority in the Assembly is a curious and unstable amalgam of Communist, neutralist, and anti-Communist states, divided by ideological incompatibilities, personal animosities, conflicting ambitions and aspirations, and political rivalries; yet it is sufficiently cemented together by a common passion against colonialism to consign the former dominant anti-Soviet majority to an ill-deserved oblivion from which it was only temporarily retrieved as a result of the Soviet intervention in the Hungarian uprising. The solid nucleus of this ascendant constellation is the Asian-African bloc of 27 states (including Japan but not Turkey), only recently intoxicated by a heady elixir of moral self-rectitude brewed at Bandung, preponderantly neutralist in sentiment, but embracing pro-Western countries like the Philippines and Pakistan as well as implacable regional rivals like Egypt and Iraq, yet excluding, for purposes of transparent expediency, the two pariah states of Israel and Nationalist China. The Asian-African bloc, which was augmented by fully one-half of the twenty-one new members, is the largest single regional grouping in the Assembly and, although not united on all issues, by itself constitutes one-third of the total membership. Without a single additional vote, this bloc can veto any important Assembly resolution as effectively as any Great Power can frustrate the work of the Security Council.

To this doctrinaire core of anti-colonial sentiment must be added the nine votes of the Soviet bloc, which enthusiastically supports the dismemberment of the Western colonial empires as the quickest way to subvert the power of the Atlantic alliance, and the vote of Communist Yugoslavia. Thus the core of the current anti-colonial majority is an irreducible minimum of 37 votes which will unwaveringly support a straight anti-colonial ticket—more than enough to stop any important resolution obnoxious to this group.

To pass a resolution it favors, the anti-colonial bloc needs to pick up only seventeen additional votes, and they are easy enough to find among the large and sprawling Latin-American contingent, the four Scandinavian states, and assorted members like Finland, Austria, and Greece, all of which are anti-colonial in sentiment, although they reserve for their own judgment the definition of a "colonial" issue. Even Israel, Nationalist China, Turkey, Eire, Spain, and Italy can be counted upon to support the principle of national self-determination in the colonial empires. Of the twenty-one new members, only Portugal can be relied upon to vote the straight colonial ticket.

After a protracted period of equivocation on colonial issues, embarrassingly reminiscent of Indian neutralism on East-West issues, the United States appears to have plunged into the anti-colonial camp in an effort to assume its leadership in order to avoid becoming its chief victim. In "this very great problem of the shift from colonialism to independence," Secretary Dulles recently explained, "the role of the United States is to try and see that the process moves forward in a constructive, evolutionary way, and does not either come to a halt or take a violent revolutionary turn." While this new policy fortuitously coincides with American oil interests, anti-colonial traditions, and longstanding faith in the virtues of national self-determination, it lamentably collides with American political commitments and attachments to the Western democracies, who, as the chief beneficiaries of the colonial system, are bound to suffer most by its liquidation.

The lodestar of American policy remains the containment and eventual recession of Soviet imperialism; this policy is the only consistent element in a bewildering profusion of indecisive, contradictory, and inept diplomatic maneuvers in the United Nations and elsewhere. With the general weakness of the Soviet position in Europe exposed by the Hungarian rebellion, the significance previously attached to NATO in American security calculations will inevitably diminish as the policy of containment shifts its geographic focus from Western Europe to the Middle East in search of new power vacuums. Only by support of the

independence movements in Africa and Asia, which invariably alienates
Western Europe and automatically dissipates the Atlantic alliance, can
the Administration hope to find an ideological foundation upon which
to erect an anti-Soviet coalition in the Middle East under the protective
umbrella of the "Eisenhower Doctrine," or hope to reshape the anti-
colonial majority in the General Assembly into its own anti-Soviet
image.

The anti-colonial majority is likely to expand further before it dimin-
ishes in influence. Aside from divided Germany and neutral Switzerland, all prospective members of the U.N. will be drawn from Asia and
Africa. Ghana (the Gold Coast) has already been admitted and Malaya
will be as soon as she is released from the paternity of the British
Colonial Office, and even if an agreement is hammered out admitting
the bifurcated states of Germany, Korea, and Vietnam together with
Outer Mongolia and that perennial bogey of American politicians, Red
China, Europe will gain only two additional representatives and Asia,
six, while the anti-colonial movement will garner at least seven additional full-time and part-time crusaders. Unless Europe and the New
World improvise some form of political mitosis as a measure of desperation, their numerical influence will continue to shrink as the U.N. is
brought into focus with demographic reality, and the General Assembly
will resemble, in the words of one exasperated European diplomat, "an
expanded version of the Bandung Conference."

Originally conceived during an anti-fascist crusade and fortified by
the prestige of a great military victory, the U.N. was brought into being
to preserve the postwar peace through a system of collective security,
resting, not upon the slender reed of "world public opinion," but upon
a foundation of power, with the Great Powers its cornerstones. Yet,
however flawless its theoretical conception, collective security under the
Charter was doomed to remain a formula shrouded in ambiguity as
long as it was impossible or inexpedient to agree upon a definition of
the peace to be preserved or an objective identification of the culprit
who threatens it. The founders purposely avoided defining aggression,
leaving this onerous task to their successors, who disbanded a special
committee which, after more than two years of inconclusive wrangling,
confessed an inability to arrive at a common definition of the most
serious international crime under the Charter.

When the ghost of fascism failed to materialize after the war, the

U.N. directed its energies into quixotic sorties against the only avowed fascist state in existence, Franco Spain. But as it became apparent that the real threat to the peace emanated from within the organization itself, the United Nations tried to wiggle out of the contradictions of the Charter and was gradually, if at first imperceptibly, transformed from an abortive anti-fascist organization, vainly scouring the world for new Hitlers, into a coalition prepared to deal with aggression inspired by one of its own police captains. Then it became evident that just as "world public opinion" failed to deter Japan, Hitler, Mussolini, and Stalin in the days of the League, so the massive numerical anti-Soviet majorities in the General Assembly failed to subdue the ambitions of a dictatorial regime whose interests conflicted with those of a majority in the Assembly.

This should have come as no surprise since Stalin told both Roosevelt and Churchill at Yalta that he "would never agree to having any action of the Great Powers submitted to the judgment of the smaller powers." Stalin's refusal to be unnerved by the moral force of public opinion led to the creation of the so-called Little Assembly in 1947 and in the following year to an advisory opinion of the World Court that the exercise of the veto in the Security Council on the admission of new members was "illegal." Both maneuvers produced only Pyrrhic victories, since the Little Assembly withered into oblivion and the World Court's advisory opinion was neither legally binding nor enforceable.

The Korean War in 1950 led to the first serious attempt in history to convert an international parliamentary majority into a military coalition. The fortuitous absence of the Soviet delegate from the Security Council made it possible to secure a condemnation, still of doubtful juridical validity, of North Korea as an aggressor, and as soon as the Soviet delegate returned to the Council, Secretary of State Acheson pushed through the General Assembly the now famous "Uniting for Peace" resolution, which openly confessed that the existing machinery of collective security under the Charter afforded more comfort to the aggressor than to the aggrieved. The formula of the Charter was jettisoned in favor of resurrecting the transparently defective machinery of the League. Once again collective security was to rely upon the moral force of "world public opinion" and the individual responsibility of the members of the General Assembly.

The "Uniting for Peace" resolution, which is the basis upon which the U.N. is acting in both the Hungarian and Egyptian crises, enables a two-thirds majority of the General Assembly to call upon its members to furnish aid to the victim of aggression, but allows each state to decide for itself, in the light of its own interests, policies, and sense of obligation, what action it should take in response to a call for "collective measures" against a declared aggressor. A total of 53 members supported the original decision of the Security Council to "furnish such assistance to the Republic of Korea as may be necessary to repel the armed attack and to restore international peace and security in the area," but as the nations divided for war in response to the call to unite for peace, the task of converting paper majorities into armed battalions foundered on the inexorable logic of the Charter and was frustrated by the implacable canons of power politics.

Instead of the single massive mobilization against the aggressor envisaged by the theory of collective security, four distinct responses, representing varying degrees of interest, conviction, capacity, and responsibility, materialized. While sixteen states participated in the action to some degree and a large bloc of members responded with unqualified verbal expressions of approval, the Soviet bloc actively aided the aggressors, while a group of Asian states expressed general approval for the principle of collective security but expressed reservations about the intervention in Korea. The principal virtue, and at the same time the greatest potential hazard, of the "Uniting for Peace" resolution is that it enables a Great Power, under the color of the U.N., to enforce the decisions of the General Assembly. This role, played by the United States during the Korean War, may be conceivably played by the Soviet Union at some future date, now that the United States no longer has undisputed command of Assembly majorities.

The Korean War not only marked the zenith of the U.N.'s anti-Soviet phase, but also prepared for the beginning of the next. The Asian states that viewed the Korean intervention with reluctance became convinced, as the war dragged on indecisively, that the United Nations was being manipulated as an instrument of an American crusade against Communism to the detriment of what they considered to be the more pressing problem of national self-determination in the colonial empires. This embryonic "neutralist" bloc gradually disassociated itself from the U.N. effort and, by its debilitating and irresponsible kibitzing, vitiated both the success of the military venture and the anti-Soviet character of the organization.

Conceived as an expedient weapon of the moment to halt Communist aggression, the American-invented "Uniting for Peace" resolution permanently shifted the center of gravity of the U.N. from the Security Council to the General Assembly. This meant that as long as the United States commanded automatic majorities in the Assembly, conflicts between American policy and that of the United Nations could be kept to a minimum, but with the recent influx of new members that era is over. The United Nations was released from the predictable whims of a few powerful lions on the Security Council only to be at the mercy of the machinations of a menagerie of lesser beasts in the General Assembly, furtively maneuvering to contrive a numerical majority purporting to be the custodian of the "conscience of mankind."

Ever since Cicero expressed the opinion that "the consensus of opinion among all nations, on whatever matter, may be taken for the law of nature," statesmen in the Western World, and particularly in Britain and the United States, have been searching for an institutionalized expression of "world public opinion" which would embody not only universal moral truth but in its transcendent omnipotence would be, in the words of Woodrow Wilson, "the mistress of the world."

Although the triple assumption that a "world public opinion" exists, that it invariably reflects moral wisdom, and that its power is irresistible is unsupported by logic and disproved by experience, this persisting illusion has been sedulously nurtured and propagated by American statesmen, whose diplomatic wisdom is often exceeded by their good intentions. Although both Moscow and Peking successfully defied the resolutions of the Assembly during the Korean War, an intrepid Dulles, unembarrassed by this dismal record or the even more wretched experience of the League, told a Senate group on January 18, 1954, that the U.N. "has become a place where world opinion can register and exert a moral authority which no nation, however powerful or despotic, publicly disdains or wholly disregards." And on September 18, 1956, less than two months before Moscow resumed her calculated contempt for Assembly resolutions, Ambassador Lodge wrote that "the U.N. has developed into the greatest single engine for mobilizing public opinion —a force which no government can withstand forever, no matter how dictatorial it may be."

Moral pressure can elicit a response only from the morally sensitive, but to the Kremlin "world public opinion" is a bourgeois myth and formal numerical majorities a cunning contrivance of bourgeois politics. Consequently, Soviet leaders, who reject the political reality of "world public opinion" and disown its moral validity, can remain cynically unresponsive to the importunings of Assembly majorities, without outraging anything but the principles of their enemies, while the Western democracies, who invented, nurtured, and popularized the notion of a "world public opinion" until it has been accepted as real by a substantial body of their articulate citizenry, are likely to be confronted with the awful alternatives of either permitting contrived majorities to subvert their national interests or violating their own principles in order to protect what they consider to be vital to their security.

Although Secretary Dulles has expressed a good deal of nonsense about "majority will" and "world public opinion," he once correctly observed that "the United States and no doubt others would be reluctant to subject itself to the will of the majority who might not represent world-wide opinion . . . but are free to act in accordance with their own views of policy and expediency." Nevertheless, American policy has placed the "conscience of mankind" in the hands of the small powers, most of which are weak, newly independent, internally unstable, not highly developed, and reflecting not a corporate conscience or wisdom but merely a spectrum of all the passions, interests, and prejudices that bless and curse mankind. Small states, no less than large, are actuated by their own national interests, not necessarily by abstract virtue, and in a world without a universally accepted code of morality or conception of truth, each state tends to identify its own interests, aspirations, and ideology with that of humanity. The true moral quality of this conglomeration of contradictory and conflicting hopes and interests can never rise above the political motives and moral judgments of the Ibn Sauds and Nassers, who are apt to confuse vengeance with justice, or the Khrushchevs and Titos, who equate eternal truth with Communism, or the Nehrus and Sukarnos, who tend to confuse their own shortcomings with exploitation, and others who happen to determine the policies of their individual countries. In an association embracing despotisms, democracies, and every cunning and subtle variation in between, it is a cruel deception to pretend that its parliamentary procedures can have any real resemblance to those in a democracy organized within a preaccepted moral and constitutional order governed by the rule of law.

In the United Nations, where majorities do not correspond to the actual distribution of population, wealth, power, or enlightenment, "majority will" is a synthetic contrivance expressing the lowest common denominator of interests and passions which temporarily and adventitiously shape it, while "majority rule," under these conditions, is an unmitigated vice.

As long as midget states like Luxembourg and San Salvador enjoy parity with Russia and the United States, juridical absurdities like Jordan and Nepal have the same vote as China and India, and outrageous fabrications like the Ukraine and Byelo-Russia have equal voice with bona fide states with legitimate interests, universality, instead of mirroring world reality and the "moral conscience of mankind," merely substitutes one illusion for another. Until the one state-one vote formula in the General Assembly is replaced with one more clearly in focus with the power and demographic realities of the world, it is better for the United Nations to function as an international forum and clearing house for disputes and discords than to be burdened with the fiction that it is an effective security organization entrusted with the wisdom of mankind.

Essentially the new anti-colonial majority is only a permutation of the old anti-Soviet majority that dominated the Assembly during most of the past decade. The old majority remains technically intact, but was rendered dormant by the bromide administered at Geneva and all but interred by the avalanche of "colonial" problems that have descended upon the organization. The prevailing mood of the Assembly remains both anti-colonial and anti-Soviet, i.e., anti-imperialist, but numerical similarities in the General Assembly can be deceiving. The two majorities are overlapping, not congruent, and their energies are far from being synchronized. Subtract the Soviet bloc and an influential cluster of Arab-Asian neutralists, add the colonial powers, and the anti-colonial majority is converted, *mutatis mutandis*, into the anti-Soviet majority.

The United States hoped, by its prompt and unequivocal denunciation of Britain and France, to assume leadership of the anti-colonial forces in the Assembly and, by the example of its own noble sacrifice, to persuade the Asian-African neutralists to abandon political expediency and national interest in favor of principle on the Hungarian question. But the Administration dangerously miscalculated by supposing that the moral pretensions of the Asian-African bloc were to be taken as a serious basis for its diplomacy, that the Egyptian and Hungarian crises would be universally viewed as identical outrages against mankind, and that its own gesture would be interpreted as an act of nobility rather than of expediency.

However, as the debates in the General Assembly and the voting alignments on the two crises show, the dent made in the "neutralist" bloc by this gesture was hardly significant enough to justify the luxury of abandoning two key and reliable allies to the mercy of the Soviet and Asian-African blocs. The neutralist Arab states clearly followed the dictates of expediency, while India and Indonesia, pretending ignorance, betrayed a massive indifference to the indignities perpetrated on the Hungarians, and it was generally conceded that the American decision was a calculated effort to compete with Moscow for the favors of the anti-colonial bloc rather than an abandonment of national interest in favor of principle, and hence both hypocritical and expedient.

Having taken the lead in both the Egyptian and Hungarian crises, the United States sought futilely to identify the interests of the anti-colonial movement with its own, in an effort to weld together the anti-Soviet and anti-colonial majorities into a monolithic crusade against all forms of imperialism and foreign domination. But since the dominant focus of American diplomacy is the Soviet threat, not colonialism, there are obvious limits to the leadership which the United States could hope to offer to the unbridled and destructive brand of nationalism represented by zealots like Nasser, dedicated to the destruction of the power and influence of our closest allies and committed to the annihilation of a state, Israel, which we are pledged to preserve. The anti-colonialists are not likely to permit themselves to become the instrument of an anti-Soviet crusade as long as they are convinced that they can utilize Moscow's anti-Western interests in pursuit of their own.

Regardless of the deceptive quantitative similarities, even a casual comparison of the voting alignments on the two crises betrays the almost unbridgeable gap which divides the anti-Soviet and anti-colonial majorities in the present Assembly. Granted the technical differences between the two events, the crises were iminently comparable since they shared the key issue of aggression, although in the case of Hungary, force was employed to preserve an existing position of power, while in Egypt it was employed to reassert one that had been tacitly surrendered. If the majorities on the Egyptian resolutions transcended purely anti-colonial sentiment, the smaller majorities on the Hungarian resolutions reflected more than a routine anti-Soviet exercise.

Although the issues in the Hungarian situation were more comprehensive in that they involved the attempt to repress and subjugate an entire nation, with correspondingly greater bloodshed and devastation, while the Egyptian affair was narrowly localized geographically, severely circumscribed in its objectives, and at least partly mitigated by the provocative actions of the Nasser regime, which invited, if not justified, retaliation by the three countries involved, the same sense of urgency did not grip the anti-colonial "neutralists," some of whom appeared convinced until almost the end that the Hungarian crisis was a contrived Western "red herring" designed to divert attention from Egypt. The very members who waxed so indignant at Britain and France now eagerly barricaded themselves behind the flimsy technicality that the Kadar regime's invitation to Soviet troops to butcher the rebels reduced the Hungarian affair to a purely internal matter beyond the purview of the United Nations. While Nehru pleaded ignorance and confusion about the "civil war" in Hungary, his delegate, Krishna Menon, was telling the General Assembly that "so far as my government is concerned . . . we would not regard them [the Hungarians] as a people struggling for independence [and] . . . we cannot deal with the problem as in the case of a colonial country." Systematically abstaining on the resolutions, Menon, during the height of the debate, betrayed an enigmatic confidence that Moscow's excesses were an unappreciated temporary aberration when he grotesquely praised the "great changes . . . taking place in the Soviet Union . . . calculated to assist in the progress of humanity and in the enlargement of human freedom."

Burma and Ceylon eventually deserted the coterie of abstainers, and India indulged in a bit of soul-searching, but the decisive and essential distinction between the two majorities remained the fact that, on the Egyptian resolutions, the majority embraced the two superpowers, India, and the heavily populated countries of Asia, with the outside support of Communist China, while on the Hungarian, a substantial and influential number of Arab-Asian neutralists, led by India, Indonesia, and Egypt, abstained, and the Soviet bloc, with the outside support of Communist China, was in opposition. This meant that countries representing well over half of the world's population and including significant centers of power were either actively opposed or refused to support the Hungarian resolutions, affording the majority only the most dubious and tenuous claim to being the expression of that elusive entity "world public opinion."

The truth is not that a country cannot defy the "moral force" of the

U.N., but that, in international affairs, it cannot defy the combined opinion of the United States and the Soviet Union. Britain and France stood virtually alone against all the major world centers of population and power and they succumbed, not because of President Eisenhower's charitable explanation that "they had a decent respect for the opinion of mankind as reflected in the General Assembly of the United Nations," which they were clearly primed to ignore, but because of the crude threats from Moscow, the American obsession with its moral rectitude, and the Indian threat to dissolve the Commonwealth. The "moral force" of a U.N. resolution, no matter how large the majority, is likely to remain an empty gesture unless it includes support of both super-powers, or the vital interests of one are so affected that it chooses to convert an international parliamentary majority into a military coalition against the other. Otherwise, both the United States and the Soviet Union, individually or together, can defy Assembly majorities with impunity.

If the Administration seriously adheres to its public commitment to equate Assembly majorities with the "opinion of mankind" as long as only the interests of others are at stake, the U.N. will be impelled to press its decisions only upon those powers most likely to be responsive to its edicts. Now that the Soviet bloc, the Arab states, and India have successfully demonstrated that they reserve for themselves the right to be the ultimate moral judges of their own actions, as well as the decisions of the world organization which impinge upon their interests, they eagerly embrace the President's curious theory that the very survival of the United Nations rests upon its willingness to impose its authority upon those members who are too weak to resist, susceptible to moral importuning, or unattached to powerful voting blocs in the General Assembly. The President's view inadvertently provides a philosophical basis for converting the world organization into a diplomatic instrument of Soviet and anti-colonial policy.

It is questionable, however, whether the Administration will be able to pursue a policy whose flimsily constructed abstract foundations are likely to collide with the requirements of practical statesmanship, though members of the anti-colonial majority will now have their exertions thrice blessed with the principles of national self-determination, "majority rule," and what Christian Pineau has aptly characterized as the principle of "inequality of actions." They will be encouraged, on the flimsiest pretexts, to wrap their interests and aspirations in the cloak of "anti-colonialism," since this appears to guarantee the widest measure of support in the Assembly.

Soviet contempt for Assembly majorities, India's defiance of the Security Council in the Kashmir dispute, and Nasser's transparent opportunism on the Israeli and Suez questions have introduced serious fissures in the Asian-African bloc, disenchanted its large circle of non-Communist sympathizers, and rendered the anti-colonial majority more unstable than before. The evolution of the United Nations from an expanded NATO alliance into an expanded version of the Bandung Conference appears to be temporarily arrested, freezing the U.N. between two stages in its now indeterminate metamorphosis.

At this juncture, the Assembly of the United Nations appears doomed to the same paralysis as exists in the Security Council, with various blocs sufficiently powerful to thwart two-thirds majorities but unable to produce them. This may be a blessing in disguise, since under present world conditions this appears to be the only way to prevent the world organization from becoming the instrument of national or ideological policy rather than the servant of an idea. If it is impossible to have a United Nations which can impose its decisions on all its members, it is better to have one which can impose them on none.

The U.N. and National Security*

by Lincoln P. Bloomfield

[1]

In 1945, when the United Nations was founded, its *raison d'être* was to provide greater security for its member nations. As the basic conflict of interests between Soviet Communism and the free nations unfolded, the cold war rapidly came to suffuse the entire organization like a sort of nerve gas, paralyzing but not killing. In a relatively short time, it was seen to be incapable of resolving or even seriously affecting the dominant world conflict. The United States and its principal allies were forced to conclude that except as it provided a forum for counter-

* From *Foreign Affairs*, Vol. XXXVI, No. 4 (July 1958), pp. 597-610. Copyright 1958 by the Council on Foreign Relations, Inc., New York. Reprinted by special permission from *Foreign Affairs*.

propaganda the United Nations was irrelevant to the over-riding short-term military and security problem posed by aggressive and expansionist Soviet Communism.

The Korean War threw a new light on the capabilities of the U.N. as a political mechanism for organizing and demonstrating world-wide resistance to limited Communist aggression. But the disproportionately large contribution which the United States had to make to that fight strengthened the doubt whether the U.N. could play a central rôle in the short-run protection of American national security. It continued to exercise a powerful attraction for the American people, since it exemplified their great will for peace. But as the custodian of the peace it seemed to be in a fiduciary relationship not to us but to an unborn generation of men who might have a capacity for managing their affairs rather more harmoniously.

Reasons for the American public to favor continued participation in the U.N. were, besides the moral attraction of the Charter ideal, the possibility of using the organization selectively in the settlement of disputes within the free world, and its "secondary" activities involving dependent areas, technical assistance and the humanitarian achievements of the Specialized Agencies. Those functions turned out to be important enough to sustain American membership. But no amount of enthusiasm for the potentialities of the organization under different circumstances could overcome the conviction that at best it must be considered to be "on ice" so far as concerned the profound and immediate security problem that preoccupied us.

Meanwhile great changes have been taking place in power relationships and in the policies designed to protect national security. The capacity of the United States to influence international events decisively has seemed to decline in recent years. We cannot afford the luxury of misusing any available means of making our influence felt. What of the United Nations? Has our estimate of its capabilities taken account of our new insights into the present realities of international political life, specifically as they relate to political and technological developments? What contribution might it make to security in the years immediately ahead?

II. THE CHANGING U.N.

Four things have happened in recent years to put in question our old basic attitudes toward the U.N. as an agency promoting our national security.

The first is the loosening of the alliance structure on both sides. In the early days of the cold war it was not uncommon for the vote in the General Assembly to be 55 to 5 on a whole range of issues. The lines were sharply drawn; the balance of power was so rigid that little flexibility for manœuvre was left within the U.N. or for that matter outside. Even so, U.N. action played a part in varying degrees in Iran, Greece, the Berlin blockade, Korea and, later, Hungary. In the over-all it was not much. There clearly was no possibility of "U.N. action" in the cold war apart from whatever the United States and its allies were themselves able or willing to do.

In view of the cold war, the presence of Soviets and Americans under one roof posed a novel problem for Western diplomacy. In a time when we were struggling to organize a world-wide defensive coalition against the Communist threat, we had to meet and negotiate with our allies in the presence of the enemy. Each issue and each vote thus came to represent a separate test of free-world unity, and often it was more important in this sense than because of the actual question involved. As time went on, the unity of the non-Communist world was put under increasing strain by the growing split between the poles of what might be called North and South, primarily on issues arising in the colonial field. But the over-all alliance held together, albeit with difficulty.

Since 1952, the tone and mode of Soviet diplomacy, in and out of the U.N., have altered. The political effect of this has been acute, coming at a time when the bipolar political world was itself beginning to splinter. With the development of something like a military standoff between the United States and the Soviet Union, forces within the two coalitions began to assert their freedom of manœuvre and to move toward positions relatively independent of the two leader states. Britain, India, Jugoslavia, Poland, Egypt, China and Germany suddenly began to emerge as foci of new independent leadership. "Automatic majorities" and "automatic leadership" in the U.N., if they had ever really existed, became things of the past. The world was changing, and the U.N. was changing with it.

A second development was the enhanced rôle of the uncommitted countries. The success of the West in gathering support from these countries through the U.N. has become increasingly dependent on the stands which Western nations take on issues of primary importance to the peoples of that "third world." These have not been such issues as capitalism vs. Communism, or German unification, or liberation of the satellites, but colonialism, "self-determination," economic development and racial discrimination. Out of the present membership of 81 countries, approximately 45 members for one reason or another see these as the crucial issues and put the United States to the test in regard to them with increasing frequency. Here again the issue often is purely symbolic; it may reflect an accumulated heritage of resentment or be designed to play off the East against the West. But in the U.N. these issues take concrete shape in resolutions and action programs in which Russian and American performance is constantly made the measure for a host of other attitudes.

The way in which we have restructured the U.N. itself has added to the American dilemma. For perfectly good reasons the United States urged a greater rôle for the General Assembly (where all nations, whatever their size, have equal votes) in order to offset the impotence of the Security Council. In the fall of 1950 it appeared essential to re-mobilize the capabilities of the U.N. for collective military action. Happily the American display of determined resistance in Korea as well as other subsequent developments have tended to discourage military risk-taking by the Communists. The Assembly's real rôle in this field therefore is still not measurable. But as part of the same development the Assembly has become a prime political forum for the nations which remain outside the East-West camps and pursue their own goals of political independence, economic improvement and racial dignity. In this situation what might be called the North-South conflict cuts across the East-West issues and makes its own powerful demands on American diplomacy, while offering magnificent opportunities for the Soviets to seize the political initiative.

The third change is in the military scene. It is by its performance here that many people would have the U.N. stand or fall. Of course, it long since became clear that the Security Council would not be able to carry out its enforcement powers. Yet in the 13 years since the Charter was drafted there has been no general war, and one of the chief reasons for this has certainly been that the important operational principles of the Charter—collective action for security and avoidance of violence in resolving disputes—have been in *general* effect. It might be said that the San Francisco principle has failed in detail but has had general validity in the sense that it has been translated into regional and self-defense arrangements which, because the Charter existed, were able to borrow from its spirit and purpose.

The U.N. has also invented new military and quasi-military functions connected with the security task. UNEF in Egypt and the earlier military observer teams in Palestine and Kashmir are cases in point. And despite waning confidence in the validity of its major premise, the U.N. displayed unforeseen capabilities in a "hard" case of Communist aggression—Korea—which could scarcely be envisaged in 1945. Both in and out of the U.N., then, many states have acted as though they had assumed an important general commitment and meant to take it seriously. In a way which the old League of Nations could never achieve, all states are involved in each successive crisis. This has obvious disadvantages in potentially widening an otherwise limited conflict. The offsetting advantage may be in keeping these crises from ending in general war.

The "failure of collective security," then, turns out to be a failure in the procedure which had been established more than in the substantive result achieved. The notion of universal collective security based on an abstract commitment to fight anyone, anywhere, anytime, on the call of a majority, has evaporated; but it had never really been a legitimate expectation, in the absence of a true world community and given the wide variety of meanings ascribed to the concept of "justice."

But something more than this must be said about the political rôle of the U.N. as an agency of military security in the period ahead. The revolution in military weapons has changed both the kind of wars most likely to be fought and the attitudes of the great Powers toward war itself. The political status quo of the West is anathema to the Soviets, and the territorial status quo of world Communism is unacceptable to us. Yet as general war becomes an increasingly unattractive proposition for both parties, the de facto line between the two worlds has hardened. When it is crossed in strength, as in Korea, the entire world appears to recognize it as a plain violation of the peace, and counter-action becomes politically feasible. Even India and Egypt voted initially to oppose the Communist aggression in Korea. On the other hand, as we saw in Hungary, a general military counter-action across the line was quite impossible politically even if we had been willing to lead it—which we were not.

Unlike the Communists, the United States through the President and Secretary of State has specifically renounced force to resolve political differences. There is no doubt that we would react vigorously to open Communist aggression, *i.e.* action across the line. But we explicitly avoid steps that could lead to general war. We have applied this self-denying ordinance to ourselves in the case of Communist China, the Berlin blockade, the crossing of the Yalu, Indochina and, most recently, Hungary. We have also applied this policy to our friends, as in the Suez crisis of 1956. It is argued that the United States could and should have blocked the shipment of Soviet arms into the Middle East, with the aim of heading off the subsequent crises, but the President was being entirely consistent in refusing to countenance a local military action that could lead directly to world war, however great the provocation to our friends. A significant result of the Suez fiasco is the realization that both the United States and the U.S.S.R. are likely to veto military action by third parties that might commit them to expanding potentially uncontrollable situations. Barring a drastic change in Soviet estimates of Western power, it would appear that the paraphernalia for all-out war has more political than military significance today. In turn, lesser instruments for exerting power assume increasing importance. The United Nations is one of them.

The fourth change is in the significance of disputes within the free world. Cases in point are the Indian-Pakistani dispute over Kashmir; Palestine, in all its ramifications, including the status of international waterways; India versus South Africa over Indian minority rights and racial discrimination; Greece, Turkey and the United Kingdom over Cyprus; and Indonesia versus the Netherlands over West New Guinea. Each might "go critical." As Suez illustrated, a dispute which did not directly involve the two great Powers can quickly pose life-and-death decisions for the entire human family. As things stand, the control rods of "the Suez pile" are held by an international brigade of U.N. troops. The chain reaction can start there again. But for the moment the world is buying time with the help of a variety of U.N. instrumentalities and functions, including UNEF, the U.N. Truce Supervision Organization and the activities of the Secretary-General. If Kashmir should be the scene of renewed fighting, and if the Soviet Union backed India and the

United States backed Pakistan, the risks that the direct Soviet-American confrontation might develop into general war would be that much greater, given the geography and the stakes.

Whenever possible, the United States has preferred to leave disputes not directly involving Communist nations to the U.N. It is within this range of issues that the U.N. machinery for the pacific settlement of disputes has been brought into play. The Suez case is an indication of how we have become prisoners of outmoded ways of thinking about the organization. Throughout the intense and futile negotiations in the summer of 1956 the United States and its partners rigidly shunned any positive use of U.N. instrumentalities. One American motive in this was to avoid the possibility of a public discussion of the Panama Canal, by association, as it were. Consequently we relied exclusively on the so-called London group. This forum was unacceptable to Egypt. At the same time we failed to avail ourselves of a wide range of possible actions through the U.N., including appointment of a U.N. mediator, or of a U.N. agent-general to operate the Canal in the interim without prejudice, or the establishment of a joint régime, or, at a minimum, recognition through a U.N. resolution that the Canal was international in character. Reasonable proposals that enlisted heavy U.N. support could conceivably have altered Egypt's intransigence. We now see that when the British and French finally went to the U.N. in early October it was to clear the way for unilateral action. Only when fighting broke out did we ourselves turn to the U.N. to stop it. And this was of course the one thing the U.N. was unable to do apart from its exertion of purely moral force and apart from whatever outside pressure individual members such as we and the Russians could apply.

Western statesmen have spoken for years, quite correctly, about the great value of the U.N. in getting the parties to a dispute around the table, substituting talk and mediation and conciliation, however endless and frustrating, for bullets, and offering a variety of institutional means for limiting the conflict and facilitating peaceful change. In the case of Suez we underestimated the preventive capacity of the U.N. before the crisis became acute, overestimated its capabilities when the crisis arrived, and again lost interest when the crisis had passed. Our attention immediately wandered to another dimension of the problem—the possibility of overt Russian military aggression. The resolutions regarding a peace settlement and the refugee problem which we introduced in the hectic early nights of the crisis were never again referred to, and instead

we brought forth the Eisenhower Doctrine for the Middle East. It may
have been worth while to post a U.S. "keep out" sign in the area, even
though the possibility of overt aggression was and is comparatively
slight. But this was our only real move to remedy a whole set of critical
local situations which did not primarily involve the Communist bloc
but which were the basic sources of conflict in the area. Because all of
these, including specifically the refugee problem, have once again been
passed over, it can confidently be predicted that the next local explosion
will be that much more potent.

III. SECURITY OBJECTIVES OF THE UNITED STATES

How should the considerations just mentioned affect American policy
toward the United Nations in the years immediately ahead? Let us first
identify some of the over-riding security goals of this policy today and
see how the U.N. might help in achieving them.

Of course, our principal and obvious security objective is to create
the kind of world order in which we and every other nation can cultivate our respective societies free from external threats of disruption.
Everything else falls within this governing purpose. Fully spelled out, it
would comprehend a wide variety of subordinate objectives in the economic, social, humanitarian and cultural fields. Here, however, we shall
concentrate on the most acute problems which determine our choice of
means and our allocation of resources.

Objective number one, then, is to reduce the generalized threat which
Soviet Communist power presents to the United States and all Western
society. This broad objective has three components. The first is to reduce the Soviet capability to inflict intolerable physical damage upon
us. The second is to moderate hostile Soviet intentions. The third is to
limit and if possible reduce present international support for the Soviet
Union.

The second objective is to find means of limiting warfare if it does
break out.

The third is to ensure, in the event of general war, that we rally maximum political support to our side, in order that we may have the best
chance of organizing the postwar world in an acceptable way.

The fourth is to reduce the possibility of a general war developing
inadvertently.

Reducing Soviet Military Capabilities Since the U.N. does not have any military force of its own it would seem of little use to us in attaining this first objective. It can provide a variety of forums for negotiating the limitation and regulation of armaments and restricting the use of outer space to non-warlike purposes. True, whether or not these questions are to be resolved depends on agreement between the United States and the U.S.S.R., and in this sense the decision will be bilateral rather than multilateral. Nevertheless the wide choice of means of negotiation offered by the U.N. should not be discounted, as was shown when Russia wanted to talk privately with us about liquidating the Berlin blockade. A summary appraisal must be, then, that the U.N. can affect Soviet military capabilities only indirectly, by furnishing a negotiating vehicle.

Affecting Soviet Intentions This objective is more complex. At its least complicated level—military intentions—Soviet policy since Korea seems to have consciously excluded the overt use of military force in favor of more profitable and acceptable techniques of political and economic warfare. Secretary Dulles has said on several occasions that if it were not for the U.N. we would be in World War III. The real significance of the commitment undertaken by 81 nations—including the Soviet Union to refrain from the threat or use of force is obviously not in its legal quality. Because any warlike act will immediately be brought before 80 other nations, the Soviet Union is faced with the fact that it must persuade an effective majority that it has not breached the existing line which neither side can properly cross, whatever it may be doing behind that line.

This deterrent is not comparable with the deterrent of our Strategic Air Command, but there have been too many examples of Soviet sensitivity to world public opinion for us to write it off as meaningless. It is not always remembered that the U.N. resolution condemning the U.S.S.R. in Hungary was supported by 15 Afro-Asian states, with none in opposition. The Soviets periodically stumble badly because of the difficulty of sustaining a soft line in the U.N. when their line outside hardens. Soviet troops are still in Hungary, but the Soviet Union's reputation in the uncommitted nations was gravely tarnished just when its efforts to woo them were at a peak. On balance, the fact that the U.N. exists can be set down as a consideration affecting Soviet calculations about the profitability of military operations, but it hardly figures as a prime factor. On the other hand, regional and collective self-defense arrangements largely embody the Charter commitment to oppose aggression, and these manifestly shape the Soviet estimate of the non-Communist world's vulnerability.

If, however, we think of Soviet intentions in the context of an evolution of Soviet society into something more tolerant and more tolerable, there are additional dimensions to the possible U.N. rôle which may not always be fully grasped. Certainly the U.N. cannot transform the nature of Soviet Communism significantly, but in various ways it might exert a favorable influence.

The fact that it is a continuous point of contact between the Communist bloc and the West may acquire special significance in a changing situation, if only by giving the Soviet Union assurance of being readily accepted into the community of nations as a great Power even though it is rejected as a messianic and apocalyptic force. Meanwhile, U.N. membership can have the effect of sustaining and encouraging the independent identity of such satellites as Poland.

Thus we should continue to offer the Soviets alternative courses of action that one day may appear realistic and attractive to them. With or without them, we should continue to work to institutionalize areas of common action and to create an international community that can compete successfully with the barren Soviet variety. We have already led the way in nonpolitical programs such as health and technical assistance, which the Russians, for many reasons, ultimately have come to join. Seen in this light, the cold war should spur us to greater experiments with multilateralism among those disposed to coöperate; it should not serve as an excuse for us to retreat into inaction and defeatism.

One further matter may be mentioned conveniently here even though it is not directly related to Soviet intentions.

The U.N. is a demonstration and testing point for the unity of the free world. When that unity increases, the Soviets have seemed to raise their estimates of Western capabilities; and conversely, Western disunity has encouraged the Soviets to calculate their opportunities as more promising. Sometimes the U.N. has been an embarrassment to us when used as a place for airing the free world's dirty linen. Sometimes the Russians have been able to use it as a place to disrupt free world unity. If we are to live successfully in the kind of U.N. that has developed, and retain majority support when it really counts, we must do a number of new things. We must be prepared to go a great deal further than we have with our close friends on issues which are of great political importance to them but of only secondary importance to us. Primarily these represent differences over essentially procedural matters such as elections or budgets or the composition of committees, which often have been the source of more inter-allied friction than any substantive policy issues except Chinese representation or Suez. We might do better not to engage the prestige of the United States on such procedural issues but to save it for the big ones. We might also gracefully accept an occasional minority position on some issues instead of insisting on having our own way, or going over the heads of friendly delegates, or threatening retaliation, however subtly.

Limiting International Support for the Soviet Union This support is coming primarily from the underdeveloped, neutralist, anti-colonial countries and territories. No actions of ours can be expected wholly to reverse this tide until it has run its course. Nevertheless, it is here that the battle is being fought, and our task is to find ways of diverting local forces of discontent into constructive channels, to furnish incentives for native leadership so that the forces of nationalism may be harnessed to tasks of building rather than destruction and hate.

The prime factor here is economic. We should estimate afresh the political and economic benefits that might stem from greater use of the U.N. in financing the development of underdeveloped countries. But there also are important psychological factors, and here the style and sensitivity of our diplomacy can be crucial. Both in and out of the U.N., our ability to command the support of an effective majority depends heavily on the way we handle the legacy of bruised feelings left by centuries of Western claims to racial superiority, and on the understanding with which we view the ambition of Asians or Latin Americans to "catch up," to become industrialized, to be less dependent on a peasant economy that offers only continued human misery and poverty.

The U.N. is the one place where all of these tensions and claims and expectations come into focus in full view of virtually all the world. There the uncommitted nations have found their place in the sun, there the concept of the legal equality of states offers them the self-respect and dignity they seek.[1] There they acquire a parliamentary

---

[1] This, incidentally, is why a weighted voting system, for all its logic, does not seem feasible unless and until genuine powers are reposed in the General Assembly.

strength entirely disproportionate to the amount of real power they command in the world. This power is used primarily to bring before the rest of the world their ambitions and grievances, incorporated in concrete issues and demands: freedom from the only kind of foreign domination they know about; generous economic assistance for development, specifically grants, low-interest loans and fair capital investment; protection of their exports from uncontrollable fluctuations in world prices; racial equality in practice; freedom for the remaining colonial possessions of Western Powers; in short, equality with the rest of the world.

If we are to have the political support of these nations we must find better ways than we have done so far to relate our own interests to their interests, aspirations and goals. Where the U.N. provides the only agency acceptable to them we must utilize it to the utmost.

Limiting Warfare If It Breaks Out   Our general military objective here has three parts. One is to avoid a direct military confrontation between the Soviet Union and the United States, as already discussed. Another is to keep such a confrontation within bounds if it happens. A third is to keep outbreaks within the non-Communist world from spreading into a general war.

The scope of hostilities between free-world and Communist nations would undoubtedly be determined by the estimates each side made of the intentions and the capabilities of the other. Given the will of each to keep them limited, the U.N. can then offer the advantages it did when the United States made its decision to resist the Russians in Korea.

These advantages are several. First, the U.N. furnishes one means for us to secure maximum world-wide political support. This support is indispensable if we are not to lose the sense of legitimacy and moral right which we as a people need in order to sustain a military effort. The second advantage is the opportunity given us by the commitment made by all U.N. members to assist the organization in any action it takes in accordance with the Charter. This does not have to mean "action" in the legal sense of Security Council enforcement. Marginal offers of bases, transit rights—even "a sharpshooter on a camel"—cannot merely demonstrate the breadth of international disapproval of a Soviet act of limited aggression but can pay important strategic dividends. The third advantage is that the mere fact that the conflict is before the U.N.

tends to discourage participants from expanding the scope of the war recklessly or setting extravagant war aims.

Perhaps the situation most likely to arise is one in which a military outbreak does not directly involve the armed forces of the United States or the U.S.S.R. Here the rôle of the U.N. is essentially political. When there is an effective majority against the continuance of hostilities, and the parties involved are responsive to it as they were in the Suez crisis, the conflict may be halted before it gets completely out of hand. An international military force such as UNEF can then play a most important rôle in helping restore conditions favorable to peaceful settlement and perhaps peaceful change.

Schemes for a standing U.N. force to counter large-scale aggression call for a relative preponderance of power at the center. Without some form of world government this is unattainable. Yet there is a more limited military rôle for the U.N. that is realistic and at the same time would serve to meet a vital contemporary need. Only the U.N. can develop and perfect the sort of limited and neutral force needed to prevent or deal with local situations which we know constitute a real and present danger to world peace. Such a force would not be supposed to undertake full-scale military action but only police functions. The response of the smaller nations in 1956 proved that they are ready, able and willing to contribute to such a force. Rather than continuing to present the U.N. as a club of like-minded states all prepared to take identical action, we should be grateful that some of them may form a "third party" available to be interposed in such situations. We ourselves have been the "third party" on occasion, as in the Indonesian Good Offices Committee, or in Algeria, and might well play such a rôle again.

A defect of various valuable suggestions recently made for establishing a permanent force along these lines lies in their failure to reckon fully with the formidable financial costs involved. One way to overcome this problem would be to set up a training command with a small permanent cadre. Selected units from member countries would be rotated there for a specified period, but would then return home to be held as a reserve.

Using the U.N. in a General War Situation   We are prone to believe that general war would mean the end of the U.N., and this may be so. Yet as we saw in the case of Korea, the U.N. can serve as an umbrella under which the United States can legitimize its military response to a Communist aggression. Our planning must not ignore this possibility. We must assume there will be a postwar world to organize. The U.N. might accord legitimacy to non-Communist representatives of peoples in the Soviet bloc while hostilities were still in progress and thus arrange a vital political focus for the forces which would coöperate to bring into being the sort of world for which we had fought. Finally, if the political war aims were defined by the U.N. rather than by a single nation this might bring hostilities to a satisfactory end more promptly.

Reducing the Possibility of General War Developing Inadvertently Since it is unlikely under present conditions that general war will be launched by the deliberate decision of any nation, the chief concern of responsible statesmen should be to prevent the outbreak of war by inadvertence. If we rule out the use of force to remedy the legitimate grievances of states, we are obliged to find other means for the solution of those problems. It is here that the U.N. has possibly its most vital future task to play in terms of our national security. But to energize the U.N. to undertake this task and to exploit its institutional potentialities fully the United States is going to have to attach a wholly new order of importance to developing better means for peacefully settling disputes and facilitating peaceful change. We must apply political muscle to the "preventive peace" about which we speak so frequently. It may mean a concentrated political and financial effort to resolve the Palestine refugee deadlock. It may mean taking the Peace Observation Commission out of mothballs and urging that it be dispatched to an unquiet frontier like that between Tunisia and Algeria. It may mean leading the way to greater use of the International Court of Justice, instead of setting an opposite kind of example by falling back on the domestic jurisdiction plea, as in the Interhandel Case. It may mean pressing for the international regulation of international waterways—including the Panama Canal. In short, it means doing what no one has ever done before in all history—expending an effort to prevent violence comparable to the effort usually made in picking up the pieces afterward.

In working with enlarged purpose and effort on the chronic causes of instability and friction, we should not find our motivation only in the Soviet threat. Persistent international tensions threaten our ability to fulfill the promises of our own society. For our own internal good our rôle in the world must be more than that of a powerful negative force. Our well-rounded development as a people has come to depend on the development of stability for other peoples. Means must be found to resolve peacefully the clash between the status quo and the dynamic forces that continuously challenge it.

In the period ahead the United Nations may have extremely important uses both in support of the national interest and in support of the common interest in a more stable peace. These uses, as indicated here, may have little to do with the stereotypes and symbols of U.N. action that we still cling to, expressed in terms of universal collective security, "misuse of the veto," overemphasis on purely military estimates of the cold war, excessive U.S. control over multilateral funds and programs, the "popularity contest" theory, and expectations about altruistic international behavior. The crisis is too grave for us to afford to misunderstand the capabilities of any instrumentality offering genuine opportunities to advance our national prospects and the prospects for a tolerable world around us.

Economic Cooperation under U.N. Auspices*

by Robert E. Asher

The economic programs of the United Nations have been jogging along for some time now. The pace, one fears, is not quite fast enough to get anywhere by sundown. Moreover, the road map, if it even existed, has been mislaid and a thick growth of underbrush has sprung up to obscure the pathway.

It may be useful, therefore, to review briefly the course of international economic cooperation during the fifteen years since the convening of the U.N. Conference on Food and Agriculture at Hot Springs, Va., in May 1943. After that, it would be logical to pause for a closer look at the accomplishments of the major U.N. economic programs. Finally, it would be desirable to ask what, if anything, can be done to provide the design, the sense of direction, and the dimensions required to rally and retain greater support in the free world for U.N. programs.

* Reprinted, with the permission of *International Organization* and of the Brookings Institution, from *International Organization*, Vol. XII, No. 3 (Summer 1958). Copyright 1958 by the World Peace Foundation. Since 1954, the author has been a member of the senior staff of the Brookings Institution. The views expressed in this article are his own. They do not necessarily reflect the views of other members of the Brookings staff or of the administrative officers of the Institution.

I. TRENDS WITHIN AND OUTSIDE THE U.N. SYSTEM[1]

In recent years the more dramatic moves appear to have been taken outside the U.N. framework, while international cooperation on economic matters has been inching forward unspectacularly within that framework. During the latter part of the war and the early postwar period, however, the opposite was true. To supplement and complement the machinery inherited from prewar days, a succession of global agencies was launched, each with fanfare and enthusiasm, each carrying with it the hopes and good wishes of important and articulate sectors of society. Not only Hot Springs, but also Bretton Woods, Chicago, San Francisco, London, and other centers served in memorable fashion as launching sites.

The United States stood at the pinnacle of its prestige and appeared to have a plan, a design, a strategy, for meeting the problems of the day. Other nations subscribed to United States thinking more readily than would later be the case. It was widely believed that, after a brief period of grants from the United Nations Relief and Rehabilitation Administration (UNRRA), international equilibrium would be re-established with the aid of loans and guarantees from the International Bank, private investment, intergovernmental agreement to reduce trade barriers, and the return, within the course of about five years, to currency convertibility. Should nations later find themselves in temporary balance-of-payments difficulties, they would be able to draw on the new International Monetary Fund (IMF). The activities of the specialized agencies would be coordinated by a principal organ of the U.N., the Economic and Social Council (ECOSOC).

The United States representative at the first meeting of ECOSOC, Ambassador Winant, did not appear to be indulging in sheer hyperbole when he said that "seldom before in human history has an organization been created with greater opportunity to save mankind than has been given to the Economic and Social Council under the Charter of the United Nations." [2] Although its specific powers were limited, the Coun-

---

[1] By "United Nations system" and "United Nations framework," is meant not only the United Nations and its councils, commissions, and subsidiary units, but also the group of autonomous specialized agencies related to the United Nations by formal agreement.

[2] Economic and Social Council *Official Records* (1st session), First Meeting, January 23, 1946, p. 14.

cil in its early years was manned by distinguished and respected representatives.

Within five years ECOSOC had under it eight functional commissions dealing with economic and employment issues, human rights, population questions, social problems, transportation and communication, statistics, narcotic drugs, and other matters. Three regional economic commissions were reporting to it. It had initiated and assumed responsibilities in connection with a number of operating programs involving the feeding of children, the provision of technical assistance, and the rendering of emergency aid to the needy. It had negotiated agreements with ten worldwide, specialized agencies dealing with labor, health, education, food and agriculture, civil aviation, telecommunications, postal services, meteorology, international investment, and monetary policy, and it was trying—gingerly—to coordinate their work.

But "summer's lease hath all too short a date." While this complex organizational structure was being erected, enthusiasm for the global, U.N. approach to international questions was beginning to wane and counter-pressures began to assert themselves. As early as March 1946, Winston Churchill had announced to the world that from "Stettin in the Baltic to Trieste in the Adriatic, an iron curtain has descended across the continent." [3]

UNRRA, conceptually and spiritually in the U.N. mold, though never formally a part of the U.N. system, was dismantled before its task was completed. The United States undertook to extend aid on a bilateral basis to certain UNRRA members not yet sealed off by the Iron Curtain, while the U.N. system fell heir to some of UNRRA's health, welfare, and refugee work.

The bilateral aid programs of the United States continued from then on to dwarf the multilateral programs. The Soviet Union, too, began extending aid on the basis of bilateral agreements, first to its satellites, and eventually to other countries as well. By late 1957, a number of underdeveloped countries were obtaining assistance from both the Soviet Union and the United States. Multilateralism has continued to receive lip service, but most of the money has been flowing through bilateral channels.

The most notable multilateral initiatives of the last decade, moreover, have—with a few exceptions—been taken outside the U.N. frame-

---

[3] *Vital Speeches,* March 15, 1946 (Vol. 12, No. 11), p. 331.

work. In the economic field, these include three concomitants of the Marshall Plan, the Organization for European Economic Co-operation, the European Payments Union (EPU), and the European Productivity Agency; three associations involving Benelux, France, Germany, and Italy, the European Coal and Steel Community (ECSC), the European Atomic Energy Community, and the European Economic Community (common market); two other European groupings, the proposed free trade area, and the proposed Nordic Customs Union; and a peculiar arrangement that includes participants from several continents and has both multilateral and bilateral features, the Colombo Plan.

The reasons for the apparent downgrading of the U.N. in the foreign economic policies of key governments are not far to seek. The true dimensions of the postwar reconstruction job were woefully underestimated. The imperialism of Soviet communism and the difficulties of negotiating with its representatives were only dimly foreseen. The need for utilizing, in addition to the new global associations in the U.N. family, every other avenue for economic cooperation among "likeminded" nations was not appreciated. The complexities of promoting economic growth, social change, and democratic self-government in the underdeveloped areas of the world were barely perceived.

To redress the damage to the international economy wrought by two world wars and a prolonged depression required larger scale, longer lasting reconstruction programs for which the United States continued to be virtually the sole source of funds. It also required a priority for Europe somewhat inconsistent with the equal treatment for all nations implicit in the global framework. It is consequently doubtful whether the European Recovery Program could have operated for long under the U.N. aegis, even if there had been no cold war.

The most pervasive factor in downgrading the U.N., however, was the cold war. When Molotov in 1947 rejected the Bevin-Bidault invitation to join in the development of the European Recovery Program, he settled any lingering doubts regarding the operation of the Marshall Plan within the U.N. framework. Not only did the cold war spur the formation of machinery that would not be paralyzed by Soviet intransigence, it also shifted the spotlight from action on the economic front to action on the defense front.

The creation of NATO in 1949 became one of a series of transcendently important steps in strengthening the military defenses of the free world. In mid-1950, the U.N. itself became engaged in repulsing communist aggression in Korea. The Korean experience, in turn, confirmed the United States in its determination to complete a network of mutual security pacts reinforcing the North Atlantic Treaty. But in today's world, a mere military alliance is as unfashionable as a marriage of convenience. To pass as true love, it must sooner or later be sweetened with an economic cooperation agreement. The United States defense pacts consequently involved the extension of economic as well as military aid, but under circumstances that have operated to keep both in bilateral channels.

Within the NATO region, an attempt to establish a European Defense Community failed, but gave added impetus to the previously-mentioned efforts of Belgium, Luxembourg, the Netherlands, France, Germany, and Italy to form a single economic community. Whereas the U.N. is a purely voluntary association of sovereign states with virtually no sanctions in the economic field other than the sanction of public opinion, the most recent treaties of the six western European nations establish some supra-national machinery authorized to exercise directly—not through national governments—certain powers that have heretofore been exercised by national governments.

Although east-west tensions have served, on balance, to impede and to deflect interest from the economic work of the U.N. system, they have not operated in one direction only. The desire of the major powers for propaganda victories, or for possible bridges between east and west, or for the good will of uncommitted nations, has also been responsible for proposals that started U.N. agencies on new and fruitful ventures. Other forces favoring continued expansion of U.N. activities include the unremitting pressures of the underdeveloped countries, the unmet needs that are constantly being revealed to both developed and underdeveloped countries, the dedicated efforts of some of the international civil servants, and the successes of certain of the programs.

The underdeveloped countries have come to regard the U.N. as a projection and protection of their sovereignty. Individually, they are in a weak position in bargaining with the industrialized nations on economic matters—unless they can convince the United States that they are peculiarly vulnerable to communism. Collectively, they can assume a more self-respecting stance and be more influential. For the underdeveloped countries, the high road to dignity and status is via the U.N. The developed countries, by contrast, now tend to view the U.N. as a mechanism for compromising their freedom of action and extracting financial aid from them. They have consequently taken a "go-slow" attitude toward any expansion of U.N. activities, usually alleging that such caution is recommended, not in self-interest, but in the interest of the underdeveloped countries.

While some bold and well-publicized programs have been initiated outside the U.N. framework, cooperation within that framework has by no means been at a standstill. The International Bank has made a secure place for itself and President Black is emerging as an international statesman of considerable repute. IMF, after a brief burst of activity and eight years of conserving its resources, has done more business in the last two years than in the preceding decade. The Expanded Program of Technical Assistance, following a faltering start and stabilization for several years at an excessively modest level, may be substantially enlarged as a result of the United States proposal adopted by the twelfth General Assembly.

The Food and Agriculture Organization (FAO), the World Health Organization, the International Labor Organization, and other specialized agencies, are carving out deeper niches for themselves. An International Finance Corporation (IFC), an International Atomic Energy Agency (IAEA), and an Intergovernmental Maritime Consultative Organization (IMCO) have come into being. Within the U.N. structure of commissions and committees, the regional economic commissions for Europe, for Latin America, and for Asia and the Far East have deepened their roots and are flourishing; in addition, an Economic Commission for Africa has just been established.

To these gains, there have been offsets. The International Trade Organization (ITO), which was to be a keystone of the international economic structure, never got off the ground. A pallid substitute, the Organization for Trade Cooperation, has been similarly stalled for nearly four years. Moreover, if and when it does come into being, it will not be a specialized agency of the U.N. Refugee work, a principal activity of UNRRA and the full-time responsibility of a short-lived specialized agency (the International Refugee Organization), is no longer a major continuing function of the U.N. The role of the U.N. High Commissioner for Refugees is limited and the fund he administers is small. The United Nations Relief and Works Agency for Palestine Refugees in the Near East is dying of financial starvation. Korean reconstruction, once envisaged as a collective effort to build a monument to the highest principles of the U.N., has petered out as a U.N. program and was almost from the beginning overshadowed by the United States program of bilateral aid.

The Economic and Social Council handles its heterogeneous functions more competently than its many critics would have us believe, but it has not become "an economic general staff" for the U.N., and its overall record lacks luster.[4]

Although continuing to allege that support of the U.N. is the cornerstone of their foreign policy, the major western powers are no longer inclined to nominate their own best men for U.N. posts, nor indeed to accept outstanding and independent men of other nationalities in key posts. With no disrespect to the hard-working directors of U.N. agencies today, and with full consciousness of the imperfections of some of their predecessors, one can call attention to the lamentable and, one suspects, not entirely necessary scarcity of men of the stature of Albert Thomas, Julian Huxley, Edward Warner, John Boyd Orr, Gunnar Myrdal, and Brock Chisholm. The unedifying procedures whereby the top posts in a new and potentially important agency, IAEA, were filled in 1957 provide a measure of the change in spirit that has occurred since the aforementioned persons served in international capacities.

II. ACCOMPLISHMENTS OF THE UNITED NATIONS SYSTEM

The economic objectives of the Charter are at the same time the objectives of most Member governments. The U.N. can assist particular governments at their request, and it provides all with basic information. It can recommend courses of action, but it cannot compel any government to follow its recommendations. In addition to providing advice, analysis, and facilities for negotiation, the U.N. system has provided material assistance on a modest scale. The total contribution of these activities to the substantial but unevenly distributed improvement in the economic situation that has occurred since 1946 cannot readily be

---

[4] For further discussion of the Economic and Social Council see, *inter alia:* A. Loveday, "Suggestions for the Reform of the United Nations Economic and Social Machinery," *International Organization*, August 1953 (Vol. 7, No. 3); Isador Lubin and Forrest Murden, "ECOSOC: Concept Versus Practice," *Journal of International Affairs*, 1955 (Vol. 9, No. 2); Robert E. Asher, Walter M. Kotschnig, and others, *The United Nations and Promotion of the General Welfare*, Washington, Brookings Institution, 1957, Chapter III; Report of the Commission to Study the Organization of Peace, *Strengthening the U.N.*, New York, Harper & Bros., 1957, p. 185-186, 191-199.

isolated and measured. Nevertheless, there is evidence enough to provide a basis for some general conclusions concerning the record to date and the outlook for the future.[5]

In appraising the record, it is tempting to fall in line with the current practice of justifying public programs because of their success in providing—not the benefits for which they were originally established—but other benefits considered valuable by the appraiser. The International Bank, it can be said, may have loaned only modest amounts of development capital, but it has driven home some important truths without offending the sensibilities of the underdeveloped countries. The International Monetary Fund has thoroughly exposed the evils of inflation and the inadvisability of multiple exchange rates. The technical assistance program has provided unexpected opportunities for underdeveloped countries possessed of expertise in particular fields to help other underdeveloped countries.

But serendipity has its deceptive side. It usually begs the question whether the incidental benefits that loom so large in hindsight could have been obtained in less costly or less cumbersome fashion. In order, for example, that sound financial advice on development might be dispensed to would-be borrowers, was it necessary to create a lending agency with subscribed capital in excess of $9 billion? Would countries have listened to an agency that lacked the wherewithal to finance approved undertakings?

Honest appraisal is further complicated because of the inability of the international agencies openly to take credit for some of the things they do. They work through member governments and, in a real sense, their most important function is to strengthen the responsible forward-looking elements in those governments. When they are successful, the forward-looking elements, not the agency, reap the credit. This is as it should be, of course, and the ultimate pay-off ought to be better administration at national and local levels and greater understanding at international levels.

In the early postwar years, the emphasis in the economic field was overwhelmingly on reconstruction, but the task proved to be beyond the capacities of the fledgling U.N. Since the inauguration of the Expanded Program of Technical Assistance in 1950, the problems of the under-

---

[5] For a more extensive discussion, see *The United Nations and Promotion of the General Welfare*, especially Part V, from which the author borrowed for this section and for portions of the next section of this article.

developed countries have moved to the center of the world stage, and the consideration of ways and means of facilitating economic growth and social change in those areas has preoccupied the U.N. Because it has focused world attention on newly-liberated forces of explosive potentialities, the priority given to the whole subject of economic development has been a constructive achievement on the part of the U.N. Aspects of the development process have been intensively explored and the U.N. has made some noteworthy contributions to the slowly emerging understanding of the nature of economic growth. The importance of investment in agriculture, education, health, and public administration, as well as in industry, is more widely appreciated; balanced growth has become the goal.

Technical assistance has become firmly established as a technique for promoting development. Much of the work financed from the regular budgets of the U.N. and the affiliated specialized agencies is essentially technical assistance—designed to facilitate better employment of the human and material resources of Member nations. Expenditures under the regular budgets have been rising and increasing amounts of technical assistance are being provided by the U.N. system outside of, as well as under, the Expanded Program of Technical Assistance. The Expanded Program, though inadequately-financed and thinly-spread, is a notably more efficient operation than it was several years ago.

Technical assistance has brought representatives of the U.N. system to the most isolated communities, where they have helped to reduce social and institutional barriers to progress within the underdeveloped countries themselves. In the process, many of the traditional distinctions between matters of international concern and matters essentially domestic have been obliterated. The development of a sense of international community has been promoted and the improvements that can be wrought without massive expenditures of capital are being demonstrated daily. Nevertheless, technical assistance is clearly not enough.

Some of the requirements for foreign capital are being met through the International Bank. Some are being met by the Export Import Bank of Washington, the International Cooperation Administration, and other agencies of the United States government. Sizable investments in dependent overseas territories are being made by certain western European nations. Still other needs for development capital are not being met at all.

The International Bank, as stated elsewhere, has increasingly become a kind of publicly managed investment fund whereby money raised in the private capital markets of the United States, Canada, and western Europe is invested for productive purposes in other regions of the world.[6] Off to a very slow start, its lending to underdeveloped countries totaled only about $1.3 billion between the time it opened its doors in June 1946 and the end of 1955. For 1956 and 1957, however, loans to underdeveloped countries rose to about $670 million, half as much during a two-year period as during the preceding nine and one-half years. Including the reconstruction loans made to western European nations in 1947, and the loans thereafter to areas such as Australia, Japan, the Union of South Africa, and other countries that, because of relatively high per capita income levels are not usually referred to in U.N. circles as underdeveloped, the grand total loaned by the Bank through March 31, 1958, amounted to more than $3.5 billion.[7] Though not a negligible total, this remains far below the target figure of $1 billion per year *to the underdeveloped countries* that was recommended by a group of U.N. experts in 1951.[8]

Underdeveloped countries have considered their problems insoluble without greater financial assistance from abroad, particularly for meeting the costs of non-self-liquidating projects such as schools, sanitation systems, hospitals, and roads, which are nevertheless basic to development. The long campaign of the underdeveloped countries for the establishment of a U.N. fund to make grants-in-aid and loans repayable in local currencies has not yet been successful. The United States at first opposed, then postponed, and lately has tried to deflect the campaign for the Special United Nations Fund for Economic Development (SUNFED).

The unending pressure for development capital on better terms than those offered by the International Bank has had important by-products, however. The first has been the establishment, as an affiliate of the Bank, of IFC, which is able to invest risk capital in private enterprises

---

[6] *Ibid.*, p. 1050.

[7] International Bank for Reconstruction and Development, *Loans at Work,* March 31, 1958.

[8] "The Bank should set itself to reach, within five years, some such target as an annual rate of lending of not less than $1 billion to the underdeveloped countries. If it shows no signs of approaching this target, the whole question of the proper international organization for the provision of adequate amounts of loan capital to the underdeveloped countries should be reviewed by the United Nations." *Measures for the Economic Development of Underdeveloped Countries,* Report by a Group of Experts Appointed by the Secretary-General of the United Nations, Document E/1986, May 3, 1951, p. 83-84.

in underdeveloped countries without the governmental guarantee required in connection with loans made by the Bank. Like other international agencies, IFC is getting off to a slow start and the record of its first two years would seem to this observer to indicate that it will not provide much risk capital during the medium-term future.

The second by-product of the campaign for SUNFED has been the substantial expansion of the technical assistance program proposed by the United States and endorsed unanimously by the General Assembly in late 1957.[9] Put forward in the General Assembly not as a "substitute for SUNFED . . . not an alternative to SUNFED . . . not an attempt to exclude the future development of SUNFED," [10] it is more frankly described in the Executive Branch's public presentation of the Mutual Security Program for 1959 as having been "advanced as an alternative to more ambitious proposals for . . . an international development fund. . . ." [11] The purposes of the United States in advancing the proposal are in a sense irrelevant. The fact is that if achieved, the expansion will provide something called "technical assistance in depth," but neither loans nor grants.

While the expansion of international machinery for financing development programs has been minuscule, the United States has unilaterally established a Development Loan Fund to offer loans on easier terms than those of the International Bank. The Soviet Union, moreover, is offering long-term loans at rates of interest lower than those available either from international agencies or from the United States. Engaged in competitive co-existence without ground rules of any kind, both the United States and the Soviet Union are exposing themselves increasingly to blackmail from underdeveloped countries in quest of foreign aid.

The promotion and protection of private international investment has been much discussed in U.N. forums. The International Bank has

---

[9] The proposal involves enlargement of the present Expanded Program of Technical Assistance from a level of about $30 million per year to $50 million and the creation of a separate Special Fund of $50 million to finance intensive surveys of water, mineral and potential power resources, the establishment of training institutes in public administration, statistics and technology, and the setting up of agricultural and industrial research and productivity centers.

[10] Walter H. Judd, Statement of November 27, 1957, in the Economic and Financial Committee of the General Assembly, United States Delegation Press Release 2824.

[11] Department of State, Department of Defense, and International Cooperation Administration, *The Mutual Security Program, Fiscal Year 1959, A Summary Presentation*, February 1958, p. 45.

been ingenious and persevering in developing techniques for associating private with public loan capital and in paving the way for a revival of private international investment. The Fund and the General Agreement on Tariffs and Trade (GATT) have exerted their influence in the direction of liberalized exchange restrictions and trade restrictions. Attempts by the U.N. system to develop a multilateral code of fair treatment for private investors have foundered, but the climate for private investment has improved notably. The U.N., despite one or two unfortunate resolutions and some abrupt actions by certain Middle Eastern members, has contributed to the improved climate.[12]

United States private investment abroad rose significantly in 1956 and early 1957. Private investment, however, does not necessarily move in accordance with the political requirements of foreign policies or with the exigencies of the international situation. It is clear that in the present world situation, public investment on a fairly sizable scale will continue to be a necessary forerunner of private investment.

Through GATT, which has operated as a partial substitute for an International Trade Organization but which does not report to ECOSOC, encouraging progress has been made in reducing and stabilizing tariff rates, in lowering other trade barriers, and in obtaining observance of a code of trade rules. GATT, moreover, is a shining example of the fact that a major intergovernmental organization can function—and function well—with a very small secretariat lacking assurance of tenure and other elements of job security, but dedicated to the production of economic reports of high quality and the summoning of meetings only when meetings are needed.

In the U.N. proper, the standard for economic analysis was similarly established, not by the permanent headquarters, but by the secretariats of the regional economic commissions during the days when the regional commissions were still an experiment and the decision to make them permanent had not yet been taken. In the early years, the regional economic surveys, especially in Europe and Latin America, were more penetrating, more sophisticated, and more enlightening than the World Economic Report and some of the other publications of the headquarters office. At present, the same generalization would be unfair to the central office.

There are potential conflicts between the regional and global ap-

---

[12] See *The United Nations and Promotion of the General Welfare*, especially p. 352-364.

proaches, especially to the solution of trade and payments problems. The most difficult problems, however, have not been posed by actions of the U.N. regional commissions, although all three have initiated work on regional trade and payment problems, and the Economic Commission for Latin America is currently involved both in promoting economic integration in Central America and in exploring the possibilities of a common market in South America. The hard problems have been those involving EPU, ECSC, and the common market. Here it can be said that conflicts between the interests of the regional groupings and of the nations not in such groupings are being adjusted in a more orderly and mutually beneficial manner than if there had been no GATT and no IMF.

IMF, whose creation seemed more important at Bretton Woods than the creation of the International Bank, played an exceedingly modest role on the international stage during the first decade of its life. It began courageously enough by selling to its members more than $600 million in dollar exchange between March 1947 and April 1948, thereby serving with the Bank as a life-line to a sinking Europe until Marshall Plan grants were mobilized. Logically enough, the Fund then ceased engaging in dollar exchange transactions with countries receiving Marshall Plan aid. Exceptional efforts were later required to meet the standards imposed by the United States Treasury and to secure a revival of Fund activity. In the meantime, new techniques were developed by the Fund to facilitate its operation. During the past two years, the Fund has again contributed impressively to international liquidity.[18] In addition, it has converted a growing proportion of its membership to the principles they theoretically accepted when they ratified the Fund's Articles of Agreement.

The specialized agencies in the field of transportation and communication—the International Civil Aviation Organization, the International Telecommunication Union, the Universal Postal Union, and the World Meteorological Organization—have, on the whole, concentrated on the provision of long-range technical services of a non-

---

[18] Total financial assistance (drawings plus outstanding stand-by arrangements) provided by the Fund from its inception to April 1958 amounted to $3.9 billion, two-thirds of which had been made available within the preceding twenty-four months. If the transactions represented by unused stand-by arrangements are excluded, the amount obtained by European countries came to $1.65 billion and the amount obtained by other member countries to $1.32 billion. (International Monetary Fund, *International Financial News Survey*, April 18, 1958, p. 323, 325-26.)

controversial character. Some of the forward-looking practices of these agencies might well be emulated elsewhere in the U.N. family. The 1956 session of the ICAO Assembly, for example,

> . . . decided that the ICAO Council should establish a special panel, composed of a small number of highly qualified persons with a broad knowledge of aviation, to consider what improvements in international air navigation facilities and services will be most necessary during the next five years. If countries, either for technical or financial reasons, cannot provide these facilities and services, the task force will discuss possible means of overcoming the difficulties with the governments concerned and then recommend ways in which ICAO might help remedy the situation.[14]

That the cumbersome U.N. system is capable of rising to the sudden challenge has been demonstrated on numerous occasions in its relief and refugee work, in the health field, and in other activities. Nowhere has this been more dramatically illustrated than in a recent episode that may be too quickly forgotten: the clearance of the Suez Canal in late 1956 and early 1957. A political as well as an economic achievement, the clearance operation was completed in less than four months—six weeks ahead of the original schedule—at a cost that proved to be only a fraction of the original estimate.

Since its re-opening, the Canal has been operating efficiently. Moreover, at the invitation of the government of Egypt, the International Bank helped to negotiate a settlement between Egypt and the former owners of the Canal and has been collaborating in plans for widening, deepening, and improving the waterway. Within the near future, the nationalized Canal may become a more modern and serviceable artery than if it had remained in the hands of its previous owners.

III. WHERE DO WE STAND TODAY?

The total of solid accomplishments creditable to the U.N. system is sufficient to have enabled me, less than two years ago, to express qualified optimism about the future.[15] A foundation seemed to have been laid during the first postwar decade for a large and well-balanced expansion of the world economy during the ensuing ten years.

Surveying the situation today, my optimism would be further tem-

[14] U.S. Participation in the U.N., Report by the President to the Congress for the Year 1956, Washington, Government Printing Office, December 1957, p. 180.
[15] The United Nations and Promotion of the General Welfare, p. 1079.

pered. The opportunity to build adequately on the existing foundation, particularly in the field of economic development, is being neglected by member governments. Remarkable progress has been made in improving the cluster of institutions through which four score and more of sovereign states—each pursuing its national interest, usually conceived in distressingly short-range terms—can develop and express a greater sense of international community. In many respects, however, that sense of community is weaker today than it was at the close of the Second World War.

It is in danger of further disintegration unless revived with a grand design, an inspiring objective, that can be pursued with vigor and zest, and that succeeds in once more identifying the U.N. with the aspirations of the common man. However naive the expectations of the United States concerning the international economy may have been in the early 1940's, they gave to the United States and to the coalition which the United States led, a sense of purpose and direction. In the creation of a steadily expanding and increasingly integrated world economy, UNRRA, the Bank, the Fund, ITO, etc. had definite roles to play. When the true dimensions of the reconstruction problem were revealed, the design had to be revised and the Marshall Plan was adopted. Although limited to western Europe and carried through outside the framework of the U.N., it was an imaginative plan, with an objective, a time limit, and a price tag.

Today there is no over-all plan, inside or outside the U.N., apart from the designs the communists harbor. There is growing recognition of the complexity of certain problems, which is wholesome—and growing cynicism about man's capacity to find solutions, which is dangerous. There are plans for eradicating malaria, for improving air transport, and for cajoling countries into further reductions of exchange restrictions, but these are not objectives around which any sizable fraction of the world can rally. The congeries of U.N. activities of aid to specific sectors of the economy or to specific geographic areas does not add up to an international program for maintaining an expanding world economy or even preventing the spread of deflationary pressures.

The international community has not been willing to increase significantly the volume of international reserves available for meeting short-term requirements. For understandable reasons, it has not been willing to guarantee the maintenance of a given level of international trade or a given flow of investment funds. Although the prices of inter-

different reasons, however, they may be interested in the U.N. as a forum for the exchange of views with underdeveloped countries.

In non-communist Asia, in the Middle East, in Africa, and in Latin America, there is need for the U.N. and opportunity galore. India, the largest country in the entire free world, stands at the threshold of a new era of self-sustaining growth, provided that a substantial financial boost is obtained from abroad. A number of countries are furnishing some assistance, but the total is insufficient to enable India to meet the relatively modest targets of its Second Five Year Plan. If assistance in the necessary volume is not obtained, the prospects for an Asia truly committed to the principles of the U.N. Charter will be considerably bleaker.

In two of the other largest countries in Asia, Pakistan and Indonesia, the situation is deteriorating; a massive galvanizing of energies will be required to reverse the process. The Arab world is seething with discontent and is entirely too likely to work out its frustrations in external adventures unless satisfying results can be obtained by focusing on domestic problems. With the exception of a few oil-rich countries, the Arab nations need considerable development capital from abroad. The Latin American republics, for the most part, did not succeed during the boom period in controlling inflation or in saving any significant portion of their increased export earnings for release during the current downswing. The hard-won advances of that area are menaced by falling commodity prices and by new restrictions on access to the United States market. Africa, last of the continents to awaken, daily grows more restive.

In these circumstances, the main goal of the U.N. system in the economic field must surely be to pursue more vigorously the challenging, unifying, and vitally necessary job of concentrating additional resources from both developed and underdeveloped countries on raising levels of living among peoples no longer resigned to poverty, hunger, disease, and subordinate status.[17] In view, however, of the difficulties besetting the U.N. at its present modest level of operations, are there good grounds for hope that it will soon be better equipped to stimulate economic growth in underdeveloped areas?

---

[17] Important as it is, the main goal should not become the sole goal. Other useful activities of the U.N.—and there are many—must, of course, be continued and new activities, where appropriate, must be undertaken.

The way to find out—and I recognize that it is infinitely easier to suggest an enlightened policy than to put one into effect—is for the United States to put forward or support some constructive proposals that will encourage countries to set their sights on realistic economic targets for a few years hence and to organize themselves to reach those targets. The preparation of national development programs covering a period of four, five, or six years must be more actively promoted and assisted. The secretariats of the regional economic commissions, the commissions themselves, independent panels of experts, or other appropriate agencies of the U.N. should be authorized to receive and analyze the national development plans of countries willing to subject their plans to such scrutiny. The purpose of the analysis would be to note the assumptions made concerning domestic investment and savings, foreign private investment, world commodity prices, population trends, internal distribution of anticipated increases in the gross national product, etc. Out of these analyses and discussions should come some sensible projections of the amounts of outside aid needed by underdeveloped countries during the ensuing three or four years in order to permit gradual improvements in local levels of living without resort to Draconian measures—albeit with real effort on the part of the countries concerned.

Concurrently, the U.N. system must be better equipped to see that the necessary aid is forthcoming. The U.N. must, of course, learn to walk before it can run, but need it be compelled to limp before it is allowed to walk? Nothing could be more paralyzing than the present system of financing, on an annual pass-the-hat basis, work that is alleged to be vitally important. This method puts far too little pressure on Member governments to contribute in accordance with their capacities.

Their capacities have changed considerably since the inauguration of the Marshall Plan when Europe was prostrate and North America was the sole source of assistance. A reinvigorated western European economy has now expanded to the point where it can again contribute to the development of non-European territories. The economic resources of the United States, greater now than in 1948, are no longer fully employed; our foreign aid programs could be vastly enlarged with no diminution in domestic levels of consumption and investment. The Soviet Union, with steel production in the first quarter of 1958 equal to that of the United States, has become a major industrial power and—in carefully selected situations—a substantial dispenser of foreign aid.

World trade has grown enormously, but the share represented by trade between industrial and non-industrial areas of the world has been declining.

The gap between levels of living in the more developed and the less developed countries has widened ominously and, in the latter, popular demand for tangible improvement is reaching flood tide proportions. The U.N. system, however, can provide only technical assistance on a small scale, short-term credit for countries in temporary balance-of-payments difficulties, and long-term loans to cover the foreign exchange requirements of bankable projects.

Expertise is always rather scarce, but it is not so heavily concentrated in the United States as is capital. The case for a larger multilateral program of technical assistance is consequently strong. The case for a significant enlargement in the resources of IMF is likewise strong. The gold and dollar reserves of countries other than the United States are larger than they were, but the growth in the liquidity of the world economy as a whole has not begun to match the expansion in trade and payments that has occurred in the last ten years. The potentialities of the Fund justify entrusting it with greater resources than it now has. Insofar as hard loans to underdeveloped countries are concerned, the International Bank is about half way toward the billion-dollar per year lending target recommended by the experts in 1951 as a goal for 1956. During the past few years, however, it has been moving ahead with commendable energy, particularly along such promising paths as assisting in the creation of the local industrial investment institutions that are popularly known as development banks.

The U.N. system is not equipped to provide grants or to make loans repayable in local currencies. United States hostility to grants-in-aid, in either United States or U.N. programs, has been based on strong feelings that grants for economic development purposes should not become a normal feature of international economic cooperation. Grants to developed countries for reconstruction purposes proved tremendously beneficial and grants for military purposes have been regarded as capable of strengthening underdeveloped countries. But grants for development purposes, it is said, would weaken their moral fiber.

The United States doctrine that development loans are good but development grants are bad is not the result of analysis of the debt-servicing capacities of the underdeveloped countries or of the rates of progress most likely to promote the general welfare. If larger investment programs are deemed essential in India, Indonesia, Burma, Ceylon, Bolivia, and other countries in which borrowing capacity is severely limited, the wisdom of foreclosing the grant channel is open to question.

Nevertheless, in deference to United States views, the countries that have pressed for the establishment of SUNFED would be well-advised to concentrate on something along the lines of the International Development Association (IDA) recently proposed by Senator Monroney, but with a capital fund of at least $5 billion in usable resources. Unlike the Children's Fund or SUNFED, the proposed IDA would not operate as a unit of the U.N. proper, but would be under the aegis of the International Bank. It would be authorized to make loans on much more flexible terms than those of the Bank, including loans repayable in local currencies, and would provide a mechanism whereby other countries could join in a job that the United States has thus far insisted on doing alone through its inadequately-financed Development Loan Fund.

To give the U.N. system a creative role in meeting the most challenging economic problem of the next few decades and to avoid the suspicion of motives and competitive blackmail inherent in present bilateral rivalries, I would favor greater reliance on multilateral channels for development assistance even if this resulted in a corresponding decrease in bilateral assistance.[18] The real problem, however, is to increase the total flow of technical assistance and development capital. Would the people of the relatively prosperous industrialized nations fail in this task if they could be reasonably confident that the national programs of the underdeveloped countries were well-conceived, the countries themselves were making adequate efforts, they intended to distribute equitably the fruits of productivity increases, they were utilizing their borrowing capacity, and they were, in the words of the Charter, promoting "social progress and better standards of life in larger freedom"?

Unless the U.N. system is given a more significant role in the unfolding drama of economic development, its contribution to economic stability and progress will be slim. The challenge of the day cannot be

---

[18] Greater reliance on multilateral machinery does not mean exclusive reliance. For some time to come, situations will arise in which the United States will wish to favor some of its friends more than others. In aid, as in trade, however, discriminatory treatment has serious disadvantages and the long-term trend is surely toward uniform ground rules and more equitable treatment for those prepared to observe the agreed rules.

met by inching along. At 63,360 inches to the mile, it takes entirely too long to pass a milepost.

International Organization and World Order*

by Inis L. Claude, Jr.

World federalists and champions of international organization can agree that the world needs techniques and institutions capable of preventing war and mobilizing human and material resources in a vast effort to create a good society which encompasses the whole earth. The fundamental difference between them is that the former think in terms of *governmental institutions* as the indispensable means for the realization of these purposes, whereas the latter emphasize the ideal of obtaining *governmental results* by whatever methods may be tried and found useful. To say that the world needs to be governed is not the same as saying that a world government must be erected.

The world requires methods and agencies adequate for performing reasonably well on a global scale the functions which governments have undertaken to perform and have occasionally managed to perform with great success in independent states; yet world government is not the only conceivable or necessarily the best possible means for meeting that requirement. To put it differently, the benefits which governments ideally and sometimes actually confer upon the societies in which they operate are desperately needed by the global society, but it is not certain that those advantages are most likely to be provided by institutions patterned after or closely analogous to the so-called "governmental" institutions of states. The instrumentalities appropriate to the solution of the world's problems may or may not constitute a system which looks like government, sounds like government, or acts like government. The test is functional performance, not institutional resemblance.

THE PROGRESS OF INTERNATIONAL ORGANIZATION

In functional terms, the process of international organization has brought greater progress toward a governed world than has been gen-

* From *Swords into Plowshares: The Problems and Progress of International Organization*, pp. 434-450, copyright, © 1956, by Inis L. Claude, Jr. Reprinted by permission of Random House and Inis L. Claude, Jr.

erally recognized, and certainly more than is acknowledged by those who adhere to the doctrinaire view that government and anarchy are the two halves of an absolute either-or formula.

The last century, and particularly the last generation, has been an era of continuous development of patterns and techniques for managing the business of the international community. The old story of the sociological lag emphasizes the important truth that mankind has far to go, but it tends to obscure the fact that we are living in a period of adventurous experiment and flourishing inventiveness in the field of international relations. The creation of such institutional innovations as the general international organization, the international secretariat, the international conference of the parliamentary type, the international field commission for investigation and supervision, the international technical assistance mission, the multilateral defense machinery of the NATO type, and the supranational functional agency of the Schuman Plan type testifies to the significance of that fact. Moreover, fruitful improvisation is being increasingly supplemented by more systematic activities. The invention of invention is not exclusively a phenomenon of the scientific world; the international community is now equipped as never before with the analytical tools, professional staff, and organizational framework for designing and instituting new instruments to meet its needs.

The achievements of international organization include notable gains in the field of noncoercive regulatory devices. The agencies of the United Nations system exercise substantial influence and control—in short, *power*—over the behavior of states through the exploitation of a variety of methods: consultation and advice; inquiry, debate, and criticism of both public and private varieties; examination of reports and conduct of inspections; granting and withdrawal of subsidies and other forms of assistance; and recommendation followed by evaluation of response to this sort of pressure and possibly by insistent reiteration.

Additionally, limited progress has been made in the development of techniques of mandatory enactment and coercive enforcement. Failure to realize the ideal potentialities of collective security does not imply the utter sterility of the effort to create a multilateral enforcement system. The general acceptance in 1945 of a paper scheme whereby the Security Council might function as an authoritative agency of the international community, for acting against flagrant violations of its standards by all except the veto-protected great powers, in itself marked a significant advance. The critical deficiencies of this scheme, both in theory and in practice, overshadow but do not obliterate the fact that a primitive enforcement mechanism has come into being. The collapse of the Security Council scheme has been a little less than total; the compensatory development of the general Assembly and the supplementary construction of extra-United Nations devices for multilateral action have provided less than adequate or ideal but more than negligible support for the project of diminishing the probability that the arbitrary use of force will evoke no organized resistance from the community of states.

Future historians may find more significance in the fact that the League tried than that it failed to organize sufficiently vigorous measures to stop Italian aggression in Ethiopia, in the fact that the United Nations was able to adopt a posture stern enough to bring the Palestinian situation under control than that it was unable to guarantee the security of all troubled areas, and in the fact that the United Nations ventured to organize military and economic sanctions against Communist intrusions into South Korea than that it offered no effective means of coping with the broader dangers of Soviet aggressiveness in the cold war era.

The tentative opening up of limited possibilities of collective coercion under the auspices of international organization does not significantly offset the conclusion that the primary resources for regulation of state behavior which have been discovered by the League and the United Nations fall into the category of persuasion and influence rather than edict and compulsion. The question of the implications to be drawn from this factual situation is of central importance for the evaluation of international organization.

The simplest and perhaps the most tempting response is to conclude that the age of international organization is, after all, only a continuation of mankind's long and dismal period of global anarchy. To say that international organization relies primarily upon regulatory devices which are noncoercive in character is to admit that it is doomed to ineffectuality. Hence, no reasonable man can avoid making a choice between two conclusions: either that statesmen should give up the illusion that a governed world is possible, and settle down to the serious business of power politics, or that leaders and peoples should recognize the imperativeness of making the jump to a genuine world federation. What is not tenable is the assumption that international organization makes sense for a world in which power is the fundamental reality. The only meaningful alternatives are the mobilization of power behind national interest, or the concentration of power in support of the law of a global government.

This response reveals a curiously narrow conception of the means by which government performs regulatory functions, and, in its world federalist version, an extraordinarily broad view of the regulatory potency of the coercive instruments which are associated with governments. The truth is that all governments rely heavily—and that the most desirable governments rely predominantly—upon noncoercive methods for producing and maintaining social order. To say that international organization has distinguished itself most notably by creating a record of persistence, flexibility, and ingenuity in the development and exploitation of devices for inducing compliance by consent rather than compulsion is not to say that it has proved absolutely either the impossibility or the indispensability of creating a world government. Rather, it is to say that some of the basic means for governing the world have been evolved and are being utilized with increasing effectiveness by agencies which do not conform to theoretical models of governmental institutions. It is surprising how many estimable people, who would recoil with horror at the thought of a purely coercive government in the United States and insist with intelligent understanding that a decent political order in the nation must rest upon processes of inducement and adjustment rather than upon sheer force, seem to picture government solely in terms of a policeman beating criminals into submission when they shift their attention to the international scene. People are being governed at other times than when they cower before a policeman or languish in prison cells. Nations are being governed at other times than when they are being prohibited, restrained, and compelled.

The obvious answer is that noncoercive techniques of social regulation are not enough, either within a nation or among the nations: a system of international organization which must rely almost wholly upon an ability to induce compliance, unsupported by a reserve capacity to command and compel obedience, is not simply an incompletely equipped agency of world order but a fatally defective one.

This observation applies equally to a system which possesses the power to enforce without the capacity to persuade. The experience of governments makes it clear that recognition of the indispensability of force must be qualified by awareness both of its inherent inadequacy and of its limited attainability. Power is not enough, and there cannot in fact be enough power to guarantee against breaches of the peace. The project of endowing a world government with sufficient power to prevent disorder is not only dangerous, but it is ultimately infeasible. Only in a thoroughly atomistic society is there a real possibility that threats to order can be put down by coercion without results which amount to a disruption of social order. Such societies exist only in the minds of theorists and in the objectives of totalitarian dictators. In the real world, national societies are characterized by a pluralism which can never be entirely ground down even by the most determined dictator, and the international society exhibits a pluralistic nature which is so striking that virtually all world governmentalists defer to it by advancing proposals for global federation rather than unitary government. To admit this is in fact to concede that governmental coercion cannot keep the civil peace; it can at best win the civil war.

The American system of government, so often cited as evidence of the desirability of global federalism, serves as an instructive illustration of this point. The creation of federal government in the United States has not produced a situation in which Washington can maintain order by coercing the states which have handed over vital portions of their sovereignty to the union.

> The experience of the Civil War illustrates the fact that in a federal system where state loyalty is strong, the federal government and the state governments must act with constant vigilance to avoid forcing any deep dividing issue to the point where armed resistance comes into view. And if that point is reached no constitutional provisions about the control of the armed forces can prevent armed resistance and a conflict of loyalties for those in the forces of the general government.[1]

The United States Government maintains order among the component groups of its richly pluralistic national society, not by the distinctively governmental method of coercion, a method which is unavailable to the United Nations so long as it remains a mere international organization, but by techniques of persuasion, compromise, and inducement—precisely the sort of method which international organization has developed for the regulation of the affairs of nations. The truth is that it has no practicable alternative; major segments of American society—be they states, organized labor, the business community, reli-

---

[1] K. C. Wheare, *Federal Government* (New York: Oxford University Press, 1947), p. 204.

gious bodies, or professional groups—are not so much subject to restraint by the threat of coercion as they are capable of forcing the initiation of a process of political adjustment by raising the threat of collective defiance of governmental authority. For practical purposes, there is no more possibility that Washington will forcibly impose its will upon the segregationist South, or the farm organizations, or the Catholic Church than that the United Nations will resort to compulsion against defiant and disorderly states. The facts of life in the United States are that the Federal Government will compromise with a recalcitrant Texas, not threaten to bomb its cities; it will consult with labor leaders and revise a controversial legislative policy, rather than send the army into pitched battle against the nationwide membership of aroused labor unions; it will probably never even consider the possibility of using armed force to break the defiance of Southern states which insist upon maintaining racial segregation in the schools. And if, in some dire emergency, it *does* resort to coercion against a major segment of the national population or a regional bloc of states, this will symbolize not the majestic operation of the governmental principle in preserving social order, but the tragic failure of government to prevent the disruption of social order; the Federal Government will not be presiding over the peace, but conducting war.

It is striking how much *can* and *must*—even in a system of federal government—be done without the pressure of legal dictate and coercive threat. There are vital differences between the United States and the United Nations, but the contrast is not meaningfully stated by saying that the federation can rule by holding the threat of force over the major groups constituting the society which it governs, while the association is dependent upon the effectiveness of noncoercive methods in dealing with analogous entities within its domain. If a bitter conflict should arise between the groups of states east and west of the Mississippi River, the United States Government would be in very much the same position as the United Nations in the period of cold war, and its response to such a situation would be essentially the same; it would rely upon political methods for resolving the issues, just as the United Nations does, and if these methods failed, American society would dissolve into war, just as might happen in the case of global society. The evidence of American federalism does not support the thesis that the critical deficiency of the United Nations is its lack of power to coerce such states as the Soviet Union and that its transformation into a federation would, by remedying that lack, emancipate it from dependence upon methods of persuasion, discussion, and conciliation for maintaining world order. In relying upon such methods, the United Nations, which is not a government, is behaving as a government would have to behave in analogous circumstances.

This argument is only partially met by the thesis that it *is* coercion, but coercion applied against individuals rather than collective entities, which serves federal regimes as the ultimate safeguard of the peace. According to this view, the key to the transcendence of international anarchy is the shift from organizational reliance upon influencing states, to governmental dependence upon enforcing the law against individuals.

American experience lends only limited credibility to this view. It is true that Washington customarily checks collective entities—when they are willing to be checked—by holding their leaders legally responsible; but when a significant element of society exhibits a solidarity of disaffection, the government undertakes to negotiate with its leaders, not to hold the law over their heads, and to placate the group, not to treat it as a mass of individual law-breakers. No reasonable man would contend that the fiasco of the Eighteenth Amendment proved the capacity of government to uphold the law by applying it on an individual basis to a mass of determined violators, and it is doubtful that federal enforcement of desegregation in Southern schools against the wishes of states is rendered feasible by the fact that Washington has the theoretical capacity to imprison all state governors, legislators, and local school officials who defy its will. Governmental authority and power to deal with individuals is important, but it does not suffice to cope with either disobedience by an amorphous mass or resistance by an organized major segment of society in the United States.

Applying this lesson to the international scene, we may well look with skepticism upon the notion that the United Nations could prevent war if only it had the power to enforce its law upon individual citizens or leaders of member states. Governmental coercion of individuals is an effective instrument against scattered criminality and against the recalcitrance of groups which are not prepared to press the issue, but it is not a means of dissolving the solidarity of organized entities which are determined to insist upon the protection and advancement of their vital corporate interests as they conceive them. When such an entity presses its claims, the community has the choice of maintaining order by initiating a process of political compromise and adjustment, or of accepting the collapse of order and submitting the issue to the arbitrament of arms. The choice lies between war against a collective entity and political settlement with a collective entity; the alternative of pretending that the collective entity is a mere fiction and that relations wih it can be dissolved into a series of relations between the massive community and the lonely individual does not realistically exist.

In the final analysis, the decisive difference between the United States and the United Nations as systems of order is to be discovered in the fact that the United States is, and the United Nations is not, a society in which the significance of constituent groups has been so reduced that they are unlikely to press their claims to the point of disrupting the social fabric. The difference lies in the nature of the communities. The United States enjoys a degree of stability far superior to that of the international community because its states, regions, interest groups, and other component parts require neither the threat nor the use of federal force to restrain them from launching civil war or revolution; they are amenable to the political settlement of most of the issues which affect them, and there is general agreement within the community that the tough residue of disputed issues will not be forced to a showdown. In contrast, the international community is composed of states which have not, to such a degree, lost the disposition to challenge the order of the community, by force if necessary. Something has happened to Texas that has not happened to the Soviet Union. It is not so much that Texas, unlike the Soviet Union, has been overshadowed by a coercive institutional superstructure, but that Texas, unlike the Soviet Union, has been incorporated in the consensual foundations of a larger community.

If this analysis is correct, then the key to a well governed world is not the endowment of the United Nations with plenary coercive capacity but the reproduction on a global scale of the conditions which have made the pluralistic society of the United States a community in which group conflicts do not normally pose the threat of violent upheavals. The difficulty is that no one can quite say how the United States got that way, but two major considerations may be suggested. One is that the dividing lines of American society have become so numerous and intertangled, the pluralism has become so complex, that no clean-cut divisions of loyalty and interest can be found; the community has not been thoroughly unified, but its divisions have been confused by a process of multiplication. Thus, Texas cannot pose the threat of civil war because there is no one who is wholly a Texan, and labor unions cannot launch a revolution because there is no one who is fully a unionist. The second consideration is that individual loyalties have not only been scattered among a variety of groups, but that some of them—including in most cases the ultimately decisive loyalties—have been detached from smaller entities and lodged in the national community itself. Texas cannot revolt against the United States because its people are more fundamentally Americans than they are Texans. These are perhaps the basic conditions which make the maintenance of order possible in the United States, and which must be reproduced in the international community if stable world order is to become a reality.

The development of these conditions in American society has occurred in large part independently of the influence of government and without conscious social direction and control. Nevertheless, it is clear that government has figured indispensably in the process of creating the foundations of the community upon which it rests. The world governmentalist is right in his rejection of the notion that nothing should or can be done about institutions until a full-fledged world community has somehow sprung into being. He is right, too, in his insistence that the relationship of the individual to the community is a factor of crucial importance. But the governmental contribution to the evolution of the American community has not been produced primarily by the coercive methods which the world governmentalist is so eager to place at the disposal of the United Nations. The United States Government has promoted the development of its social underpinnings by serving the people of the nation in a thousand ways, protecting their rights, welfare, and safety, facilitating mobility, communication, and free association among them, mobilizing them in common enterprises of war and peace, and cultivating a nationalist ideology. These methods have been more significant and effective in "making Americans" than the method of enforcing federal law against private citizens throughout the length and breadth of the land. The helping hand of federal service is a more impressive argument for national allegiance than the long arm of federal justice.

The conclusion to be drawn from this is that what the United Nations most needs for the purpose of helping to create a meaningful world community is not new instruments of coercion, but precisely the variety of tools for doing useful work in the world which it has been busily shaping. In these terms, a world which has recently devoted itself to creating and setting into operation an unprecedentedly elaborate system of international service agencies is not guilty of fatuous unconcern with the problem of escaping anarchy. It is conceivable that the development of a public service corps is a more essential contribution to the creation of a community fit for law and order than the establishment of a police force.

In short, the conception of government as an agency which maintains order simply by commanding and compelling, prohibiting and punishing, has little relevance to a pluralistic national society and still less to a global society which is chiefly characterized by the depth of its divisions, the simplicity of its pluralistic pattern, and the underdevelopment of its capacity to superimpose a universal allegiance upon national loyalties. Given this kind of international community, the realization of the theoretical ideal of subjecting the world to unchallengeable authority would require the creation of an inordinately powerful world government; the fulfillment of the practical task of maintaining order in such a world involves the assiduous application of methods of compromise and adjustment. Here is a real paradox: the international community is so deficient in consensual foundations that it must theoretically be held together more by force than by consent, but it is marked by such decentralization of the resources of political and physical power that it must in practice be managed by agencies, whether they be called instruments of international organization or of world federation, which operate more by persuasion than by coercion. In the world as it is, there is no real alternative to efforts to achieve regulation of state behavior by noncoercive methods, and no more appropriate collective task than the provision of international services which may ultimately prove conducive to the breaking down of those features of the community structure which make reliance upon consent rather than coercion at once so necessary and so precarious. The regulatory methods and functional emphases of international organization may not conform to the image of government concocted by those who are impatient to abolish the problem of war by creating an entity which can, by definition, knock any and all national heads together, but they do correspond closely to the actual approach to the problem of maintaining order in a pluralistic society which the Federal Government of the United States has found essential. It is less significant that international organization is not a federal world government than that it is engaged in the effort to do the sort of thing that must be done, by the sort of method that can be used, to produce the sort of community that can, with proper management, sustain a peaceful existence. In this sense, the experiment of governing the world is now in operation, and the task of making the world governable is already being undertaken.

International organization has not been unaffected by the urge to solve the problem of world order by developing potentialities of coercion; the recurrent efforts of statesmen to create an effective system of collective security testify to this point. However, even this project is suffused with the spirit of voluntary cooperation rather than that of governmental compulsion, for collective security involves the collaboration of independent states in joint enforcement action, not the brandishing of sovereign power by a central regime. In the final analysis, international organization is primarily dedicated to the proposition that the nature of international society makes the preservation of peace dependent upon the stimulation of voluntary cooperation, the mobilization of moral restraint, the enlightenment of national self-interest, and the development of mutual understanding. The most urgent question of our time is not how to escape from the necessity of relying upon such methods as these, but how to make that necessity more tolerable. It is doubtful that the cause of world order is better served by agitated obsession with the danger that the essential consent of states to accept restraint and responsibility may not be forthcoming, than by constructive devotion to the task of developing more effective means for inducing that consent.

THE PROSPECTS OF INTERNATIONAL ORGANIZATION

To say that international organization does not represent a fundamentally mistaken approach to the problem of world order is not to assert that it is destined to succeed. The tough reality of the national divisions of world society makes the quest for agreed solutions of international problems a necessary enterprise, but the conflicting interests and purposes of national entities also make that quest a difficult one. Mankind is blessed by no cosmic guarantee that all its problems are soluble and all its dangers are avoidable.

The danger of imminent conflict between states possessing vast power is the overwhelming reality of our time. Only the coldest of comfort is to be derived from the observation that the existence of this danger is attributable to the nature of the international community rather than to the nature of the international architecture which was contrived in 1945. In this situation, it is all too clear that the United Nations can offer no guarantee of peace and security; at best, it can facilitate the balancing of power against power, and mobilize the resources of political adjustment. In the long run, international organization may transform the working of the multistate system. In the short run, it is inevitably more affected by the circumstances of international relations than effective in altering those circumstances.

There can be no guarantee that international machinery will in fact be utilized for the high purposes to which it may be formally dedicated. The establishment of an international organization does not involve the creation of an autonomous will, inexorably set upon the pursuit of the ideal of peace in a prescribed manner. Rather, it involves the creation of a mechanism to be placed at the disposal of states, which may use it for whatever purposes their agreements or their disagreements dictate. In practice, international organization may serve as the institutional framework for the joint exploration of approaches to peace, but it is also capable of serving as an arena for the conduct of international political warfare, or as an instrument for the advancement of the political objectives of a particular state or group of states.

International organization does not emancipate the world from dependence upon the quality of its statesmanship. Structural apparatus cannot generate its own supply of political decency, discretion, wisdom, and moderation. In the final analysis, both the possibilities and the limitations of international organization are set by political forces operative within and among member states. The deficiencies of the United Nations indicate a greater need for review and revision of national policies than of the Charter itself.

The most casual observer of the international scene can see that the problem of world order has not been solved. The most careful student of international organization can see that no world-saving miracles have been wrought, no infallible formula for solution of fundamental problems has been drafted, and no glorious certainty of a brave new world has been projected before the troubled eyes of modern man. But there is more to be seen than continued anarchy, unsolved problems, unresolved conflicts, and unparalleled dangers of chaos and destruction. Fallibility is not the same as futility; limited achievement is not the same as unlimited failure; danger is not the same as doom.

The development of international organization represents both a realistic response to the requirements of doing national business in an increasingly complex international setting and an idealistic attempt to modify the operation of the multistate system so as to make civilized living possible in an increasingly interdependent world. For better or for worse, the world has abjured the Hobbesian solution of throwing up hastily contrived institutional structures resting upon nothing more substantial than desperate fear of mutual destruction, adopting instead the Ciceronian ideal of establishing institutions of common life upon the limited but solid foundations of *consensus juris* and *utilitatis communione*. The builders of international organization have on occasion overestimated the extent of international agreement upon fundamental issues of right and justice and international preparedness to sustain joint approaches to mutual advantage, but they have not subordinated considerations of foundational adequacy to conceptions of architectural grandeur.

The proliferation of agencies in the United Nations system, the simultaneous exploration of approaches to peace ranging from collective security to technical assistance and from regulation of civil aviation to dissemination of artistic masterpieces, is evidence not merely of a weakness for indiscriminate experimentation but also of a growing recognition of the multifaceted character of the problem of world order and of the essential interconnectedness of the parts of its solution. The world is truly beginning to see its problems "in the round";[2] international organization provides "a world's eye view"[3] of basic problems which can hardly fail to affect the perspectives of governments. Awareness of the scope and complex interrelatedness of the problems at hand is the necessary starting point for satisfactory solutions.

The world is not only developing a more sophisticated conception of its problems, but it is also beginning to recognize that global problems require global solutions. International organization is something more than a gathering of national governments; it is, in a very rudimentary sense, an expression of the concept that there is an international community which bears responsibility for dealing with matters which refuse to be confined within national boundaries. Statesmen assemble at the United Nations to promote the interests of their national constituencies,

---

[2] Feller, *United Nations and World Community*, p. 119.
[3] Philip V. Cardon, "The Earth's Resources in the Service of Man," *United Nations Review*, July 1955, p. 20.

but they cannot altogether escape the tendency to feel that they compose a collective body whose constituency is mankind. The international community has become a little bit more than a dream of idealists. There is a limited sense in which it is meaningful to speak of a United Nations which imposes a principle of international accountability upon its member states, asserts its jurisdiction in areas previously encompassed by the functional boundaries of sovereignty, and assumes responsibility for doing as much of what must be done as can be done, on behalf of humanity.

The long-range effects of international organization upon the multistate system cannot be confidently predicted. It may be regarded as a process of evolutionary unification; yet, it functions now to support the fragmentation of empires into groups of newly independent states. It may be regarded as a process of gradual replacement of national governments as the major agencies for the management of human affairs; yet, it operates now less to deprive governments of their domestic functions than to assist them in acquiring the competence to do their jobs more effectively. It may be regarded as a process leading to the eventual transcendence of the multistate system; yet, its immediate function is to reform and supplement the system, so as to make the maintenance of legal, political, and administrative pluralism compatible with the requirements of an interdependent world.

It is perhaps necessary to stress again the distinction between international *organizations* and international *organization*. Particular organizations may be nothing more than playthings of power politics and handmaidens of national ambitions. But international organization, considered as an historical process, represents a secular trend toward the systematic development of an enterprising quest for political means of making the world safe for human habitation. It may fail, and peter out ignominiously. But if it maintains the momentum which it has built up in the twentieth century, it may yet effect a transformation of human relationships on this planet which will at some indeterminate point justify the assertion that the world has come to be governed—that mankind has become a community capable of sustaining order, promoting justice, and establishing the conditions of that good life which Aristotle took to be the supreme aim of politics.

This is the conception of international organization that Arthur Sweetser had in mind when, on the occasion of his retirement after thirty-four years of active membership in the first generation of international civil servants, he addressed his colleagues of the United Nations staff:

You were born out of the labor and travail of these older days [of the League]; you are the successors of those who tried to build before you, got swept temporarily away, but still left foundations to which you could anchor. You have built prodigiously upon them; I would not, in those first days of 1920, have dared dream you would get so far so fast. Don't underestimate this progress.

The great lesson of all this effort and suffering, even frequent disappointment, is that you are right, eternally right, in the fight you are making. You have got hold of the big things of life; you are on the road to the future; you are working for all the ends that make life worth while on this planet—for peace, for the eradication of war, for human advancement, for human rights and decencies, for better living standards, better education, better health, better food, better homes, better labor conditions, better travel and communications—in short, for the world as it ought to be.

This is the highest secular cause on earth. You deserve to be immensely proud of what you are doing, especially that you are privileged to be part of the permanent staff. During your low and grim moments, lift your eyes, I beg you, to these vaster horizons beyond; rise up out of the irritations and anxieties of the moment and realize that you have opportunities permitted to very few indeed.

You cannot feel too strongly that the right is on your side and that your cause will win in the long run; it is your opponents who are wrong and on the losing side.[4]

Sweetser's words proved nothing. They were an expression of faith—that faith in the moral capacity and the rational capacity of man which provides the philosophical underpinning of international organization. That faith may be mistaken, but it is not wrong, or ignoble, or unworthy of any man. It represents modern man at something very near his best.

---

[4] *United Nations Bulletin*, February 1, 1953, p. 123.

FOR FURTHER READING:

Robert E. Asher and others, *The United Nations and the Promotion of the General Welfare* (Washington, D.C.: The Brookings Institution, 1957).

Lawrence S. Finkelstein, *Somaliland Under Italian Administration: A Case Study in U.N. Trusteeship* (New York: Woodrow Wilson Foundation, 1955).

Leland M. Goodrich, *Korea: A Study of U.S. Policy in the United Nations* (New York: Harper and Brothers, 1956).

Leland M. Goodrich and Anne P. Simons, *The United Nations and the Maintenance of Peace and Security* (Washington, D.C.: The Brookings Institution, 1955).

H. Field Haviland, *The Political Role of the General Assembly* (New York: Carnegie Endowment for International Peace, 1951).

Howard C. Johnson and Gerhart Niemeyer, "Collective Security—The Validity of an Ideal," *International Organization*, Vol. VIII, No. 1 (February, 1954), pp. 19-35.

Bronislaw E. Matecki, *Establishment of the International Finance Corporation and United States Policy: A Case Study in International Organization* (New York: Frederick A. Praeger, 1957).

H. G. Nicholas, *The United Nations as a Political Institution* (London: Oxford University Press, 1959).

Gerhart Niemeyer, "Balance Sheet of the League Experiment," *International Organization*, Vol. VI, No. 4 (November, 1952), pp. 537-558.

Robert E. Riggs, *Politics in the United Nations: A Study of United States Influence in the General Assembly* (Urbana: The University of Illinois Press, 1958).

Walter R. Sharp, "The United Nations System in Egypt: A Country Survey of Field Operations," *International Organization*, Vol. X, No. 2 (May, 1956), pp. 235-260.

Eric Stein, *Some Implications of Expanding United Nations Membership* (New York: Carnegie Endowment for International Peace, 1956).

Kenneth W. Thompson, "Collective Security Reexamined," *The American Political Science Review*, Vol. XLVII, No. 3 (September, 1953), pp. 753-772.

Arnold Wolfers, "Collective Security and the War in Korea," *The Yale Review*, Vol. XLIII, No. 4 (Fall, 1954), pp. 481-496.

Index

746

The Divided World

Areas covered by United States mutual defense pacts or executive agreements

Soviet bloc

Areas not covered by either U.S. or Soviet defense agreements